Spain For Dummies, 1st Edition

A List of Handy Spanish Words and Phrases

English	Spanish	Spanish Pronunciation
Thank you	Gracias	grah-thee-yahs
Please	Por favor	por fah-bohr
Yes/No/and	Sí /No/y	see/no/ee
Do you speak English?	Habla usted inglés?	ah-blah oo-sted een-glais
I don't understand	No comprendo	no cohm-pren-doh
I'm sorry	Lo siento	lo see-yen-toh
Good day/Good evening	Buenos días/ Buenos tardes	bway-nohs dee-ahs/ bway-nohs tar-days
Excuse me (to get attention)	Perdóneme	pair-dohn-eh-meh
Excuse me (to get past someone)	Perdón/Disculpe	pair-dohn/dees-kool-pay
How much is it?	¿Cuánto cuesta?	kwan-toh kway-stah
Where is . . .?	¿Dónde está?	dohn-day eh-stah
. . . the bathroom	el servicio/ el baño/ el lavabo	el sair-bee-thee-yo/ el bahn-yoh/ el lah-vah-boh
. . . train station	la estación	lah es-tah-thee-yon
to the right/to the left	a la derecha/ a la izquierda	ah lah deh-ray-chah/ ah lah eeth-kyair-dah
straight ahead	siga derecho	see-gah deh-ray-cho
ticket	un billete	oon bee-yay-tay
first class/second class	primera classe/ segunda classe	pree-mair-ah klah-say/ seh-goon-dah klah-say
one way/round trip	ida/ ida y vuelta	ee-dah/ee-dah ee bwehl-tah
a double room for X nights	una habitación doble por X noches	oo-nah ah-bee-ta-thee-yon doh-blay pore X noh-chays
1/2/3	uno/dos/tres	oo-noh/dohs/trays
restaurant	un restaurante	oon res-taur-ahn-tay
I would like . . .	Quisiera	kee-see-yair-ah
. . . some of this/that	unos de éste/ ése	oo-nos day eh-stay/eh-seh
. . . a glass of	un vaso de	oon bah-soh day
. . . sparkling water/still water	agua con gas/ sin gas	ah-gwah cohn gahs/ seen gahs
. . . red wine/white wine	vino tinto/ vino blanco	bee-noh teen-toh/ bee-noh blahn-coh
. . . beer	una cerveza	oo-nah thair-bay-thah
The check, please	La cuenta, por favor	lah kwain-tah por fah-bohr
Is service (tip) included?	¿Está incluido el servicio?	eh-stah een-clu-ee-doh el sair-bee-thee-yo

For Dummies™: Bestselling Book Series for Beginners

Spain For Dummies,® 1st Edition

Cheat Sheet

Spanish Wine and Recommended Vintages

I recommend seeking out the following wines (listed here by type) while touring Spain.

- ✔ **Rioja Reds:** Viña Ardanza, Artadi, Imperial, Marqués de Arienzo, La Rioja Alta 890 (or 904), Castillo de Ygay, Beronia.
- ✔ **Rioja Whites:** Marqués de Riscal.
- ✔ **Ribera del Duero Reds:** Pesquera, Valbuena, Mauro, Vega Sicilia (but prohibitively expensive), Condado de Haza, Roda I, Protos.
- ✔ **Penedès Reds:** Gran Sangre de Toro, Jean León, Torres Gran Coronas.
- ✔ **Priorato Reds:** Cims de Priorato, Clos Martinet, Clos Dofí.
- ✔ **Cava (sparkling wine from Catalonia):** Juvé y Camps.
- ✔ **Sherry:** San León (manzanilla); Tío Pepe (fino).
- ✔ **Others:** Raimat, Marqués de Griñon Syrah, Castillo de Perelada, Chivite.

Recommended Vintages for Rioja and Ribera del Duero Wines

Year	Rioja	Ribera del Duero
1987	Very good	Good
1988	Good	Very good
1989	Good	Excellent
1990	Good	Excellent
1991	Very good	Very good
1992	Good	Good
1993	Good	Average
1994	Excellent	Very good
1995	Excellent	Excellent
1996	Very good	Excellent

For Dummies™: Bestselling Book Series for Beginners

Spain FOR DUMMIES®

1ST EDITION

by Neil E. Schlecht

Hungry Minds™

HUNGRY MINDS, INC.

New York, NY ◆ Cleveland, OH ◆ Indianapolis, IN

Spain For Dummies,® 1st Edition

Published by:
Hungry Minds, Inc.
909 Third Avenue
New York, NY 10022
www.hungryminds.com
www.dummies.com

Library of Congress Control Number: 00-110786

ISBN: 0-7645-6195-2

ISSN: 1533-7162

Printed in the United States of America

10 9 8 7 6 5 4 3 2 1

1B/SR/QT/QR/IN

Distributed in the United States by Hungry Minds, Inc.

Distributed by CDG Books Canada Inc. for Canada; by Transworld Publishers Limited in the United Kingdom; by IDG Norge Books for Norway; by IDG Sweden Books for Sweden; by IDG Books Australia Publishing Corporation Pty. Ltd. for Australia and New Zealand; by TransQuest Publishers Pte Ltd. for Singapore, Malaysia, Thailand, Indonesia, and Hong Kong; by Gotop Information Inc. for Taiwan; by ICG Muse, Inc. for Japan; by Intersoft for South Africa; by Eyrolles for France; by International Thomson Publishing for Germany, Austria and Switzerland; by Distribuidora Cuspide for Argentina; by LR International for Brazil; by Galileo Libros for Chile; by Ediciones ZETA S.C.R. Ltda. for Peru; by WS Computer Publishing Corporation, Inc., for the Philippines; by Contemporanea de Ediciones for Venezuela; by Express Computer Distributors for the Caribbean and West Indies; by Micronesia Media Distributor, Inc. for Micronesia; by Chips Computadoras S.A. de C.V. for Mexico; by Editorial Norma de Panama S.A. for Panama; by American Bookshops for Finland.

For general information on Hungry Minds' products and services please contact our Customer Care department; within the U.S. at 800-762-2974, outside the U.S. at 317-572-3993 or fax 317-572-4002.

For sales inquiries and resellers information, including discounts, premium and bulk quantity sales and foreign language translations please contact our Customer Care department at 800-434-3422, fax 317-572-4002 or write to Hungry Minds, Inc., Attn: Customer Care department, 10475 Crosspoint Boulevard, Indianapolis, IN 46256.

For information on licensing foreign or domestic rights, please contact our Sub-Rights Customer Care department at 650-653-7098.

For information on using Hungry Minds' products and services in the classroom or for ordering examination copies, please contact our Educational Sales department at 800-434-2086 or fax 317-572-4005.

Please contact our Public Relations department at 212-884-5174 for press review copies or 212-884-5000 for author interviews and other publicity information or fax 212-884-5400.

For authorization to photocopy items for corporate, personal, or educational use, please contact Copyright Clearance Center, 222 Rosewood Drive, Danvers, MA 01923, or fax 978-750-4470.

Hungry Minds™ is a trademark of Hungry Minds, Inc.

About the Author

A writer, photographer, and cycling fanatic who has lived in Spain, Brazil, and Ecuador, **Neil E. Schlecht** now resides in rural Connecticut. His first exposure to Spain was as a college sophomore teaching English at Col.legi Sant Ignasi in Barcelona. He returned to Barcelona just before the 1992 Summer Olympics and stayed for most of the past decade, working as a consultant on social and economic development projects for the European Union and as a contributing writer for a Spanish art and antiques magazine. The author of a dozen travel guides, as well as articles on art and culture and art catalogue essays, Neil is especially keen on assignments that take him back to Spain.

The author counts among the highlights of his Spanish travels a few treasured road miles cycling in the Navarra countryside alongside Miguel Indurain, Spain's five-time Tour de France champion. Neil's favorite reminder of Spain is his Labrador Retriever, who hails from a farm on Ibiza, one of the Balearic Islands. Despite her relocation to the U.S., she refuses to obey any commands not in Spanish.

Dedication

To Keny, who immersed me in the ways of Spain, and Solà, whose wine-fueled *charlas* in his studio helped me interpret them.

And to Sharon, who makes me want to hurry home.

Author's Acknowledgments

A special thanks (and *abrazo muy fuerte*) to Pilar Vico and José Carlos Fernández of the Tourist Office of Spain in New York. Their generosity and good-natured assistance proved essential to the completion of this book.

Publisher's Acknowledgments

We're proud of this book; please send us your comments through our Hungry Minds Online Registration Form located at www.dummies.com

Some of the people who helped bring this book to market include the following:

Editorial

Editors: Kelly Regan, Alissa Schwipps

Copy Editor: Billie A. Williams

Cartographer: Elizabeth Puhl

Editorial Manager: Jennifer Ehrlich

Editorial Assistant: Jennifer Young

Senior Photo Editor: Richard Fox

Assistant Photo Editor: Michael Ross

Cover Photos: Front Cover: Anthony Cassidy/Tony Stone Images; Back Cover: Robert Frerck/Odyssey

Production

Project Coordinators: Leslie Alvarez, Dale White

Layout and Graphics: Amy Adrian, Joe Bucki, LeAndra Johnson, Jacque Schneider, Julie Trippetti

Proofreaders: David Faust, Angel Perez, Marianne Santy, York Production Services, Inc.

Indexer: York Production Services, Inc.

Special Help: Carol Strickland

General and Administrative

Hungry Minds, Inc.: John Kilcullen, CEO; Bill Barry, President and COO; John Ball, Executive VP, Operations & Administration; John Harris, CFO

Hungry Minds Consumer Reference Group

Business: Kathleen A. Welton, Vice President and Publisher; Kevin Thornton, Acquisitions Manager

Cooking/Gardening: Jennifer Feldman, Associate Vice President and Publisher

Education/Reference: Diane Graves Steele, Vice President and Publisher; Greg Tubach, Publishing Director

Lifestyles: Kathleen Nebenhaus, Vice President and Publisher; Tracy Boggier, Managing Editor

Pets: Dominique De Vito, Associate Vice President and Publisher; Tracy Boggier, Managing Editor

Travel: Michael Spring, Vice President and Publisher; Suzanne Jannetta, Editorial Director; Brice Gosnell, Managing Editor

Hungry Minds Consumer Editorial Services: Kathleen Nebenhaus, Vice President and Publisher; Kristin A. Cocks, Editorial Director; Cindy Kitchel, Editorial Director

Hungry Minds Consumer Production: Debbie Stailey, Production Director

◆

The publisher would like to give special thanks to Patrick J. McGovern, without whom this book would not have been possible.

◆

Contents at a Glance

Cartoons at a Glance

By Rich Tennant

page 7

page 71

page 119

page 467

page 249

page 347

Cartoon Information:
Fax: 978-546-7747
E-Mail: richtennant@the5thwave.com
World Wide Web: www.the5thwave.com

Maps at a Glance

Table of Contents

bar

Introduction

*I*f you've been considering a trip to Europe, but weren't sure which country best fits your interests and budget, I'm convinced that Spain is an excellent choice for just about everyone. It appeals to the art lover, ecotourist, historian, pop culture scholar, gourmet, backpacker, and unrepentant hedonist; it even appeals to the cheapskate.

One of Europe's oldest countries, Spain has architecture dating back to the Romans and Moors, several of Europe's most spectacular art museums, warm people, vibrant festivals, fantastic food, and brilliant weather. These things make it ideal for year-round vacations, where you can soak up the good life at outdoor cafés, hit the beaches, and join sports-mad Spaniards in everything from golf and boating to cycling and skiing.

Though you may have to trot out a little beginner's Spanish when visiting, Spain is one of the easiest and most rewarding European countries in which to travel, as well as one of the most affordable. You don't have to kiss your retirement fund goodbye for a two-week jaunt to Spain. Throughout the late 1990s, Spain ranked as one of the most affordable European destinations in nearly every respect. So far this millennium, prices have steadily dropped for most international travelers.

Spain is one of Europe's largest countries, though, so it's unlikely that you can go everywhere you wish — at least on this trip. You've got to pick and choose carefully, and that's where this book comes in handy. Rather than try and pack the entire country into a book that's too heavy to carry around, I began with the best of the best, the top destinations for a first- or second-time traveler to Spain: the places you've got to see, the best places to stay and eat, and easy ways to design regional trips instead of trying to scurry all over Spain and lose valuable time in the process. I also give you tips for saving money and make careful selections and recommendations in every crucial category, from small inns to great *tapas* bars (bars that serve Spanish appetizers) to choosing the best seat at a bullfight. And I steer you away from the places that really aren't worth your time.

This book differs from other guides. It doesn't just dump the information in your lap and expect you to sort it all out, somehow unearthing the gems in all that rough. I've traveled throughout Spain for nearly two decades now, and in this book, I list places and things to do that I recommend to close friends. Spaniards are famous for their spontaneity, but if you've never been there, landing in the Madrid or Barcelona airport and just winging it would be pretty daunting. I've done the homework so that you can hit the ground running — or relaxing, if that's more your speed.

I've loaded *Spain For Dummies,* 1st Edition, with easy-to-understand information and advice about Spanish customs, culture, and language. The
best place to start, though, may be with two simple phrases you're likely
to hear frequently in Spain: *Bienvenido* (Welcome) and *¡Salud!* (Cheers!).

About This Book

Spain for Dummies, 1st Edition, is designed for use as a reference text.
You don't have to plow through all the chapters like a novel from front to
back; the chapters function independently of each other, allowing you to
pick up with any planning section or city or regional chapter without
worrying about losing out on information placed elsewhere in the book.

Please note that travel information is subject to change at any time —
this is especially true of prices. Therefore, in this book, I suggest that
you write or call ahead for confirmation when making your travel
plans. The authors, editors, and publisher cannot be held responsible
for the experiences of readers while traveling. Your safety is important
to us, however, so we encourage you to stay alert and be aware of your
surroundings. Keep a close eye on cameras, purses, and wallets, which
are all favorite targets of thieves and pickpockets.

Conventions Used in This Book

In this book, I use some standard terminology to help you access information quickly and easily. For starters, all prices are given first in
Spanish pesetas (abbreviated *pta.*) and then in U.S. dollars ($), rounded
to the nearest five cents. Though the exchange rate fluctuates daily, the
rate I use in this guide is $1 = 180 pta.

I also use the Spanish method for providing street addresses. Using this
style, the building number comes after the street name, not before. For
example, if a hotel has a building number of 22 and is located on *Calle
Atocha* (Atocha Street), the address is written *Calle Atocha, 22.* Likewise,
in many small towns, you often come across an address in which the
building has no number. In these cases, the address is written *Calle
Atocha, s/n,* where *s/n* stands for *sin numero* (without number).

I've compiled my favorite hotels, restaurants, and attractions across
Spain. Especially for the hotels and restaurants, I include abbreviations
for commonly accepted credit cards. Take a look at the following list
for an explanation of each:

- AE — American Express
- DC — Diners Club
- MC — MasterCard
- V — Visa

In the larger destinations, I divide hotels and restaurants into two categories: my personal favorites (in a variety of price categories) and those that don't quite make the standout list but are still very much worth a stay or a meal. Don't be shy about considering these "runners-up" if you're unable to get a room or a reservation at one of my favorites or if your preferences diverge from mine.

I also include general pricing information to help you as you decide where to unpack your bags or dine. I use a system of dollar signs to show a range of costs for one night in a hotel (a double room) or a meal at a restaurant (included in the cost of each meal is a standard appetizer, main course, and dessert). With restaurants in particular, I also include, where applicable, information about fixed-price meals. With this option, you order from a special menu; select an appetizer, main course, dessert, and beverage; and pay a set price for the whole thing. These fixed-price meals (called *menú del día,* or "menu of the day," in Spain) often represent excellent value, and are a great way to eat cheaply in more expensive restaurants.

Check out the following table to decipher the dollar signs:

What the Dollar Signs Mean

Cost	Hotel	Restaurant
$	less than 8,000 pta. ($45)	less than 2,000 pta. ($11)
$$	8,000–17,000 pta. ($45–$95)	2,000–3,000 pta. ($11–$17)
$$$	17,000–25,000 pta. ($95–$140)	3,000–5,000 pta. ($17–$28)
$$$$	25,000–35,000 pta. ($140–$195)	5,000–8,000 pta. ($28–$45)
$$$$$	more than 35,000 pta. ($195)	more than 8,000 pta. ($45)

Foolish Assumptions

As I wrote this book, I had to make a few assumptions about you and what your needs may be as a traveler. I assume the following:

✔ You're an inexperienced traveler looking for guidance when determining whether to take a trip to Spain and how to plan for it.

Or . . .

✔ You're an experienced traveler, but you don't have a lot of time to devote to trip planning, or you don't have a lot of time to spend in Spain once you get there. You want expert advice on how to maximize your time and enjoy a hassle-free trip.

Or . . .

> ✔ You're not looking for a book that provides every last bit of information available about Spain or one that lists every hotel, restaurant, or attraction available to you. Instead, you're looking for a book that focuses on the places that will give you the best or most unique experience in Spain.

If you fit any of these criteria, rest assured that *Spain For Dummies,* 1st Edition, gives you the information you're looking for!

How This Book Is Organized

Spain For Dummies, 1st Edition, is divided into six major parts, beginning with introductory information about the country and planning advice and then moving on to the major regional sections, which contain individual destination chapters.

Part 1: Getting Started

The first part introduces you to the glories of Spain and helps you decide exactly where and when to go. It outlines some great itineraries, gives tips on planning your budget, and offers tailored tips to travelers with special interests — everything you need to consider before planning a trip to Spain.

Part 11: Ironing Out the Details

The second part helps you with all the nitty-gritty stuff — everything from what documents you need to searching the Web for more information and choosing and booking the best airfare and hotel (or package tour), to how to get around Spain, how to budget and pay for your trip, and figuring out exactly what you need to pack.

Part 111: Northern Spain: Barcelona, the Costa Brava, and the Basque Country

Part III covers the best of Northeastern Spain, including Barcelona, the Costa Brava, and the Basque Country.

Part IV: Central Spain: Madrid and Castile

Central Spain includes Madrid, Spain's capital, and the best of the surrounding region of Castile — Segovia, Salamanca, and Toledo, all easy side trips from the capital.

Part V: Southern Spain

This part is all about the region of Andalusia: Seville and Córdoba; Ronda, the so-called *Pueblos Blancos* (white villages), and the sunny coasts; and Granada.

In each of Parts III–V, you'll find a chapter on each major destination in the region. Each chapter includes all you need to know about getting there and getting around; information on the top hotels and restaurants; the top attractions and what to do, including shopping and nightlife; and easy side trips in the area.

Part VI: The Part of Tens

With a nod to my habit of making and keeping lists, the final part is a couple of Top 10 lists — a compendium of both my personal faves and curious tidbits about Spain.

You also find a few other elements near the back of this book. I include a few appendixes. Appendix A, "Quick Concierge," contains lots of handy information that you may need when traveling in Spain, such as phone numbers and addresses for emergency personnel or area hospitals and pharmacies, contact information for babysitters, lists of local newspapers and magazines, protocol for sending mail or finding taxis, and more. Check out this appendix when searching for answers to the many little questions that may come up as you travel. Appendix B, "A Guide to Spanish Art and Architecture," runs you through the major building styles and most famous artists to come from and out of Spain. You also find here a list of common architectural terms that may pop up as you visit Spain's many historical landmarks.

I also include a bunch of worksheets to make your travel planning easier. Among other things, you can determine your travel budget, create specific itineraries, and keep a log of your favorite restaurants so you can hit them again next time you're in town. You can find these worksheets easily because they're printed on yellow paper.

The Index cross-references the information in ways that let you see at a glance your options in a particular subcategory: for example, Basque restaurants, downtown hotels, and family-friendly attractions.

Icons Used in This Book

Keep your eyes peeled for these icons, which appear in the margins:

Discover ways to avoid hassles, wastes of time, and advice on how to schedule your time wisely as you travel in Spain when you see the Tip icon.

This icon steers you away from tourist traps, rip-offs, overrated activities, and places that aren't worth the trouble, as well as other pitfalls of traveling. On occasion, Heads Up icons also indicate words to the wise aimed to make you look and feel less like a *guiri* (foreigner).

A Kid Friendly icon identifies hotels, activities, attractions, and establishments that are especially suited to people traveling with children.

Keep an eye out for this icon for tips on pinching *pesetas* and cutting corners to make your trip more affordable, as well as things to do and see that are, in my opinion, great deals.

This icon designates those destinations and attractions that may be just off or even considerably beyond the beaten track. Such attractions are well worth seeking out if you have a bit of extra time and interest in seeing more than only the big-name greatest hits that most people have heard of. This symbol designates authentic doses of Spanish culture and *España* at its most authentic, from customs to food and drink.

Where to Go from Here

At this point, you're ready to dive into Spain and design the trip that best suits you. Doing so is not as tough as it sounds. If you're stressing about finding time to brush up on your Spanish, visit travel agents, research Spain, and plan your trip at the same time, relax. Planning your trip doesn't have to be a hassle, and daydreaming about all the cool stuff you'll see and do can actually be fun.

If you're not sure yet what part(s) of Spain you want to visit, check out the first three chapters of this book, which give you an overview of the cities, regions, and highlights, as well as the best times to go. If a particular city or region strikes your fancy, you may want to skip ahead to the corresponding chapters to read about it in more detail (see the Contents at a Glance page, near the front of the book).

However, if you already have a good idea of when and where you'd like to visit, perhaps you'd rather begin with the nitty-gritty of planning your budget (Chapter 4) and looking into airfare, accommodations, and package tours, or transportation and money particulars (all found in Chapters 6 through 10 of Part II). Either method of research is perfectly acceptable. It is your trip, after all!

Part I
Getting Started

The 5th Wave   By Rich Tennant

"And how shall I book your flight to
Spain – First Class, Coach, or Medieval?"

In this part . . .

I give you a concise overview of Spain, including its
people, history, culture, and some of its biggest attractions region by region. I also outline some possible itineraries and cover the preliminaries for your trip to Spain,
including planning a budget, keeping costs down, and
providing specific advice for families, seniors, and other
travelers with individual needs.

Use the information in this part to help you decide where
and when to go; you'll not only get started, you'll be on
your way to Spain in no time.

Chapter 1

Discovering the Best of Spain

*E*ven though images of Spanish culture are pervasive, Spain is, of course, a foreign country, with different customs, laws, and cultural assumptions than the United States. Because you don't want to hit the ground knowing nothing about Spain, I address — very briefly — Spanish history, language, art, and architecture. Likewise, I also discuss the fun stuff like dining, drinking, and shopping.

Welcome to España

The saying goes that it never rains in Spain, but this southern European country of 40 million people (and even more annual visitors) reigns on the pop-culture radar. Don't believe me? Think about these examples: Don Quixote; Don Juan; bullfights (Hemingway's famous *Death in the Afternoon*) and the Running of the Bulls; and Pablo Picasso and Salvador Dalí, towering figures as inimitable as their groundbreaking art.

Those are just a few images of Spain, and I haven't yet mentioned the fiery rhythms of gypsy flamenco, miles of sun-drenched beaches, lazy mid-afternoon siestas, costumed religious festivals, and raucous bars flowing with wine and tantalizing *tapas* (small plates of appetizers). In the language used to write travel brochures and promote study-abroad programs, Spain has become shorthand for sun, fun, and passion.

Spain

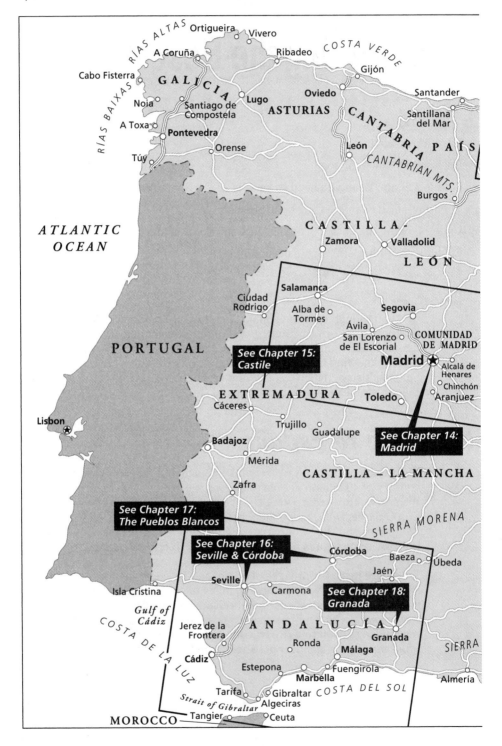

ATLANTIC
OCEAN

RIAS ALTAS

Ortigueira · Vivero

A Coruña · Ribadeo

Cabo Fisterra

COSTA VERDE

Gijón

GALICIA

Santander

RIAS BAIXAS

Noia · Lugo · Oviedo

Santiago de Compostela

ASTURIAS

CANTABRIA

Santillana del Mar

A Toxa · Pontevedra

PAÍS

Orense

León

Túy

CANTABRIAN MTS.

Burgos

CASTILLA-

Zamora · Valladolid

LEÓN

Salamanca

Ciudad Rodrigo

Segovia

Alba de Tormes

Ávila

San Lorenzo de El Escorial

COMUNIDAD DE MADRID

PORTUGAL

See Chapter 15: Castile

Madrid ★

Alcalá de Henares

Chinchón

EXTREMADURA · Toledo · Aranjuez

Cáceres

Trujillo · Guadalupe

See Chapter 14: Madrid

Lisbon ★

Badajoz

Mérida

CASTILLA – LA MANCHA

Zafra

See Chapter 17: The Pueblos Blancos

SIERRA MORENA

See Chapter 16: Seville & Córdoba

Córdoba · Baeza · Úbeda

Jaén

Isla Cristina

Seville · Carmona

See Chapter 18: Granada

Gulf of Cádiz

COSTA DE LA LUZ

Jerez de la Frontera

ANDALUCÍA

Ronda · Granada

SIERRA

Cádiz

Málaga

Estepona · Fuengirola

Marbella

Almería

Tarifa · Gibraltar

COSTA DEL SOL

Strait of Gibraltar · Algeciras

MOROCCO

Tangier · Ceuta

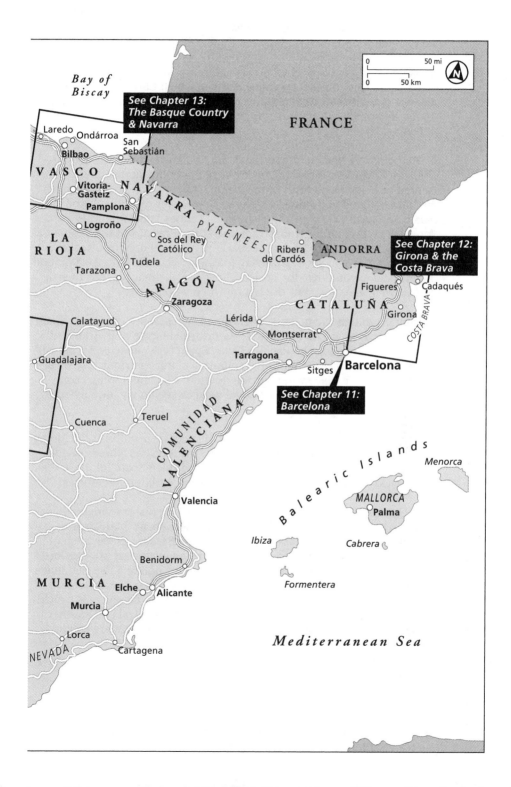

Bay of
Biscay

FRANCE

0   50 mi
0   50 km

**See Chapter 13:
The Basque Country
& Navarra**

Laredo
Ondárroa
San
Sebastián
Bilbao

V A S C O

Vitoria-
Gasteiz
Pamplona

N A V A R R A

Logroño

**L A
R I O J A**

Sos del Rey
Católico

Tudela

Tarazona

P Y R E N E E S

Ribera
de Cardós

ANDORRA

**See Chapter 12:
Girona & the
Costa Brava**

Figueres
Cadaqués

A R A G Ó N

Zaragoza

Lérida

C A T A L U Ñ A

Girona

C O S T A   B R A V A

Calatayud

Montserrat

Guadalajara

Tarragona

Sitges

Barcelona

**See Chapter 11:
Barcelona**

Cuenca

Teruel

**C O M U N I D A D
V A L E N C I A N A**

B a l e a r i c   I s l a n d s

Menorca

Valencia

M A L L O R C A
Palma

Ibiza

Cabrera

Benidorm

Formentera

M U R C I A   Elche
Alicante

Murcia

Lorca

NEVADA
Cartagena

M e d i t e r r a n e a n   S e a

But Spain is much more than one big cliché. Though a little smaller than Texas, Spain is a remarkably varied nation, with five indigenous languages, people with their own unique cultures and histories, and an astounding geographical diversity. Spain's geography ranges from 11,000-foot peaks to parched plains and rainy green hills that look more like Ireland than the stereotypical Spain in which Carmen (heroine of the opera of the same name) once strutted her stuff. Wherever you touch down, Spain is a fascinating country, a place to plunge into and return again and again.

Perhaps you've been dying to check out Spain ever since the 1992 Summer Olympics splashed cutting-edge Barcelona across the TV screen or because pictures of the gleaming new Guggenheim Museum in Bilbao piqued your interest. Maybe a coworker recently visited Spain and hasn't shut up about the great castles and cathedrals, Moorish monuments, art masterpieces at the Prado, and the Spaniards' unparalleled ability to forego sleep. Or, maybe you're a thrill-seeker and every July you get a hankering to run for your life with 2,000-pound bulls chasing you down the street. Those are all great reasons to visit Spain (well, maybe all but the last one, in my opinion).

During its golden age in the sixteenth and seventeenth centuries, Spain was the most powerful nation in the world, an empire that stretched from the Americas to the Pacific. Today Spain is dynamic and modern, but also starkly traditional, with reminders of its illustrious history at every turn. It's a place where ultramodern design and a robust economy come face-to-face with medieval villages seemingly untouched by the passing centuries.

Ancient Spain was inhabited by waves of successive cultures, including the Romans, Visigoths, Celts, and Moors (the Muslims who crossed into Spain from North Africa and lived in and ruled Spain for more than 700 years). Today Spain continues as a nation of different cultures.

The *Catalans* in the northeast corner have a long history independent of the rest of Spain, and for the most part, they speak Spanish as a second language, after Catalan. Up north, the *Basques* are an ancient people who have preserved an inscrutable language that boggles linguists, and many Basques continue to argue for political independence from Spain. *Gallegos,* the people of Galicia, a region in the extreme northwest of Spain, descended from the Celts; their language is a melding of Portuguese and Spanish. The Spaniards of central and southern Spain speak the national language, but their regional ties are just as strong as those felt by the Basques and Catalans. Despite these distinct cultures and disparate points of view, Spain seems incapable of disintegrating into small factions of independent states like some other European nations. (To get an idea of where these regions are located, see the "Spain" map in this chapter.)

That's one Spain, a historic and complex European nation. But Spain is also a vacation wonderland. Northern Europeans flock to the far south for its vastly superior year-round weather. Enticed by 300 days a year of sunshine, they crowd the beaches all along Spain's east and south coasts, as well as on the islands — and turn a pretty shade of pink in the process. You can go boating, golfing, hiking, cycling, or take part in virtually any outdoor activity that ends in –ing, including skiing. Although Spain may not quite rank with the Alps, you can hit the slopes in winter in the Pyrenees in the north and the Sierra Nevada down south.

Spanish History 101

Spain, one of the oldest inhabited places on Earth, has a long and complicated history of conquerors and cultures. Cave-dwellers and hunters-gatherers — perhaps the forefathers of the Basque people — arrived on the Iberian Peninsula, around 800,000 B.C. The prehistoric cave paintings of animals in **Altamira,** in the north of Spain, date from at least 13,000 B.C. and are possibly the world's oldest.

Some 5,000 years ago, at the beginning of recorded history, a people known as Iberians occupied parts of Spain. By 1100 B.C., a series of Mediterranean invaders began a pattern of conquests. First came the Phoenicians, followed by the Greeks and Carthaginians. The Romans conquered Iberia around 200 B.C., and it remained part of their massive empire until A.D. 414, when they ceded the Peninsula to the Visigoths, who remained in Spain some 300 years.

The next group of invaders had a huge and lasting impact on Spanish culture, language, and architecture. The **Moors** crossed the Strait of Gibraltar from North Africa in A.D. 711. In 756, they founded an independent Muslim emirate in Córdoba, Europe's most advanced city during the ninth and tenth centuries. The Moorish occupation of Iberia — which endured for nearly eight centuries — extended all the way to the Basque Country in the north of Spain and resulted in a prosperous civilization, **Al-Andalus** (today's Andalusia).

By the eleventh century, though, Muslim dominance weakened, and Christian kingdoms ruled the north of Spain in Navarra, León, Castile, Aragón, and Barcelona. About this time, pilgrims began to make their way from all over Europe along the St. James trail across northern Spain to Santiago de Compostela, in Galicia. Factions developed in the Moorish Caliphate and eroded the emirate's power and influence. The Moors suffered losses to the Christians in many parts of Spain, and the sphere of Moorish control shrank to the Nazarid kingdom in **Granada,** site of the spectacular Alhambra palace. *Los Reyes Católicos,* the Catholic Monarchs Ferdinand and Isabel, captured Granada in 1492, capping the **Reconquest** campaign to rid Spain of the Moors. The year was the beginning of perhaps the most important phase — certainly the best documented — in Spanish history.

The **Spanish Inquisition,** a campaign of religious fervor and severe
repression of Jews, Moors, and Protestants, was instituted several
years before the end of the Reconquest. After their victory, the
Catholic kings declared Catholicism the national religion of Spain. All
Jews were expelled in 1492, and Moors were given the choice to con-
vert to Christianity or meet with the same fate. The same year, Italian-
born Cristóbal Colón — also known as Christopher Columbus — was
credited with discovering the Americas. Spain, under the Catholic
Monarchs, then entered a period of glory during the sixteenth century.
Carlos, a Hapsburg and the son of Queen Juana (called Juana the Mad)
and King Philip (called Philip the Fair), became king and was named
Carlos V, Holy Roman Emperor in 1519. Riches flowed back to Spain
from the unabashed pillaging of the New World. Under Carlos (Charles)
V and Felipe (Philip) II, Spain flourished, extending its colonies
throughout the Americas and as far as the Pacific. Madrid became the
capital of Spain in 1561, but an economic crisis of inflation and debt
rocked the country, the result of a succession of wars against France
and other European countries.

By the end of the sixteenth century, political and economic decline
beset Spain, even as it entered its greatest artistic period. The seventeenth century is known as Spain's "Golden Age," because the art
patronage of the Hapsburgs gave rise to brilliance of painters such as
Velázquez, El Greco, Zurbarán, Ribera, and Murillo. Felipe V and the
Bourbon dynasty assumed the throne in the 1700s, but additional wars
and unenlightened leadership further weakened the country. Another
artistic genius, the wildly talented court painter Francisco de Goya,
emerged. Napoleon invaded Spain in the early nineteenth century, and
Spain lost its American colonies to wars of independence. In Barcelona
and then Paris, Pablo Picasso became an art world star, basically defining twentieth-century modern art.

Spain was neutral during the first World War (1914–1917), but political
instability reigned. By the 1920s, Spain found itself under a military dic-
tatorship (though the king remained on the throne); in 1931, a revolution led to the formation of a republic, forcing King Alfonso XIII to flee
the country. In 1936, the army ended the five-year-old Second Republic,
and civil war broke out. Ultraconservative Nationalist troops led by
General Francisco Franco stormed the country and fought Republican
and Anarchist factions for three years, defeating them in horrific bat-
tles that drew volunteers to the Republican side from England and the
United States. Franco emerged as the military victor. He ruled as a
repressive dictator for almost 40 years.

After the end of World War II, Franco was the only remaining fascist
head of state in Europe, and he isolated Spain from the rest of Europe,
severely impeding economic development. After his death in 1975,
Juan Carlos, the hand-picked successor to Franco, became king of
Spain, and democracy was restored. Spain's budding democracy suffered a grave threat on February 23, 1981, when the military struck a

coup, even firing shots in Parliament. But King Juan Carlos interceded, putting the military in its place and preserving Spain's post-Franco democracy.

Spain entered the European Economic Community (now called the European Union) in 1986 and announced its growing international presence with the celebration of the Summer Olympics in Barcelona and the World Expo in Seville, both in 1992. The Socialist Prime Minister Felipe González failed to get elected for a third term, and the center-right Popular Party candidate José María Aznar was elected in 1996. Tourism, one of the country's most important industries since the late 1960s, continued to grow exponentially, and by the beginning of the twenty-first century, Spain had catapulted to second place among the most visited countries in the world.

Touring with Your Taste Buds in Mind

One of the primary pleasures of visiting Spain is eating and drinking. The predominantly Mediterranean diet is rich in olive oil, garlic, tomatoes, and peppers. The Moors introduced Middle Eastern elements, like rice and saffron, to Spanish cooking. You've probably heard of, and maybe even tried, *paella* (the huge rice-based seafood dish), *gazpacho* (cold vegetable soup) and *tapas* (see the sidebar "Talking tapas," later in this chapter).

But Spanish food is much more than those signature dishes. If you're expecting to eat only heavy, medieval-like cooking, or if you assume Spain produces spicy Latino dishes, you're in for a big surprise. In Spain, you can find fresh seafood as well as classic Castilian dishes like roast suckling pig. In general, you receive fresh and fine-quality ingredients.

Spanish food has really started to make its mark around the world, with *tapas* bars sprouting like mushrooms in the U.S., Canada, and the U.K. At some places abroad, *tapas* are just an excuse to serve a tiny bit of food for a big price, but that's not the case in Spain. *Tapas,* which cover everything from free little snacks like olives, chips, slices of spicy chorizo sausage, and cubes of cheese to haute-cuisine mini-meals, are a longtime Spanish tradition. Joining a jubilant *tapeo,* or *tapas* crawl, is one of the finest eating experiences in Spain. People refer to *tapas* bars by a variety of names — *tascas, mesones, bodegas, tabernas* — but they all serve small amounts of food and abundant quantities of beer and wine. Like ravenous Spaniards, you can saunter from bar to bar, nibbling on an amazing array of snack foods laid out before you, and wash it all down with sherry, wine, or beer. *Tapas* are meant to be shared among friends — or new acquaintances. My advice: Grab a toothpick and dive in.

Beyond *tapas* and the ubiquitous *tortilla española* (a potato-and-onion omelet, served either hot or cold), speaking of a national Spanish cuisine is nearly impossible. Instead, Spain has a number of unique regional cuisines. With Catalonia's rich Mediterranean diet, both sophisticated and rustic; the Basque Country's delicate preparations; Central Spain's roasted meats and game; Galicia's fresh seafood; and Andalusia's revered cured hams and refreshing cold vegetable soups, you'll find a culinary variety in Spain that would be hard to match anywhere else in the world.

Spain is surrounded on almost all sides by water, and fresh seafood forms a fundamental part of the Spanish diet. But meat is equally important. Except in restaurants that specialize in shellfish by the pound (and I include only a couple of that variety in my suggestions throughout this book), you can get meat and non-meat appetizers and entrees everywhere. Spaniards especially love pork and cured ham. In fact, *jamón serrano* (cured ham) is one of Spain's true delicacies. Spaniards also eat a lot of chicken, salads, and fresh fruits and vegetables. Spain is not the easiest place for vegetarians (and is harder still for vegans); vegetarian restaurants are few and far between. But nearly every restaurant has a good selection of salads, non-meat soups and vegetables.

Knowing what to expect when you're eating out

The first thing you should know is that Spaniards are passionate about food. Dining — whether at home in the kitchen, at a tavern, or at an elegant restaurant — is an important social affair, a time to relax and an event to prepare for, savor, and talk about afterwards. Spaniards eat little or no breakfast, snack a lot, and consume full three- and four-course meals for lunch and often dinner (though dinner is more frequently a much lighter affair — perhaps salad and a *tortilla*). Lunch is the main meal of the day, and it's always cheaper to savor a fine meal at this time than it is at night. Look for the fixed-price *menú del día* (menu of the day), which usually includes an appetizer, main course, dessert, bread, and wine or water for a very reasonable price (often around $10 or so).

One of the highlights of eating in Spain is sampling regional specialties — *suquet de peix* (seafood stew) in Catalonia; *cordero asado* (roast baby lamb) in Castile; *pulpo a feira* (octopus with paprika) in Galicia; *bacalao al pil-pil* (salt cod in garlic sauce) in the Basque Country; *gambas al ajillo* (garlic-soaked shrimp) in Andalusia, and many more. In each chapter, I highlight some of the typical regional dishes. Look for the sections titled "Eating Like A . . ." and try what I recommend.

Talking tapas

The hunt for *tapas* is called a *tapeo*. The term *tapas* covers all manners of snacking, but there's actually an entire vocabulary to go along with finger foods. A *ración* ("rah-*thyone*") is a full serving, a plate to be shared with one or more *amigos* (friends). You may, however, consume a *media-ración* (half-ration) solo. A *tapa*, strictly speaking, is either a tiny morsel served free along with your beverage, or a slightly more substantial single serving, also called a *pincho* ("*peen*-choh").

The word *tapa* means "lid," and *tapas* the snacks emerged from a tradition of placing scraps of food on top of wine jugs in taverns. Patrons drank the wine and then downed the lid, too. Pretty soon, tavern owners started setting snack-filled saucers on top of drinks. The *tapeo,* the often boisterous bar-to-bar snack cruising, has its own curious origin. After church, men would gather at the tavern while the women went home to prepare the Sunday meal. The men would stroll from tavern to tavern, meeting up with friends and scarfing down finger foods and wine on their way home, marking time until dinner.

You'll find a whole range of restaurants in Spain, from informal taverns and family-owned joints to elegant European dining rooms. In the cities, finding a wide variety of cuisines — French and Italian are common, and more diverse ethnic choices, such as Vietnamese, Mexican, and Indian, are also beginning to take hold — won't present a problem. In this book, however, I focus mostly on the best Spanish restaurants (though Spanish is really a misnomer, because it's really regional Spanish cooking that you'll sample).

Tasting Spanish vino

Spain's excellent wines are finally earning a deserved worldwide acclaim and are popping up in restaurants that have nothing to do with *tapas*. If you're a wine drinker, you may find heaven in Spain. Not only will you get to try wines you won't find at home, you'll also adore the prices. Wine is a staple of the Spanish diet, and Spain doesn't burden it with ridiculous taxes. Even fine wines are amazingly affordable in restaurants; you can have a splendid bottle for $10. However, keep in mind that Spain is predominantly a red wine drinking country, and across the board, reds are the country's standouts.

When sampling Spanish wines, you can choose from *vinos tintos* (rich reds, made predominantly from the tempranillo grape) from wineries in **Rioja** and **Ribera del Duero** (north of Madrid), as well as **Penedès** and **Priorato** (south of Barcelona). Several *vinos blancos* (white wines) from **Penedès** and **Rioja** are quite good, too. The young and fruity whites of

Galicia, Albariños and **Ribeiros,** are excellent with shellfish. And there's *jerez* (sherry) from the south and the world's best-selling bubbly, *cava,* the sparkling wine of Catalonia. If you're confused and not really much of a wine connoisseur, you usually can't go wrong with the *vino de la casa,* the house wine. (In small restaurants the house wine is a carafe or bottle of regional wine, while in fine restaurants it may be a bottle selected by the sommelier or a wine made especially for the restaurant.)

You've probably had *sangria,* and many tourists who go to Spain sit down to a fruity pitcher of it at every stop. But most sangria is a tourist concoction, little more than wine-based Kool-Aid. Many restaurant owners know foreigners want it, so they trot out their cheapest wine, dilute it, and toss in a couple of thin orange slices. Voilà! *Sangria.* Maybe you'll be lucky, though, and enjoy splendid, fruity sangria that actually tastes like wine at a small tavern or restaurant. However, I don't order it at one of those obviously touristy places with menus in six languages splayed on sandwich boards.

Enjoying other drinks

Spaniards drink nearly as much wine as their neighbors, the French, but if you're not a wine drinker (or you don't drink, period), don't worry. All the familiar American soft drinks are available, as well as fruit juices — primarily fresh-squeezed orange juice from Valencian oranges. Wherever you see *zumo* ("*thoo*-moh"), that means "juice." Bottled water is available in every restaurant and snack shop, but don't expect to get huge jugs of iced tea. If you ask for *té* (tea), you'll receive it hot, the way the Spaniards drink it.

The price is right

If you eat wisely in Spain, you can keep your costs down and eat wonderfully for much less than you would spend in most other parts of Europe. However, if you eat like a Spaniard — four-course meals twice daily with a bottle of wine each time — you may find your food budget becoming as tight as your belt. At lunch, a cheap *menú del día* (menu of the day) costs $8 or less; at a mid-range restaurant, expect to pay between $8 and $15; and an upscale restaurant costs between $15 and $25. At lunch, paying much more than that is rare. You generally spend more at dinner, when *menús del día* are much less common, because in Spain, you almost always order dinner *à la carte* (menu items priced separately). An inexpensive restaurant likely costs between $10 and $17 for a full dinner; at the moderate range, between $17 and $30; and at upscale restaurants, dinner starts around $30 per person and goes up from there. At even the very finest Spanish restaurants, though, you're unlikely to spend much more than $75 a head — something that seems ridiculously easy to do in London, Paris, or New York.

Siesta!

The *siesta*, a post-lunch nap, used to be one of the defining characteristics of Spain. Yet only 20 percent of Spaniards, according to a study by Barcelona's Dexeus Institute, continue to find time for daily siestas. However, although businesses and shops slowly conform to American or European work schedules, many continue to close between 1:30 or 2 and 4 p.m.

A *siesta* in the afternoon follows natural sleep patterns. Doctors recommend that you limit your *siesta* to approximately 20 minutes on the sofa, and not in bed (which can trick you into expecting a full night's sleep). If you sleep for more than 20 minutes, watch out: You're likely to wake up on the cranky side.

Chow time: Knowing when and what to eat

The rhythm of the day corresponds to meals in Spain, rather than the inverse. Spaniards eat late, and meals are leisurely, compared to many northern countries. You may want to try and adopt the rhythm of later mealtimes before you go, if you don't want to feel continually frustrated and hungry. Face it, Spain isn't going to adapt itself to your desire to eat lunch at noon and dinner at 6 p.m. (though a handful of tourist-oriented restaurants may).

Breakfast (Desayuno)

For *desayuno* (breakfast), most Spaniards eat little — perhaps just a *café con leche* (coffee with milk) and a few *tostadas* (toast with jam, cheese, or sometimes ham and olive oil) or *churros* (fritters) — on their way to the office. They more commonly get to the office and then, around 10am, drop down to the local bar or café for a croissant and coffee. (Don't be surprised if you see men powering back beer, sherry, or sneaking a shot of something stronger in their coffee.)

Lunch (Almuerzo; Comida)

Membership in the European Union is slowly but surely changing Spaniards' daily routines and eroding some long-held traditions. Today fewer and fewer people return home from the office for the midday meal and quick *siesta*. Sandwich shops are making inroads, and many bars and cafes sell *bocadillos* (cheese, ham, tortilla, and chorizo sandwiches). However, *almuerzo* (lunch — known as *comida,* too) remains the centerpiece of the day, and many offices close between 1:30 p.m. or 2 p.m. and 4 p.m.. Few Spaniards bring food from home and eat at their desk. Those that can, go home and eat lunch with their family. Most restaurants open for lunch business at 1 p.m., but only begin to see crowds just after 2 p.m. (Sneaking in before the 2 o'clock rush is wise.)

The midday fixed-priced menu, which has all but disappeared in France and other countries, remains one of Spain's best deals. For a fixed price (usually around 10 bucks), you can enjoy a three-course meal, often including a bottle of house wine.

Few Spaniards in a restaurant opt for a small salad for their meal. Even after a round of pre-lunch *tapas,* most native people have a salad, soup, or other appetizer to begin their meal, a meat or fish entrée as a main course, and coffee or dessert (often fruit) to finish. Wine is usually included in fixed-price *menús del día,* and Spaniards not only share a bottle of wine over lunch, but they may very well have a cocktail before or cognac after the meal, too. If you're a single traveler, don't be surprised if you get a full carafe or bottle of house wine placed in front of you with the *menú del día.* You decide whether you want to knock off the whole thing, but if you do, don't expect to do much sightseeing in the afternoon!

Dinner (Cena)

In Spain, the *tarde* (afternoon) lasts until 8 p.m. or so, so if you sit down to supper at 6 or 7 p.m, you'll be eating dinner in the afternoon, a most peculiar concept in Spain. People in Spain eat dinner uncommonly late, usually from 9 p.m. to 11 p.m. or even later (when I lived in Spain, I frequently sat down to dinner with friends at midnight).

For most North Americans and northern Europeans, Spain's dinner hours are absurdly late. You don't have to eat quite as late as locals, however. Restaurants generally open for dinner at 8 p.m., though you can expect to be one of the few people ordering dinner at that hour. Everybody else is in the bar enjoying *tapas* and cocktails. The best plan is to down some *tapas* at your normal dinnertime to pace yourself for the late hours.

In Spanish homes, dinner is often a light and late meal — perhaps some leftovers from the main meal, lunch, or a salad and a wedge of tortilla. When dining at restaurants, though, most Spaniards can't resist doing the full-course trot: 1-2-3-coffee.

The coffee buzz

Spaniards love coffee, and stopping for *café* is a several-times-a-day ritual. If you order *un café* in Spain, you'll get a small cup of espresso, rich, strong, and delicious. If you're not an espresso drinker, ask for either a *café con leche* (coffee with milk, which is half milk) or a *café americano* (yes, they're sort of making fun of us gringos, but you get a weaker cup of coffee — they dilute it with water).

No Comprendo: Making Yourself Understood in Spanish (Or Inglés)

Until recently, Spaniards mostly studied French and spoke little English. That has changed since the country's introduction into the European Union and the increasing globalization of MTV, ESPN, and HBO English. English is now the foreign language of choice, and even if only few people over the age of 40 or 50 speak it, many young people do. And, of course, most major hotels have staff fluent in English.

However, Spain remains profoundly Spanish, and, in some ways, resistant to global homogenization. Only in primary tourist areas and tourist restaurants is English flung around with impressive ease. Knowing (or remembering from high school or college) some *español* (Spanish) will provide great assistance on your trip. You can talk to more people, get clearer directions, and you won't be quite as surprised when plates are set down in front of you.

If conjugating verbs is way beyond you and all you want is the ability to utter a few basic pleasantries and ask a few pointed questions, you shouldn't have too much trouble. The most important words and phrases to learn are: *por favor* (please), *gracias* (thank you; "*grah*-thee-ahs"), and *¿Habla inglés?* (Do you speak English?, "*ah*-blah *een*-glayse"). Never assume automatically that someone speaks your language. You win big points by asking politely if he or she does.

Speaking Spanish in Spain

Two features most distinguish Iberian Spanish (the type spoken in Spain) from Latin American Spanish. One is the lisp-heavy pronunciation of the letters *c* and *z*. Thus, in Spain, *cerveza* (beer) is pronounced "thare-*bay*-tha," and the native population uses the third-person *vosotros* (you) form, rather than the *Ustedes* form common throughout Latin America. So in Spain, "What are you doing?" becomes "*¿Qué hacéis?*" ("kay ah-*thace*") rather than "*¿Qué hacen?*" ("kay *ah*-then").

Beyond these minor differences, Spanish is one of the rare languages that is perfectly phonetic, so don't worry about lisping and give it your best shot. Pronounce every letter, and don't worry about missing accents and confusing masculine and feminine articles and objects. Spaniards aren't at all like the notoriously snooty French (okay, Parisians), who sometimes look down on foreigners mangling their language. Natives amply appreciate any effort to speak Spanish, and you will receive a warm response. Check out the handy Cheat Sheet in the front of this book for some more phrases and important menu terms. Also, check out *Spanish For Dummies* by Susana Wald (Hungry Minds, Inc.) if you're interested in broadening your foreign-language abilities.

Sounding like a Spaniard

Spaniards are wonderfully expressive. Their voices are deep — most Spanish women sound as though they're speaking straight from the sternum. If you know some Spanish, and especially if you know the kind they never taught you in high school, you'll marvel at how widely everyone swears. A foreigner prone to parroting the locals can run into difficulties. Don't repeat anyone unless you know what they're saying — and you mean to say the same. Table 1-1 includes some other words that'll make you sound like a native.

Table 1-1	Dang-nabit! A Few Phrases to Know	
Exclamation	*Pronunciation*	*Meaning*
¡Hombre!	("ohm-bray")	"Man!" A common exclamation with a zillion applications and intonations. You'll see men and women exclaiming it when they've cut into a great steak, seen an old friend, or when they don't believe a word that the old friend says.
Vale	("*ball*-ay")	"Okay, yeah, right, I'll do it, yep, okay, no problem, I said okay, all right?" Spaniards are capable of uttering *vale* up to eight times in a single sentence — saying it more than once makes it a slightly more forceful pronouncement.
¡Ostras!	("*owe*-struhs")	Literally "oysters," it's a substitute expletive, something like "fudge!"
¡Miércoles!	("mee-*yayr*-koh-lace")	Translated as Wednesday, it's another good Spanish substitute swear word, for the already inoffensive (in Spain, anyway) *mierda* (the s-word in the U.S.).

Taking Notes on Nightlife

Spaniards are true creatures of the night — they often don't finish dinner until well after midnight and most visitors can't really hope to compete when it comes to owning the wee hours. If you conform to a Spanish schedule, a night out may not consist of much more than going to dinner and maybe having a nightcap somewhere (that is if you want to get up the next day at a reasonable hour). To really make a night of it — going dancing and to bars and clubs — the action doesn't heat up in most places until well after 1 a.m.

Smoked out

As soon as Spaniards get off a plane, most will light up, especially after international, nicotine-depriving flights. While waiting for your baggage, you receive a fine introduction to smoke-heavy Spain. Sometimes it seems like a smoldering cigarette in hand is as much part of the school uniform as a bookbag for teen (and even pre-teen) school kids. Don't go to Spain — or any part of Europe for that matter — expecting a slew of no-smoking signs and separate non-smoking sections in restaurants. A North America-like smoke-free environment is nearly impossible to find. Yes, many top hotels have nonsmoking rooms and floors, and legally you can't smoke on subways and buses, but be prepared for a waft of cigarette smoke to envelop you in more places than not. Among men in the European Union, the percentage of smokers in Spain trails only Greece. A total of 35.7 percent of Spaniards over the age of 16 smoke (44 percent of men, a number that has slowly declined, compared with 27 percent among women, a figure on the rise). If you're severely affected by second-hand cigarette smoke, do your best to stay out of bars, especially late at night, and look for airy restaurants with outdoor seating and high ceilings. Some Spaniards are beginning to respect others' polite requests for them to refrain from smoking, but don't count on it. Cigarette smoke, and lots of it, comes with the territory.

Bringing Back the Loot: Shopping in Spain

Your dollars may go much farther in Spain than you expect, thanks to a favorable exchange rate and the continued decrease of the euro, the European Union's common currency (see Chapter 9). So get ready for some good deals (barring, of course, a major crash in the dollar or sudden surge of the euro between the writing of this book and your trip). In this section, I give you a few ideas for what to pick up and the best places to score big.

 In Spain, sales are coordinated by law, with twice-annual sell-offs of inventory that all begin at the same time: the second week of January and the last week of July. Signs announcing *rebajas* (sales) are plastered over store windows. Prices continue to drop when stores move from first to second and finally, ultimate *rebajas* (like the final clearance sale).

Good shopping can be found throughout the country. For antiques and flea markets, check out Barcelona, Girona, Madrid, and Seville. Big pieces are tough to lug home, but Spain's a great place for antique odds and ends. Barcelona reigns supreme for design and home objects. The Catalan capital is on the cutting edge; if you're fascinated by cool design and works of art, it's definitely the place to drop some bucks. For clothing by Spanish designers, save your *pesetas* for Barcelona, Madrid, and Seville, all of which have excellent local designers and the shops of the country's big names, such as Roberto Verino and Adolfo Domingo. See Chapter 9 for a discussion of the *peseta,* Spain's national currency.

You can find nice jewelry throughout Spain, but several places offer particularly good indigenous stuff. Look for *azabache* (jetstone) in Santiago de Compostela, and Majorca pearls (the brilliant fakes) in Palma de Mallorca (as well as in the major mainland cities). For quality ceramics, plan on shopping stops in Palma de Mallorca, the Costa Brava (especially La Bisbal), Madrid, Talavera de la Reina, Toledo, and Seville. If you're looking for something for your *señorita* (lady) or if you're the *señorita,* pick up Spanish fans, shawls, and flamenco dresses in Seville and Córdoba. The top crafts centers are Toledo (for such damascene objects as swords, letter openers, and jewelry), Córdoba (leather, silver filigree), and Granada (iron objects, leather, guitars).

Embroidery is big in Palma de Mallorca, Toledo, and two small towns outside of Toledo, Lagartera and Oropesa. Another good gift, best purchased at the end of your trip to avoid lugging the weight, is Spanish wine. Look for Penedès wines in Barcelona, Albariños in Galicia, Riojas in Navarra, and sherries, such as *fino* and *manzanilla* throughout Andalucía, but particularly in Jerez de la Frontera.

Enjoying Sports and the Great Outdoors

Spain is sports-mad, and Spaniards are equally passionate participants and spectators. *Fútbol* (soccer) is hands-down the national obsession, but cycling, golf, tennis, hiking, and water sports are also extremely popular. If you're a soccer fan, check out a *fútbol* game in Barcelona (FC Barça) or Madrid (Real Madrid) to see madness take possession of 100,000 people. If you're a recreational golfer, sunny Spain is one of the best countries in Europe for a golf vacation. With top pros like Seve Ballesteros, José María Olazábal, and Sergio García, Spaniards have gone for golf in a big way. There are nearly 200 courses, most in sunny Andalusia and Catalonia. Several tour operators and hotels, including some national *paradors* (government-owned inns), offer golf packages. (See Chapter 6 for packagers and Chapters 12 and 17 on Catalonia and Andalusia for more information on golfing in Spain).

Witnessing the Raging Bull

To many Spaniards, bullfighting is art, high drama, cultural tradition, delicate choreography, and a respected ritual with all the solemnity of midnight mass — anything but sport. I've been to a number of bullfights and had friends explain it and praise its virtues with great passion, but I still don't see the appeal. To me, it remains the slaughter of innocent and magnificent creatures, no matter how you spin it. Despite the foreigners who became fans of the sport — most famously, Ernest Hemingway and Orson Welles — everybody else probably needs Spanish blood coursing through their veins to really appreciate the drama of life-and-death struggle. The rest of us see it only as a life-and-death struggle for the bull.

Even though you're unlikely to fully grasp its nature, a *corrida* — bullfight — in Madrid, Seville, or Ronda is something to see once in your life (but not if you're squeamish). The bullfight is all about the pageantry, bravery, and risking death for one's art, which underlines the Spanish obsession with mortality and their fascination with violence and blood. Practiced since the Middle Ages and once unleashed in town squares, bullfighting, once on the wane, is again enjoying renewed popularity in Spain. Top *matadors* (bullfighters) are national celebrities whose spotlights eclipse even matinee idols.

There are three basic chapters in a bullfight. In the first, the matador appraises his opponent and entices the fighting bull with a large pink cape. *Picadores* (horsemen) use long lances used to weaken the 1,000-pound bull's brute shoulders (so his head will drop and allow the matador to kill him eventually). In the second stage, *bandilleros* (assistants on horseback) plunge colorful pairs of darts into the bull, further weakening him for the matador. (You begin to grasp what a fair "fight" this really is.) In the final stage, the matador, in his brilliant *traje de luces* ("suit of lights," so named for its vivid colors that seem to glow in the sun) orchestrates showy passes at the bull with his *muleta* (red cape), and choruses of *¡olé!* resound throughout the ring. It's all dramatic buildup to the kill — the moment of truth in which the matador plunges (in theory, precisely) his sword between the bull's shoulders. If the lance drives straight to the heart, the bull drops in a heap, dead. Bullfights go through six bulls; a spectacular kill earns the matador the doomed bull's ear or tail.

The art of the paseo: The stroll Español

In towns small and large, you see Spaniards in constant motion, walking to and fro. Where are they going? Often, nowhere in particular. They're strolling. The stroll Español — the *paseo* — is a time-honored tradition, an inescapable component of Spanish social life. There's the lovers' stroll, the family paseo, and the takin' care of business stroll. Not only good exercise, they're expressions of Spanish life at full tilt. The *paseo* is usually timed around meals, coming before or after lunch or coinciding with prime *tapas* hour at the end of the work day. People meet up with old friends, stop at a café, have a drink and a few *tapas,* and move on. Join the *paseo,* or pull up at a sidewalk café and watch Spanish life lazily roll on by.

Checking Out Spanish Art and Architecture

From religious art of the Middle Ages to the latest revelations of the contemporary art scene, Spain has produced more great artists than virtually any other country. Several — Veláquez, Goya, El Greco, and Picasso — are among the finest artists the world has ever seen. Spain abounds with Romanesque and Gothic masterpieces, but the masterworks of Spain's Golden Age, the seventeenth century, and the twentieth century are what most visitors come to see. Don't miss the Prado, Thyssen-Bornemisza, and Reina Sofía museums in Madrid (see Chapter 14); the Museu d'Art de Catalunya, Museo Picasso, and Fundació Miró in Barcelona (see Chapter 11); the Theatre-Museu Dalí in Figueres (Catalonia) (see Chapter 12); and the Museo de Bellas Artes in Seville (see Chapter 16). Those museums are the biggest and finest, but I also highlight other eminently worthwhile repositories of Spanish art throughout the country in individual destination chapters. See Appendix B for a pared-down list of some of the greats whose work you should seek out if you have at least a passing interest in art.

The wealth of architectural styles on display throughout Spain is astounding; the country is like a survey of architecture from the fifth century B.C. to the present. With relatively little effort, your trip to Spain can encompass everything from **Roman** and **Romanesque** to **Moorish** and **Mudéjar, Gothic** and **Renaissance** to **Baroque** and Catalonia's unique **Modernismo** architecture, not to mention the latest in avant-garde design and works by some of the finest contemporary international architects, such as Frank O. Gehry's revolutionary Guggenheim Museum in Bilbao. For a cheat sheet on architectural periods and terms, see Appendix B.

Experiencing Música Española

Spain is a splendidly musical country, and incorporating some musical evenings into your itinerary will add greatly to your trip and understanding of Spain. If you like what you hear, pop into a record shop and ask the clerks for their current faves.

You won't just hear flamenco music in Spain, though that passionate sound, which developed among the *gitanos* (Gypsies) in Andalusia, has crossed over into the pop and jazz fusion fields and is widely appreciated throughout Spain. Music, like cuisines, is largely regional. There are Celtic sounds and bagpipes, traditional folk music, and rock en español, a once-boring category of English and American rock sounds sung in Spanish, but increasingly creative hybrid that has really taken off, both in Spain and throughout Latin America. Jazz is extremely popular, as evidenced by the major jazz festivals in San Sebastián and

Vitoria (as well as in Madrid and Barcelona). Several of the world's top opera stars are Spanish, including Plácido Domingo, José Carreras, and Montserrat Caballé. Opera has a large following, especially in Barcelona, Madrid, and Seville.

However, flamenco is what Spain is famous for, and rightly so. An ancient musical form thought to have its origins in India and Eastern Europe, flamenco developed among the marginalized Gypsy populations deep in Andalusia, beginning in the Middle Ages but taking on its present form in the eighteenth century. Flamenco forms the musical soul of the Andalusian people. The staccato handclaps, the masterful rhythmic guitar work, and above all, the passionate and expressive *cante jondo* (deep-throated song) vocals can be entrancing. One element above all defines great flamenco, an intangible quality that artists and fans speak of reverentially. *Duende,* an untranslatable term that means something akin to "spirit" or "magic," is something that, to hear artists tell it, inhabits the body of a flamenco singer or dancer, and creates a riveting performance from deep within the Gypsy soul.

Flamenco dance has evolved every bit as much as the music, drawing popular raves and intense criticism from purists who deride its more accessible incarnations. While I highly encourage you to experience a *tablao* (club) performance of music and dance in Madrid, Córdoba, or Seville, you should also try to see a highly stylized dance theater performance if one is on when you're in town. **Antonio Canales** and **Joaquín Cortés** are both riveting *bailaores* (flamenco dancers), and their shows have drawn fans worldwide.

Spain in literature and film

To get a feel for Spain before you go, here is a very brief (and undeniably haphazard) sampling of some books and films to check out:

Spaniards: A Portrait of the New Spain by John Hooper is an excellent depiction of contemporary Spain. Washington Irving's *Tales of the Alhambra* is the 1832 classic that, although rife with cultural and historical error, colorfully revives all the legends and myths of the great Moorish dynasty and palace in Granada. *Homage to Catalonia* is George Orwell's classic about revolution in Barcelona and the Spanish Civil War. Ernest Hemingway, an admirer and devotee of Spanish machismo, is a prime reason so many people run with the bulls, and gorge on red wine and suckling pig once they realize their dream of coming to Spain. Read his classic works set in Spain, including *The Sun Also Rises, Death in the Afternoon,* and *For Whom the Bell Tolls.* Miguel de Cervantes wrote what is considered by many the first and greatest novel, *Don Quixote,* about the idealistic title figure and his side-kick Sancho Panza. (If you take it along to read on trains or the beach, you're much more ambitious than I.) *The Life of Saint Teresa of Ávila* (autobiography by St. Teresa) is one for the devoted flocks and New-Age mystics. Federico

(continued)

(continued)

García Lorca, Spain's great modernist poet and playwright, shot to death by literature-fearing Falangists, also wrote many enduring works. One to start with is the haunting *The House of Bernarda Alba.* Camilo José Cela is Spain's recent winner of the Nobel Prize for Literature. Have a look at *The Family of Pascual Duarte.*

For those with an interest in architecture, and particularly the Catalan *modernismo* movement led by Antoni Gaudí, *Barcelona* (Vintage, 1993) by Robert Hughes is indispensable, and hugely enjoyable. John Richardson's three- and going on four-part *A Life of Picasso* (Random House, 1996) is generally believed by art scholars to be the definitive work on the life of the greatest painter of the twentieth century. A nicely edited compendium of articles about Spanish culture (and many about its quirkier aspects), *Travelers' Tales: Spain* (ed. Lucy McCauley, Travelers' Tales, Inc., 1995) makes good pre-trip reading. And a good primer on what you'll eat and drink once you reach your destination is *The Foods and Wines of Spain,* by Penelope Casas (Random House, 1982).

Pedro Almodóvar singularly reinvented Spanish cinema in the 1980s, at the head of *la Movida,* the name given to Madrid's craziness and cultural renaissance. Antonio Banderas (who stunned Spaniards by dumping his wife and going completely Hollywood) was one of his early discoveries. Almodóvar's films are widely available on video, but make sure you get subtitled and not badly dubbed versions; all of them display a cheeky wit and provide an exuberant (if skewed) look at life in modern Spain. *Women on the Verge of a Nervous Breakdown* is a hoot; *Matador* is a smoky film noir study of sex, death, and bullfighting. Almodóvar's latest opus, *All About My Mother,* is perhaps his most brilliant feature. The other bad boy of Spanish movies is the Catalan Bigas Luna. His *Jamón, Jamón* ("Ham, Ham") is very nearly a scratch-and-sniff picture about the passions and food of Spain. Rent it if only to see Penélope Cruz as a steamy hitchhiker and tortilla-eater. *Belle Époque* is Fernando Trueba's Oscar-winning (for Best Foreign Film) romantic comedy about a small town and four sisters, a bevy of Spanish beauties. It's an enjoyable romp and smart period piece that captures some stunningly beautiful landscape on film.

For the smoldering passions of Andalusia, you can hardly do better than Carlos Saura's dance-centric films *Carmen, Flamenco,* and *Blood Wedding.* If you're in the mood for classics, don't miss the films of the surrealist Luis Buñuel. *Un Chien Andalou* — a short film Buñuel made with Spanish artist and fellow surrealist Salvador Dalí in 1929 — broke new ground with its use of bizarre and shocking imagery (one famous shot shows a man slicing an eyeball open with a razor); his other most famous film is *The Discreet Charm of the Bougeoisie,* a pointed critique of middle-class tastes.

Chapter 2

Deciding When and Where to Go

. . . .

. . . .

*Y*ou can do almost anything in this complex, delightful, and scenically rich country. But what do you *want* to do? Storm the Prado and every other art museum in a country that has produced a disproportionate number of masters, including Velázquez, El Greco, Goya, Picasso, and Dalí? Indulge in seafood *paella* (a rice and seafood casserole) and red wines from Rioja? Attend a bullfight or colorful festivals? Relive Spain's past in great palaces, castles, and cathedrals? Hit cosmopolitan cities or small villages where time seems to stand still? Or bask in the beach culture that has made Spain a magnet for sun-starved northern Europeans? One of the hardest things about planning a trip to Spain is that it offers so much, so how do you decide where to go?

And when's the best time to go? What's the best time to enjoy Spain's great weather? Maybe there are special festivals that you want to be a part of, like *Semana Santa* (Easter) or the *San Fermín* (the Running of the Bulls). Or, maybe you prefer traveling off-season to avoid crowds and high prices.

If all you know about Spain is that it's in southern Europe, and it's where Don Quixote tilted with windmills on the plains, use this section to help you figure out which region is best suited to your interests.

Introducing Spain, Region by Region

Perhaps you think that choosing which part or parts of Spain you travel to doesn't matter that much. After all, all of Spain is sunny, hot, full of castles and cathedrals, pretty flat, and close to beaches, right?

Mapping it out

On a map of Europe, Spain lies in the southwestern corner. France (with which it shares the Pyrenees Mountains) borders it in the north, and its southernmost point is just 8 miles across a narrow straight from Morocco, in North Africa. To the west is the Atlantic Ocean, to the north the Bay of Biscay, and to the east, the Mediterranean Sea. Spain makes up the majority of the Iberian Peninsula that it shares with Portugal, and the only Western European country larger than Spain is France.

Two island groups are also part of Spain: the Balearics, in the Mediterranean off the eastern coast, and the Canary Islands, far south in the Atlantic Ocean, much closer to Morocco than to Spain. To see these regions pinpointed on a map, see the map of Spain in Chapter 1.

And all Spaniards speak Spanish, right, so what's to figure out? Sorry to burst your bubble, but as they say in Spain, ¡No!

Much of Spain, it's true, is sunny and hot, parts are flat, and much of the country is lined with great beaches. However, you can also see a Spain that is the opposite of hot, dry plains, where the coast is a plane flight — not an easy drive — away. And while Spanish is obviously the national language, the locals in four regions of the country speak a language other than Spanish (though they also speak *castellano,* Castilian Spanish). For a brief overview of Castilian Spanish, see Chapter 1.

Which Spain do you want to visit? Finding colossal cathedrals isn't hard no matter where you go, but the cultures, cuisine, customs, traditions, and attractions are vastly different across the country. Perhaps you've decided to concentrate on a single region and see some of the diversity within it, or maybe you have more wanderlust and time and you want to experience two or more regions of Spain.

When planning a trip to a big country, you not only choose where to go, you also choose where *not* to go. So that you can start narrowing down your own choices, here's info on Spain's regions, following the order in which I discuss them in greater detail in later chapters.

Northeastern Spain: Barcelona, the Costa Brava, and the Basque Country

Catalonia may not be familiar to you, but I'm sure Barcelona is. The site of the 1992 Summer Olympics, **Barcelona** ("Bar-*thay*-loh-nah") is a 2,000-year-old city, founded by the Romans, that is also a thoroughly modern place with rich architectural and artistic legacies. Barcelona is the capital of **Catalonia,** a region of six million people whose first language is Catalan (though almost everybody also speaks Spanish). The region is Spain's most prosperous.

Catalonia (Catalunya in Catalan) borders France in the north and has a long Mediterranean coastline, including the rocky **Costa Brava** north of Barcelona. The interior of Catalonia is a largely agricultural region of beautiful, fertile plains and small medieval villages, which is very sedate and pastoral, until you realize that this is the region that gave birth to Salvador Dalí's mad genius.

The *País Vasco* (the Basque Country; pronounced "pie-*ees boss*-koh") begins just west of the French border and the Pyrenees, hugging the northern coastline and inhabiting the remote interior above the River Ebro. (For simplicity's sake, I lump Navarra in with the Basque Country, though strictly speaking it's no longer Basque. My apologies to geographical purists.) The Basque Country is primarily agricultural, hilly, and full of emerald meadows, small villages, and rustic farmhouses. Fishing villages line the sparsely developed coastline along the Bay of Biscay. Historically, the region's topography and rainy weather have rendered it inaccessible and rather inhospitable.

Spain's sixth-largest city, **Bilbao,** was, for most of the twentieth century, a grimy industrial city. It now, however, possesses the shiny Guggenheim Museum and has suddenly become one of Spain's top tourist attractions. **San Sebastián** (called *Donostia* in Basque) is a summer resort and one of Spain's prettiest cities, with serene beaches framing a perfect shell-shaped bay. **Navarra** (often spelled Navarre in English) is an ancient region that was once an independent kingdom. People in some parts of the province still speak the Basque language.

Navarra is a mountainous region, dominated by the Pyrenees, and like most of the north, very agricultural. The capital, Pamplona, is a conservative place that rockets to life once a year, during its famous summer festival, **San Fermín** — the Running of the Bulls. You can drink especially well in Navarra; the famous red-wine region, La Rioja, is just a few kilometers southwest.

The main attractions in this region are:

- ✔ Barcelona's medieval **Gothic Quarter,** mind-altering early twentieth-century architecture (including Gaudí's Sagrada Familia), and sparkling urban beaches.

- ✔ Super side trips from Barcelona — a mountain monastery, a lazy beach resort, and Catalan wine country— as well as short scenic drives around Catalonia.

- ✔ **Girona,** a quiet medieval city on a hill with a Jewish past and the **Dalí Triangle** — three towns touched by surreal Salvador.

- ✔ The beaches, piney coves, and icy blue waters of the **Costa Brava.**

- ✔ Bilbao's mind-blowing **Guggenheim Museum,** universally acclaimed as one of the standout buildings of the twentieth century.

- ✔ **San Sebastián,** a leisurely small city perched on a perfect bay — with Spain's greatest concentration of haute cuisine restaurants.

- ✔ **Pamplona,** a reserved city where hysteria reigns once a year when one-ton bulls rule the streets.

- ✔ Basque cuisine — Spain's most sophisticated and inventive. In other places, eating is a complementary activity; in the Basque Country, everything else takes a back seat.

But keep in mind . . .

- ✔ Barcelona's very hot with tourists now, and its hotels and restaurants do a good job helping you part with your *pesetas.*

- ✔ Street signs and menus in Catalan (a language unfamiliar to most visitors) can throw you for a loop.

- ✔ In the Basque Country, it's rain, rain go away. If you only get mist while in the area, it's the equivalent of brilliant sunshine anywhere else.

- ✔ Historically, the Basque Country and Navarra haven't really been on the international tourist's radar. Therefore, much of the region's services, hotels, and restaurants are playing catch-up.

- ✔ Pamplona during the Running of the Bulls is an expensive nightmare if you don't have reservations.

Central Spain: Madrid and Castile

When most people think of Spain, what they're picturing is most likely the central and southern parts of the country. The plains of Central Spain are arid, predominantly flat, and topped by dozens of castles and palaces marking ancient kingdoms and conflicts. The most prominent geographical feature is the *meseta,* a broad plateau that consists of Madrid, Old and New Castile, and Extremadura, and makes up about 40 percent of the Iberian Peninsula.

Madrid is the capital of and largest city in Spain, even though it wasn't much more than a backwater stuck in the middle of the country until Felipe pronounced it the new capital. In addition to occupying the geographic middle, Madrid is the political center of Spain and the core of the Spanish cultural world. It claims several of the finest art museums in Europe, with the world-famous Prado leading the way.

The previous Spanish capital was **Toledo,** south of Madrid. Toledo's fascinating juxtaposition of Arab, Christian, and Jewish culture has made it one of Spain's top draws for decades. Toledo, along with

Segovia and **Salamanca,** are the top day trips (or better yet, "couple-of-days" trips) from Madrid. Their proximity to the capital makes it extremely easy to design a Central Spain visit.

The main attractions in this region are:

- ✔ Madrid and its many parts: *Viejo Madrid* (Old Madrid), Hapsburg Madrid, and Bourbon Madrid. Across the board, the capital is lively, full of world-class art and the most frenetically paced nightlife scene in Spain.

- ✔ Right on the outskirts of town: the somber — but still eye-popping — palace **El Escorial;** and **Aranjuez,** the regal garden retreat of royals.

- ✔ **Segovia,** a town molded like a medieval dreamscape, with a 2000-year-old Roman aqueduct and a picturebook castle on a hill.

- ✔ **Salamanca,** one of Spain's most architecturally inviting cities — a classic university town, much the same as Oxford in England.

- ✔ **Toledo,** the labyrinthine city on a hill where the artist El Greco thrived, as well as Romans, Visigoths, Christians, Jews, and Muslims.

But keep in mind . . .

- ✔ Guess what? An arid, flat plain like the *meseta* is unforgivably hot in summer and brutally cold in winter.

- ✔ Much of Central Spain, especially Toledo, is a tourist magnet; it's tough to visit the cities of Old and New Castile and not get trampled by boisterous bus groups.

- ✔ Madrid has fine hotels and restaurants, but it's also the most expensive (and probably most chaotic) city in Spain.

Southern Spain: Andalusia

Andalucía ("*ahn*-dah-loo-*thee*-ah"; Andalusia) is the sultry, passionate Spain of posters: flamenco-dancing Gypsies, bloody bullfights, blistering sun, and scorching *señoritas*. Clumps of olive groves are sprawled across unending acres of khaki-colored earth, producing golden Extra Virgin olive oil for much of the world.

Andalusia (*Al-Andalus* to the Arabs that once inhabited this region) is also the part of Spain that the Moors influenced most distinctly. They ruled Spain for seven centuries, and their dominance and sophistication is evident in the alluring Alhambra palace in **Granada,** the magnificent Great Mosque in **Córdoba,** and the arresting *Alcázar,* or palace-fortress, in **Seville.** You also see a distinctive Moorish presence in the white villages perched in the Andalusian mountains. After Spain's discovery and looting of the New World, the riches passed through Seville first.

The southern coast of Spain is also an international playground land for the rich, famous, and often tacky. The glitzy **Costa del Sol** was Spain's jet-setting beach getaway for decades, but you can find better, less crowded and less expensive beaches — on the **Costa de la Luz,** for example. If Andalusia's abundant sun is too much for you, come in winter, when you can ski on Spain's highest mountain range, the Sierra Nevada.

The main attractions in this region are:

✔ Seville, Córdoba, and Granada — the three pillars of Moorish Andalusia — and their great monuments: Seville's **Cathedral,** the world's largest Gothic building; the awe-inspiring **Great Mosque** in Córdoba; and Granada's **Alhambra,** a miracle palace of light and legend.

✔ Andalusia's famous spring festivals: Seville's Holy Week and April Fair, Córdoba's decorated patios and May Festivals, and the pilgrimage to Rocío.

✔ The delicious art of the *tapas* crawl, invented by Andalusians, who still practice it with unequaled flair (see Chapter 1).

✔ The **Pueblos Blancos,** medieval whitewashed villages perched on the peaks of the southern mountain ranges.

✔ The leisurely south: Andalusia's famed coasts.

But keep in mind . . .

✔ I'm melting, I'm melting! In summer (and to a lesser extent year-round), there are few places hotter on earth.

✔ Those great spring festivals draw crowds from around the world and push prices through the roof.

✔ To see much of the south, you have little choice but to rent a car.

Discovering the Secret of the Seasons

Almost any time of year is the right time to go to Spain, which has, along with Portugal, the best year-round weather in Europe. Though it's renowned and revered for its sun — and rightly so, there's certainly lots of it — you want to avoid some sunny areas in the deadly-hot summer. Fortunately, no matter when you go, you can find a part of Spain tailor-made for the time of year you're visiting.

Even in winter you can find the warmth of the Spanish sun. Spring and fall are overall perhaps the most enjoyable seasons, when you can enjoy festivals, fewer crowds than in summer, and a respite from scorching summer heat. If you visit Spain in the summer, you may want to do as Spaniards themselves do and head north.

Spring

Spring (especially late spring, from mid-April to mid-May) is ideal for Central Spain, Andalusia, the Mediterranean coast, and the Balearic Islands. The sun hasn't cranked up its full potential yet, flowers are in dazzling bloom, and Spaniards, who love to be outside, fill sidewalk cafes. You can also find some of the best festivals occurring in spring.

But keep in mind: The north can be pretty rainy, and the festivals in Andalucía put hotel accommodations at a premium.

Summer

Summer is an excellent time to hit Northern "Green" Spain, which is usually very rainy in winter and spring. From the Basque Country to Galicia, the temperatures are the peninsula's coolest, averaging around 70°F.

Keep the heat and crowds in mind, however. Madrid and Andalusia are extremely dry, like an oven at 450°F. Barcelona's pretty humid, so even though temperatures may only be in the mid-80s, you can feel sticky and uncomfortable. Summer is when Europeans pour into Spain, especially the coastal regions, and August is when 90 percent of Spaniards are on vacation. Much of the country (inland, at least) closes up for the month. During the last week of July and first week of August, highways crisscrossing Spain clog with expatriate Moroccans returning home from northern Europe for the summer holidays.

Fall

Fall may be the best time to visit Spain as a whole. Days are sunny and comfortable around the Iberian Peninsula, skies are clear, and the crowded days of summer are over.

Although fall offers great weather for traveling in Spain, the Atlantic coast gets a good bit of rain in autumn, and the summer heat may still linger in the south.

Winter

Winter is a good time to travel to the southern Mediterranean and the mountains in both the north and south for snow sports. Crowds are nonexistent, and prices drop for hotels and airfares.

But keep in mind that some coastal resorts, especially on the Costa Brava, virtually shut down during this slow season. And in Central Spain, winter can be as cold as it is hot in summer, because the center of the country specializes in extremes.

Table 2-1   Spain's Average High and Low Temperatures in Degrees Fahrenheit

Area of Spain	Jan	Feb	Mar	Apr	May	June	July	Aug	Sept	Oct	Nov	Dec
Barcelona (and the Costa Brava)	55/42	57/44	61/48	67/51	74/55	77/61	84/65	84/69	77/64	69/58	61/50	55/44
Bilbao	55/42	57/43	60/44	62/46	67/51	72/57	77/60	76/58	69/53	62/48	57/45	55/43
Northern Coast (Basque Country)	50/39	55/40	59/42	61/43	66/43	70/59	75/59	75/59	69/53	60/48	55/45	53/42
Madrid	47/34	51/35	59/41	65/45	73/50	83/57	88/57	88/63	91/62	78/57	64/49	50/35
Seville	60/42	63/44	69/48	74/52	80/56	89/63	96/68	95/68	89/64	78/57	68/50	60/44
Granada	53/44	57/35	63/40	68/43	74/48	86/57	92/62	90/62	90/62	84/57	71/48	53/39
Málaga (Costa del Sol)	60/46	64/46	69/50	75/56	78/57	82/64	86/67	87/70	84/65	77/59	70/53	65/48

Getting a handle on crowds and prices

Spain gets many more visitors every year than it has citizens, which is pretty incredible, if you think about it. And it means that during much of the year, parts of Spain are quite crowded and expensive. You can find the best bargains during the shoulder (fall and the beginning of spring) and off-seasons. Prices are lower at hotels; getting a reservation and doing just about everything else — going to a restaurant, visiting a museum or cathedral, traveling by train or on the highway, and so on — is much less difficult. As a general rule, prices in Spain are lowest November through February. The shoulder seasons are cheaper than summer (but don't expect the kind of bottom-drawer prices you'd find in Mexico or the Caribbean; there's a drop, but it won't halve your vacation costs).

Usually prices in Spain are lowest November through February and highest in July in August. If a bargain trip is high on your list, keep this in mind when making your reservation.

Besides July and August, prices are also highest during Easter Week. Avoid these times also if you don't want rushes of Spanish and European tourists to sweep you away. Traditionally, Europeans, en masse, take off the month of August and try to beat each other to the beaches (as it happens, they end up squeezing in next to each other). Most Europeans don't yet have the vacation flexibility that many North Americans enjoy (that said, though, most Europeans get a full month or more of vacation!). So take advantage of your greater flexibility if you can visit Spain in fall, winter, or early spring.

Knowing when you shouldn't go

You've probably already figured out that August is a deadly month in Spain. The sun bakes the heck out of everything in sight, major cities become ghost towns as wise Spaniards flee to the coasts, and the most desirable places where water or cooler temperatures are within reach are packed with Spanish and European tourists. You may find it very frustrating, with short hours and closings and few restaurants from which to pick.

Christmas and Easter holidays can be great times to visit Spain as long as you know what you're getting into: lots of holidays and closings of museums and businesses. But that's the trade-off to see Spain at its religious and folkloric best. Many Spaniards have the entire Holy Week (Easter) off, so coasts, ski resorts, and popular Easter cities like Seville and Málaga are packed not only with Spaniards but also with people from the rest of the planet too.

Prices follow the law of demand and go through the roof when everybody wants to visit a particular place, which means April and May during the celebrated festivals of Seville and Córdoba and summer (July and August) in the Balearics, Northern Spain, and along the Mediterranean coasts. If you don't want to run with the bulls, or watch other people perform the original extreme sport, don't go to Pamplona in early July (July 6–14). In fact, if masses of people and high costs make you squirm, make sure that you avoid Pamplona during the Running of the Bulls at all cost.

Parties and Prayers: Enjoying Rowdy and Religious Festivals

Spain's special *fiestas* (celebrations) are what make it unique. No other European country has maintained the variety of vibrant expressions of culture and color like Spain. However, if you want to plan your vacation around them, keep in mind two important words: *plan ahead.* Several of the festivals are extremely popular with national as well as international travelers, and unless you're partial to sleeping on the street, they require reservations way in advance.

 Every city and town in Spain also celebrates a patron saint's feast day. These days are pretty difficult to keep track of (strike that — impossible), so understand that you may arrive in a place and discover that it's a holiday, even though we don't list it in this with the rest of Spain's major holidays, later in this chapter. Therefore, in Spain, where people still use paper money to for pay many things, it's a good idea to have some cash on you at all times in case banks are closed and you can't change money. For a more comprehensive list of the patron saints' feast days consult the Web site for the **Spanish National Tourist Office,** www.tourspain.es.

Spain's national holidays

National holidays celebrated in Spain include January 1 (New Year's Day), January 6 (Feast of the Epiphany), March 19 (Feast of St. Joseph), Good Friday, Easter Monday, May 1 (May Day), June 10 (Corpus Christi), June 29 (Feast of St. Peter and St. Paul), July 25 (Feast of St. James), August 15 (Feast of the Assumption), October 12 (Spain's National Day), November 1 (All Saints' Day), December 8 (Immaculate Conception), and December 25 (Christmas).

A calendar of special events

Note that with most of these events, exact dates change from year to year, according to the calendar. Therefore, make sure that you confirm the dates with the National Tourist Office of Spain (see "Where to Get More Info" in Appendix A) if you want to make sure that you're in town for a specific event.

Every dog has his day

If you're in Spain on January 17, the Feast Day of St. Anthony, you'll see an odd sight all over the country: churches full of animals. Saint Anthony is the saint of household pets, and, following a sixteenth-century tradition, people bring their pets to Mass for a member of the clergy to bless. I've seen pigs and even rats blessed by the local *padre* (father).

January

✔ **Día de los Reyes (Three Kings Day),** throughout Spain, January 6. Spain has traditionally celebrated the gift-giving of Christmas on King's Day (though Santa Claus, also known as *Papa Noel,* is starting to visit Spanish kids). In most cities, elaborately dressed kings and their entourages parade through the city. Eating a King's cake, which has a miniature baby doll buried in the batter, is also a tradition. Odd as it sounds, the one who gets the baby in his mouth has to pay for a party.

February/March

✔ **Carnaval,** Cádiz, late February or early March, depending on dates of Easter. Spain's best and most flamboyant carnival celebration is also the oldest. This is the closest Spain comes to Rio, but southern Carnival has a flavor all its own. See Chapter 17 for more information.

April

✔ **Semana Santa (Holy Week),** Seville, Mid-April. Spain's most revered religious celebration is Easter, and nobody celebrates it like Seville. Dead-serious processions run round the clock, from Palm Sunday until Easter Sunday. Brotherhoods of men carry *pasos* (floats) of Virgins or Christ and shuffle through the streets to the eerie wail of the *saeta,* a religious funeral hymn. Cloaked and hooded penitents accompany the float-carrying men. Make hotel reservations three months to a year in advance. See Chapter 16 for more information.

✔ **Feria de Abril (April Fair),** Seville, third week of April. *Sevillanos* pull out all the stops for their spring fair, which follows the solemn Easter celebrations. Women dazzle in brightly colored, polka-dotted flamenco dresses; men play the part of country *caballeros* (gentlemen). Coaches are decked out with so many flowers they look like floats in the Rose Bowl parade, and the streets rock with all-night flamenco dancing, bullfights, and horseback riding. Feria de Abril fills Seville to the rafters. For exact festival dates, contact the

Spanish National Tourist Office in your home country (see "Where to Find More Information" in Appendix A). For more information about the fair itself, see Chapter 16.

May

- ✔ **Festival de los Patios (Patio Festival),** Córdoba, first two weeks in May. Cordobeses, known for the beauty of their whitewashed patios and courtyards, go all out every May, daring their neighbors to better their flower-bedecked displays. You can pick up a schedule of competing patios and judge for yourself. Get more information in Chapter 16.

- ✔ **Romería del Rocío (Pilgrimage of the Virgin of the Dew),** El Rocío (Huelva), Mid- to late-May. You must see Romería del Rocío, (also called simply El Rocío), Spain's most famous religious procession, to believe it. A million people go south to see a large group of men carry the statue of the Virgin 10 miles to Almonte, through the marshes of Coto Doñana, for consecration. Massive crowds do their best to touch the Virgin and feel her healing power.

- ✔ **Fiesta de San Isidro,** Madrid, mid-May. San Isidro is the patron saint of Madrid, and locals throw a 10-day celebration to honor San Isidro. You can enjoy daily bullfights at Las Ventas, food fairs, folklore, parades, parties, concerts, and lots of food and drink. Make hotel reservations early. See Chapter 14 for more information.

- ✔ **Feria de los Caballos (Jerez Horse Fair),** Jerez de la Frontera, May 13–20. Classic Andalusian horses are the focus of this traditional fair, though women decked out in their finest flamenco dresses certainly give the horses a run for their money. See Chapter 17 for more information.

June

- ✔ **Corpus Christi,** all over Spain, June 14. Another major religious holiday, big processions hit "cathedral cities," such as Toledo, Málaga, Seville, and Granada.

- ✔ **International Music and Dance Festival,** Granada, June 21–July 7. For 50 years, Granada has put on a great international program of dance and music at incredible venues: the Alhambra and Generalife palaces, among others. This festival is a great way to see those places enlivened by top-notch talent. Reserve at least a couple of months in advance. See Chapter 18 for more information.

- ✔ **Battle of Wine Festival,** Haro (La Rioja). In one of Spain's top wine regions, *vino* becomes ammo as people douse each other with 70,000 liters of red wine — then they stumble around a lot. June 29.

July

✔ **San Sebastián Jazz Festival,** San Sebastián, last two weeks in July. Spain's oldest and most prestigious jazz party gets some of the international biggies together for smooth jazz and soulful bebop every July. Enjoy big-ticket shows (Wynton Marsalis and Pat Metheny were recent performers), as well as some freebies. Get more information in Chapter 13.

✔ **Fiesta de San Fermín (Running of the Bulls),** Pamplona, July 6–14. You may have known all about the Running of the Bulls before you even picked up this book. Popularized by Hemingway, massive beasts race through the streets of Pamplona, while joyful and crazy humans try to outrun them. Those that don't run get swept up in the revelry just the same. This is the most popular celebration in Spain. Reserve months, or at some hotels, years in advance. See Chapter 13.

✔ **Festival de la Guitarra (Guitar Festival),** Córdoba, first two weeks of July. Spanish classical and flamenco guitar fuels the rhythms of everyday life in Andalusia, and Córdoba gets some of the finest national and international guitar heroes to town for a series of concerts. See Chapter 16 for more information.

September

✔ **Feria de Pedro Romero (Pedro Romero Fair),** Ronda, first week of September. The site of Spain's oldest bullfighting arena and the home of a legendary matador, Ronda dips back in time every September. Its *corrida goyesca* recreates the atmosphere of an eighteenth-century bullfight from the era of Spain's great painter, Francisco Goya. Men and women decked out in fancy dress ride through the streets on horse carriages, and bullfighting aficionados come from all over the world to see classical exhibitions. Check out Chapter 17 for more information.

✔ **Wine Harvest Festival,** Logroño and throughout La Rioja, June 29. One of Spain's most famous wine regions celebrates the great grape, with dancing, bullfighting, music, and parades. Oh yeah, and drinking, too. See Chapter 13.

✔ **La Mercé,** Barcelona, September 24. Barcelona rolls out the *cabezudos* — big papier mâché heads — that roam the streets, fascinating (or frightening) kids and honoring Our Lady of Mercy. See Chapter 11 for more information.

✔ **Autumn Festival,** Madrid, late October to late November. Acclaimed Spanish and international artists participate in this wide-reaching cultural program, with opera, ballet, dance, music, and theatrical performances. A great opportunity for culture vultures. Make hotel reservations early, and write for a schedule and tickets to Festival de Otoño, Plaza de España, 8, 28008 Madrid (☎ **91-580-25-75**). See Chapter 14.

✔ **International Film Festival,** San Sebastián, second half of September (dates vary). Spain's top film festival shakes up this beautiful resort city. You can find nearly as many screenings and stars as in the Cannes Film Festival in France. See Chapter 13 for more information.

December

✔ **Noche Vieja (New Year's Eve),** throughout Spain, December 31. People stuff grapes into their mouths, one at the sound of each of 12 chimes at midnight, to ring in the New Year. In Madrid, people crowd into the Puerta del Sol plaza and cheer on the clock tower.

Trip-Planning Tips

If you've never been to Spain and think of it as a small European country, you may believe that you can cover Barcelona, the Basque Country, Madrid and the castles of Castile, and all of Andalusia in a couple of weeks. Although it's theoretically possible to do that (and easier than ever with faster trains and cheaper flights), you'd have to endure a blitzkrieg bop across Spain, and quantity doesn't often equal quality when you're traveling.

Many travelers today instead focus on one particular region, concentrating on the big and small attractions of that area and (I think) getting a better overall flavor of the country. I encourage you to do that as well, and not get too manic about seeing *every*thing. The hassles of transportation can eat into your vacation; if you spend more time getting places than experiencing them once you're there, you may return from your trip feeling that you need a vacation to recover from the one you just had. Especially if you think there's a chance you may return to Spain some day, I advise that you plan a regional-based trip (for suggested itineraries, see Chapter 3).

Because you can get a huge dose of Spanish flavor in any region, I always tell friends to start with a list of what they absolutely must see or experience, and then build an itinerary around that. If you're a certified art head and you can't step foot in Spain without seeing the great Spanish masters at the Prado, plan a couple of days in Madrid and then decide on day trips to Castile or a visit to the south of Spain. If you're a disciple of Gaudí and are dying to see Barcelona's famed *modernista* architecture, focus on the Catalan capital and add the Costa Brava, perhaps. Food junkies may want to take a seat at the splendid tables of San Sebastián and Bilbao and then walk it off touring northern Spain.

Spain is pretty easy to get around, whether by public transportation or rental car — though distances can be significant, and you've got to factor in travel time. You can't just bop from Barcelona to Madrid to Seville to Bilbao unless you fly. Some Spanish trains still aren't up to par with northern Europe, but they are to major destinations, and Spain has fantastic high-speed rail (abbreviated in Spanish as AVE) between Madrid and Andalucía.

Dealing with the daily tourist grind

As exciting as it is to see a new place (and a new country), be careful that you don't overdo it. There's a reason that people who go on "if it's Tuesday, it must be Belgium" trips can't usually remember what Belgium looked like. Their visit was a blur because they'd packed too much into too little time. Build some time into your schedule to get into the rhythm of Spanish life. Taking time to relax and absorb your stay in Spain — listening to the exuberant Castilian Spanish all around you, checking out the fashions, and so on — is, for most people, more important than seeing that one last cathedral or museum.

The easiest way to dive into the culture is to get off your feet and plunk yourself down at an outdoor café. Cafés are a Spanish institution, a daily ritual. Not only will you be able to reflect on what you've seen so far, you'll also be able to watch Spanish life all around you. Realizing how much you glean from a few slow-sipped espressos or *cafés con leche* will surprise you. In smaller towns, take time to stroll the central promenade — also a time-honored element of Spanish life — and hit the local *tapas* joints. Look for signs of Spanish life, such as grandparents babysitting their grandchildren, young mothers comparing toddler notes, senior citizens talking about the latest *fútbol* (soccer) game over a glass of wine.

Chapter 3

Six Great Spain Itineraries

*I*f you're making your first trip to Spain, you may be inclined to try to see everything in a two-week period (I know that's what I wanted to do the first time I went). Spain abounds with so much to see in virtually every corner of the country, though, that you have to have to be realistic about how much ground you can cover without skimming over too much.

One of the most important things I've learned in two decades of travel is the wisdom and value of regional trips. If you don't try to do too much and dart from one end of the country to the next, you can very often have a more enjoyable trip and gain a greater variety of experiences than if you try to see absolutely everything. A regional trip also allows you to base yourself in one spot and set out on day trips from there, which means you don't have pack up your suitcase every morning before breakfast.

Keep in mind that the following itineraries are mere examples; you can just as easily design a week in the Basque Country. (In fact, the chapters on those regions give you hints for creating your own regional trips.) Whatever you decide to see and do, be realistic. Spain is large and 14 cities in 14 days just isn't feasible.

The Best of Barcelona and Catalonia in One Week

For more information on these destinations, see Chapters 11 and 12, as well as the suggested itineraries for Barcelona in Chapter 11.

- ✔ Fly directly to **Barcelona** and stay there three days.

- ✔ **Day 1:** Visit the Gothic Quarter, including the Museu Picasso and the cathedral. Hit the Rambla for a late-afternoon stroll.

- ✔ **Day 2:** See the *modernista* architecture in the Eixample district, including Gaudí's Sagrada Familia cathedral and Parque Güell, and the Manzana de la Discórdia on Passeig de Gràcia.

- ✔ **Day 3:** Spend this day checking out the Museu Nacional d'Art de Catalunya, the Fundació Miró, and Olympic installations on Montjuïc hill in the morning, and stroll the Waterfront in the afternoon.

- ✔ **Day 4:** Take a trip out of town and see a few destinations in Catalonia. Head first to **Montserrat,** the Benedictine monastery built into a jagged mountain. Combine your visit with one to the **Penedès** wine country (if you have a car), or spend the day at the charming beach town of **Sitges.**

- ✔ **Day 5:** Travel to **Figueres** to see the Dalí museum.

- ✔ **Day 6:** Spend this day in the beautiful medieval city of **Girona** or at a beach town along the **Costa Brava.** Return to Barcelona late in the day, or better yet, stay the night in Girona to soak up some charming, small-town atmosphere.

- ✔ **Day 7:** Return to Barcelona in time for your flight.

The Best of Madrid and Castile in One Week

For more information on the destinations in this itinerary, see Chapters 14 and 15, as well as the suggested itineraries for Madrid in Chapter 14.

- ✔ **Days 1–2:** Spend your first two days in **Madrid,** visiting the Prado and Thyssen-Bornemizsa museums and exploring Viejo Madrid, around the Plaza de Mayo. Visit the Royal Palace and use the evenings to participate in a *tapas* crawl or two, traveling from bar to bar to sample a variety of *tapas* (small plates of Spanish appetizers).

- ✔ **Day 3:** Head out to Segovia for the day, seeing the Alcázar, cathedral and Roman Aqueduct. If you have a car, spend the night in **Segovia.**

✔ **Day 4:** Drive to **El Escorial,** the austere monastery/fortress that's home to some beautiful art and is the primary burial place for Spanish kings. Spend the night back in Madrid.

✔ **Days 5–6:** Head south to **Toledo** and spend two days exploring the ancient city, with its Moorish, Jewish, and Christian monuments. Spending the night here allows you some quiet time to really soak up the city's history and atmosphere.

✔ **Day 7:** Return to Madrid in time for your flight. If there's time, catch a bullfight if you want or do some shopping in the capital's elegant Salamanca district.

If you can squeeze in an extra couple of days on your trip, don't miss **Salamanca,** the pristine university town a couple of hours west of Segovia. Or, for a quick taste of Andalusia, take the high-speed train down to **Seville** for two days (see the following section for details).

The Best of Andalusia in One Week

Because there's so much to see in this region, I've "cheated" a little with my one-week itinerary, extending it to nine days to cover the weekends on either end of a one-week trip. For more information on the destinations in this itinerary see Chapters 14, 16, 17, and 18, as well as the suggested sightseeing itineraries for Madrid (in Chapter 14), Seville, and Cordóba (both in Chapter 16).

✔ **Day 1:** Arrive in **Madrid** and take it easy after your flight strolling around Viejo Madrid and the Plaza de Mayo.

✔ **Day 2:** In the morning, visit the Prado before catching a high-speed (AVE) train to **Seville** in the afternoon.

✔ **Days 3–4:** Now that you're in Seville, visit the Santa Cruz Quarter, the cathedral, and the Reales Alcazares, and make sure that you hit a flamenco performance, called a *tablao,* one night.

✔ **Days 5–6:** Rent a car and explore a couple of the **pueblos blancos** (white villages), starting with Arcos de la Frontera and ending with Ronda, staying overnight there. Take in the refreshing whitewashed architecture and tour a few sherry *bodegas* (wine cellars). Then head east to **Granada.**

✔ **Days 7–8:** Spend the first day visiting the magnificent Alhambra palace, and the second seeing the cathedral and Albaycín, the old Arab neighborhood. From Granada, head to **Córdoba.**

✔ **Day 9:** See the Great Mosque and Jewish Quarter in the morning. Return to Madrid for your flight back home.

If you can add a couple extra days to your trip in Andalusia, spend them on the beach or golfing (after your time in either Seville or Ronda). Head south from Arcos for a day at the beach on the **Costa**

de la Luz near Cádiz or do the same on the **Costa del Sol** after visiting Ronda. Spend the night at one of the *paradors* (government-run hotels) near the coast. See Chapter 17 for more information on the Costa de la Luz and Costa del Sol.

The Greatest Spots of Spain in Two Weeks

With such a surplus of choices, constructing a best of, whirlwind tour of Spain is difficult — but here goes. (Don't expect a lot of rest or quiet, local color, but do expect the world-class showcases of Spain.) You can fly into either Madrid or Barcelona. Let's say you fly to Madrid. Here's a sample itinerary:

- ✔ **Days 1–2:** Spend these two days exploring **Madrid.** (See "The Best of Madrid and Castile in One Week," earlier in the chapter.)

- ✔ **Day 3:** Head out to **El Escorial** for the day. Return to Madrid for the night.

- ✔ **Day 4:** Take the bus to **Toledo.** Return to Madrid later that evening.

- ✔ **Day 5:** In the morning, catch an AVE train to **Córdoba,** stopping off to see the Great Mosque. Afterward, get back on the AVE to **Seville.**

- ✔ **Days 6–7:** Spend these two days exploring **Seville** (see "The Best of Andalusia in One Week," earlier in this chapter).

- ✔ **Days 8–9:** Travel by train or car to **Granada** (reserving the most time for the Alhambra palace).

- ✔ **Days 10–11:** Return to Madrid and catch a shuttle flight to **Barcelona** on Day 10. Spend Days 10 and 11 in the Catalan capital (see "The Best of Barcelona and Catalonia in One Week," earlier in this chapter).

- ✔ **Day 12:** Fly to **Bilbao** to see the gleaming new Guggenheim Museum and enjoy an indulgent Basque lunch. That evening, return by plane to Madrid.

- ✔ **Day 13:** Spend the day shopping or visiting the **Royal Palace** or another of the Golden Triangle of art museums — perhaps the Reina Sofía or Thyssen-Bornemizsa — in the capital.

- ✔ **Day 14:** Depart for home.

Exploring Spain with Kids

Spaniards are overwhelmingly family-oriented, and you can easily construct a rewarding and fun trip with kids in pretty much any city or region of Spain. In my opinion, though, two places are particularly well stocked with family diversions, and I mention them in the following paragraphs. However, if you have your heart set on traveling with children to other parts of Spain, by all means check the individual destination chapters in this book for attractions that I highlight with the Kid Friendly icon.

Barcelona

Three to five days should give you enough time to introduce the kids to this cosmopolitan city. Strolling along La Rambla — where gaily costumed human statues (people performing, or rather staying frozen in place, for tips) stake out a spot every hundred yards or so — is a joy with kids, as is a walk through the pedestrian-only streets of the atmospheric **Gothic Quarter.** Children aren't usually all that impressed with grown-up architecture, but the works of Barcelona's early twentieth-century visionary architect Antoni Gaudí — particularly the Parc Güell and the rooftop and interactive museum of **La Pedrera** — are very appealing to kids of all ages.

The waterfront, with its nice beaches, yachts, and kid-friendly diversions, such as the giant L'Aquarium and Imax theater, is a place to spend a fun-filled day. The hills around Barcelona are also alive with opportunities for children: **Tibidabo** has a fun, easygoing theme park (Parc d' Attracions) with great views of the city; **Montjuïc** also has a theme park, as well as the Pueblo Espanol, a theme-park like representation of all of Spain. Kids also enjoy taking the aerial cable car from Montjuïc down to the waterfront.

Side trips to the monastery of **Montserrat,** which you can reach via aerial cable car, and the pleasant seaside town of **Sitges,** are also good ideas for kids.

The Basque country

You may not have considered northern Spain for a trip with kids, but I think it can be an ideal destination. **San Sebastián** is a relaxed, small city on a brilliant bay. Its beaches along La Concha are heaven to most kids, and in the summer, you can take boat trips out to the small island in the bay. You can visit a pretty good aquarium that makes for a fun diversion. Unfortunately, the city's gourmet restaurants aren't likely to appeal to children. Although I normally don't recommend taking kids to bars, they'll enjoy eating snacks for dinner, as will you, scarfing down wonderful *tapas* (called *pintxos* in this neck of the woods) in the countless small bar/restaurants in the Old Quarter (Parte Vieja).

Just outside the city, older kids may enjoy a visit to the outdoor sculpture park of Eduardo Chillida or a lunchtime visit to the tiny town of **Pasajes de San Juan;** you take a small boat to get there, and it's home to excellent seafood restaurants.

Bilbao stands out for families for a single reason: The curving, wavy Guggenheim museum, both inside and out, inspires awe in parents and children. You've never seen young people have so much fun at an art museum; they can ring the colorful techno chimes in the cathedral-like atrium, enjoy wonderfully tactile modern art exhibits, and play with the giant, cuddly, and flower-bedecked *Puppy Dog* sculpture out front.

The brightly colored and oddly shaped restaurant at the Guggenheim is even a treat for tots. As in San Sebastián, *pintxos* bars in the Old Quarter make for fun snacking. After lunch, take the elevator up to the upper town and Basílica de Begoña for a panoramic view of the river and the "Guggy."

Touring Spain's Great Works of Art in One Week

If you're a committed art lover, you can pack the high points of the world-class Spanish art scene into one week if you're willing to fly among Spanish cities. An international flight that allows you to fly into Madrid and leave from Barcelona (or vice-versa) is a good option. Beginning in **Madrid** — you may as well start at the top — follow this itinerary to see Spain's great works of art:

- ✔ **Day 1:** Spend the day at the Museo del Prado seeing the Spanish, Italian, and Flemish old masters (if you're a connoisseur, you're likely to need more than a single day here).

- ✔ **Day 2:** Complete the Golden Triangle, with visits to the Thyssen-Bornemizsa and Centro de Arte Reina Sofía, both just minutes away from the Prado (basing yourself in a nearby hotel is a good idea).

- ✔ **Day 3:** Take a bus or train to **Toledo,** the city forever linked with El Greco. See his masterpiece, *The Burial of Count Orgaz* at the church of Santo Tomé and visit the Casa El Greco, considered by most only to be a reasonable facsimile of the house he once occupied in the Jewish Quarter. For a view of Toledo like El Greco famously painted, take a taxi across the river to the *parador,* and spend the night before returning to Madrid.

- ✔ **Day 4:** In the morning, fly to **Bilbao.** Few art fans can resist seeing the groundbreaking Guggenheim Museum. Even if the permanent collection isn't all that much to speak of (though lovers of contemporary art will find interest in the traveling exhibits and pieces loaned from the Guggenheim Museum family), Frank Gehry's building is itself a remarkable work of art. Nearby, you can also check out the excellent Museo de Bellas Artes, with a range of past and modern masters. Fly to **Barcelona** in the evening.

✔ **Days 5–6:** Start with the Museu Picasso in the Gothic Quarter and then visit the Romanesque and Gothic art at the Museu Nacional d'Art de Catalunya and Fundació Joan Miró (both on Montjuïc). If you're an art aficionado, take the chance to visit the eccentric *modernista* buildings of Antoni Gaudí and his cohorts, especially La Pedrera, El Palau de la Música, and La Sagrada Familia. Killing two birds with one stone, see the Fundació Antoni Tàpies — the third of Barcelona's museums dedicated to a single artist — housed in a landmark *modernista* building by Domènech i Muntaner.

✔ **Day 7:** Take the train to **Figueres,** north of Barcelona, to see Salvador Dalí's idiosyncratic Museu-Teatre. Return to Barcelona that night (and onto Madrid if necessary to catch your return flight).

Lunchtime is the best time to visit many popular museums like the Bilbao Guggenheim. Spaniards, as well as most Europeans, disappear for lunch between 2 p.m. and 4 p.m. A week-long art tour necessarily makes it hard to escape Monday, when most museums are closed (the major exception is the Reina Sofía in Madrid). If your time is tight, you may want to arrive in Madrid that day after an international flight, so that you're rested the next morning to storm the Prado. Or, schedule your flight out of Spain on a Monday.

Getting off the Beaten Path

You may not want to focus only on the greatest hits (the places all your office mates and neighbors have already visited) while in Spain. Many of the places that I include in this book already qualify as off-the-beaten-path stops for first-time visitors — white villages in Andalusia, medieval stone villages in the interior of Catalonia, and so on. Although they're not exactly the Spanish boonies, they are slightly beyond the international tourism mainstream, and visits there allow you to see a Spain far removed from the museums of Madrid or the bullfights of the south. It's trite to say, but in these places, you may find you've come closer to finding the real Spain.

Drawing Up a Daily Itinerary

A good way to plan your time and keep track of what you want to do in each place is to draft a daily itinerary. You can either scratch them out in your calendar, approximating the amount of time you need to spend at each sight (not forgetting the time between attractions for transportation, rest, and nourishment). Or better yet, the worksheets in the back of this book are excellent trip-planning tools if you want to put your schedule on paper.

Foot traffic alert

Spaniards tend to flood the streets just before lunch time (1 p.m. to 2 p.m.) and again right afterwards (4 p.m. to 6 p.m.). If you're trying to get somewhere on foot or do some shopping, these are not the best times to get around. However, they are good times to snack on a few *tapas* (Spanish appetizers).

Tips on Sightseeing Guides and Day Trips

I think guided visits and escorted day trips are most useful if you're extremely limited on time. If you only have three hours in Barcelona, for example, hopping aboard a city bus tour and seeing the sights mostly from the bus window may be the best way to get an overview of the city. A bus tour is also useful if you want to get a general introduction to a city and then revisit on your own the places that were most appealing.

Guided walking tours are excellent ways to get to know a foreign place. A good guide points out buildings and supplies you with anecdotes that you wouldn't discover on your own. Also, walking — though often tiring — is a lovely way to see a city as its residents do (well, this goes for Spain; obviously in Los Angeles, to see the city as Angelenos do, you'd have to hop behind the wheel of a convertible and cruise the interstate). Escorted day trips are a good way to get away on a short day trip without the hassle of managing it yourself — important in a place where you don't speak the language.

Save guided tours for the museums in which you're extremely interested; otherwise, you may find yourself spending too much time in a place that may not deserve such emphasis. Also, judging your guide's credentials is tough. A great (and potentially overwhelming) museum such as the Prado in Madrid is perfect for hiring an expert to take you around. You can find them inside; just negotiate the amount of time and money you want to spend, and notify the guide of your main interests.

A good, flexible alternative to hiring a guide are the excellent hand-held digital recordings available in museums such as the Bilbao Guggenheim, Seville's Alcázar, Granada's Alhambra, and so on. You can go at your own pace, switch it off when you want, and skip over anything that's not interesting. They're very affordable (generally 400–700 pta., or $2.25–$4), and you can even share them.

Chapter 4

Planning Your Budget

● ●

In This Chapter

▶ Developing a realistic budget

▶ Looking out for hidden expenses

▶ Keeping costs down

▶ Checking out sample budgets for one- and two-week tours

▶ Finding out what things cost in Spain

● ●

*Y*ou're probably at least curious — if not yet clutching a calculator — to know approximately how much a vacation to Spain will set you back. Of course, that amount depends on what kind of trip you're taking — an anniversary or honeymoon blowout, or a more economical taste-of-Spain trip?

The good news is that Spain is one of the most affordable countries in Europe: Travelers are the beneficiaries of a very favorable exchange rate. You may find that many things in Spain are cheaper than they are in your home country. When I moved to Spain in 1992, the exchange rate for the U.S. dollar was around 89 pesetas, making Spain ridiculously expensive. More recently, however, it edged past 180 pesetas (and continued to climb as the euro lost value). So barring any sudden economic turnarounds, you're in for some pleasant purse-string surprises. The big cities, nicer hotels, and fancy restaurants are still expensive (but below par for most of Europe), but many hotels and restaurants, not to mention modes of transportation, are downright bargains. See Chapter 9 for more on money issues.

Adding Up Your Budget Elements

Budgeting a trip to Spain depends on where you go and what you plan to do on your trip. Your major expenditures are airfare and accommodations; you can find reasonable dining, but if you want to sample the best in big cities, expect to pay. Where and when you go also affects your budget. A room in Barcelona or Madrid, Pamplona during the

Running of the Bulls, or Seville during Easter or April Fair, costs a lot more than what you'd pay in a smaller city during the shoulder or off seasons; ditto for all other expenses (meals and so on) down the line.

Use the budget worksheets at the end of this book to help you figure out where (and how far) your money will go. So that you don't encounter any (okay, many) surprises, start the numbers game from the moment you walk out of your home's door: In your head, walk through your trip. Begin with transportation costs to the airport, your airfare (see Chapter 6 for tips on getting to Spain for less), the price of getting to your hotel once in Spain, and then all your daily expenses: the hotel, local transportation, meals, and admission and entertainment costs. The number at which you arrive is your base cost. If you're a thrifty traveler, add another 10 percent to this base cost for good measure; if you're more relaxed about spending money, add 15 to 20 percent to the base cost to cover unknown expenses that, hard as you try, may get away from you. Tables 4-1 and 4-2 give you a sampling of what things cost in a few Spanish cities — one more expensive big city (Barcelona) and one less expensive smaller city (Ronda).

Table 4-1   What Things Cost in Barcelona

Item	Cost in U.S. dollars
Taxi from airport to Plaça de Catalunya	$17
One metro or bus ride (not discount ticket)	85¢
Café (coffee)	$1
Beer at *tapas* bar	$2
Scotch at nightclub	$7
Local phone call	20¢
Double Room at Hotel Astoria	$125
Ticket to concert at Palau de la Música	$11–$55
Movie ticket (*versión original,* in English)	$6
Admission to the Picasso Museum	$4
Dinner at Casa Calvet	$40
Lunch at La Dentellière	$10
Cover charge at Tablao Flamenco Cordobés, one drink included	$23

Table 4-2	What Things Cost in Ronda
Item	*Cost in U.S. dollars*
Taxi from train station	$2.75
Café (coffee)	85¢
Beer at *tapas* bar	$1.50
Scotch at nightclub	$5
Local phone call	20¢
Double room at Parador de Ronda	$85
Admission to Plaza de Toros (bullfighting ring)	$2
Dinner at Restaurante Tragabuches	$35
Lunch at Casa Santa Pola	$15
Horseback riding, one hour	$22

Figuring out transportation costs

Assume that airfare is one of your biggest expenses, even after you apply all the cost-cutting tips that I give you later in this chapter. Airfares fluctuate year round, with special deals offered during low travel season and prices hiked up for holidays. Of course, fares vary widely depending on your point of origin and your destination. For example, if you live in New York, with the shorter distance and greater frequency of flights, you may pay anywhere from $450 to $800 for a round-trip ticket to Madrid or Barcelona. The price range from the West Coast of the U.S. and much of Canada goes up from the New York–based prices. If you're flying from London, you're in especially good luck, because there are tons of special flight deals and charters.

Most transportation costs on the ground are reasonable — even surprisingly affordable — in Spain. Within major cities (like Barcelona, Bilbao, and Madrid), the *metro,* or subway, is efficient and a great deal, especially if you purchase a multi-trip ticket. Buses are just as affordable, and even taxis won't bust too many budgets (most in-town trips cost less than 1,000 pta./$5.50).

As for transportation in a specific region or around Spain, your choices are air, rail, or rental car. Unless you're in a real hurry, or you need to cover a lot of ground (say, Barcelona to Seville or Madrid to Bilbao), you probably don't need to fly. Flights around Spain are expensive, though the Barcelona-Madrid shuttle flight, once prohibitively costly, is now somewhat affordable (about $100). Spanish trains are punctual and attractively priced.

The most costly option is to rent a car, which, at $70 and up per day, you should only consider in areas where good public transportation options don't exist, you need to cover a lot of ground in a short period of time, or, of course, where the flexibility of your own car really adds to the trip (the Pueblos Blancos in Andalusia is a good example). In each region's chapter, I discuss whether a rental car is a good idea. *Petrol* (gasoline) is one of the major expenses in European countries, and the same is true in Spain. At this writing, a gallon of unleaded gasoline costs 150 pesetas (83¢) per liter, which is more than $3 per gallon.

Finding affordable accommodations

Unless you book a package that combines the costs of airfare and accommodations (see Chapter 6 for details), lodging vies with (or may possibly exceed) the costs of flying. An economy hotel runs 8,000–17,000 pta. ($45–$95) per night for a double room. A moderately priced hotel costs between 17,000–30,000 pta. ($95–$165). Expensive hotels run 30,000 pta. ($165) and up. However, only the famous palace-like hotels in Spain (like the Ritz in Madrid; see Chapter 14) cost upwards of $300. Many hotels include buffet breakfast but not the 7 percent IVA tax in their rates; make sure you inquire about both items. (See Chapter 9 for a discussion of IVA.)

Searching for the right restaurants

Next to airfare and hotels, meals are next in line as potential budget breakers. What you work to save on hotel rooms, you'll probably eat up in meals (but that's not such a bad thing; you *were* planning to eat, weren't you?). You can snack on cheap *tapas* or fast food, or break the bank with fancy, multi-course dinners at restaurants specializing in seafood or Basque Country cuisine. Sensible *tapas* munching (heck, sometimes you can put a small meal together with the free snacks that you get with glasses of wine and beer) and fixed-price *menús del día* (daily menus that are usually available for lunch) can really keep down your costs. You can often score a good, hearty meal with wine, appetizer, and dessert for little more than $10–$15, and if you eat lunch late like Spaniards do (between 2 and 4 p.m.), you may not need much of a dinner — perhaps some *tapas* will suffice.

The bottom line is, eating out in most of Spain is nowhere near as expensive as it is in England or France. So what does an average Spanish dining experience cost? A typical three-course dinner in a popular neighborhood, low-key restaurant runs about 2,000–4,000 pta. ($11–$22) a head. You can also find restaurants serving satisfying two- (or more) course meals for as little as 1,500 pta. ($8). (Check out the good options at this price range that I include in every region's chapter.) Lunch is always cheaper than dinner, so follow the Spaniards and eat a full lunch (when most sites are closed anyway) and go light at dinner.

Is there no such thing as a free munch?

All *tapas* are not created equal. You can enjoy the free variety — small snacks that you get to nibble along with a *vinito* (glass of wine) or *cerveza* (beer) — and the slightly larger *tapas* and *raciones* (full portions) that you must pay for but are inexpensive (unless you order the king-sized prawns). However, beware of the place that sets down a too-good-to-be-true salad or whopping plate of food next to your glass of wine. It may be none-too-good to your wallet. Ask about any unsolicited food if you're unsure if additional charges apply.

A note about breakfast: As a rule, Spaniards don't eat a whole lot more than some toast or a croissant and coffee for breakfast. Those boffo breakfast buffets at hotels usually aren't included in the cost of your room, and if you blindly stumble into the breakfast room each morning, you may find that you're tacking as much as $20 onto your daily lodging bill.

If you're traveling with kids, fast food is an option, and you can find your share of McDonald's and Burger Kings across Spain. Their prices don't differ much from what you'd pay in North America at the same chains.

Estimating sightseeing costs

Entry fees to museums and other sights aren't individually too expensive in most parts of Spain, but they can quickly add up, especially if you're a museum maniac. (Museum and monument admissions generally range from 200–1,000 pta. or $1.10–$5.50.) In the places that you intend to go, making a list of must-dos to get a ballpark figure of how much money you need to set aside for sightseeing may help you plan your budget. Many museums offer free admission on certain days; when applicable, I list deals along with hours and admission costs in attraction listings throughout this book.

Shopping

Shopping is the most elastic part of your budget, and the part most dependent on your own tendencies, because you can buy nothing at all or enough to fill a dozen suitcases. Spain is not exactly Mexico — a haven for inexpensive crafts — but with the favorable exchange rate, you may want to bring home Spanish fashions, crafts, or ceramics. Like most of Europe, Spain holds biannual sales in January and July. Steering clear of most items that you can buy at home is a good idea. While the clerk won't physically add on a tax to your purchase price, you can rest assured that it's built-in. If you live outside the E.U. (European Union), you may be able to reclaim part of the 16 percent value-added sales tax (VAT, or *IVA* in Spanish), but only if you meet certain requirements. See Chapter 1 for details.

Enjoying nightlife and entertainment

The price of your evening entertainment depends on your finances and stamina level. See Table 4-3, later in this chapter, for a general idea of what tickets and cover fees cost around town. Although beer and wine are rather affordable, alcoholic drinks in nightclubs and special bars can make even a New Yorker weep. If you're planning on lots of late nights out, budget big if you plan to paint the town *rojo* (red).

If you enjoy pricey extras such as golf, expect to pay a pretty *peseta*. Greens fees can run from 7,500–15,000 pta. ($42–$83).

Keeping a Lid on Hidden Expenses

Unless you plan for hidden costs, you're likely to return from your trip over budget. Among costs that you must consider are: 7 percent hotel taxes; additional rental car costs (surcharges such as a $10 airport pickup, value-added tax — IVA — of 15 percent if you don't pre-pay for the car; and gasoline costs); tipping (though probably less than you're accustomed to); and costs of communicating with folks back home, either through international phone calls or internet café. You can't avoid some of these costs, of course, but keeping them in mind can certainly inform the decisions you make on your trip to Spain.

Tipping tips

Many Americans over-tip in Spain. The difference is most noticeable in a Spanish restaurant, where a gratuity is officially figured into the bill — but none of that goes to the server. In nice restaurants, adding about 10 percent to the cost of the bill is customary. If you're a New Yorker and you leave a 20 percent tip, you may see your picture hanging on the wall the next time you come back. Don't tip bartenders for each round of drinks; leave 100–250 pta. (55¢–$1.35) at the end of the night to show your appreciation. Give 100 or 200 pta. (55¢–$1) per bag to a bellhop and 150 pta. (85¢) per night for a maid. Doormen receive 100 pta. (55¢) per bag. Pay a concierge who's gone out of his or her way to help you or procure something for you between 500–2,000 pta. ($2.75–$11). Tipping taxi drivers isn't necessary; just pay the meter (though a driver who is especially helpful should receive 100–200 pta.). Likewise, give ushers that help you to your seat in a theater or bullring a few coins, perhaps 50 or 100 pta.

Ten — okay, eleven — tips for cutting costs

Throughout this book, Bargain Alert icons highlight money-saving tips and/or great deals. Here are some additional cost-cutting strategies:

1. **Go in the off-season.** If you can travel at non-peak times (October through March), hotel prices and flights cost less (often by 20 percent or more) than during peak months. The best thing about traveling during the off season is that you also avoid the major rush of European visitors, who may make your long-awaited vacation a crowd-filled headache. Major holidays and local festivals are the exceptions to the cheaper off-season rules — on those occasions, you may see hotel prices double.

2. **Travel during off days of the week.** Airfares vary depending on the day of the week. If you can travel on a Tuesday, Wednesday, or Thursday, you may find cheaper flights to your destination. When you inquire about airfares, ask if flying on a different day can get you a cheaper rate.

3. **Try a package deal.** For many destinations, you can make one call to a travel agent or packager to book airfare, hotel, ground transportation, and even some sightseeing tours for a lot less than if you tried to put the trip together yourself. (See "Understanding Escorted Tours and Package Tours," in Chapter 6 for specific companies to call.)

4. **Always ask for discount rates.** Membership in AAA (American Automobile Association), frequent-flyer plans, trade unions, AARP (American Association of Retired Persons), or other groups may qualify you for discounted rated on car rentals, plane tickets, hotel rooms, and even meals. Ask about everything; the answer you receive may pleasantly surprise you. When you're quoted a hotel rate, politely ask, "Are you sure that's the best rate you can offer?"

5. **Ask if your kids can stay in your room with you.** A room with two double beds usually doesn't cost any more than one with a queen-size bed. And many hotels won't charge you the additional person rate if the additional person is pint-sized and related to you. Even if you have to pay $10 or $15 for a rollaway bed, not taking two rooms can save you hundreds.

6. **Travel with a friend.** This reminds me of a t-shirt my older sister had in the '70s that said "Save water. Shower with a friend." You don't have to go that far, but a tandem approach saves money. Traveling alone can up your costs, because single rooms are often almost the price of doubles. If you've got a friend in tow, splitting the cost of the double is much more affordable, and many Spanish hotel rooms feature two single beds rather than a double or queen bed (called a *cama matrimonial*), anyway.

7. **Bright lights, big costs:** Get out of the big city. Big cities and resorts are by nature more expensive. If you're concerned about costs, minimize your time in big cities and resorts and visit the Spanish countryside. Doing so allows you to find the soul of the country, as well as some very pleasantly priced hotels and restaurants in small towns. For an illustration of this, compare the prices listed in Table 4-1, "What Things Cost in Barcelona" (a big city), versus the prices quoted in Table 4-2, "What Things Cost in Ronda" (a smaller town). Both tables appear earlier in this chapter.

8. **Walk a lot.** Spaniards love to stroll, so you'll fit right in pursuing one of their pastimes. A good pair of walking shoes can save you a lot of money in taxis and other local transportation. As a bonus, you get to know your destination more intimately and you can explore at a slower pace.

9. **Sit in the sol and not the sombra.** At bullfights, the cheap seats are in the *sol,* or sun. Sitting in the *sombra* (shade) costs more. Pull out your baseball cap and sunblock and enjoy the savings. You can apply a similar principle when attending concerts staged at concert halls known for their architecture. If you're going more to see the inside of the hall rather than to hear a particular program, go for the nosebleed seats; they're often around 900 pesetas ($5).

10. **Skip the souvenirs.** Your photographs and memories should be the best mementos of your trip. If your money situation worries you, do without the endless t-shirts, keychains, salt-and-pepper shakers, Mexican sombreros (why they sell those in Spain, I don't know), and other trinkets.

11. **Do lunch.** Lunch is the main meal in Spain, and prices are usually a fraction of what dinner may cost at a top restaurant. Plan to load up on midday menus — lunchtime fixed-price meals are a Spanish classic — and you can get a full meal for approximately 1,800 pesetas ($10) or so. Also, order house wine. Spanish wine in a restaurant is much more affordable than it is in the U.S., but if you really want to save money, you usually can't go wrong with the sometimes ridiculously cheap *vino de la casa* (house wine). A pitcher or bottle often costs little more than a pop.

Table 4-3   Sample Budgets: Average One- and Two-Week Tours

Expense	Cost for One Week	Cost for Two Weeks
Airfare (round trip NYC–Madrid)	$600	$600
Individual rail tickets (based on train trips of average length, $30 each)	$60 for two trips	$150 for five trips
A tank of gas ($35)	$35	$60
Overnight in hotels ($60 per person per night)	$420	$840
Meals per person (assuming breakfasts at $5, lunches at $10, and dinners at $30)	$315	$630
Sightseeing admission ($15 per day)	$105	$210
City transportation ($5 per day)	$35	$70
Souvenirs, postcards, miscellaneous ($10 per day)	$70	$140
Total	**$1,640**	**$2,710**

Chapter 5

Tips for Travelers with Special Needs or Interests

In This Chapter

▶ Traveling tips for families, seniors, and students

▶ Accessing Spain for travelers with disabilities

▶ Getting out and about in Spain for gays and lesbians

▶ Touring Spain with a special interest in mind

*W*hether you're retired or a student, traveling with the kids in tow or looking for hotels with special facilities, you may have special needs that you need to consider for your trip abroad.

Advice for Families

Spaniards are extremely family-oriented, and they dote on children. The biggest problem you may encounter is meeting parents and grandparents of all ages who want to talk to, play with, and spoil your kids.

Too bad that the Spaniards' love for children doesn't necessarily mean that your kids will immediately adopt all things foreign about Spain. The food and mealtimes are different, the language is strange, and travel is — let's face it — often exhausting, even for adults with long legs. Therefore, make sure that you think about how your kids will adjust to Spain before you arrive.

One of your main considerations while in Spain is feeding your kids. Will they like *tapas?* If not, finding food that your kids will eat (although what kid doesn't like finger foods?) shouldn't be a problem; you can find American-style fast-food restaurants in every Spanish city. However, the late Spanish lunch and dinner hours may cause a problem, as well as the fact that very few restaurants provide anything that remotely resembles a kiddie menu (though most are happy to provide smaller portions).

Many Spanish hotels offer special deals for children — at least allowing you to put a cot in your room for a nominal fee. At Spain's 86 national *paradors* (historic government-run hotels), children under the age of 14 receive a free supplementary bed when sharing the room with adults, as well as a 50 percent discount off the price of the buffet breakfast.

When traveling with your family, public transportation is also a major consideration. Most Spanish buses and metro systems are free only for children under 5; Spaniards encourage their kids slip under turnstiles to solve this problem — an example of getting around the law that you may not want to impart to your kids just yet.

If you need a break from the kids, arranging day care and babysitting in the larger cities, either through your hotel or tourist information offices, is pretty easy. Barcelona, for example, offers at least four babysitting agencies, whose services range from 600 to 1,000 pta. ($3–$5.50) an hour. Many agencies can provide an English-speaking caregiver upon request.

Family Travel Times is a newsletter about traveling with children ($40 for four issues). Contact **TWYCH** (Travel with Your Children), 40 Fifth Ave., New York, NY 10011 (☎ **212-447-5524**). Another organization and newsletter worth checking out is **Have Children Will Travel** (☎ **877-699-5859;** Internet: http://havechildrenwilltravel.com). Their Web site features "Ask the Travel Agent," and you can purchase the newsletter for $29 per year.

Traveling with the kiddies

To help your kids feel at home when traveling, take along a few of their favorite toys, even if doing so makes packing a little bulkier. (However, don't bring any expensive electronic gizmos that can get stolen.) If your kids encounter foreign kids at the hotel who've never seen playthings like your children's before, your child can use his or her toys as good conversation starters.

Study some Spanish with your kids before your trip. (The phrases on the Cheat Sheet at the front of this book are a good place to start, and you may also want to check out *Spanish For Dummies,* Hungry Minds, Inc.) Most children pick up languages with amazing quickness. Trying out their new words is exciting for kids. In fact, you may end up using them as translators.

Likewise, if they're old enough, ask your kids to read up on whatever aspects of Spain — or your specific destination within Spain — interest them. You can find plenty of books about the country for all reading levels. Asking your kids to help you research your destination makes your kids feel more engaged in your trip.

Using the top family tour operators

Dorothy Jordon of TWYCH (Travel with Your Children), 40 Fifth Ave., New York, NY 10011 (☎ **212-447-5524**), recommends the following family tour operators:

- ✔ **Rascals in Paradise** ☎ **800-U-RASCAL,** 415-978-9800; Fax: 415-442-0289; 650 Fifth St., Ste. 505, San Francisco, CA 94017.

- ✔ **Journeys** ☎ **800-255-8735** or 313-665-4407; Fax: 313-665-2945; 4011 Jackson Road, Ann Arbor, MI 48103; Internet: www. journeys-intl.com.

- ✔ **GrandTravel** ☎ **800-247-7651** or 301-986-0790; Fax: 301-913-0166; 6900 Wisconsin Ave., Ste. 706, Chevy Chase, MD 20815; Internet: www.grandtrvl.com.

Advice for Seniors

Spain has long been a favorite of retirees, who take to the country's good weather and relaxed pace of life. Likewise, the Spanish respect for family extends to the older generation; Spaniards view grandparents as pillars of the family, and they treat the elderly and not-quite-ready-to-be-called-elderly with dignity and deference.

People over the age of 60 travel more than ever. And why not? Being a senior citizen entitles you to some terrific travel bargains (virtually every Spanish museum and attraction offers senior discounts).

Iberia Airlines' **Senior Plus Program** offers travelers 62 years of age or older a 10 percent discount on most airfares, including some promotional discounts. If a hotel or attraction doesn't explicitly list a discount for seniors, never hesitate to ask: *¿Existe un descuento para mayores de edad?* (Is there a discount for seniors?) For more information, contact Iberia Airlines (see Appendix A for a list of airline toll-free numbers and Web sites).

If you're not a member of **AARP (American Association of Retired Persons),** 601 E St. NW, Washington, DC 20049 (☎ **202-434-AARP**), do yourself a favor and join. Joining entitles you to discounts on car rentals and hotels.

In addition, most major domestic airlines, including American, United, Continental, US Airways, and TWA all offer discount programs for senior travelers — make sure you ask whenever you book a flight. In most cities, if you're over the age of 60, you can take advantage of reduced admission at theaters, museums, and other attractions, and you can often receive discount fares on public transportation. Carrying identification with proof of age can pay off in all these situations.

The Mature Traveler, a monthly newsletter focusing on senior citizen travel is a valuable resource, available by subscription ($30 a year). For a free sample, send a postcard with your name and address to GEM Publishing Group, Box 50400, Reno, NV 89513 (E-mail: maturetrav@aol.com). GEM also publishes *The Book of Deals,* a collection of more than 1,000 senior discounts on airlines, lodging, tours, and attractions around the country. Call ☎ **800-460-6676** to purchase it for $9.95.

Another helpful publication is *101 Tips for the Mature Traveler,* available from **Grand Circle Travel,** 347 Congress St., Suite 3A, Boston, MA 02210 (☎ **800-221-2610;** Internet: www.gct.com). Grand Circle Travel is also one of the literally hundreds of travel agencies that specialize in vacations for seniors. But beware: Many agencies specialize in tour-bus vacations, with free trips thrown in for people who organize groups of 20 or more. If you're a senior seeking more independent travel, consult a regular travel agent. **SAGA International Holidays,** 222 Berkeley St., Boston, MA 02116 (☎ **800-343-0273**), offers inclusive tours and cruises for people 50 and older.

Advice for Travelers with Disabilities

In some respects, Spain, which lagged behind Europe's most developed countries for decades, is still catching up with regard to facilities that accommodate travelers with disabilities. For example, in subways and trains, you still find a glaring lack of ramps and elevators. Many of Spain's ancient towns were constructed a millennium or more before legislation was introduced to create a level public playing field for those with disabilities, so you may find that mobility is a problem, especially in small, hilly towns. Expect uneven streets, unending stairs, and narrow entryways without the standard American facilities that ease access.

However, conditions and awareness are steadily improving (one of Spain's best-known public organizations is **ONCE,** a society for the blind that sponsors a top cycling team and is known throughout Spain). If you're a traveler with a disability, look for the newest hotels and restaurants and perhaps stick to the larger cities, such as Barcelona, Seville, and Madrid. Keep in mind, however, that many hotels claiming to offer facilities and services for disabled visitors are likely less well equipped in regard than hotels in the U.S. or your native country.

But, don't let a disability stop you from traveling. More options and resources are available than ever before to help you plan your vacations. *A World of Options,* a 658-page book of resources for disabled travelers, covers everything from biking trips to scuba outfitters. You can purchase it for $45 from Mobility International USA, P.O. Box 10767, Eugene, OR 97440 (☎ **541-343-1284,** voice and TDD; Internet: www.miusa.org). For more personal assistance and general information about traveling with a disability, call the **Travel Information Service** at ☎ **215-456-9603** or 215-456-9602 (for TTY).

Hotel discounts for seniors

Spain's national network of *parador* (government-run) hotels offer a great deal for seniors. The *Días Dorados* (Golden Days) program gives a 35 percent discount on accommodations and breakfast for the over-60s set at almost any *parador* in Spain. (If you're a senior, the same discount applies to your roommate, regardless of age.) Certain dates apply (most are October through March), and the discount is not valid for the parador in Granada, the most popular one in the country. Request the *Días Dorados* brochure from **Marketing Ahead** (☎ **800-223-1356**) or log on at www.parador.es. See Chapter 8 for more information on *paradors*.

You may also want to consider joining a tour that caters specifically to travelers with disabilities. One of the best operators is **Flying Wheels Travel,** 143 West Bridge (P.O. Box 382), Owatonna, MN 55060 (☎ **800-535-6790**). They offer various escorted tours and cruises, as well as private tours in minivans with lifts. Another good company is **FEDCAP Rehabilitation Services,** 211 W. Fourteenth St., New York, NY 10011. Call ☎ **212-727-4200** or fax 212-721-4374 for information about membership and summer tours.

Contact the **American Foundation for the Blind,** 11 Penn Plaza, Suite 300, New York, NY 10001 (☎ **800-232-5463**), for information on traveling with seeing-eye dogs.

Advice for Gay and Lesbian Travelers

Spain, still a very Catholic country, has been pretty slow in accepting openly homosexual expression — even though it legalized homosexuality after repressive dictator Francisco Franco's death in 1978. Progressive film director Pedro Almodóvar *(Women on the Verge of a Nervous Breakdown, Tie Me Up! Tie Me Down!),* came of cinematic age during *la Movida,* the artistic renaissance that flourished in Madrid and elsewhere after Franco's death; Almodovar's outrageously campy (and wildly popular) films have gone a long way toward bringing homosexual relationships into Spain's cultural mainstream.

Public affection by same-sex couples still raises eyebrows in most parts, and it may even provoke hostility in small towns. In Madrid and Barcelona, you can find many gay clubs and bars, though if you're looking for a specifically gay-friendly vacation, you may head to Sitges, the beach resort just south of Barcelona, or Ibiza, the Balearic island in the Mediterranean where an everything-goes attitude reigns. The Web site www.pangea.org/org/cgl/guiagaie.html covers gay life in Spain, including an amazingly complete run-down of events, hotels, restaurants, bars and nightclubs, shops, health clubs, bookstores, and information services.

In Madrid, the area around Plaza de Chueca is where much gay nightlife is centered; Café Figueroa (Augusto Figueroa, 17) is one of the longtime pillars of gay life in the capital. For more information, contact the **Coordinadora Gay de Madrid** (Espíritu Santo, 37; ☎ 91-523-00-70). Look for the free magazines *Shangay Express* and *Revista Mensual,* available at kiosks, which both offer information and listings for clubs, restaurants, and other entertainment options.

A good general resource for gay travelers is *Out and About* (www. outandabout.com), which lists gay travel sites, gay tour operators, and gay-friendly hotels and clubs throughout the world. Also look for *Frommer's Gay & Lesbian Europe,* which covers Madrid, Barcelona, Sitges, and Ibiza.

Advice for Students

The best resource for students is the **Council on International Educational Exchange,** or CIEE (☎ 800/226-8624; Internet: www.ciee.org). They can set you up with the student traveler's best friend, the **International Student Identity Card** (ISIC). It's the only officially acceptable form of student identification, good for discounts on rail passes, plane tickets, and other items; it also provides for basic accident and sickness insurance. Cost for the card is $22 per year. CIEE's travel branch, Council Travel Service (www.counciltravel.com), is the largest student travel agency operation in the world.

Not only is Spain a big destination for students traveling across the continent with a Eurail train pass, it's also one of the biggest study-abroad countries in the world. American and other students flood Madrid, Seville, and Salamanca for language and university semester programs. (Spain receives more North American students for study-abroad semesters and language courses than any other European country.)

Students receive discounts on public transportation and almost all attractions, including museums. Carry your ISIC with you at all times, and never hesitate to ask: *¿Existe un descuento para estudiantes?* (Is there a student discount?) The relative affordability of Spain is especially gratifying for students. Sleeping, eating, and, yes, drinking are easy to do while pinching *pesetas.* Low-cost hotels (in Spain, chiefly *hostales* and *pensiones*) and restaurants abound.

The ABCs of Special-Interest Tours: Architecture, Bikes, and Cruises

There are dozens of tour companies that cater to travelers with a specific active or cultural interest. I've just sampled a few in this section.

✔ **Archetours, Inc.** (☎ **800-770-3051** or 646-613-1846; E-mail: info@ archetours.com; Internet: www.archetours.com). This company concentrates exclusively on architecture and design tours, which the organizers call "intelligently hip vacations." "Art and Architecture of Bilbao and Barcelona" ($2,795 per person) is a Spanish tour that the company offers. Archetours targets travelers with an insatiable cultural and architectural interest. Expect expert guides, pre-trip reading materials (including an architecture reading list), architecturally correct hotels, and no stops at souvenir shops. The Web site advertises a $100 savings if you register before certain dates.

✔ **Camino Tours** (☎ **800-938-9311**; E-mail: caminotour@aol.com; Internet: www.Webtravel.com/caminotour). Use this tour company if you're an active traveler who wants to visit Spain via bike or on foot. They offer customized biking trips in the south of Spain, and a La Rioja Wine Tour (which sounds potentially dangerous!), all on Specialized brand hybrid bicycles. Walking trips through the Picos de Europa, Pyrenees, and Canary Islands are equally attractive. The trips are not all work, though; tours include accommodations in *paradors,* luxury hotels, and quaint inns; dinners concentrate on regional foods and wines; and sweep vans (which will pick you up if you get tired along the way). Tours are limited to groups of 6 to 20 people. Trips range from $1,995 to $3,995.

✔ **Renaissance Cruises** (☎ **888-800-7144**; Internet: www. renaissancecruises.com). This company offers 16-day cruises to Mediterranean and Coastal Spain, including two-night hotel stays in Barcelona and Lisbon (in Portugal!), aboard the new *R2* ship. Stops include Barcelona, Mahon (in Menorca, Balearic Islands), Palma de Mallorca, Almería, Málaga, Gibraltar, Tangier, Casablanca (the cruise also goes to Morocco!), Cádiz, and Lisbon. Prices range from $3,299 to $6,999 for a suite with balcony. When the ship is in port, hotels are cream of the crop: Barcelona's Hotel Arts and the Four Seasons in Lisbon.

Part II
Ironing Out the Details

The 5th Wave   By Rich Tennant

In this part . . .

*U*se the information in this section to get down to the nitty-gritty and start planning. To have a successful trip, you need all the facts at hand so you can tackle issues such as dealing with travel agents, deciding on (or discarding) package tours, and handling money matters.

The biggest questions you probably have at this point, though, are the following: What's the best way to get to Spain? How do I get around once I've landed? Where the heck am I going to stay? Don't worry, we'll get to that and sort it all out. This section lays the best resources on the line (including many that are online). I also explain the basics for step-one stuff, such as passports and visas, Customs, travel insurance, and packing tips.

Chapter 6

Getting to Spain

● ●

In This Chapter

▶ Weighing the pros and cons of using a travel agent to plan your trip

▶ The bundle: Finding out what you need to know about package tours

▶ Booking the airfare that's right for you

● ●

*T*he saying goes that getting there is half the fun — but before you make plans to get to Spain, you need to do a little homework sorting out travel agents, package and escorted tours, and finding a good airfare on your own. Fear not, however. This homework isn't as complicated as it sounds.

Using a Travel Agent

The best way to find a good travel agent is the same way you find a good plumber, mechanic, or doctor — through word of mouth.

Any travel agent can help you find bargain airfare, a hotel, or rental car. A good travel agent stops you from ruining your vacation by trying to save a few dollars. The best travel agents can help you budget your time, find a cheap flight that doesn't require you to change planes in Atlanta and Chicago, get you a better hotel room for about the same price, arrange for a competitively priced rental car, and give you restaurant recommendations.

 To get the most out of your travel agent, do a little homework. Read up on your destination (you've already made a sound decision buying this book) and pick out some accommodations and attractions that you like. If necessary, check out other comprehensive travel guides such as *Frommer's Spain* (Hungry Minds, Inc.). If you have Internet access, check prices on the Web before visiting a travel agent (see "Getting the best airfare," later in this chapter for ideas) to get a sense of ballpark prices. You can then take your guidebook and Web information to the travel agent and ask him or her to make the arrangements for you.

Because travel agents can access more resources than even the most complete Web travel site, travel agents should be able to get you a better price than you can get by yourself. Likewise, they can issue your tickets and vouchers on the spot. If they can't get you into the hotel of your choice, they can recommend an alternative, and you can look for an objective review in your guidebook while you're waiting.

Travel agents work on commission. The good news is that you don't pay the commission; the airlines, accommodations, and tour companies do. The bad news is that unscrupulous travel agents try to persuade you to book the vacations that snap them the most money in commissions. However, over the past few years, some airlines and resorts have started limiting or eliminating travel agent commissions altogether. The immediate result is that travel agents don't bother booking certain services unless the customer specifically requests them, and some travel agents have started charging customers for their services. When the practice of travel agents charging customers for their services becomes more commonplace, the best agents may prove even harder to find.

Understanding Escorted Tours and Package Tours

Do you like letting a bus driver worry about traffic while you sit in comfort and listen to a tour guide explain everything? Or, do you prefer to rent a car and follow your nose, even if you don't catch all the highlights? Do you like to plan events for each day, or would you rather improvise as you go along? The answers to these questions will determine whether you should choose a guided tour or travel a la carte.

Joining an escorted tour versus traveling on your own

Some people love escorted tours. The tour company takes care of all the details and tells you what to expect at each attraction. You know your costs up front, and you don't encounter many surprises. Escorted tours can take you to the maximum number of sights in the minimum amount of time with the least amount of hassle.

Other people, however, hate escorted tours; they need more freedom and spontaneity. You may prefer to discover a destination by yourself, and you don't mind getting caught in a thunderstorm without an umbrella or finding that a recommended restaurant is no longer in business. These minor instances are just part of your adventure.

If you decide you want an escorted tour, think strongly about purchasing travel insurance, especially if the tour operator asks to you pay up front. But don't buy insurance from the tour operator! If the tour operator doesn't fulfill its obligation to provide you with the vacation you've paid for, you have no reason to think that they'll fulfill their insurance obligations either. Get travel insurance through an independent agency. See "Buying Travel and Medical Insurance," later in Chapter 10.

Selecting the best escorted tour for you

When choosing an escorted tour, ask a few simple questions before you buy:

- ✔ **What is the cancellation policy?** Do you have to put a deposit down? Can the tour operator cancel the trip if they don't get enough people? How late can you cancel if you're unable to go? When do you pay? Do you get a refund if you cancel? Do you get a refund if *they* cancel?

- ✔ **How jam-packed is the schedule?** Does the tour operator try to fit 25 hours into a 24-hour day, or will you have ample time to relax by the pool or shop? If getting up at 7 a.m. every day and not returning to your hotel until 6 or 7 p.m. sounds like a grind, you may want to avoid certain escorted tours. (Make sure you review their itinierary!)

- ✔ **How big is the group?** The smaller the group, the less time you spend waiting for people to get on and off the bus. Tour operators may be evasive about this information, because they may not know the exact size of the group until everybody makes their reservations, but they should be able to give you a rough estimate. Some tours have a minimum group size, and they may cancel the tour if they don't book enough people.

- ✔ **What exactly is included?** Don't assume anything. You may have to pay to get yourself to and from the airport. The tour may include a box lunch in an excursion but drinks may cost extra. Or, they may include beer but not wine, for example. How much flexibility do you have? Can you opt out of certain activities, or does the bus leave once a day, with no exceptions? Are all your meals planned in advance? Can you choose your entree at dinner, or does everybody on the tour receive the same chicken cutlet?

Boarding the magic bus: Escorted tour operators

Check out the following tour operators to take you through Spain:

- ✔ **Petrabax Tours** (☎ **800-634-1188;** Internet: www.petrabax.com) has organized escorted motorcoach tours of Spain for 25 years. Its long list of holiday tours include bus tours, fly/drive packages combining stays at *paradors* (a government-run chain of hotels; see Chapter 8) and locally hosted city packages. Its *Spain and the*

Paradors trip is a ten-day, nine-night trip to Madrid, Ávila, Segovia, Salamanca, Cáceres, Mérida, Seville, Córdoba, Granada, Úbeda, Almagro, and Toledo (whew!); if that's not enough for you, try the 17-day, 16-night *Grand Tour of Spain* package. Ask about their Value Season 50 percent discount for a second person sharing a double room (which also requires that you purchase your roundtrip airfare from Petrabax).

✔ **Trafalgar Tours** (☎ **800-352-4444;** Internet: www.trafalgartours. com) is the world's biggest-selling escorted tours operator. This fact is neither a compelling argument to call 'em up or to flee; but it does mean pretty attractive prices. Trafalgar has operated motor-coach tours for more than half a century, and their tours to Spain include a 16-day *Best of Spain* trip, which visits Madrid, Santander, Pamplona, Barcelona, Valencia, Granada, Mijas, Seville, and Córdoba — an awful big chunk of Spain. Prices range from $1,335 for land only (not including airfare) to $1,980 for land and air, including 21 meals — not to mention a stylish travel bag and wallet! If you're more ambitious than the *Best of Spain* tour, you can jump aboard a 17-day Spain, Portugal, and Morocco trip for $1,804, including airfare.

Choosing a package tour

Package tours aren't the same as escorted tours; they're simply a way of bundling together the cost of your airfare and accommodations in order to save money.

For the most popular, tourist-oriented destinations in Spain, like Costa del Sol or Madrid, package tours are a smart way to save money. In many cases, a package that includes airfare, hotel, and transportation to and from the airport will cost less than just your hotel if you book each part separately, because packages are sold in bulk to tour opera-tors, who resell them to the public. Compare package tours to buying your vacation at one of those membership-discount clubs. The differ-ence is that the tour operator is the person who buys the 1,000 options (hotel rooms, airline tickets, and so on) and resells them ten at a time for a cost that undercuts what you'd pay at your average neighborhood supermarket.

Package tours can vary as much the weather, too. Some offer a better class of hotels than others. Some offer the same hotels for lower prices. Some offer flights on scheduled airlines; others book charters. Some packages may limit your choice of accommodations and travel days. Some let you choose between escorted vacations and independ-ent vacations; others allow you to add a few excursions or escorted day trips (also at discounted prices) without booking an entirely escorted tour.

You can buy a package at any time of the year, but the best deals usually coincide with low travel season — May through early December — when room rates and airfares plunge. Your may find your flight dates more limited during this time, because airlines cut back on their schedules during the slow season, but if you're flexible and don't mind a little rain or chilly weather, you can get some great bargains.

Consider these questions when comparing packages:

✔ Is airfare included?

✔ Is the flight direct? If not, how many stops are there?

✔ How many nights are covered?

✔ What facilities does the hotel have?

✔ Is the hotel right on the beach or out in the boonies?

✔ Will I have a view of the street, ocean, or a brick wall?

✔ Is the price based on double occupancy or is it per person?

✔ What is the cost for kids?

✔ Are all transfers, airport user fees, and taxes included?

✔ How far in advance do I have to purchase the tickets?

✔ What happens if I need to cancel?

Finding the perfect package deal

Almost every destination on the map has one or two packagers that are cheaper and offer better value than the rest because they buy in larger bulk quantities than their competitors. You'll be well rewarded for the time that you spend shopping around for the best package deal.

The best place to start looking for package deals is the travel section of your local Sunday newspaper. Also check the ads in the back of travel magazines such as *Travel & Leisure, National Geographic Traveler,* and *Condé Nast Traveler.* Likewise, **Liberty Travel** (☎ 888-271-1584 to find the branch nearest you; Internet: www.libertytravel.com) is one of the biggest packagers in the Northeastern U.S., and usually boasts an ad in Sunday papers. **American Express Vacations** (☎ 800-346-3607; Internet: http://travel.americanexpress.com/travel/) is another option.

Another good resource to check out is the airlines, which often package their flights together with accommodations. When you pick your airline, choose one that offers frequent service to your hometown and one on which you can accumulate frequent flyer miles. Although disreputable packagers are uncommon, they do exist; but if you buy your package through an airline, you can be pretty sure that the company will still be in business when your departure date arrives.

Among airline packages, your options include: **American Airlines Vacations** (☎ 800-321-2121; Internet: www.aavacations.com); **Continental Airlines Vacations** (☎ 888-898-9255; Internet: www.coolvacations.com); **Delta Vacations** (☎ 800-872-7786; Internet: www.deltavacations.com); and **US Airways Vacations** (☎ 800-455-0123; Internet: www.usairwaysvacations.com).

Most European airlines also offer competitive packages (see Appendix A for their Web sites and toll-free numbers). Likewise, the biggest hotel chains, casinos, and resorts also offer packages. If you already know where you want to stay, call the hotel or resort and ask if they offer land/air packages (airfare, hotel room, and sometimes car rental, depending on the deal).

Sometimes *peseta*-pinching packages pop up right before your trip. To get the latest on last-minute package deals, log on to the Frommer's Web site (www.frommers.com) and check out deals for Spain. You may find a $299 roundtrip airfare or a $599 hotel and air package.

Picking a packager

If you want to design your own trip to Spain but you aren't willing to just turn yourself over to the travel decisions and destinations of a mega-packager, check out the following companies:

- **Marketing Ahead** (433 Fifth Ave., New York, NY 10016; ☎ 800-223-1356 or 212-686-9213) is the Spanish specialist that has been designing travel packages to Spain for three decades. They're the original booking agents for the national *parador* hotels, and they also represent a long roster of the finest and most character-filled three- and four-star hotels in Spain (and Portugal), like Salamanca's Hotel Rector. Marketing Ahead impressed me with their patient and personalized service, as well as their ability to tailor the right Spanish vacation to the needs of their clients.

- **Solar Tours** (☎ 800-388-7652 or 800-727-7652; Intenet: www.solartours.com; E-mail: land@solartours.com) is a wholesaler specializing in European and Latin American tours. They have a number of interesting packages, including city packages to Madrid, Barcelona, and Seville, beach packages, themed tours like *Regal Spain* and *Verdant Spain,* and self-drive packages through Andalusia and Northern Spain. Full packages include roundtrip air on Spain's Iberia Airlines, transfers from the airport, accommodations, some meals, hotel taxes, and English-speaking assistance.

  A 7-day train tour of The Magic of Al-Andalusia visits Madrid, Córdoba, Seville, and Granada, and costs $720 per person without airfare; a self-drive 11-day package (which includes a 9-day car rental) of Northern Spain costs $954. Solar Tours only accepts bookings from travel agents, but you can suggest that your agent look at what they offer.

Surfing the Web for packages

For one-stop shopping on the Web, visit www.vacationpackager.com, an extensive Web search engine that links you up with enough package-tour operators to make your eyes glaze over (more than 305 package deals to Spain, offered by 252 companies, at press time). To save time, skip over prices and destinations don't interest you.

The Spanish National Tourist Office of the United States includes a tour package search feature on its Web site, www.okspain.org. Go to *Plan Your Trip* and search for desired activities and either land-only or land-and-air package. The search engine spits out a wealth of companies and their packages, including prices.

✓ **Escapade Vacations** (Isram World of Travel) (☎ **800-223-7460** or 212-661-1193; Internet: www.escapadevacations.com; E-mail: info@escapadevacations.com) offers a whole slew of options for package and escorted travel to Spain, Portugal, and Morocco. Besides group bus tours, they offer air and land packages (with flights on Iberia, TWA, and TAP Air Portugal), unique private car tours (with private drivers and city guides), and mix-and-match tours that allow you to customize your trip to Spain by combining independent city, island, and coastal tours. Deluxe *Ultimate Spain* tours (those with the private driver and guides) have ultimate price tags: Expect to drop close to $5,000 for an 11-day car tour with stays at deluxe hotels (like the Ritz in Madrid and Parador San Francisco in Granada). You can save about $1,000 if you travel via minivan rather than a car.

If you're worried about being stuck in some crummy, tour-bus hotel by the side of the highway, Escapade Vacations may be for you. They focus on some of the better hotels each destination has to offer — I recommend many of them in this book.

✓ **Spanish Heritage Tours** (☎ **800-456-5050**; Internet: www.shtours.com; E-mail: info@shtours.com) specializes in low-cost airfares to Spain. They advertise affordable airfares (Madrid and Barcelona $429 roundtrip, Málaga and Mallorca $529; both are for flights from the East Coast of the U.S.), and also offer hotel/airfare packages to Madrid and Barcelona at good, reputable hotels. Packages include roundtrip air from New York on Air Europa, transfers, three- or six-night hotel accommodations, and daily buffet breakfast. Tours range from $915 to $1599 per person for a Barcelona to Madrid tour.

Making Your Own Arrangements: The Independent Traveler

Because Spain lies across a body of water for everyone but continental Europeans, you're probably going to fly there. In this section, I give you information on flying to Spain.

Knowing who flies where

Spain is the second most popular destination in the world, so most of the big airline carriers fly there from North America, the U.K., and Australia and New Zealand. Most travelers fly into either Madrid or Barcelona, although several European airlines also fly directly to Málaga as well as several other, smaller Spanish cities.

Flying from North America

Iberia Airlines (☎ 800-772-4642), the national carrier of Spain, has the most routes into and within Spain. It offers a daily nonstop flight from New York to Barcelona, as well as daily flights from New York, Miami, and Chicago to Madrid and then on to Barcelona. You can also catch flights from Los Angeles (with a brief stop in Miami). Iberia also offers daily service to Madrid from Montreal.

Air Europa (☎ 800-327-1225), another Spanish carrier, offers nonstop service from New York's JFK airport to Madrid (and on to Barcelona after switching planes) every day except Wednesday or Sunday, and it flies once a week from New York to Málaga. A third Spanish airline, **Spanair** (☎ 888-545-5757), based in Palma de Mallorca, has five non-stop flights per week from Washington, D.C. (Dulles International Airport) to Madrid.

Many North American airlines also fly to Spain. **American Airlines** (☎ 800-433-7300) offers daily nonstop service to Madrid from Miami and New York. **Delta** (☎ 800-241-4141) maintains daily nonstop service from Atlanta and New York to both Madrid and Barcelona (separate flights). **Trans World Airlines (TWA)** (☎ 800-221-2000) operates separate daily nonstop flights to Madrid from New York, as well as daily flights to Barcelona that touch down first in Lisbon. **Continental Airlines** (☎ 800-231-0856) has daily nonstop flights from Newark, New Jersey to Madrid. **US Airways** (☎ 800-428-4322) offers daily nonstop service between Philadelphia and Madrid. The Spanish charter airline **Air Plus Comet** (☎ 800-234-1700 or 877-999-7587) flies weekly non-stops to both Madrid and Málaga from New York.

Flying from the U.K.

British Airways (☎ **0345-222-747** or 0181-759-5511 in London) and **Iberia** (☎ **0171-830-0011** in London) are the two major carriers that fly from London's Heathrow and Gatwick airports. British Airways flies to Barcelona, Bilbao, Madrid, and Málaga. Iberia offers daily service to several points in Spain from London, including Madrid, Bilbao, Seville, and Barcelona. **Air Europa** (☎ **411-712-338-111** in London) flies from London to Madrid and **Spanair** (☎ **902-13-14-15** in Palma de Mallorca; no offices in London) offers twice-weekly service on the same route.

More Britons go to Spain than anyone else, and a very high percentage of them hop aboard charter flights, often scoring some real flight deals. Delays aren't unheard of, though, and booking conditions can be severe — read the fine print carefully. Ads for slashed fares to Spain usually pack British newspapers. A good source is *Time Out,* a weekly London magazine.

Flying from Australia and New Zealand

British Airways (☎ **02-8904-8800** in Sydney) flies to Spain after touching down in London (see "Flying from the U.K.," earlier in the chapter). You can also fly **Quantas** (☎ **008-112-121** in Sydney; Internet: www.quantas.com) to London and catch a British Air flight on to Spain from there.

Deciding which airport to fly into

Most international flights go to Madrid's **Barajas** or Barcelona's **El Prat** airports. Which airport you fly into should depend upon the itinerary you wish to follow in Spain. If you plan to see Catalonia (including Barcelona), the Balearic Islands, or the north of Spain, flying into Barcelona's El Prat is your best bet. For most other parts of Spain, including Castile, Galicia, and Andalusia, you're better off flying into Madrid's Barajas, which offers more direct train and air service to those destinations. Madrid also includes easy connections to the Basque Country and Navarra. If you're flying from the U.K., you can also fly directly to Andalusia (Málaga) or the Basque Country (Bilbao) on British Airways.

Getting the best airfare

Competition among the major U.S. airlines is unlike that of any other industry. A coach seat is virtually the same from one carrier to another, yet the difference in price may run as high as $1,000 for a product with the same basic value.

Business travelers who need the flexibility to purchase their tickets at the last minute, change their itinerary at a moment's notice, or who want to get home before the weekend pay the premium rate, known as *full fare*. Passengers who can book their ticket long in advance, who don't mind staying over Saturday night, or who are willing to travel on a Tuesday, Wednesday, or Thursday pay the least, usually a fraction of the full fare. On most flights, even the shortest hops, full fare is close to $1,000 or more, but a 7-day or 14-day advance purchase ticket costs around $200 to $300. Obviously, planning ahead pays.

The airlines also periodically hold sales in which they lower the prices on their most popular routes. These fares have advance purchase requirements and date-of-travel restrictions, but you can't beat the price, which is usually no more than $400 for a cross-country flight. Keep your eyes open for these sales as you plan your vacation. (The sales tend to take place in seasons of low travel volume.) You almost never see a sale around the peak summer vacation months of July and August or around Thanksgiving or Christmas, when people have to fly, regardless of fare.

Consolidators, also known as *bucket shops,* are a good place to check for the lowest fares. Their prices are much better than the fares you can get yourself, and they're often even lower than rates that your travel agent can find. You can find consolidator ads in the small boxes near the bottom of the page in your Sunday travel section. Some of the most reliable consolidators include **Cheap Tickets** (☎ 800-377-1000; Internet: www.cheaptickets.com), **1-800-FLY-CHEAP** (www.flycheap.com), and **Travac Tours & Charters** (☎ 877/872-8221; Internet: www.thetravelsite.com). Another good choice, **Council Travel** (☎ 800-226-8624; Internet: www.counciltravel.com), caters especially to young travelers, but people of all ages can take advantage of their bargain basement prices.

Booking your ticket online

Scouring the Internet is another way to find the cheapest airfare for your trip. The number of virtual travel agents on the Internet has increased exponentially in recent years.

There are too many Internet travel-booking sites to mention, but a few of the better-respected (and more comprehensive) ones are **Travelocity** (www.travelocity.com), **Microsoft Expedia** (www.expedia.com), and **Yahoo Travel** (http://travel.yahoo.com). Each site has its own little quirks, but all provide variations of the same service. Simply enter the dates you want to fly and the cities you want to visit, and the computer looks for the lowest fares. Several other features are standard to these sites, too: the ability to check flights at different times or dates in hopes of finding a cheaper fare, E-mail alerts when fares drop on a route that you've specified, and a database of last-minute deals that advertises super-cheap vacation packages or airfares for those who can get away at a moment's notice.

An excellent way to take advantage of several Internet travel booking services at once is to use **Qixo** (www.qixo.com). Qixo is a search engine that offers real-time airfare price comparisons for more than ten online booking sites, including several airline sites, Expedia, Lowestfare, Travelocity, Cheap Tickets, Travelscape, and Trip.com. Qixo also plans to offer hotel and rental car comparisons.

You can also access great last-minute deals directly from airlines through a free E-mail service called **E-savers.** Each week, the airline sends you a list of discounted flights, usually leaving the upcoming Friday or Saturday, and returning the following Monday or Tuesday. Log on to **Smarter Living** (www.smarterliving.com) or go to each individual airline's Web site to sign up for all the major airlines at once. These E-savers sites offer schedules, flight booking, and information on late-breaking bargains.

Save with air passes

Iberia's **Visit Spain Airpass** allows you, for as little as $240, to hop from one destination to another within Spain. The Airpass is good for all of Spain's most popular mainland destinations as well as the Balearic Islands. And for only $60 more, you can add the Canary Islands. Every Airpass contains four travel coupons good for flights within Spain on either Iberia or Aviaco airlines, valid for 60 days after you use the first coupon (additional coupons are $50 each). The Airpass is available year round, but you must purchase it prior to departure and in conjunction with a round-trip transatlantic ticket to Spain on Iberia.

Another sweet Iberia deal is the **Europass** (not to be confused with the well-known **Eurail** train pass). When you book a flight to Madrid or Barcelona on Iberia, you can add London, Paris, Berlin, Rome, and many other European cities for $125 each way. You can purchase the EuroPass as a part of an Iberian Air itinerary from your home country only. For information, call ☎ 800-772-4642.

A similar program is the **Europe by Air Pass,** which allows you to create customized flight itineraries within Europe for $99 per flight (plus tax). The Europe by Air Pass works with Spanair and other European carriers. For information call: ☎ 888-387-2479 or visit their Web site at www.europebyair.com.

Chapter 7

Getting around Spain

● ●

In This Chapter

▶ Jetting across Spain via plane

▶ Riding the country's rails

▶ Boarding a bus to select destinations

▶ Renting a car and saving money while you do it

● ●

Spain is pretty easy to get around. Compared to the U.S., Spain isn't a huge country, but it's probably larger than you think. If you plan to cover a lot of ground once you're in Spain — say from Barcelona to Bilbao and then on to Seville — you may want to travel those long legs of your trip by air. Otherwise, if you're planning a regionally-based trip, rail and road are the best ways to travel. In the destination chapters that follow, I describe what I think is the best way to travel a given region.

Flying around Spain

Flying between distant points sometimes makes sense in Spain. By European standards, Spain's domestic flights are priced favorably, but they're still not cheap, so consider carefully where you need to fly. The following carriers fly domestic routes within Spain:

- ✔ **Iberia** and its smaller cousin, **Aviaco** (☎ **800-772-4642** in the U.S.)
- ✔ **Spanair** (☎ **888-545-5757** in the U.S.)
- ✔ **Air Europa** (☎ **800-327-1225** in the U.S.)

Taking the Train

Unless you're traveling in a region in which renting a car for a driving tour makes sense (see "Cruising via Car" later in this chapter), the most economical — and generally the most enjoyable and relaxing — way to travel in Spain is on the **Spanish State Railroad** (abbreviated RENFE in Spanish). The network of trains crisscrosses the whole of Spain, allowing you to travel to all but the smallest of towns. Once slow and inefficient, RENFE trains have improved in recent years. They now enjoy a 98 percent punctuality rate. Primary long-distance routes are served by night express trains with first- and second-class seats as well as *literas* (bunks) serving primary long-distance routes. High-speed trains include TALGO and AVE trains, which are tops in their classes. Although TALGO and AVE trains are slightly more expensive than regular *largo recorrido* (long distance) trains and *regionales* (regional) and *cercanías* (local) trains, they are vastly superior and faster.

Spain's train fares are some of the cheapest in Europe. Discounts are available for students and seniors. Purchase tickets at the *estación de tren* (train station) or *estación* RENFE ticket office, or *taquilla* ("tah-*key*-yah"). Many stations are equipped with automatic vending machines. Generally, reservations are only necessary for overnight sleeper berths and the high-speed AVE trains in high service. Make reservations in person at the train station or call the local RENFE office (see specific destination chapters) or their toll-free number.

You can find timetables at any train station or travel agent in Spain. You can also log on to the RENFE Web site (www.renfe.es) to download schedules and fares.

Two vintage trains, reminiscent of the Oriental Express, operate in Spain. One is **El Transcantábrico,** which runs across the green north of Spain, from San Sebastián to Santiago de Compostela. The other is **Al Andalus Expreso,** which travels through romantic Andalusia. For reservations and brochures, contact **Marketing Ahead,** 433 Fifth Ave., New York, NY 10016 (☎ **800-223-1356** or 212-686-9213).

Saving money with rail passes

Rail Europe offers the **Iberic Flexipass,** a discounted rail pass, offering prices that start at $205. The pass permits any three days of travel within a two-month period for first-class train travel in Spain and Portugal — including the high-speed AVE train from Madrid to Seville. You can purchase additional days, up to a maximum of seven, for an additional $45 per day. A **Spain Flexipass** allows second-class travel, which costs $155 for three days travel plus $30 for additional days (up to seven extra days). Children under age 4 travel free, and children ages 4 to 11 pay half the adult fare. You can only purchase passes outside of Spain, prior to your departure. For more information, consult **Rail Europe, Inc.** (☎ **800-4-EURAIL** in the U.S., 800-361-RAIL in Canada; or visit Internet: www.raileurope.com/us/rail/passes/spain_portugal_index.htm; **E-mail:** info@ileurope.com).

Knowing the language of el tren

You don't need to know much Spanish to ride the trains in Spain, but a few short words will help. When reserving your ticket, ask for either *ida* ("*ee*-da"; one-way) or *ida y vuelta* ("*ee*-da ee *bwel*-tah"; roundtrip). Economy class is *turista* ("too-*ree*-stah"), and first class *primera clase* ("pree-*mair*-ah *class*-ay").

Getting around by Bus

Reserve bus travel mostly for places that you can't get to by train. Though buses are often cheap as dirt and go everywhere, in my opinion, they're a less preferable mode of transportation, because they can be hot, crowded, uncomfortable, and smoke-filled. The biggest exceptions to this rule are the buses to Toledo and around the Basque Country, which are faster and more frequent than the trains. For information about bus travel to and from specific locations, see the relevant destination chapters later in this book.

Cruising via Car

A car gives you the greatest amount of flexibility to travel throughout Spain, allowing you to reach small towns, make detours, and stay the amount of time that you want, independent of public transportation. On the other hand, renting an auto is more expensive than the train or bus, and you need to worry about the business of driving in Spain — for example, reading maps, extricating yourself from traffic and one-way streets, and following street signs in Spanish (or Catalan) if you wander into a large city. Generally, I'd save car rentals for the following regions:

- ✔ Catalonia outside of Barcelona, including the Costa Brava.
- ✔ Quick side trips from Madrid to Segovia, Salamanca, and Toledo.
- ✔ The Pueblos Blancos, or White Villages, of Andalusia.

If you're planning on renting a car for any of the regions that I describe in this section, arrange your rentals before leaving home. Arriving in Spain with vouchers and reservations in place is both more convenient and more economical. Otherwise, you risk not getting a car (or the car of your choice) during the high season in popular areas.

Most of North America's biggest car-rental companies, including Avis, Budget, and Hertz, maintain offices throughout Spain. You can also find Spanish car-rental companies, but you're better off going with a name and company familiar to you, especially when dealing with billing matters and insurance claims.

Singing the stick shift blues

If you're used to driving monster sport utility vehicles and Cadillacs with automatic transmissions on wide roads, you need to prepare yourself for small cars, narrow lanes, expensive gas, and standard transmissions. Almost all Spanish cars are stick shifts. If you can find an automatic transmission car, it's likely not only a larger and more luxurious car, but more expensive as well — significantly so. If you don't drive a stick, make your rental reservations well in advance, because most agencies have access to very few automatic cars. If it's been a while since you last drove a four- or five-speed standard transmission, doing some brushing up before arriving on Spanish soil may be a good idea, lest you wind up on a steep, narrow one-way street, nervously absorbing the impatient honks of a stream of drivers behind you.

Auto Europe (☎ 800-223-5555) may not be familiar to you, but it's a wholesaler that reserves cars for you in any Spanish city through their agreements with Avis or Europcar. I found their service excellent and prices very competitive; I left home with all my vouchers and when I had the slightest problem, their toll-free, English-speaking line solved my problems in the smallest of towns.

Even if you prepay after making your reservations, you must still fork over money for local tax and insurance matters at the local rental agency in Spain. Your cost is a 15 percent value-added tax (IVA tax in Spanish) plus any insurance that you decide to take out. If you're pulling out of an airport lot, expect to pay a surcharge of between 1,000–1,500 pta. ($5.50–$8).

Companies require that drivers be at least 18 years of age (some may stipulate 21). To rent a car, you must have a passport and a valid driver's license; you must also have a valid credit card or a prepaid voucher. Your home-country driver's license is sufficient; no international license is necessary.

The American Automobile Association (AAA) (☎ 800-222-4357) publishes a regional map of Spain available free to members at most AAA offices in the U.S. Also available free to members is a guide of approximately 60 pages, *Motoring in Europe,* that gives helpful information about road signs and speed limits, as well as insurance regulations and other relevant matters. For more information on obtaining maps for your trip to Spain, consult the "Maps" section of the Quick Concierge in Appendix A of this book.

Saving money on your rental

Car rental rates vary even more than airline fares. The price you pay depends on the size of the car, the length of time you keep it, where and when you pick it up and drop it off, where you take it, as well as a host of other factors.

Asking a few key questions can save you hundreds of dollars. For example, you may find that weekend rates are lower than weekday rates. Ask if the rate is the same for pickup Friday morning as it is Thursday night. If you're keeping the car five or more days, you may find that a weekly rate is cheaper than the daily rate. Likewise, some companies assess a drop-off charge if you don't return the car to the same renting location; others don't. Ask if the rate is cheaper if you pick up the car at the airport or at a location in town (in Spain, picking the car up at the airport is usually more expensive). If you see an advertised price in your local newspaper, make sure that you ask for that specific rate; otherwise, you may be charged the standard (higher) rate. Don't forget to mention membership in AAA, AARP, frequent-flyer programs, and trade unions. These usually entitle you to discounts ranging from 5 to 30 percent. Ask your travel agent to check any and all of these rates. You usually get the best rate if you reserve at least two weeks in advance and prepay.

Many car rentals are worth at least 500 miles on your frequent-flyer account. Also, check into fly/drive and other package deals, which may include car rentals, and are almost always a cheaper option (see "Understanding Escorted Tours and Package Tours" in Chapter 6).

As with other aspects of planning your trip, using the Internet can make comparison shopping for a car rental much easier. All the major booking sites — **Travelocity** (www.travelocity.com), **Expedia** (www.expedia.com), **Yahoo Travel** (www.travel.yahoo.com), and **Cheap Tickets** (www.cheaptickets.com), for example — have search engines that can dig up discounted car-rental rates. Simply enter the size of the car you want, the pickup and return dates, and the city where you want to rent, and the server returns a price. You can even make your reservation through these sites.

Gas facts

In Spain, unleaded gasoline is called *sin plomo.* Americans find that gas (*petrol* in Spanish, pronounced "*pay*-trol") is very expensive in Spain — about three times as much as in the U.S. It's also sold by the liter (a little more than a quart). Few Europeans drive the big, gas-guzzling automobiles that are popular in America, probably because they can't afford to — gas costs are higher, due to national taxes that Americans won't tolerate in their home country. To fill up, tell the attendant (whom you should tip a few coins): "*lleno, por favor*" ("*yea*-no, por fah-*vohr*"). Many Spanish gas stations, especially off highways, are now automated self-service stations, so you don't need to unleash your Spanish.

Demystifying renter's insurance

On top of the standard rental prices, other optional charges apply to most car rentals. The *Collision Damage Waiver (CDW),* which requires you to pay for damage to the car in a collision, is covered by many credit card companies. Check with your credit card company before you go so you can avoid paying this hefty fee (as much as $15 a day).

Car rental companies also offer additional liability insurance (if you harm others in an accident), personal accident insurance (if you harm yourself or your passengers), and personal effects insurance (if your luggage is stolen from your car). If you have insurance on your car at home, you're probably covered for most of these unlikelihoods. If your own insurance doesn't cover you for rentals, or if you don't have auto insurance, consider the additional coverages (the car rental companies are liable for certain base amounts). However, make sure that you weigh the likelihood of getting into an accident or losing your luggage against the cost of these coverages (as much as $20 a day combined), which can significantly add to the price of your rental.

If you decline the insurance offers by rental car companies because your credit card covers it (be *very* sure that your credit card does cover such things), keep in mind that, according to Spanish law, you're held liable for damage or theft to the car until your credit card covers the charges. This means that *you're held responsible for up to the full value of the car* (in Europe, easily $20,000 to $30,000 or more) *until you file a claim with your credit card company and they pay the claim.* This Spanish law has never stopped me from relying on my credit card's policy of insurance, but I've also never had an accident or a car stolen, so I hesitate to say unequivocally that you should follow my precedent, too. Think about the consequences, and ask your credit card company about its coverage (and response time) in such a situation.

Understanding the rules of the road

Most traffic signs are international and easy to understand. Spaniards drive on the right side of the road, and they drive fast. When they pass on the left, they often zoom up quite close before darting around the car in front of them. They may also honk their horns as they move to pass you. So, don't panic if you see a car in your rear-view mirror close to your bumper.

Spain has two types of express highways: *autopistas,* which sometimes charge exorbitant tolls *(peajes),* and *autovías,* which are free. The prefix A- or E- (the latter a European Union designation) precedes *autopista* numbers on road signs. Exits are labeled *salida,* except in Catalonia, where the sign reads *sortida. Carreteras nacionales* are countrywide main roads designated by N- and a Roman numeral. To turn around and go the other direction on a highway, look for the sign that reads *Cambio de Sentido* (change of direction) or shows a U-turn arrow.

Spaniards tend to drive as though the entire country was one big southern European racetrack, but in fact, speed limits do exist. Routinely ignored but in force just the same, speed limits are: 120 km/hr (74 mph) on motorways and highways; 100 km/hr (62 mph) on main roads; 90 km/hr (56 mph) on secondary roads; and 50 km/hr (31 mph) in urban areas.

If you're from the U.S., another thing you may notice about Spanish streets, in both big cities and small villages, is that they're very narrow. Also, drivers don't worry too much about staying strictly within the painted lines. Driving in such intimate company may take you some time to get used to.

Parking your car facing oncoming traffic is illegal. Many cities have *zona azul* (blue zone) areas where you can park in a metered spot. The meter is a few paces away; put in 100-pta. coins for the time desired (about 200 pta., or $1.10 per hour) and place the printed receipt on the dash inside your car (face up so parking police can see how long you're legally parked). Parking hours are 8 a.m. to 2 p.m. and 4 p.m. to 8 p.m., Monday to Saturday. Non-metered parking is virtually impossible to find. In underground parking areas, collect the ticket and pay upon exiting.

Never leave anything inside your car in full view. Break-ins and theft of rental cars, especially in Madrid and Andalusia, are not uncommon in Spain. You'd be surprised how many travelers park their cars on the streets or in lots with cameras, suitcases, and other tell-tale "please rob me" possessions visible. What you can't leave in the hotel you should lock securely in the trunk.

Breakdown!

In the event of a vehicle breakdown, look for emergency phone boxes on major motorways. On secondary roads, call for help by asking the operator to locate the nearest *Guardia Civil* (police station), which will direct you to a garage or repair shop.

AAA maintains an association with the **Real Automóvil Club de España** (Royal Automobile Club of Spain), José Abascal, 10, Madrid (☎ 91-447-32-00), which provides helpful information about road conditions and travel data, as well as limited emergency road service.

Chapter 8

Booking Your Accommodations

. . . .

In This Chapter

▶ Considering your options, from hotels to castles to paradors

▶ Understanding everything you need to know about rack rates

▶ Looking for deals and making reservations

▶ Recommending the best paradors, small hotels, and luxury splurges

. . . .

*W*hen I backpacked around the globe as a college student, where I slept was usually one of my last considerations — I camped out in train stations and on the floors of new acquaintances. Those days are long gone. For obvious reasons, where you stay is a significant part of your trip to Spain, because you'll spend important hours there after long days of sightseeing. Where you stay can also have a significant impact on your trip: In Spain, you have the chance to stay in everything from family-run inns to sixteenth-century monasteries and palaces.

This chapter homes in on the essential questions about accommodations, including what you get for your money (and how to get more) and a rundown of some of my favorite hotels in Spain.

Understanding Rack Rates (And Why You Don't Have to Pay Them)

The *rack rate* is the maximum rate that a hotel charges for a room, and it's also the rate that you get if you walked in off the street and asked for a room for the night. You sometimes see the rack rate printed on the fire/emergency exit diagrams posted on the back of your door. Because the rack rate is a hotel's official price for a room, it's also the price that I give you when I quote the cost of a room in this book.

Hotels are happy to charge you the rack rate, but you don't have to pay it! In fact, at larger hotels, few people do. Perhaps the best way to avoid paying the rack rate is surprisingly simple: Ask for a cheaper or discounted rate. The answer you get may pleasantly surprise you. (Exceptions to this rule are smaller, more modest hotels, where rates are usually fixed, and *paradors,* which may offer a promotional discount in off-season, but otherwise charge the same official rate.)

Getting the best room at the best rate

In all but the smallest accommodations, the rate you pay for a room depends on many factors — chief among them is how you make your reservation. A travel agent may negotiate a better price with certain hotels than you can get by yourself. (Hotels often give travel agents a discount in exchange for steering his or her business toward that hotel.)

Reserving a room through the hotel's 800-number may also result in a lower rate than if you call the hotel directly. On the other hand, the central reservations number may not know about discount rates at specific locations. For example, local franchises may offer a special group rate for a wedding or family reunion, but they may neglect to tell the central booking line. Your best bet is to call both the local number and the 800-number and see which one gives you a better deal.

Room rates also change with the season, as occupancy rates rise and fall. If a hotel is close to full, it's less likely to extend discount rates; however, if it's close to empty, it may negotiate. Resorts are most crowded on weekends, so they usually offer discounted rates for midweek stays. The reverse is true for business hotels in downtown locations. Room prices are subject to change without notice, so the rates that I give you in this book may differ from the rate you receive when you make your reservation. Likewise, make sure you mention membership in AAA, AARP, frequent flyer programs, and any other corporate rewards programs when you make your reservation. You never know when you can get a few dollars off your room rate.

Racking up the rates come festival time

Occasionally in Spain, you're not only asked to pay the rack rate — you're asked to pay it twice over or more! This situation occurs when you make reservations in Pamplona during the *San Fermín,* or Running of the Bulls, Festival, and in Seville during Easter and the city's *Feria de Abril* (April Fair). Don't think they're taking you for a sucker, though — the hotels charge what they legally can and what they know they can get. Even at those rack-rates-plus, you may still have a hard time getting a room during such festivities.

After you've made your reservation, asking one or two more pointed questions can go a long way toward making sure you have the best room in the house. Here are a few suggestions of questions to ask:

✔ Always ask for a corner room — they're usually larger, quieter, closer to the elevator, and have more windows and light than standard rooms, and they don't always cost any more.

✔ Ask if the hotel is renovating; if it is, request a room away from the renovation work.

✔ Inquire about the location of the restaurants, bars, and discos in the hotel — these can be a source of irritating noise.

If you aren't happy with your room when you arrive, talk to the front desk. If they have another room, they should be happy to accommodate you, within reason.

Surfing the Web for hotel deals

Although major travel booking sites (Travelocity, Expedia, Yahoo Travel, and Cheap Tickets; see Chapter 6 for details) offer hotel booking, you may find better deals using a site devoted primarily to lodging, because you may find properties that aren't listed on more general online travel agencies. Some lodging sites specialize in a particular type of accommodations, such as bed and breakfasts, which you won't find on the more mainstream booking services. Other services, such as TravelWeb (described in the following list), offer weekend deals on major chain properties, which cater to business travelers and thus have more empty rooms on weekends. Try the following services:

✔ Although the name **All Hotels on the Web** (www.all-hotels. com) is something of a misnomer, the site does offer tens of thousands of listings throughout the world. Bear in mind that each hotel listed paid a small fee (of $25 and up) to be listed, so it's less of an objective list and more like a book of online brochures.

✔ **hoteldiscount!com** (www.180096hotel.com) lists bargain room rates at hotels in more than 50 U.S. and international cities. The cool thing is that hoteldiscount!com pre-books blocks of rooms in advance, so sometimes you can find rooms — at discount rates — at hotels that are "sold out." Select a city, input your dates, and you get a list of best prices for a selection of hotels. This site is notable for delivering deep discounts in cities where hotel rooms are expensive. The toll-free number is printed all over this site (☎ 800-96-HOTEL); call it if you want more options than those listed online.

✔ **InnSite** (www.innsite.com) has B&B listings in all 50 U.S. states and more than 50 countries around the globe. Find an inn at your destination, see pictures of the rooms, and check prices and availability. This extensive directory of bed and breakfasts only includes listings if the proprietor submitted one (getting an inn listed is free). Innkeepers write the descriptions, and many listings link to the inn's own Web sites.

✔ **TravelWeb** (www.travelweb.com) lists more than 26,000 hotels in 170 countries, focusing on chains such as Hyatt and Hilton, and you can book almost 90 percent of these online. TravelWeb's Click-It Weekends, updated each Monday, offers weekend deals at many leading hotel chains.

Determining Your Hotel Needs

If you play your cards right, you can make your accommodations as evocative as the museums, castles, and flamenco shows that you visit. From converted medieval castles and Renaissance palaces to sixteenth-century and art nouveau mansions, Spain has an unrivalled network of atmospheric — and surprisingly affordable — places to stay. If the options I mention sound too grandiose, you can also find regular hotels and guesthouses. However, don't dismiss where you'll lay your head as a place that you'll see only in the dark for a few hours a night. A unique hotel can equal the experience of visiting a special museum, as well as enhance your appreciation of Spain.

Because hotel accommodations are more reasonable across the board in Spain than in almost all other European countries, in this book, I focus on moderate to expensive hotels and the national *paradors* (a chain of state-owned properties that are discussed later in this chapter). Most of the small and very inexpensive *pensiones* (pensions), *hostales* (hostels), and *albergues* (guesthouses) have few amenities (such as private bathrooms) and even fewer personnel who speak English, so with a few exceptions, I stay away from this category. Instead, I include the best-value hotels in each city and region, while making a special effort to include hotels with convenient locations (so you're not stuck in the boondocks away from the majority of attractions) and hotels with special Spanish character or architectural distinction. I also include a few high-priced hotels in several places because they're simply worth the splurge.

Spain doesn't yet have bed-and-breakfast options on the same scale as the U.K. or U.S. (I include just one in this book, in Madrid). Self-catering options — staying at *casas rurales* (rustic farmhouses) or week-long rentals, for example — are mostly available in the countryside of Navarra and the Basque Country or in the Balearic Islands. If you want to stay in a house and cook for yourself, I also provide information on how to do so in these areas (later in this chapter).

I think you'll find that most Spanish hotels are a delight. Don't expect them all to have 24-hour room service, coffee makers, fax machines,

E-mail, and other American-style conveniences, however. In Spain, most people still eat in restaurants, have their coffee at a café, and conduct business at the office. What you can expect from most hotels is personal service and a willingness to help you with directions, travel advice, and personal recommendations. At the more pricey properties, you can almost universally expect hotel personnel to speak fairly fluent English. At smaller hotels, however, you need a little patience, because employees may sometimes not understand you. Spaniards are wonderfully patient and eager to help, though, and communicating in simple English or with sign language is part of the fun of traveling abroad.

Finding affordable accommodation isn't a huge problem in most parts of Spain, though Barcelona and Madrid are considerably more expensive than the rest of the country. Determining how much to budget for a hotel depends not only on your finances, but also on how much time you plan to spend in your room. If you're happy with a clean but functionally furnished double hotel room with a private bathroom and cable TV, expect to pay about 6,000–12,000 pta. ($33–$67). This price won't get you luxury; it's strictly budget territory. Rooms for this price are no frills where decor is concerned, but it's a livable and perfectly inoffensive environment. Occasionally you can get a great location, but doing so is a rarity.

If you're willing to part with 14,000–20,000 pta. ($78–$111), in most cities and towns you can get a room with a good deal of comfort and, often, some Spanish charm. You can also land a desirable, convenient location. Naturally, the more you're willing to spend, the better the service and more luxurious the accommodations. However, be extremely careful about extras like telephone calls and minibar goodies, for which Spanish hotels, just like their counterparts all over the world, charge highway robbery prices. (Avoid calling home from your hotel without a calling card at all costs.)

Remember that breakfast most often costs extra and a 7 percent value-added tax (IVA tax in Spain) is added to the cost of your room and anything else you consume (including breakfast, telephone calls, laundry, and mini-bar items).

In general, you should make your hotel reservations up to a couple of months in advance (desirable, smaller hotels fill up fast). If you're traveling in high season (April to October) or to places that are swamped for special events, make your reservations even earlier. Many hotels in Seville and Córdoba during Easter Week, as well as *Feria de Abril* and May festivals, respectively, recommend making reservations six months or more in advance. For Pamplona's Running of the Bulls in July, making your reservations a year in advance may not be soon enough.

Staying at a luxury hotel

The top-flight hotels in Spain are, for the most part, less expensive than their counterparts in other parts of Europe. But make no mistake about it: Spain has some of the finest luxury hotels on the continent. Here are my picks for the top splurges (even though several aren't all that much more expensive than an average-cost hotel):

- **Claris, Ritz** and **Hotel Arts,** Barcelona (see Chapter 11)
- **Mas de Torrent,** Girona (see Chapter 12)
- **Hotel Carlton** and **López de Haro,** Bilbao (Chapter 13)
- **Santo Mauro, Villa Real,** and **Ritz,** Madrid (Chapter 14)
- **Ciudad de Toledo,** Toledo (Chapter 15)
- **Hotel Residencia Rector,** Salamanca (Chapter 15)
- **Alfonso XIII, Casa Imperial** and **Hacienda Benazuza,** Seville (Chapter 16)
- **Alhambra Palace,** Granada (Chapter 18)

Introducing paradors, Spain's historic government-run hotels

Foremost among Spain's hotel offerings is the state-owned chain of national *paradors,* which you can find sprinkled throughout Spain. Many are former castles, convents, or palaces restored and furnished with period pieces and modern amenities. Staying at a couple of the top *paradors* really adds to the flavor of your Spanish vacation. The first *parador* opened in 1928, and several of these establishments are among the finest places you can stay anywhere, at prices far below most deluxe hotels. *Paradors* haven't raised prices in more than two years, despite the steadily declining rate of exchange for the peseta versus several currencies, the dollar included — so they're more of a bargain than ever.

The best of the *paradors* rank as both great experiences and bargains. Among the stars of the 86-member network is Granada's **Parador de San Francisco,** but even if you can't get into that one, you can find others nearly as historic and beautiful. *Paradors* are not uniform in cost, but with a couple of exceptions, they run about 15,000–18,000 pta. ($83–$100) per night for a double. For reservations at any of the *paradors,* call **Central de Reservas** (☎ **91-516-66-66;** Fax: 91-516-66-57; Internet: www. parador.es). You can also go through the North American booking agent, **Marketing Ahead,** 433 Fifth Ave., New York, NY 10016 (☎ **800-223-1356;** Fax: 212-686-0271).

Not all *paradors* are alike. Most are in historic buildings, but a few are modern and unattractive. Pretty much across the board, though, they've got dynamite locations. Here's my selection of the best national *paradors* in the regions that I cover in this book:

- ✔ **Parador Príncipe de Viana,** Olite (Chapter 13)

- ✔ **Parador de Toledo,** Toledo (Chapter 15)

- ✔ **Parador Casa del Corregidor,** Arcos de la Frontera (Chapter 17)

- ✔ **Parador de Ronda,** Ronda (Chapter 17)

- ✔ **Parador de San Francisco,** Granada (Chapter 18)

Enjoying the charm of Spain's smaller hotels

One of the best accommodation choices in Spain is the smaller, charming hotels that are full of character. These hotels are usually tied to a city or region, and they're often converted mansions, old Arab *cármenes* (houses with enclosed orchards and gardens), and rustic farmhouses. Expect to pay between 12,000–18,000 pta. ($67–$100) for a double at these smaller accommodations, though some are cheaper.

The following is my partial list of hotels unique in their purely Spanish charm:

- ✔ **Hotel Niza,** San Sebastián (Chapter 13)

- ✔ **Hotel Monaco,** Madrid (Chapter 14)

- ✔ **Hotel Infanta Isabel** and **Hotel Los Linajes,** Segovia (Chapter 15)

- ✔ **Hotel Residencia Rector,** Salamanca (Chapter 15)

- ✔ **Hostal del Cardenal,** Toledo (Chapter 15)

- ✔ **Las Casas de la Judería, Las Casas de los Mercaderes,** and **Taberna del Alabardero,** Seville (Chapter 16)

- ✔ **Hotel Amistad Córdoba,** Córdoba (Chapter 16)

- ✔ **Cortijo Fain,** Arcos de la Frontera (Chapter 17)

- ✔ **Hotel San Gabriel,** Ronda (Chapter 17)

- ✔ **Hotel Carmen de Santa Inés** and **Hotel Palacio de Santa Inés** (Granada, Chapter 18)

Receiving paramount deals at paradors

Spain's *paradors* have a special **Two-Night Stay** promotion during certain dates at almost any of the hotels. If you stay two or more nights half-board (breakfast and one other meal included), you receive a 20 percent discount on the price of the room, the buffet breakfast, and menu of the day for the second meal you choose. Children 14 and under receive a 50 percent discount July through October and during Easter week; and they can stay for free during rest of year. Another great deal is the **Five-Night Discount Book,** which contains five vouchers that you can use to stay at any *parador* included in the promotion for 10,500 pta. ($58) for a double room (certain dates apply). At some *paradors,* this is a savings of nearly $50.

Other deals available include a 50 percent discount on the price of adult buffet breakfast; 50 percent off the price of adult *menú del día* (menu of the day) in parador restaurants; and a free cot for children up to age 2. Likewise, seniors receive especially good deals at *paradors* (see "Advice for Seniors" in Chapter 5). For more information, visit the Web site, www.parador.es, or contact Marketing Ahead (☎ **800-223-1356**).

Chapter 9

Money Matters

In This Chapter

▶ Winning the exchange rate game

▶ Everything you need to know about the peseta and euro

▶ Deciding which is best: ATMs, traveler's checks, or credit cards

▶ Understanding IVA (value-added tax) and how to get a refund

*B*y introducing a single common currency for member nations, the European Union is doing its best to make currency-exchange headaches a thing of the past. But until 2002, if you're visiting Spain, you still need to get your hands on *pesetas* and understand the local currency. What's the best way to deal with money matters while you're traveling in Spain? With traveler's checks? Using local ATM machines to withdraw cash, just like at home? Or whipping out plastic across the country? This chapter answers your questions about dishing out your dough.

Making Sense of the Peseta

Spanish currency is the *peseta* ("pay-*say*-tah"), usually abbreviated pta. or ptas. (and occasionally PTE.). Coins come in denominations of 5, 10, 25, 50, 100, 200 and 500 pesetas; banknotes in 1,000, 2,000, 5,000, and 10,000 pesetas.

You can exchange foreign currency for *pesetas* at all banks, open Monday to Saturday from 8:30 a.m. to 2 p.m. (except in summer, from June to September, when they close on Saturdays), as well as at *casas de cambio* (exchange bureaus) in the main cities. A good number of hotels and travel agencies also exchange money. In addition, most hotels, restaurants, and shops accept traveler's checks and leading international credit cards.

Breaking down the exchange rates

For the latest exchange rates, log on to CNN's travel Web site, www. cnn.com/travel/currency, which features a convenient convertibility tool. Plug in any world currency against the Spanish *peseta* and instantly receive the current, official exchange — pretty cool.

Once you're in Spain, you find that quick calculations are easier if you figure out approximately how much 1,000 pta. is worth. For example, if 1,000 pta. is about $5, something that costs 5,000 pta. is $25 (5 × $5 = $25).

Keep in mind that all prices in this book are calculated at 180 pta. to one U.S. dollar, but it's likely that the rate has fluctuated by the time you reach Spain. At press time, here are the latest exchange rates for Spanish *pesetas:*

> 1 British pound = 273 *pesetas*
>
> 1 U.S. dollar = 180 *pesetas*
>
> 1 Canadian dollar = 131 *pesetas*
>
> 1 euro = 166 *pesetas*
>
> 1 New Zealand dollar = 81 *pesetas*
>
> 1 Australian dollar = 106 *pesetas*

Dealing with Spanish currency

Take some time at the beginning of your trip to familiarize yourself with Spanish currency. Bank notes differ in design and color. In simple terms, the green notes are worth 1,000 pta.; the red, 2,000 pta.; the brown, 5,000 pta.; and the blue, 10,000 pta. If you ever come across any large bills — too large to fit into your wallet — they are old notes that will eventually be taken out of circulation.

As for Spanish coins, they come in all shapes and sizes. If someone asks for a *duro,* he or she means five *pesetas.* Or a clerk may say *veinte duros* ("*vain*-tay *duhr*-ohs"), meaning 20 fives, or 100 pta. Count your coins carefully — they are worth more than you think. The most common coin, about the size of a U.S. quarter, is worth 100 pta. (55¢), and a large gold coin is 500 pta. ($2.75), so you may want to think twice before handing it out as a routine tip. By the way, the little 25-peseta coins with the holes in the middle aren't play money or the victims of some teenage vandals with a drill. They're real coins and they are supposed to have a hole. (My wife asked me to collect them on my trips to Spain; she put some fishing line through about 50 of them and made a pretty funky necklace.)

Choosing among Traveler's Checks, Credit Cards, ATMs, and Cash

You can exchange money in Spain at three places: banks, *casas de cambio* (exchange houses), and hotels. Banks (including *Banco de España,* BBV, and Barclays), even those that charge a 1 percent commission, almost always offer more advantageous rates. If you can avoid exchanging money at *casas de cambio* and hotels, do; their rates are much worse. Likewise, be careful of exchange houses that advertise no commission; their rates are so low that you lose money. Also, don't exchange very much money into pesetas before leaving for your trip. The rates are always considerably lower than those that you find in Spain.

Using Spanish ATMs

Traveler's checks are something of a relic from the days when people wrote personal checks instead of going to an ATM (automated teller machine). Because you can replace traveler's checks if lost or stolen, they were a sound alternative to filling your wallet with cash at the beginning of a trip.

These days, most cities have 24-hour ATMs linked to a national network that almost always includes your bank at home. **Cirrus** (☎ 800-424-7787; Internet: www.mastercard.com/atm/) and **PLUS** (☎ 800-843-7587; Internet: www.visa.com/atms) are the two most popular networks; check the back of your ATM card to see the network to which your bank belongs. (The 800 numbers and Web sites give you specific locations of ATMs where you can withdraw money while on vacation.) Using ATMs allows you to withdraw only as much cash as you need every couple of days, which eliminates the insecurity (and the pick-pocketing threat) of carrying around a big wad of cash.

ATMs are just about as ubiquitous in Spain as they are in the U.S., Canada, and other places. Look for signs advertising *Cajero Automático* or *Cajero 24 horas* (24-hour ATM). As long as your bank card uses a four-digit PIN (Personal Identification Number), you can most likely use your card at ATMs abroad to withdraw money directly from your home bank account. Instead of withdrawing U.S. or Canadian dollars or British pounds like you do on your home turf, you get Spanish *pesetas.* The exchange rate is usually the best you can get; it's calculated at the current rate, and ATMs (and their affiliated banks) don't usually charge a commission.

Spanish ATMs only accept four-digit PIN (Personal Identification Number) codes. If your PIN is more than four digits, make sure you change it before leaving, or you won't be able to withdraw money from any ATM on Spanish soil. Check with your bank to see if you need to reprogram your PIN code for usage in Spain.

PLUS, Cirrus, and other ATM networks operate in Spain. Before leaving home, contact your bank to see if your card will work in Spain, if there are frequency limits for withdrawals, and if you're assessed any fees for usage abroad. For specific Cirrus and PLUS locations abroad, call the 800 numbers or check out the Web sites listed previously in this section.

 Another important reminder: Many banks now charge a fee ranging from 50 cents to three dollars whenever a non-account-holder uses their ATMs. Your own bank may also assess a fee for using an ATM that's not one of their branch locations. These fees mean that in some cases, you're charged twice for using your bankcard. And although an ATM card can be an amazing convenience when traveling in Spain (put your card in the machine and out comes foreign currency at an extremely advantageous exchange rate), banks are also likely to slap you with a foreign currency transaction fee for making them do the pesetas-to-dollars math conversion. Given these sneaky tactics, you may find it cheaper (though certainly less convenient) to revert to using traveler's checks.

Using traveler's checks

If you prefer the security of traveler's checks, you can get them at almost any bank. **American Express** offers checks in denominations of $20, $50, $100, $500, and $1,000. You pay a service charge ranging from 1 to 4 percent on the total amount you purchase, though AAA members can obtain checks without a fee at most AAA offices. Call ☎ **800-221-7282** to purchase American Express traveler' checks.

Visa (☎ **800-227-6811**) also offers traveler's checks, available at Citibank locations across the country and at several other banks. The service charge ranges between 1.5 and 2 percent; checks come in denominations of $50, $100, $500, and $1,000.

Using credit cards

Credit cards are invaluable when traveling; they're a safe way to carry money and provide a convenient record of all your travel expenses when you arrive home. You can get cash advances from your credit card at any bank, and you don't need to go to a teller; you can receive a cash advance at the ATM if you know your PIN number (in Spain, ATMs accept only a four-digit PIN). If you've forgotten your PIN number or didn't know that you had one, call the phone number on the back of your credit card and ask the bank to send it to you. Receiving your PIN usually takes five to seven business days, though some banks will give you the number over the phone if you tell them your mother's maiden name or some other security clearance.

Babes in euroland

You may have read about the *euro*, Europe's new single currency. Introduced in January 1999 as the single currency of Germany, Belgium, France, the Netherlands, Italy, Spain, Portugal, Ireland, Austria, Finland, and Luxembourg, the euro has fallen fast against the U.S. dollar almost since its inception. But don't go to Spain expecting to find your pockets full of euros. You'll find some prices quoted in euros (in Spain, pronounced "*aird*-ohs"), but new euro bank notes and coins won't begin to circulate until the beginning of 2002. When you receive cash or pay with cash in Spain, you're using *pesetas*. However, when you use your credit card, you're charged in euros — which are then converted to dollars (or your home currency) when you receive your statement. Don't worry, though; you're spending the same amount of dollars whether you're charged in euros or *pesetas*.

 A hidden expense to contend with when receiving a cash advance from your credit card is that interest rates for cash advances are often significantly higher than rates for credit-card purchases. More importantly, you start paying interest on the advance the moment you receive the cash. Likewise, on an airline-affiliated credit card, a cash advance doesn't earn frequent-flyer miles.

The most commonly accepted credit cards in Spain (in order of most widely accepted to least widely accepted) are Visa, American Express, Diner's Club, and MasterCard (called Eurocard in Spain). Don't bother taking your Discover Card — it's only good in the U.S.

 When you use your credit card abroad, the exchange rate you receive is the rate that is in place when the charge actually goes through — as much as a month after the fact. Therefore, you're essentially functioning as a foreign-exchange trader, betting on an exchange rate. If you want to bet on the dollar (or pound, and so on) getting stronger against the euro, use plastic. If you prefer the current exchange rate to a future one, use cash. Don't sweat this decision, though. Unless you're purchasing Picassos, the difference in exchange rates between when you make the purchase and when your transaction goes through is likely to be negligible.

Dealing with a Stolen Wallet

Almost every credit card company has an emergency number you can call if your wallet or purse is stolen. They may wire you a cash advance off your credit card immediately, and in many instances, they can give you an emergency credit card in a day or two. The best thing to do is to call you credit-card company before you leave and ask them for the specific number to call to report a lost or stolen card once you are in Spain. **Citibank Visa's** U.S. emergency number in Spain is ☎ 605-335-22-22 (call collect). If you're an **American Express** cardholder and or you have American Express traveler's checks, call ☎ 91-322-53-00 in Spain. If you use **MasterCard,** call toll-free in Spain ☎ 900-97-12-31.

If you opt to carry traveler's checks, keep a record of their serial numbers in a safe place so you can handle just such an emergency.

Odds are that if your wallet is gone, you've seen the last of it, and the police aren't likely to recover it for you. However, after you realize that it's gone and you cancel your credit cards, call to inform the police — either the *Policía Municipal* (municipal police) or *Policía Nacional* (national police). You may need the police report number for credit card or insurance purposes later.

Getting Your Value-Added Tax Back

In Spain, the only thing you need to worry about tax-wise is something called *IVA* (pronounced "*ee*-vah") — Spanish for value-added tax (often abbreviated VAT in English). Confused? VAT is a tax, assessed on virtually everything you consume, from clothing to hotels to meals. The good thing for non-residents of the European Union (sorry, Brits) is that you can back get much of the tax heaped on items you're likely to buy — with a few conditions.

Europe's value-added tax is hefty — ranging from 6.5 to 25 percent, depending on the item being taxed — but if you maintain your primary residence outside of the European Union, you have a right to get most of it back on many purchases. Spain's IVA on most consumer goods is 16 percent. Hotels and restaurants charge 7 percent IVA, but that's money that won't be refunded. To get money back, you have to be vigilant. Global Refund, a company that acts as a third-party agent for IVA refunds, says that Americans lose an estimated $50 million a year in unclaimed refunds.

When shopping, look for the blue-and-gray "Tax Free Shopping" or "Tax Free for Tourists" signs in the windows of stores. Such a sign means that the store participates in the IVA Refund Program, and therefore, it can provide you with the necessary forms. The required paperwork — filled out at each store and then signed and stamped by Customs officials at the airport on your way out of the country — can be a pain, though, so hold on to all your receipts and forms. (Fortunately, personnel in many stores accustomed to dealing with tourists are well-versed in IVA refund matters, and most can walk you through the steps.)

You are only eligible for a refund if you spend a minimum of 15,000 pta. (approximately $80) in a single store. At the departing airport (or border crossing), present the refund request forms at Customs and get them stamped. Afterward, go to the "Cash Refund" office and show the receipt for the purchase and, if requested, the actual items bought, and surrender the stamped tax-free slips and receipts. (You can also mail receipts and slips from your home country; when you get the forms from each store, an envelope is included for doing this.) Global Refund is the major company facilitating refund transactions in Europe. At its airport kiosk, it accepts stamped receipts and gives immediate cash refunds in the local currency or in the currencies used for the purchases. It can also issue a credit to a major credit card (your refund amount is converted to your home currency). Global Refund claims a fee of approximately 3 percent, and if you want your refund in dollars, you must pay another fee. In the end, your refund is less than the 16 percent VAT — usually around 13 percent.

Be sure to leave a little extra time to complete the necessary bureau-cratic steps at the airport if you wish to receive a refund. For more information before you go, consult the Global Refund Web page (www. globalrefund.com) or call ☎ 203-326-8881.

Chapter 10

Last-Minute Details and Other Things to Keep in Mind

● ●

In This Chapter

▶ Securing your passport and getting into Spain

▶ Dealing with Customs and immigration

▶ Getting the skinny on travel and health insurance

▶ Staying healthy — and what to do if you don't

▶ Packing tips

● ●

*Y*ou can probably taste the *tapas* (snacks) and imagine the beautiful castles on the plains right now. Fret not, they are just a flight away. But before you start to pack your bags, consider a few odds and ends — passports and Customs, insurance, health questions, safety, making advance reservations, and especially what to pack. In this chapter, I help you sift through all the last-minute details you need to think about before jetting off to Spain.

Getting into Spain

Traveling to Spain is simple. Citizens of the U.S., U.K., Canada, Australia, and New Zealand (adults and children) need only a valid passport to enter Spain (and stay for up to 90 days). As members of the European Union, the process is especially harmless for British citizens: You don't need to get your passport stamped (though you still need to carry it).

Citizens of South Africa, however, need a visa in order to visit Spain. Contact the Spanish embassy or consulate in the city closest to you. Visit the **Spanish Embassy** at 169 Pine St., Arcadia-Pretoria 0083 Pretoria (☎ 27-12-344-38-75). **The Spanish Consulate** is in Cape Town: 37 Shortmarket St., Cape Town 8001 (☎ 27-21-22-24-15), and you can find an **Honorary Spanish Consulate** in Johannesburg (7 Coronation Road, Sandhurst, Sandton-Johannesburg 2196; ☎ 27-11-783-20-46).

Obtaining a Passport

The only legal form of identification recognized around the world is a valid passport; besides clothing, it's the only item you absolutely *must* have in order to travel. In fact, you can't cross an international border without it (land borders in Europe are notoriously lax, but authorities definitely request your passport if you arrive by plane or ferry). In the U.S., a driver's license is an all-purpose ID card. Abroad, it only proves that some American state permits you to drive. Getting a U.S. passport is easy, but completing the process takes time. If you're applying for a passport for the first time, you need to apply in person at one of 13 passport offices throughout the U.S., or at many federal, state, or probate courts, or major post offices. Not all of these locations accept applications; to find the ones that do, consult the State Department Web site (http://travel.state.gov) or call the **National Passport Information Center** (☎ **900-225-7778**; 35¢ a minute for automated service; $1.05 a minute to speak with an operator). You need to bring proof of citizenship, which means a certified birth certificate. Bring along your driver's license, state or military ID, and any other identifying documents. You also need two *identical* passport-sized photos (2 x 2 inches) taken within the last six months. You can get these taken at just about any corner photo shop; they have a special camera to make the pictures identical. Please note, however, that you *cannot* use the strip photos from one of those photo vending machines.

When you get your passport photos taken, have the photo shop make six to eight total. You need them to apply for an International Driving Permit and student or teacher IDs. Take the rest of your photos with you. Heaven forbid you lose your passport, but if you do, you can use one as a replacement photo.

For people 16 years of age and over, a U.S. passport is valid for 10 years and costs $60 ($45 plus a $15 handling fee); for children 15 years old and under, the passport is valid for five years and costs $40 total. If you're over 15 and have a valid passport issued less than 12 years ago, you can renew it by mail by filling out the passport application, which is available at the places I described earlier in this section or at the State Department Web site (http://travel.state.gov). If you renew your passport by mail, you bypass the $15 handling fee and it costs just $45.

Allow plenty of time — at least two months, preferably longer — before your trip to apply. The processing takes four weeks on average but can run longer in busy periods (especially spring). You can help speed things along if you write on the application a departure date within the next three weeks. To expedite your passport — and get it in five business days — visit an agency directly (or go through the court or post office and have them submit your application by overnight mail) and pay an additional $35 fee. For more information and to find your regional passport office, consult the State Department Web site (http://travel. state.gov) or call the **National Passport Information Center** (☎ **900- 225-7778**; 35¢ a minute for automated service; $1.05 a minute to speak with an operator).

Keep your passport with you (securely in your money belt) at all times. The only times you need to hand over your passport are at the bank (for them to photocopy when they change your traveler's checks), at borders for the guards to peruse (or the conductor on overnight train rides), of course if any police or military personnel ask for it, and briefly to the concierge when you check into your hotel.

Hotel front desks in Spain often want to keep your passport overnight. Because the hotel must register you with the police, the front desk clerk piles up all the passports in a drawer until the evening so he or she can fill out all the guest slips at once. Smile and ask politely whether the clerk can do the paperwork on the spot or at least whether you can come by in an hour or two to retrieve your passport. If you lose your passport while abroad, go directly to the nearest Embassy or Consulate. Bring all forms of ID that you have, and they'll start generating you a new passport. However, try to avoid this hassle at all costs. Keep your passport in a safe place — either on your person or in your hotel room safe, if your room has one.

Dealing with Spanish Customs and Immigration

On the plane you need to fill out a form for Spanish Customs. (See Appendix A for information on what you can bring into Spain.) In the airport, you first go through Immigration. There are separate lines for members of the European Union (EU) and lines for citizens of other countries. (Pay attention to the signs; if you're not a member of the EU and you get in that line by mistake, count on being turned around at the front and redirected to end of the proper line.) Hand the attendant your passport and the form you filled out on the airplane. Afterward, you can go pick up your bags. Exiting the baggage area, you pass Customs officials (who in truth don't pay all that much attention to incoming flights of tourists from places like the U.S. and the U.K.). They are legally allowed to rifle through your bags if they choose, but they seldom do.

Technically, there are no limits on how much loot you can bring back into the U.S. from a trip abroad, but the Customs authority does limit how much you can take in for free (the limits are mainly for taxation purposes, to separate tourists with souvenirs from importers).

U.S. residents can bring home $400 worth of goods duty-free, providing you've been out of the country for at least 48 hours and haven't used the exemption in the past 30 days. The $400 limit includes one liter of an alcoholic beverage (you must, of course, be over 21), 200 cigarettes, and 100 cigars. Anything you mail home from abroad is exempt from the $400 limit. You may mail up to $200 worth of goods to yourself (marked "for personal use") and up to $100 to others (marked "unsolicited gift") once each day, as long as the package doesn't include alcohol or tobacco products. You must pay an import duty on anything over these limits. Art purchases are exempt from U.S. Customs and tax considerations, so if you're thinking about snapping up that long dreamt-about Dalí or perfect Picasso, go for it.

Coming back from Spain, Customs officials often ask a few questions about where you've been. Mostly, they want to know whether you've visited places other than Spain — North Africa, for example. Customs officials ask these questions because people have been known to make hashish detours to Morocco from Spain. In addition to being illegal, taking controlled substances across international borders is extremely foolish.

If you're a U.S. citizen, note that buying items at a duty-free shop before flying home *does* count toward your Customs limits (monetary or otherwise). The duty that you avoid in those shops is the local tax on the item (like state sales tax in the U.S.), not any import duty that the U.S. Customs office may assess.

For further questions, or for a list of specific items that you cannot bring into your home country, contact your Customs office. In the U.S., look in the phone book (under U.S. Government, Department of the Treasury, U.S. Customs Service,) or check out the Customs Service Web site at www.customs.ustreas.gov/travel/travel.htm.

Buying Travel and Medical Insurance

If you're looking for a little security in the event that your plans fall through, consider purchasing one or more of the three primary kinds of travel insurance: trip cancellation insurance, medical insurance, and lost luggage insurance. Trip cancellation insurance is a good idea if you've paid a large portion of your vacation expenses up front, but the other two types of insurance — medical and lost luggage — don't make sense for most travelers.

Your existing health insurance should cover you if you get sick while on vacation. (However, always check to see whether you're fully covered when away from home, especially if you belong to an HMO.) Home-owner's insurance should cover stolen luggage if you have off-premises theft. Check your existing policies before you buy any additional coverage. The airlines are responsible for $2,500 on domestic flights (and $9.07 per pound, up to $640, on international flights) if they lose your luggage; if you plan to carry anything more valuable than that, keep it in your carry-on bag.

Some credit cards (American Express and certain gold and platinum Visa and MasterCards, for example) offer automatic flight insurance against death or dismemberment in case of an airplane crash. If you feel you need even more insurance, try one of the companies in the following list, but don't pay for more insurance than you need. For example, if you only need trip cancellation insurance, don't purchase coverage for lost or stolen property. Trip cancellation insurance costs approximately 6 to 8 percent of the total value of your vacation. Reputable issuers of travel insurance include

- ✔ **Access America,** 6600 W. Broad St., Richmond, VA 23230 (☎ **800-284-8300;** Fax: 800-346-9265; Internet: www.accessamerica.com);

- ✔ **Travelex Insurance Services,** 11717 Burt St., Ste. 202, Omaha, NE 68154 (☎ **800-228-9792;** Internet: www.travelex-insurance.com);

- ✔ **Travel Guard International,** 1145 Clark St., Stevens Point, WI 54481 (☎ **800-826-1300;** Internet: www.travel-guard.com);

- ✔ **Travel Insured International, Inc.,** P.O. Box 280568, 52-S Oakland Ave., East Hartford, CT 06128-0568 (☎ **800-243-3174;** Internet: www.travelinsured.com).

Being Prepared If You Get Sick Away from Home

Apart from how getting sick can ruin your vacation, finding a doctor you trust when you're away from home can be difficult. Bring all your medications with you, as well as a prescription for more in case you lose the bottle or run out. Likewise, bring an extra pair of contact lenses in case you lose one, and don't forget meds for common travelers' ailments like upset stomach or diarrhea.

I strongly recommend that you pack any medications in a carry-on bag, just in case the airline loses your luggage.

If you have health insurance, check with your provider to find out the extent of your coverage outside of your home area. Always carry your identification card in your wallet. If your existing policy isn't sufficient, purchase medical insurance for more comprehensive coverage (see "Buying Travel and Medical Insurance," earlier in this chapter).

If you suffer from a chronic illness, talk to your doctor before taking your trip. For conditions such as epilepsy, diabetes, or a heart condition, wear a Medic Alert identification tag to immediately alert any doctor to your condition and give him or her access to your medical records through

Medic Alert's 24-hour hotline. Membership is $35, with a $15 renewal fee. Contact the **Medic Alert Foundation,** 2323 Colorado Ave., Turlock, CA 95382 (☎ **800-432-5378;** Internet: www.medicalert.org).

Spain has a national (meaning socialized) health care system, which provides mostly free care to all Spanish citizens. A system of private clinics, hospitals, and insurance exists that's similar to what you find in the U.S., and many Spaniards choose this option (for what they perceive to be better, or at least more efficient, service), even though private health care is considerably more expensive. As a foreigner, you're in a position to take advantage of either socialized or private medical treatment; the socialized national system is considerably more bureaucratic and time consuming. Long waits are not at all unheard of, even in emergency situations.

If you do get sick and your situation isn't an emergency, your best bet is to do as Spaniards do: Consult a pharmacist. Spanish pharmacists are allowed to prescribe medicine and are usually quite adept at treating run-of-the-mill illnesses. You can easily identify *farmacias* ("far-*moth*-ee-ahs"; pharmacies) by their illuminated red or green crosses. Every pharmacy posts an after-hours list of other pharmacies in the area that are open at night. The schedule is on a rotation basis and the hours vary, so read the list carefully and don't hesitate to ask someone to help you find the nearest *farmacia de turno* or *farmacia de guardia* (night pharmacy).

In the event of a more serious situation, call your local embassy or consulate if there is one near you (specifically, if you're staying near Madrid and Barcelona). The embassies and consulates maintain lists of recommended English-speaking doctors in the area. In other cities and regions, ask the concierge at your hotel to recommend a local doctor — even his or her own doctor if necessary. This is probably a better recommendation than any recommend-a-doctor hotline you may come across.

If you can't get a doctor to help you right away, try the emergency room at the local hospital. Many hospital emergency rooms have walk-in-clinics for non-life-threatening emergency cases. Emergency rooms at public hospitals are free, but if the waiting room is crowded, you may have to wait longer as a foreigner than a Spanish citizen. In fact, you may be directed to a private hospital, where you will have to pay (check with your insurance carrier to determine its policy on over-seas treatments).

Remember that not all health care insurance policies cover their insured when traveling abroad, and your coverage may differ when used in a foreign country. You may have to pay all costs up front and collect reimbursement — often only after supplying official translations of all medical reports — after you land safely back in your home country. Even if you think you know your policy, call your insurer to make sure that you understand what will happen if you get sick in Spain.

Making Reservations and Getting Tickets in Advance

For most activities, events, and dining, you don't need to make advance reservations — at least not from home before you set out for Spain. You can usually pick up last-minute tickets to music and theater performances, however you may prefer knowing what is on before you go and reserving tickets by phone or via the Internet before arriving in Spain.

To find out what's showing during your visit, check out the Web sites of the leading cultural guide in Spain, *Guía del Ocio.* It offers both Madrid (www.guiadelociomad.com; not yet up-and-running at press time) and Barcelona (www.guiadelociobcn.com) editions; the sites cover music, art, theater, cinema, and so on. You need some basic knowledge of the Spanish language to navigate the site, but it's not too difficult. In a similar vein is LaNetro Madrid (http://madrid.lanetro.com), also in Spanish. English-language stops on the Web include www.timeout.com/barcelona and www.timeout.com/madrid. See Appendix A for a list of other informational Web sites, including those of Spanish tourist information offices and individual cities and regions.

Big-ticket shows for which I advise getting advance tickets include the **opera houses** in Madrid (www.teatro-real.com) and Barcelona (www.liceubarcelona.com), the **Palau de la Música** concert hall (www.palaumusica.org) in Barcelona, and the popular **Summer Music Festival** in Perelada (www.festivalperalada.com). If you're a soccer fan and you want to check out Barcelona's popular *fútbol* (soccer) squad, **FC Barcelona,** log onto www.fcbarcelona.com for information and schedules (call ☎ 93-496-36-00 for tickets). Madrid's top team, **Real Madrid,** also has a Web page (www.realmadrid.es); call **Caja Madrid** (☎ 902-488-488) for tickets.

If you're a jazz fan, catch one of Northern Spain's summer jazz festivals, which are excellent and well attended. You can get a schedule and reserve tickets in advance for the festivals in **Bilbao** (☎ 944-91-40-80; Internet: www.getxo.net), **San Sebastián** (☎ 943-48-11-79; Internet: www.jazzaldia.com), and **Vitoria** (☎ 945-14-19-19; Internet: www.jazzvitoria.com).

Serviticket (www.lacaixa.es) handles online ticket sales in Barcelona and Catalonia. In Madrid, **Caja Madrid** (www.cajamadrid.es/entradas) lists a wide series of events, including bullfights, *fútbol* (soccer), music, theater, opera, dance, and more. At press time, however, only reserving and purchasing tickets is possible by telephone (☎ 902-488-488).

Very few Spanish restaurants require a reservation before you visit in order to get in. (However, if a restaurant particularly interests you, and especially if you hope to dine late on a Friday or Saturday night, you may want to call for a reservation as soon as you hit town.) A few of the highly sought-after restaurants in the Basque country provide major exceptions to this rule. In Bilbao, dining at Martín Berasategui's **Restaurante Guggenheim Bilbao** (☎ 94-423-93-33), within the museum, usually requires a reservation at least two weeks in advance. If you have your heart set on a dinner in San Sebastián at either **Arzak** (☎ 943-27-84-65; Internet: www.juanmariarzak.jet.es) or **Akelarre** (☎ 943-21-20-52) in high season (July and August), make the reservation from home to avoid getting there and not gaining entry.

Packing for Spain

Take everything you think you need and laying it out on the bed to start packing for your trip to Spain. Now get rid of half of it. Sure, the airlines let you take it all — with some limits — but why get a hernia from lugging half your belongings around with you?

One thing to make sure you bring with you is extra film for your camera. Buying it at home before you leave is almost always cheaper. Nothing puts a damper on your sightseeing faster than paying highway-robbery prices for a roll of film from a souvenir trinket cart.

What are the bare essentials for traveling in Spain? Comfortable walking shoes, a versatile sweater and/or jacket, a belt, toiletries and medications (pack these in your carry-on bag so you have them if the airline loses your luggage), a camera, and something in which to sleep. Unless you attend a board meeting, the opera, or one of the city's finest restaurants, you probably don't need a suit or a fancy dress. You can get more use out of a pair of jeans or khakis and a comfortable sweater or sport coat.

When choosing your suitcase, think about the kind of traveling you do. If you walk with your luggage on hard floors, a bag with wheels makes sense. If you carry your luggage over uneven roads or up and down stairs, wheels don't help much. A foldover garment bag helps keep dressy clothes wrinkle-free but can be a nuisance if you pack and unpack a lot. Hard-sided luggage protects breakable items better but weighs more than soft-sided bags. When packing, start with the biggest, hardest items (usually shoes) and then fit smaller items in and around them. Pack breakable items in between several layers of clothes, or keep them in your carry-on bag. Put things that can leak, such as shampoos, suntan lotions, and so on, in sealable plastic bags. Lock your suitcase with a small padlock (available at most luggage stores, if your bag doesn't already have one), and put a distinctive identification tag on the outside of your bag so can easily spot it on the carousel.

If the airlines lose your luggage, expect them only to pay out a maximum of $2,500 — and that's only for a flight within the U.S.; the international lost-luggage allowance pays out a maximum of $650— so don't pack your jewelry in your suitcase. In fact, don't pack your jewelry, period.

Because lost-luggage rates are at an all-time high, many travelers bring their possessions on board to try to divert disaster. However, planes are also more crowded than ever, and overhead compartment space is at a premium. Airlines have started cracking down, and some limit you to a single carry-on for crowded flights and impose size restrictions to the bags that you bring on board. The dimensions vary, but the strictest airlines say that carry-ons must measure no more than 22 x 14 x 9 inches, including wheels and handles, and weigh no more than 40 pounds. Many airports are already furnished with X-ray machines that literally block any carry-on bigger than the posted size restriction. The restrictions sound drastic, but keep in mind that many of these regulations are enforced only at the discretion of the gate attendants. However, if you plan to bring more than one bag aboard a crowded flight, make sure that you consolidate your medications, documents, and valuables into one bag in case you must check the second one.

Deciding what and how much to bring

Spaniards are generally very stylish and fashion-conscious. Visitors usually need smart casual clothing to feel like they fit in. Men are expected to wear a jacket in better restaurants and nightclubs. Jeans and sport shirts (and sandals and Bermuda shorts in summer) are acceptable in informal bars and restaurants. In fact, you see very few locals eating out wearing shorts or tennis shoes, except during the summer in casual outdoor cafés.

If you head to the north of Spain, don't forget some rain gear — a lightweight, water-resistant jacket or poncho. For the rest of the country, consider sunscreen and a cap or hat essential gear also.

On international flights from North America to Spain, passengers can carry two pieces of checked luggage, not to exceed 70 pounds each. The third bag must be a carry-on, but weight limits vary according to the airline, from 20 pounds to 70 pounds (though no one ever checks). Carry the following in your carry-on:

- ✔ A book (perhaps this one!)

- ✔ Any breakable items that you don't want to put in your suitcase

- ✔ A personal headphone stereo

- ✔ A snack (in case you don't like the airline food)

- ✔ Any vital documents that you don't want to lose in your luggage (return tickets, passport, wallet, and so on)

- ✔ Empty space for the sweater or jacket that you stow away while waiting for your luggage in an overheated terminal

Knowing what items to leave at home

Leave electrical devices at home. Your curling iron and hair dryer likely require an adaptor; so do without them if you can. (Many hotels now have hairdryers as standard amenities anyway.) Unless you're hosting a Web journal of your trip, you can probably do without the laptop, too — it's just more weight, as well as a safety concern and ISP (Internet service provider) headache. Hit a *café Internet* (cybercafé) instead. Likewise, although traveling with a selection of your own music is great, lugging a personal CD player and notebook of 25 discs is more bother and weight than it's worth (I take CDs with me everywhere *except* on trips overseas). Enjoy hearing a lot of live Spanish music instead.

The standard for electricity in Spain is 220 volts, but some hotels have a voltage of 110 to 120 in bathrooms as a safety precaution. Sockets (outlets) take round, two-pin plugs, so you may need to pack an international adapter plug. North Americans also need a transformer unless they have dual-voltage travel appliances.

Part III
Northern Spain: Barcelona, the Costa Brava, and the Basque Country

The 5th Wave   By Rich Tennant

RUNNING WITH THE VERY TENACIOUS BULLS IN PAMPLONA

509

"Get your room key ready, Magaret!"

In this part . . .

The north might challenge your preconceptions of Spain. For example, in Catalonia, of which Barcelona is the capital, Spanish isn't the main language (Catalan is). Catalonia has long been considered more European and faster-paced than the rest of Spain, and though this part of Mediterranean Spain is definitely unique, it has just about everything for which you come to Spain: history, culture, unique architecture, incredible landscapes, and spectacular coastlines. From the 2,000-year-old but cutting-edge city of Barcelona to the fertile lands of Girona province and the beach coves of Costa Brava, Catalonia is very nearly what Catalans say it is: a country unto itself.

The Basque Country and Navarra, on the other hand, are remote and primarily rural areas, isolated by harsh climates and rugged terrain. The people living here today trace their roots to some of the earliest inhabitants of Spain, and they stick to their traditional ways. However, these facts don't mean there aren't exciting things happening up north. The Guggenheim Museum has single-handedly revitalized industrial Bilbao. San Sebastián is a gourmet paradise — the finest restaurant scene in Spain. And Pamplona, of course, is where the bulls charge through the streets.

Whether you want a relaxing trip to traditional Spain or you're looking for more adventure, you can find it in the little-discovered north.

Chapter 11

Barcelona

● ●

In This Chapter

▶ Everything you need to know about getting to and around Spain's style capital

▶ Choosing a hotel, from art nouveau palaces to chic design hotels

▶ Tasting Barcelona — *tapas,* country cooking, and Mediterranean haute cuisine

▶ Keeping busy in Barcelona

▶ Day tripping to a secluded mountain monastery, a lazy beach resort, and Catalan wine country

● ●

*B*arcelona has been around since the Romans dubbed it *Barcino* 2,000 years ago, but it was the 1992 Summer Olympic Games that thrust it onto the world stage. In a flash, Barcelona became one of Europe's hottest destinations.

Barcelona has a tradition of embracing visionary artists like Picasso, Miró, and Dalí, but the city's favorite eccentric son was Antoni Gaudí, whose wildly imaginative architecture is an appropriate symbol for this ancient yet futuristic city. Though you can still see parts of the Roman wall and the Gothic Quarter remains fundamentally unchanged since the Middle Ages, Barcelona has reinvented itself several times in the past century. Today, Barcelona is as modern a city as you'll find in Europe, one that sports a newly invigorated waterfront.

The people of Spain's second-largest city are hard-working, pragmatic, and serious about their Catalan identity, with its strong ties to the countryside. On weekends, Barcelonans rush out to renovated sixteenth-century *masías* (farmhouses) or head to the hills in search of wild mushrooms. When visiting Barcelona, following suit with the natives is a terrific plan. Spend a few days in this head-turning, cosmopolitan city, as well as a couple in the countryside or on the beaches of Costa Brava (for more on the Costa Brava, see Chapter 12). In this chapter, I give you all the information you need to make your stay in Barcelona enjoyable.

The guru of *modernismo*

Antoni Gaudí, a pious man with a devil of an imagination, was run over by a tram in 1926, but he remains a celebrated figure in Barcelona. The eccentric architect of several of Barcelona's most mind-bending masterpieces was the foremost creator of *modernismo,* or Catalan Art Nouveau. In Barcelona, you see buildings molded like ocean waves, roofs tiled like dragon scales, and chimneys straight out of *Star Wars* — and that's just Gaudí. Around the turn of the century, a whole band of *Modernistas* in Barcelona dreamed up the most fanciful buildings their imaginations and rich patrons allowed.

Gaudí's creative cohorts were Lluís Domènech i Montaner and Josep Puig i Cadafalch, among many others. You can see their unique take on art nouveau in its fantastic forms, decorative flourishes (in wrought iron, metal, colorful tiles, and stained glass), and signature elements like Gaudí's bizarre chimneys. This group also introduced convention-defying structural innovations like parabolic arches and spirals. In fact, the futuristic buildings they left in Barcelona, such as the Sagrada Familia church, La Pedrera apartment building, and the Palau de la Música concert hall, still wow visitors as aesthetic and technical marvels.

Just the Facts: Barcelona

Barcelona is the capital of the province of the same name and the capital of Catalonia — an autonomous region in the northeast of Spain. But this chapter deals only with Barcelona the city.

- ✔ **The name game.** In Spanish, Barcelona is pronounced with a lisp: "Bar-thay-*loh*-nah." In Catalan, the pronunciation has a soft *c,* as it does in English. The region of which Barcelona is the capital is spelled Catalonia in English, Cataluña in Spanish, and Catalunya in Catalan. Street signs and place names appear in both Spanish and Catalan.

- ✔ **Cómo se dice? Talking the talk.** In bilingual Barcelona, everyone speaks Spanish and Catalan. The primary language of Catalonia — Catalan — isn't a dialect of Spanish but a nasal Latin-derived language that sounds something akin to a cross between French and Castilian Spanish.

- ✔ **What's for dinner?** Sit at a table or stand at the bar for fresh seafood and wild mushrooms with a Mediterranean twist (lots of olive oil, tomatoes, and fresh vegetables). Top it all off with local Penedès or Priorato red wines, or *cava,* Spain's excellent sparkling wine.

- ✔ **The forecast.** The weather in Barcelona is very mild and sunny much of the year, but humid — think northern California crossed with Washington, D.C.'s high humidity.

✔ **When to go.** Avoid the summer heat and humidity and head to Barcelona in spring, early summer, or fall, when this Mediterranean city thrives. Winter is mild by North American standards and not a bad time to visit, either. Barcelona doesn't really have a high and low travel season; hotel rates remain relatively constant throughout the year, though some hotels offer slightly lower prices when Barcelonans escape the city in droves (during Easter, the month of August, and Christmas).

✔ **How long before moving on?** You need at least two days to sample Barcelona's highlights. Plan a third day for excursions or some time off at the beach. If you're an architecture and/or history buff, you can easily spend a week or your entire vacation in the city and its environs.

Arriving in Barcelona

Only a decade ago, North American visitors arrived in Barcelona only by car or train. Back then, you could only fly into Madrid from the U.S. and Canada. Today, several airlines offer direct international flights to Barcelona from North America and all over Europe. If you're bent on traveling around Catalonia, it's a good bet that you fly into Barcelona, either from abroad or on a shuttle from Madrid. However, you can be an old-school traveler, rolling into town in rented wheels or aboard a RENFE train, Spain's national train service. At any rate, Barcelona is now considerably more accessible than it was at the end of the last century.

By air

Airlines that fly into Barcelona from North America include TWA, Delta, and Iberia. Barcelona's international airport, **El Prat de Llobregat** (☎ **93-478-50-32**) lies 12 km (7 miles) south of the center of the city. The international terminal is Terminal A; Terminals B and C handle domestic and European flights. If you've flown in from overseas, you must go through customs first (you'll see two lines, one for European Union (EU) members and another for everyone else) and then go downstairs for your luggage.

Carts are free; grab one, sling your bags on it and wheel past the disinterested guards (who theoretically are allowed to inspect your bags if they choose, which they almost never do) out to the soaring, glass-enclosed lobby, which even has palm trees growing under the roof. You can find rental car agencies, an ATM machine, and a tourism information booth just a few feet from where you emerge from baggage claim. Drop in at the tourism counter to pick up a map and get easy directions to the buses, trains, and taxis going into the city.

If you're flying in from Madrid, shuttle flights run on the hour (and more frequently during prime businesspeople hours) on **Iberia**

(☎ 93-325-73-58), **Air Europa** (☎ 93-298-33-28), and **Spanair** (☎ 93-298-33-62).

You have three options for getting from the airport into Barcelona (and for returning to the airport) — the train, bus, and taxi. All three methods from the airport to downtown take between 30 to 45 minutes. If you have transportation questions, call **Airport Information, ☎ 93-358-11-11.**

✔ **RENFE (☎ 93-490-02-02)** runs trains just outside the airport terminal. Trains leave every half hour, stopping at Estació de Sants and Plaça Catalunya, and hours of operation are Monday through Friday, 5:43 a.m. to 10:13 p.m.; cost is 310 pta. ($1.75), 355 pta. ($2) on holidays. A new feature with RENFE is that you can use the multi-use T-1 ticket (see the sidebar entitled "Multi-trip ticket bargains," later in this chapter) on the airport train.

✔ The bus service, **Aerobus (☎ 011)**, departs every 15 minutes for Plaça Catalunya, passing some principal addresses in route, including Plaça de Espanya, Gran Vía, and Passeig de Gràcia. (Buses run Monday through Friday 6 a.m. to 11 p.m.; weekends 6:30 a.m. to 10:50 p.m., every 30 minutes.) Aerobus buses return to the airport from Plaça Catalunya, leaving every half hour between 5:30 a.m. and 10:15 p.m. (on weekends and holidays, from 6 a.m. to 10:15 p.m.). The price is 500 pta. ($2.75).

✔ White **taxis,** lined up outside the terminals, will take you to the center of the city for about 3,000 pta. ($17).

The inexpensive Aerobus (500 pta./$2.75) is your best option from the airport, because most of the hotels I recommend are close to the many stops that it makes. The train makes only two stops, meaning that you most likely need a taxi to complete your journey. Likewise, taxis won't necessarily get you to the city much quicker than Aerobus, because traffic in Barcelona is sometimes a real drag. However, taxis will deposit you at your the hotel — an important consideration if you're feeling ragged after a long flight or not traveling especially light. Note that cabbies charge an airport supplement of 300 pta. ($1.75), as well as a 100-pta.-per-suitcase (55¢) supplement.

By train

Trains are one of the best ways to get around Spain, even if they don't have the reputation of trains in Switzerland or Germany. **RENFE (☎ 93-490-02-02)** is the Spanish national train service. Most national and international trains arrive at **Estació Sants (☎ 93-490-02-02;** Metro: Sants). Trains with international destinations also leave from **Estació França (☎ 93-319-32-00;** Metro: Arc de Triomf). **Ferrocarrils Generalitat de Catalunya (FGC) (☎ 93-205-15-15;** Internet: www.fgc.catalunya. net), runs the local trains in Catalonia.

By car

The highways outside of Barcelona are generally excellent — even though everyone drives at warp speed. The A-7 highway leads to Barcelona from France and northern Catalonia — the Costa Brava and Girona. The A-2 leads to Barcelona from Madrid, Zaragoza, and Bilbao. From Valencia or the Costa del Sol, take the E-15 north.

When you get close to the city, look for one of two signs into downtown Barcelona: **Centre Ciutat** takes you downtown, into the Eixample district, while the **Ronda Litoral** is a beltway that takes you quickly to the port area.

Autopistas are toll roads, and in Catalonia, they're among the costliest in Spain. They were either very expensive to build or the tolls collected pay for something other than road upkeep. A friend of mine who drove to Barcelona from a beach near Valencia was flabbergasted that he had had to shell out about $80 on tolls. If you've got more time than *pesetas,* look for the local highways (designated by *N,* as in N-1), which are not as direct but are a heck of a lot cheaper. The word you want to stay away from, the one that makes you dig into your pockets, is *peatje* or *peaje* (toll).

By bus

Buses are generally cheaper than trains, but they're not the most comfortable or relaxing way to travel. You often feel squeezed in your seat, and if you're a nonsmoker stuck in the rear smoking section, woe is you. (If you do get stuck in the smoking section, ask someone to change seats with you; many Spaniards, even those who don't smoke, don't mind doing so.)

Several coach operators including **Enatcar** (☎ 93-245-25-28), **Julià** (☎ 93-490-40-00), and **Sarfa** (☎ 93-265-11-58) offer bus service to Barcelona from cities and towns in Catalonia and further afield. Most Spanish buses arrive at and depart from **Estació del Nord** (☎ 93-265-65-08; Metro: Arc de Triomf); international buses use **Estació Autobuses de Sants** (☎ 93-490-40-00; Metro: Sants), next to the Sants train station.

By ferry

Seemingly out of nowhere, Barcelona has become Europe's top cruise port, and shiploads of tourists now stream into the city from across the Mediterranean. Barcelona's newfound popularity as a cruise port began with the Olympics, when the city made a concerted effort to renew its maritime past.

If you're arriving by boat into Barcelona's port (Estació Marítim), you're either steaming in on a huge Mediterranean cruise ship or aboard the ferry that runs to Palma de Mallorca. **Buquebus** is the fastest Mallorca ferry (3 hours; 9,100 pta. /$51 adults, 4,700 pta./$26 children one-way). Buquebus departs from Barcelona daily at 8 a.m.; Friday and Saturday at 8 a.m. and 4 p.m. Return trips from Palma leave Friday and Sunday at 8 p.m. and midnight. All other days, the ferry leaves at 7:30 p.m. Contact Buquebus at ☎ **902-41-42-42** (Fax: 93-412-35-90; Internet: `www.buquebus.com`; E-mail: `reservas@buquebus.es`) for further information and bookings. **Transmediterránea (☎ 93-443-25-32)** also operates ferries to the Balearic Islands, though most of the year they take about 8 hours. In summer, Transmediterránea operates an express ferry that takes about 4 hours to Palma de Mallorca.

Orienting Yourself in Barcelona

A city with a metropolitan population of 4 million, Barcelona doesn't seem nearly that large. It's surrounded by natural barriers — the Mediterranean Sea and the low-slung mountains Montjuïc and Tibidabo. However, Barcelona is also one of Europe's densest cities; cars and one of the continent's highest concentrations of motor scooters choke the streets.

Barcelona's major neighborhoods tend to overlap (which is why many guidebooks say the Picasso Museum is in the Gothic Quarter, when it's really in La Ribera). A focal point of the city is **Plaça de Catalunya,** which neatly divides the Old City from the modern expansion. **Ciutat Vella** loosely encompasses much of the Old City, including the once-walled Barri Gòtic (Gothic Quarter), La Ribera, La Rambla, and El Raval. The elegant shopping avenue Passeig de Gràcia bisects **El Eixample** (the modern city). Parallel to Passeig de Gràcia is Rambla de Catalunya, a tree-lined extension of the old town's famous boulevard La Rambla (which is in fact five separate Ramblas, but I explain that later in the chapter). The Waterfront area comprises a number of smaller areas: Barceloneta, Port Vell, Moll de la Fusta, Port Olímpic, and Vila Olímpica (see "Exploring Barcelona by neighborhood," later in this chapter).

Much of Barcelona, especially the Gothic Quarter, is a hair-raising maze. How people got mail in the tenth century is beyond me. Even in the modern city's geometric grid, street numbers can be a confusing mess. Odds and evens don't progress logically or even chronologically on opposite sides of the street; No. 10 may be across from No. 323. When giving addresses, locals often designate *mar o montaña* (sea or mountain side). This designation makes directions easy, because in most parts of the city, all you have to do is look up to see Tibidabo mountain to orient yourself. To begin, figure out if an address is above or below Plaça de Catalunya, and then figure out on which side of Passeig de Gràcia or La Rambla it falls. Your next step may be supplementing the maps in this book with a more detailed one from a kiosk.

Calling all linguistics majors

The Catalan language has some idiosyncratic features. A period in the middle of a word (Paral.lel) isn't a misprint, but a construction used to separate the double letter. The letter *i* (as in *Antoni Gaudí i Cornet*) often separates a person's last name; meaning "and," the letter *i* joins the surnames of both the person's mother and father.

During dictator Francisco Franco's 40-year reign, the Catalan language and culture were harshly repressed in Barcelona; speaking Catalan in public could've landed you in jail. Since the dictator's death and Spain's rapid consolidation of democracy, Barcelona has reasserted its proud heritage, and Catalan is again what you hear on the streets. The language sounds a bit like a mixture of Spanish and French — which makes sense, because Catalan is a descendent of the Provençal language of southeastern France.

Most street signs in Barcelona are in Catalan. If you're hoping your high-school Spanish will rescue you, well, you probably didn't learn terms like *carrer* (*calle,* or street); *avinguda* (*avenida,* or avenue); *passeig* (*paseo,* or boulevard). Still, locals often refer to streets interchangeably by their Catalan and Spanish names. The city's most famous street variously appears as La Rambla, Las Ramblas, or, in Catalan, Les Rambles. The modern grid-like area of downtown is most often called El Eixample (Extension), though some Spanish-speakers still call it the Ensanche. Passeig de Gràcia is also often called Paseo de Gracia, in Spanish. Consell de Cent (Catalan) is the same as Consejo de Ciento (Spanish). Oh, and *modernismo,* the style of architecture on virtually every corner, is the same as *modernisme.*

Confused yet? Relax. You'll get the hang of it. (Even if you don't, it won't detract from your enjoyment of the city in the least.)

Exploring Barcelona by neighborhood

Check out the sites in the following neighborhoods as you tour Barcelona.

Eixample

When Barcelona grew beyond its old Roman walls in 1860, the city came up with a hyper-rationalist expansion plan: a major grid of equal-sized blocks. Building took place when industrial and shipping wealth flowed into the city, and the *modernismo* style of architecture took. *Eixample* ("eye-*shahm*-pluh") is home to fine strolling boulevards, designer shops, and most offices (pinstriped lawyers and bankers have some of the coolest art nouveau digs). El Eixample's the best *barrio* (neighborhood) for hotels and shopping, but you may also spend much of your sightseeing time here, because most of the *modernismo* buildings are here. Here you'll find:

- ✔ **Plaça de Catalunya,** a square that's really a circle, as well as the geographic heart of the city.

- ✔ **Passeig de Gràcia,** Barcelona's boulevard of ultrachic shops, and Gaudí's masterpiece, the apartment building **La Pedrera** (also called *Casa Milà*).

- ✔ **Manzana de la Discórdia,** the "block of discord," a collection of some of the finest *modernista* buildings in Barcelona.

- ✔ **La Sagrada Familia,** Gaudí's visionary, still unfinished church, begun in the early twentieth century; expect to find construction crews here midway through this millennium.

Ciutat Vella (Old City)

The Ciutat Vella encompasses a couple of neighborhoods. The *Barri Gòtic* (Gothic Quarter) is where Barcelona was born. Once enclosed by Roman walls, the *barrio* gets its name for its collection of thirteenth to fifteenth century buildings and medieval atmosphere — it's the true heart of the city. *La* Ribera is next to, but in many people's minds part of, the Gothic Quarter. It's very fashionable, with tons of art galleries and bars. The Ciutat Vella vies with the Eixample for the highest concentration of attractions, but the Old Quarter offers more restaurants and nightlife options. Here you'll find:

- ✔ **Catedral,** a Gothic landmark and heart of the neighborhood.

- ✔ **Palau de la Música,** a surreal concert hall designed by a Gaudí contemporary, Domènech i Montaner.

- ✔ **Carrer Montcada,** a street of Gothic palaces — one of which is the **Museu Picasso.**

- ✔ **Santa María del Mar,** the greatest Catalan Gothic church.

La Rambla

Technically part of the Ciutat Vella and one of the world's most famous streets, La Rambla is always overflowing with people, newsstands, bird and flower sellers, and mimes dressed up like Don Quixote and Greek statues. This neighborhood is a great place to do like the locals — stroll without a care in the world, occasionally ducking into a bar or restaurant along the way.

La Rambla, and especially around Café Zurich, which is where the boulevard begins, is the best place in the city for people watching. Most visitors to Barcelona storm La Rambla as soon as they set down their bags. Though hotels (and tons of knick-knack stores) line La Rambla, I don't think it's the best place to stay — it's very noisy and a little rough-and-tumble in the wee hours. Here you'll find:

- ✔ **Gran Teatre del Liceu,** Barcelona's great opera house, rebuilt for 2000 after a horrific fire.

- ✔ **Mercat de la Boquería,** one of Europe's liveliest food markets.

✓ **Monument à Colom,** the statue of Columbus pointing out to sea at the end of La *Rambla.*

Waterfront

In 1992, Barcelona remembered it was a port city and reoriented itself back toward the Mediterranean Sea. The city rebuilt the unsightly and dangerous port. It developed a scenic marina and cleaned up its urban beaches. Today, the waterfront is one of the prime places to live and party. You can find most of the city's new restaurants here, but there's only one major hotel. As a base, the area is not the most convenient, but it's great for shopping and entertaining kids. The beaches are so convenient that you can spend the morning sightseeing in the Gothic Quarter and the afternoon swimming in the Mediterranean. Here you'll find:

✓ **Vila Olímpica,** a planned neighborhood inaugurated by Olympic athletes in 1992.

✓ **Port Olímpic,** a popular port area with more bars and restaurants than boats.

✓ **Platja de Barcelona,** the city's beaches (yep, they're topless).

✓ **Port Vell,** the old port transformed into a swank mall, with restaurants, shops, an aquarium, and an Imax theater.

Montjuïc

Montjuïc, a mountain whose name means "Hill of the Jews," offers amazing views of the city below. Olympic TV cameras couldn't get enough shots of divers doing half-gainers from high platforms on the hill, the city forming the backdrop for their twisting, arching bodies. Montjuïc has two top art museums, the Olympic installations, nice gardens, and an amusement park for kids. There are no hotels or restaurants to speak of, though. Here you'll find:

✓ **Museu d'Art de Catalunya,** one of the world's top collection of Romanesque art.

✓ **Estadi Olìmpic,** the Olympic stadium.

✓ **Fundació Miró,** a museum housing native son Joan Miró's surrealist works.

✓ **Poble Espanyol,** a kitschy theme park of make-believe Spanish houses.

Tibidabo

Barcelona's other mountain provides perhaps even more spectacular views of the city than Montjuïc — that is, when the smog lifts. You can take a tram up the mountain to bars and restaurants and see the sea and the block formation of the modern city. A visit here is best for the panoramic views at sundown. Here you'll find:

- ✔ **Parc d'Attracions,** a retro amusement park high above the city.

- ✔ **Carretera de les Aigues,** a dirt path that winds along the mountain for several miles, which is a great place to walk, jog, ride bikes, or walk the dog (my dog practically lived here).

Barrios Altos

Barcelona's upper neighborhoods — **Sarrià, Pedralbes,** and **Gràcia** — were once isolated villages where people had summer homes. Today, they're residential areas. If you're pressed for time, skip the *Barrios Altos* — except for a quick trip to *Parc Güell,* one of Barcelona's must-sees. Here you'll find:

- ✔ **Parc Güell,** Gaudí's fantastic park city bathed in mosaics and perfectly integrated with nature.

- ✔ **Monasteri de Pedralbes,** a monastery that houses part of the impressive Thyssen-Bornemisza art collection (the major part is in Madrid; see Chapter 14).

Getting info after you arrive

Turisme de Barcelona, Plaça de Catalunya, 17 (underground), ☎ 906-301-282, is open daily 9 a.m. to 9 p.m. **Informació Turística de Catalunya,** which provides information on both the city and the entire autonomous region, is in Palau Robert, Passeig de Gràcia, 107 (☎ 93-238-40-00). You can also find tourism information offices at Estació Sants train station and the airport. Call ☎ 010 for general visitor information; operators speak English and other languages.

Getting around Barcelona

Hemmed in by mountains and sea, Barcelona is compact and easy to manage. You can do most everything by Metro (subway) and on foot, with a few taxis thrown in for convenience, out-of-the-way sights, and late nights (the Metro stops running right about the time that Barcelona's nightlife cranks up). The **El Eixample** neighborhood is constructed on an easy-to-negotiate grid system, while the **Ciutat Vella** is nowhere near as organized.

By Metro

The **Metro** (☎ 010 or 93-486-07-52; Internet: www.tmb.net) is Barcelona's excellent, modern, and clean subway. Its five lines are by far the fastest and easiest way to navigate the city. (The Metro has begun implementing tri-lingual directions and audio — in Spanish, Catalan, and English.) Red diamond symbols mark stations. (You can find good pocket-sized maps at all Metro stations.) Single-ticket fares are 150 pta. (85¢), although you can get ten-trip tickets for 825 pta. ($4.50), a nearly half-price bargain. The Metro runs Monday to Thursday from 5 a.m. to 11 p.m.; Friday and Saturday from 5 a.m. to 2 a.m.; holidays from 6 a.m. to 11 p.m.; and Sunday from 6 a.m. to midnight. However, if you want to keep up with the locals at night, you can't rely on the Metro. It goes to bed long before they do.

Besides the Metro, you can also ride something called FGC Trains. Run by the provincial government, not the city, these subway trains share some terminals (it costs the same as the Metro, and you can pay for it using the same Metro multi-trip tickets). Two different FGC lines connect the city center to the upper neighborhoods and suburbs, including Sarrià, Vallvidrera, Tibidado, and Gràcia. The only real problem you encounter is if you want to switch between a FGC train to a regular Metro train. To do so, you have to exit the first and reenter the second — paying each time.

By bus

About 70 bus lines crisscross Barcelona. Though lines and hours are clearly marked, for first-timers, using the bus isn't the best option. You may have trouble figuring out where you are, and few bus drivers speak English. With the subway, you can at least clearly identify your stop. Buses run Sunday to Thursday from 5 a.m. to 11 p.m. and Friday and Saturday from 5 a.m. to 2 a.m. (fare is 150 pta./85¢). Special night buses run less frequently (believe me!), from 10:30 p.m. to 5 a.m. For route information, call ☎ **010.**

By taxi

Black-and-yellow taxis are affordable and everywhere. Few journeys will cost more than 1,000 pta. ($5.50). During the day, taxis aren't usually your best option, because traffic is very heavy in the city — you can end up paying for the pleasure of watching the meter tick. At night, though, especially if you've dined in the Ciutat Vella, taxis are the best way to return to your hotel or continue with the night (have the restaurant call a taxi if you don't feel comfortable waiting for one on the street). You can either hail a cab in the street (the little green light on the roof means you can hop in) or get one where they're lined up (usually outside hotels). Fares begin at 295 pta. ($1.65) and go up 101 pta. (55¢) per km. Cabs charge a slightly higher rate from 10 p.m. to 6 a.m. and on Saturdays and holidays. Reliable taxi companies include **Radio Móvil** (☎ **93-358-11-11**), **Barnataxi** (☎ **93-357-77-55**), and **Radio Taxi** (☎ **93-490-22-22**).

Multi-trip ticket bargains

Your best value option for traveling around Barcelona are bargain-basement multi-tickets for the Metro and buses. You can purchase these *tarjetas* (tickets) in automated Metro ticket offices, *estancos* (tobacco shops on the street), newspaper kiosks, and branches of the *La Caixa* and *Caixa de Catalunya* banks. The best deal is the **T1** ("tay-uno"), good for ten trips on all metros and the bus (it costs 825 pta./$4.50); several passengers can share the same ticket. You can also share a T-10x2, valid for ten trips on Metro, FGC, and buses, with free transfer among all three except from one bus to another; it costs 1,325 pta. ($7.50). One-day, three-day and five-day tickets are also available: **T-Dia/1 day** is good for unlimited travel for one person on Metro, FGC, and buses for one day (625 pta./$3.50); **3 Dies/3 days** allows unlimited travel for one person on the Metro and buses (not FGC) for three days (1,600 pta./$9); **5 Dies/5 days** is valid for five days of travel (2,400 pta./$13). Finally, the **Aerobús+Bus+Metro** pass allows for bus travel to and from and back to the airport in addition to unlimited bus and subway travel. Valid for three (1,900 pta./$10.50) or five days (2,400 pta./$13), you can buy it on board the *Aerobús* (see "By air" earlier in this chapter).

Multi-day passes only make sense if you're really zigzagging around the city on public transport, because much of what you want to see in Barcelona is best done of foot. Call ☎ 93-318-70-74 for further information.

By car

Trying to negotiate Barcelona's unfamiliar, traffic-clogged streets will put a definite damper on your vacation. The calmest of drivers loses his or her nerve driving in Barcelona, and parking is an expensive nightmare (finding parking on the street is only for the most agile and confident). However, a car is useful if you plan to head out on day trips to Sitges, Montserrat, or the Penedès wine country or travel to the Costa Brava and Girona (see "Side Trips from Barcelona," later in this chapter and in Chapter 12).

On foot

Compact Barcelona is ideal for walking. Strolling, especially along La Rambla, is a pastime ingrained in the local culture. Barri Gòtic, the Gothic Quarter, is not only a great place to walk and make discoveries — just don't panic if you get turned around! — it's virtually the only way to get around the labyrinthine district. If you have trouble finding your way, ask someone to direct you to La Rambla or La Catedral (the cathedral). From there, you should have no problem finding your way. You can comfortably cover most of the city on foot, from Avinguda Diagonal (the main traffic artery in the Eixample) down to the port.

Look out for people zipping through red lights on motor scooters. No matter what the law says, pedestrians definitely do not have the right of way in Spain. You may even find yourself dodging annoying *motos* (scooters) on sidewalks.

Bunking in Barcelona: The Hotel Scene

Barcelona went hog wild building and refurbishing hotels in time for the 1992 Olympics, and today you can find an amazing assortment of hotels, from historic *modernista* buildings to the latest in the high-tech design for which the city is known. You have to shell out more money in Barcelona than you will in most parts of Spain, though. I hesitate to recommend some of the cheaper places, because they're mostly located in areas that, even if pretty safe on the whole, may seem a little dubious to you if you're unfamiliar with the city. For a further explanation on the price breakdowns that I use in this book, see Chapter 5.

Most of Barcelona's top attractions, restaurants, and nightlife are concentrated in Eixample, around the Rambla and in the Ciutat Vella, so that's where you want to stay. Many visitors choose to stay on or near the Rambla, though it can prove a noisy choice. Most mid- to upscale-level hotels are either along La Rambla or in El Eixample.

 Turisme de Barcelona operates a hotel-booking service at its office in *Plaça de Catalunya* (bookings, ☎ **93-304-32-32** and 93-304-33-26).

Barcelona's top hotels

Gran Hotel Havana

$$$$ Eixample

High-tech design reigns in Barcelona. Don't believe me? Step into a few hotels built for the 1992 Olympics for proof. This is one of the best. In a totally hollowed-out 1872 mansion on Gran Via, the Havana is deluxe at a fairly reasonable (for Barcelona) price. Every detail, from Italian marble baths to Catalan lamps and headboards, has Barcelona's design mantra plastered all over it. If your idea of luxury is English-style patterns and French antiques, this isn't your kind of place: The very comfortable rooms offer lots of funky-style touches and peculiar shapes.

Gran Vía de les Corts Catalanes, 647. ☎ *93-412-11-15. Fax: 93-412-26-11. E-mail:* silken@hoteles-silken.com. *Internet:* www.hoteles-silken.com. *Metro: Diagonal. Parking: 2,200 pta. ($12). Rates: 31,000–45,000 pta. ($172–$250) double. AE, DC, MC, V.*

Barcelona Accommodations, Dining & Attractions

ACCOMMODATIONS ■
Gran Hotel Havana **22**
Hotel Allegro **30**
Hotel Arts **47**
Hotel Astoria **5**
Hotel Avenida Palace **20**
Hotel Balmes **7**
Hotel Claris **13**
Hotel Colón **37**
Hotel Condes de Barcelona **15**
Hotel España **60**
Hotel Gaudí **62**
Hotel Gótico **40**
Hotel Granvía **21**
Hotel Jardí **35**
Hotel Majestic **14**
Hotel NH Calderón **19**
Hotel Oriente **61**
Hotel Regente **16**
Hotel Ritz **23**
Hotel Rivoli Ramblas **27**

DINING ◆
Agua **48**
Agut **54**
Botafumeiro **4**
Can Culleretes **58**
Casa Calvet **24**
El Gran Café **55**
Els Quatre Gats **29**
La Dentellière **53**
Les Quinze Nits **57**
Los Caracoles **56**
Lungomare Ristorante **45**
Mordisco **9**
Quo Vadis **33**
Restaurante 7 Portes **51**
Senyor Parelleda **42**
Taktika Berri **6**
Talaia Mar **46**
Tragaluz **8**
Travi Mar **50**

ATTRACTIONS ●
Estadi Olímpic (Olympic Ring) **66**
Casa de la Caritat **25**
Casa de les Puntxes **12**
Catedral de Barcelona **38**
Fundació Joan Miró **64**
Fundació Tàpies **17**
Gran Teatre del Liceu **59**
Hospital Sant Pau **2**
La Boquería **32**
La Pedrera (Casa Milà) **10**
La Rambla **31**
La Sagrada Familia **1**
Manzana de la Discórdia **18**
Maremagnum **49**
Monument à Colom **52**
Museu d'Art Contemporani
 de Barcelona **26**
Museu d'Historia de la Ciutat **39**
Museu de la Música **11**
Museu Nacional d'Art
 de Catalunya **65**
Museu Picasso **43**
Palau Güell **63**
Palau de la Música **28**
Parc Güell **3**
Plaça del Pi **34**
Plaça del Rei **39**
Plaça de Sant Jaume **41**
Plaça Sant Felip de Neri **36**
Santa María del Mar **44**

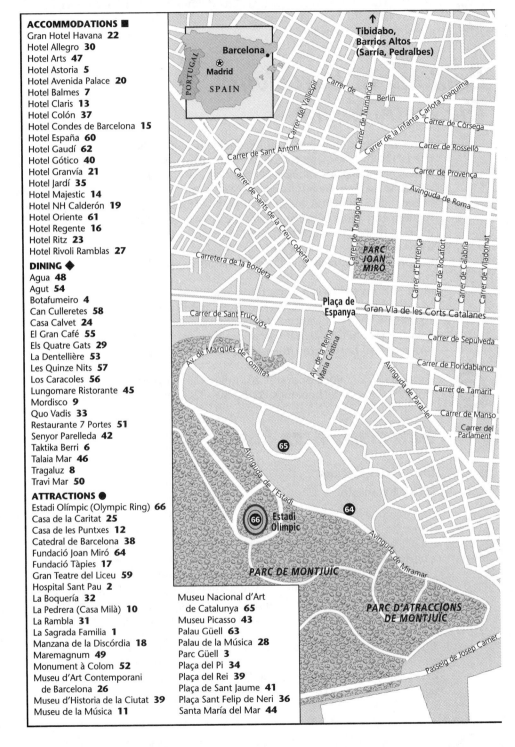

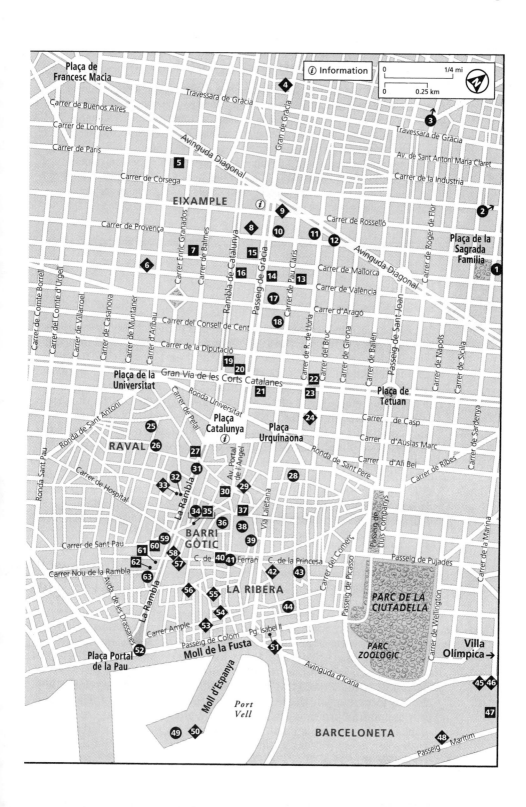

Plaça de
Francesc Macià

Carrer de Buenos Aires

Carrer de Londres

Carrer de Paris

Travessera de Gràcia

Gran de Gràcia

Avinguda Diagonal

Travessera de Gràcia

Av. de Sant Antoni Maria Claret

Carrer de la Indústria

Carrer de Còrsega

EIXAMPLE

Carrer de Rosselló

Avinguda Diagonal

Plaça de la
Sagrada
Família

Carrer de Provença

Carrer Enric Granados

Carrer de Balmes

Rambla de Catalunya

Passeig de Gràcia

Carrer de Pau Claris

Carrer de Mallorca

Carrer de Roger de Flor

Carrer de València

Carrer d'Aragó

Passeig de Sant Joan

Carrer de Napols

Carrer de Sicília

Carrer de Comte Borrell

Carrer del Comte d'Urgell

Carrer de Villarroel

Carrer de Casanova

Carrer de Muntaner

Carrer d'Aribau

Carrer del Consell de Cent

Carrer de la Diputació

Carrer de R. de Llúria

Carrer del Bruc

Carrer de Girona

Carrer de Bailèn

Plaça de la
Universitat

Gran Via de les Corts Catalanes

Ronda Universitat

Plaça de
Tetuan

Carrer de Sardenya

Ronda de Sant Antoni

Plaça
Catalunya

Plaça
Urquinaona

Carrer de Casp

Carrer d'Ausiàs Marc

Carrer de Ribes

RAVAL

Ronda Sant Pau

Carrer de Pelai

Av. Portal de l'Àngel

Ronda de Sant Pere

Carrer d'Alí Bei

Carrer de Hospital

La Rambla

Via Laietana

Passeig de Lluís Companys

Carrer de la Marina

BARRI
GÒTIC

Carrer de Sant Pau

C. de Ferran

C. de la Princesa

Carrer del Comerç

Passeig de Pujades

Carrer Nou de la Rambla

La Rambla

LA RIBERA

Passeig de Picasso

PARC DE LA
CIUTADELLA

Carrer de Wellington

Avda. de les Drassanes

Carrer Ample

Passeig de Colom

Pg. Isabel II

Moll de la Fusta

PARC
ZOOLÒGIC

Villa
Olímpica →

Plaça Portal
de la Pau

Moll d'Espanya

Port
Vell

Avinguda d'Icària

BARCELONETA

Passeig Marítim

ⓘ Information

0   1/4 mi
0   0.25 km

Is Catalonia Spain?

Barcelonans boast that their fiercely independent region has for centuries been more European — by that they mean more *continental* — than the rest of Spain. Although you can find bullfights and the occasional tourist-oriented flamenco show, Barcelona really isn't the place for such typically Spanish arts. The city takes pride in its stubborn sense of self and identity — and how un-Spanish it feels. You may see t-shirts proclaiming that "Catalonia is not Spain," and hear shopkeepers responding to Spanish-speakers in Catalan. While there are some who'd prefer Barcelona to be the capital of an independent, Catalan-speaking nation, mostly these hard-working people are just frustrated that so much of the region's wealth is rerouted to Madrid.

Hotel Arts
$$$$$ Waterfront (Vila Olímpica)

Barcelona has only two skyscrapers, and this high-tech, high-rise wonder is one of them. Built for the 1992 Olympics but not opened until 1994 (oops), the Arts is on the beach, in the heart of the *Vila Olímpica* (Olympic Village). Don't expect to find any old-world flavor here, but rather the ultimate in sophistication and privacy. Rooms are light and airy, with incredible views of the Mediterranean and the city. The luxurious bathrooms, with sit-down showers and family-sized tubs, are larger than most compact cars. Of course, to live like a king, you need royal pockets. A Ritz-Carlton hotel, this is the hands-down favorite of most Americans.

Carrer de la Marina, 19–21. ☎ *800-241-3333 in the U.S. or 93-221-10-00. Fax: 93-221-10-70. Internet:* www.ritzcarlton.com. *Metro: Ciutadella–Vila Olímpica. Parking: 3,200 pta. ($18). Rates: 50,000 pta. ($278) double; weekend rate 27,500 pta. ($153) double; family package 45,000 pta. ($250), allows one child under 12 to sleep free in parents room; breakfast buffet included. AE, DC, MC, V.*

Hotel Astoria
$$$ Eixample

$133 per night
5 nights

I love this classy, quiet hotel — so much so that I put up friends and family here when my apartment in Barcelona was too small for guests. The Hotel Astoria is an excellent value, and definitely one of the top three-star hotels in Barcelona. It's just a few blocks from the top of *Rambla de Catalunya* and minutes from prime shopping territory on *Diagonal*. Around since the '50s, the Astoria was recently refurbished, and it's more elegant than ever, without being at all stuffy. The sound-proofed rooms are modern and elegant, done mostly in cremes and blacks, and some have small sitting rooms (perfect for a kid's cot) or garden terraces. You can choose between black-and-white tile or hardwood floors.

París, 203. ☎ *93-209-83-11. Fax: 93-202-30-08. E-mail:* info@derbyhotels.es. *Internet:* www.derbyhotels.es. *Metro: Diagonal. Parking: Nearby, 2,300 Pta. ($13). Rates: 22,200 pta. ($123) double. AE, DC, MC, V.*

[handwritten: Derby]

Hotel Balmes

[handwritten: $96 per night 5 nights Hotel 4 Barcelona]

$$$ Eixample

The hotels in Barcelona's Derby chain have perfected a winning formula: good-value and supremely tasteful hotels with character. Like its older cousin the swanky Astoria, the Balmes has large, comfortable, and understated rooms with cool designer touches. An interior patio pool is a real bonus, as is its perfect location: smack in the middle of El Eixample, only steps from Rambla de Catalunya and Passeig de Gràcia. Even though you're in the thick of Barcelona, this hotel feels like a mini-retreat.

Mallorca, 216. ☎ *93-451-19-14. Fax: 93-451-00-49. E-mail:* info@derbyhotels. es. *Internet:* www.derbyhotels.es. *Metro: Diagonal. Parking: 2,000 Pta. ($11). Rates: 24,400 pta. ($135) double. AE, DC, MC, V.*

Hotel Claris

$$$$$ Eixample

Behind the nineteenth-century palace façade and the for-guests-only museum of Egyptian art is a surprise: one of the most modern, design-oriented hotels in Spain. High-tech elevators cruise to the rooms overlooking an interior foyer. Rooms, many of which are split-level and even two-story, are a mix of cool chic and warm sophistication: They have parquet floors, bold color schemes (for example, royal purple), rich fabrics, and furnishings that combine antiques and Catalan design. Each room has original artwork, often a beautiful Nepalese, Indian, or Egyptian piece. The top-floor terrace, which has a small pool, offers sweet views of the surrounding Eixample neighborhood. (Insider's tip: A bellboy once told me that the hotel's popular with supermodels, for whatever that's worth.)

Carrer de Pau Claris, 150. ☎ *800-888-4747 in the U.S., or 93-487-62-62. Fax: 93-215-79-70. E-mail:* info@derbyhotels.es. *Internet:* www.derbyhotels. es. *Metro: Passeig de Gràcia. Parking: 2,000 pta. ($11). Rates: 42,900 pta. ($239) double; weekends 25,000 pta. ($139) double, including breakfast. AE, DC, MC, V.*

Hotel Condes de Barcelona

$$$$ Eixample

Occupying two grand former palaces on opposite corners of chic Passeig de Gràcia, this is yet another Barcelona hotel in love with design. (It's a favorite with architects, and designers.) The hotel is in the middle of the Quadrat d'Or, the section of town famed for its funky *modernista* houses, and is just a block from Gaudí's La Pedrera apartment building. Rooms are modern, large, and elegant, decorated in bright but tasteful colors.

Passeig de Gràcia, 73–75. ☎ *93-467-47-80. Fax: 93-467-47-85. E-mail:* reservas@condesdebarcelona.com. *Internet:* www.condesdebarcelona.com. *Metro: Passeig de Gràcia. Parking: 2,000 pta. ($11). Rates: 31,000–42,000 pta. ($172–$233) double. AE, DC, MC, V.*

Hotel España

$$ Ciutat Vella (Ramblas)

Do you hate homogenous modern hotels? Sleep better surrounded by a bit of local history and character? Right off the lower part of La Rambla, the Hotel España was decorated by one of *modernismo's* star architects, Domènech i Montaner (designer of the Palau de la Música and Casa Lleó Morera). His colorful stamp in the terrific public rooms is what makes this place special. Guest rooms, on the other hand, are simple — even plain. However, they're clean and large, which is all you can ask for in a budget hotel, much less one with the pedigree and location of this one. The hotel doesn't have air conditioning, though, and to get to the hotel, you must pass an assortment of humanity (equal numbers tourists, prostitutes, and immigrants). A dose of adventurous, "Hey we're in Europe!" spirit is required, but even that may not inspire you to stay here in the heat of summer.

Carrer Sant Pau, 11. ☎ *93-318-17-58. Fax: 93-317-11-34. Metro: Liceu or Drassanes. Parking: Nearby, 3,000 pta. ($17). Rates: 10,700 pta. ($59) double. AE, DC, MC, V.*

Hotel NH Calderón

$$$ Eixample

The NH chain is famous in Spain for efficient, nicely decorated hotels with all the right amenities and excellent service (even if the hotels all do tend to look the same). The Calderón is no exception, and it's located on Rambla de Catalunya — one of the best spots to situate yourself in the whole city. Rooms are modern and high-tech, with well-chosen light woods and bold fabrics. Though built for businessmen who expect functionality and order, it's also great for tourists and families. A bonus is the rooftop pool, which is great in the midsummer heat.

Rambla de Catalunya, 26. ☎ *93-301-00-00 or 91-398-44-00 for NH hotels throughout Spain. Fax: 93-412-41-93. Internet:* www.nh-hoteles.es. *Metro: Passeig de Gràcia or Plaça de Catalunya. Parking: 2,000 pta. ($11). Rates: 26,100 pta. ($145) double; weekend rate 22,500 pta. ($125); occasional promotional rate 18,500 pta. ($103); Children under 12 sharing parents' room stay free. AE, DC, MC, V.*

Hotel Ritz

$$$$$ Eixample

The Ritz is on its way to regaining its stature as the classiest address in Barcelona, a splendid tree-lined avenue in El Eixample. If you're Old Money (or just want to pretend that you are), this is the place to come for white-glove treatment. Spacious public rooms are grand, aristocratic, and richly decorated, and the guest rooms are large and formal. Some rooms have marble fireplaces, and, befitting an emperor, a select few offer Roman-style baths with rich mosaics.

Gran Vía de les Corts Catalanes, 668. ☎ *93-318-52-00 or 93-318-48-37 for reservations. Fax: 93-318-01-48. E-mail:* ritz@ritzbcn.es. *Internet:* www.ritzbcn.com. *Metro: Passeig de Gràcia. Parking: 3,500 pta. ($19). Rates: 45,000 pta. ($250) double; contact hotel for special offers. AE, DC, MC, V.*

Barcelona's runner-up hotels

Hotel Allegro

$$$ **Gothic Quarter** This hotel, on one of Barcelona's busiest pedestrian shopping streets, has large rooms, a nice garden patio, and a dose of urban. *Portal de l'Àngel, 17.* ☎ *93-318-41-41. Fax: 93-301-26-31. E-mail:* cataloni@hoteles-catalonia.es. *Internet:* www.hoteles-catalonia.es.

Hotel Avenida Palace

$$$$ **Eixample** Wonderfully ornate, elegant, and a little fussy — a luxurious hotel for the anti-minimalist crowd. *Gran Vía de les Corts Catalanes, 605.* ☎ *93-301-96-00. Fax: 93-318-12-34. E-mail:* avpalace@husa.es.

Hotel Colón

$$$$ **Barri Gòtic** This hotel is right across a plaza from Barcelona's soaring cathedral, in the absolute heart of the Barri Gòtic. If you score one of the sixth-floor rooms with large terraces and dramatic cathedral views, you won't care that the rooms have sickly floral and pastel color schemes. *Avenida de la Catedral, 7.* ☎ *93-301-14-04. Fax: 93-317-29-15. E-mail:* colon@ncsa.es. *Internet:* www.nexus.es/colon/.

Hotel Gaudí

$$ **La Rambla** A clean and comfortable (if a tad dull) hotel right across from one of Gaudí's earliest buildings, the *Palau Güell*, on the *Raval* side of *La Rambla*. However, if you're at all squeamish about street life and its colorful denizens, you may want to look elsewhere. *Nou de la Rambla, 12.* ☎ *93-317-90-32. Fax: 93-412-26-36. E-mail:* gaudi@hotelgaudi.es. *Internet:* www.hotelgaudi.es.

Hotel Gótico

$$$$ **Barri Gòtic** This hotel was handsomely renovated from the ground-up in 1999 and is now one of the Gothic Quarter's best places to stay, just paces from the *Plaça de Sant Jaume,* considered the heart of the

neighborhood. *Jaume 1, 14.* ☎ *93-315-22-11. Fax: 93-310-40-81. E-mail:* gotic@ gargallo-hotels.com. *Internet:* www.gargallo-hotels.com.

Hotel Granvia

$$ Eixample Located in a nineteenth-century palace, this is a good choice and great deal; the clean, charming rooms aren't large, but they have nice antiques. *Gran Via Corts Catalanes, 642.* ☎ *93-318-19-00. Fax: 93-318-99-97.*

Hotel Jardí

$ Gothic Quarter A small hotel that overlooks two of the prettiest plazas in Barcelona; rooms are nicer than you'd expect for the cheap price. *Plaça Sant Josep Oriol, 1.* ☎ *93-301-59-00. Fax: 93-318-36-64. E-mail:* sgsllosa@encomix.es.

Hotel Majestic

$$$$ Eixample This hotel has large rooms, done in bright colors and patterns, and is up to par with the great location on Passeig de Gràcia. However, it's big with tour groups and a tad impersonal. *Passeig de Gràcia, 68.* ☎ *93-488-17-17. Fax 93-487-97-90. E-mail:* recepcion@hotelmajestic. es. *Internet:* www.hotelmajestic.es.

Hotel Oriente

$$ La Rambla A charmingly nostalgic place right on the *Rambla,* this was Barcelona's first official hotel. The large but simple rooms are probably best for backpackers and travelers with a sense of adventure. *Ramblas, 45–47.* ☎ *93-302-25-58. Fax: 93-412-38-19. E-mail:* horiente@husa.es. *Internet:* www.husa.es.

Hotel Regente

$$$$ Eixample This great-looking 1913 *modernista* townhouse has a superior location, but rooms are a little disappointing given the hotel's winningly original façade. *Rambla de Catalunya, 76.* ☎ *93-487-59-89. Fax: 93-215-31-57. E-mail:* hcc@hoteles-centro-ciudad.es. *Internet:* www. hoteles-centro-ciudad.es/en/regente.

Hotel Rivoli Ramblas

$$$–$$$$ La Rambla This busy, gleaming townhouse hotel is on the front lines of the never-ending pedestrian bustle just beyond the front door on La Rambla; rooms are a little small but, thankfully, soundproofed. *La Rambla, 128.* ☎ *93-302-66-43. Fax: 93-317-50-53. E-mail:* rivoli@alba. mssl.es.

Dining in Barcelona

Catalans love to eat, and they enjoy one of the best and most imaginative cuisines in all of Spain. Barcelona is the best place to sample the rich variety of food that Catalan cooking offers. You can find both haute cuisine and the traditional rustic dishes that has fed Catalans for centuries. Most restaurants are in the Ciutat Vella and Eixample, though the most popular dining area is along the Waterfront and in the new port. The focus of the food scene is farther along, toward the Hotel Arts and beaches.

Barcelona is only 90 miles from the French border, so it's not surprising that lots of restaurants serve French cuisine, as well as regional Spanish cuisines, like Basque. (Basque *tapas* — hors d'oeuvres — bars pop up like the wild mushrooms that Catalans love so much; for more on Basque cuisine see Chapter 13.) About the only difficulty you may have eating your way across Barcelona is ordering at the handful of restaurants that feature menus printed only in Catalan.

For more on Spanish dining customs, including mealtimes, taxes, costs, and tipping, see "Knowing what to expect when you're eating out" in Chapter 1.

Eating like a Catalan

Catalan cooking is equal parts Mediterranean and mountain — well prepared but with little stuffiness. So expect fresh seafood, *all i oli* (garlic and virgin olive oil), produce from the countryside, and *setas* (wild mushrooms) — an object of obsession for people all over Catalonia. The basis of rustic Catalan food is *pa amb tomàquet,* literally, bread and tomato. But I'm not talking bread, mayo, and beefsteak tomatoes. *Pa amb tomàquet* are long slices of rustic bread rubbed with halves of beautiful fresh tomatoes, doused with virgin olive oil, and sprinkled with salt. Another typical Catalan dish is *espinacs a la catalana,* which is spinach prepared with pine nuts, raisins, bacon, oil, and garlic. Others you may run across include: *escudella* (Catalan stew); *suquet de peix* (fish and shellfish soup); *butifarra* (white Catalan sausage, often with white beans) and *fuet* (long, dry sausage); *fideus* (long, thin noodles with pork, sausage, and red pepper); *escalivada* (grilled peppers, eggplant, tomato, and onion); and *amanida* (salad with meat, fish, shellfish, and cheese). For dessert, try *crema catalana,* an egg custard with grilled sugar on top.

Drinking like a Catalan

The wines from the **Penedès** region are excellent and worthy rivals to **Riojas** (Spain's beloved reds). Among Penedès reds, try *Torres Gran Coronas, Raimat,* and *Jean León.* The wines from the **Priorato** region are big, fine, expensive reds that rival those from **Ribera del Duero,** the best in Spain. You may have heard of *Freixenet* and *Codorniu,* the two top-selling *cavas* (sparkling wines) in the world. Both are from Penedès, just a half-hour from Barcelona. *Cava* is a perfect accompaniment to the seafood and lighter fare that you can enjoy in Barcelona.

Barcelona's top restaurants

Agua

$$ Waterfront (Port Marítim)   MEDITERRANEAN/SEAFOOD

Agua (water) is one of the latest additions to a Waterfront restaurant scene that's really blossomed. A mod-looking, relaxed place on the beach, it's got a great outdoor terrace that is perfect for people-watching. Fish, rice dishes (such as risottos), and vegetarian dishes are all well-prepared and affordably priced. I'm a big fan of this relaxed place, which let me bring my dog in for dinner (she recommends the grilled sardines).

Passeig Marítim de la Barceloneta, 30. ☎ *93-225-12-72. Reservations recommended. Metro: Barceloneta. Main courses: 850–2,500 pta. ($5–$14). AE, MC, V. Open: Lunch and dinner daily.*

Agut

$ Ciutat Vella (Barri Gòtic)   CATALAN

This 75-year-old restaurant, tucked away on a small street in the Gothic Quarter, is a real find — great looking (in a homey way) and dripping with local flavor. Best of all, it's a bargain. The crowd is a cool mix of artists and suited professionals; you won't find any tour groups here. You can't go wrong with the daily specials, whether homemade *canelones* (canneloni), fish, or game. The excellent rice dishes are giant — order them only if you want to share.

Gignàs, 16. ☎ *93-315-17-09. Reservations not necessary. Metro: Drassanes or Liceu. Main courses 750–2,500 pta. ($4–$14); Lunch menú del día 1,275 pta. ($7) Tue–Fri. AE, MC, V. Open: Lunch and dinner daily.*

Botafumeiro

$$$$ Eixample   SEAFOOD

One of the king of Spain's favorite restaurants (his preferred table is on the second floor), this is the place for perfectly prepared seafood. It's large, informal, and often a little rambunctious. Much of the incredibly fresh seafood is flown in daily from Galicia, where the owner is from. The shellfish are amazing, and the long seafood bar was recently named the best in Spain (you can make a great meal of seafood *tapas* here, and keep costs down if you're conscientious). Because Botafumeiro doesn't close after lunch, go at off hours — 1 p.m. for lunch and 7:30 p.m. for dinner. It's the only time you'll be able to walk in and get a table — or even a seat at the bar — if you haven't reserved a table well in advance.

Language primer: Catalan menu basics

Refer to the following list when translating a Catalan menu.

English	Catalan	English	Catalan
bread	*pa*	salmon	*salmó*
cheese	*formatge*	shellfish	*marisc*
chicken	*pollastre*	soup	*sopa*
dessert	*postre*	steak	*carn*
eggs	*ous*	sugar	*sucre*
fish	*peix*	toast	*torrada*
fruit	*fruita*	veal	*vedella*
ham	*pernil*	beer	*cervesa*
hake	*lluç*	coffee	*café*
ice cream	*gelat*	juice	*suc*
mussels	*musclos*	milk	*llet*
oil	*oli*	tea	*te*
omelette	*truita*	water	*aigua*
rice	*àrros*	wine	*vin*
salad	*amanida*		

Gran de Gràcia, 81. ☎ *93-218-42-30. Reservations recommended (not necessary at bar). Metro: Fontana or Diagonal. Main courses: 2,500–8,500 pta. ($14–$47). AE, MC, V. Open: Lunch and dinner daily without interruption.*

Can Culleretes

$ Ciutat Vella (Barri Gòtic)   CATALAN

The oldest restaurant in Barcelona (open since 1786), Can Culleretes continues serving traditional, filling Catalan food. In fact, you may feel as if the Ciutat Vella grew up around this restaurant. This homey spot is the place to try standards like *espinacas a la catalana* (spinach with pine nuts and raisins) and *butifarra* (white sausage). You can choose from fixed-price menus both day and night during the week.

Carrer Quintana, 5. ☎ *93-317-30-22. No reservations. Metro: Liceu. Main courses: 675–1,900 pta. ($4–$11). AE, MC, V. Open: Tues–Sat lunch and dinner; Sun lunch only.*

Casa Calvet

$$$–$$$$ Eixample   CATALAN

Housed on the first floor of one of Antoni Gaudí's emblematic apartment buildings (with the oldest elevator in Barcelona), the sumptuous white-brick and stained-glass *modernista* décor alone is enough to recommend a visit. The welcome surprise is that it's an excellent and fairly priced Catalan restaurant. Give the *raviolis de ostras gallegas en salsa de cava* (Galician oyster raviolis in champagne) a whirl. Dining at Casa Calvet is a great, non-touristy way to get up close and personal with a *modernista* classic.

Casp, 48. ☎ *93-412-40-12. Internet:* www.gulliver.es/casacalvet.htm. *Reservations recommended. Metro: Jaume 1. Main courses: 1,825–2900 pta. ($10–$16). AE, MC, V. Open: Lunch and dinner Mon–Sat; closed holidays.*

La Dentellière

$–$$ Ciutat Vella (Barri Gòtic)   MEDITERRANEAN/FRENCH

You can't beat the fixed-price menus at this cozy and charmingly rustic French restaurant. The entire menu is well conceived and prepared, with a good selection of affordable wines. The French owner, Sue, insists on good food and good value. If there's another place in Spain where you can find an artistically presented three-course meal (with homemade desserts like *profiteroles* — small cream puffs) for $7, please write and tell me. For a while when I lived nearby, my Lab Retriever and I came here at least three times a week for lunch. (I have a weakness for dog-friendly restaurants.)

Carrer Ample, 26. ☎ *93-319-68-21. Reservations recommended. Metro: Drassanes. Main courses: 900–2,400 pta. ($5–$13); midday menú del día 1,300 pta. ($7); dinner menú del día 2,300 pta. ($13). AE, DC, MC, V. Open: Lunch and dinner Tues–Sat.*

Quo Vadis

$$$ Ciutat Vella (Ramblas)   SPANISH

This inviting place near the Boquería food market is a Barcelona mainstay. Barcelonans speak in reverential tones about the fried goose liver with prunes, and in season, people practically line up for the wild mushroom *ragout* (a highly seasoned stew). With several small and casually elegant dining rooms, the feeling is intimate and relaxed.

Carme, 7. ☎ *93-302-40-72. Reservations recommended. Metro: Liceu. Main courses: 1,700–3,800 pta. ($9–$21); menú del día 3,750 pta. ($21). AE, MC, V. Open: Lunch and dinner Mon–Sat.*

Restaurante 7 Portes

$$$ Waterfront (Port Vell)   SEAFOOD/CATALAN

This Barcelona institution and national monument, which has seven doors facing the street (hence the name), has been hosting large dining parties since 1836. (It was the first place in Barcelona with running water.) Barcelonans drop in to celebrate special occasions. *Sete Portes,* as it is also known, is famous for its rice dishes; my favorite is the black rice with squid in its own ink. All the *paellas* are tremendous. Portions are huge, and very reasonably priced. The dining rooms — some semi-private — are classically elegant, with beamed ceilings, checkerboard marble floors, and antique mirrors and posters, and there's plenty of room between tables.

Passieg Isabel II, 14. ☎ *93-319-68-21. Reservations recommended. Metro: Drassanes. Main courses: 1,400–4,500 pta. ($8–$25). AE, DC, MC, V. Open: Lunch and dinner daily, without interruption.*

Taktika Berri

$$–$$$ Eixample   BASQUE

Basque cooking is the finest in Spain, and this is one of the best in Barcelona: an intimate but lively Basque family-owned-and-operated *tapas* bar and restaurant with excellent food. The *pintxos* (Spanish appetizers) are so splendid here, you may not make it to the entrees. Try the blood sausage (much better tasting than it sounds) or *tapas* of *bonito* (tuna), and wash it all down with a Basque *txacolí* ("*cha*-koh-lee," a fruity white wine). Loosen your belt, though; you've *got* to save room for pastry chef Keny Núñez's heavenly desserts.

Carrer Valencia, 169. ☎ *93-453-47-59. Reservations required (except at bar). Metro: Provença. Main courses: 2,200–3,800 pta. ($12–$21). AE, MC, V. Open: Lunch and dinner daily without interruption.*

Talaia Mar

$$$–$$$$ Waterfront (Port Marítim)   MEDITERRANEAN/SEAFOOD

The dining scene around the port is bustling and borderline frenetic, but most restaurants there are mediocre, homogenous, and rowdy. But at Talaia Mar, Chef Carles Abellán creates an innovative, seafood-dominated menu. Try the lamb sweetbreads with cuttlefish and white beans or the grilled fish of the day. The restaurant is one of the best examples of Barcelona's avant-design. The dining room — a glass-enclosed circular room that mimics a watchtower — has a sweeping bay window overlooking the port.

Marina, 16. ☎ *93-221-90-90. Reservations recommended. Internet:* www.talaia-mar.es. *Metro: Barceloneta. Main courses: 1,950–3,800 pta. ($11–$21). AE, DC, MC, V. Open: Lunch and dinner daily.*

Barcelona's runner-up restaurants

El Gran Café

$$ Gothic Quarter This café looks like an English pub on the outside, but has a handsome art nouveau interior and standard French/Catalan menu; try the *canelones de pescado* (fish canelloni) or the stuffed shrimp. *Carrer Avinyó, 9.* ☎ **93-318-79-86.**

Els Quatre Gats

$$–$$$ Barri Gòtic This restaurant, a landmark *modernista* building, is where Picasso, Ramón Casas, and other bohemian artists used to hang out, draw, and dream; today it serves up a pretty good *menu del día* (menu of the day) of simple Catalan fare, such as shrimp crepes and filet of sole, along with tasty *tapas. Carrer de Montsió, 3.* ☎ *93-302-41-40.*

Les Quinze Nits

$ Ramblas/Barri Gòtic This place often has long lines of folks hungering to pay fast-food prices for surprisingly well-prepared Catalan and Mediterranean dishes. To beat the crowds, do the *gringo* thing and come early. A nearby sister restaurant, **La Fonda,** on Carrer dels Escudellers, 10 (☎ **93-301-75-15**), offers nearly the same menu and décor. *Plaça Reial, 6.* ☎ *93-317-30-75.*

Los Caracoles

$$–$$$ Barri Gòtic This eatery has existed since 1835 and fed both John Wayne and Dick Nixon; tourists love to trek through the raucous kitchen to their tables for classic Catalan and Spanish fare, such as *caracoles* (snails), roasted chicken, rabbit, and lamb ribs. *Carrer Escudellers, 14.* ☎ *93-302-31-85.*

Lungomare Ristorante

$$–$$$ Waterfront (Port Marítim) Perched high above the port with great views of anchored yachts, this refreshingly simple place is great for pizzas and pastas, as well as more exotic dishes like duck breast with black truffle sauce. *Marina, 16–18.* ☎ *93-221-04-28.*

Mordisco

$ Eixample This is a good place for a fast lunch (there's even a sandwich called the "Speedy Gonzalez") and a break from visits to *La Pedrera* and all the nearby *modernista* monuments. *Rossellón, 265.* ☎ *93-415-76-76.*

Senyor Parellada

$$–$$$ **Barri Gòtic** A good-value and good-looking restaurant that's popular with locals of all ages, it's down-to-earth, but quietly sophisticated and serves excellent, authentic Catalan fare. *Carrer Argentaria, 37.* ☎ *93-310-50-94.*

Tragaluz

$$$$ **Eixample** On a tiny passageway off Passeig de Gràcia, this restaurant is wildly colorful — a monument to Barcelona's design craze. The Mediterranean cooking keeps pace with excellent fish (such as sole stuffed with red peppers) and meat, plus low-fat and veggie dishes and a separate sushi restaurant downstairs. *Pasaje Concepción, 5.* ☎ *93-487-01-96.*

Travi Mar

$$$ **Port Marítim** This seafood restaurant nearly drowns in its nautical theme, but the fish and shellfish are very well prepared, and the views of the surrounding port are outstanding. *Maremagnum (Moll d'Espanya), Local 110, first floor.* ☎ *93-225-81-36.*

Enjoying tip-top tapas

Barcelona may not have the reputation for *tapas* grazing that Madrid, San Sebastián, and Seville have, but it's a wonderful city to eat on the run — and tide yourself over until those late meal times at most restaurants. Here's a brief sampling of some of the best *tapas* joints in the Catalan capital.

- ✔ **Bar Pinotxo** (no phone) may look like a nondescript bar, but it's a legend, right in the heart of the sensational La Boquería food market on La Rambla (see "Strolling La Rambla," later in this chapter). Grab a bar stool and point to whatever looks good (the fish is as fresh as anywhere in the city).

- ✔ The *tapas* at **Bar Turó,** Tenor Viñas, 1 (Parc Turó; ☎ 93-200-69-53) are famed the city over, but it's mostly a beautiful-people crowd that frequents the place. You can also choose from a good-value midday menu for 1,500 pta. ($8).

- ✔ **Irati,** Casanyes, 17 (Barri Gòtic; ☎ 93-200-69-53), a Basque *tapas* joint just off La Rambla, is always at standing-room only capacity. The *tapas* (called *pintxos* in Basque) are set out on the bar, and they keep coming. Keep track of how many you eat and pay when you're done.

- ✔ **La Bodegueta,** Rambla de Catalunya 100 (Eixample; ☎ 93-215-48-94), is an easy-to-miss, simple step-down bar that's ideal for a snack and a glass of *Rioja* red wine or a *cava* (sparkling wine).

Exploring Barcelona

Barcelona has a greater diversity of things to see and do than any other city in Spain (something folks from Madrid are loath to admit). When visiting, concentrate on neighborhoods, which is how I lay out the attractions in this section. The works of Gaudí and his imaginative *modernista* cohorts are perhaps the most obvious highlight, but the rich medieval Gothic Quarter and newly robust harbor provide enjoyable contrasts. Best of all, Barcelona is among Europe's great strolling cities, with secluded plazas, open-air cafés, tree-lined boulevards, and an inexhaustible supply of nooks to stop and have coffee, a beer, or *tapas* during your meanderings.

If you're planning to wear out your shoes sightseeing in Barcelona, you may want to get a discount card offered by the city tourism office. Available in 24-, 48-, and 72-hour versions, the *Barcelona Card* offers free public transportation and discounts of up to 50 percent at 70 sites in the city, including museums, bars, shops, and restaurants. La Pedrera, La Sagrada Familia, and Fundació Joan Miró are all included, as well as the Aerobus to the airport. The 24-hour card includes a free 10-journey travel card for the Metro and bus, and the 48- and 72-hours cards include a pass offering unlimited travel on the Metro and bus. Cards cost between 2,500 pta./$14 (2,000 pta./$11, for children ages 6 to 15) and 3,500 pta./$19 (3,000 pta./$17 for children). You can purchase the Barcelona Card at **Turisme de Barcelona** information offices in *Plaça de Catalunya* (☎ **93-304-31-35**), *Plaça de Sant Jaume,* and *Estació de Sants* (Sants Railway Station).

Seeing the top sights: Mega modernismo attractions

La Sagrada Familia
Eixample

Barcelona's landmark is Antoni Gaudí's unfinished legacy and testament to his singular vision, the art of the impossible. Hordes of people come to gawk at this mind-altering creation, and it's not anywhere near completion. Begun in 1884 after Gaudí took over from another architect — who was making an ordinary Gothic cathedral — the father of *modernismo* transformed the project with his fertile imagination. Even though Gaudí abandoned all other works to devote his life to this cathedral, which would be the world's largest if completed, he knew he could never finish it in his lifetime. Although he intended for future generations to add their signatures (he left only general plans), he probably didn't plan on resigning from the project when he did: Gaudí was run over by a tram in 1926.

A modernista treasure hunt

Barcelona is so littered with art nouveau sights that keeping track of them all can prove difficult. The city's **Ruta del Modernisme** (Modernist Route) gives you a hand — and a discount. For 600 pta. ($3.30) adults, 400 pta. ($2.20) students and seniors, free for children under 10, you receive a ticket with a map of sites and a 50 percent admission discount, good for 30 days, at each of nine *modernista* buildings that allows visits (including La Sagrada Familia, Palau de la Música Catalana, Fundació Tàpies, La Pedrera, Palau Güell, the Casa-Museu Gaudí at Parc Güell, and Museu de la Música). You tour on your own, though guided visits are mandatory if you visit Casa Lleó Morera, Palau de la Música, Palau Güell, or Museu d'Art Modern. The complete tour probably takes a full week or more, but even if you only hit the highlights, the pass pays for itself after just a few stops. The route includes all of Barcelona's celebrated landmarks as well as the landmarks you may otherwise overlook. If visiting 50 sites seems overwhelming, check out my suggestions on a handful of other *modernista* sights — a Group B, if you will — in "More cool things to see and do in Barcelona," later in this chapter.

Get tickets and information at **Casa Lleó Morera**, Passeig de Gràcia, 35 (second floor); ☎ **93-488-01-39.** You can purchase tickets Monday through Saturday from 10 a.m. to 7 p.m., and Sunday and holidays from 10 a.m to 2 p.m.

A private foundation works furiously to finish the church (amid protests from some that say it should be left unfinished as a memorial to Gaudí), but it remains only a façade. (It's a wonderful, otherworldly façade, however!) The eight bejeweled spires (plans called for 12, one for each of Jesus's disciples) drip like melting candlesticks. Virtually every square inch of the surface includes intricate spiritual symbols. The Barcelona sculptor Josep Maria Subirachs's additions on the west side depicting the life of Christ have been derided as disastrous kitsch, but the feelings they provoke keep with the church's design. Love it or hate it, you can't deny that the church is the work of a unique visionary.

The best stuff at La Sagrada Familia is what you see on the outside. In fact, you won't waste your trip to Barcelona if you skip going in and save your five bucks. The inside is hollowed out anyway. All you miss if you don't go in is an elevator to the top for the views and a fairly skimpy museum, which pales in comparison to the one at Gaudí's true masterpiece, the La Pedrera apartment building. Of course, your money does contribute to the continued construction of the church (uh-oh, guilt trip). If you only want to see the outside, you can do so in 20 minutes; otherwise, allow about an hour.

La Sagrada Familia is prime turf for thieves relieving tourists of their belongings, because most visitors are too busy looking bug-eyed at the sky. Someone offering you a carnation may have an accomplice eyeing your camera or wallet. See tips on safety in Appendix A.

Carrer Majorca, 401. ☎ *93-455-02-47. Metro: Sagrada Familia. Admission: 800 pta. ($4.50); additional 200 pta. ($1.10) for elevator to the top. Open: Nov–Feb, daily 9 a.m.–6 p.m.; Mar and Sept–Oct, daily 9 a.m.–7 p.m.; Apr–Aug, daily 9 a.m.–8 p.m.*

La Pedrera (Casa Milà)
Eixample

Gaudí's most fascinating and inspired civic work is officially called *Casa Milà,* named after the patrons that allowed him to carry through with such an avant-garde project back in 1910. However, everyone always refers to the apartment building as *La Pedrera,* which means "stone quarry" — a reference to its immense limestone façade. Gaudí's unfinished church *La Sagrada Familia* may be better known, but *La Pedrera* represents the crowning glory of *modernismo.*

The exterior undulates like ocean waves around the corner onto Provença street; on the roof are a set of chimneys that look like the inspiration for Darth Vader. On the first floor (near the entrance on Provença) is a great exhibition space for temporary art shows. The building was given a head-to-toe facelift in the mid-1990s. The apartments inside had suffered unspeakable horrors, and Gaudí's beautiful arched attics had been sealed up, but the painstaking restoration has revealed its author's genius in new ways. The attic floor is now a high-tech Gaudí museum (called *Espai Gaudí*), with cool interactive exhibits, terrific slide shows, and access to the roof, where you can hang out with the warrior chimneys (which, according to some, represent Christians and Moors battling for Spanish turf).

In late 1999, *El Pis,* one of the original Gaudí apartments — all with odd shapes, handcrafted doorknobs, and idiosyncratic details — opened to the public. The apartment was meticulously outfitted with period furniture, many pieces of Gaudí's design. Allow at least a couple of hours to browse this work of art (though visitors have hung out, mesmerized, on the roof until they're kicked out!).

You can enjoy flamenco, opera, and jazz evening concerts *(La Pedrera de Nit)* on the fantastic roof of *Casa Milà,* Friday and Saturday nights from July to the end of September (1,500 pta./$8).

Passeig de Gràcia, 92 (at Provença 261–265). ☎ *93-484-59-95. Metro: Diagonal or Provença. Admission: Attic (Espai Gaudí) and terrace, 600 pta. ($3); modernista apartment (El Pis), 600 pta. ($3) (350 pta./$1.75 for students and seniors); combination ticket, 1,000 pta. ($5.50), (500 pta./$2.75 for students and seniors). Open: Daily, 10 a.m.–8 p.m. (closed Dec. 25–26 and Jan. 01–06). Tours available in English, Spanish, and Catalan.*

Manzana de la Discórdia
Eixample

The so-called *Block of Discord,* a single block of the chic boulevard *Passeig de Gràcia* between *Aragó* and *Consell de Cent,* is the best place for a crash course on modernista architecture. At No. 35 is **Casa Lleó Morera,** a gorgeously ornate corner house built in 1906 by Lluís Domènech i Montaner, a serious rival to Gaudí. Up the block, on the same side of the street (No. 41), is **Casa Amatller** (1900) with its distinctive Flemish roof. The medieval-looking façade, a creation of the architect Puig i Cadafalch, has great carved stone and ironwork. Although you can't visit the interior, you can take a peek inside the Gothic entrance if the door's open.

Next door, at No. 43, is **Casa Batlló** (1906), which many people say is their favorite Gaudí building (he, in fact, only remodeled it). Its façade glimmers with fragments of colorful ceramics, the roof curves like the blue-green scales of a dragon's back, and the balconies resemble either carnavalesque masks or menacing monster jaws. Casa Batlló is now owned by the company that produces Chup-a-chups, Spain's famous lollipops. Again, you can only visit the interior of the house if you have been invited to a board meeting, party, wedding reception, or other private function.

For a bonus, look around the corner (Aragó, 225) at the **Fundació Antoni Tàpies** (☎ 93-487-03-15; open Tuesday through Sunday, 10 a.m. to 8 p.m.; 700 pta./$4), a museum dedicated to the contemporary Catalan painter Antoni Tàpies. The building, former publishing headquarters, is another terrific example of modernista architecture by Domènech i Montaner. The giant tangle of steel on the roof is a sculpture called *Cloud and Chair* by Tàpies. Allow about an hour (more if you're a fan of contemporary art and wish to visit the Tàpies museum in depth).

Passeig de Gràcia, 35–43. Guided visits in English at Casa Lleó Morera, which also takes you to Paseo de Gràcia and includes a nice explanation of the other two houses. ☎ *93-488-01-39. Metro: Passeig de Gràcia. Admission: 200 pta. ($1.10). Open: Mon–Sat 10 a.m.–7 p.m.*

Palau de la Música
Eixample

Domènech i Montaner's magnificent music hall (1908) is so over-the-top ornate that it may take you some time to appreciate it. After attending my second concert, I liked it; by my third, I was in love with the place. Apartment buildings hem in the Palau tightly (though a nondescript church next door was demolished to give the hall greater breathing space), and the relatively sedate exterior does little to prepare you for what's inside. The interior is a wild fantasy of ceramics, colored glass, and carved pumice, crowned by an enormous yellow, blue, and green stained-glass dome that looks like a swollen raindrop. The building is one of Barcelona's great *modernista* masterpieces. I rearranged a trip to see a concert here once, but if you can't manage to see a performance — it almost doesn't matter what or who is playing — you can take a guided tour, which I highly recommend. The tour lasts about an hour.

Sant Francesc de Paula, 2. ☎ *93-268-10-00 or 93-315-11-11. Internet:* www.palaumusica.org. *Metro: Urquinaona. Admission: 700 pta. ($4). Open: Guided visits daily, 10 a.m.–3:30 p.m. (on the half-hour in Spanish, Catalan, and English; on the hour in English).*

Parc Güell
Bairros Altos (Upper Barcelona)

This whimsical park, removed from downtown but still relatively easy to reach, is another of Gaudí's signature creations. Envisioned as a housing development for Gaudí's faithful patron, Eusebi Güell, the garden city was never fully realized. Gaudí originally planned to design every detail of the 60 houses; however, only one was finished, in which Gaudí lived as he struggled to complete the park. (The house is now the **Casa-Museu Gaudí.**) The parts that Gaudí did finish look something like an idiosyncratic theme park, with a mosaic-covered lizard fountain, Hansel and Gretel pagodas, and undulating park benches swathed in broken pieces of ceramics, called *trencadis*. Gaudí was so intent on the community's total integration into nature that he built part of it into a hill, constructing a forest of columns that look like tree trunks. On clear days, you can see much of Barcelona, making out the spires of *La Sagrada Familia* and the twin towers on the beach. Although that the park doesn't include much required sightseeing to check off a list, you can easily linger for hours on end. Allow at least one hour to take in the full flavor of the park.

Olot s/n. ☎ *93-284-64-46. Metro: Vallcarca/Lesseps (and six-block walk uphill). Bus: 24 or 28 (Visiting by taxi is easiest and quickest). Open: Park, May–Sept, daily 10 a.m.–9 p.m.; Oct–Apr, daily 10 a.m.–6 p.m. Casa-Museu, daily 10 a.m.–8 p.m. Admission: Park, free; Casa-Museu Gaudí, 300 pta. ($1.75).*

Exploring the Ciutat Vella (Old City)

Barcelona's *Barrio Gótico* (Gothic Quarter) — below *Plaça de Catalunya* and between *Las Ramblas* and *Vía Laietana* — is the oldest part of the city. Segments of the original Roman walls that once contained the whole of the city still survive. The district today is an intricate maze of palaces and treasures from the eleventh through fifteenth centuries. Although some late weeknights and quiet Sunday mornings it may seem as though you've been transported back in time, the Gothic Quarter is not a time-forgotten museum. People live and work — and especially go to restaurants and bars — here. Though there are a number of monuments to see, don't forget to take a sightseeing time-out and enjoy one of Barcelona's greatest pleasures, an idle wander among the Quarter's narrow streets, past alleys filled with hanging laundry and quiet plazas.

Baby Jesus, wise men, and ... who's that?

Barcelona's flair for the unusual is quite apparent in its avant-garde architecture. But nothing is more unusual than the *caganer,* a figure who creeps into most nativity scenes at Christmas time. The little guy, outfitted with a traditional red Catalan peasant's cap, appears squatting down and ... defecating. He's not meant to cause offense; locals explain that he's a symbol of the fertile earth. Today, you can find the *caganer* marketed in all kinds of variations (priests, nuns, Bart Simpson — all assuming the position).

The cathedral and Picasso Museum (covered later in this chapter) are the major sights, but also worth a visit is the noble **Plaça del Rei,** the courtyard of the fourteenth-century palace of the kings of Aragón (the Catholic Monarchs received Columbus here after his successful voyage to the Americas). Inside the palace is the **Capella de Santa Àgata** (Chapel of St. Agatha). Climb the lookout tower of King Martin for great views of the neighborhood and Waterfront.

Just off the plaza is the **Museu d'Historia de la Ciutat** (City History Museum; ☎ 93-315-11-11). The chief attraction is in the basement, where excavations have uncovered the foundations, including sculptures, walls, a bathing pool, and cemeteries of the ancient city of the Romans and Visigoths. You can also view a multimedia show that brings Barcelona's unique history to life. The museum is open Tuesday through Saturday, 10 a.m. to 2 p.m. and 4 to 8 p.m., Sunday and holidays 10 a.m. to 2 p.m. (650 pta./$3.50). Admission is free the first Saturday of every month from 4 p.m. to 8 p.m.

On your strolls through the Quarter, don't miss the **Roman walls** at Plaça Nova; **Plaça de Sant Jaume,** the heart of the Roman city and today site of municipal and regional governments; **Plaça del Pi,** the district's liveliest square, with outdoor cafes and a weekend art market; peaceful **Plaça Sant Felip de Neri** (though walls ravaged by shrapnel indicate it wasn't always so quiet); and the lovely winding streets **Carrer de la Palla** and **Carrer Banys Nous,** known for their antiques dealers.

Contrary to what someone who visited Barcelona a decade ago may tell you, walking around the Gothic Quarter is safe. The area was cleaned up considerably, but of course you need to exercise caution, especially at night. Purse snatchings and pickpockets do occur, so make sure you put your wallet in your front pocket, and don't carry either a camera or a bag.

Allow at least a full morning or afternoon — more if you've got it — to take in the Gothic Quarter and its myriad highlights.

Sardana and fútbol: Catalan classics

On Sundays at noon, people perform that quintessential (but to foreign eyes, quaint) expression of the Catalan spirit, the *sardana,* in front of the cathedral. The dance looks pretty medieval. People place their bags in the middle of an ever-widening circle, join hands, and hop and skip to the music. Feel free to throw your backpack in and give it a whirl.

Likewise, Spaniards are rabid *fútbol* (soccer) fans, and Barcelona is a legendary club in Europe. The team's known as Barça ("*bar*-sa"), or Fútbol Club Barcelona (www.fcbarcelona.com). For tickets to a game at Camp Nou (Avenida del Papa Joan XXIII; Metro:Maria Cristina/Palau Reial) that will surely double as a sociology lesson, visit the ticket office at Carrer Aristides Maillol, 12–18; ☎ 93-496-36-00. You can also visit Camp Nou's Barça Soccer Museum, which is (believe it or not) one of the most visited museums in Spain.

Catedral de Barcelona

This Catalonian Gothic cathedral, the focal point of the Old City, is actually a mix of architectural styles. Though construction began in 1298, most of the structure dates from the fourteenth and fifteenth centuries. The façade was added in the nineteenth century. Inside, check out the handsome carved choir and surprisingly lush cloister. With its magnolias, palm trees, pond, and white geese, the cathedral is a lovely oasis in the midst of the Medieval Quarter. (In the Middle Ages, geese functioned as guard dogs, their squawks alerting priests to intruders.) Try to visit at least once at night, when the cathedral is illuminated and birds soar in the floodlights. A half-hour is sufficient to see the cathedral.

Plaça de la Seu, s/n (Barri Gòtic). ☎ *93-315-15-54 or 93-310-71-95. Metro: Jaume I. Admission: Cathedral free; rooftop visits 200 pta. ($1.10); cloister museum 100 pta. (55¢). Open: Cathedral, daily 8 a.m.–1:30 p.m. and 4–7:30 p.m., Sat and Sun open 5–7:30 p.m. Rooftop, Mon–Fri 9:30 a.m.–12:30 p.m. and 4–7:30 p.m.; Sat 9:30–12:30 p.m. Museum, daily 10 a.m.–1 p.m.*

Museu Picasso

Pablo Picasso, though born in Málaga in the south of Spain, spent much of his youth in Barcelona before making the requisite artistic pilgrimage to Paris, where he soon became the most famous artist of the twentieth century. Barcelona's Picasso museum, the second most-visited museum in Spain, after the Prado in Madrid, can't compete with the superior collection in Paris, but it is the largest collection of his works in his native country. Picasso donated 2,500 paintings and sculptures to the museum, many of them early pieces, including several from his blue period. If you're a fan, you're likely to love the museum, even though few works are considered among Picasso's masterpieces. His loopy series based on

Velázquez's renowned painting *Las Meninas* is a trip, though, evidence of Picasso's playful genius. After a recent expansion, the museum now occupies several exquisite fifteenth-century palaces on a pedestrian street lined with medieval mansions. Even if you're convinced you despise Picasso, visit the museum just to see the interior and patios of the distinguished palace — and, you may change your mind, at least about his early work. Plan on spending a couple of hours here.

Montcada, 15–19. ☎ *93-319-63-10. Metro: Jaume I. Admission: 725 pta. ($4) adults, 400 pta. ($2.20) students, free for children 12 and under; free first Sunday of month. Temporary exhibits, 800 pta. ($4.50); combined entrance to permanent collection and temporary exhbit, 1,250 pta. ($7). Open: Tues–Sat 10 a.m.–8 p.m., Sun 10 a.m.–3 p.m.*

Santa María del Mar

I'm wowed every time I duck into this fourteenth-century Catalan Gothic church. It's not opulent and jewel-encrusted, and it doesn't have amazing cloisters or a fabulous art collection — it's a simple and solemn but wholly inspired space. The church is gorgeously conceived, with perfect proportions in its three soaring naves, wide-spaced columns, and handsome stained-glass windows. Architects understandably wax poetic about Santa María del Mar. The cathedral once sat on the waterfront, and sailors and fishermen (and their wives) would come to pray for safe returns. You can take a ten-minute walk-through, though even the non-religious tend to linger in this supremely serene space. Occasionally there are music concerts here, which are unforgettable experiences.

Plaça de Santa María (Ribera). ☎ *93-215-74-11. Metro: Jaume I. Admission: Free. Open: Mon–Sat 9 a.m.–1:30 p.m. and 4:30–8 p.m., Sun 9 a.m.–2 p.m. and 5–8:30 p.m.*

Strolling La Rambla

Victor Hugo extolled Barcelona's La Rambla as "the most beautiful street in the world," and the Spanish poet García Lorca said it was the "only street he wished would never end." La Rambla is more than just an attractive street; it's an interminable street parade. With its variety of people, vendors, markets, and historic buildings, La Rambla is the perfect introduction to the city. Many locals practice the fine art of the *paseo* (stroll) every day of their lives along this mile-long pedestrian avenue.

Almost any hour of the day, La Rambla is an intriguing and occasionally uplifting expression of life in Barcelona. It's a feast of sounds, smells, and activity. Subdivided into five separate *ramblas,* each of different character and attractions, are a succession of newspaper kiosks, fresh flower stands, bird sellers, and mimes in elaborate costumes and face paint hoping for a few *pesetas.* In many ways, La Rambla may be the highlight of your trip to Barcelona (to ensure that it is, keep a keen eye on your bag and camera). You can walk the length of La Rambla in a half-hour, but allow one or two hours (or several more) if you want to make pit stops for refreshments, shopping, and exploring along the way.

Begin your stroll at the very top of La Rambla, near Plaça de Catalunya, where you can find a number of chairs that are usually filled with older men talking about football and Spanish politics. To sit in a chair, you have to part with a few *pesetas* — they're for rent. The water gurgling from the **Calanetes Fountain** that's on the upper Rambla is not only safe to drink, but is also said to confer instant "native of Barcelona" status to its drinkers.

Farther down La Rambla is a noisy bird market. Continuing toward the water, you come upon bustling flower stalls. Look for a gorgeous *modernista* bakery, **Escribà,** on the right side. Nearby is one of the highlights of La Ramblas, the **La Boquería** food market. If you aren't already suffering from sensory overload, take a detour in here to see and smell an amazingly lively scene: the selling, slicing, and dicing of fresh fish, meats, produce, and just about everything your tummy could want. If you begin to feel intense hunger pains, hunt down **Bar Pinotxo** inside the market for excellent *tapas.*

Back on La Rambla is **Gran Theatre del Liceu,** Barcelona's great opera house that went up in flames in 1994 and reopened in late 1999. The international opera stars José Carreras and Montserrat Caballé, both from Barcelona, paid their dues here at the Liceu ("lee-*say*-oo"). In the middle of La Rambla is a mosaic by Joan Miró, while across the street is a great nineteenth-century café-bar, **Café de la Ópera,** long a gathering spot for opera-goers and literary types and now a hangout for gays, tourists, and old-timers. A little farther down La Rambla, off the left side as you face the sea, is the **Plaça Reial,** a grand plaza with palm trees, arcades, and lampposts designed by none other than Antoni Gaudí. In the past, the Plaça Reial was a drug haven and a place you definitely wouldn't want to frequent. However, the square has been drastically cleaned up, and it's now full of cafés and bars dealing legal stimulants.

The character of the strip changes again in the last section of La Rambla, near the water. At night, the area feels pretty seedy, but by day it's perfectly safe. Look for an artisans' fair on your way to the **Monument à Colom** (Columbus Monument), which stands at the bottom of La Rambla at the harbor, punctuating the end of this preeminent stroller's avenue. (Don't tell anyone, but Columbus, ostensibly pointing to the Americas, is turned in the wrong direction. He's pointing out at the Mediterranean, which isn't exactly the way to get to Florida.)

Montjuïc Hill: More than Olympics

If a taxi or subway's too boring for you, you can take a *teleférico* (aerial cable car) or funicular to the top of Montjuïc. The funicular leaves Avenida Paral.lel (250 pta./$1.40). The *teleférico* crosses the port; climb aboard in Barceloneta or Port Vell for 525 pta. ($3) oneway or 675 pta.

($3.75) roundtrip. Call ☎ **010** for more information. While visiting Montjuïc Hill, check out the following sights:

Museu Nacional d'Art de Catalunya (MNAC)

If you want to get a sense of Catalonia's history, this splendid medieval art museum — one of the best in the world — is a vital stop (though overlooked by many rushed visitors). At the top of the stairs and fountains leading up to Montjuïc, housed in the domed **Palau Nacional** (National Palace), the museum is anything but a stale repository of religious art. The collection of Romanesque works, salvaged from churches all over Catalonia, is unequaled. Here you can view superb altarpieces, polychromatic icons, and treasured frescoes displayed in apses, just as they were in the country churches in which they were found. The museum also holds paintings by some of Spain's most celebrated painters, including Velázquez, Ribera, and Zurbarán. Plan on spending a couple of hours at the MNAC.

Leading to the Palau Nacional is the terrace of the **Font Màgica** — the Magic Fountain. On Friday and Saturday evenings, from 8 p.m. to midnight May through October (7 to 9 p.m. March and April), the fountains perform a tricky ballet of rising and falling jets bathed in a mist of changing colors — all programmed to music.

Mirador del Palau, 6 (Palau Nacional, Parc de Montjuïc). ☎ *93-423-71-99 or 93-622-03-60. Internet:* www.gencat.es/mnac. *Metro: Espanya. Admission: 800 pta. ($4.40) adults, 400 pta. ($2.20) children 7–18, children under 7 free; combined entrance to MNAC/MAM (Museu d'Art Modern), 900 pta. ($5). Open: Tues–Wed and Fri–Sat 10 a.m.–7 p.m., Thurs 10 a.m.–9 p.m., Sun 10 a.m.–2:30 p.m.*

Fundació Joan Miró

Joan Miró was a Catalan surrealist painter and sculptor who became one of the twentieth century's most celebrated artists. Though his work may look like colorful doodles to the uninitiated, Miró was one of the rare artists successful in creating his own artistic language. The museum displays more than 200 of his canvases, as well as a wealth of drawings, graphics, and sculptures. Likewise, it has a real knack for landing some of the city's most interesting temporary exhibitions. Be sure to check local listings in the *Guía del Ocio* to see what's on when you're there. Seeing the full museum requires a couple of hours, but if you find Miró's work a series of incomprehensible squiggles, you may jog through it in a quarter of that time.

Avenida Miramar, 71/Plaça de Neptú (Parc de Montjuïc). ☎ *93-443-94-70. Internet:* www.bcn.fjmiro.es. *Metro: Espanya (then take the escalator from Palau Nacional); alternatively, take bus No 50. Admission: 800 pta. ($4.50) adults, free for children 14 and under. Open: July–Sept, Tues–Sat 10 a.m.–8 p.m., Thurs 10 a.m.–9:30 p.m., Sun 10 a.m.–2:30 p.m.; Oct–June, Tues–Wed and Fri–Sat 10 a.m.– 7 p.m., Thurs 10 a.m.–9:30 p.m., Sun 10:30 a.m.–2:30 p.m.*

Estadi Olímpic

The Estadi Olímpic (Olympic Stadium) that served as the setting for much of the 1992 Summer Olympics is on Montjuïc Hill. You can take a peek at the track-and-field stadium, originally built in 1929 for the World's Fair, or see Arata Isozaki's sleek *Palau d'Esports Sant Jordi,* the indoor stadium that hosted the gymnastics and volleyball events. Visiting the sights takes about half an hour.

Avenida del Estadi (Parc de Montjuïc). Metro: Espanya (then take the escalator from Palau Nacional); alternatively, take bus No 50.

More cool things to see and do in Barcelona

✔ **Hanging out at the Waterfront.** In 1992, taking advantage of the upcoming Olympics (and incoming government funds) for an excuse to remake the city, Barcelona completely revamped its port, which was unsightly and dangerous. The formerly polluted urban beaches are now quite clean — though the water isn't always — and the Waterfront is now one of the hottest places to live and party. Check out **Vila Olímpica,** an award-winning neighborhood and medley of conceptual architecture, where swimmers, ice-skaters, weight-lifters and other Olympic athletes were the first to inhabit the apartments, which were later sold and rented to the public. The two towers on the beach, Barcelona's only skyscrapers (one is the chic Hotel Arts, the other an office complex), were initially very controversial, but Barcelonans now accept them as another component of their forward-looking city. **Port Olímpic,** the new harbor, swims with bars and restaurants, while **Port Vell** (the old port) is a hyper-developed entertainment and shopping area. (Metro: Drassanes, Barceloneta, or Ciutadella – Vila Olímpica.)

✔ **Trekking up Tibidabo.** Climb Tibidado mountain (well, you don't have to actually climb; you can take the tram, taxi, or funicular) for marvelous views of the city below. Locals swear that they've seen the island of Mallorca on a clear day. I'd love to believe them, but . . . I don't. The tram takes you to an overlook with bars and restaurants with enviable panoramic views of the city and the ocean. A bit farther up the mountain is **Carretera de les Aigues,** a long and winding exercise path popular on weekends. On top of Tibidabo, you find the odd juxtaposition of a neo-Gothic church and a 1950s-ish amusement park, **Parc d'Atraccions Tibidabo** (the gentle swing ride is spectacular; it seems to suspend you over the city).

Tibidabo is a storied and strangely poetic name. It comes from Latin, meaning "I will give you" — words the devil reputedly used to tempt Jesus Christ when he took him up on a mountain and showed him the glory below.

To get there: By Blue Tram & Funicular: Take the historic Tramvia Blau (Blue Tram) — the only existing tram in Barcelona — to Mirablau on the way to Tibidabo. (275 pta./$1.50). From Plaza Kennedy (Metro: Tibidabo), the tram connects with the Funicular Tibidabo, a cable car that completes the trek to the top of the mountain (closed mid-October to the end of March; 400 pta./$2.20). Call ☎ **010** for more information.

✔ **Toasting your trip with *cava*.** *Tapas* bars are everywhere in Spain, but a Catalan specialty is the champagne bar, called a *xampanyería*. These bars serve *cava* (sparkling wine) as well as *tapas*. *Penedès,* an area half an hour from Barcelona, is the world's largest producer of sparkling wine. A few good bars to try are the elegant La Cava del Palau (Verdaguer i Callis, 10 near Palau de la Música; Metro: Urquinaona), the more down-to-earth El Xampanyet (Montcada, 22; Metro: Jaume I), or Xampú Xampany (Gran Via, 702; Metro: Girona).

✔ **Searching out *más* (more) *modernismo*.** If your first peeks at Gaudí have piqued your interest, there's much more *modernismo* to see in Barcelona. The easiest way to organize more architecture visits is with the *Ruta del Modernisme* pass (see the "A modernista Treasure Hunt" box, earlier in the chapter). You're unlikely to have time to see the full roster of sights, but here's the best of the second-tier group: **Hospital Sant Pau,** Domènech's incredible hospital city, down Avinguda Gaudí from **La Sagrada Familia** church (Cartagena at Sant Antoni Maria Claret); **Palau Güell,** one of Gaudí's earliest works, its roof a surprising forest of tiled chimneys (Nou de la Rambla 3–5); **Museu de la Música,** a cool music museum in a wonderful palace (Avinguda Diagonal 373); and the fairytale-like **Casa de les Punxes** (Avinguda Diagonal, 416).

✔ **Touring the *Barrios Altos*.** Once summer villages reachable only by horse but now wholly integrated into the city, Barcelona's upper neighborhoods, at the base of Tibidabo Mountain, are residential districts that hold a few interesting sights and real insight into what living in Barcelona is like. **Pedralbes** is chic and leafy, **Sarrià** is a 1,000-year-old Catalan village, and **Gràcia** is a working-class neighborhood with lively bars and restaurants. The **Monasteri de Pedralbes** (Pedralbes Monastery), the one essential visit in the Barrios Altos, displays Barcelona's medieval holdings of the renowned Thyssen-Bornemisza Art Collection, the major portion of which is displayed in Madrid.

Monasteri de Pedralbes: Bajada del Monasterio, 9; ☎ **93-280-14-34;** admission 500 pta.($2.75); Metro (FGC): Reina Elisenda, Sarrià, and Gràcia.

✔ **Barcelona from a kid's point of view.** There's plenty for kids and parents to do in Barcelona. Besides beaches, the Port Vell waterfront has the second-largest aquarium in Europe: **L'Aquàrium de Barcelona,** Moll d'Espanya (☎ **93-221-74-74;** Open September through June, 9:30 a.m. to 9 p.m. Monday through Friday, and

9:30 a.m. to 9:30 p.m. Saturday, Sunday, and public holidays; July through August, 9.30 a.m. to 11 p.m. daily; Admission: 1,400 pta. ($8) adults, 950 pta.($5) children 4 through 12 and seniors, and free for children under 4). You can also find an **IMAX theater** and lots of diversions in the **Maremagnum Mall** — just crossing the funky drawbridge, *Rambla del Mar,* to get there is fun. Near the Columbus statue at the end of La Rambla is the **Museu Marítim** (Maritime Museum), an old shipyard with replicas of huge royal ships. In the Parc de la Ciutadella, the **Parc Zoológic** (Zoo) (☎ 93-221-25-06; Open November February 10 a.m. to 5:30 p.m., March and October 10 a.m. to 6 p.m., April and September 10 a.m. to 7 p.m., and May through August 9:30 a.m. to 7:30 p.m. daily; Admission 1,500 pta. ($8), 950 pta.($5) children under 12 and seniors, free under 3) has the world's only albino gorilla in captivity, named *Copito de Nieve* Snowflake.

In the *Barrios Altos,* the **Museu de la Ciència** is a hands-on science museum with children's workshops (Calle Teodor Roviralta 55-C/ Cister 64; ☎ 93-212-60-50; Open 10 a.m. to 8 p.m. Tuesday through Sunday; Admission 500pta.($2.75) adults, 350pta.($1.90) students under 25 and senoirs, free for children under 7). **Poble Espanyol** in Montjuïc Park is a recreation of a Spanish village with architectural styles from all over Spain. You may find it a little cheesy, but it's a nice place for families to visit. (Avinguda del Marqués de Comillas; ☎ 93-508-63-30; Mon 9 a.m. to 8 p.m., Tuesday through Thursday 9 a.m. to 2 a.m., Friday through Saturday 9 a.m. to 4 p.m., Sunday 9 a.m. to 12 p.m.; Admission 950 pta.($6.35) adults, 525 pta.($3.50) children 7–14, free for children under 7.) If Poble Espanyol isn't enough to wear out your kids, check out the amusement parks on both Montjuïc and Tibidabo. Children also enjoy attending some of the kid-friendly and fireworks-heavy festivals in Barcelona, such as La Mercé, Festa Major da Gràcia, and Sant Joan (see the Calendar of Events in Chapter 2), as well as **Parc Güell,** which Gaudí built with the uninhibited imagination of a child.

✔ **Trolling the other side of *La Rambla.*** If you're eager to see Barcelona in transition, and the slightly seedy side of life doesn't make you nervous, check out the Raval neighborhood (to the right of *La Rambla* if you're facing the sea). For decades a mostly under-class and immigrant neighborhood, Raval was also home to clus-ters of starving artists, down-and-out hookers, and junkies. Today the *barrio* (neighborhood) is a curious mix of rough-around-the-edges and avant-garde design. In the last couple years, the city razed buildings, installed pedestrian streets and plazas, and com-missioned big projects in an effort to revitalize the district. See Richard Meier's glistening white **Museu d' Art Contemporani de Barcelona** (MACBA, or Museum of Contemporary Art), on Plaça dels Angels, 1. The **Casa de la Caritat,** an old hospital behind MACBA, was intriguingly revamped as a city museum.

Although the Raval area is definitely on its way up, you need to be careful and mindful of your belongings, especially at night. Don't take anything you couldn't live without. (Metro: Liceu or Plaça de Catalunya.)

And on Your Left, La Sagrada Familia: Seeing Barcelona by Guided Tour

If you don't have a lot of time, sometimes the best way to see as much as possible is on an organized tour. Here are some of the best.

By bus

Barcelona Bus Turístic. Hop aboard for a tour of 24 city sights. You can take either or both of the Red and Blue Routes, and get on and off as you please. Both depart from *Plaça de Catalunya* at 9 a.m. daily; all stops have full timetables. Complete journey time is about 3½ hours. The bus runs daily throughout the year, except December 25 and January 1. Price: One-day, adults 2,000 pta. ($11), children 4 though 12 1,200 pta. ($6.50); two-day, 2,500 pta. ($14). Booking: Purchase tickets on board or in advance at **Turisme de Barcelona,** Plaça de Catalunya, 17 (☎ **93-315-11-11**).

 Walking tours of El Eixample are best left to weekends to avoid the overbearing traffic congestion and noise that overtakes the area during the work week. Nighttime is also a good time for a walking tour, because many of the star *modernista* monuments, including La Pedrera and Casa Battló, are illuminated. (The area around Passeig de Gràcia is safe at night.)

By foot

Barcelona Walking Tours. You can join English-speaking, guide-led tours of the Gothic Quarter every Saturday at 10 a.m. Walks (90 minutes in length) begin at **Turisme de Barcelona,** Plaça de Catalunya, 17. Information: ☎ **93-315-11-11.** Price: 950 pta. ($5); children 4–12, 500 pta. ($2.75).

 If you'd like a personal guide to escort you around Barcelona (no, not *that* kind of escort!) and explain *modernismo* and Gaudí, contact Carmen Turiera-Puigbò of **Barcelona Guide Bureau** (BGB). She can tailor-organize a walking tour of the city to your needs. The BGB office is at Via Laietana, 54; ☎ **93-310-77-78;** E-mail: bgb@bcn.servicom.es.

By bike

Un Cotxe Menys. This company (the name means "one fewer car" in Catalan) offers a pair of enjoyable Barcelona-by-bike tours around the Old City and the Waterfront (one tour includes dinner). These tours aren't for hardcore cyclists, however; the jaunts include drinks and even dinner. Information: ☎ **93-268-21-05** or 93-207-08-96.

By balloon

Barcelona Globus Turistic, a passenger balloon inaugurated in 2000, allows visitors to get a panoramic view of the city from a height of 120 m (393 feet). Capacity is 35 people. Cost is 2,000 pta. ($11). Paseo de la Circunvalación. (☎ **93-597-11-40** for information, 93-342-97-90 for reservations.)

Suggested One-, Two-, and Three-Day Sightseeing Itineraries

On **Day One** in Barcelona, stroll along La Rambla, making sure you take in the sights and smells of the *La Boquería* market, and meander the medieval alleyways in the Barri Gòtic, including visits to the Museu Picasso and the Catedral de Barcelona. In the afternoon, view some of the city's fabulous *modernista* architecture, including La Sagrada Familia, La Pedrera, and the Manzana de la Discórdia.

Spend **Day Two** along the lively Waterfront and urban beaches or visiting Montjuïc (and the Museu Nacional d'Art de Catalunya and Fundació Joan Miró museum) and Tibidabo. You can also squeeze in a visit to Gaudí's Parc Güell. All of these attractions offer spectacular lookouts over the whole of Barcelona.

On **Day Three,** if you're an architecture buff, you can round out your roster of emblematic *modernista* buildings in *El Eixample,* hitting the highlights of the *Ruta del Modernisme* (see sidebar "A modernista treasure hunt," earlier in this chapter). However, if you're restless, you can hop aboard a train for a daytrip to Montserrat, Sitges, or the wine region of Penedès (see "Side Trips from Barcelona," later in this chapter).

Shopping in Barcelona

Barcelona's fascination with design makes it a great place to load up on unique art objects and home furnishings. Likewise, Barcelona is noted for its fashion and jewelry. For the quality that Barcelona offers, prices are pretty reasonable (especially with a high dollar). Although

Barcelona has added a couple of mega-malls in recent years, small, often family-owned stores still dominate the city. Window shopping along the city's picturesque boulevards is an art here.

Finding the best shopping areas

Tour these shopping areas to find the best that Barcelona has to offer:

- **Passeig de Gràcia** and **Rambla de Catalunya.** You can find some of Barcelona's finest boutiques on these two chic streets above *Plaça de Catalunya.* For fashion, jewelry, and home design, these are great window-shopping streets — as are nearby Mallorca, Valencia, and Provença.

- **Avinguda Diagonal.** This avenue, which cuts across Barcelona, has some of the finest and most expensive stores in Barcelona. Check it out if your tastes run to Armani, et al.

- **Carrer Consell de Cent.** Barcelona has a thriving art scene. In the heart of *El Eixample,* between *Passeig de Gràcia* and *Aribau,* this is the city's major art avenue.

- **Plaça de Catalunya.** The entrance to the Old City is the jumping off point for some of its principal shopping streets: Avinguda Portal de l'Angel and Carrer Portaferrisa always swarm with shoppers.

- **Gothic Quarter.** Deep in the oldest part of town is one of the best spots for antiques and art galleries. Check out the streets Banys Nous, Carrer de la Palla, and Petritxol.

- **La Rambla.** Many of the shops on this street focus on tourist trinkets, but you can still find amazing little pastry and jewelry shops.

- **Old Port.** Barcelona's newest shopping mecca is Maremagnum, a mall teeming with restaurants and all kinds of shops. It's open every day of the year and until 11 p.m.

Knowing what to look for and where to find it

From antiques to cigars to fashion and more, Barcelona has it all. The following sections give you the info you need to find the items you want.

Antiques

Carrer de la Palla and Banys Nous in the Gothic Quarter are home to innumerable antiques dealers; many of the shops are as interesting as their wares. **Bulevar dels Antiquaris** (Passeig de Gràcia, 57; Metro: Passeig de Gràcia) is a storefront that hides a maze of at least 70 antiques dealers, but keep in mind that dealers sometimes randomly disappear for long breaks — and not just at siesta time.

L'Arca de L'Àvia (Banys Nous, 20; ☎ 93-302-15-98; Metro: Jaume I), an inviting little shop that specializes in antique clothing and lace, is reportedly the shop where the costume designer for *Titanic* found the clothes on which that movie's costumes were based.

Art

Two areas worth exploring are Consell de Cent, in El Eixample, and Passeig del Born, which is a hot gallery area. In particular, keep an eye out for **Sala Parés,** Barcelona's oldest art gallery, specializing in traditional art (Carrer Petritxol, 5; ☎ 93-318-70-20; Metro: Liceu) and **Galería Maeght,** a huge and prestigious contemporary gallery down the street from the Picasso Museum (Carrer Montcada, 25; ☎ 93-310-42-45; Metro: Jaume I).

Books

Barcelona headquarters Spain's publishing industry; you can find a wide array of titles in English and other foreign languages. You can find excellent art books, books on Spanish culture, cookbooks, and lots of discounted titles — many in English — at **Happy Books,** which has branches on Passeig de Gràcia (Metro: Passeig de Gràcia) and Ronda de la Universitat (Metro: Plaça de Catalunya). **Llibrería Francesa,** on Passeig de Gràcia at Provença (Metro: Passeig de Gràcia), has many books in English, particularly travel titles and, as the name implies, French titles. The **Crisol** chain, with a branch on Rambla Catalunya, 81 (Metro: Passeig de Gràcia), is also very well stocked, as is the huge French department store, **FNAC,** on Plaça Catalunya.

Cigars and tobacco

Gimeno (Rambla de les Flors, 100; ☎ 93-302-09-83), a specialist in all sorts of tobacco products, has a natural cellar and, yes, lots of Cubans (cigars, not the people). Americans have to smoke 'em before returning home, though.

Department stores

El Corte Inglés (located at Plaça de Catalunya and a new branch on Avinguda Portal de l'Angel and Santa Anna) is the big daddy of Spanish department stores; it carries everything from perfume to bikes, and people swarm the store at all hours of the day and night. If crowds make you nervous, stay away.

Design

Vinçon (Passeig de Gràcia, 96; ☎ 93-215-60-50; Metro: Passeig de Gràcia) is Barcelona's premiere design store, with everything that is, in the estimation of founder Fernando Amat, well designed — including lamps, watches, furniture, kitchen utensils, toys, writing instruments, and so on. The display windows are whimsically avant-garde and worth checking out even if you don't have time for shopping. The shop occupies the former house of the great Catalan painter Ramón Casas (this was the first building in Barcelona built with a car garage). **BD Ediciones de Diseño** (Carrer Mallorca, 291-293; ☎ 93-458-69-09; Metro: Diagonal), housed in a marvelous *modernista* house, sells the high end of Catalan design, including reproductions of Gaudí and Dalí furniture. Check out this store if you've got style and *pesetas* to burn.

Fashion

One of the foremost young Catalan designers, **Antonio Miró's** fashions for men and women are exquisite, but they're for people with a serious interest in fashion. The actor John Malkovich has been known to wear Miró's stuff. His signature shop is at Consell de Cent, 349 (☎ 93-487-06-07; Metro: Passeig de Gràcia). Look for his other store, **Groc,** on *Rambla de Catalunya.* **Adolfo Domínguez** is a Galicia-born designer who has successfully marketed fashion to the masses; he has shops across Spain. Besides the store at Passeig de Gràcia, 32 (☎ 93-487-41-70; Metro: Plaça de Catalunya), you can also shop at Diagonal 570 and another at Passeig de Graci, 89. A Galician fashion phenomenon, **Zara** has affordable but stylish clothes for men, women, and children. The stores have sprouted like the European Gap; look for branches on Rambla de Catalunya at Aragó and on Avenida Portal de l'Angel.

Flea market

If you're a junk-hound, convinced that you'll uncover that special thing you didn't even know you had to have, check out **Els Encants,** Barcelona's biggest and best flea market. Vendors hawk their goods and your finds all day every Monday, Wednesday, Friday, and Saturday at Plaça de les Glóries Catalanes (Metro: Glóries).

Foodstuffs

Colmado Quílez offers packaged goods, fine wines, cheeses, and imported beer in a bustling and atmospheric shop. After you place an order, the attendant gives you a ticket; you go pay, and then return to the counter to collect your items. Find it at Rambla de Catalunya, 63 (☎ 93-215-87-85; Metro: Passeig de Gràcia). **Escribà** (Rambla de les Flors, 83; ☎ 93-487-06-07; Metro: Liceu) is a classic pastry-and-chocolates shop in a lovely *modernista* place on a corner along Las Ramblas. Eyeball the window; I defy you to resist stepping inside. **Caelum** means "heaven" in Latin; accordingly, what you find here are all sorts of products, such as Trappist-monk beer, candles, cheeses, and honey, made by monasteries and religious orders. Downstairs is a great tea room in what were fourteenth-century baths. Find Caelum on *Carrer de la Palla,* 8 (☎ 93-302-69-93; Metro: Jaume I). You can also visit **E&A Gispert,** a 150-year-old, great little shop known for its roasted nuts, dried fruits, coffee, and spices (Sobrerers, 23; ☎ 93-319-75-35). The place, which smells absolutely wonderful, is just around the corner from the Santa María del Mar Church in La Ribera.

Gifts

You can find ceramics and handcrafts, much better quality than the souvenir trinkets you find along *Las Ramblas,* at **Art Escudellers** (Carrer Escudellers, 23–25; ☎ 93-412-68-01; Metro: Drassanes). Like-wise, **BCN Original** offers a very nice selection of gifts, such as t-shirts, paper products, and much more, with the Barcelona stamp — all conveniently located next to the Tourism Information Office at Plaça de Catalunya 17 (Metro: Plaça de Catalunya). If you're looking for *Lladró* china figurines, **Mils** (Passeig de Gràcia; ☎ 93-412-17-94; Metro: Passeig de Gràcia) is one of many places to find them. **La Pedrera's Giftshop** (Provença, 261–265) offers Gaudí souvenirs and knock-offs, including coasters and chocolates designed to look like the octagonal tiles that form the sidewalk on *Passeig de Gràcia.* (Gaudí was obsessed with details; he often designed the furniture, door knobs, and lamps for his houses.)

La Noche: Checking Out Barcelona's Nightlife

Barcelona really hops at night, and though the city doesn't have quite the crazed reputation that Madrid does, Barcelonans are only too happy to stay up all night. To get a grip on what's hip, what's hot, and what's happening, pick up a copy of the weekly *Guía del Ocio,* a guide to all entertainment in Barcelona (available at newsstands, in Spanish) or *Barcelona Olé!,* the monthly guide distributed by Barcelona Tourism. *Barcelona Olé!'s* not as up-to-date or detailed as *Guía del Ocio,* but it carries the big shows and performances, and offers a bunch of useful information (the kind you'd be lost without if you didn't have your trusty *Dummies* guide!).

Opera and classical music

If you're into music, be sure to check out the following venues while touring Barcelona.

- ✔ **Palau de la Música.** For spectacular experience, see a concert in this *modernista* wonderland. It's really loosened up in recent years; besides classical music, I've seen concerts by Lou Reed, Tindersticks, and David Byrne here. (Sant Frances de Paula 2; ☎ 93-268-10-00; Metro: Urquinaona.)

- ✔ **Gran Teatre del Liceu.** Barcelona's grand opera house, was completely gutted by fire in January 1994, but the city raced to rebuild it, and it reopened in October 1999. (Carrer Sant Pau, 1; ☎ 93-41-235-32; Metro: Liceu.)

- ✔ **L'Auditori (Barcelona Auditorium).** This splendid new addition to the music scene, the work of the famed Spanish architect Rafael Moneo, features two halls for classical music concerts. It's high

tech all the way. (Carrer Lepant, 150; ☎ **93-247-93-00;** Internet:
www.auditori.com; E-mail: info@auditori.com; Metro: Marina
or Glóries.) Tickets at box office (open Mon–Sat from 10 a.m. to
9 p.m.) or by calling ☎ **902-10-12-12** or 34-93-479-99-20 from abroad.

Flamenco shows

Barcelona can't compare with Madrid or Andalusia for *tablaos* ("tah-*blah*-
ose") — live flamenco performances — but there is a handful of rather
touristy shows. One is **Tablao Flamenco Cordobés,** Las Ramblas 35
(☎ **93-317-66-53;** Metro: Liceu). The show, with one drink, costs 4,200
pta. ($23). **El Patio Andaluz,** Aribau, 242 (☎ **93-209-33-78;** Metro: Gràcia)
puts on *flamenco* shows (4,175 pta,/$23) as well as *sevillanas* ("seh-vee-
yah-nahs," more traditional southern-style singing and dancing).

Cafés and bars

Two places to drink in the local atmosphere are **Café de la Ópera,**
La Rambla, 74, and **Els Quatre Gats,** Montsió, 3 (☎ **93-302-41-40;** Metro:
Urquinaona). Tiny **Mesón del Café,** Llibreteria, 16 (☎ **93-315-07-54;**
Metro: Jaume I) gets my vote for coolest café and best coffee. Another,
which looks unearthed from 1940s Havana, is **Boadas,** Carrer Taller 1
(☎ **93-318-95-92;** Metro: Plaça de Catalunya). **Schilling,** Ferran 23
(☎ **93-317-67-87;** Metro: Jaume I), is a cool bar that beautiful people —
almost every one of them smokers — frequent. **El Born,** the area near
Santa María del Mar, and the **Olympic Port** near the Hotel Arts are two
of the city's hottest nightlife areas. You can't walk without stumbling
into a bar.

Live music

You can find a wild night of campy cabaret at **Bodega Bohemia,**
Lancaster, 2 (☎ **93-302-50-61;** Metro: Liceu). **El Molino,** Vila i Vila, 99
(☎ **93-329-88-54;** Metro: Paral.lel), is another legendary place — one of
the city's oldest cabarets. **Harlem Jazz Club,** Comtessa de Sobradiel
(☎ **93-310-07-55;** Metro: Jaume I.), is probably the city's best jazz club,
a tiny affair tucked away in the Gothic Quarter. **Los Tarantos,** Plaça
Reial (☎ **93-318-30-67;** Metro: Liceu), frequently has flamenco or pop
flamenco shows.

Dancing

Antilla Cosmopolita, Muntaner, 244 (Metro: Muntaner), bills itself as a
salsateca (salsa club). The nightclub **Nick Havanna,** Rosselló, 208
(Metro: Provença), was one of Barcelona's first sleek design-oriented
bars. **Luz de Gas,** Muntaner, 246, and **Otto Zutz,** Lincoln, 15, are among
the hottest late-night dance places.

Good Grec: Barcelona's summer festival

If you find yourself in the Catalan capital in the heat of summer, check out the listings for **Grec,** an annual festival of international dance, music, and theater. For six weeks, from the last week of June to the end of the first week in August, Grec showcases scores of stuff — everything from American blues to Brazilian samba and avant-garde Belgian dance. Call ☎ **93-301-77-75** or check the Web site (www.grecbcn.com) for a schedule of events and ticket information.

Side Trips from Barcelona

If you've got some extra time in Barcelona, the following side trips are well worth your while.

Montserrat: The holy jagged mountain

Montserrat is Barcelona's peculiarly formed and sacred mountain. *Montserrat,* which means "sawtooth mountain," cuts a dramatic, jagged line across the Catalan sky.

Getting there

Montserrat is 50 km (30 miles) northwest of Barcelona. You can go by car, bus, or rail, but the most dramatic approach to Montserrat is via train and a cable car that ascends to the top (though the cycling club I used to belong to biked to the mountain, and that wasn't bad, either). The FGC train (see "By train," earlier in this chapter) offers a **TransMontserrat** ticket (2,900 pta./$17, children under 10 1,500 pta./$8 roundtrip) that leaves from Barcelona's *Plaça d'Espanya* Station and connects to the aerial cable car (☎ **93-205-15-15;** Internet: www.fgc.catalunya.net). **Autocares Juliá** (☎ **93-490-40-00**) travels by bus direct from Barcelona, leaving daily at 9 a.m. and returning at 5 p.m. The trip costs 1,140 pta. ($6).

The only other way to visit the mountain is by car, especially if you want to combine the journey with a visit to the Penedès Wineries (see "Penedès: Spain's cava country," later in this chapter). You can easily do both in a single day if you're driving. By car, take the A-2 out of Barcelona towards Tarragona and Martorell, or the Barcelona-Terrassa highway via the *Túneles de Vallvidrera.* The signs to Montserrat are clearly marked.

The **Tourist Information Office** is on Plaça de la Creu (☎ **93-835-02-51**).

Seeing the sights

Friends and I once took a Swedish visitor to see Montserrat, but she was wholly unimpressed. "It's just a mountain," she said, but I beg to differ. This is no ordinary 4,000-foot mountain, either in appearance or symbolism. The setting for Wagner's opera *Parsifal,* Montserrat is home to an eleventh-century **Benedictine monastery,** which is spectacularly tucked into its ridges. In the sixteenth-century basilica is a shrine to the famous *Black Madonna,* the patron saint of Catalonia. Pilgrims come from all over to worship her, and you'll see her reproduced image everywhere in Barcelona.

Besides visiting the monastery and appreciating the incredible views of the Catalan countryside, time your visit to see the **Esolanía,** one of the oldest boys' choirs in Europe (dating to the thirteenth century). The choir performs every day at 1 p.m. and 6:45 p.m. On Sundays and holidays, you can hear them at morning mass (11 a.m.).

Avoid making your pilgrimage to Montserrat on April 27 and September 8. Those holy days draw pilgrims from all over Spain, and the place is a zoo.

Stylin' Sitges: A beach resort

Sitges is a pretty beach town along the so-called *Costa Daurada* (Golden Coast), with an attractive Old Quarter and two important Modernista-era museums. Sitges is also one of Spain's top gay resort areas, drawing many Europeans and Spaniards. Sitges makes an easy day-trip from Barcelona if you set out early.

Getting there

Sitges is 35 km (21 miles) southwest of Barcelona. The trip is 40 minutes by train, with frequent departures from Barcelona Sants station (330 pta./$1.80); drive along coastal road C-246 to get there by car. However, on weekends, opt for toll highway A-7 to avoid heavy traffic. (Allow 45 minutes to an hour.)

The **Tourist Information Office** (☎ **93-984-12-30**) is at Passeig De Vilafranca.

Seeing the sights

Tiny Sitges has long been a cultural center, drawing the painters Santiago Rusiñol and Salvador Dalí, as well as the poet Federico García Lorca to its enclave. **Museu Cau Ferrat** (on Carrer del Fonollar s/n) was the home of Rusiñol (who converted two sixteenth-century fisherman's houses), and it is today as it was in his lifetime — chock full of *modernista*-period paintings, other artworks by the likes of El Greco, and personal knick knacks. You can also browse through nice collections of ceramics and wrought iron (☎ **93-894-03-64;** 400 pta./$2.20 adults, 200 pta./$1.10 students, free for children under 16; open 10 a.m. to 1 p.m., 4 to 6 p.m.). The other museum of note is **Museu Maricel del Mar** (Carrer del Fonollar s/n) is a handsome palace displaying Gothic and Romantic artworks (☎ 93-894-03-64; 500 pta./$2.75, 250 pta./$1.30 students, free children under 16; open 10 a.m. to 1 p.m., 4 to 6 p.m.).

As enjoyable as these two museums are, the lazy lifestyle of beaches and seaside restaurants are Sitges's main draw. The beach in town is lovely, while beaches further west draw some less inhibited behavior. Unless you want an eyeful (of skin and more), stick to the beaches in or near town, which are those most popular with families. When night falls, the best plan is to check out the constant beachfront stream of humanity along the promenade. Otherwise, the *Sant Bonaventura* section in the town center sizzles with gay party spots.

Where to stay and dine

You can find a number of good restaurants on *Paseo de la Ribera*. For example, try **El Velero de Sitges,** at No. 38, or **Mare Nostrum,** at No. 60. If you want to hang out for a couple of days in Sitges, I suggest checking into either **Capri/Veracruz** (Avinguda De Sofía, 13–15; ☎ 93-811-02-67; $$$) a calm and charming old palace, or **El Xalet** (Isla de Cuba, 33–35; ☎ 93-811-00-70; $$) a *modernista* house with many original furnishings.

On the Sunday after Corpus Christi (June 21), Sitges is laid out with thick carpets of fresh flowers. Likewise, during the first weekend in March, the city serves as the endpoint of the Barcelona-Sitges Vintage Car Rally.

Penedès: Spain's cava country

Catalonia's sparkling wine, called *cava,* comes from Penedès, a pretty region just outside of Barcelona. You can tour the wineries and admire the *modernista* architecture.

Getting there

Penedès is 40 km (25 miles) from Barcelona. By car (40 minutes), take A-2 in the direction of Tarragona/Lleida; Exit 27 is Sant Sadurní d'Noia, and Cordoniu is clearly marked. If you want to get on a bus, **Autocares La Hispano Llacunense** (☎ 93-891-25-61) makes the trip, leaving from the corner of Avenida de Sarrià and Urgell. Eight buses a day go to *Sant Sadurní* Monday through Friday, and just two on Saturday and Sunday. The fare is 500 pta. ($2.75) Monday through Saturday and 605 pta. ($3.30) on Sundays.

Seeing the sights

Several wineries are in the main town, *Sant Sadurní del Noia.* Try a tour of **Codorniu,** which, though it's still family-owned, is Spain's largest producer of *cava.* The visit to the winery is an excellent addition to the *modernista* sightseeing you may have already done in Barcelona. The main buildings on the Codorniu campus, the 1898 work of Gaudí contemporary Puig i Cadafalch, are a National Artistic and Historic Monument. More than 150,000 people a year visit the winery, the highlight of which is a theme-park-like cart ride through 16 miles of atmospheric underground cellars.

Codorniu's friendly staff are happy to point out local restaurants for lunch ask them about **Fonda Neus,** a popular place; family-owned *Sol i Vi;* and the more upscale **El Mirador de las Cavas,** which offers great views of the surrounding wineries. Codorniu is open year-round (except Christmas and New Year's), and guided visits in English are free during the week. On Sundays, visitors receive a champagne glass along with their tasting; the visit costs 200 pta. ($1.10). Call ☎ **93-301-46-00** for more information.

Fast Facts: Barcelona

Area Code

The area code for telephone numbers within Barcelona is **93**. Even within the city, you must dial the prefix first.

American Express

Ramblas, 74; ☎ **93-301-11-66**. It's open Mon–Fri from 9:30 a.m. to 6 p.m. and Saturday from 9 a.m. to noon.

ATMs/Currency Exchange

You can exchange currency either at banks or *casas de cambio* (exchange houses). You can also find currency exchange offices at the Sants rail stations and El Prat airport. Major Spanish banks include *La Caixa, Caixa de Catalunya, BBV,* and *Central Hispano.* Branches of these banks are located near Plaça Catalunya. Most banks offer 24-hour ATM machines. Currency exchange houses include BCN World and BCN Change & Transfer.

Doctors

To locate a hospital, dial ☎ **93-427-20-20**. The Hospital Clínic is at Villarroel, 170 (☎ **93-454-60-00**).

Embassies/Consulates

The U.S. Consulate is located at Paseo Reina Elisenda, 23 in Sarrià (☎ **93-280-22-27**); Canadian Consulate, Passeig De Gràcia, 77 (☎ **93-215-07-04**); U.K. Consulate, Aviguda Diagonal, 477 (☎ **93-419-90-44**); Australian Consulate, Gran Vía Carles III, 98 (☎ **93-330-94-96**); and New Zealand Consulate, Travessera de Gràcia, 64 (☎ **93-209-03-99**).

Emergencies

For medical emergencies, dial ☎ **061**. The National Police emergency number (in and outside Barcelona) is ☎ **091**. For local police, call ☎ **092**. Call ☎ **93-300-20-20** to request an ambulance. For fire, call ☎ **080**.

Hospitals

To locate a hospital, dial ☎ **93-427-20-20**. The Hospital Clínic is at Villarroel, 170 (☎ **93-454-60-00**).

Information

Call ☎ **010** for general visitor information. Turisme de Barcelona, Plaça de Catalunya, 17 (underground), ☎ **906-301-282**, is open daily 9 a.m. to 9 p.m. Informació Turística de Catalunya, which provides information on

Barcelona and the entire autonomous region, is located in Palau Robert, Passeig de Gràcia, 107 (☎ 93-238-40-00). There are also tourism information ofices at Sants train station and the airport. For transit information (metro, bus, and so on), call ☎ 010 or 93-486 07 52. Internet: www.tmb.net.

Internet Access and Cyber Cafés

The Internet Gallery Café is down the street from the Picasso Museum (Calle Barra de Ferro, 3; ☎ 93-268-15-07).

E-Mail from Spain is at La Rambla 42/Passatge Bacardí 1 (☎ 93-481-75-75; E-mail: info@emailfromspain.es Metro: Liceu). Open 10 a.m. to 8 p.m. Mon–Sat, 600 pta.($3) half hour.

La Web a Ciutat Vella Carrer Sant Pere Més Baix 14 (☎ 93-295-40-07; Metro: Urquinaona). Open 11 a.m. to 10 p.m. Mon–Sat; 5 to 10 p.m. Sun, 450 pta.($2.50) half hour.

Mail

The Central Post Office is at Plaça de Antoni López, at the end of Via Laietana (☎ 93-318-38-31). It's open Mon–Friday 8:30 a.m. to 9 p.m. and Saturday from 8 a.m. to 8 p.m. The yellow sign "Correos" identifies branches of the post office. Those at Aragó 282 and Ronda Universitat 23 are open 8:30 a.m. to 8:30 p.m.

Maps

Get free maps at Turisme de Barcelona, Plaça de Catalunya, 17 (underground), or purchase city, regional, and country maps at any kiosk along *La Rambla.*

Newspapers/Magazines

The best sources for national and international press are the kiosks along La Rambla, which are open virtually around-the-clock.

Pharmacies

Pharmacies operate during normal business hours but there is always one in every district that remains open all night and on holidays. The location and phone number of this *farmacia de guardia* is posted on the door of all the other pharmacies. You can also call ☎ 010 or 93-481-00-60 to contact all night pharmacies.

Police

For municipal police, dial ☎ 092; for national police, ☎ 091. The main police station is at Vía Laietana, 43 (☎ 93-301-66-66).

Safety

Be careful around any major tourist sight, but especially: *La Rambla* (especially the section closest to the sea); *Barri Gótic; Raval* neighborhood; and *La Sagrada Familia.* Your primary danger is from pickpockets and purse snatchers.

Telephone

For national telephone information, dial ☎ 003. For international telephone information, dial ☎ 005.

Chapter 12

Girona and the Costa Brava

● ●

In This Chapter

▶ Getting to and around northern Catalonia

▶ Wandering the walled city of Girona

▶ Following the strange footsteps of Salvador Dalí

▶ Exploring the medieval stone villages of the Empordà and the beach towns of the Costa Brava

● ●

*B*efore you bolt out of Barcelona for another region of Spain, take a look at other areas within Catalonia. Sandwiched between Barcelona and the French border, the province of Girona is a scenic, historic, and delightful area. Adding a few days of exploration onto a visit to Barcelona, which is only an hour or two from most of the places that I describe in this chapter, makes for a terrific and varied regional trip.

The seductive and surprising city of Girona is one of Spain's most historic towns (the Romans first stepped foot on the Iberian Peninsula here), but one North American travelers rarely visit. Nearby is the Costa Brava, the "untamed coast," a stretch of rocky coves and small beaches, intensely blue Mediterranean waters, and whitewashed fishing villages. The trick is steering away from overdeveloped areas where mass-market tourism has marred the coastline's natural beauty. (Don't worry; I give you some pointers for doing just that, later in this chapter.) Inland from the coast are movie-set medieval villages with ancient stone houses, many of which have been purchased as weekend and summer homes by wealthy Barcelonans.

When in Girona, you can also explore the case of Spain's famous madman, the surrealist painter Salvador Dalí. Dalí hailed from these rural parts, and while his art and antics earned him fame in New York and Paris, he lived much of his life in the Costa Brava. You can visit the three points of the Dalí Triangle, tracing the artist's life from his birthplace and the agreeably loony museum he designed as his legacy to his legendary Costa Brava homes. These visits are a must for anyone with an interest in Dalí and contemporary art.

In this chapter, I give you information on everything you want to see and do while in Girona and the Costa Brava.

Just the Facts: Girona and the Costa Brava

Wedged in the extreme northeast corner of the Iberian Peninsula, Girona province is part of Catalonia. The province extends from just north of Barcelona up to the Spanish Pyrenees and the French border. The capital city is also called Girona.

- ✔ **The way to go.** Girona and most spots on the Costa Brava are within one to two hours from Barcelona.

- ✔ **The name game.** *Girona* ("jeer-*oh*-nah") is the Catalan name. In Spanish, you spell it *Gerona* ("hair-*oh*-nah"). The region is *Catalonia* in English, *Cataluña* in Spanish, and *Catalunya* in Catalan. Street signs and names are mostly in Catalan. The plains area inland from the Costa Brava is *L'Empordà* in Catalan and *El Ampurdán* in Spanish.

- ✔ **¿Cómo se dice? Talking the talk.** Catalan — not a dialect of Spanish but a Latin-derived language that sounds a bit like a cross between French and Castilian — is the first language of this area. Catalan is more prevalent here than in Barcelona, but almost everyone also speaks Spanish.

- ✔ **What's for dinner?** Girona is known for its creative country cooking, seafood, and fresh produce. Natives cook virtually everything in virgin olive oil. Trekking through the mountains in search of wild mushrooms is also good fun.

- ✔ **The forecast.** Blissfully Mediterranean (temperate) most of the year. Winter can be chilly but sunny.

- ✔ **When to go?** You can go year-round, though the Costa Brava closes up shop in mid-winter. In summer, especially July and August, the Costa Brava is only for the brave because it's overrun by Northern Europeans. As a result, hotel prices are highest — and the need for advance bookings greatest — at these times, as well as during Easter.

- ✔ **How long before moving on?** When visiting, allow one day for Girona capital, another day to see the Dalí Triangle, and a day or two for the Costa Brava.

Exploring the Major Attractions of Girona and the Costa Brava

Unless you're Dutch or German on a blitz to the beach, you're most likely coming to Girona and the Costa Brava from Barcelona. You can easily access the entire region from Barcelona by car, train, and bus, but a car is the best way to maximize your time.

Your first visit to Catalonia (beyond Barcelona) ought to include the better part of a day in the city of Girona and another full day to see the Dalí sights (though many people visit only the museum in Figueres, which you can do in a couple of hours). If you're a beach bum, only you can decide how many sunny beach days on the Costa Brava you need. Otherwise, try to spend a day or two in the Empordà, visiting medieval villages. The Empordà (*El Ampurdán* in Spanish) is a beautiful plains area inland from the Costa Brava.

Girona

Everything in this chapter belongs to the province of Girona, but the first section refers to the inland capital, a quietly stunning city with a pristine medieval core. Girona the city is about equidistant from Barcelona and France. Here you'll find:

- ✓ **El Call**, the ancient Jewish Quarter.
- ✓ The **walled city,** with its impressive cathedral and museums.

The Dalí Triangle

In the northernmost area of Girona province, within easy reach of one another and the provincial capital Girona, are three sites that were fundamental to the strange life and work of Salvador Dalí. Here you'll find:

- ✓ **Figueres,** Dalí's birthplace and home to his unique legacy, the Dalí Museum-Theater.
- ✓ **Cadaqués,** a pretty and peaceful fishing village transformed by the artist's presence next door at Port Lligat.
- ✓ **Púbol,** where Dalí bought his eccentric Russian bride a medieval castle.

The Costa Brava and the Empordà

The Costa Brava is one of Spain's most popular tourist destinations. Many urban dwellers in Barcelona keep beach houses here, but in the summer months a stampede of pale northern Europeans arrives and takes over large stretches of the coast, refusing to leave until they've turned an alarming shade of pink. The Empordà is the beautiful plains region dotted with a number of medieval towns that are worth visiting.

Girona & the Costa Brava

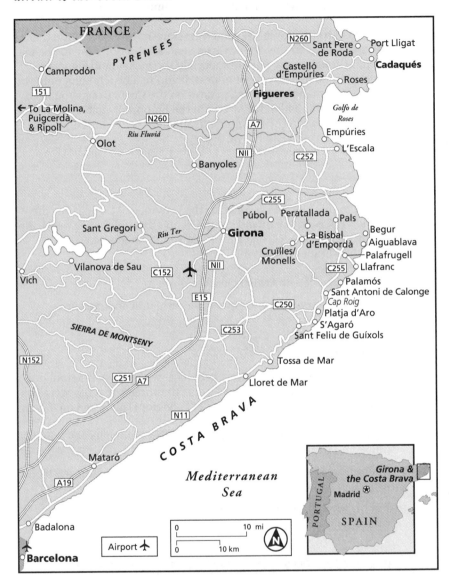

 Don't be confused if you see the terms *Alt Empordà* and *Baix Empordà;* they merely distinguish between the upper and lower regions of the Empordà. Here you'll find

 ✔ Fine beaches, fishing villages, and pine-forested coves.

 ✔ Medieval villages of the Empordà.

 ✔ **Empúries,** the site of Spain's most impressive Greco-Roman ruins.

Get out the clubs: Golfing in Girona

With 11 well-kept courses, Girona is one of the top golfing regions in Spain. Two courses at which you are welcome to play are **Club de Golf Costa Brava** (Santa Cristina de Aro, 5 km from San Feliú de Guíxols, 18 holes; ☎ **972-83-71-50**; green fees 4,200–6,000 pta./$23–$33) and **Club de Golf de Pals** (Playa de Pals, 7 km from Bagur, 18 holes; ☎ **972-63-60-06**; green fees 6,000–10,000 pta/$33–$56).

Discovering Girona: A Little-Known Medieval Treasure

Girona is one of the unsung jewels of not only Catalonia, but of all Spain. Its beauty surprises many visitors, who wonder why they hadn't heard of Girona before — especially since it's just 60 miles from Barcelona. Girona is also one of Spain's most historic cities. The Old Quarter, steeped in the layered histories of the Romans, Moors, and Jews, is a compact jumble of narrow stone streets, dark alleyways, and the medieval arches of *El Call* — the ancient Jewish neighborhood.

The city of Girona is perched on a hill, beckoning athletic climbers with wonderful views of the surrounding countryside. The modern section of town lies across the Onyar River, itself a picturesque district. Multicolored laundry flaps in the breeze from the balconies of yellow and orange sun-drenched apartment houses. In one long day, you can see most of the historic city, but at night the city empties of shoppers and tourists, and its silent streets exude medieval atmosphere.

Girona has a reputation as a provincial, emphatically Catalan city and province. True to that reputation, the Catalan language is much more dominant than it is in Barcelona (and in the Girona countryside, you might find that people speak very little Spanish). When people do speak Spanish, they often do so with a heavy Catalan accent and nasal tone.

Getting to Girona

Most people still choose to visit Girona as a day trip from Barcelona or the Costa Brava, so the bus, train, and car directions that I give in this section reflect that supposition.

By air

Girona has an international airport, and you can fly in from the U.K., Germany, and some other European cities. If you're coming in from a

European country, contact the airport at ☎ **972-47-43-43.** Taking a taxi to the city is your best bet. If you are flying in from the U.S., you will need to go through Barcelona first.

By bus

Many buses leave daily for Girona from Barcelona's Estació Nord. From Girona, buses leave for Figueres and several spots along the Costa Brava. Call ☎ **972-20-17-96.**

By car

From Barcelona, take the *ronda* (beltway) in the direction of France and then the A-7 to Girona. The 60-mile journey should take about an hour, unless you set out during morning or evening rush hour. Figueres is about two hours north of Barcelona (on A-7) and a half-hour north of Girona (N-II). C-255 and C-252 go along the coast and to principal towns in the Empordà.

By train

Frequent RENFE service connects Girona, Figueres, Port Bou, and Barcelona. You can choose from 27 daily trains. Trains leave from Barcelona's Estació Sants station between 6 a.m. and 9:30 p.m., and arrive at Girona's Plaça Espanya. For train information, call ☎ **902-24-02-02** (Internet: www.renfe.es; 790–910 pta./$4.40–$5). Trains take between one and two hours, depending on the service.

From Girona, you can take trains to the Costa Brava towns of Llança, Blanes, and Colera (the last, a town whose name presents a serious public relations problem!). For more, see "The Costa Brava," later in this chapter.

Getting around Girona

Girona is a tiny town; you'll need only your feet as transportation once you've arrived. You may require an occasional taxi to take you to a restaurant or hotel that may be outside the center of the Old Quarter. If you've driven to Girona and are staying at a hotel removed from the center, you can easily drive to the Old Quarter and park there.

By bus

Sarfa (☎ **93-265-11-58**) buses operate throughout the Costa Brava, traveling to Girona, Figueres, and Cadaqués. Call ☎ **972-20-70-93** in Girona and ☎ **93-490-02-02** in Barcelona for bus service throughout the region.

By car

If you plan on visiting more than just the city of Girona or Figueres, a car is very helpful, if not downright essential. Distances are short, but you can't rely on train and bus service because it's too spotty. With a car, you can easily see a bit of everything — medieval villages, beaches, and Dalí's haunts — in a few short days. You're probably best off renting a car in Barcelona (see Chapter 8 for car-renting tips).

By train

Trains connect Girona to Llança, Blanes, and Colera on the Costa Brava, with increased service in summer. The RENFE station is on *Plaça d'Espanya* (☎ **972-20-70-93**).

Knowing where to stay in Girona

Girona draws mostly daytrippers from Barcelona and the Costa Brava. Consequently, it's not overflowing with hotels and *pensions* (boarding-houses), but it's a comfortable place to stay overnight. (Staying over-night allows you to wander the silent Old Quarter at night.) The Tourism Information Office (☎ **972-22-65-75;** Rambla de la Llibertat, 2) can help with accommodations if you arrive without a reservation.

Costabella

$$

The name *Costabella* means "beautiful coast," but this hotel is nowhere near a beach. This hotel sits at the northern entry to the city, removed from the modern commercial district of Girona, but just a five-minute drive from the Old Quarter, across the River Onyar and near the La Devesa Park. A simple and comfortable hotel, the rooms are functional in design and fine for an overnight stay.

Avenida de França, 61. ☎ *972-20-25-24. Fax: 972-20-22-03. Near the N-11 Highway to Figueres. Parking: 1,000 pta. ($5.50). Rates: 13,455 pta. ($75) double. AE, MC, V.*

Hotel Carlemany

$$$

By far the best (but also the most expensive) option in Girona, this modern, mirrored new hotel is a ten-minute walk across the Onyar river from the Old Quarter. Rooms are nicely appointed, spacious, and very comfortable. The hotel, large for Girona, is where all the cell-phone busi-ness travelers camp.

Plaza Miquel Santaló (three blocks west of Estació Renfe). ☎ *972-21-12-12. Fax: 972-21-49-94. E-mail: carlemany@grn.es. Internet: www.grn.es/carlemany. Parking: 1,000 pta. ($5.50). Rates: 15,800 pta. ($88) double. AE, MC, V.*

Hotel Ultonia

$$

This small hotel is centrally located, not far from the main square, or the *Plaça Independencia,* and the River Onyar — and thus, close to the historic quarter. The rooms aren't anything special, and I don't recommend spending your entire summer vacation here, but the hotel is more than adequate for a short stay.

Gran Via de Jaume I, 22. ☎ *972-20-38-50. Fax: 972-20-33-34. Parking: Free. Rates: 15,000 pta. ($83) double. AE, MC, V*

Dining in Girona

Some of Girona's most celebrated restaurants are along the Costa Brava or in the countryside. But the restaurant scene continues to improve in the capital, where you can find several good places to sample authentic Catalan cooking. All of the restaurants listed below can be found in the Old Quarter. For more on Spanish dining customs, including mealtimes, costs, and tipping, see "Knowing what to expect when you're eating out" in Chapter 1.

Eating like a Gironès

The cuisine in the Girona region is ancient, Mediterranean, and based equally on the sea and the region's rolling farmlands. A Catalan staple is *pa amb tomàquet* — rustic bread raked with fresh tomatoes and doused with virgin olive oil. Likewise, native people talk about hunting for wild mushrooms with the same passion usually reserved for soccer. On menus, you find lots of *ali-oli* (olive oil and crushed garlic sauce); *fuet* (long, thin, dried sausage), and *butifarra* (Catalan white sausage). *Escalivada* is a great country dish made with baked eggplant, onions, and sweet peppers. For dessert, don't miss out on *crema catalana* (crème caramel with a burnt sugar top).

Catalans are almost as wild about leeks as they are about wild mushrooms. During the month of March, *calçotada* madness arrives. *Calçots* are specially grown leeks that are grilled and served with romesco sauce and broiled meat. It's a messy dish, but if you pass a roadside restaurant advertising *calçots* or a *calçotada* (essentially an onion BBQ), most of the diners you see are decked out in bibs and slurping on long and tasty leeks.

Drinking like a Gironès

Good wines come from Peralada and the Penedès region just south. If you didn't have any crisp *cava* (Catalan sparkling wine) in Barcelona, try some in Girona; it tastes great with *tapas* (appetizers or small snack foods).

Cal Ros

$$ CATALAN

This historic hangout is a favorite with locals; it's centrally located and a very good value. The kitchen prepares classic Catalan cooking, with simple, local ingredients. Try the *arroz a la cazuela con sepia, mejillones y coliflor frita* (rice casserole with squid, mussels, and fried cauliflower).

Cort Reial, 9. ☎ *972-21-73-79. Reservations recommended. Main courses: 700–2,000 pta. ($4–$11). V. Open: Lunch and dinner daily.*

El Celler de Can Roca

$$$–$$$$ CATALAN

Two brothers (the Rocas of the restaurant's name) own and operate this family restaurant, widely considered the best restaurant in the capital. Joan heads the kitchen and creates carefully executed, imaginative dishes like *lubina* (sea bass) with a sauce of hazelnuts and lemon peel in a cabernet sauvignon vinaigrette.

Carretera Taialá, 40. ☎ *972-22-21-57. Reservations recommended. Main courses: 1,500–3,100 pta. ($8–$17); tasting menu, 5,500 pta. ($31). AE, MC, V. Open: Lunch and dinner Tues–Sat.*

Largada

$$ CATALAN

A good place to take a break from all the climbing that you do in the steep Old Quarter, this comfortable, relaxed restaurant specializes in grilled meats. Largada has a nice brick interior with a large wood-burning grill that makes clear just what you should order: meat. The restaurant is just across the plaza from the Central Post Office.

Avenida Ramon Folch, 7. ☎ *972-21-84-05. Reservations recommended. Main courses: 1,300–2,500 pta. ($7–$14). AE, MC, V. Open: Lunch and dinner Tues–Sun.*

Exploring Girona

Girona is compact — virtually everything you want to see is in the heart of the Old Quarter — but there are many things to see.

The **Tourist Information Office** offers two-hour guided visits to the historic center of Girona at 11:30 a.m. on Saturdays and Sundays of most months. The cost is 1,000 pta. ($5.50). Call the tourism office (☎ 972-22-65-75), or stop by the office on Rambla de la Llibertat, 2, for additional information. (The language in which the tour is given depends on the group assembled.)

Enjoying the top attractions

El Call

Girona's Jewish ghetto (*El Call* in Catalan), according to many observers the best preserved in Western Europe, is a tangle of narrow, dark, atmospheric streets tucked within the Old Quarter. Girona was home to a prosperous Jewish community for over six centuries, until its members were expelled in 1492. Visit the sections along Carrer de la Força, where buildings date from the thirteenth to fifteenth centuries. Make a point of seeing the two synagogues and the **Centre Bonastruc Ça Porta** (a history center documenting the Jews of Girona); the fascinating story it tells is a little-known piece of Spanish history. Allow an hour to walk around the old Jewish Quarter.

Bonastruc Ça Porta, on Carrer Santa Llorenç. ☎ *972-21-67-61. Admission: Free. Open: Tues–Sun 10 a.m.–2 p.m. and 4–7 p.m.*

Catedral

Girona's dazzling cathedral, atop the fortress-like hill overlooking the city, is a can't-miss sight in the Old Quarter. Seeing the Baroque stairs — all 90 of them — may tempt you to look for a less challenging visit, but don't shy away. The cathedral, a work-in-progress for seven centuries, is worth the effort. The cloister and tower are the only surviving elements of the original, early-eleventh-century Romanesque building. The single Gothic nave — there are no aisles — is reputed to be the widest in the world. Don't miss the cathedral's treasury, which houses a magnificent collection of religious art. Of special interest is the gorgeous copy of the *Beatus*, St. John's eighth-century treatise on the Apocalypse. The curiously shaped twelfth-century *claustro* (cloisters) contain fine columns with beautifully etched *friezes* (a series of decorations forming an ornamental band around a room). You can climb the eleventh-century bell tower named for Charlemagne, but only if you can find someone manning the tower and willing to take you up — not always an easy task. Anticipate spending a half-hour or so here, more if you climb the tower.

Plaça de la Catedral. ☎ *93-21-44-26. Admission: Cloister and museum, 400 pta. ($2.20). Open: Cathedral daily 9 a.m.–1 p.m. and during cloister and museum visiting hours, which aren't strictly adhered to, but in general are 10 a.m.–8 p.m. in summer and 10 a.m.–2 p.m. and 4–6 p.m. in winter; closed Mon.*

Kissing *culo*

Locals like to point out the statue of a lioness in the Old Quarter near the Sant Nicolau church. An old refrain in this ancient town says that anyone coming from Barcelona need only kiss the *culo* (rear end) of the lioness to consider themselves a *Gironí* (native of Girona). (I sense that natives are playing a less-than-subtle prank on unsuspecting outsiders.)

Stopping to smell the flowers

May is a great time to visit Girona, and not only because you beat the summer heat. For two weeks, the streets of the Old Quarter are ablaze with colorful flowers in full bloom. Private patios that are off-limits the rest of the year open in celebration of the season's exuberance.

Cases de l'Onyar

Cases are houses, and the ones along the River Onyar are a magical sight. They shimmer in the water's reflection, and laundry flutters in the breeze. Despite the picturesque Mediterranean colors, many of the houses date to the Middle Ages — they were outside the original walls of the old city. Take a stroll along the river and walk across the iron bridges at sunset. A visit here requires little more than a quick drive-by.

Along the River Onyar, at edge of Old Quarter.

Banys Àrabs

The Moors made their presence known in Girona; however, the Arab Baths are one of the only reminders of that important community. Constructed in the twelfth century, the Romanesque baths are among the best-preserved in Spain, receiving significant restoration in the 1920s. Light streams in from the central dome, and it's easy to imagine the central role the baths must have played in the Middle Ages. If you're lucky, you may catch a cool underground art exhibit here. Allow a half-hour for your visit here.

Carrer Ferran el Católic. ☎ 93-21-32-62. Admission: 200 pta. ($1.10). Open: Apr–Sep, Mon–Sat 10 a.m.–7 p.m., Sun 10 a.m.–2 p.m.; Oct–Mar, daily 10 a.m.–2 p.m.

Museu d'Art

Housed in a former Episcopal palace, Girona's Art Museum covers almost 1,000 years of history and art. It features excellent Catalan Romanesque and Gothic paintings, as well as a significant collection of contemporary art. Among the highlights is a fifteenth-century altarpiece, *Sant Miquel de Cruïlles*, one of the finest works of Catalan Gothic art anywhere. If you missed Barcelona's Museum of Romanesque and Gothic Art, the Museu d' Art is the next best thing. Plan on spending at least an hour here.

Pujada de la Catedral, 12. ☎ 972-20-95-36. Admission: 200 pta. ($1.10) adults; free for students, adults over 65, and children; free on Sun and holidays. Open: Mar–Sept, Tues–Sat 10 a.m.–7 p.m. (in June–Aug, Wed hours are 10 a.m.–2 p.m.), Sun 10 a.m.–2 p.m.; Oct–Feb, Tues–Sat 10 a.m.–6 p.m., Sun 10 a.m.–2 p.m.

More cool things to see and do

- ✔ **Roaming La Rambla.** Girona's La Rambla is shorter and less grand than Barcelona's, but it plays just as central a function in the city. The tree-lined pedestrian street in the Old Quarter is packed with shops and cafes, many under the ancient arches. (In the medieval city, this was the central marketplace.) La Rambla begins near the Tourist Information Office, Carrer Nou, at River Onyar.

- ✔ **Checking out Girona's churches. Sant Pere de Galligans,** Santa Llúcia, 1 (☎ 972-20-26-32) is a handsome twelfth-century Benedictine monastery that was once a fortress, its belltower serving as a watchtower. The church houses the city archaeology museum, with several items culled from the Roman ruins at nearby Empúries. Admission is 300 pta. ($1.70); hours are Tuesday through Saturday 10 a.m. to 1 p.m. and 4:30 to 7 p.m., Sun 10 a.m. to 1 p.m. **Església de Sant Feliu,** Pujada de Sant Feliu (☎ 972-20-14-07), includes an imposing bell tower, important *retablos* (altarpieces), and the tomb of Saint Narciso, the patron saint of Girona. Admission is free; hours are daily 9 to 10:30 a.m., 11:30 a.m. to 1 p.m., 4 to 6:30 p.m., and holidays 4 to 6:30 p.m.

- ✔ **Stepping into the celluloid past.** Girona recently inaugurated Spain's only cinema museum, the **Museu del Cinema,** Sèquia, 1 (☎ 972-41-27-77), which houses the private collection of Tomàs Mallol. Film buffs dig seeing the original camera of the Lumière brothers. Admission is 400 pta. ($2.20); hours are Tuesday through Sunday, May through September, 10 a.m. to 8 p.m.; October through April, 10 a.m. to 6 p.m.

Shopping in Girona

Girona is one of the wealthiest towns in Spain, and it has a surprising number of chic design and home furnishings shops sandwiched near *El Call.* One such design store you shouldn't miss, if only because the way it's installed in the Old Quarter is so cool, is **Pabordia** (Catedral, 4; ☎ 972-20-17-04). An attractive antiques store is **La Cononja Vella,** at the end of Plaçeta de L'Institut Vell, next to the Cathedral. The nearby town of **La Bispal** is famous for its ceramics; in Girona, you can find a good selection of what you'd find in La Bispal (at slightly lower prices) at **Vila Clara** (Vallesteries, 40; ☎ 972-22-37-78).

La Noche: Checking out Girona's nightlife

Girona was once written off as a deadly quiet town that forced all the local kids to drive to Barcelona for some weekend action. No more — though the utter stillness during the week is amazing. The Old Quarter has a number of interesting bars along La Rambla and back toward the Jewish ghetto. **Plaza de la Independencia** and **Zona La Dehesa** are both popular areas lined with cafes, bars, and discos. Two bar/pubs worth checking out are **Sidharta** (Pedret, 116) and **Dig-Higt** (Ramón Folch).

The tiny hamlet of Perelada, near Girona, is famous for its castle (site of a popular casino), wines and summer concert series. Some of the world's most prestigious opera singers, symphonies, and dance troupes come here every summer to perform under the stars outside the castle. (I've seen Plácido Domingo and the Argentine ballet star Julio Bocca here.) The setting, under a canopy of stars in the gardens of the castle makes for a magical evening. Call the festival organizers at ☎ 972-53-81-25 or fax 972-53-80-87 for further information and directions.

Taking a side trip to the Greco-Roman ruins of Empúries

Near the summer resort town of L'Escala are the extensive ruins of a Greco-Roman city, **Museu d'Empúries** (☎ 972-77-02-08), one of the most fascinating archaeological finds in Spain. Three different civilizations settled on the coast here between the seventh and third centuries B.C.: the Indigetes, the Greeks, and the Romans. (Empúries is the only place in Spain with incarnations as a Greek village, an Iberian settlement, and a Roman town.) The sea wall is an important engineering achievement, and the Roman mosaic floors are equally impressive.

Hitting the Catalan ski slopes

People tend to think of Spain as hot, flat, and lined with topless beaches. But Spain also offers some great skiing, and the Pyrenees of Girona province is one of the top skiing destinations in the country. The region called *La Cerdanya,* only 1½ hours from Barcelona, has several resorts, including **La Molina,** the site of Spain's first chair lift. La Molina is within easy striking distance of several other excellent resorts in the French Pyrenees and tiny Andorra, which for my money, offers the best skiing in the region. You can even zip up from Barcelona in the morning, ski a half day, and make it back in time for dinner.

The closest town with a reasonable number of places to stay is the unpronounceable town of Puigcerdá (try "pooch-chair-*dah*"). If you want a special treat, line up a night's stay at **Torre del Remei,** a splendidly designed modernista palace property just down the road in Bolvir. Torre del Remei is a funky luxury haven of haute-design, and it has one of the best chefs in all of Catalonia. Contact Torre del Remei at ☎ 972-14-01-82; Fax: 972-14-04-49; E-mail: torreremei@relaischateaux.fr; Internet: www.relaischateaux.fr/torreremei (27,000 pta./$150 double). For more information on skiing in the Catalan Pyrenees and where to stay, contact the tourism board, **Patronat de Turisme Costa Brava/Girona** (☎ 972-20-84-01; Fax: 972-22-15-70; E-mail: cbrava@cbrava.es; Internet: www.cbrava.es/girona/.).

To visit Museu d'Empúries, take N-II north and make the turn-off toward the coast and L'Escala (signs indicate the Museu d'Empúries). To take the bus, call ☎ **972-20-17-96** in Girona for information. Admission is 400 pta. ($2.20) adults and free for children under 12. Hours are June 1 to September 21, daily from 10 a.m. to 8 p.m.; September 22 to May 31, daily from 10 a.m. to 6 p.m.

Connecting the Dots of the Dalí Triangle

Along the Costa Brava and the interior of Girona province, you can trace the artistic, kooky, and ultimately permanent stamp Salvador Dalí left on his native Catalonia. The *Dalí Triangle* includes his appropriately surreal Museum-Theater in **Figueres,** the home he shared with his controversial wife Gala in **Port Lligat,** near the beautiful fishing village of **Cadaqués,** and the 900-year-old castle he bought Gala in **Púbol.** By car, you can easily see these sights in a day or two, using Girona, a beach town along the Costa Brava, or an inland site in the Empordà as a base. Following Dalí around the region is a great way to get to know this beautiful and intensely individualistic region of Spain.

Figueres

Dalí's Museum-Theater in Figueres is the third-most visited museum in Spain, which isn't surprising; Dalí's eccentric genius and personality infiltrated pop culture throughout North America and Europe. His surrealist paintings of melting watches and dreamscapes continue to exert a strong, strange hold on artists and novices alike. Likewise, the museum Dalí himself designed (and wished to be buried in) is part theater, part crazy amusement park.

Though unassuming Figueres (*Figueras* in Spanish) was a historically important town, it's now all about Dalí. The artist was born here, and he was determined to build his unique museum here. Crowds flock to the museum and then quickly depart for more appealing destinations.

 Figueres isn't really worth exploring. This is one of the few times I advise you to follow the crowd. Do like the tour buses: Stop at the Dalí Museum and then get the heck out of town.

Getting there

Figueres is about two hours north of Barcelona (on A-7) and a half-hour north of Girona (N-II). Frequent RENFE trains run from Barcelona's Sants Station to Figueres (Barcelona–Port Bou line); the Dalí museum is approximately a ten-minute walk from the train station. SARFA buses

(☎ 972-20-17-96 — ☎ 93-265-11-58 in Barcelona) serve Figueres, Girona, the Costa Brava, and Barcelona.

Visit the **Figueres Tourism Office** on Plaça del Sol (☎ 972-50-31-55).

Dining in Figueres

Even though few visitors stick around long enough for a real meal, Figueres has a reputation as a great restaurant town. If you stay for lunch or dinner, you can eat well. **Empordà** (Antigua Ctra. a Francia, s/n; ☎ 972-50-05-62; $$$), is not only one of the best restaurants in Catalonia, but also one of the top places in all of Spain. As the name suggests, the restaurant focuses on the creative cooking and ingredients of the surrounding Empordà countryside. Dalí was a regular here. Another standout restaurant is **Durán** (Lasauca, 5; ☎ 972-50-12-50; $$$), in the center of Figueres. The price-quality ratio at Durán is a little less favorable than that at Empordà, however.

Exploring Figueres

Teatre Museu Dalí

To some, Dalí was a genius; to others, he was a freak. In my opinion, he was both. One of the world's most famously eccentric artists certainly left a museum befitting the stature he earned as an international art celebrity. The museum is idiosyncratic, maddening, and witty. If you think of museums as dry, dusty places that make your lower back ache, this one should change your notion altogether. Dalí's own notion — he designed the museum himself — was closer to theater.

As an artist, Dalí was famous for surreal and highly charged imagery; as a personality, he was famous for his eccentricity and exhibitionism. The museum, like Dalí himself, means to provoke and please. It presents a variety of Dalí's works and installations, many of which feature his flamboyant, outrageous Russian wife, Gala. The red building, modestly topped by giant white eggs and a glass dome, and decorated with glazed ceramic loaves of bread, is every bit as understated as the pieces displayed inside. There, you can find a salon that uses furniture to teasingly re-create Mae West's face (with a sofa fashioned like soft red lips), as well as a circular central patio that displays an attention-getting work he presented in New York called *Rainy Taxi* — a long black Cadillac with sprinklers inside. (They go off if you drop a 100-peseta coin in the box — Dalí's untethered commercialism is alive even in death.) Dalí himself is buried in a crypt here, next to a series of gold cobra statues.

Given the crowds and theatrical peculiarities of the museum, expect to spend the better part of a morning or afternoon here.

Plaça de Gala-Salvador Dalí, 5. ☎ *972-51-18-00. Internet:* www.dali-estate. org. *Admission: 1,000 pta. ($5.50) adults; 800 pta. ($4.40) students and adults over 65; free for children under 9. Open: July–Sept, Tues–Sun 9 a.m.–7:15 p.m.; Oct–June, daily 10:30 a.m.–5:15 p.m.*

Museu del Joquet (Toy Museum)

Paling in comparison with favorite son Dalí, but fun for kids and kids at heart, is Spain's largest and oldest Toy Museum. The museum just reopened after years of extensive renovations and an expansion of its original site, the Hotel Paris. Here you can find some 3,500 toys, mostly from the nineteenth and early twentieth centuries, including Dalí's childhood teddy bear (also displayed are letters the poet Garcia Lorca, a close acquaintance of Dalí, wrote to the toy bear, named Don Osito Marquina).

Carrer Sant Pere 1. ☎ *972-50-45-85. Admission: 750 pta. ($4) adults; 600 pta. ($3) children 5–11; free for children under 5. Open: daily 10a.m.–1p.m. and 4–7p.m.*

Cadaqués and Port Lligat

Even after he became an international superstar, Dalí continued mixing with the wizened fishermen in Cadaqués. The town gained international fame when Dalí groupies sought out the artist here and next door at Port Lligat. Cadaqués certainly looks the part of the perfect seaside Mediterranean village. Even when bands of playboys and would-be artists decided to set up camp (and swim in Dalí's pool), the town didn't change all that much. In summer, the area attracts chichi Catalans in fancy cars, but Cadaqués remains small and cozy, a function of its isolation.

Access to the town is via a long and winding (by that I mean tortuous) road, so development, like resorts farther down the coast, hasn't spoiled Cadaqués. It's still a scenic little town — a sun-dappled cluster of whitewashed houses tucked into the hills with a pretty waterfront. (The beaches, though, are unspectacular by Costa Brava standards.) Cadaqués is ideal for a day trip combined with a visit to Port Lligat — or an even longer stay. (I've met Europeans who came on vacation 20 years ago, determined to follow the path of Dalí, and have yet to leave.) Cadaqués remains a working fishing village; you can watch the fishermen take the day's catch right to the restaurant kitchens.

Getting there

Take C-260 from Figueres, and then a twisting, maddening road down to Cadaqués (38 km, or 23 miles). The Cadaqués tourism office is located on Cotxe 2–A, ☎ **972-25-83-15.**

Hello Dalí: Egghead or *señor* dollars?

Few art figures have been as controversial — adored, puzzled over, and reviled — as Salvador Dalí. Was he a genius with a special insight into human psychology or a self-promoting fake?

The artist claimed that recurrent motifs in his work, such as melting watches and rubbery eggs, sprang from the subconscious, which is why giant white *huevos* (eggs) top both the museum in Figueres and his house in Port Lligat. Dalí maintained that he remembered being an embryo inside his mother's womb, and his interest in eggs (and soft-boiled wrist watches) served as a metaphor for his fetal experience. Whatever their artistic merit (there are many art scholars who assert that Dalí was a trailblazing master), the surreal images certainly grab your attention.

When Dalí split from the surrealist movement and became, in the eyes of many, a blatant publicity hound with an unerring commercial streak, he was branded "Avida Dollars" by the surrealist poet André Breton. The cruelly on-target nickname, an anagram, stuck — at least among Dalí's detractors.

Where to stay in Cadaqués

Cadaqués doesn't offer a whole lot in terms of hotels and restaurants — just a few standard places that, while unexciting, are agreeable enough if you don't want to drive the twisting road out of town just yet.

Playa Sol

$$$

This tranquil and modern hotel has 50 comfortably furnished rooms and nice views of the Cadaqués Bay and the town. Half the rooms have air conditioning. Run by the owners, the hotel also offers tennis courts and a pool.

Pltaja Pianc, 3. ☎ 972-25-81-00. Fax: 972-25-80-54. Parking: 1,000 pta. ($5.50). Rates: 13,900–18,500 pta. ($77–$103) double. AE, MC, V. Closed Jan 10–Feb 15, Nov 15–25.

Port Lligat

$$

This small, isolated hotel is 1 km outside of Cadaqués proper. The 29 comfortable rooms have tile floors that keep things cool in summer. The hotel has a terrace overlooking the harbor, and a number of the accommodations offer fine sea views. On the grounds is a refreshing pool with *cabanas* (poolside dressing rooms).

Playa de Port Lligat. ☎ 972-25-81-62. No fax. Rates: 13,200 pta. ($73) double. AE, MC, V.

Dining in Cadaqués

La Galiota
$$$ CATALAN/FRENCH

The best restaurant in town, La Galiota has been here since Dalí was the star attraction — some 30 years now. Pictures of the artist on the walls attest to his patronage. Near the cathedral, La Galiota operates a straightforward, quality-driven kitchen. Good choices include the marinated salmon *al sueco* (Swedish style) and beef tenderloin in Port wine sauce.

Carrer Narciso Monturiol, 9. ☎ 972-25-81-87. Reservations required. Main courses: 1,800–3,000 pta. ($10–$17); menú del día 1,800 pta. ($10). AE, DC, MC, V. Open: Daily lunch and dinner. Closed Mon–Fri in Nov–May.

Sa Gambina
$$ CATALAN/FRENCH

This no-frills restaurant, where European bohemians mix with local year-round residents, is known for its rice dishes and fish stews. Enjoy its nice terrace out back.

Riba Nemesi Llorens, s/n. ☎ 972-25-81-87. Main courses: 1,000–2,200 pta. ($7–$15). V. Open: Daily lunch and dinner; closed Mon–Fri in Nov–May.

Exploring Cadaqués and Port Lligat

Dalí's house in Port Lligat is the top attraction in the area, but **Cadaqués** is its rival. Taking in the relaxed and extraordinarily pretty town and its lovely views is the prime activity — if you can call that an activity. If you're moved to do more, visit the cathedral, the seventeenth-century **Església de Santa Maria,** and the **Museu Muncipal de Arte Contemporáneo** (Municipal Contemporary Art Museum, on *Carrer Narcis Monturiol*) for works by Dalí and Picasso. The museum is open Monday through Saturday, 11 a.m. to 1 p.m. and 4 to 9 p.m.

Casa-Museu Salvador Dalí

Dalí built his first home with Gala, his equally eccentric Russian-born bride, in Port Lligat, a tiny fisher's village on a secluded cove along the Costa Brava (1 mile north of Cadaqués). The views of the bay are still as gorgeous as those that seduced Dalí early in his career, and the village remains isolated — except for the nearby, wildly incongruous Club Med (where Dalí would no doubt be a regular if he were still living).

Dalí's house in Port Lligat, which climbs a small hill overlooking the bay, opened to the public in 1997. Dalí and his wife, Gala, began to acquire property in the early 1930s, cobbling together several modest fisher's residences. What became their seaside home is rustic, but the décor lives up to Dalíesque standards — living spaces sport stuffed swans, a lip sofa, and Dalí-designed chimneys. Gala's bathroom, filled with photos of the couple and famous people, is worth a look. . She died here in 1982.

Having such an eccentric character as Dalí living among them must have been peculiar for villagers in this remote part of Northeastern Spain. But apparently the artist forged good relationships with the people of Port Lligat and Cadaqués. To this day, local fishers speak of *Señor Dalí*, using the Spanish term of respect.

Advance reservations are required to visit; verify hours when making reservations. Only small groups of eight at a time, with a maximum of 300 people per day, are allowed entry. A visit lasts about an hour.

Port Lligat (Cadaqués). ☎ *972-25-80-63 or reservations,* ☎ *972-67-75-00. Admission: 1,300 pta. ($7) adults; 800 pta. ($4.40) students and adults over 65. Open: mid-Mar–mid-June and mid-Sept to Jan 6, 10:30 a.m.–6 p.m. Tues–Sun. Mid-June–mid-Sept, daily 10:30 a.m.–9 p.m.*

La noche: Cadaqués nightlife

In summer you find a very agreeable atmosphere along Passeig Marítim (the promenade) at the water's edge. Cadaqués slips out of its quiet skin and gets surprisingly wild at night. A little jazz club on the main drag, **L'Hostal,** has an illustrious history. Dalí once strode in with Mick Jagger on his arm. The club showcases reputable jazz musicians in prime tourist season and often stays open until 5 a.m. For drinks, try **Marítim** (also on the promenade), a bar that's been around since the '50s. Enjoy its nice terrace that overlooks the beach.

Púbol

The only reason to visit this tiny, isolated village on the plains of L'Empordà is to experience the medieval castle Dalí bought for his beloved princess, Gala.

Casa-Museu Castell Gala Dalí

Dalí gave this eleventh-century castle to his wife Gala in the late 1960s. Given the decidedly peculiar marital history of Gala and Dalí, and the fascinating rooms tucked inside the castle's stone walls, the residence is perhaps even more interesting than Port Lligat. During the 1970s, Gala lived here for long stretches of time, while Dalí stayed at the couple's house in Port Lligat. Gala allowed Dalí to visit only when she invited him — which was practically never. The castle, which lords above the town of Púbol, is considerably more austere than anything people associate with Dalí — although a stuffed horse greets visitors in the entrance and other odd Dalíesque touches pop up throughout. In the garden, giant cement elephants (standing awkwardly on spindly giraffe's legs) spray water through their snouts, and a small pool is adorned with an assortment of colorful busts of the composer Wagner. A bit of graffiti reads "Dalí was here."

Dalí wasn't of noble lineage, though he pretended otherwise. The king of Spain did him a bigger favor than he may have known when he decreed Dalí the *Marqués of Púbol.* Dalí designed a golden throne for his wife, but he often used it to entertain journalists' questions.

Substantiated rumors state that the Púbol castle served as Gala's love palace. Even into her late 60s, she entertained a bevy of considerably younger men, including one young actor/hanger-on whom Gala and Dalí picked up at a performance of the musical *Hair* in New York.

After Gala died, and Dalí no longer needed his wife's permission to come, he lived in the castle for two years. In 1984, a mysterious, dangerous fire erupted in the bedroom where Dalí lay asleep. The enfeebled artist barely escaped with his life, and he never returned to the castle, even though he once hoped to be buried there alongside Gala.

Anticipate spending an hour at the castle, and make sure that you figure in transportation time, depending upon where you're coming from.

Carrer Gala Salvador Dalí, s/n (Púbol is about 25 miles south of Figueres along high-way C-252 follow signs to Parlava; It's 10 miles east of Girona along C-255. Drive into town, park below the castle, and walk up.). ☎ *972-48-82-11. Admission: 700 pta. ($3.90) for adults; 500 pta. ($2.75) for students; and free for children under 9. Open: mid-Sept to Nov 1 and mid-Mar–mid-June, daily 10:30 a.m.–6 p.m. (guided visits at 12 p.m. and 4 p.m., in Catalan and Spanish); mid-June–mid-Sept, daily 10:30 a.m.–8 p.m. (guided visits at 12 p.m. and 5 p.m.).*

Visiting the Medieval Villages of the Empordà

Several small villages of the *Baix Empordà,* or Lower Plains, are beauti-fully maintained medieval gems. The plains are dotted with small towns, but I suggest visiting **Pals, Peratallada** ("pear-ah-tie-*yada*"), **Monells,** and **Cruïlles** — in that order, depending upon your time. They're all close together, and you don't need to allot much time to see them — only long enough to walk around and have coffee or lunch.

You can find hotel and restaurant information for these towns under "Where to stay and dine in the Costa Brava and Empordà," later in this chapter.

Getting there and getting around

The only reasonable way to see the small villages of the Baix Empordà is by car (public transportation is spotty, and it would take you days to see what you can see in a morning in a rental car). From Barcelona, take highway A-7 to C-253 and C-255; from Girona, hop on C-255. The towns are clearly signposted, but if you blink, you'll miss them, so make sure you pay attention.

For information on Pals, contact the tourist office of Pals, Carrer Aniceta Figeres, 6 (☎ 972-66-78-57); for Peratallada, the Peratallada Town Hall, Carrer La Roca (☎ 972-63-40-05); and for Cruïlles and Monells, the Tourist Office of La Bisbal d'Empordà, Plaça del Castell s/n (☎ 972-64-25-93).

Exploring the Baix Empordà

You can easily visit all of the towns I mention in this section in a half-day trip.

Pals

A picture-perfect medieval town, Pals sits atop a rise, its silhouette visible from miles around on the plains. It's a pristine place, almost too perfect to be real. The tiny alleys and thick stone walls look movie-set medieval. All kinds of Gothic details, such as windows and wells, adorn Pal's immaculate mansions. Look for the circular Romanesque tower **Torre de les Hores,** and the **Church of Sant Pere.** Climb to the lookout point **Mirador del Pedró** for unequaled views of the countryside and coast (on clear days, you can see the Medes Islands).

Peratallada

Pals is pretty, but I like Peratallada even better. More rugged and less slick, its history is more apparent. An old fortified nucleus, the town grew up around an unusual castle. The castle today houses a fine restaurant and tiny, charming hotel (see "Where to stay and dine in the Costa Brava and Empordà," later in this chapter). Walking along Peratallada's twisting stone streets, you discover a fourteenth-century palace, a porticoed main square, and houses rich with Gothic details. The town, a favorite of in-the-know city dwellers from Barcelona, also has a handful of interesting antiques dealers.

Cruïlles and Monells

These two quiet villages, connected administratively, are the kind of low-key places to which most people would like to retire. (But maybe not once you see the prices for these old stone houses.) The villages, handsome and sturdy enclaves of medieval stonework, are completely unassuming. Monells's main feature is a handsome porticoed main square, while at the center of Cruïlles, which was once enclosed by walls, is a Romanesque eleventh-century monastery.

The Costa Brava: Resorts and Rugged Beauty

The fabled Costa Brava, the sandy playground of thousands upon thousands of Europeans, is about 200 km (125 miles) long, extending from Blanes, just north of Barcelona, all the way to the French border. The coast is an enticing mix of mountains, plains, long sandy stretches, and tiny, gorgeous coves thick with pine trees.

But in several places — especially the lower half, nearest Barcelona — some of the most overcrowded, overdeveloped, and repugnant tourist ghettoes in Spain (comparable only to Benidorm, near Valencia, and the Costa del Sol in the south) have unforgivably wrecked the natural beauty of the coast. Unless you want to be sorely disappointed, you need to pick and choose carefully where you will base yourself on the Costa Brava.

The undisputed megawatt star of the European package tour is **Lloret de Mar,** about 35 miles north of Barcelona. An overdeveloped and rather crass, commercial beach resort, it's the equal of Cancún or worse. Luckily, there are other spots tucked among small coves that are well worth exploring for their beauty and seclusion. Near the resort towns Palafrugell and Palamós is **Begur.** Nestled at the foot of a former castle, Begur (*Bagur* in Spanish) enjoys fine panoramic views of the coast. The town is just minutes from a number of pretty coves, including **Aiguablava, Sa Tuna,** and **El Racó.** Look also for **Llafranc** and **Sant Antoni de Calonge,** both relatively quiet spots. You can easily access all of these spots from Girona and the medieval towns of the Baix Empordà that I describe earlier in the chapter.

Northern Europeans — Germans, Dutch, French, and, increasingly, monied Eastern Europeans like Czechs and Russians — overrun parts of the Costa Brava in summer. If you don't want to feel like you've landed unwittingly in a Euro Club Med, stay away from Lloret de Mar, Platja d'Aro, and, to a slightly lesser degree, Tossa de Mar. The clifftop road that passes these towns, however, makes for a splendidly scenic coastal drive.

Getting there and getting around

Except for the major destinations, a car remains your best bet for seeing the Costa Brava without waiting for public transportation. For more information once you arrive, contact the tourist information offices in **Begur** (Plaça Església, 1; ☎ **972-62-40-20**); or **Llafranc** (Carrer Roger de Llúria; ☎ **972-30-50-08**).

Beach watch

The Costa Brava's got some beautiful beach spreads, but many of them suffer from overdeveloped tourism. The following is a list of beaches awarded blue flags (the top rating for best swimming conditions) by the European Union.

Town	Best swimming beach(es)
Begur	Sa Riera, Aiguablava
Palafrugell	Tamariu, Llafranc, Canadell, Port Bo
Palamós	Platja Gran, La Fosca
Sant Antoni de Calonge	Torre Valentina, Torretes
Sant Feliu de Guíxols	Platja de Sant Feliu

The following beaches get five stars, the top rating, from the Catalonian government for environmental protection.

Town	Beach(es)
Begur	Racó, Sa Tuna
L'Escala	Les Muscleres, La Platja
Pals	Platja Gran de Pals
Palafrugell	Tamariu, Canadell
Palamós	La Fosca, Margarida
Sant Feliu de Guíxols	Sant Pol, Sant Feliu

By car

The main road C-255 travels along the lower coast and darts inland; C-252 is the principal road for the northern half of the Costa Brava. From these, you need to get off onto local, signposted roads, which lead to individual coastal villages and resorts.

By bus

Sarfa (☎ **972-20-17-96** in Girona, ☎ **93-265-11-58** in Barcelona) buses operate throughout the Costa Brava from Girona and Figueres. Getting to the archaeological site **Empúries** by bus is a bit complicated. You have to take the Sarfa **Girona–L'Escala** bus and ask the driver to let you off at Empúries, which is a ten-minute walk from the main road.

By train

Trains leave from Girona's **Plaça d'Espanya** and make their way to several points along the Costa Brava, including Llançà, Blanes, and Colera, with increased service in summer. For more information concerning trains along the coast, call ☎ **972-20-70-93**.

Where to stay and dine in the Costa Brava and Empordà

While in the high summer months (July and August) you can have the hardest time finding a hotel room along the Costa Brava, in the dead of winter (when the area is actually quite beautiful, and not all that cold), you have trouble finding hotels and restaurants that are open. Much of the coast, including Cadaqués, pretty much boards up the windows.

Aigua-Blava
$$$ **Aiguablava (Costa Brava)**

Next to the water and surrounded by a remarkable expanse of private gardens, this mid-size hotel is one of the best options and values along the Costa Brava. It's much preferable to the nearby *parador* (government-run hotel). Rooms are large and airy, and the service is personal and gracious. Enjoy the tennis court, pool, and superb views of the cove from the garden. The restaurant (same phone number) serves local Ampurdanés cuisine, and is fairly priced.

Platja de Fornells, s/n. ☎ *972-62-20-58. Fax: 972-62-21-12. Internet:* www. aiguablava.com. *E-mail:* hotelaiguablava@aiguablava.com. *Rates: 21,000 pta. ($117) double. Parking: Free. AE, MC, V. Closed second week Nov–mid-Feb.*

Castell de Peratallada
$$–$$$ **Peratallada (Empordà)**

A tenth-century medieval castle (on a site inhabited during the Bronze Age) that dominates a stately plaza, this is a charming little privately owned hotel. It's a tiny and much more personal version of the state-run *paradors*. Rooms (five of which are in the noble section of the castle; the other three are situated off the gardens) are nicely outfitted with period pieces. The ambience and furnishings are more castle than hotel. Because the hotel has so few rooms, advance reservations are essential. The rustic dining room of the restaurant (same phone number), once a principal salon in the fortress, serves traditional Catalan country cooking.

Plaça Castell. ☎ *972-63-40-21. Fax: 972-63-40-11. E-mail:* casteperat@ aplitec.com. *Internet:* www.castelldeperatallada.com. *Rates: 25,000–30,000 pta. ($139–$167) double. Parking: Free. AE, DC, MC, V. Open weekends only Oct–May; does not close Jul–Sept.*

Hostal de la Gavina
$$$–$$$$ **S'Agaró (Costa Brava)**

One of the most famous hotels on the Costa Brava is this luxurious retreat located in popular and touristy S'Agaró (between Sant Feliu and

Cap Roig). Indulging Spaniards and international guests with perfect service and abundant comfort since 1932, Hostal de la Gavina is a place to go and lose yourself for an entire vacation. Doing so is beyond the financial reach of most people, though, so view it as a one-night splurge. Despite the high prices, its elegant rooms overlooking S'Agaró Beach are in consistently high demand.

If you can't squeeze in an overnight stay, or prefer to indulge your taste buds, the hotel's restaurant (☎ **972-32-11-00**) is also one of the finest on the Costa Brava. The elegant dining room serves fine Catalan cuisine, while the more informal terrace offers lighter, but still excellent dishes.

Plaça de la Rosaleda, s/n. ☎ ***972-32-11-00****. Fax: 972-32-15-73. E-mail:* gavina@ iponet.es. *Internet:* www.iponet.es/gavina. *Parking: Free. Rates: 42,000 pta. ($233) double. AE, DC, MC, V. Restaurant (main courses 1,800 pta.–4,500 pta./$10–$25) closed mid-Oct to Easter week. Parking: 2,600 pta. ($14).*

Hotel El Far de Sant Sebastià

$$$–$$$$ Palafrugell (Costa Brava)

The owners of Mas de Torrent (see the following review) recently opened another hotel on a historic site near Llafranc (hence the name). The hotel is perched on a coastal hill next to an old lighthouse, with just nine splendid rooms and unbeatable views.

Platja de Llafranc. ☎ ***972-301-369****. Fax: 972-304-328. E-mail:* hotelfss@intercom. es. *Internet:* www.elfar.net. *Parking: Free. Rates: 22,000–26,000 pta. ($122–$144) summer, Easter, and Christmas; 19,000–22,000 pta. ($105–$122) rest of year, double.*

Mas de Torrent

$$$$$ Torrent (Empordà)

If you spring for a splurge, this is the kind of hotel and restaurant that makes your trip to Spain memorable. It's not just the best hotel in Girona, it's one of the best in Spain (named 1998 Hotel of the Year by Spain's prestigious *Gourmetour*). A 1751 *masía* (Catalan farmhouse), the hotel is an exercise in rustic elegance. It's charming, peaceful, and geared toward the pleasure-seeker. The gardens and pool are splendid, and the expensive but exquisite restaurant is as famous as the hotel. Mas de Torrent is perfectly placed for car or bicycle explorations of the surrounding Empordà (the medieval towns mentioned previously in the chapter are just minutes away) and the Costa Brava. Try to get one of the suites in the main house, because they are infinitely more charming than the bungalows in the newer wings and at these rates, are worth the extra money.

The restaurant is one of the region's best, serving fresh fish from the coast (like *dorada al romero,* or John Dory in romero sauce) and meats from the countryside (try the *solomillo de ternera al foie con salsa de setas* — beef sirloin with foie gras and wild mushroom sauce). The wine cellar has an outstanding selection of Spanish and French wines.

Afueras de Torrent, s/n (in Torrent, 6 km, or about 3 miles from Palafrugell). ☎ *972-30-32-92. Fax: 972-30-32-93. E-mail:* mtorrent@intercom.es. *Internet:* www.mastorrent.com. *Parking: Free. Rates: 40,000–45,000 pta. ($222–$250) Jul–Aug.; 32,000–39,000 pta. ($178–$217) rest of year, double. Open year-round (the restaurant is closed to the public, but open to guests, from Jan 15–Feb 15). AE, DC, MC, V.*

Parador de Aiguablava
$$$ Aiguablava (Costa Brava)

This modern white box perched on a tiny peninsula above the sea is a favorite with many travelers, but it isn't what I expect from the generally excellent *parador* chain (see Chapter 8 for more information on paradors). The views are astonishing, but I find it a heck of a blight on the surrounding cliffs and forest. This hotel may be the best place to learn that Spanish *paradors* don't always occupy castles and palaces. Staying here means choosing modern, well-kept, and plain rooms.

The restaurant (same phone number) serves local Ampurdanés cuisine, and is very fairly priced. Its young chef, Lluis Ferrés, is quickly gaining a reputation for his creative local dishes, like *suquet de rape* (monkfish stew). The wine cellar is one of the better ones on the coast.

Platja de Aiguablava, s/n. ☎ *972-62-21-62. Fax: 972-62-21-66. E-mail:* aiguablava@parador.es. *Internet:* www.parador.es. *Parking: Free. Rates: 19,500 pta. ($107) double. AE, DC, MC, V. Open year-round.*

Sa Punta
$$$–$$$$ Platja de Pals (Empordà)

About a half-mile from the beach, and just outside the perfect medieval ensemble of Pals, this small hotel and restaurant is a great place for lunch if you're touring the Costa Brava beaches or inland villages. If you're staying overnight nearby (or here — it has 25 comfortable rooms), it's a great place for a romantic dinner. The setting, amid pine trees and tranquil gardens, is lovely. The menu, like most good restaurants in the area, focuses on traditional specialities of the Empordà, such as *Rosejat de arroz con colitas de gambas* (a baked rice dish with shrimp tails). For dessert, don't miss the *helado de crema catalana* (Catalan custard ice cream).

Urbanización Sa Punta, s/n (Platja de Pals). ☎ *972-66-73-76. Fax: 972-66-73-15. Parking: free. Rates: 14,000–20,000 pta. ($78–$110) double. AE, DC, MC, V. Restaurant: Open daily for lunch and dinner; main courses 1,400–2,900 pta. ($8–$16).*

El Ruso's private garden

High up on **Cap Roig**, a peninsula near Calella de Palafrugell, is an incredible estate that once belonged to a Russian army general (referred to as "El Ruso"). It is now a botanical garden (☎ 972-61-45-82) with extraordinary Mediterranean gardens and super views of the coast. In July and August, the garden hosts the Costa Brava Jazz Festival.

La Xicra
$$$ Palafrugell (Empordà)   CATALAN

For fine local Catalan cooking in the heart of the Empordà region, La Xicra ("shee-kra") is well worth a stop. The kitchen continually comes up with creative dishes that bring in both regulars and tourists. From fish soup to *calçats* (long green leeks, a Catalan specialty) and *merluza al cava* (hake — a white fish — in Catalan sparkling wine), it's tough to choose an unsatisfying dish here.

Carrer Estret, 17 (In Palafrugell, near Llafranc). ☎ *972-030-56-30. Main courses: 1,500–2,800 pta. ($10.50–$19). MC, V. Open: Lunch and dinner Thur–Mon, Tue lunch only. Closed Nov.*

Fast Facts: Girona and the Costa Brava

Area Code
The area code for telephone numbers throughout the province of Girona is **972**. Because the prefix is three digits, only six numbers follow — making a total of nine digits, as throughout Spain. You must dial all of them, even when making local calls.

Currency Exchange
Downtown Girona near the tourist information office has a number of banks and *casas de cambio* (exchange houses). Stop by the office at Rambla de la Llibertat, 2, along the river, or call the tourism office, ☎ 972-22-65-75, for specific locations.

Emergencies
Dial ☎ **091** or ☎ **092**.

Hospitals
Figueres: Hospital de Figueres (☎ 972-50-14-00); Blanes: Hospital Comarcal de la Selva (☎ 972-35-32-64); Lloret de Mar: Hospital Lloret de Mar (☎ 972-36-47-36).

Information
Girona has two *Turisme* (tourism information) offices: at the train station and at Rambla de la Llibertat, 2. Contact both at ☎ 972-22-65-75. They're open weekdays from 8 a.m. to 8 p.m., Saturday from 8 a.m.

to 2 p.m. For broader provincial information, contact Patronat de Turisme Costa Brava/Girona (☎ 972-20-84-01; Fax: 972-22-15-70; E-mail: cbrava@cbrava.es; Internet: www.cbrava.es/girona/).

The Figueres tourism office is on Plaça del Sol (☎ 972-50-31-55).

The Cadaqués tourism office is on Cotxe 2-A (☎ 972-25-83-15).

Police

Dial ☎ 092 in most towns; in Girona, the police station is on Avenida Jaume I, 18 (☎ 972-20-50-50). In Figueres, contact the Policía Municipal at ☎ 972-51-01-11.

Post Office

The Central Post Office in Girona is on Av. d'En Ramon Folch (☎ 972-20-16-87). It's open from Mon–Fri from 8:30 a.m. to 9 p.m. and Sat from 8 a.m. to 8 p.m.

Chapter 13

The Basque Country and Navarra

- -

In This Chapter

▶ Getting to and around the Basque Country and Navarra

▶ "Basque"-ing in art at the Guggenheim Museum in Bilbao

▶ Dining and relaxing in San Sebastián

▶ Joining the stampede in Pamplona

▶ Sampling Basque food — Spain's top cuisine

- -

Spain's great, green north — *España Verde* — begins with the Basque Country and Navarra. Historic regions wedged between the Pyrenees Mountains and the Cantabrian Sea, they're characterized by rugged terrain and reserved, independent-minded people. Yet they're also famous for star attractions with all the quiet and reserve of a Hollywood Oscar bash: Bilbao's Guggenheim Museum and Pamplona's Running of the Bulls. The former is the world's latest and greatest architectural marvel; the latter a daredevil dash made legendary by Ernest Hemingway's enthusiastic tales of man-versus-beast heroics.

The gateway to the Basque Country is **Bilbao.** Until recently, it was a grim industrial capital to be avoided on a tour of Spain. Today, newly revitalized, it tops the agendas of many travelers to Spain — all due to a futuristic art museum. More than a landmark building, the Guggenheim has become a cultural ambassador, exposing the Basque Country to an international public.

The other Basque city of great interest is **San Sebastián,** one of Spain's loveliest cities. It's an easy-going, sparkling resort town on Spain's northern coast, just downwind from Biarritz in southwestern France.

Pamplona, the capital of Navarra, continues to revel in its fame as host of the original extreme sport. Seventy-five years after Hemingway, the town is still a powerful magnet for tourists young and old, irrational and merely curious, to test themselves — or just get drunk and fantasize about the bravado they wish they had — against one of the emblematic images of Spain: the charging bull.

The Basque Country (País Vasco) & Navarra

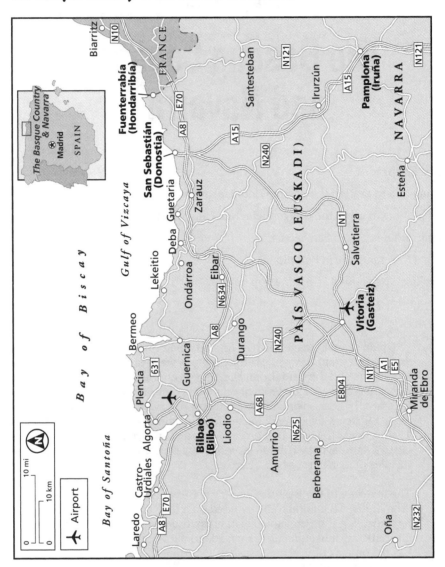

Just the Facts: The Basque Country and Navarra

Bilbao is the industrial center of the Basque Country, the largest city in the region, and the capital of Vizcaya province. **San Sebastián** is the capital of Guipuzcoa province. **Pamplona,** not technically part of the Basque Country, is the capital of Navarra province.

✔ **The best way to go.** Bilbao, San Sebastián, and Pamplona are all within two hours of each other by road or rail. All are roughly an hour's flight from Madrid or Barcelona.

✔ **The name game.** As in Catalonia, street signs get a little confusing up north. The Basque Country is called *País Vasco* in Spanish, *Euskadi* in the Basque language (called Euskera). In Euskera, Bilbao is written *Bilbo;* San Sebastián is *Donostia,* Pamplona is *Iruña,* and Navarra is *Nafarroa. Sanfermines* ("san-fair-*mean*-ez") is the summer festival with the Running of the Bulls; the actual sprint is called an *encierro* ("en-*thee*-air-oh"). And, most important, *tapas* are called *pintxos* ("*peen*-chos") up north.

✔ **¿Cómo Se Dice? Talking the talk.** The complicated, mysterious Basque language is enjoying a renaissance, but Spanish is still the primary language for most. See the "Basque-ing in obscurity: Language and politics" sidebar, later in this chapter, for more on Euskera.

✔ **What's for dinner?** Gastronomes delight in Basque cooking, the most accomplished in Spain; half the reason (or more) to come here is the food. Basque cuisine means impossibly fresh seafood, delicate sauces, and *pintxos,* the stacked *tapas* of the Basque Country. Top things off with *txakoli,* a young, fresh, fruity white wine that's slightly fizzy.

✔ **The forecast.** The weather here is gray and misty or rainy much of the year — think coastal Scotland. It's spectacularly green all of the time.

✔ **When to go.** Spring, summer, and fall are all super seasons to visit the north. In July and August, San Sebastián is full of vacationing Spaniards and French. The Running of the Bulls in Pamplona is the second week in July. During these times, prices skyrocket and hotels are packed to the rafters.

✔ **How long before moving on?** One day in each city, a day or two extra if you want to explore the countryside.

Major Attractions in the Basque Country and Navarra

Thanks in large part to the Guggenheim Museum's popularity, travelers are discovering a region that has been a secret kept by a select few: brawny green hills, a rocky coastline, and an imaginative cuisine that many consider the finest in all of Spain.

Bilbao

Bilbao, Spain's biggest commercial port, is the political capital of the Basque Country, an inhospitable region that repelled both the Romans and the Moors. The city stretches more than 10 miles along the River Nervión. Once known only for its shipping and steelworks prowess, today it's experiencing an architectural and cultural renaissance. Here you find:

- ✔ The **Guggenheim Bilbao,** Frank Gehry's modern masterpiece
- ✔ The **Old Quarter,** the lively heart of the city
- ✔ **Pintxos** (*tapas* or Spanish appetizers) and superb Basque dining

San Sebastián

San Sebastián's aesthetic and culinary delights have held vacationing Spaniards and French in thrall for more than a century. The small city has an incomparable setting — the city curves deliciously around a half-moon bay, and hills frame it at either end — perfect for panoramic pictures. Here you find:

- ✔ **La Concha,** Spain's best urban beaches and esplanade
- ✔ The mouth-watering *tapas* bars of the **Old Quarter**
- ✔ **Gourmet dining** at Spain's best restaurants

Pamplona

Although Pamplona (and its province Navarra) is not technically part of the Basque Country, it shares ancient roots with the Basque people. For example, in certain parts, locals still speak Basque. The ninth-century fortified capital of the Kingdom of Navarra, Pamplona is a modest, provincial city with few attractions. However, it's known the world over for its annual July eruption of daring — people running through the streets with harried bulls at their heels. Here you find:

- ✔ **San Fermín and the Running of the Bulls,** Europe's liveliest and most dangerous street party
- ✔ The **Cathedral,** a Gothic landmark
- ✔ The impressive **Navarra Museum,** near the city's medieval walls

Basque-ing in obscurity: Language and politics

Within Spain and the rest of Europe, the Basque Country is perhaps best known for a secretive terrorist group, known by its Basque-language acronym *ETA*. For decades, ETA (which stands for "Basque Nation and Liberty") has demanded independence from Spain and the establishment of a Basque nation. They have pursued this goal with extreme violence; many police, military personnel, and politicians have been assassinated on behalf of the cause. The group's terrorist actions in recent years have provoked public repudiation across Spain. I've met Spaniards visiting the Basque Country who half-expected to find a police state, but as a tourist, you're extremely unlikely to see any signs of the shadowy group. And, almost none of the terrorist acts are committed on home turf.

The Basque people are one of the oldest in Europe. Some theorists believe that they're indigenous Iberian people descended from Cro-Magnon man. Others propose that the Basques are the living link to the lost city of Atlantis. Modern Basques don't feel the least rootless, however; they revel in their unknown origins, a distinction that sets them even farther apart from the rest of Spain.

The Basque language, called *Euskera* (also spelled *Euskara*), completely baffles linguists and ethnologists. Wholly unrelated to any living language, scholars believe that Euskera pre-dates all Indo-European tongues. Heck, just looking at the preponderance of letters *k, t, x,* and *y* mystifies you. Despite its ancient roots, Euskera is taught in schools, and local TV and radio are broadcast in the language (but only about a third of the population actively speaks it). If you know Spanish, don't expect to catch even a few words — Basque is insanely difficult to pronounce and learn. Knowing a language such as Hungarian or Finnish would provide you with a better warmup!

Euskera is remarkable not only because no one can identify its origins, but also because the language has no swear words. Basques must dip into Spanish when they want to curse.

Bilbao

Bilbao, just 10 miles from the Cantabrian Sea, is split down the middle by the Nervión estuary — what locals call the *ría*. Founded in 1300, the city's *Casco Viejo* (Old Quarter) sits on the right bank, connected by four bridges to the much larger modern section on the left bank. Between the Casco Viejo and the river is a wide promenade, the Arenal. The main commercial street, Gran Vía, bisects the modern (new) part of the city, a grid called the Ensanche (the Enlargement). The new Guggenheim Museum hugs the riverbank on the northern side of modern section.

Bilbao

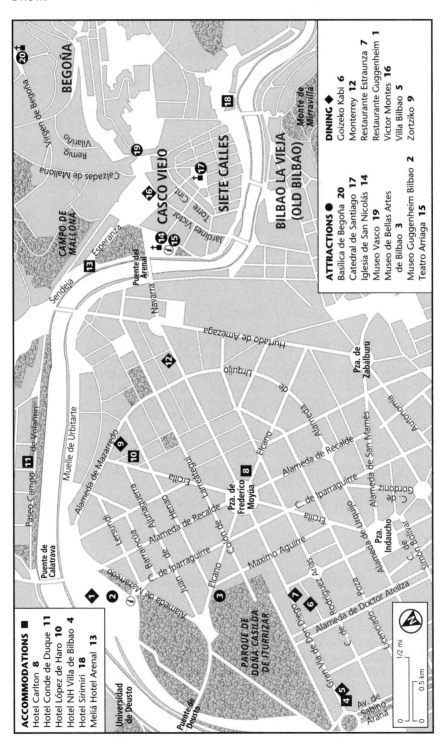

ACCOMMODATIONS ■
Hotel Carlton **8**
Hotel Conde de Duque **11**
Hotel López de Haro **10**
Hotel NH Villa de Bilbao **4**
Hotel Sirimiri **18**
Meliá Hotel Arenal **13**

ATTRACTIONS ●
Basílica de Begoña **20**
Catedral de Santiago **17**
Iglesia de San Nicolás **14**
Museo Vasco **19**
Museo de Bellas Artes
de Bilbao **3**
Museo Guggenheim Bilbao **2**
Teatro Arriaga **15**

DINING ◆
Goizeko Kabi **6**
Monterrey **12**
Restaurante Estraunza **7**
Restaurante Guggenheim **1**
Victor Montes **16**
Villa Bilbao **5**
Zortziko **9**

Arriving in Bilbao

For information on quick trips to Bilbao from either Madrid or Barcelona, see the sidebar entitled "Traveling to Bilbao and back in a day."

By plane

Bilbao's airport, **Aeropuerto Internacional de Bilbao-Sondica** (☎ 94-453-23-06), lies 10 km (6 miles) north of the city. **Iberia, Spanair,** and **Air Europa** all fly to Bilbao from other Spanish cities. The airport is pretty small and easy to get around. Check out the very helpful tourism office (open 7:30 a.m. to 1 p.m.) right after you pick up your bags and visit the car rental agencies, if you want to get wheels for the País Vasco.

The **airport bus** (140 pta./75¢; ☎ 94-420-79-40) just out in front of the airport takes you along the river to the city in about 30 minutes. (Note, though, that even if a bus is waiting to depart, surly drivers don't let you board until they're good and ready to go. You have to stand on the curb, so you may want to have your umbrella handy, because downpours are frequent.) The bus drops you off next to the river, at the open-air bus station across from the *Ayuntamiento* (City Hall). The bus returning to the airport is No. 3247, marked "Bilbao-Aeropuerto." It leaves every 40 minutes starting at 6 a.m.

A taxi from the airport to downtown costs about 2,500 pta. ($14). Taxies line up out front where you catch the bus (most taxis are pretty fancy rigs in northern Spain — Mercedes and Audis).

By car

You can easily access Bilbao by national highway from both Barcelona (the A2) and Madrid (the A1), as well as France (the A8) and Pamplona (the N-240).

By bus

The main bus terminal is **Estación Autobuses Garellano** (☎ 94-439-50-77; Gurtubay, 1). *Transportes Pesa* buses travel between San Sebastián and Bilbao (1¼ hours); Autobuses *La Únion* and *La Burundesa* arrive from Pamplona (2 hours). The ANSA bus line connects Bilbao to Madrid and Barcelona.

By train

The **RENFE** train station is located at **Estación de Abando** (Plaza España, 1; ☎ 94-423-86-35). Long-distance trains come and go to Madrid (a 6- to 7-hour trip) and Barcelona (a 12-hour trip).

Traveling to Bilbao and back in a day

The new **Guggenheim Museum** has proved so popular that people fly to Bilbao from Barcelona and Madrid early in the morning, visit the museum, and returning at night. If you want to insert a Guggenheim day into your itinerary, you can catch the first and last flights on **Iberia** (☎ 800-772-4642) or **Air Europa** (☎ 800-238-7672) from either of those cities. Easier still is a single-day tour from **Tecnic Viajes,** which includes transfers from the airports, a panoramic tour of Bilbao, museum tickets, and an English-language tour of the Guggenheim. For information, call ☎ 91-388-16-36 or e-mail: tecviamad@cambrabcn.es.

Getting around Bilbao

In Bilbao, you can cover almost all points of interest by foot or on the new, efficient Metro (subway). If you're traveling to other city destinations in the region, you don't need a car (buses are considerably cheaper and easier to ride to both San Sebastián and Pamplona).

By car

To explore the countryside around Bilbao, a car is your best option. The roads are among the best in Spain, but highway tolls are high. You can find major rental companies at the Bilbao airport, including **Europcar** (☎ 94-471-01-33) and **Hertz** (☎ 94-415-36-77).

By bus

The line of **city buses** is extensive, but with the easily managed distances and Metro, you probably won't need to take a bus. If you do, call ☎ 94-475-82-00 for information. A single ticket is 125 pta. (70¢), and a ten-trip ticket (Bonobus) is 715 pta. ($4).

By metro

The new **Metro Bilbao** (☎ 94-425-40-25), designed by Sir Norman Foster, the recent Pritzker Architecture Prize winner, is exceedingly clean and efficient. You can't miss the unmistakable entryways, fanciful Plexiglas domes. Trains run from 6 a.m. to 10 p.m. Monday through Thursday, 6 a.m. to 1 a.m. Friday; 6 a.m. to 5 a.m. Saturday; and 6 a.m. to 11 p.m. Sunday. A single ticket costs 135 pta. (75¢); a ten-journey ticket is 825 pta. ($4.50).

By taxi

Bilbao's **taxis** are plusher than in other parts of Spain, but they're also more expensive. The meter starts at 500 pta. ($2.75), so don't hail a cab for very short journeys if you can walk. Recommended operators include **Radio Taxi** (☎ 94-444-88-88); **Radio Taxi Bizkaia** (☎ 94-426-90-26); or **Tele Taxi** (☎ 94-410-21-21).

Staying in Bilbao

Until the Guggenheim Museum landed like a shiny spaceship on the Nervión River, business travelers were Bilbao's most frequent visitors. Today, the construction of new hotels is catching up with tourists' sudden interest in the city. However, because Bilbao is still a business capital with tons of conventions and fairs, you can get weekend deals at most hotels.

Hotel Carlton

$$$$ **New City (Abando)**

Over the years, the Carlton has been occupied by the glamorous and powerful: Orson Welles, Ava Gardner, and the Republican Basque government during the Spanish civil war (I imagine the latter group got a great discount). A grand, gleaming building right on handsome Plaza Moyúa, the Carlton is the city's most prestigious hotel. Constructed in 1925 in the Belle Époque style (an elegant architectural style popular around World War I) and recently refurbished from head-to-toe, the continental-style rooms are elegant and spacious, with boldly patterned drapes and bedspreads. The Guggenheim is only a ten-minute stroll away.

Plaza Federico Moyúa, 2. ☎ *94-416-22-00. Fax: 94-416-46-28. E-mail:* jegana@ hcarlton.tsai.es. *Internet:* www.codeconet.com/aranzazu. *Metro: Moyúa. Parking: 2,000 pta. ($11). Rates: 26,500 pta. ($147); July–Sept, 16,000 pta. ($89) double. Deals: weekend rate, 16,000 pta. ($89). AE, DC, MC, V.*

Hotel Conde Duque

$$$ **Along river (Uribarri)**

Facing the space-age Calatrava Bridge and walking distance downriver from the Guggenheim, this comfortable, mid-size hotel is very well located. The top-floor rooms used to have great views of the "Guggy" until an sprawling modern building was erected next door. But, some rooms still have good views of the river. Rooms are often whimsically decorated in bright colors, but vary greatly in size (some are huge, some are tiny; ask to see a few upon arrival). The baths, however, are uniformly large. Unusual in Spain, certain rooms are said to be "tastefully designed" specifically for women. I'm still trying to figure out what that means (the rooms in question were bright and colorful), and whether that's a progressive or disparaging policy.

Paseo Campo Volantín, 22. ☎ *94-445-60-00. Fax: 94-445-60 66. E-mail:* reservas@ hotelcondeduque.com. *Internet:* www.hotelcondeduque.com. *Metro: Abando. Parking: 1,500 pta. ($8). Rates: 24,500 pta. ($136) double; weekend rate, 12,000 pta. ($67) (two-night minimum; including breakfast). Children under 2 free, and a 3rd adult 20 percent discount. AE, MC, V.*

Hotel López de Haro
$$$$ **New City (Abando)**

For discrete elegance, this is the place to be in Bilbao. Tucked away on a quiet street in the modern section of town near the river, this is a fine, small hotel that opened in 1990 and has been robbing the city's other top hotels of clients ever since. It's intimate and handsome, with a clubby feel, but not fussy. The restaurant, Club Nautico, is excellent. The rooms and baths are five-star elegance all the way.

Obispo Orueta, 2-4. ☎ *94-423-55-00. Fax: 94-423-45-00. E-mail:* lh@ hotellopezdeharo.com. *Internet:* www.hotellopezdeharo.com. *Metro: Moyúa. Parking: 2,100 pta. ($11). Rates: 30,700 pta. ($171) double; weekend rate (includes breakfast buffet), 23,600 pta. ($131). AE, DC, MC, V.*

Hotel NH Villa de Bilbao
$$$ **New City (Abando)**

This large and slick hotel, part of Spain's NH hotel chain, is popular with business travelers. It's at the far end of Bilbao's main drag — close to both the Museum of Fine Arts and the Guggenheim, but a little far from the Old Quarter. Rooms are professional: modern and unpretentious. They have light woods, navy blue-and-polkadot bedspreads and curtains, parquet floors, modern furnishings, and good-sized baths. The restaurant, La Pergola, has a good 3,000-pta. ($21) *menú del día* (fixed-price menu).

Gran Vía, 87. ☎ *94-441-60-00. Fax: 94-441-65-29. E-mail:* nhbilbao@ nh-hoteles.es. *Internet:* www.nh-hoteles.es. *Metro: Moyúa. Parking: 1,700 pta. ($9). Rates: 22,000 pta. ($122) double; weekends, 16,500 pta. ($92); Children under 12 sharing parents' room stay free. AE, DC, MC, V.*

Hotel Sirimiri
$$ **Old Quarter**

This small hotel in the *Casco Viejo* (Old Quarter) is rather poetically named: *Sirimiri* means "light drizzle," which is the kind of weather you're almost certain to find in Bilbao — though I don't know if it accurately describes this functional, clean hotel. Rooms are good size, with yellow walls; bathrooms are sparkling, with pearly gray tile. With good, personal service, this hotel is a pretty good deal — but a hike from the Guggenheim, if that's all you want to see in Bilbao.

Plaza de la Encarnación, 3. ☎ *94-433-07-59. Fax: 94-433-08-75. E-mail:* hsirimiri@ euskalnet.net. *Internet:* www.adi.es/hsirimiri. *Metro: Casco Viejo. Parking: 1,000 pta. ($5.50). Rates: 11,000 pta. ($61) double. MC, V.*

Meliá Hotel Arenal
$$$ Old Quarter (near the Arenal promenade)

One of Bilbao's newest establishments (it opened in July 1998), this small hotel is aimed at tourists and businessmen who balk at bulky hotels. With just 40 rooms, it's much more personal than the other members of Spain's Meliá hotel chain. Near the river and on the edge of the Old Quarter, it's still not far from the Guggenheim. Rooms are good size and very comfortable.

Fueros, 2. ☎ *94-415-31-00. Fax: 94-415-63-95. E-mail:* melia.confort.arenal@ solmelia.com. *Internet:* www.solmelia.es. *Metro: Abando. Parking: Nearby, 1,800 pta. ($10). Rates: 21,500 pta. ($119) double; weekend rate, 14,000 pta. ($77) (including breakfast). AE, DC, MC, V.*

Dining in Bilbao

Say you want to travel to Spain for the sole pleasure of eating — not at all an absurd notion. A culinary tour could begin and end in the Basque Country. Eating is an inalienable fixture of Basque culture. From tantalizing *tapas* — works of art called *pintxos* in these parts — to nine-course tasting menus at three-star restaurants, fine dining is an everyday affair. At private gastronomic societies, members get together to cook for each other, eat, and philosophize about food. Basques talk about food even more than they talk politics.

The Basque Country is lodged between the Bay of Biscay and the rugged Pyrenees, so it's unsurprising that the cuisine is inspired in equal parts by the mountains and the sea. Basques delight in succulent lamb and game, but they adore the day's catch: *bacalao* (salt cod), grilled clams, squid, tuna, and baby eels. The Basque love of sauces is second perhaps only to the French; their passion for food is second to none.

Bilbao ranks second only to San Sebastián in terms of great Basque restaurants — which means that it's one of the two or three best places to eat in Spain. While it's not cheap to eat at the more celebrated Basque restaurants — in fact, it's downright pricey — you can eat very well focusing solely on delectable *pintxos* ("*peen*-chose"), or *tapas*. The ritual is easy: Muscle up to the bar of any place with a lot of noise and hungry mouths inside, and grab the tastiest morsel within your reach. Ask for a *vino tinto* (glass of red wine), *cerveza* (beer), or *txacolí* ("*cha*-koh-li"; Basque white wine) and keep track of how many drinks and *pintxos* you have. This informal style of snacking or dining operates strictly on the honor system. Finger counting and pointing does fine when you need to calculate the bill.

At 200 pta. ($1.10) or so a pop, *pintxos* seem like a cheap way to eat. And they can be, if you exercise restraint, but they're so good that doing so is a tall order. It's nearly impossible to resist reaching for one more . . . then one more . . . and one last one. Pretty soon, your meal of snacks turns into a full meal, cost included. Be careful if you're watching your wallet — or your weight!

Bilbao's got a few classic old cafés, which are good places to get a jolt of espresso or a *cerveza* and talk about the Guggenheim (or take a breather from a *tapas* crawl). **Café Iruña** (Jardines de Albia; ☎ 94-423-70-21), full of Moorish-looking, colorful tiles, dates to 1903. **Café Boulevard** (Arenal, 3; ☎ 94-415-31-28), on the perimeter of the *Casco Viejo* and just down the street from the *Teatro Arriaga,* is the oldest café in Bilbao. Since 1871, literary sorts have come to this art deco place, which, in addition to a full lineup of caffeine and drinks, has a pretty good assortment of *pintxos* and cheap *platos combinados* (combination platters), ideal for a quick lunch. Finally, **Café La Granja** (Plaza Circular, 3; ☎ 94-423-18-13), around since the 1920s, is one of the old-time, simple coffee shops frequented for *merienda,* the term for a late-afternoon snack.

For more on Spanish dining customs, including mealtimes, costs, and tipping, see "Knowing what to expect when you're eating out" in Chapter 1.

Goizeko Kabi

$$$$ New City (Abando) BASQUE

One of the best known restaurants in Bilbao, this rustic-looking chalet looks like a gussied-up ski lodge. It's a place to snuggle up and try tremendous traditional Basque dishes — especially if you're unfamiliar with Basque cooking. The chef, Fernando Canales, performs what amounts to a daily primer of the food of his hometown. For starters, try homemade *chorizo* (a spicy Spanish pork sausage) or wild *perrichico* mushrooms. Main courses include *entrecote* (a boned rib steak) with foie gras (goose-liver pate), langoustines (prawns) with oyster ravioli, and sea bass with tomato vinaigrette and artichoke. A specialty that makes Bilbao natives weep are *kokotxas al pil-pil* (fresh cod filets from the "chins" of the fish, cooked in a bubbling and salty green sauce). Desserts are every bit as elaborate and wonderful as main dishes.

Particular de Estraunza, 4–6 (New City). ☎ *94-441-50-04. Reservations required. Metro: Moyúa (one short block south of Gran Vía). Main courses: 1,900–3,400 pta. ($11–$19); menú del día 5,200 pta. ($29). AE, MC, V. Open: lunch and dinner Mon–Sat.*

Monterrey

$$$ New City (Abando) BASQUE

A long, narrow restaurant on Bilbao's principal commercial avenue, Monterrey disarmingly proclaims itself a *cafetería* on the awning. In fact, it's a small, inviting, and fairly priced place for a traditional Basque meal. The 12 tables go straight back, parallel to the bar. Try fresh artichokes for a starter before sampling the *solomillo* (beef tenderloin) stuffed with *foie gras* or hake (a white fish) served with *angulas* (baby eels).

Gran Vía, 6 (New City). ☎ *94-424-84-90. Reservations required. Metro: Moyúa. Main courses: 1,400–4,600 pta. ($8–$26); menú 2,500 pta. ($14). AE, MC, V. Open: Lunch and dinner Tues–Sat.*

Restaurante Estraunza
$$$$ New City (Abando)   BASQUE

The entrance to this unassuming place, on Bilbao's main drag in the modern part of town, looks more like a modest café than a fine restaurant. But don't despair; the quality of the kitchen far outpaces the lackluster décor. Try monkfish cooked in *txakolí* (the local Basque white wine) with almonds and bacon, or lamb sweetbreads with mushrooms.

Gran Vía, 59. ☎ *94-442-23-72. Reservations recommended. Metro: Moyúa. Main courses: 1,750–3,250 pta. ($10–$18); menú del día, 5,500 ($31). AE, MC, V. Open: Daily lunch and dinner.*

Restaurante Guggenheim Bilbao
$$$ New City (Abando)   BASQUE

Dining at the Guggenheim Museum reveals, appropriately, the art of Basque cooking. Carved out of the museum's peculiarly shaped interior is an excellent restaurant that opened to glowing reviews and has been jam-packed every night since. The menu, the work of rising star Martín Berasategui (and carried out by his protégé, Bixente Arrieta), has as much flair as the playful dining room. Choose from items *del mar* (from the sea) or *del campo* (from the countryside). You can't go wrong on the menu, but you may start with the large and chunky lobster salad, perhaps followed by duck cannelloni. The dessert sampler is heaven for those with a sweet tooth.

The restaurant is so popular that you need to call ahead of your visit to Bilbao, because the wait is up to two weeks or more (if that fails, try the more accessible lunch cafeteria, which has an affordable *menú del día*).

Abandoibarra Etorbidea, 2 (within Guggenheim Museum, New City). ☎ *94-423-93-33. Reservations required. Metro: Moyúa. Main courses: 1,800–2,600 pta. ($10–$14). AE, MC, V. Open: Lunch and dinner Tues–Sat; Sun lunch only.*

Victor Montes
$$–$$$ Old Quarter   BASQUE/TAPAS

Planted on Plaza Nueva in the Casco Viejo, this is a classic Basque restaurant and *pintxos* bar. Basque Tourism could just set up cameras during *tapas* hour and film a winning ad for Bilbao here. Lined with wine bottles, the restaurant is like a cross between an art nouveau pharmacy and a wine cellar. It has a small dining room downstairs that opens onto the bar, and a more intimate room upstairs. The real action is at the bar, however, where amazing *pintxos* (of cod, squid, spinach tortilla — you name it) are piled high. They fly off the bar into the hands of impatient, but good-natured, regulars.

Plaza Nueva, 8. ☎ 94-415-70-67. Reservations recommended. Metro: Casco Viejo. Main courses: 1,400–2,900 pta. ($8–$16). AE, MC, V. Open: Lunch and dinner Mon–Sat; Sun lunch only. Closed Easter week and August 1–15.

Villa Bilbao

$ New City (Abando)   SPANISH

If you're just looking for a good, simple midday meal, this small restaurant serves a very affordable and respectable three-course *menú del día*. That may mean cannelloni or fish soup to begin, followed by a nice portion of baked *hake* or scrambled eggs with wild mushrooms and shrimp. The price includes bread, homemade dessert, and a bottle of decent local wine. The crowds of nearby office workers recognize a good deal when they see one, so you may want to arrive early. It's not all that far from the Guggenheim, making it a good place to go before or after your visit there.

Gran Vía, 87. No phone. Metro: San Mamés. Main courses: 700–1,500 pta. ($4–$8); menú del día 1,200 pta. ($7). No credit cards. Open: Breakfast, lunch, and dinner Mon–Sun.

Zortziko

$$$$$ New City (Abando)   BASQUE

Around the corner from the Guggenheim, in a chic neighborhood, this is one of the hottest restaurants in Bilbao. The sophisticated kitchen combines innovative dishes and traditional Basque items. Choose from sea bass roasted in Rioja red wine, prawns with mushroom risotto, or rare pigeon breast in a sweet red wine sauce. The tasting menu isn't cheap, but it's a memorable smorgasbord, which is a good move if everyone at your table is willing (and able — it's a ton of food) to go that route. Zortziko is elegant and more formal than most other restaurants in Bilbao, so you may want to dress up a bit.

Alameda Marzarredo, 17. ☎ 94-423-97-43. Reservations recommended. Metro: Abando. Reservations required. Main courses: 1,700–3,800 pta. ($9–$21); tasting menu, 7,500 pta. ($42). AE, MC, V. Open: Lunch and dinner Tues–Sat; Mon lunch only. Closed last week Aug.

Exploring Bilbao

No question about it: Sightseeing in Bilbao is now the Guggenheim Museum and everything else. By all means, beeline it to the wondrous museum, which meets and beats expectations, but don't miss out on exploring Bilbao's other attractions, including its atmospheric *Casco Viejo* (Old Quarter).

For a bird's-eye view of Bilbao, take the elevator near the *Ayuntamiento* (City Hall) by the river — at Calle Esperanza, 6 — to the upper town. You can reach the massive Gothic church *Basílica de Begoña.* Aim your camera down river for the space-age Calatrava Bridge and Guggenheim Museum.

Casco Viejo
Old Quarter

Just east of the Nervión River is Bilbao's Old Quarter. Though Bilbao dates to the Middle Ages, it isn't rich in medieval buildings and monuments. However, the small Casco Viejo — a national historical and artistic monument — is a great and lively part of the city. One section is known as *Siete Calles,* named for the seven parallel streets that begin at the river. They're packed with restaurants and bars, and any day of the week after work, large groups spill noisily into the streets as they pursue a Basque ritual dear to their hearts and stomachs: the *tapeo,* or *tapas* crawl.

The best thing to do is wander the Old Quarter as the mood strikes, stopping here and there for small glasses of wine or beer and assorted *pintxos.* At the edge of the *barrio* (neighborhood) are the impressive **Teatro Arriaga,** a nineteenth-century theater, and the neighborhood's most important church, **Iglesia de San Nicolás.** Don't miss **Plaza Nueva** (on Plaza Arenal)**,** the spiritual heart of old Bilbao, which has 64 arches and only slightly fewer *tapas* bars. Also nearby is the **Catedral de Santiago,** originally constructed in the fourteenth century, then restored in the sixteenth century after a fire.

You can take a good walk around the district in under two hours.

East of the River Nervión, bounded by Puente del Arenal on the north side and calle Zabalbide on the south. Metro: Casco Viejo. Or, walk across the Arenal bridge from Gran Vía.

Museo Guggenheim Bilbao
New City (along River Nervión)

Frank Gehry's critically lauded, much-photographed museum has been called the "greatest building of our time" by Philip Johnson, the legendary New York architect. Imagining a more exciting art and architecture experience than the one Gehry crafted, improbably, on the banks of the River Nervión in Bilbao is impossible. When the Guggenheim Foundation announced its plans to build another European branch in this rough-and-tumble industrial city in Spain, the art world was shocked. What's more shocking is the commanding success of the museum's design and execution. It's as if Gehry took the bet of Frank Lloyd Wright (the architect of the Guggenheim in New York) and said "I'll raise you one." The museum is just about perfect: daring, inspired, conceptual. More than a building, it deserves to be considered a sculpture on a monumental scale. As revolutionary as it is, its detractors are few — if any exist. (Locals affectionately call it *Guggy* — pronounced "*goo*-ghee" — or "El Guggen.") Like a giant fish, the building is sheathed in a metallic skin: Its 30,000 thin titanium panels shimmer in the sun. The structure's sensual curves give it impressive movement, as does the soaring atrium; as you wind your way through the structure, you keep returning to the building's heart. Except for Richard Serra's sensational sculpture, "Snake" (perfectly in tune with the long fish gallery), the museum is almost wholly given over to itinerant exhibitions and works on loan from the other Guggenheims — but, frankly, it could be empty and still be a spectacular art experience.

And there's no denying the Bilbao Guggenheim's wild popularity. In its very first year, the museum pulled in 1.4 million people — more than three times the projected attendance, and more than the two Guggenheim museums in New York combined. By mid-2000, 2.5 million people already visited the museum.

Allow at least two hours to see the museum, and more if the temporary exhibits interest you (in that case, expect to spend the better part of a full morning or afternoon). See the sidebar entitled "Getting the most out of the Guggenheim" for advice on tours and discounted admission.

Avenida Abandobiarra, 2. ☎ *94-435-90-80. Internet:* www.guggenheim-bilbao. es. *Metro: Moyúa. Admission: 1,000 pta. ($5.50); 500 ($2.75), students and seniors; free for children under 12. Open: Tues–Sun 10 a.m.–8 p.m.; July 4–August 31 open every day 9 a.m.–9 p.m.*

Museo de Bellas Artes de Bilbao
New City

The Guggenheim's not the only art show in town, though it does over-shadow the excellent Fine Arts Museum, founded in 1908. The latter's rich and varied collections include paintings by the old masters El Greco, Zurbarán, and Goya; contemporary artists like Francis Bacon and Antoni Tàpies; and a survey of nineteenth- and twentieth-century Basque artists. Eduardo Chillida's large-scale *Monument to Iron* is a good introduction to the work of this tremendous Basque sculptor. The museum, exempt from the crowds across the way at the Guggenheim, is nicely quiet most of the time.

Art fans may need a couple of hours here; those with moderate interest can make do with an hour.

Getting the most out of the Guggenheim

Listen up: The Guggenheim offers excellent hand-held audio tours (700 pta./$4), which allow you to go at your own pace, hear an analysis of the building's revolutionary architecture, and listen in on comments from the architect himself. The same tour leads you through the current exhibitions.

Guided tours: The Guggenheim offers free guided visits in English, Tuesday through Sunday at 11 a.m., 12:30 p.m., 4 p.m. and 6:30 p.m. A special family visit, at this writing in Spanish only, is Saturday at 5 p.m. Visits focus on current temporary exhibitions and the museum's architecture and permanent collection. To reserve a guided tour, call ☎ **94-435-90-90.**

Art bargain: Combined entrance to the the Guggenheim Museum and the next-door Bilbao Museum of Fine Arts is just 900 pta. ($5 — less than admission to the Guggenheim alone) with the Artean Joint Voucher, which you can purchase at the box office of either museum.

Go when everyone's having lunch: To have the Guggenheim virtually to yourself, eat an early lunch and go to the museum when it clears out of Spaniards and many European visitors, from 2 p.m. to 4 p.m. In summer and on weekends, though, youhave a harder time buying yourself this lunchtime peace and quiet.

Plaza del Museo, 2 (Doña Casilda Iturriza Park). ☎ *94-439-60-60. Internet:* www.museobilbao.com. *Metro: Moyúa. Admission: 400 pta. ($2.20) adults, 200 pta. ($1.10) seniors and students, children under 12 free; free Wed. Combined entrance with Guggenheim (Artean Voucher) 900 pta. ($5). Open: Tues–Sat 10 a.m.–1:30 p.m. and 4–7:30 p.m.; Sun 10 a.m.–2 p.m.*

Museo Vasco
Old Quarter

This museum of Basque archaeology and ethnography occupies a handsome Jesuit *colegio* (high school) and its beautiful cloisters in the old town. Interesting exhibits address the ancient history of the Basque people, including carved stonework, prehistoric utensils, furniture, and ceramics. Allow an hour, at least.

Cruz, 4. ☎ *94-415-54-23. Metro: Casco Viejo. Admission: 300 pta. ($1.67) adults, 150 pta. (85¢) children and students. Open: Tues–Sat 10:30 a.m.–1:30 p.m. and 4–7 p.m.; Sun 10:30 a.m.–1:30 p.m.*

And on your left, the Guggenheim: Seeing Bilbao by guided tour

The Bilbao Tourism Office offers free, guided **"Panoramic and Monumental Bilbao"** walking tours every Wednesday and Saturday at 9:30 a.m. The language of the tour depends upon the linguistic leanings of the group assembled. Contact **Bilbao Iniciativas Turísticas,** Plaza Arriaga, 1 (☎ **94-416-00-22**). **Bilbao en Autobús** (Bilbao by Bus) offers 90-minute bus tours of the city (passengers can get on and off throughout the day). Daily departures are at 10 a.m., 12 p.m., 3 p.m., and 5 p.m. (Calle Marqués del Puerto, 9; ☎ **94-415-36-06**; E-mail: bisertur@ bisertur.com; Internet: www.bisertur.com). Adults 1,000 pta. ($5.50)/children and seniors, 500 pta. ($2.75). **Bilbao Paso a Paso** (Bilbao Step-by-Step) leads walking tours (90 minutes) of the Old Quarter that depart from the Tourism Office (Paseo del Arenal, 1; ☎ **94-473-00-78**; E-mail: bilbao.pap@clientes.euskaltel.es) and end at Teatro Arriaga. Tuesday, Saturday, and Sunday in English at 10:30 a.m.; 500 pta. ($2.75), children under 10 free. Get tickets (at tourism office) 30 minutes before the tour. A company named for a famous Basque dish, **Pil Pil** (☎ **94-424-59-21**), offers not culinary tours but boat trips past Guggenheim and other new developments along the river. Trips last 50 minutes, leaving Tuesday through Sunday in summer, 12 p.m., 1 p.m., 5 p.m., and 6 p.m.; in winter, Saturday and Sunday only 12 p.m., 1 p.m., 4 p.m., and 5 p.m. (Cost: adults 1,500 pta./ $8, children 750 pta./$4). A four-hour dinner, dancing, and drinks tour leaves Friday and Saturday at 9 p.m. (6,000 pta./$33).

Shopping in Bilbao

Bilbao's best shopping areas are the Old Quarter and along Gran Vía, the main drag in the modern section of town. Fine clothing shops abound, but one of the most emblematic things you can buy here is an authentic Basque *boina* (beret). The oldest hat shop in town, run by seven brothers who are fourth-generation hat makers, is **Sombreros Gorostiaga** in the Old Quarter (Victor, 9; ☎ **94-416-12-76**). If the talkative brother, Emilio, is there, he can tell you more than you ever wanted to know about berets, including how to prop one on your head like a Basque. A good beret, durable enough for daily wear in Bilbao's constant mist, runs about $20.

The Basques make a fashion statement with their berets; few men of a certain age dare leave the house without their favorite *boinas* artfully perched atop their heads. Emilio Gorostiaga, a gregarious 4th-generation Bilbao hatmaker, says that *abuelos* (old timers) buy a new beret and stick it under the mattress for a year, until they deem it wearable. The lesson? Never fold your beret; you must store it perfectly flat. And never, never buy a *boina* that's not 100 percent wool. Such a beginner's mistake is considered sacrilege in these parts.

Gettin' jazzed

Be-boppers dig the Basque Country in summer, when three major jazz festivals play the north of Spain. The **Bilbao Getxo Jazz Festival,** which got its start in 1976, hits the stage the first week of July with names such as Phil Wood. **Jazzaldia,** the San Sebastián Jazz Festival, has grown steadily since the mid-'60s. Branching out with performers like Branford Marsalis and Van Morrison, it happens the last week in July. A short drive from either of those cities is Vitoria, which hosts a highly touted festival in mid-July. In past summers, Pat Metheny, Chick Corea, and Wynton Marsalis have all dropped in on the **Vitoria-Gasteiz Festival de Jazz.**

You can obtain schedules and ticket information for the Basque Country Jazz Festivals at the following numbers and Internet addresses: in **Bilbao** (☎ 94-491-40-80; Internet: www.getxo.net); in **San Sebastián** (☎ 943-48-11-79; Internet: www.jazzaldia.com); in **Vitoria** (☎ 945-14-19-19; Internet: www.jazzvitoria.com).

Enjoying tapas bars and more: Bilbao's nightlife

Bilbao's best nightlife scene is the one spilling out of the *tapas* bars in the *Casco Viejo.* Basques are enthusiastic about food, and all that excited noise you hear is probably people talking about what they've just eaten. Crammed in the *Siete Calles* district of the Old Quarter are more bars than you can ever visit; stick your head in any that seem appealing and snatch some snacks off the bar. Join the flow as it rolls on to the next spot and repeat steps one through three.

Tapas in the Basque Country are so elaborate that they are named for the toothpicks — *pintxos* — that you use to control the small stacks of smoked salmon, marinated squid, tortilla, salt cod, and pastries stuffed with chicken and capers. Walk into a bar, and you may think you've stumbled onto the world's best party — only no party serves hors d'oeuvres like this.

If you've had your fill of *pintxos,* or you're looking for something more sedate, check out the **Teatro Arriaga,** Bilbao's monument to high culture. Opera, dance, and a wide variety of concerts play at the theater, a nineteenth-century gem renovated and reopened in the 1980s. Call ☎ 94-416-33-33 for program information. Bilbao also has the **Gran Casino Nervión** (Calle Navarra, 1; ☎ 94-424-00-07), open daily from 5 p.m. to 5 a.m.

Fast Facts: Bilbao

Area Code

The area code for telephone numbers in Bilbao is **94**. You must dial it with all local numbers.

Currency Exchange

You can exchange currency either at banks downtown, near Gran Vía and Plaza Moyúa, or at *casas de cambio* (exchange houses). The Bilbao airport also has a currency exchange.

Emergencies

For medical emergencies, contact Servicio Vasco Salud (☎ **94-410 00 00**). For police emergencies, call ☎ **092**.

Hospitals

Hospital de Basurto is found at Avenida de Montevideo, 18 (☎ **94-441-88-00**).

Information

Call ☎ **010** to obtain general visitor information. Bilbao Tourism Offices are located at the airport and just outside the Guggenheim Museum. Their hours are Mon–Fri 11 a.m. to 2 p.m. and 4 to 6 p.m.; Saturday 11 a.m. to 2 p.m. and 5 to 7 p.m.; Sunday 11 a.m. to 2 p.m.

Police

The main police station is located at Calle Luís Briñas, 14. Call ☎ **092**.

Post Office

The Central Post Office is at Calle Avenida Urquijo, 19 (☎ **94-422-05-48**). It's open Mon–Fri 8:30 a.m. to 9 p.m. and Saturday from 8 a.m. to 8 p.m.

San Sebastián

San Sebastián (called *Donostia* in the Basque language) is the capital of tiny *Guipúzcoa* province. Sandwiched between two hills (*Monte Urgull* and *Monte Iguelda*) and fronting a beautiful half-moon bay *(Bahía de la Concha)*, the city is one of Spain's most beautifully situated. Two long beaches, La Concha and Ondarreta, follow the gentle curve of the bay. Those beaches are why San Sebastián, a city of just 180,000 residents, swells with summer vacationers and French weekenders from just across the border.

San Sebastián, once a quiet fishing village, became a fashionable resort for aristocrats and royalty in the late nineteenth century, after Queen Isabel II headed to this coast in search of a cure for a pesky skin ailment. The royal court, including her son King Alfonxo XII and Queen María Cristina, followed, building the Miramar Palace and transforming the *Bahía de la Concha* into one of Spain's chicest spots.

The city retains much of its past grandeur. Besides the handsome esplanade and beaches, the most interesting section of town is the **Parte Vieja,** the Old Quarter. San Sebastián also hosts important annual jazz and film festivals, which attract big-name international stars of both arts.

San Sebastián

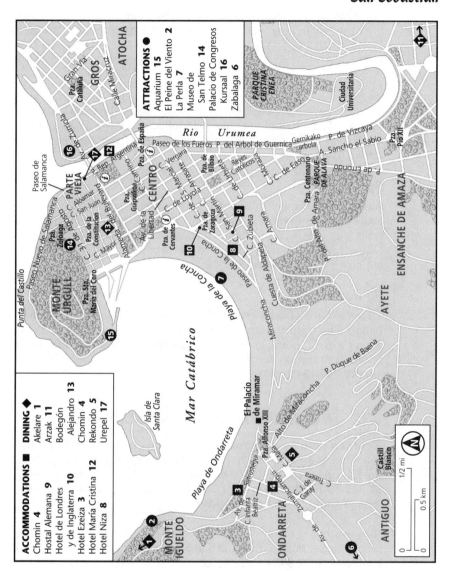

ATTRACTIONS ●
Aquarium **15**
El Peine del Viento **2**
La Perla **7**
Museo de
San Telmo **14**
Palacio de Congresos
Kursaal **16**
Zabalaga **6**

ACCOMMODATIONS ■
Chomin **4**
Hostal Alemana **9**
Hotel de Londres
y de Inglaterra **10**
Hotel Ezeiza **3**
Hotel María Cristina **12**
Hotel Niza **8**

DINING ◆
Akelare **1**
Arzak **11**
Bodegón
Alejandro **13**
Chomin **4**
Rekondo **5**
Urepel **17**

Arriving in San Sebastián

Unless you're embarking on a route through the Basque Country, take the bus between Bilbao and San Sebastián instead of renting a car. The toll roads in the Basque Country are among the highest in Spain — between the two cities you have to shell out nearly 3,000 pta. ($17). The bus costs just 1,120 pta. ($6) and takes only an hour.

By air

The city's airport, **Aeropuerto de San Sebastián,** is 20 km (12 miles) from the city in Fuenterrabia (☎ 943-66-85-00). Frequent **Bizcai Buses** (6 a.m. to 10:30 p.m.) travel to San Sebastián from the airport (130 pta./ 75¢).

By car

You can reach San Sebastián from Bilbao along the main coastal highway, A-8. From Pamplona, take A-15 followed by N-1. From Barcelona, the fastest route is through Pamplona (A-15); from Madrid, through Bilbao (A-68).

By bus

San Sebastián is well connected with major cities. The routes are especially painless in the Basque Country, where the bus is faster than the train. The city is an hour and 15 minutes from Bilbao and just over 1½ hours from Pamplona (buses leave every half hour). The bus station is at Plaza Pío XII; ☎ 902-10-12-10.

By train

Trains to San Sebastián roll in from Madrid and Barcelona, as well as Bilbao. The train station, **Estación el Norte** (for RENFE trains), is at Avenida de Francia s/n (☎ 943-28-30-89). **Estación de Amara** (for Eusko Tren trains), for Basque Country trains, is found at Plaza Easo, s/n (☎ 943-45-01-31).

Getting around San Sebastián

A car is a good way to explore the Basque Countryside, but San Sebastián is small enough that you can walk virtually everywhere but the hilltop lookouts. Rental car agencies include: **Hertz** (Zubieta, 5; ☎ 943-46-10-84); **Europcar** (Estación de RENFE; ☎ 943-32 23 04); and **Avis** (Triunfo, 2; ☎ 943-46-15-27).

Frequent buses are available to other major cities in the region (see the preceding section "Arriving in San Sebastián,"); bus service also runs to Funterrabia (☎ 943-64-13-02), Guernica (☎ 94-454-05-44), and many other small towns in the Basque Country. Buses depart from Plaza Pío II.

If you need to hail a cab, try either **Taxis Donosti** (☎ 943-46-46-46) or **Vallina** (☎ 943-40-40-40).

Staying in San Sebastián

A popular summer destination, San Sebastián has tons of hotels for its small size (but that doesn't mean they don't fill up — note my use of the word *popular*). The most desirable are near either of the two main beaches or right on La Concha promenade, and you have a good range of options — from comfortable, family-run, small hotels to grand, Belle Époque places.

Avoid San Sebastián in July and August if you can, when hotels fill to capacity and charge special supplements (if you do come during this time, make reservations far in advance).

Chomin
$$ Ondarreta (beachfront)

With just eight rooms in a quiet residential neighborhood, this is like staying at a friend's house — if you had a friend lucky enough to live in a chalet a short walk from San Sebastián's perfect beach. Rooms are simple but charming and very comfortable, and the restaurant of the same name is an excellent value (it takes precedence, in fact; the rooms are merely a bonus). No breakfast, though. (So make do with a croissant on the street, go to the beach, and then come back for a shower and lunch. Problem solved.)

Avda. Infanta Beatriz, 16. ☎ *943-21-07-05. Fax: 943-21-14-01. E-mail:* chomin@ facilnet.es. *Parking: free, on street. Rates: 8,000–10,000 pta. ($44–$55) double. MC, V.*

Hostal Alemana
$$ Playa de La Concha

One flight up in a handsome downtown building, this small, friendly little hotel with large rooms is perfect for kids. It's one of San Sebastián's better bargains if you're looking for something simple and straightforward, and rooms are surprisingly large for the price (Room 203 is downright huge). And they're sparkling, as are the bathrooms.

San Martín, 53 (first floor). ☎ *943-46-25-44. Fax: 943-46-17-71. Parking: 1,300 pta. ($7) nearby. Rates: 8,500–10,500 pta. ($47–$58) double. AE, DC, MC, V.*

Hotel Ezeiza
$$ Ondarreta (beachfront)

A small, modern, and clean hotel in a residential neighborhood, the Ezeiza ("ay-*thay*-tha") doesn't exactly bubble over with personality, but it's virtually on top of fashionable Ondarreta beach. Some rooms have views of Montes Urgull and Igueldo, and the place features a nice restaurant and terrace, as well as free parking.

Avenida Satrustegui, 13. ☎ *943-21-43-11. Fax: 943-21-47-68. Parking: Free. Rates: 11,900–15,000 pta. ($66–$83) double. AE, MC, V.*

Hotel de Londres y de Inglaterra
$$$–$$$$ **Playa de La Concha**

The name of this nineteenth-century hotel (translated as "Hotel of London and of England") loudly proclaims its stately English character. Known simply as the Hotel Londres, it has one of San Sebastián's best locations: It faces the bay and La Concha beach, and is a short walk from the Old Quarter. The hotel was recently remodeled, and guest rooms are tasteful, formal, and spacious with modern marble bathrooms. Rooms with gorgeous views of the bay cost more but are worth it in a place as pretty as San Sebastián.

Zubieta, 2. ☎ *943-44-07-70 or 900-42-90-00. Fax: 943-44-04-91. E-mail:* h.londres@paisvasco.com. *Internet:* http://paisvasco.com/hotl/londres. *Parking: 2,000 pta. ($11) nearby. Rates: 21,600–23,700 pta. ($120–$132) double. AE, DC, MC, V.*

Hotel María Cristina
$$$$$ **New City**

This is your place of refuge if you want to live like a queen or a pampered film star (and really, who doesn't?). The María Cristina now hosts all the A-list stars during the San Sebastián Film Festival, but the Belle Époque hotel has been the choice of aristocrats and the merely wealthy since its opening in 1912. As befitting as the Queen it's named after, the hotel is grand and graceful, with opulent halls and lavish rooms, but to some it may feel overly formal, or even snooty, in a town as unfussy as San Sebastián. It's perched on the banks of the River Urumea but not right on the bay, as are some other hotels.

Paseo República Argentina, 4. ☎ *888-625-5144 in the U.S., or 943-42-49-00 in Spain. Fax: 943-42-39-14. E-mail:* hmc@ittsheraton.com. *Internet:* www.sheraton.com. *Parking: 2,500 pta. ($14). Rates: 31,000–67,200 pta. ($172–$373) double. AE, DC, MC.*

Hotel Niza
$$$ **Playa de La Concha**

The Niza is the perfect hotel for San Sebastián. It's small, family-run (owned by relatives of the great Basque sculptor Eduardo Chillida), and absolutely charming. A hotel since the 1920s, it's dead center in the middle of La Concha, with incomparable views of the entire bay and the promenade. The hotel is warmly decorated, with antiques, bright modern colors, and a cool, old elevator. Rooms aren't huge, but the whole place is so comfortable and *encantador* (enchanting) that I prefer it to many of the fancier hotels in town. Try to snag a room with sea views (make reservations as far in advance as possible). Breakfast is served in a café right on the promenade, part of a cute pizzaria run by the hotel.

Zubieta, 56. ☎ *943-42-66-63. Fax: 943-44-12-51. E-mail:* niza@adegi.es. *Internet:* www.adegi.es/hotelniza. *Parking: 1,700 pta. ($9) nearby. Rates: 14,100–16,500 pta. ($78–$92) double. AE, DC, MC, V.*

Dining in San Sebastián: An unrivaled restaurant scene

Basques, other Spaniards say, live to eat. And San Sebastián is the pinnacle of that culinary universe, the home of *nueva cocina vasca* (nouvelle Basque cuisine). San Sebastián has as many top-rated restaurants as Madrid and Barcelona, both of which dwarf this coastal city in size. In fact, it has more Michelin-starred restaurants than anywhere else in Spain. This is the one city to indulge your appetite and inflate your budget (but hopefully not your waistline!).

Nothing demonstrates what food nuts the locals are like the private, all-male gastronomic societies that flourish in this small city. Born in San Sebastián in the nineteenth century, more than 100 of these societies (called *txokos*) still exist, still reveling in the culinary creativity of the coast, still eating to their hearts' contents, and, alas, still not allowing in women except for special occasions.

Eating in San Sebastián is considerably more expensive than other places in Spain, but what can I say? It's worth it. A less expensive, but in many ways equally excellent way to dine is to join the *poteo* (nightly *tapas* crawl). See "Out on the poteo: San Sebastián's nightlife" later in this chapter.

Eating like a Basque

You don't have to look hard for local specialties, including: *bacalao al pil-pil* (salt cod in garlic and red pepper sauce); *marmitako* (tuna and potato stew); *besugo* (sea bream); *bacalao a la viscaína* (stewed salt cod in fresh tomatoes); *angulas* (baby eels in garlic); *kokotxas* (hake cheeks — Basques swear they're a delicacy — in green sauce); and *txangurro* (stuffed spider crab).

In other parts of Spain, a *tapas* (hors d'oeuvres) crawl is called a *tapeo*. In the Basque Country, where *tapas* are more commonly called *pintxos,* the crawl goes by another name: *poteo* ("poe-*tay*-oh"). Whatever you call it, it's a great way to assemble a great meal on your feet and barhop at the same time. See "Out on the poteo: San Sebastian's nightlife" later in this chapter for some tasty recommendations.

Drinking like a Basque

The drink of choice up north is *txakolí* ("cha-koh-*lee*"), a young white wine produced only in the Basque Country and typically poured with dazzling dexterity, from high above the barman's head. Txakolí goes especially well with pintxos. If this fizzy wine doesn't do it for you, choose from among many excellent Rioja and Ribera del Duero red and white wines. *Sidra,* or low-alcohol cider, is also popular with the locals.

Akelare

$$$$$ Monte Igueldo (just outside San Sebastián)   BASQUE

In a chalet perched on Igueldo Hill overlooking the Bay of La Concha and the Cantabrian Sea, this classic restaurant's sweeping views are every bit as spectacular as its menu. By most accounts, chef-owner Pedro Subijana is neck-and-neck with or just trails his rival Arzak (see the following description). Whether you opt for classic dishes, like sea bass with green peppers, or more innovative preparations, like puff pastries stuffed with anchovies, you're sure to find the experience memorable. The in-house pastries are delectable. The restaurant is about 5 miles west of San Sebastián, in Barrio de Igueldo on Monte Igueldo.

Paseo del Padre Orcolaga, 56. ☎ *943-21-20-52. By car, drive up Paseo del Faro to Monte Igueldo and continue west for about 4 miles. The restaurant is on your right. Reservations required. Main courses: 2,400–4,900 pta. ($13–$27); menú del día 8,700 pta. ($48). AE, DC, MC, V. Open: lunch, Tues–Sun; dinner, Tues–Sat. Closed Feb and Oct 1–15.*

Arzak

$$$$$ East of San Sebastián (on way to Pasajes)   BASQUE

Juan Mari Arzak is San Sebastián's diplomat in a chef's coat. His restaurant, a simple-looking cottage (built by his grandparents in 1897) on the outskirts of town, has earned the praises of presidents and queens, not to mention three Michelin stars. It is, simply, exquisite in every detail. From the classic dishes on the back of the menu to the creative flourishes he continually comes up with, this is the place to go if you're only going to have one Basque meal. From *puding de krabarroka* (rockfish terrine) to roasted gamecock and wild boar, it's so hard to choose among the mouth-watering appetizers and entrees that the fixed-price tasting menu may be the only way to go.

Alto de Miracruz, 21 (east of San Sebastián on N-I, on way to Pasajes). ☎ *943-27-84-65. Internet:* www.juanmariarzak.jet.es *(also at* www.paisvasco.com/donostia/ingles/indexi.htm*). Reservations required. Main courses 2,800–4,950 pta. ($16–$27); fixed-price tasting menu 9,500 pta. ($53). AE, DC, MC, V. Open: Lunch, Tues–Sun; dinner, Tues–Sat. Closed last two weeks of June, first three weeks of Nov.*

Bodegón Alejandro

$$$ Parte Vieja (Old Quarter)   BASQUE

Run by one of the celebrated new generation of Basque chefs called the "Berasategui boys" (see Martín B's restaurant later in this section), this charming restaurant focuses on excellent fixed-price menus. It's easily one of the best bargains in San Sebastián. The menu changes daily and always features a healthy number of mouth-watering choices. You can start with artichokes with clams and follow it up with *bacalao de la Isla de Feroe con pimientos* (salt cod, which the restaurant claims is the "Rolls Royce of cod" in red peppers). For dessert, how about the literal and linguistic mouthful, *tarteleta de chocolate con naranja amarga y helado de chocolate* (chocolate cake with orange marmalade and chocolate ice cream)? There are two inviting dining rooms with bright yellow walls and colorful *azulejos*, or tiles.

Fermín Calbetón, 4. ☎ 943-42-71-58. Reservations required. Main courses: 1,200–2,400 pta. ($7–$13); menú del día, weekdays lunch 1,850 pta. ($10); evening and weekends, 2,900 pta. ($16). AE, MC, V. Open: Lunch, Tues–Sun; dinner, Tues–Sat. Closed last two weeks Dec.

Chomin

$$$ Ondarreta   BASQUE

Some top Basque restaurants threaten to burst your vacation budget. Not Chomin. Prices at this comfortable, friendly restaurant on the first floor of a private chalet are extremely reasonable given the quality of the cooking and service. Near Ondarreta beach in a quiet neighborhood, Chomin's worth seeking out, especially for the mid-day lunch deal, a real steal. The *brocheta de rape y langostinos* (kebab of monkfish and prawns) and steak tartare are especially savory. A standard, the *merluza Chomin* (white fish with clams) amounts to comfort food for spoiled locals.

Infanta Beatriz, 16. ☎ 943-21-21-59. Reservations required. Main courses: 1,975–2,850 pta. ($11–$16); tasting menu 3,000 pta. ($17); midday, 1,600 ($9). AE, MC, V. Open: Lunch, Tues–Sun; dinner, Tues–Sat. Closed last two weeks in Dec, first week in Jan.

Martín Berasategui

$$$$$ Lasarte-Oria (outskirts of San Sebastián)   BASQUE

The restaurant bearing the name of one of the new generation's star chefs is just outside San Sebastián on the way to Fuenterrabia. Berasategui, still in his 30s, has amassed a number of restaurants, including the one at the Guggenheim in Bilbao, and even more accolades (including the Euskadi Gastronomy Award for best Basque chef). He's one of the Basque Country's most innovative chefs. Try the smoked-eel soup or grilled tuna, served in a crème of artichokes, asparagus, clams, and squid. For a superlative culinary experience, order the nine-course tasting menu — a meal that will make the highlight reel of your trip to Spain.

Loidi, 4. In Lasarte-Oria, 4 miles from San Sebastián. ☎ 943-36-64-71. By car, take the N-1 highway south to the small town Lasarte-Oria and ask anyone for the well-known restaurant (pronounced "mahr-teen bear-ah-sah-tay-ghee"). Reservations required. Main courses: 2,000–3,900 pta. ($11–$22); menú del día 8,500 pta. ($47). AE, DC, MC, V. Open: Lunch, Tues–Sun; dinner, Tues–Sat. Closed Dec.

Rekondo

$$$$ Above San Sebastián (near Miramar Palace) BASQUE

Just up the hill from San Sebastián proper, beyond the Miramar Palace, Rekondo is the kind of place that draws everyday diners and families and couples celebrating special occasions. The menu is terse and focuses on the Basque basics: squid in their own ink, lamb chops, and fish dishes of turbot and sea bream. The kitchen's great, but many savvy diners here are wine lovers who come for the wine cellar. One of Spain's best, it boasts more than 100,000 bottles, including some very rare vintages. It's the kind of place you can blow a big wad of cash on a special *Gran Reserva* wine from your birthday year.

Paseo Igueldo, 57. ☎ *943-21-29-07. Reservations required. Main courses: 1,950–3,600 pta. ($11–$20). AE, DC, MC, V. Open: lunch and dinner, Thur–Tues (July–Aug, daily). Closed last two weeks in June and first three weeks of Nov.*

Urepel

$$$$ New City BASQUE

Classically decorated, with dark wood and flowered wallpaper, this handsome, intimate restaurant serves some of the best food in San Sebastián. It's great for classic dishes like grilled sea bass in tomato vinaigrette or roasted venison, but Urepel's team of chefs continues to introduce new, innovative fare. Though a little formal looking, the restaurant draws a diverse crowd — from seniors to hipsters. It's prices are reasonable, at least for the five-star crowd.

Paseo Salamanca, 3. ☎ *943-42-40-40. Reservations required. Main courses: 1,800–3,100 pta. ($10–$17). AE, DC, MC, V. Open: Lunch and dinner, Wed–Sat; lunch only, Tues. Closed mid-June–mid-July, last two weeks Dec, Easter week.*

The cider house rules

After you have your fill of fancy Basque restaurants, you may need something a little down-n-dirty to bring you back to earth. Soaring in popularity are rustic *sidrerías* ("seed-ray-*ree*-ahs"), or cider houses, on the slopes of the hills overlooking San Sebastián. From mid-January to the end of March, you can grab a simple meal and as many glasses of fresh, low-alcohol cider as you can drink, served from the spigots of giant oak vats. You sit at long wooden picnic tables; the simple fare — a codfish omelet, beef or *bacalao* (salt cod) with green pepper — is brought out on metal trays with an enormous baguette. The cider is the real star, though its slightly sour taste may not be for everyone. In truth, the meal is mainly an excuse to have something to do between trips back to the vat room to fill up your glass. If it's really crowded, the owner may come around, authorizing tables one at a time to rise and ritualistically collect their cider. Contact the **Tourism Office** (Calle Reina Regente, s/n; ☎ 943-48-11-66) for a list of *sidrerías* open in season.

Exploring San Sebastián

San Sebastián is a great walking city, but if you want to make the rounds quickly and conveniently, the city recently introduced a tour bus, **Donostia Tour** (Bus Turístico). It offers 27 stops throughout the city and allows passengers to get on and off as many times as they wish during a single day. The route begins twice daily, Tuesday through Sunday, at 12 p.m. and 2 p.m. The entire route takes 1 hour, 50 minutes. It leaves from CAT (*Centro de Atracción y Turismo,* the Center of Attractions & Tourism) Calle Reina Regente s/n, though you can purchase tickets on board at any of the 27 stops.

Want a great overview of the city? For gorgeous perspectives of San Sebastián laid out beneath you, drive or take the *funicular* (cable car) up to the top of Monte Igueldo (the hill on the left as you face the bay). (The funicular leaves from Plaza del Funicular, 4; ☎ **943-21-05-64;** 10 a.m. to 8 p.m. in summer, 11 a.m. 6 p.m. in winter.) You can visit a small theme park (with a turn-of-the-century roller coaster) and a rather bland hotel up here, but the main thing is the spectacular view of the town and its perfect shell-shaped beach, promenade, leafy avenues, and Belle Époque buildings. Early evening is the best time, because the city lights begin to sparkle. If you're driving, you may want to consider eating at top-rated Akelare, farther along the coast (see description of Akelare in the preceding restaurant section).

At the base of Monte Igueldo and the end of Ondarreta Beach is a small plaza and one of Basque artist Eduardo Chillida's most famous sculptures, *El Peine del Viento* (The Wind Comb). Rust-colored iron pieces thrust out of the rock, just above the crashing surf of the Cantabrian. It's an evocative work — and a beautiful spot at the edge of the sea.

The grounds and gardens of **Palacio Miramar,** the former summer palace of the royal family, sits on a small hill above the two main beaches and is also a lovely, relaxing spot with pretty views. A leisurely stroll, including a funicular ride, may take two to three hours.

Strolling the Promenade

As much as the Basques of San Sebastián love to eat, it's not surprising that people are always out walking. The **Paseo de la Concha/Paseo Nuevo Promenade,** along the beach, is one of the most inviting places for a stroll you're likely to step foot upon. Even in the dead of winter, I couldn't resist taking the steps down to the beach and kicking off my shoes. People are out at all hours, but particularly before and after mealtimes. A white iron railing, tamarind trees, and turn-of-the-century apartment buildings line the walkway. As you near the *Parte Vieja,* you come upon the *Ayuntamiento* (City Hall) and a plaza with an old-time carousel.

Another tempting place to stroll is along the left bank of the **River Urumea,** which stretches from the neighborhood of Amara down to the

Old Quarter. You pass the Victorian-looking María Cristina Hotel and Victoria Eugenia Theater. Allow an hour or two for strolling.

Prowling the Parte Vieja

Around the curve of the bay, just before Monte Ugull, is the *Parte Vieja* (Old Quarter), where San Sebastián was born. It's a handsome tangle of small streets and fishermen houses that really comes alive in the afternoon and evening, when people flood the *tapas* bars. (Don't miss performing your own *pintxo* crawl.) The heart of the Old Quarter is **Plaza de la Constitución,** a handsome yellow-and-white arcaded square affectionately called "La Consti." The other important old town site is the **Museo de San Telmo** (Plaza Zuloaga, 1; ☎ 943-42-49-70; free admission; Tuesday through Saturday, 10 a.m. to 1 p.m. and 4 to 8 p.m.). A museum of Basque culture, it's housed in a sixteenth-century convent and features European and Basque art from the fifteenth to nineteenth centuries. Perhaps most notable, however, are the spectacular canvas panels by José María Sert that decorate the interior of the church. The canvasses depict episodes in Basque history.

San Sebastián dates back to the Middle Ages, but much of the city has been repeatedly destroyed by 12 major fires. The worst was in 1813, when Anglo-Portuguese liberators wrestled the city from Napoleon's troops and, like football hooligans who won the game, ended up sacking and burning the city. People who live on 31 de Agosto Street, near the *Basilica de Santa Maria* in the *Parte Vieja,* commemorate the episode by lighting candles in their windows every August 31. You can peek around the Old Quarter in less than an hour, unless you get hungry and start ducking in a few *tapas* bars.

More cool things to see and do

 ✔ **Getting a fish-eye view.** San Sebastián's recently revamped **Aquarium,** with an underwater walkway that provides a 360-degree view of marine life swimming around you, is a good spot for kids. It's not the biggest or best aquarium you'll ever see, but I'd give kids at least an hour here. It's in the port, near the Parte Vieja (Paseo del Meulle, 34; ☎ 943-44-00-99). Hours are Monday through Sunday 10 a.m. to 8 p.m. Admission for adults 1,100 pta. ($6); children ages 5–10 550 pta. ($2.70); children under 5 free.

 ✔ **Visiting Zabalaga, Chillida's Sculpture Museum.** Eduardo Chillida, born in San Sebastián in 1924, is arguably Spain's foremost living artist and definitely one of the world's great sculptors. In 1998, he received the International Sculpture Center's Lifetime Achievement Award. Zabalaga, the sixteenth-century *caserío* (farmhouse) he bought and restored, is a magnificent showcase — as are the bucolic acres of wooded grounds — for his architectural sculptures in stone and iron. Inside the house are several smaller pieces, including early works, and the artist's famous works on paper, called *Gravitations.* The museum, finally opened after a two-year delay, is a private initiative of the Chillida family, with the support of the Basque government. Allow a couple of hours, including transportation (the farmhouse is in the suburbs of San Sebastián).

Cacería Zabalaga, Barrio Jauregi, 66, in Hernani. ☎ **943-33-60-06.** Admission: 850 pta. ($4.75). Open: Wed – Mon 10:30am– 2pm. To get there: Take the bus marked "Hernani" from downtown San Sebastián; the bus stop is just after the Campsa gas station after the turnoff from the highway. Inquire at the **Tourism Office** (Reina Regente, s/n; ☎ **943-48-11-66** or 943-27-12-79) for additional transportation information.

↳ **Relaxing at a spa.** If you're the type who comes back from vacation needing a vacation, then **La Perla,** one of Europe's top spas, is a must-visit. La Perla's ample facilities, including the soothing water therapy circuit, sit smack in the middle of Paseo de la Concha area. Tired after a long day of walking and sightseeing? Try the amazingly restorative series of pool stations that isolate parts of your tired body against water jets; allow you to relax on waterbeds or beneath waterfalls; and massage your aching feet in thick-grained, sand-bottom pools. There's even direct beach access, so you can dart out for a swim in the bay and come back for more therapy. Day visits are welcomed (and if you just can't tear yourself away, La Perla also has a gym and café-restaurant overlooking the bay). Single visits range from 2,300 pta. ($13) for a one-hour-and-45-minute session to 3,000 pta. ($17) for a five-hour session — a real deal. **The Perla Café-Restaurant** overlooking the bay is also a good stop for lunch after you spendthe morning taking the waters (☎ **943-45-88-56;** E-mail: info@la-perla.net; Internet: www.paisvasco.com/donostia/ingles/indexi.htm).

↳ **Basking at the Beaches.** Beach-loving Spaniards from the sultry center and south of the country flock to San Sebastián in summer. The city has three beaches right in the middle of the City: **La Concha, Ondarreta,** and **La Zurriola.** La Concha, one of the most splendid urban beaches in Europe, became famous in the mid-nineteenth century, when Queen Isabel made pilgrimages there for skin treatments. Ondarreta, at the foot of Monte Igueldo, features aristocratic villas and gardens overlooking sunbathers. In the mid-'90s, San Sebastián inaugurated a new beach, La Zurriola, on the right of the river Urumea (near the striking Palacio de Congresos Kursaal).

During summer, if the beaches get too crowded (or the number of bare breasts on display becomes overwhelming), you can hop a boat out to the city's fourth beach, on **Santa Clara Island** in the middle of the bay. It's less crowded and more family-oriented. Inquire along the beach or at the central tourism office for information about ticket prices and times for boats traveling to the island (it's all very informal, and there are no set schedules).

✔ **Giving Kudos to *Los Cubos*.** That attention-getting angled white box of a building on the Zurriola Beach and the banks of the Urumea River is the **Palacio de Congresos Kursaal,** San Sebastián's new convention center. Affectionately, or perhaps quizzically, known to locals as *Los Cubos* (The Cubes), the startling building is the work of the renowned prizewinning architect Rafael Moneo, who's also been entrusted with the enlargement of the Prado Museum in Madrid. It's a great place to drop in for lunch: The restaurant and cafeteria in the building are the work of the renowned Basque chef Martín Berasategui (see "Dining in San Sebastián," earlier in this chapter for an overview of the restaurant).

Shopping in San Sebastian

As a destination for summering Spaniards and across-the-border weekenders, San Sebastián has plenty of chic shops all along the bay and throughout the new city. Yet your best bet may be to pick up something authentically Basque, like the classic berets worn by older gentlemen year-round. Pick up a *boina* (beret) at **Casa Ponsol,** the oldest hat shop in San Sebastián, founded in 1838. It's at the corner of Narrica and Plaza de Sarriegui.

Out on the poteo: San Sebastián's nightlife

Hands down the best nighttime activity in San Sebastián is joining the rowdy, famished natives on a *poteo* (*tapas* crawl) in the Parte Vieja neighborhood. Locals say that San Sebastián's Parte Vieja holds the world record for most bars per square meter. (It's a wonder no U.S. party schools offer study-abroad programs in San Sebastián.)

The Old Quarter near the waterfront positively swims with appetizing little taverns, each offering bar counters full of the best little meals on a toothpick you've ever seen. Calling these *objets d'art* mere snacks is hardly fair; they beat the pants off of cocktail weenies. Among the popular *pintxo* spots in the Parte Vieja are **Bar Martínez** (31 de Agosto, 13); **Ganbara** (San Jerónimo, 21); and **La Cepa** (31 de Agosto, 7).

Starting to feel like all you do in Spain (and especially San Sebastián) is eat, eat, eat? You can lose a couple pounds sweating it out at a disco — check out **Rotonda,** on Paseo de la Concha, 6 — or just watch your wallet get thinner at the **Casino de San Sebastián,** in the swank Hotel Londres (Zubieta, 2; ☎ 943-42-92-15), which has been around since the turn-of-the-century.

Lights, camera, actors!

Ever since Queen Isabel II, San Sebastián has courted royalty. Now it's royalty of a different sort that hits the Cantabrian coast. While not as well known as Cannes, Berlin, or Venice, the annual **San Sebastián International Film Festival** is one of the most important in Europe. Every September, the silver screen's firmament showers this small Basque city — past guests have included Bette Davis, Johnny Depp, and Martin Scorsese. If you're here then, join the paparazzi party at the María Cristina Hotel.

Taking side trips from San Sebastián

If you're looking for a small package tour to explore some of the Basque Country or sample the great outdoors, **Green Services Tours** organizes a bundle of visits throughout the Basque Country. Their guided tours and excursions include the Guggenheim in Bilbao, Fuenterrabia, and horseback and hot-air balloon rides. Contact them through **Viajes Olatz,** (Calle Fermín Calbetón, 44; ☎ **943-27-77-33**).

Pasajes de San Juan

Visiting this fishing village (called *Pasaia Donibane* in the Basque language) doesn't actually get you too far out of town — it's only 6 miles from San Sebastián. But it's a very popular, charming spot to spend half a day and have lunch at one of the famous fish restaurants. From the neighboring village, *Pasajes de San Pedro,* you can walk or take a little blue boat across the harbor to the town. Pasajes de San Juan is a pretty (if touristy in summer) collection of balconied houses along one main street — where Victor Hugo lived in the mid-1800s. Two family seafood restaurants worth checking out are: **Casa Cámara** (San Juan, 7; ☎ **943-52-36-99**), a historic place where the lobster and crab pots are hoisted up through the floor of the dining room; and **Txulotxo** (San Juan, 82; ☎ **943-52-39-52**), an attractive stone restaurant overlooking the harbor.

To get there: Take a bus marked "Pasaje de San Pedro" from Calle Aldamar in San Sebastián or a taxi. Even if you have a car, travel by bus or taxi because the area is a bottleneck waiting to fill up.

Fuenterrabia

About 15 miles along the coast on the way to France — through spectacular mountain countryside — is this historic and pretty seaside resort (called *Hondarribia* in Basque). The town, extremely popular in summer, has thick medieval walls, stone houses with coats of arms and colorful balconies, and a tenth-century castle that today is a *parador.* It also has a nice, long beach and marina.

If you want to stay overnight, the **Parador de Hondarribia Carlos V** is one of the best of the *parador* bunch (Plaza de Armas, 14; ☎ 943-64-55-00; Fax: 943-64-21-53; Internet: www.parador.es; Rate: 15,500–19,500 pta./$86–$108). Much smaller, but also in an attractive medieval structure, is **Hotel Obispo** (Plaza del Obispo; ☎ 943-64-54-00; Fax: 943-64-23-86; E-mail: bidasoa@camerdata.es; Internet: www.camerdata.es/bidasoa/obispo). A cool, atmospheric little restaurant is **Sebastián** (Mayor 9–11; ☎ 943-64-01-67), while the fanciest place to dine is **Ramón Roteta**, just outside the city (Irún, Villa Ainara; ☎ 943- 64-16-93).

Fast Facts: San Sebastián

Area Code

The area code for telephone numbers within San Sebastián is **943**.

Currency Exchange

Currency exchange houses include Change (Avenida de la Libertad, 1; ☎ **943-43-14-93**); Agencia de Cambio (Easo, 35; ☎ **943-45-17-55**); and Change Baraca (Ijentea, 4; ☎ **943-42-06-90**).

Emergencies

Contact SOS Deiak, ☎ **112**.

Hospitals

Hospital Nuestra Señora Aranzazu is at Dr. Begiristain, 114 (☎ **943-44-70-00**). On the same street is Hospital de Guipuzkoa (Dr. Begiristain, 115; ☎ **943-45-40-00**).

Internet Access

If you need an e-mail fix, pay a visit to NET LINE (☎ **943-44-50-76**) Calle Urdaneta 8, in the center of town. Prices are: 15 minutes, 250 pta. ($1.40); 30 minutes, 400 pta. ($2.20); one hour, 750 pta. ($4). It's open from Mon–Sat 10 a.m. to 10 p.m.

Information

The main city tourism office is Centro de Atracción y Turismo de San Sebastián (Calle Reina Regente, s/n; ☎ 943-48-11-66). Open Mon–Sat 9 a.m. to 2 p.m. and 3:30 to 7 p.m.; Sunday 10 to 1 p.m. Oficina de Turismo del Gobierno Vasco, the provincial office, is at Fueros, 1 (☎ 943-42-62-82) and is open from 9 a.m. to 1:30 p.m. and 3:30 to 6:30 p.m. Mon–Fri 9 a.m. to 1 p.m. and 3:30 to 6:30 p.m. on Sat.

The Tourism Office puts out a handful of good, useful brochures: *Donostia in Two Hours* (which to my mind really undersells the appeal of the city) and *Donosti Aisia — The Guía del Ocio de San Sebastián,* which gives you all the goods on what's happening day and night.

Police

For municipal police, dial ☎ **092**. For national police, ☎ **091**. The main police station is located at Easo, 41 (☎ **943-45-00-00**).

Post Office

The Central Post Office is located at Urdaneta s/n (☎ **943-46-34-17**).

Pamplona

The principal city of the Spanish Pyrenees, **Pamplona** is the ancient fortified capital of the independent kingdom of Navarra. The province shares borders with the Basque Country, Aragón, and France.

But what everybody everywhere knows about Pamplona is that it's the site of the legendary Running of the Bulls, called the *encierro* ("en-thee-*air*-oh"), an adrenaline rush of popular culture that dramatizes Spain's up close and personal relationship with death. Ernest Hemingway wrote enthusiastically about the festival in *The Sun Also Rises,* published in 1926, and the world's been coming here in droves ever since.

The **Festival of San Fermín** (also called **Sanfermines**), during which the daily *encierros* take place, is the kind of exhilarating experience that stays with you (and you don't have to actually hit the streets ahead of the bulls to live it to the hilt). The oddest thing about one of Europe's great party scenes is that Pamplona is, the rest of the year, one of Spain's more conservative cities. Indeed, outside of the bedlam of *Sanfermines* (held every July 6–14), Pamplona doesn't rank as one of Spain's top attractions. When bulls aren't in the streets, there's not all that much to see. And when the bulls are stampeding, well, there's no place to sleep. If you're not here for the Running of the Bulls, you've probably got more on your mind — perhaps a day or two in Pamplona and some time in the countryside or the more interesting towns of the neighboring Basque Country.

Arriving in Pamplona

Most people roll into Pamplona by road or rail from other parts in the north, or perhaps from Madrid or Barcelona. You can also fly in, if you're only coming for *Sanfermines.*

By air

Flights from Madrid and Barcelona arrive at **Aeropuerto de Noáin** (☎ **948-16-87-00**), about 3 miles from Pamplona. You have to take a taxi into town (about 1,500 pta./$8). A bus does exist, but it's only a local bus that goes to the town of Noáin, and it has no luggage compartments. Take a cab.

By car

From San Sebastián, N-240 leads to Pamplona. Take the route through San Sebastián or Vitoria (N-1) from Bilbao.

By bus

Estación de Autobuses (the bus station) — a messy place guaranteed to give you bus-fume headaches — is located at Avenida Conde Oliveto, 8, at the corner of Yanguas and Miranda (☎ **948-22-38-54**), just beyond the Old Quarter. Buses arrive from most major cities and the smaller ones in Navarra and the Basque Country.

By train

The **RENFE** train station is at Avenida San Jorge s/n (☎ **948-13-02-02**). Several trains a day steam in from Madrid and Barcelona, as well as San Sebastián and Bilbao.

Pamplona

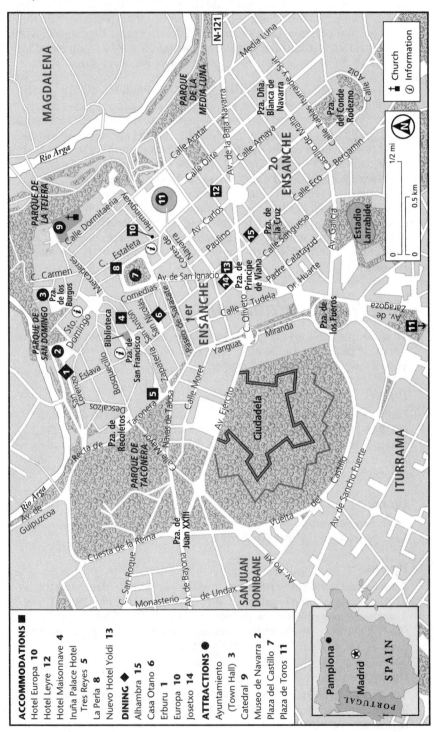

N-121

MAGDALENA

Media Luna

ENSANCHE

Pza. Dña.
Blanca de
Navarra

Pza.
del Conde
Rodezno

✝ Church
ⓘ Information

Calle Arata

*PARQUE
DE LA
MEDIA LUNA*

Calle Olite

Calle Amaya

Av. de la Baja Navarra

1/2 mi

0.5 km

Rio Arga

*PARQUE DE
LA TEJERA*

Calle Dormitaería

Av. Carlos

Paulino

Pza. de
la Cruz

Calle Sangüesa

Av. Galicia

Estadio
Larrabide

C. Carmen

C. Estafeta

ⓘ

Av. de San Ignacio

Pza. de
Príncipe
de Viana

Padre Calatayud

Dr. Huarte

*PARQUE DE
SAN DOMINGO*

Pza.
de los
Burgos

Comedias

Calle Oliveto Tudela

Pza. de
los Fueros

Av. de Zaragoza

Sto. ⓘ
Domingo

Biblioteca

Pza. de
San Francisco

Miranda

Yanguas

ENSANCHE

1er ENSANCHE

Paseo de Sarasate

Calle Moret

Av. Ejército

Ciudadela

ITURRAMA

Recta de

*PARQUE DE
TACONERA*

Cuesta de la Reina

Pza. de
Juan XXIII

Av. de Bayona

de Undax

**SAN JUAN
DONIBANE**

Monasterio

Rio Arga
Av. de
Guipuzcoa

ACCOMMODATIONS ■
Hotel Europa **10**
Hotel Leyre **12**
Hotel Maisonnave **4**
Iruña Palace Hotel
   Tres Reyes **5**
La Perla **8**
Nuevo Hotel Yoldi **13**

DINING ◆
Alhambra **15**
Casa Otano **6**
Erburu **1**
Europa **10**
Josetxo **14**

ATTRACTIONS ●
Ayuntamiento
   (Town Hall) **3**
Catedral **9**
Museo de Navarra **2**
Plaza del Castillo **7**
Plaza de Toros **11**

SPAIN

Pamplona ●
Madrid ✪

PORTUGAL

Getting around Pamplona

The Old Quarter of Pamplona is so small that you don't need more than your feet to explore it. The heart of the old city is **Plaza Castillo,** also the hub of *Sanfermines* when bulls aren't running through the streets or dodging *matadors* in the bullring. Calle Estafeta is the main street; well known to the hundreds that run in the *encierros* each year; it leads right to *the Plaza de Toros,* or bullring (well known to the bulls). Parks bound the Old Quarter: Parque de la Media Luna to one side, and Parque de La Ciudadela and Parque de La Taconera to the other.

You'll most likely only need to call a taxi to get to the bus station or airport. Whether you're getting out of town or going to dinner, though, try **Teletaxi** (☎ **948-23 23 00**); **Radio Taxi Association of Pamplona** (☎ **948-22 12 12**); or **Asociación Teletaxi Pamplona** (☎ **948-23 21**). On entering the taxi, the meter starts at 450 pta. ($2.50).

Staying in Pamplona

Pamplona has only a tiny fistful of decent hotels, a couple of which have historically been associated with the *encierros.* The following list (with the exception of the runner-up choices that may have beds during San Fermín; see the sidebar entitled "I see lotsa bulls, but where are the hotels?") describes hotels all within or very near the old center of the city. The high rate listed is always the special festival rate (often triple or more the regular rack rate). Pamplona has a centralized number for hotel reservations; call ☎ **948-20-65-41;** Fax: 948-20-70-32; E-mail: central.reservas@cfnavarra.es.

Hotel Europa

$$$

A small, charming, and family-owned hotel — originally built as a private house in the 1930s — the Europa has a great location and real intimacy. Twenty-one nicely decorated rooms (in soft pinks and purples) are tucked away upstairs, past the excellent restaurant (even the owners consider their operation a restaurant with rooms on the side). Several rooms overlook Calle Estafeta, which the bulls rumble down during the *encierros.* Oh, if you can just get a reservation during the festival. (Well, you can't. Don't even try.)

Calle Espoz y Mina, 11. ☎ *948-22-18-00. Fax: 948-22 92 35. E-mail:* heuropa@ cmn.navarra.net. *Internet:* www.sanfermin.com/europa.html. *Parking: nearby, 1,200 pta. ($7). Rates: 15,000–33,500 pta. ($83–$186) double; weekend rate 8,200 pta. ($46) double. AE, MC, V.*

I see lotsa bulls, but where are the hotels?

Pamplona's Running of the Bulls is one of Spain's greatest hits. But finding a hotel during the festival is bull . . . er, a real pain. You've either got to make a reservation six months or more in advance and dish up an absurd sum of money, or be care-free enough to try your luck at scoring a *pensión* (guesthouse) when you arrive. A mediocre $60 hotel can easily set you back $200 during Sanfermines. That's if you're lucky enough to score a reservation. Some better-known hotels in Pamplona are sold out three and four years in advance of the annual San Fermín festival, with rooms occupied by perennial bull aficionados. Even for less popular spots, you need to make reservations six months to a year in advance.

Visiting Pamplona during the Running of the Bulls is one of those situations that demands you take a good, realistic look at your budget. If you're dying to attend the week-long mayhem in July, and you don't have a reservation or a pile of dis-posable income, check with the Tourism Office for a list of some 50 *pensiones* — prices are probably double the 3,000–6,000 pta. ($17–$33) they get the rest of the year. Locals looking to make a buck also open up their homes, and it's not that difficult to score a spare bedroom for a price that, compared to what hotels are charging, is a bargain. Inquire at the tourist office or look around town for signs posted.

If the hotels with listings in this section are full, you can try these runners-up:

NH El Toro. Three miles from Pamplona, the name ("the bull") is fitting. And it's a reliable entry in the NH hotel chain. Location: Carretera de Guipúzcoa, km 5. ☎ **948-30-22-11.** Fax: 948-30-20-85. E-mail: nh@nh-hoteles.es. Internet: www.nh-hoteles.es. Rates: 12,000–24,000 pta. ($67–$133) double. AE, MC, DC, V.

NH Ciudad de Pamplona. In the modern section of town, this is a good, functional choice. Location: Iturrama, 21. ☎ **948-26-60-11.** Fax: 948-17-36-26. E-mail: nh@nh-hoteles.es. Internet: www.nh-hoteles.es. Rates: 9,700–26,900 pta. ($54–$149) double. AE, MC, DC, V.

Tryp Burlada. This major chain hotel is in Burlada, about 2 miles from Pamplona. Location: Calle La Fuente, Burlada. ☎ **948-13-13-00.** Fax: 948-12-23-46. E-mail: hotel@tryp.es. Rates: 10,475–17,200 pta. ($57–$96) double. AE, MC, DC, V.

Casa Otano. A chaotic family-run *residencia* (residence) on bar-lined San Nicolás right in the Old Quarter of Pamplona. Rates double during *Sanfermines,* but they're still cheap. You have to pay for rooms in advance. Don't expect too much (any?) sleep during the festival. Location: San Nicolás, 5. ☎ **948-22-70-36.** Fax: 948-21-20-12. Rates: 5,500–10,000 pta. ($31–$55) double. No credit cards.

Hotel Leyre

$$

A good-looking, mid-sized option not far from the Plaza de Toros (where the bulls end up after their dash through town), the Leyre is extremely comfortable. Carefully renovated in the mid-1990s, rooms have hardwood floors and colorful headboards and curtains. The hotel is associated with two of the better restaurants in town, Europa and Alhambra, and offers a deal at the first for guests. The hotel itself is a deal.

If you stay at the hotel, you can score a deal at one of Pamplona's finest restaurants, Europa: a special fixed-price menu for 2,925 pta. ($16), including wine, water, bread, and dessert. (See "Dining in Pamplona," later in this chapter.) Ask at the hotel; they'll give you an invitation with the menu selections printed on it.

Calle Leyre, 7. ☎ *948-22-85-00. Fax: 948-22-83-18. E-mail:* hleyre@cmn. navarra.net. *Internet:* http://webs.navarra.net/hleyre. *Parking 1,200 pta. ($7). Rates: 15,000–32,000 pta. ($83–$178) double; weekend rate, 9,000 pta. ($50) double. AE, DC, MC, V.*

Hotel Maisonnave

$$

A large and stylish hotel on a nice street in the Old Quarter, near Plaza de San Francisco, the Maisonnave is a fine place to crash during Sanfermines. Completely renovated in the late 90s, rooms are a bit small-ish but attractive, decorated in clean beige, white, and black tones. The hotel's calling card says it's "very personal," and for a large place, that's not far from the truth. It's a good value all year, except for that brief busy time in July.

Calle Nueva, 20. ☎ *948-22-26-00. Fax: 948-22-01-66. E-mail:* información@ hotelmaisonnave.es. *Internet:* www.hotelmaisonnave.es. *Parking: 1,200 pta. ($7). Rates: 15,700–30,000 pta. ($87–$167) double; weekend rate 8,100 pta. ($45) double. AE, DC, MC, V.*

Iruña Palace Hotel Tres Reyes

$$$

Large and modern, the Tres Reyes (Three Kings) is a good choice for anyone looking for convenience and comfort. It's downtown Pamplona's biggest and finest hotel. The cement block exterior is a little less than charming, and if the place doesn't drip with personality, it's a pretty fair value, especially on weekends. Rooms are contemporary and tasteful, and the hotel has a nice swimming pool (a plus for kids), pretty garden, and excellent gymnasium. It's located just outside the Old Quarter, on the edge of La Taconera Park, but within easy walking distance — an important factor during the all-hours craziness of San Fermín.

Jardines de la Taconera, s/n. ☎ *948-22-66-00. Fax: 948-22-29-30. E-mail:* hotel3rayas@abc.ibernet.com. *Parking: 1,500 pta. ($8) indoors; free out-side. Rates: 21,000–39,500 pta. ($117–219) double; weekend rate 14,000 pta. ($78). AE, DC, MC, V.*

La Perla

$$

La Perla (The Pearl) is old-fashioned — a kind way to say that it's a little dumpy — but it's still a classic Pamplona hotel. (I'm sure it was once classy.) The oldest in town, inaugurated in 1880 on Plaza del Castillo, the main square, it overlooks Calle Estafeta. In its glory years, it hosted Ernest Hemingway and continues to draw legions of fans of the annual *encierros.*

Plaza del Castillo, 1. ☎ *948-22-77-06. Fax: 948-22-15-19. No parking available. Rates: 9,000–33,000 pta. ($50–$183). AE, DC, MC, V.*

Nuevo Hotel Yoldi

$$

The Yoldi is a simple, quiet, and functional hotel that only comes to life during the San Fermín Festival. Very near the Plaza de Toros, it hosts just about all of the best-known bullfighters in attendance for the *corridas* (bullfights). They stay here year after year (they're a superstitious bunch) as do their obsessed followers. The Yoldi ranks, along with La Perla, as *the* San Fermín hotel. Don't even dream of getting a booking during the party, though; it's booked four years in advance.

Avenida San Ignacio, 11. ☎ *948-22-48-00. Fax: 948-21-20-45. E-mail:* hyoldi@ cmn.navarra.net. *Internet:* http://webs.navarra.net/~hyoldi. *Parking: 1,000 pta. ($5.50). Rates: 16,000–28,500 pta. ($89–158) double; weekend rate 7,200 pta. ($40) double. AE, DC, MC, V.*

Dining in Pamplona

You can eat very well in Pamplona; the haute cuisine of the nearby Basque Country and more rustic dishes from the mountains of Navarra influence the fine dining.

During Sanfermines, *always* make advance dinner reservations so that you won't waste time in line or risk not getting into the restaurant of your choice. Fortunately, lots of places are open around the clock. All of the restaurants I recommend in this section are within walking distance of Plaza del Castillo in the Old Quarter.

Eating like a Navarrese

Several of the dishes you find in the Basque Country are also stars of restaurants in Pamplona. But in general, the food in Navarra is simpler, with a greater emphasis on game, lamb, and trout. Dishes to try include: *pimientos rellenos* (spicy red pepper stuffed with fish, meat or shellfish); *trucha a la Navarra* (grilled or fried trout, stuffed with cured ham); and *cochifrito* (lamb stew). When you've got the munchies, get your hands on *queso Roncal* (cured sheep's milk cheese) and *chistorra* (a local variety of chorizo sausage).

Drinking like a Navarrese

Choose one of the fine reds from Ribera del Duero or La Rioja, the famed grape-growing region just south of Pamplona. Riojas are prestigious reds made from *tempranillo* grapes. Riojas to look for include: CUNE Imperial, Viña Ardanza, Marqués de Arienzo, Faustino, Muga, and Artadi.

Alhambra

$$$$ NAVARRESE/SPANISH

Pamplona is pretty far north for a restaurant named for the Moorish palace in Granada, especially considering that the restaurant in question focuses mainly on regional Navarrese and Basque dishes. No matter. Now owned by the same local company that owns Hotel Leyre and Europa, Alhambra has long been a Pamplona favorite. Slickly handsome to begin with, it underwent a thorough remodeling in early 1999 and is now back up and running, better looking than ever. For an appetizer, try a warm salad of foie gras and duck *confit* (duck cooked and preserved in its own fat). For a main course, the risotto of mushrooms, truffles, and shrimp is a winner.

Calle Bergamín, 7. ☎ 948-24 50 07. Reservations recommended. Main courses: 2,625–3,475 pta. ($15–$19); menú del día 3,875–5,850 pta. ($22–$33). AE, DC, MC, V. Open: Mon–Sat lunch and dinner. Closed last week July, first week Aug.

Casa Otano

$$ NAVARRESE/SPANISH

Otano's the kind of good-value, unpretentious restaurant that you may find yourself eating at several times during a stay in Pamplona. On the second floor above an informal *pension,* along one of the city's busiest bar streets, the dining room is surprisingly large and attractive. It's got just the right Spanish feel, with exposed brick walls and dark woods. The local Navarrese dishes and grilled meats aren't surprising, just very well done for the reasonable prices. A standard is the *merluza al cantábrico en salsa verde con almejas* (Cantabrian hake in green sauce with clams). The midday menu, at 1,600 pta. ($9), is a good deal. If you need a place to crash, ask about the simple, inexpensive rooms upstairs (see the sidebar titled "I see lotsa bulls, but where are the hotels?" earlier in this chapter).

San Nicolás, 5. ☎ 948-22-50-95. Reservations recommended. Main courses: 1,100–2,500 pta. ($6–$14). AE, MC, V. Open: Mon–Sat lunch and dinner; Sun lunch only.

Erburu

$$ NAVARRESE/SPANISH

On a busy street bursting with *tapas* bars (and regular, old, drinking bars), this is a good place for simple, home-cooked fare. The dark wood dining room, with just a few tables, is at the back, past the long bar decorated with hanging hams and *chiles* (peppers). Check out the lunch menu for a good, hearty meal.

San Lorenzo, 19–21. ☎ *948-22-51-69. Main courses: 1,100–1,900 pta. ($6–$10). MC, V. Open: Tues–Sun lunch and dinner. Closed second half of July.*

Europa

$$$$ SPANISH

This sophisticated restaurant is a stone's throw from the bullring and Plaza del Castillo. The place for perhaps Pamplona's finest dining experience, Europa is classic with modern touches. The several small dining rooms began life as a private house in the 1930s. Also a small hotel, it has 21 rooms (see the Hotel Europa listing reviewed earlier in this chapter). The restaurant, though, is the undisputed star. It serves creative regional dishes, such as grilled salmon in olive vinaigrette, roasted lamb with mint *cuajada* (curd), and *lomo de rape asado con guisantes frescos y espárragos verdes fritos* (grilled monkfish with fresh peas and fried green asparagus). Desserts are elaborate; you must order several, such as the chocolate soufflé with mint sauce, at the beginning of your meal.

Calle Espoz y Mina, 11. ☎ *948-22-18-00. Reservations recommended. Main courses: 2,650–3,450 pta. ($15–$19); menú del día 3,875–5,875 pta. ($22–$33). AE, DC, MC, V. Open: Mon–Sat lunch and dinner.*

Josetxo

$$$$ BASQUE

Excellent, if a little fussy and stuffy, Josetxo is where families and dates come for special celebrations. The formal dining room is everything you want in an Old World European restaurant, with service to match. As a Basque restaurant, the best dishes are from the sea — the shellfish pastry and lobster salad are terrific, but don't pass up the super goose liver.

Plaza Príncipe de Viana, 1. ☎ *948-22-20-97. Reservations recommended on weekends. Main courses: 1,975–3,675 pta. ($11–$20); tasting menu 6,500 pta. ($36). AE, DC, V. Open: Mon–Sat lunch and dinner. Closed Aug.*

Exploring Pamplona

Whether you come to sprint with bulls snorting at your heels or see the historic city of Pamplona (with no one snorting anywhere in your general vicinity), you want to stick to the Old Quarter. Modern Pamplona, while flush with gardens, isn't terribly attractive. You can easily see the small number of sights in a single day.

The Encierro: Running of the Bulls

Few international visitors to Pamplona's Fiesta de San Fermín are likely to know or care that Spain's biggest street party is actually religious in origin and dates to at least 1591. The experts who run ahead of the bulls pray to Pamplona's patron saint to keep them out of hooves' way. For most people, Sanfermines is eight days of mayhem highlighted by a daily running of the bulls through the streets.

The party begins at noon on July 6 (and lasts through July 14), when a swarm of people dressed all in white except for red sashes and kerchiefs, gathers at the Town Hall. With a cry of "Citizens of Pamplona: Viva San Fermín!" a rocket explodes, and so does the city. Each day begins (it's tempting to say ends, because virtually no one goes to bed) with the *diana*, a 6 a.m. marching of bands through the streets, and the 8 a.m. *encierro*.

If you're one of the smart ones, determined to watch the *encierro* from the safety of the barricades along Calle Estafeta, you've got to get up early (or do like everyone else and stay up all night). The crowd stakes out their places at 6 a.m. for the 8 a.m. running.

People crowd balconies and climb the barricades that have been set up along the route. Experts and foolish novices crowd the area near the gates. The most daring actually run *toward* the gates just before the shot rings out and the gates fly open, releasing the beasts. The mad rush begins, runners inevitably stumble, and the six bulls hurtle over bodies and cobblestones toward the unseen goal: the bullring. If a bull becomes separated from the pack, he is apt to freak out and look to run down anything that moves. Minutes later, a second pistol signals that all the bulls have entered the Plaza de Toros. Everyone heads to the Plaza del Castillo for breakfast and excited (no doubt inflated) tales of near misses.

Late in the afternoon is the day's bullfight, which draws some of Spain's top matadors. If you want to score some first-come, first-serve tickets to that afternoon's bullfight, go directly to the ticket office at the Plaza de Toros. Tickets go on sale at 6:30 a.m., but you need divine intervention to score one. They sell out weeks and months in advance, mostly to locals. Try asking your hotel concierge if he or she knows how to get a ticket, but be prepared to pay the premium scalper's rate.

The party cranks up again afterwards, with marching bands, spontaneous dancing, and parades of costumed figures — literal giants and big heads. And the daily revelry begins anew. The pattern repeats each day until the 14th, when the closing song is a lament: "Poor me, poor me," the

Pamploneses sing, "San Fermín is finished." See the sidebar "Taking the bull by the horns: To run or not to run?" as well as the official Web sites, www.sanfermin.net and www.encierro.com, for practical information on enjoying the festival.

The top attractions

Catedral
Old Quarter

The Gothic cathedral, built in the fourteenth century on the foundations of a former Romanesque church, is the single most important sight in Pamplona. The squat interior houses a marble tomb of Charles III, the last great king of Navarra, and his queen, Leonor. The delicate medieval cloisters, considered among the finest in Spain, feature an intricately carved door with scenes from the Bible. A small museum (the Museo Diocesano) occupies the former refectory and kitchen, and exhibits religious objects, including a series of 13 virgins (er, that's polychrome virgins). You can conduct a decent visit in a half hour or so.

Taking the bull by the horns: To run or not to run?

Should you try to outrun annoyed, one-ton animals rushing madly through the medieval streets of Pamplona? Even if you're the adventurous sort, this is a no-brainer. Every year a number of people get maimed and gored running, and it's never the locals (who know how much distance to maintain and where to hide). It's almost always the out-of-towners, often young and inebriated, who join the *encierro* (the Running of the Bulls) and get trampled. Sure, fatal gorings are rare (there were 15 or 16 in the last 100 years), but a college student from Chicago was killed in the mid-1990s. My advice for most people? Don't do it. Come, drink too much if you wish, but climb the barricade and get a good look at the madness from a safe distance.

Oh, one other thing: The *encierro* is regarded as a male-only event (boys and bulls only). Here, women are viewed as either the fairer or the slower sex, and are prohibited from trying to outrun the charging bulls. (I maintain that most women are simply too smart to try to outrun bulls, although some disregard the rules and run anyway.)

You've probably heard people who've done it and say it's a terrific rush. If you're one of those who will never be dissuaded, all I can say is: *suerte!* (good luck!).

Here's a tip for the brave souls who do run: If a bull comes anywhere near you, check the photography stores near the Plaza del Castillo. Photographers snap pics to sell as souvenirs. You may just spot your harried self with a bull at your heels — proof for those tales of *machismo* you'll no doubt spin back home.

Plaza de la Catedral. ☎ *948-22-46-67. Admission: (including museum) 400 pta. ($2.20). Open: Winter daily 8 a.m.–11:30 a.m. and 6–8 p.m.; summer daily 10:30 a.m.–1:30 p.m. and 4–6 p.m. Guided visits in Spanish 11:30 a.m., 12:30 p.m., and 5:30 p.m. daily.*

Museo de Navarra
Old Quarter

Pamplona's other major sight, its excellent museum, occupies a sixteenth-century charity hospital in the Old Quarter. It was handsomely remodeled a decade ago. Of great interest are the fourth- and fifth-century Roman mosaics, several in pristine condition, and the Gothic and Romanesque pieces. Look for the unusual French Gothic statue of the Virgin with child. The collection of paintings includes Goya's expressive portrait of the Marqués de San Adrián. Allow a couple of hours here.

Cuesta de Santa Domingo, s/n. ☎ *948-10 64 92. Admission: 300 pta. ($1.67), seniors free, and students 150 pta. (85¢); Sat afternoons and Sun mornings, holidays and December 3, free. Open: Tues–Sat 10 a.m.–2 p.m. and 5–7 p.m., Sun 11 a.m.–2 p.m.*

More cool things to see and do

✔ **Exploring the Old Quarter on foot.** A short walk around Pamplona's Old Quarter gives you a good feel for the town. Beyond the cathedral, up cobblestoned Calle Bedin, is a nice view of the city and river below, and the medieval walls that once enclosed Pamplona. Check out the baroque City Hall, where the rocket signaling the beginning of the San Fermín festival, in Plaza de los Burgos, fires. On 10 Calle Ansoleaga is the thirteenth-century Cámara de Comptos (General Accounting Office, the oldest in Spain), a beautiful example of Gothic civic architecture. Plaza Castillo is the heart of Pamplona, built in 1651 and a zoo during festival time. Leading from it are several streets famous for their *tascas* (*tapas* bars). You can take a brief walk around the small *casco histórico* (historic district) in an hour.

✔ **Taking the no-bull route.** If you're not in Pamplona during the San Fermín festival, you can trace the well-worn *encierro* route — just please don't hold your fingers on your head and run through the streets snorting like a bull. The police will arrest and deport you. (Okay, maybe they won't, but I will.) The bulls leave the gates from their corrals just outside the Old Quarter; they precede along Cuesta de Santo Domingo, race past the Ayuntamiento (Town Hall), and down the long stretch of Calle Estafeta. The bulls and staggering runners cross Paseo Hemingway and flood into the Plaza de Toros, the bullring.

Can you guess which macho American writer is represented by a bust on Pamplona's Paseo Hemingway? Yep, Ernest Hemingway, the author of *The Sun Also Rises,* the novel that brought Sanfermines to a worldwide audience. Papa is depicted in a thick Irish sweater, above an inscription that reads, "A friend of the people of Pamplona and an admirer of their festivals." During San Fermín, he'll almost certainly be wearing a red kerchief around his neck, just like the locals.

✔ **Catching a game of flying balls.** If you want to see a professional game of *jai alai,* also known as *pelota,* you can catch one at the **Frontón Eskal Jai Berri** in Huarte, about 4 miles from Pamplona. Games are generally Thursdays, Saturdays, and Sundays. Call ☎ 948-33-11-59 for more information and directions.

Getting adventurous: Navarra outdoors

If you're looking for something different (and running with the bulls just wasn't enough), check out the services of these tour companies, which organize food and wine trips, balloon excursions, and adventure sport outings in beautiful, rural Navarra.

✔ As well as guided tours in Pamplona, **Erreka** offers a wide program of routes through Navarra, including food and wine tours. Location: Calle Curia, 18. ☎ **948-22 15 06.** E-mail: erreka@cmn.navarra. net. Internet: http://webs.navarra.net/erreka.

✔ **Nattura** organizes aquatic and mountain activities in the Pyrenees accompanied by trained guides. Activities include rafting, canoeing, spelunking, cross-country skiing, and snow-shoe walks. Location: Calle Marcelo Celayeta, 75. Edificio Iwer, B-1. ☎ **948-13-10-44;** E-mail: nattura@masbytes.es.

✔ **Novotur's** mantra is *Unusual Navarra,* which means this tour company offers musical itineraries as well as trips to wine cellars and amateur bullfights. If San Fermín whetted your appetite for more, they can set up tests of bravery with young bulls. Location: Avda. de Bayona 9, second floor, left entrance. ☎ **948-26-76-15.**

Roaming the tascas: Pamplona nightlife

San Fermín notwithstanding, Pamplona's a conservative, fairly quiet town. At night the thing to do is wander the streets of the Old Quarter, visiting the *tascas (tapas* bars). The liveliest streets are San Nicolás, San Lorenzo, and Jarauta. The bars in the main square, Plaza del Castillo, are also good watering holes; **Café Iruña** (No. 44) is a legendary art deco hangout.

Taking side trips from Pamplona

To explore a bit of the province of Navarra, a car is the best way to go, although several trains per day also run to **Olite;** call ☎ 948-70-06-28 for schedules and fares.

The major car rental agencies in Pamplona are: **Avis,** Monasterio de la Oliva, 29 (☎ **948-17-00-36**); **Budget,** Polígono Iturrondo, 2 (☎ **948-13-17-00**); **Europcar,** Avenida Pío XII, 43 (Hotel Blanca de Navarra; ☎ **948-17-60-02,** or 948-31-27-98 at the airport); and **Hertz,** Avenida de Navarra, 2 (☎ **948-26-12-56,** or 948-16-87-67 at the airport).

The government of the province of Navarra pretty much invented the idea of rural homestays (staying in farmhouses and small rustic *hostales,* or hostels) in Spain. If you want to get away from it all, losing yourself in the intensely green, hilly Navarrese countryside makes for a terrifically restorative and cheap, vacation. (I did it one summer near Ochagavia, and wound up in an amazing, quiet old farmhouse — a week there cost me about what two nights in a city hotel would've cost). You go on hikes, bike and, most of all, eat at simple local restaurants, where the food's good and the Rioja wines are even better. For information, including a comprehensive book with photos of each rural house, contact the Centralized Reservations bureau of the **Navarra Tourism Office:** ☎ **948-22-93-28;** Fax: 948-21-20-59; E-mail: `turnavarra@cfnavarra.es.`

Alternately, if you want to explore other Navarrese towns, I recommend trying one of the following day trips.

Olite, a Gothic town

Just over 25 miles south of Pamplona, Olite ("oh-*lee*-tay") was a favorite of the king of Navarra, Charles III. The town's most notable feature is the thirteenth-century castle and fairytale-like French Gothic castle, the royal palace, with cone-shaped turrets. The church next door, **Santa María la Real,** the former royal chapel, is a lovely example of Navarra Gothic.

The **Parador Príncipe de Viana** occupies three towers of the fifteenth-century castle. The rooms in the castle are a bit gloomy, but perfect if you're looking for true Gothic immersion. (☎ **948-74-00-00;** Fax: 948-74 02 01; Internet: `www.parador.es`). Rates: 15,000–17,500 pta. ($83–$97).

To get there: By car take N-121 south. Two bus companies run the Pamplona-Olite route: **Conda** (☎ **948-22-10-26**) and **Tafallesa** (☎ **948-22 28 86**). Each outfit has four to five buses a day (400 pta./$2.20 each way).

Haro: Rioja wine tastings

Red wines in Spain have long been synonymous with the Rioja wine-producing region. Just south of Pamplona, the region is a lovely area to explore if you've got a car and are interested in visiting *bodegas* (wineries). Check out the **Old Quarter of Haro** ("*ar*-oh"), full of aristocratic mansions and wine taverns, and then visit a *bodega* (wine cellar) or two. Check about visits to **Bodegas Muga** (☎ 941-31-04-98), **C.V.N.E.** (☎ 941-31-06-50) and other wine cellars with the tourist information office (Plaza Monseñor Florentino Rodríguez; ☎ 948-30-33-66).

If you're looking to stay the night, check out **Los Agustinos,** a sixteenth-century convent magnificently converted into a hotel (Calle San Agustín, 2, Haro; ☎ **941-31-13-08;** Fax: 94-30-31-48; Internet: www.codeconet.com/aranzazu/agustinos.html). Rates: 11,00–13,300 pta. ($61–$74).

If you're going by car, take N-111 west to N-232 to get there. Likewise, **La Estellesa** (☎ **948-22-22-23**) runs daily buses from Pamplona to La Rioja.

Fast Facts: Pamplona

Area Code

The area code for telephone numbers within Pamplona is **948.**

Emergencies

In case you get gored by the bulls, call S.O.S. Navarra, ☎ **112.** For medical emergencies, call ☎ **061.** After-hours pharmacies ☎ **948-22-21-11.**

Hospitals

Three hospitals are located on Calle Irunlarrea (all s/n, or unnumbered): Hospital de Navarra (☎ **948-42-21-00**); Hospital Virgen del Camino (☎ **948-42-94-00**); and Clínica Universitaria (☎ **948-25-59-00**).

Information

The main tourism office is located at Calle Eslava, 1; ☎ **948-20 65 40;** E-mail: oit.pamplona@cfnavarra.es. Open Sep–June, Mon–Fri 10am. to 2 p.m., 4 to 7 p.m., and Sat 10 a.m. to 2 p.m. (July–Aug, Sat also open 10 a.m. to 2 p.m., 4 to 7 p.m.); during San Fermín, daily 10 a.m. to 5 p.m.

Police

For municipal police, dial ☎ **091.**

Post Office

The Central Post Office is located at Paseo de Sarasate, 9 (☎ **948-22-12-63**).

Part IV
Central Spain: Madrid and Castile

The 5th Wave   By Rich Tennant

BOB'S FIRST TRIP TO SPAIN

@RICHTENNANT

"Please stop yelling 'Ole' everytime the bartender spears an olive for a martini."

In this part . . .

*I*f you've dreamed of legendary castles rising from the plains and groundbreaking Spanish art, make sure that you spend time dead center in the middle of Spain: Madrid and the star attractions of Castile — Toledo, Segovia, and Salamanca.

Besides being the capital of the country, Madrid is hands-down Spain's cultural epicenter. Few cities in the world can challenge Madrid when it comes to civic art collections, with its world-famous Prado and other stellar museums. Though Madrid is a relatively new city, the great art on view is testament to Spain's storied past. But nowhere are the glories and ignominies of Spanish history — from the Middle Ages through the Spanish Inquisition and Golden Era — so present as they are in several towns on the plains just outside Madrid. Likewise, Castile was the land of kings and conquerors, and it's here that you find cathedrals and citadels, as well as a mind-boggling Roman Aqueduct and one of the world's earliest and greatest universities.

Chapter 14

Madrid

- -

In This Chapter

▶ Choosing the best places to stay

▶ Dining out: haute cuisine, tantalizing *tapas,* and more

▶ Keeping busy in Madrid

▶ Everything you need to know about Madrid's non-stop nightlife

▶ Getting out of town

- -

*W*hat comes to mind when you think of Spain? Picasso and the Prado Museum? Bulls charging red capes? A rowdy nightlife and going to bed when you normally would be getting up? These are all images of Spain, but more importantly for you Madrid-bound folks, they are images of the Spanish capital. On a target of Spain, Madrid is the bullseye, the geographic and political center of the country. Today, Madrid is also the cultural capital of Spain and one of the foremost art centers in Europe.

Although Madrid is mostly a modern creation, it was the site of a Moorish fortress in the ninth century. Captured by Alfonso VI, it remained a small medieval town until Spain's Golden Age (the sixteenth and seventeenth centuries), when it grew rapidly. In 1561, the height of the Golden Age, Felipe II moved the court from Toledo to Madrid, which makes it one of Europe's youngest capital cities.

Madrid has grown unrelentingly since the 1970s, and especially since Spain became a member of the European Community in the mid-1980s. For some, Madrid has lost much of its classic flavor — but you don't have to look hard to find it still. Sipping on a *vino tinto* (red wine) or sherry and munching a morsel of *tortilla española* (Spanish omelet) in the heart of the Old City, or stumbling back to your hotel at dawn, you can still discover the Madrid that inspired legions of artists and writers. This is the Madrid that invented *la marcha* — the revelry that roars louder and later here than anywhere else in Spain.

You can hit the major museums by day, take a sidetrip to El Escorial or Aranjuez, and soak up theater, opera, and flamenco by night. Madrid is Spain's undisputed nightlife champion, renowned for its relentless party-all-night-long attitude. The city's atmospheric *mesones* and *tascas* — cave-like restaurants and taverns — get the night started. When the sun goes down, you find that *Madrileños,* the people of Madrid, are among the most open and gregarious in Spain.

Just the Facts: Madrid

Madrid, located in the middle of the country, is Spain's political and administrative capital and home to the Royal Family. Madrid is also the capital of the province of the same name.

- ✔ **The name game.** Madrid is pronounced "mah-*dreeth*" by the locals, but you can get away with using a hard "d": "mah-*drid.*" Locals are called *Madrileños* ("mah-dree-*lay*-nyos").

- ✔ **Cómo se dice? Talking the talk.** Unlike Catalonia, the Basque Country, and Galicia, there is no tricky secondary language in Madrid — just the king's *castellano* (Spanish).

- ✔ **What's for dinner.** Feast on Castilian specialties such as suckling pig, lamb, and pheasant. The capital has some of Spain's finest restaurants, and Madrileños claim that the seafood flown in daily is fresher even than that found on the coasts. Snacking on *tapas* and *copas* at all hours is a part-time job for most locals.

- ✔ **The forecast.** The weather here operates in extremes: cold in the winter, very hot and dry in the summer (think Dallas in the U.S.).

- ✔ **When to go.** The best times to visit Madrid are spring and fall. If you must go in summer, avoid August. Not only is it fry-an-egg-on-the-sidewalk hot, the city's dead. Most Madrileños take the entire month off and escape to cooler climes. Many, if not most, shops and restaurants are closed. Hotel occupancy and rates are pretty consistent all year, except in August, when no one wants to be in Madrid, and during the San Isidro (mid-May) and Autumn Festivals (late October through November), when everyone does. If you want to be a part of Madrid at its most festive during these celebrations, book several months in advance.

- ✔ **How long before moving on?** If you only want a taste of Madrid, you still need at least a couple of days to visit the Prado, see some of *Viejo* (old) *Madrid,* and check out the capital's dizzying nightlife.

Getting There: All Roads Lead to Madrid

For many years, Madrid was about the only place you could fly into from North America. And even now with Barcelona on the way up as an international destination, the lion's share of overseas flights still touch down in Madrid. All roads and flight paths in Spain lead to Madrid. You can jump on a quick shuttle flight from Barcelona, or the high-speed train from Seville.

By plane

Most international airlines, including **Iberia, American, TWA, Delta,** and others, offer direct flights to Madrid. Madrid's international airport, **Barajas** ("Bah-*ra*-hass") (☎ **91-393-60-00** or 91-305-83-43) is 15 km (9 miles) from the center of the city. Passing through Customs can involve waiting in a long line, but is otherwise hassle-free. Be sure you don't get in the line that says "UE" (which indicates members of the European Union), unless, of course, you hold a passport from one of the EU countries. Look instead for the sign that says *"Otros Países"* (other countries) or *"Otras Nacionalidades"* (other nationalities).

Barajas airport is large but simple enough to navigate, even though a new terminal was added. In the international terminal, you can find major auto rental agencies, an ATM machine, and a **Tourism Information Office** (☎ **91-305-86-56;** open Monday to Friday, 8 a.m. to 8 p.m. and Saturday 9 a.m. to 1 p.m.). Carts are available for tossing your luggage on, for free.

Travel time from the airport to downtown is about 30 to 45 minutes. You now have three options for transport to the city (and returning to the airport). The yellow **Airport Bus** service (☎ **91-431-61-92**) leaves from the curb right outside the terminal. A bus passes every 15 to 20 minutes for Plaza Colón, making several stops on the way; it runs Monday through Friday from 6 a.m. to 11 p.m. and weekends from 6:30 a.m. to 11 p.m. The same bus returns to Barajas from the underground station at Plaza Colón. The price either way is 385 pta. ($2.15); you pay on board (exact change is not necessary). Taxis, lined up outside the terminals, charge about 2,500 pta. ($14) to the center of Madrid; the airport supplement is 400 pta. ($2.25), and each suitcase is worth an extra 50 pta. (30¢).

Line 8 (the pink line) of the Madrid **Metro** (subway), a long-awaited project, is finally running between Barajas airport and downtown (connecting with Line 4, the brown line). Stop by the Tourism Information booth for a subway map and determine the closest stop to your hotel (check out the Metro Web site, www.metromadrid.es, beforehand and arrive with a plan in hand). Given Madrid's awful traffic, the subway may be your best bet into the city, though you have to change lines at least once (and unless you're weighted down by several pieces of luggage, you may then have to spring for a taxi).

When you make reservations, ask your hotel about the **Aero City Service** — an airport shuttle service that picks you up at the airport and delivers you to your hotel, or vice-versa. The price is 1,600 pta. ($9) for one person or 1,800 pta. ($10) for two — which is at least 1,000

pta. less than a taxi. Participating hotels have reservation forms to fill out if you want a lift back to the airport.

By car

Spain's major highways (Roman numerals I through VI) radiate outward from Madrid, which is measured as kilometer zero on the national highway system. The N-II highway from Barcelona leads to Madrid, as does N-VI from Santiago and N-IV from Andalusia.

Nearing the city, look for signs reading *Centro* (center) that take you into downtown Madrid.

By train

Madrid splits its train service among three stations. **Atocha** (Glorieta del Emperador Carlos V; Metro: Atocha RENFE) is the station for destinations in south and southeast Spain and Portugal. The high-speed **AVE train** (for information call ☎ 91-534-05-05) departs for (and arrives from) Córdoba and Seville at Atocha. **Charmartín** (Calle Agustín de Foxá; Metro: Charmartín), the most modern train station, covers most destinations in north and northeastern Spain, in addition to most European capitals. **Estación Príncipe Pío** (also called Estación Norte; Paseo del Norte, 30; Metro: Norte) is the station for trains to and from northwestern Spain, including Salamanca and Galicia. For all train information, call ☎ 91-328-90-20. **RENFE** is the Spanish national train service; its main office, open weekdays only, is located at Alcalá, 44 (Metro: Banco de España; ☎ 91-328-90-20).

For several years now, travelers have been surprised to know that a high-speed (AVE) train links Madrid and Seville, but not the capital and the second-largest city, Barcelona. Evidently the situation seemed weird to Spanish officials as well, and the train is now in the works. An AVE high-speed railway can make the trip from Barcelona to Madrid in just 2½ hours (currently, it takes 6½ hours!) — too bad you have to wait until 2004 to ride that rapid rail route.

By bus

Madrid's main bus terminal, for national and international departures, is **Estación Sur de Autobuses** (Calle Méndez Álvaro; ☎ 91-468-42-00; Metro: Palos de la Frontera). The **La Sepulvedana** line travels between Madrid and Segovia (**Estación de la Sepulvedana,** Paseo de la Florida, 11; Metro: Príncipe Pío; ☎ 91-530-48-00 or 91-547-52-61). **Empresa Larrea** (Estación Sur; Metro: Méndez Álvaro; ☎ 91-547-52-61) goes between Madrid and Ávila. **Empresa Auto Res** buses make the journey between Madrid and Salamanca (**Estación de Auto Res,** Calle Fernández Shaw, 1; ☎ 91-551-72-00). **Galliano Continental** (Estación Sur; Metro: Méndez

Álvaro; ☎ **91-527-29-61**) travels back and forth between Madrid and Toledo.

Orienting Yourself in Madrid

 Madrid doesn't have any natural landmarks useful for getting your bearings. Street numbers are frequently confusing; also, as throughout Spain, the numbers of addresses do not often follow logically, and some are labeled *s/n,* or unnumbered. Your best bet is to orient yourself using the Metro (subway) map, because most destinations are close to a Metro stop.

After it was named Spain's capital, Madrid took off in successive waves of growth from the sixteenth to nineteenth centuries, expanding east and north from the River Manzanares. But getting a fix on the city and its neighborhoods is easy. You want to spend most of your time in Old Madrid (near the Plaza Mayor) and Bourbon Madrid (including the Prado Museum and Retiro Park). The northern and eastern neighborhoods are where many hotels, restaurants and shops are located. The periphery, the urban sprawl of Madrid, is beyond the interest of most visitors.

The main arteries of Madrid are Calle Mayor, which runs the length of the old center (and becomes Calle de San Jerónimo as the city becomes more modern); Gran Vía and Alcalá, the main commercial streets that border the newer northern neighborhoods; and Paseo del Prado/Paseo de la Recoleta, which run perpendicular to Gran Vía and Alcalá along Madrid's museum mile (from the Atocha train station past Plaza de Cibeles). Heading north, beyond Plaza de Colón, Paseo del Prado becomes the chic, tree- and café-lined Paseo de la Castellana.

Madrid by neighborhood

There are three Madrids, really. There's **Old Madrid,** the city of the Hapsburgs, between the Royal Palace and Plaza Mayor. There's **Bourbon Madrid,** the city expansion encouraged by the Bourbon monarchs in the eighteenth century. And there's **modern Madrid** — an urban sprawl that began with the northern neighborhoods like Barrio Salamanca in the nineteenth century, and which now radiates out from the center and seems equal parts Los Angeles and Brussels.

Viejo Madrid (Old Madrid)

Viejo Madrid is the heart of the city. The Moors established a fortress near the river, and Madrid grew up there in the sixteenth and seventeenth centuries. The Old City, the Madrid of the Hapsburg royal family, extends from the Palacio Real (which is actually a much later addition) to Madrid's version of Times Square, Puerta del Sol. The old district is a warren of historic buildings and crooked cobblestone streets. This neighborhood is where to go for *tascas* (*tapas* bars), restaurants, and historical sightseeing. Here you find:

- ✔ The **Royal Palace** and the Old City's historic buildings and churches
- ✔ Bustling **Plaza Mayor** and **Puerta del Sol**
- ✔ **Monasterio de las Decalzas Reales,** Madrid's most important convent
- ✔ Atmospheric **taverns** and *tapas* **bars**

Bourbon Madrid

No, a bunch of Kentucky distilleries didn't suddenly take up residence in Madrid. East of Viejo Madrid, the expansion overseen by Carlos III of the Bourbon dynasty is an area of grand boulevards, plazas, and fountains, but also thick layers of eighteenth-century apartment buildings. Bourbon Madrid is home to Madrid's major museums and its most popular park, and many of the city's finest hotels and restaurants. Here you find:

- ✔ The art world's Big Three: **The Prado, Thyssen-Bornemisza,** and **Reina Sofía** museums
- ✔ **Retiro Park,** Madrid's splendor in the grass

Modern Madrid

Beginning in the nineteenth century, Madrid expanded yet again, north and south and every which way. Modern Madrid is an ever-expanding succession of residential neighborhoods filled with elegant shops, cinemas, restaurants, banks, and smaller museums. You can find a number of fine hotels in these neighborhoods, and they make for a quieter stay if you don't mind taking the subway to get to Madrid's star attractions. Here you find:

- ✔ **Barrio de Salamanca,** the ninteenth-century neighborhood of elegant, expensive apartments and superchic boutiques
- ✔ **Chueca,** a slightly rough-around-the-edges, bohemian *barrio* (neighborhood) chock full of restaurants, bars and funky clothing and design shops
- ✔ **Paseo de la Castellana,** a wide boulevard lined with trees and cafés, where Madrileños strut their stuff
- ✔ **Plaza de Toros de las Ventas,** one of Spain's best-known bullfighting arenas

Where to get info after you arrive

Municipal Tourism Offices are located at Plaza Mayor, 3 (☎ 91-366-54-77; open Monday through Saturday, 10 a.m. to 8 p.m. and Sunday and holidays, 10 a.m. to 3 p.m.); Duque de Medinaceli, 2 (☎ **91-429-49-51;** open Monday through Friday, 9 a.m. to 7 p.m. and Saturday 9:30 a.m. to 1 p.m.); Puerta de Toledo Market, 1–6 (☎ **91-364-18-75;** open Monday through Friday, 9 a.m. to 7 p.m. and Saturday, 9:30 a.m. to 1:30 p.m.); and Barajas Airport (International Arrivals Terminal; ☎ **91-305-86-56;** open Monday through Friday, 8 a.m. to 8 p.m. and Saturday, 9 a.m. to 1 p.m.). Call ☎ **902-20-22-02** or 901-30-16-00 for tourism information.

Getting around Madrid

Madrid is large and sprawling, but the places of interest to most visitors are in a fairly compact area. In fact, you can walk much of Madrid, and what you can't, the Metro system is easy to use and goes just about everywhere you need.

By subway

The **Metro** (☎ **010** or 91-486-07-52; Internet: www.metromadrid.es), marked by red and blue diamond-shaped signs, is Madrid's subway system. Operating 11 lines with 127 stations, this is by far the fastest and easiest way to navigate the city. Stops are almost everywhere you want to go. Single-ticket fares are 135 pta. (75¢). Hours are Monday to Sunday from 6 a.m. to 1:30 a.m. You can find handy maps at Metro stations.

A ten-trip ticket **(Metrobus)** is available for 705 pta. ($4), a nearly half-price bargain. It pays for itself with just five journeys on the Metro, and you can pass it back to another passenger. You'll use it up in no time, and it also works on the bus.

By bus

The bus proves a bit complicated for first-time visitors. Conductors generally don't speak English, and with all the traffic on the wide avenues and tiny streets, it's tough to get a read on the city from the window of a bus. I usually stick to the airport bus on the way in, and go with the subway (Metro) and my own two feet until I catch the bus back to the airport. If you prefer your travel above ground, though, about 150 bus lines (called **EMT**) cover Madrid. Buses run from 6 a.m. to midnight. daily (fare, 135 pta./75¢); special night buses, (called *buhos,* or night owls) run much less frequently, from midnight to 6 a.m. For information, call ☎ **010.**

By taxi

Few taxi journeys cost more than 1,000 pta. ($5.50). You can hail a cab in the street (the little green light on the roof means you can hop in) or pick one up where they line up (usually outside hotels). Fares begin at 175 pta. ($1). A slightly higher night rate is charged from 11 p.m. to 7 a.m. If you need to call a cab, taxi companies include **Tele-Taxi** (☎ 91-445-90-08), **Radio Teléfono Taxi** (☎ 91-547-82-00) and **Radio Taxi Independiente** (☎ 91-405-12-13).

Taxi rates in Madrid are pretty reasonable, and most drivers are honest, but a few try to rip off tourists left and right. I have had several taxi drivers in Madrid (but only in Madrid — not in any other Spanish city) try to jack up the fare on me (one even slyly placed his street guide over the meter in an attempt to claim it wasn't working). Check the fare at the beginning of the journey so that you don't end up paying for the last guy's ride. Ask about any suspicious supplements to your fare. If a driver says his meter isn't working, get in another cab. And get a receipt; if you have a problem, write down the taxi driver's name and license number and the number of the cab company and have your hotel call to inquire about the fare. A taxi driver who sees you writing down his license number will give you a fair deal.

By car

Don't drive in Madrid unless you're forced to. Trust me on this one — traffic is horrendous, and you can't park anywhere. A car is really only useful for getting out of the city. Rental car companies include: **Europcar** (☎ 91-721-12-12) at the Atocha and Chamartín train stations; **Avis,** Gran Vía 60 (☎ 91-348-03-48); and **Hertz,** Gran Vía, 88 (☎ 91-542-58-05). You can also find all of these companies at the airport.

On foot

Madrid isn't the classic walking city that Barcelona is, although people walk everywhere around Viejo Madrid and love to stroll the Paseo del Prado and Paseo la Castellana on summer evenings. But, as sprawling as the city is, you can still cover much of the city on foot. Just don't overdo it. Your feet are in demand at all of those museums, and the city gets very hot in summer. Hop on the efficient and inexpensive Metro (subway) to pop around the city. When you do walk, be very careful crossing streets. Even more so than in other parts of Spain, pedestrians have few rights.

Staying in Madrid

Madrid has reigned as Spain's top tourist destination for decades, so expecting the capital to be flush with hotel options of every stripe is logical. Although you've got plenty of choices, from a surfeit of inexpensive *pensiones* and *residencias* to some of the finest white-glove

palaces in Europe, hotels in Madrid are more expensive than any other
city in Spain, including Barcelona. But don't panic: I include some money-
wise tips in this section so you don't have to worry about taking out a
loan for your trip to Madrid (unless you're determined to stay at the
Ritz or Palace, in which case you may; see the "Splurging at Madrid's
grandaddy hotels" sidebar later in this chapter).

Most traditional hotels are either located in Old or Bourbon Madrid,
while you can find newer accommodations in the residential neighborhoods beyond the center. Proximity to the Prado and other attractions
is important, but so is the noise factor, and many otherwise nice hotels
can be noisy affairs. Also keep in mind that many large hotels that
target groups and business travelers are somewhat impersonal
sometimes.

If you arrive in Madrid with no place to stay, try calling **Brújula** (☎ 91-
559-97-05), a reservation company. They've got a long roster of hotels
and can probably set you up for at least your first night.

Many of Madrid's hotels cater to business travelers, so weekend rates
and special deals are available at many hotels — always ask. Unless it's
high season and the hotel's near capacity, you can probably get a break.
Also look for the word "Deals" at the end of the following hotel reviews,
where I list the best rates.

Most hotels rates don't include breakfast or IVA, the 7 percent value-
added tax. So you aren't shocked by the bill at the end of your stay,
make sure you ask about these when booking your room.

The top hotels

Gran Hotel Reina Victoria
$$$$ Viejo Madrid/Puerta del Sol

A massive, historic hotel on hopping Plaza Santa Ana, the Reina Victoria
has been around forever. Built in the 1920s, it definitely has an older feel
to it, but it's been very well maintained. The hotel was once very popular
with bullfighters, who hung out in the clubby bar. Rooms are large and
classically decorated; though some of the best ones overlook the plaza;
if you're noise-sensitive, go for an interior room to escape the late-night
bar noise from below.

Plaza Santa Ana, 14. ☎ *91-531-45-00. Fax: 91-522-03-07. E-mail:* hotel@tryp.es.
Internet: www.tryp.es. *Metro: Tirso de Molina or Puerta del Sol. Parking: 1,750
pta. ($10). Rack rates: 30,000 pta. ($167) double; weekend rate 14,400 pta. ($80)
double. AE, DC, MC, V.*

Hotel Monaco
$$ Chueca

Warning: this small, funky hotel, a former brothel that looks the part, demands a sense of humor. It's a kitschy delight — all pink marble, ornate columns, neon lights, and faux-Louis XIV furniture. Every room is different — but they all feel as though you're playing in a human-sized dollhouse. (Double rooms, that is. Singles are pretty dismal, and best skipped.) Room 123 has a giant carved-wood ceiling mirror, while Room 127 is an exercise in Pepto Bismal pink with an absolutely fabulous bathroom. Monaco is in the heart of Chueca, a bohemian hood with tons of bars. (Straitlaced travelers take note: The *barrio* (neighborhood) has its share of slightly shady characters.)

Calle Barbieri, 5. ☎ *91-522-46-30. Fax: 91-521-16-01. Metro: Chueca. Parking: 1,750 pta. ($9.70) nearby. Rack rates: 10,000 pta. ($55) double. AE, DC, MC, V.*

Hotel NH Nacional
$$$ Bourbon Madrid

The smoothly professional NH chain, with several hotels in Madrid, leaves nothing to chance. They're designed for business travelers, who want things just so, but those demands also make them perfect for tourists. And who cares if NH hotels are predictable, when that only means excellent execution? Expect spacious, well-decorated rooms with light woods, bold colors, and original art, nice bathrooms, and good service. This one, opened in 1997 in a historic 1920s building, is on Paseo del Prado, right on the museum mile between the Thyssen and the Reina Sofía.

Paseo del Prado, 48. ☎ *91-429-66-29. Fax: 91-369-15-64. Internet:* www.nh-hoteles.es. *Metro: Atocha. Parking: 2,000 pta. ($11). Rack rates: 24,100 pta. ($139) double; weekend rate 21,900 pta. double ($122) children under 12 sharing parents' room stay free. AE, DC, MC, V.*

Hotel Paris
$$ Viejo Madrid/Puerta del Sol

Bohemian enough to justify the name, this place reeks (fortunately not literally) of Old World flavor. If you're accustomed to bright and cheery rooms, it may seem a little gloomy, but others will feel as though they ought to jot down notes for a novel at breakfast. Right in the thick of the Puerta del Sol action, the Paris has a nice interior patio (onto which the breakfast room looks). Rooms are a tad bare, but they're clean, and the bathrooms have been remodeled. It's a cool place, and a steal as well — some clients have been coming here for decades. Come to think of it, it would make a great setting for that novel. . . .

Alcalá 2. ☎ *91-521-64-96. Fax: 91-531-01-88. Metro: Puerta del Sol. Parking: 2,290 pta. ($12) per day. Rack rates: 12,840 pta. ($71) double (breakfast and taxes included). AE, MC, V.*

Splurging at Madrid's granddaddy hotels

Madrid has two granddaddy, super-luxe hotel options. The Ritz and the Palace Hotel are storied, famous, and well-located places, but both cost an arm and a leg (and perhaps even more body parts). I list them because they're classics, and they're often listed among the best hotels in Europe; but for my hard-earned bucks, I go with the newer and more intimate, if slightly less convenient, Santo Mauro (see "The top hotels" in this section).

The turn-of-the-century **Ritz Madrid** is glamour incarnate, but it's also extremely formal (jacket and tie? In this heat?). If you want a hotel that revels in a European sophistication fit for kings, this is it — if you're willing to shell out the money. Plaza de la Lealtad, 5. ☎ **800-225-5843** in the U.S. and Canada, or 91-701-67-67; reservations, ☎ **91-701-68-02.** Fax: 91-701-67-89. E-mail: reservas@ritz.es. Internet: www.ritz.es. Metro: Banco de España. Parking 4,000 pta. ($22).Rack rates: 64,000 pta. ($356) double; check Web site for "Especial Offers." AE, DC, MC, V.

The massive **Palace Hotel,** across the Paseo del Prado, is almost as stylish and elegant as the Ritz — especially its glitzy public rooms. Madrileña society, well-heeled foreigners, and celebrities are fixtures here. A long-awaited renovation was carried out in 1998. Plaza de las Cortés, 7. ☎ **800-325-3535** in the U.S., 800-325-3589 in Canada, or 91-360-80-00. Fax: 91-360-81-00. E-mail: Madrid@sheraton.com. Internet: www.palacemadrid.com. Metro: Banco de España. Parking: 2,500 pta. ($14). Rack rates: 63,000 pta. ($350) double. AE, DC, MC, V.

If the Ritz and Palace Hotels are too ritzy and regal for your wallet (they certainly are for mine), you can still get a taste of their all-out luxury. Check out the sumptuous lobby of the Palace, with its spectacular glass cupola, or the refined bar of the Ritz — just make sure you're properly dressed. In the case of the Ritz, that pretty much means jacket and tie for men, a skirt, dress, or nice pants for women. Stop by on your way to a nice dinner elsewhere in Madrid.

Hotel Santo Domingo
$$$–$$$$ Viejo Madrid/Gran Vía

A short walk from the atmospheric streets of Viejo Madrid — but also from the chaotic rush of Gran Vía — this 1994 hotel seems smaller and more personal than its 120-room size indicates. Though you wouldn't expect it from the plaza outside, the morning-yellow lobby and rooms are classically elegant, with handsome furnishings and fabrics in warm tones. Rooms vary greatly in size; some fourth and fifth floor superior doubles have small terraces. If you arrive with a reservation and the hotel's not full, ask to see several rooms.

Plaza Santo Domingo 13. ☎ *91-547-98-00. Fax: 91-547-59-95. E-mail:* reserva@ hotelsantodomingo.com. *Internet:* www.hotelsantodoming.com. *Metro: Santo Domingo. Parking: 2,475 pta. ($14). Rack rates: 19,075–29,900 pta.($106–$166) double; weekend rate 19,075–23,475 pta. ($106–$130) double, breakfast included. AE, DC, MC, V.*

Madrid Accommodations, Dining & Attractions

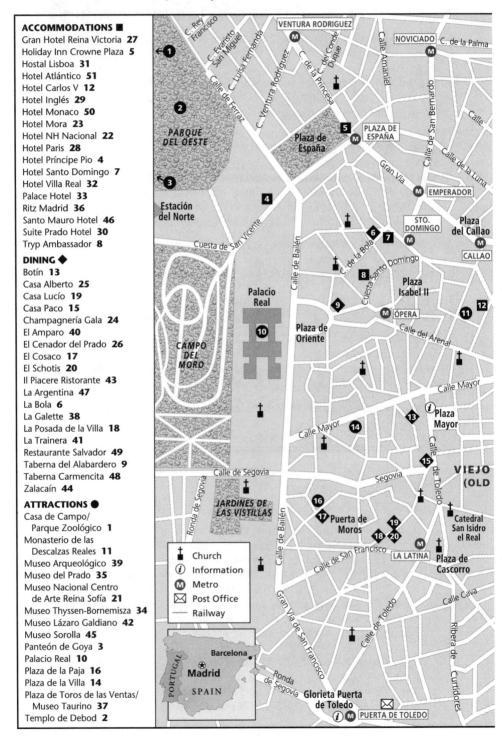

ACCOMMODATIONS ■
Gran Hotel Reina Victoria **27**
Holiday Inn Crowne Plaza **5**
Hostal Lisboa **31**
Hotel Atlántico **51**
Hotel Carlos V **12**
Hotel Inglés **29**
Hotel Monaco **50**
Hotel Mora **23**
Hotel NH Nacional **22**
Hotel Paris **28**
Hotel Príncipe Pio **4**
Hotel Santo Domingo **7**
Hotel Villa Real **32**
Palace Hotel **33**
Ritz Madrid **36**
Santo Mauro Hotel **46**
Suite Prado Hotel **30**
Tryp Ambassador **8**

DINING ◆
Botín **13**
Casa Alberto **25**
Casa Lucío **19**
Casa Paco **15**
Champagnería Gala **24**
El Amparo **40**
El Cenador del Prado **26**
El Cosaco **17**
El Schotis **20**
Il Piacere Ristorante **43**
La Argentina **47**
La Bola **6**
La Galette **38**
La Posada de la Villa **18**
La Trainera **41**
Restaurante Salvador **49**
Taberna del Alabardero **9**
Taberna Carmencita **48**
Zalacaín **44**

ATTRACTIONS ●
Casa de Campo/
   Parque Zoológico **1**
Monasterio de las
   Descalzas Reales **11**
Museo Arqueológico **39**
Museo del Prado **35**
Museo Nacional Centro
   de Arte Reina Sofía **21**
Museo Thyssen-Bornemisza **34**
Museo Lázaro Galdiano **42**
Museo Sorolla **45**
Panteón de Goya **3**
Palacio Real **10**
Plaza de la Paja **16**
Plaza de la Villa **14**
Plaza de Toros de las Ventas/
   Museo Taurino **37**
Templo de Debod **2**

VENTURA RODRIGUEZ

NOVICIADO C. de la Palma

PLAZA DE ESPAÑA

Plaza de España

EMPERADOR

Gran Via

STO. DOMINGO

Plaza del Callao

CALLAO

PARQUE DEL OESTE

Estación del Norte

Cuesta de San Vicente

Plaza Isabel II

Palacio Real

Plaza de Oriente

ÓPERA

Calle del Arenal

CAMPO DEL MORO

Calle Mayor

Plaza Mayor

Calle Mayor

VIEJO (OLD

Calle de Segovia

Segovia

JARDINES DE LAS VISTILLAS

✝ Church
ⓘ Information
Ⓜ Metro
✉ Post Office
— Railway

Puerta de Moros

Catedral San Isidro el Real

LA LATINA

Plaza de Cascorro

PORTUGAL

Barcelona

⊕ Madrid

SPAIN

Ronda de Segovia

Glorieta Puerta de Toledo

PUERTA DE TOLEDO

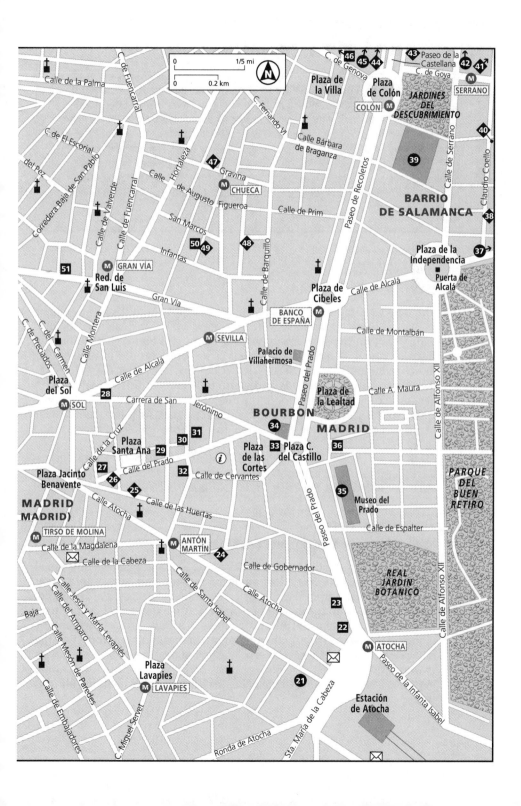

Bed and breakfasts in Madrid

B&Bs aren't common in Spain like they are in England and Ireland. But a California-based organization, **European B&B,** has started to uncover private family residences (as well as some unhosted apartments) in Madrid that offer a nice alternative to the standard hotel scene. Prices are reasonable, but so far they only have about ten listings in the capital. The Web site has detailed information on the service as well as each house or apartment, including several photos of each. You may find European bedrooms smaller than what you're accustomed to, and not all buildings have elevators. Prices range from $90–$120 per night (double occupancy), breakfast and taxes included. Contact **European B&B** at: ☎ **800-872-2632** or visit them on the Web at www.madridbandb.com.

Hotel Villa Real

$$$$$ **Bourbon Madrid**

The Derby chain has just this one hotel in Madrid, and it's just as classy as its excellent Barcelona hotels. A new building designed to look historical (you have to make up your own mind about that; to me it's tasteful kitsch, if such a thing exists), the four-year-old hotel is much more traditional than the daring Hotel Claris in the Catalan capital. Richly decorated with dark woods and warm tones and suffused with a quiet elegance, rooms are superior to the functional lobby. Many are split-level, with separate sitting areas. Bathrooms are plush, with fine linens. Best of all, you can't get a better location, just a short walk from the Prado.

Plaza de las Cortés, 10. ☎ *91-420-37-67. Fax: 91-420-25-47. E-mail:* info@derbyhotels.es. *Internet:* www.derbyhotels.es. *Metro: Plaza de la Cibeles. Parking: 1,600 pta. ($9). Rack rates: 41,600 pta. ($231) double. AE, DC, MC, V.*

Santo Mauro Hotel

$$$$$ **Modern Madrid (north of Plaza Colón)**

Breathing down the old-money necks of the Ritz and Palace is this small upstart, an upscale retreat of superior service and luxury in a quiet residential neighborhood a mile or so from the old center. It's a splendid, intimate hotel, with the kind of personal attention that matches the steep prices. This ten-year-old hotel occupies a swank turn-of-the-century mansion that was formerly the Philippino Embassy, and before that, the palace of the duke of Santo Mauro. The mix of design and antique pieces is perfectly balanced. Rooms are large and very chic, with full audio systems. The restaurant (which occupies the mansion's beautiful library) is also good.

Calle Zurbano, 36. ☎ *91-319-69-00. Fax: 91-308-54-77. Reservations,* ☎ *902-29-22-93. E-mail:* santo-mauro@ac-hoteles.com. *Internet:* www.ac-hoteles.com. *Metro: Rubén Darío or Alonso Martínez. Parking: 1,950 pta. ($11). Rack rates: 46,200–69,300 pta. ($257–$385) double. AE, DC, MC, V.*

Suite Prado Hotel
$$$ Viejo Madrid/Puerta del Sol

If you think only the superrich staying at the Ritz and Palace get to have large rooms in Madrid, think again. Tucked away on a small street not far from Plaza Santa Ana, this tiny hotel (just 18 rooms) with a pale pink exterior has almost shockingly large suites, perfect for the whole family. That means unheard-of kitchenettes and comfortable salons for the price of a standard room. Rooms are decorated with contemporary furniture in bright colors. Triples have sofa-beds. It's obviously no budget hotel, but this is still one of the best deals in Madrid, if you can get a room. Call a few weeks in advance.

Calle Manuel Fernández y González, 10 (around corner from Teatro Español, off Calle de las Huertas). ☎ *91-420-23-18. Fax: 91-420-05-59. E-mail:* hotel@suiteprado.com. *Internet:* www.suiteprado.com. *Metro: Banco de España. Parking: nearby, 2,000 pta. ($11). Rack rates: 20,475 pta. ($114) double. AE, DC, MC, V.*

Tryp Ambassador
$$$$ Viejo Madrid

A classy hotel near the Royal Palace and opera house, the Ambassador, opened in 1991, occupies two separate, thoughtfully renovated buildings. One is a magnificent palace, the other a converted monastery. The conservative rooms are large and elegant, especially in the four floors of the former palace. The hotel's on a quiet, sloping old street within easy striking distance of Viejo Madrid's principal attractions.

Cuesta Santo Domingo 5–7 (near Palacio Real). ☎ *91-541-67-00. Fax: 91-559-10-40. E-mail:* hotel@tryp.es. *Internet:* www.tryp.es/e-ambas.htm. *Metro: Opera or Santo Domingo. Parking: 2,500 pta. ($14) per night. Rack rates: 30,000 pta. ($167) double. AE, DC, MC, V.*

Madrid's runner-up hotels

Holiday Inn Crowne Plaza

$$$$ Viejo Madrid   This massive, glittering, and pricey high-rise isn't your standard Holiday Inn — it looks more like the house that Donald Trump built; rooms facing the Plaza have amazing views of the Royal Palace. *Plaza de España, 8.* ☎ *800-465-4329 or 91-454-8500. Fax: 91-548-23-89. E-mail:* reservas@crowneplaza.es. *Internet:* www.crowneplaza.com.

Hostal Lisboa

$ **Viejo Madrid/Puerta Del Sol** One of the best of the small, affordable *residencias* (pensions), with large rooms and spacious bathrooms. *Ventura de la Vega, 17, off Calle Jerónimo.* ☎ *91-429-98-94.* Fax: 91-429-46-76.

Hotel Atlántico

$$$ **Viejo Madrid** A mid-size basic right on the Gran Vía; soundproofed rooms are frighteningly heavy on the floral prints. *Gran Vía, 38.* ☎ *800-528-1234 in the U.S. and Canada, or 91-522-64-80.* Fax: 91-531-02-10. E-mail: info@hotel-atlantico.com. *Internet:* www.hotel-atlantico.com.

Hotel Carlos V

$$ **Viejo Madrid** An older-style, but still very comfortable and affordable place wedged in a pedestrian street between the Puerta del Sol and Gran Vía. *Maestro Victoria, 5 near the Gran Vía.* ☎ *91-531-41-00.* Fax: 91-531-37-61. *E-mail:* recepcion@hotelcarlosv.com. *Internet:* www.hotelcarlosv.com.

Hotel Inglés

$$ **Viejo Madrid/Puerta Del Sol** This hotel has a lobby that outclasses the nondescript rooms, but it still makes for a comfortable, economical stay, and it's about equidistant from the Prado and the Plaza Mayor. *Calle Echegaray, 8, off Calle Jerónimo.* ☎ *91-429-65-51.* Fax: 91-420-24-23.

Hotel Mora

$ **Bourbon Madrid** This 1930s hotel, has simple standard rooms, but it's a bargain and the location is good, just down the street from the Prado and around the corner from the Reina Sofía museum. *Paseo del Prado, 32.* ☎ *91-420-15-69.* Fax: 91-420-05-64.

Hotel Príncipe Pío

$$ **Viejo Madrid** This large, once-grand place, located on an unappealing multi-lane street, is a good value if you're in the market for spectacular views of the Royal Palace. Old-style rooms — with carpets the off-putting color of pea soup — are well maintained. *Cuesta de San Vicente, 16, near Casa de Campo.* ☎ *91-547-08-00.* Fax: 541-11-17. E-mail: hotelppio@futurnet.es.

Dining in Madrid

Madrid is one of the top places to eat out in Spain. It has all the regional specialties, a wide variety of international cuisines, fresh seafood flown in from the coasts, and charming Viejo Madrid-style places where you can easily imagine macho Hemingway chomping on a big suckling pig.

Classic Madrileña dishes are *cocido* ("koh-*thee*-do," a slow-cooked pork and chickpea soup/stew) and *callos* ("*kigh*-yos," or tripe).

You can eat formal, haute cuisine, or haunt the redolent tascas (*tapas* restaurants) and *mesones* (cave-like taverns), ideal places to stop in for a *vinito* ("bee-*nee*-toe," small glass of red wine), *jerez* ("hair-*eth*," sherry), and a smattering of *tapas*. Although you can easily put together a good meal from one, a *tapas* crawl in Madrid is really a cultural itinerary. Making the rounds of these bars and cave-like places is one of the highlights of Madrid — a perfect complement to afternoons viewing great paintings in the Prado. For a list of a few worth hopping into, see the section on Madrid's nightlife later in this chapter.

Eating like a Madrileño

Because it's the capital (and Madrileños love to eat), you can find any type of cuisine you want in Madrid, from the freshest fish to the most sophisticated Basque preparations. Among the regional Spanish dishes are some tried-and-true Madrid favorites. Try *cocido madrileño* (chickpea stew with beef, chicken, pork belly, and ham); *callos* (tripe with chorizo sausage); *rabo de buey* (oxtail); *sopa de ajo* (garlic soup); *cordero asado* (roasted baby lamb); and *jamón serrano* (cured ham). There's nothing like having hot chocolate and *churros* (fritters) after a late night — a night that, in all probability, began with rounds of *tapas,* all-hours snacks.

Texans have their barbecue, New Yorkers have their pizza, and New Englanders have their clam chowder. And Spaniards? Well, Spaniards wax poetic about ham. *Jamón serrano,* cured ham, is a national obsession. Aficionados of thin Iberian ham — especially *jamón de Jabugo* and *pata negra* — claim it's Spain's greatest delicacy. A *ración* (portion) of dry, razor-thin shavings of the stuff sets you back a few thousand pesetas ($20 or more), but that matters little to the Spaniards who talk about it the way others rhapsodize about caviar. In Madrid, good places to try some deluxe ham are **Cinco Jotas** (Serrano, 118; ☎ **91-562-27-10**), **Casa Lucío** (Cava Baja 35; ☎ **91-365-32-52**) and **Museo del Jamón** (Vitoria, 1), which is not (as the name implies) a Ham Museum, but a temple dedicated to cured hams from all over Spain.

Many Madrid restaurants serve *callos* at least once a week for the midday menu. Before you blindly say, "I'll try it" — as I once did and then immediately regretted my decision — you should know that this classic Madrileña dish is tripe and various other innards, which I think is only for the brave.

Wondering why *tapas* bars seem crowded at all hours of the day and night? Spaniards love to take little snack breaks. During the course of a day, people typically roll into the office and maybe run downstairs for a café and a croissant. By 11, it's time for a wedge of *tortilla española,* perhaps, and a beer or even something stronger. They may stop by another bar on their way to lunch around 2 p.m. for a *tapa* or two. And then stop again after work, and on into the night. The most amazing thing about this continual snacking is how few overweight Spaniards you see. Hooray for olive oil, I guess.

For more on Spanish dining customs, including mealtimes, costs, and tipping, see Chapter 1.

The top restaurants

Botín

$$$ Viejo Madrid   SPANISH

You want classic Madrid? You can find it at this restaurant: roast suckling pig and roast leg of lamb prepared in ancient wood ovens. Prepare to meet your neighbors in this crowded spot, though, and there are lots of 'em. Somehow, everyone seems to know that Botín has the reputation of being the oldest restaurant in the world (it hasn't closed its doors since 1725). But if you miss the one in Madrid, you can check out the considerably newer branch in Miami, Florida. How's this for pedigree? Francisco de Goya, the legendary painter, was once a dishwasher at the restaurant Botín. Not good enough? Okay, how about the fact that Hemingway set a scene in *The Sun Also Rises* at the same restaurant?

Calle de Cuchilleros, 17. ☎ 91-366-42-17. Reservations required. Metro: Ópera. Main courses: 950–3,200 pta. ($5–$18); fixed-price menu 3,900 pta. ($22). AE, DC, MC, V. Open: Daily, lunch and dinner.

Casa Lucío

$$$ Viejo Madrid   CASTILIAN '

A historic tavern on one of Madrid's famous night-crawler streets, this is one of the spots I regularly took foreign visitors during the short time I lived in Madrid. Right after the Prado, we'd head to Casa Lucío. With its cinematic, cave-like ambience and hanging forest of cured hams, it's the kind of place that has you considering a sabbatical in Spain before you finish the first bottle of wine. The famous faces and sharp-dressed crowd only add to the buzz. The food is top-quality comfort food — like the house *merluza* (hake, a white fish similar to cod), shrimp in garlic sauce, roasted lamb, and scrambled potatoes and eggs.

Cava Baja 35. ☎ 91-365-32-52. Reservations recommended. Metro: La Latina. Main courses: 2,400–3,800 pta. ($13–$21). AE, DC, MC, V. Open: Sun–Fri lunch; dinner daily. Closed Aug.

El Amparo
$$$$$ Modern Madrid   BASQUE

Martín Berasategui, the 30-something wonderkind of Basque cooking in San Sebastián, has brought his creative ways to Madrid, in the form of this rustically elegant restaurant in the chic Salamanca neighborhood. There are traditional Spanish dishes with interesting touches, like the roast lamb chops with garlic purée; but the really special ones are innovative nouvelle Basque cuisine items. That can mean sea bass with clams and cauliflower raviolis or tomato-layered salt cod. The restaurant occupies a charming former nineteenth-century stable with country wooden beams.

Puígcerdá, 8 (at corner of Jorge Juan). ☎ *91-431-64-56. Reservations required. Metro: Goya. Main courses: 3,000–5,000 pta. ($17–$28); fixed-price menu 10,000 pta. ($55). AE, MC, V. Open: Mon–Fri lunch, dinner daily. Closed the week before Easter and in Aug.*

El Cenador del Prado
$$$ Bourbon Madrid   INTERNATIONAL

In the heart of Bourbon Madrid, off of Plaza de Cortés, this elegant restaurant puts gourmet delicacies on your plate for less than most places of this caliber. You can either dine in a formal salon or a light, airy garden room. The menu, overseen by the Herranz brothers, focuses on *nueva cocina española* — nouvelle Spanish cuisine. A number of preparations are more adventurous than what you find in most Spanish restaurants, and you can detect subtle Asian influences. Try the salmon and shellfish *ceviche* (marinated in lime juice) to start, or black rice with squid. The menu continually changes, while the desserts are reason enough to come back.

Prado, 4. ☎ *91-429-15-61. Reservations recommended. Metro: Puerta del Sol. Main courses: 1,400–2,500 pta. ($8–$14); fixed-price menu 3,500 pta. ($19). AE, DC, MC, V. Open: Mon–Fri lunch and dinner, Sat dinner only. Closed third week in Aug.*

La Bola
$$$ Viejo Madrid   MADRILEÑO

This 120-year-old place is one of the old-school Madrid taverns, with flavor to spare. The bull's-blood red exterior wraps around a street corner; inside, the walls are decorated with photographs of the famous who've sat at these tables over the last century. The house specialty is a six-hour *cocido,* the famous everything-but-the-kitchen-sink stew (it takes six hours to make, not to eat). Other good comfort food includes grilled meats and fish, *ropa vieja* (a Latin American dish of spicy shredded meat), and squid in their own ink.

Dinner theater

I'm not talking dinner-and-a-show, but rather dining within the head-to-toe reconstructed Madrid Opera House. The **Restaurante Teatro Real**, Felipe V, s/n (☎ 91-516 06 70; Metro: Opera), is a little overproduced for minimalist tastes, like the theater itself, but if the idea of an upscale theme restaurant appeals to you, this is one way to get in the opera house without shelling out for a performance. The décor features the costumes of famous operas and a sparkling star canopy on the ceiling.

Calle de la Bola, 5 (at Guillermo de Rolland). ☎ *91-547-69-30. Reservations required. Metro: Plaza de España or Ópera. Main courses: 1,350–3,200 pta. ($7.50–$18); fixed-price menu 2,125 pta. ($12). No credit cards. Open: Mon–Sat lunch and dinner.*

La Posada de la Villa
$$$ Viejo Madrid   SPANISH/STEAK

Here's a way not only to see the Old Madrid, but to feel it in your bones. This inn, founded in 1642, is famed for its Castilian roasts. Come for the historic ambience, and while you're at it, dig into the exquisite roast lamb and cured pork.

Cava Baja, 9. ☎ *91-366-18-60. Reservations required. Metro: La Latina. Main courses: 1,800–3,800 pta. ($10–$21). Open: Mon–Sat lunch and dinner, Sun dinner only. Closed Aug.*

La Trainera
$$$$–$$$$$ Modern Madrid   SEAFOOD

Madrileños storm this simple-looking, multi-room restaurant in Barrio Salamanca for some of the freshest and best-prepared seafood in the city. You won't find a roast or suckling pig on the menu, but you will find heaping platters of *mariscos* (shellfish), divine filet of sole, and Galician-style hake. The shellfish is sold by weight. Close your eyes, and you may think you've suddenly landed in one of coastal Galicia's swimming-in-seafood restaurants. Open them, and you're in land-locked Madrid.

Calle Lagasca 60. ☎ *91-576-80-35. Reservations recommended. Metro: Serrano. Main courses: 3,000–7,000 pta. ($17–$39). AE, DC, MC, V. Open: Mon–Sat lunch and dinner.*

Taberna del Alabardero
$$$ Viejo Madrid   CASTILIAN

Just around the corner from the reconstructed Teatro Real opera house, and a mere echo away from the Royal Palace, this 25-year-old tavern is much more than the *tapas* bar in front implies. The restaurant in back wins raves from locals in the know, serving fresh fish, much of it Basque preparations, and delectable meat entrees, like *solomillo ibérico* (Iberian pork tenderloin) in three types of peppers.

Felipe V, 6. ☎ *91-547-25-77. Reservations required (not necessary in bar). Metro: Ópera. Main courses: 1,800–3,500 pta. ($10–$19); Bar, tapas 450–1,200 pta. ($2.50–7); menú, 5,500 pta. ($31). AE, DC, MC, V. Open: daily lunch and dinner.*

Taberna Carmencita

$$ Chueca   SPANISH/BASQUE

One of the city's classic tavern restaurants, this place has Viejo Madrid written all over it. It's been here since 1840 and was a hangout for the poet García Lorca and other cultural movers and shakers. The small dining room is charmingly decorated with lace and vivid tiles. Given the ambience, it ought to be filled with tourists, but it's remained a popular spot with locals. Try the sole in *txakolí* (the Basque wine), or *bacalao a la Vizcaina* (Biscay-style salt cod), or the duck in cognac and prunes.

Libertad, 16. ☎ *91-531-66-12. Reservations recommended. Metro: Chueca. Main courses: 900–2,800 pta. ($5–$16); weekday menú del día 1,300 pta. ($7). AE, MC, V. Open: Lunch Mon–Fri, dinner Mon–Sat.*

Zalacaín

$$$$$ Modern Madrid   BASQUE

North of downtown Madrid, this celebrated culinary temple has been one of the top restaurants in Spain for a quarter century. It's the place to go if you're in Spain celebrating a special occasion, or if you just want to eat like a king. The ambiance is supremely elegant without being stuffy. The food, plainly, is the star. The chef is Basque — true of many top kitchens in the capital — and the menu follows traditional Basque and Navarrese lines. Everything is spectacularly presented, and the taste justifies the small loan you may have to take out to eat here. It's a good place to try the six-course *menú de desgustación* (tasting menu), although its sheer quantity may put a damper on your desire to tackle the small volcano of chocolate dessert.

Álvarez de Baena, 4. ☎ *91-561-48-40. Reservations required. Metro: Rubén Darío. Main courses: 3,200–5,500 pta.($18–$31); fixed-price menu 11,500 pta. ($64). AE, DC, MC, V. Open: Mon–Fri lunch and dinner, Sat dinner only. Closed week before Easter and in Aug.*

Madrid's runner-up restaurants

Casa Alberto

$$ Viejo Madrid   This 1827 *taberna* (tavern) with a front *tapas* bar and charming little restaurant in back serves classic Madrid fare like meatballs, cod stew, roasted lamb, and ox. Don Quixote's creator, Cervantes, once lived at this address. *Calle de las Huertas, 18, near Antón Martín Metro stop.* ☎ *91-429-93-56.*

Casa Paco

$$$ Viejo Madrid Madrid's version of a Texas steak house — a place for big ol' cuts of meat, priced according to weight and seared in oil and served, usually, very pink; Madrileños like their meat almost mooing. *Puerta Cerrada, 11, in the heart of Viejo Madrid.* ☎ *91-366-31-66.*

Champagnería Gala

$ Viejo Madrid A cheery place specializing in *paellas* and a long list of other classic rice and meat dishes, it's got great patio in back and is an amazing bargain (but no credit cards). *Calle Moratín, 22 in the Huerta district.* ☎ *91-429-25-62.*

El Cosaco

$$ Viejo Madrid A fairly priced and romantic Russian restaurant, on one of the city's prettiest and most serene plazas, which has served good Stroganoff Imperial and a long list of vodkas since 1969; a good spot to take a break from *jamón serrano* and *vino tinto. Plaza de la Paja, 2, near La Latina.* ☎ *91-365-35-48.*

El Schotis

$$ Viejo Madrid An attractive little restaurant is in the heart of Viejo Madrid's happening *tasca* (*tapas* restaurant) scene. Have a few *tapas* nearby and come here for *churrasco* (grilled meats) or Basque-style fish dishes. *Cava Baja, 11.* ☎ *91-365-32-20.*

Il Piacere Ristorante

$$$ Modern Madrid/Plaza De Colón This place, just north of Plaza de Colón, is far from your average pizza-and-pasta joint; it's upscale Italiana, lovingly prepared. *Paseo de la Castellana, 8.* ☎ *91-578-34-87.*

La Argentina

$ Modern Madrid/Chueca A tiny, family-run restaurant with an emphasis on hearty food at economical prices. Try the cannelloni and roast veal, accompanied by french fries or mashed potatoes. *Gravina, 19, in Chueca.* ☎ *91-531-91-17.*

La Galette

$$ Modern Madrid A refuge for vegetarian in meat-mad Madrid; it's not entirely veggie, but the most inventive dishes are. *Conde de Aranda, 11, in Barrio Salamanca, near Retiro Park.* ☎ *91-576-06-41.*

Restaurante Salvador

$$$ **Modern Madrid/Chueca**   As nondescript as possible from the outside, but behind the door is a classic Madrid restaurant, its walls plastered with cinematic photos of bullfighters; intimate dining rooms are a place to enjoy Madrid basics like *rabo de toro* (oxen tail), fresh fish, and stuffed peppers. *Barbieri, 12 in Chueca.* ☎ *91-521-45-24.*

Exploring Madrid

A visit to Madrid should concentrate on two things: gorging on great art and stuffing yourself silly with *tapas* and small glasses of wine, beer, and sherry. If you're a fan, or just curious, attend a sun- and blood-drenched bullfight. Most people have side trips on their mind, but if you have more time in Madrid, take a crack at some smaller museums and graceful parks, and then get to the great shopping and fine dining.

Madrid has the greatest concentration of important museums in Spain — and more first-class paintings by Spanish masters including El Greco, Velázquez, Goya, and Picasso (among others) than anywhere else. If you can hit only the top two or three, begin with the Prado and the Royal Palace (which is a museum of sorts). Allow a full morning or afternoon for the Prado, and a couple of hours for the Royal Palace. The Thyssen and Reina Sofía also require a couple of hours each — more if their enviable collections hook you. Also, allow some extra time to explore the neighborhoods around the museums on foot. In Viejo Madrid, around the Plaza Mayor, spend a couple of hours (preferably in the early evening, when *tapas* crawlers are out and about) and discover the soul of the city in its cinematic *mesones* and *tascas*. Then again, this could easily become an all-night affair.

If you're a serious art lover and are banking on hitting the Madrid's Big Three — the Prado, the Thyssen Bornemisza, and the Reina Sofía museums — all within hours of landing in Madrid, make sure that your visit isn't on a Monday or Tuesday. The first two museums are closed on Monday, and the Reina Sofía collection shuts its doors on Tuesday. None of them closes for lunch, though, and occasionally, this is the best time to visit (when everyone else takes a break, from 1 p.m. to 4 p.m. or so).

A three-museum pass, called the *Paseo del Arte* (Art Stroll), entitles you to visit the Prado, Thyssen-Bornemisza, and Reina Sofía, for 1,275 pta. ($7.10) — a 25 percent discount over regular admission prices. Note that it's not such a good deal if you're a student or senior because you get price breaks anyway, or if you plan to hit the Reina Sofía and Prado on Saturday afternoon and Sunday morning, when they're free.

In addition to both the Prado and Reina Sofía museums, many smaller museums throughout the city, offer free admission on Saturday afternoons (2 p.m. to closing) and Sunday mornings. However, those are the most crowded times. If you hate crowds, go during the week when the museums are much less crowded. Or, take advantage of the free periods by going Saturday during lunch time (2 p.m. to 4 p.m.); the museums really clear out then.

Be extremely careful around the Prado and other museum tourist haunts, where thieves artfully prey upon unsuspecting tourists. If someone offers to clean mustard or some other substance off your clothing, recognize it as a trick and refuse assistance: The thief is the one who put the mustard there, and he or she will proceed to rob you after distracting you.

The top attractions

Museo del Prado
Bourbon Madrid

If you were to count the great museums of classical paintings on one hand, the Prado might be, say, your index finger. It holds the world's richest and most complete collection of Spanish Old Masters, making it one of the top attractions in Spain. You simply should not miss it, unless the thought of classical painting makes your skin crawl (in which case Spain's going to be a real drag unless you stick to the three Bs: bars, bull-fights, and beaches). The Prado began as the initiative of Spanish kings, great art collectors all, who sought a suitable place to hang the paintings they had amassed. The Prado's twelfth- through nineteenth-century collection of the Spanish school includes masterpieces by Velázquez, Goya, El Greco, Murillo, Ribera, and Zurbarán. The Velázquez and Goya collections are the star draws; so go directly to the galleries featuring their works if your time or interest is limited. Expect the crowds there, though; as you approach the room where Velázquez's masterpiece, *Las Meninas,* hangs, you can hear the rumble of guides and groups build. The Prado also possesses extraordinary works by Venetian masters — including Titian, Fra Angélico, Raphael, and Botticelli — and Flemish greats Hieronymous Bosch, Peter Paul Rubens, and Brueghel the Elder.

To try and beat the crowds at the Prado, enter through the Velázquez door (facing Paseo del Prado), and go early (9 a.m.) or during the Spanish lunch hour (2 p.m. to 4 p.m.).

The museum is so large, and it possesses so many great works, that a single visit can only scratch the surface. But don't let that deter you. Head for the highlights first (see the sidebar entitled "Must-sees: A Prado primer" for more) and proceed from there, according to your time and energy. The ground floor features Goya's Black Paintings, the fifteenth- and sixteenth-century Flemish School, and El Greco. On the first floor are Velázquez, Goya, fifteenth- and sixteenth-century Italian works, and the seventeenth-century Dutch and Flemish Schools. The Prado is in the midst of a massive expansion and restoration program, and you may find several exhibition rooms closed during your visit, though all the greatest works will remain on view. New galleries dedicated to the work of Velázquez opened in 1999 — the 400th anniversary of the great artist's birth. If you're an art aficionado, purchasing a room-by-room guide is a good idea to follow along or find particular paintings or artists.

You can spend several days at the Prado, but because few people have that kind of time or interest, leave at least a half-day to see what will amount to a small fraction of its immense collection; plan on taking a couple of back-saving breathers at the cafeteria.

 For the next few years, the Prado is continuing a massive restoration program. Several exhibition rooms will be closed, but don't worry: all the greatest hits will remain on view. The museum is also embarking on a long-awaited and debated expansion plan, which will more than double the number of paintings exhibited, from 1,200 to 2,600. The Prado chose the esteemed Spanish architect Rafael Moneo, in a politicized and controversial selection process, to design the long-awaited, $25 million expansion.

Paseo del Prado. ☎ *91-330-29-00. Internet:* http://museoprado.mcu.es/. *Metro: Banco de España or Atocha. Admission: 500 pta. ($2.75); students and seniors, 250 pta. ($1.40); free admission Sat 2:30–7 p.m., Sun 9 a.m.–2 p.m. Open: Tues–Sat 9 a.m.–7 p.m., Sun 9 a.m.–2 p.m.; closed Jan 1, Good Friday, May 1, and Dec 25.*

Museo Thyssen-Bornemisza
Bourbon Madrid

The museum with a tongue-twister of a name has quickly become a premier attraction in Madrid. In 1993, the Spanish government acquired the spectacular private collection amassed by the Baron Thyssen-Bornemisza and his son, two generations of German industrial magnates. (When Baron Thyssen-Bornemisza went shopping for a country deserving of his precious art collection, Spain held a trump card. The Baron is married to a former Miss Spain, and she apparently used her charms to convince him to give Spain the collection, making it the third jewel in Madrid's art crown.)

The Spanish government renovated the early nineteenth-century pink Villahermosa palace to show its new bounty. The impressive collection includes some 800 stylistically diverse works in Madrid (Barcelona's Pedralbes Monastery houses another 80 medieval, Renaissance, and Baroque works). Begun in the 1920s, the Thyssen collection aims to be no less than a survey of Western Art, from primitives and medieval art to twentieth-century Avant Garde and Pop Art. Displayed chronologically (starting from the top floor) and heavy on Impressionism and German Expressionism, the collection reads like a roster of the greatest names in classical and modern art: Caravaggio, Rafael, Titian, El Greco, Goya,

Rubens, Degas, Gauguin, Cézanne, Manet, Van Gogh, Picasso, Chagall, Miró, and Pollock. Some observers tout it as the greatest private collection ever assembled, but others criticize it as a showy collection of minor works by major artists. Though the museum has only been open since 1993, it's already showing some wear and tear — they're having a devil of a time matching the peach wall paint where pictures were moved or replaced.

Paseo del Prado, 8 (Palacio de Villahermosa). ☎ *91-369-01-51. Internet:* www. museothyssen.org. *Metro: Banco de España. Admission: 700 pta. ($4), 400 pta. ($2.20) students and seniors, free for children 11 and under. Temporary exhibits, 500 pta. adults ($2.75), 300 pta. ($1.75) students and seniors. Open: Tues–Sun 10 a.m.–7 p.m.*

Museo Nacional Centro de Arte Reina Sofía
Bourbon Madrid

The third address on Madrid's celebrated Art Avenue — the Paseo del Prado — is the Queen Sofía contemporary art museum. Housed in the former General Hospital, the center's makeover for its 1992 inauguration included the risky addition of two exterior, glass-enclosed elevators. The permanent collection includes the most famous painting of the twentieth century, Pablo Picasso's *Guernica.* The massive canvas in gray, black, and white is a moving anti-war protest (Picasso painted it after the Nationalist bombing of a small Basque town during the Civil War). Picasso's *Guernica* was housed for many years in New York's Museum of Modern Art, and Picasso stipulated that his most visceral painting not return to his homeland until the dictator Franco died and democracy was restored in Spain. Franco died in 1975, but the work remained in New York until 1981. Ironically, even though Picasso felt that the Prado, his country's greatest museum, was the only logical place for the painting to reside, the painting never made it to the Prado proper. *Guernica* had its own gallery in the Prado annex, Casón del Buen Retiro, before officials moved it to the Museo Nacional Centro de Arte Reina Sofia down the street.

The Reina Sofía is especially strong in early twentieth-century works by artists like Picasso, Miró, Dalí, and Julio González, as well as contemporary movements like Abstract Art, Pop Art, and Minimalism. The museum organizes some of the finest temporary exhibits of any museum in Spain; check the schedule at the entrance to see what's exhibited when you're there. If you're a contemporary art lover, you'll want to spend almost as much time here as at the Prado; allow three hours at a minimum for your visit.

Calle Santa Isabel, 52 (at Paseo del Prado, opposite Atocha train station). ☎ *91-467-50-62. Internet:* http://museoreinasofia.es. *Metro: Atocha. Admission: 500 pta. ($2.75), 250 pta. ($1.40) students and seniors, free for children 11 and under; free admission Sat 2:30–9 p.m. and Sun 10 a.m.–2:30 p.m. Open: Mon and Wed–Sat 10 a.m.–9 p.m., Sun 10 a.m.–2:30 p.m; closed Tues.*

Must-sees: A Prado primer

Diego Velázquez y Silva's *Las Meninas* (Maids in Waiting) is the Prado's most popular and probably greatest painting. The painting, a masterful achievement of perspective, spatial depth, and lighting, perennially appears on lists of the greatest works in art history. In *Las Meninas,* the Infanta Margarita is depicted in the artist's studio (Velázquez himself, who appears in the lower left corner of the work) along with her maids and two dwarfs. The Infanta's parents, the king, Felipe IV, and his queen are sitting for a portrait; however, they appear only as reflections in a mirror in the background. As you look at the painting, notice how it draws your eyes from the Infanta toward the back of the room, climbing the terraces to the mirrored reflection. In addition to this famed work, I've assembled a partial list of the museum's greatest hits.

From the Spanish School (sixteenth through eighteenth century)

✔ Diego Velázquez: *Las Meninas; The Spinners; Christ Crucified; Surrender of Breda; The Triumph of Bacchus; The Fable of Arachne*

✔ Bartolomé Murillo: *Immaculate Conception*

✔ José Ribera: *The Martyrdom of St. Felipe; The Trinity*

✔ Francisco de Goya: *The Naked Maja* and *The Clothed Maja;* the *Black Paintings,* including *Saturn Devouring His Son; The Second of May; Executions at Moncloa; The Family of Carlos IV*

✔ El Greco: *Adoration of the Shepherds*

✔ Zurbarán: *Still Life*

From the Italian School (fifteenth through seventeenth century)

✔ Titian: *Venus with the Organist; Self-Portrait*

✔ Fra Angelico: *The Annunciation*

✔ Sandro Boticelli: *Tale of Nastagio degli Honesti*

✔ Tintoretto: *The Lavatory*

From the Flemish School (fifteenth through seventeenth century)

✔ Hieronymous Bosch: *Garden of Earthly Delights; The Hay Cart*

✔ Pieter Breughel the Elder: *The Triumph of Death*

✔ Raphael: *The Holy Family with Lamb; Portrait of a Cardinal*

✔ Peter Paul Rubens: *The Three Graces*

From the German & Dutch Schools (sixteenth through seventeenth century)

✔ Albrecht Dürers: *Adam and Eve; Self-Portrait*

✔ Rembrandt: *Artemis*

Monasterio de las Descalzas Reales
Viejo Madrid

A visit to this former royal palace and splendid example of Renaissance architecture is a retreat from Madrid's modern madness. Converted into a convent for women in the mid-sixteenth century, it's anything but plain. A grand, fresco-lined staircase takes visitors to an upper cloister gallery with a series of extravagant chapels. The convent's collection of religious art by the old masters is exceptional. The highlights are Breughel's *Adoration of the Magi,* Zurbarán's *Saint Francis,* Titian's *Caesar's Coin,* and a priceless collection of sixteenth-century tapestries. Visitation hours at the convent, where a small group of cloistered nuns still live, are peculiar and not always adhered to.

Translated as the Monastery of the Royal Barefoot Franciscans, this place has a past as fascinating as its name. The daughter of the Emperor Carlos V, Juana of Austria, founded the convent of Poor Clares in a noble palace. The women of noble families that entered the nunnery brought sizable dowries, mostly great works of art. Nobles also squirreled away their young illegitimate daughters here to be reared by the nuns.

Admission to the convent is by 45-minute guided tour only.

Plaza Descalzas, 3. ☎ *91-542-00-59. Metro: Sol or Opera. Admission: 650 pta. ($3.50) (Joint admission with Monasterio de la Encarnación, 825 pta./$4.50). Open: Tues–Thur and Sat 10:30 a.m.–12:45 p.m. and 4–5:45 p.m., Fri, 10:30 a.m.–12:45 p.m., Sun 11 a.m.–1:45 p.m.; closed Jan 1, Easter week (Wed–Sat), May 1, 2, 11, 15, Aug 11, Nov 9 and Dec 25.*

Palacio Real
Viejo Madrid

Occupying the site of a ninth-century Moorish *alcázar* (fortress), the Royal Palace built by Spain's Bourbon monarchs makes a grandiose statement about Madrid's place in the world, circa 1750. Each room is an exercise in megawatt wealth, and taste flies out the window. Construction of the huge neoclassical palace — it has 2,000 rooms — took nearly three decades and incorporated the lavish tastes of both Carlos III and Carlos IV. The official residence of the Royal Family until 1931, it is now used only for state functions, because King Juan Carlos and Queen Sofía live in more modest digs, the Zarzuela Palace just beyond Madrid. Allow two to three hours to see the Palace in its entirety (or at least what they let you see!).

Of special note are the **Throne Room,** with its scarlet wall coverings, Baroque gilded mirrors, and a Tiepolo fresco on the ceiling; the regal **Gala Dining Room,** which shows off a spectacular dining table and jaw-dropping tapestries; and the **Porcelain Room,** covered floor to ceiling in a garish display of green, white, and purple porcelain. Check out the old **Royal Pharmacy** (near the ticket office), which has Talavera pottery jars and old recipe books of medications. In the **Real Armería** is a fine display of arms and armor. Wander to the edge of the large Plaza de la Armería (Royal Armory Square) that faces the palace, and you see how abruptly Madrid ends and the plains begin. Look also for the new temporary exhibits hall, part of what will eventually become the **Museum of Royal Collections** (with a permanent display of carriages, tapestries, paintings, silver, and crystal belonging to Spain's long lines of monarchs).

After your visit to the Royal Palace, step across Calle Bailén to the statue-lined **Plaza de Oriente,** where generations of monarchs and politicos have addressed the masses. The square, a good spot to take a breather, faces the recently remodeled **Teatro Real,** the Royal Opera House.

If you visit the Royal Palace on the first Wednesday of the month, you have a chance to see the ceremonial changing of the guards (at noon for free). And if you're carrying a European Union passport, you can get into the Royal Palace for free, too (on Wednesdays).

Calle de Bailén, 2. ☎ *91-547-53-50. Metro: Ópera or Plaza de España. Admission: 850 pta. ($4.75); 950 pta. ($5.25) for guided tour. Open: Mon–Sat 9:30 a.m.–5:30 p.m.; Sun and holidays 9:30 a.m.–2:30 p.m.*

Panteón de Goya (Ermita de San Antonio de la Florida)
Parque del Oeste

If you find that you're a fan of Goya, particularly his dark works, you may want to pay your respects by making a detour out to his pantheon (a bit out of the way beyond Estación Norte train station). King Carlos IV commissioned Goya, his court painter, to create frescoes for the cupola and vaults of the chapel, *Ermita de San Antonio,* in 1798. Some consider the romantic works among Goya's best. Fittingly, Goya is entombed in the chapel beneath his frescoes of Madrid society, of which he was a master of depicting. Goya's remains were exhumed and brought to Madrid in 1908 from the Bordeaux region of France. It's rumored, though, that the artist's head was inexplicably missing.

Glorieta de San Antonio de la Florida, 5. ☎ *91-542-07-22. Metro: Norte. Admission: 300 pta. ($1.75). Open: Tues–Fri 10 a.m.–2 p.m. and 4–8 p.m., Sat–Sun (and holidays) 10 a.m.–2 p.m.*

Madrid's classic corners

Parque del Buen Retiro

If your feet and back ache from doing overtime at the museums, peaceful Retiro Park beckons. A pretty expanse of green lawns, lush gardens, fountains, and tree-lined promenades, this is prime strolling and sunning ground for Madrileños of all ages. Do as they do: kick off your shoes, smoke lots of cigarettes (just kidding), and take a siesta (but attach your belongings to your one of your limbs so you don't wake up without your camera or purse). Or, rent a rowboat and paddle at the small lake in the center of the park. In summer, the park comes alive with vendors of ice cream and handcrafts, musicians, tarot-card readers, and lovers rolling around in the grass. The Palacio de Cristal (Crystal Palace), a nineteenth-century iron and glass solarium that houses a sculpture garden, is finally open again after years of renovations.

Location: Bordered by streets Alfonso XII and Alcalá, with main entrances on both. If you enter at the corner by Puerta de Alcalá, you can head right down Avenida de México to the park lake.

Plaza Mayor

Madrid's Main Square is one of the most famous and attractive plazas in Spain. The early seventeenth-century arcaded plaza today hosts restaurants, outdoor cafés, shops, and student hangouts, but its past is like a microcosm of Spain itself. The Plaza Mayor was the scene of lively marketplaces and theater festivals, bullfights and coronations of kings, religious processions and public executions, and trials during the Spanish Inquisition. Colorful frescoes above the arcades adorn the The Casa de la Panadería (the Bakery). In the center of the plaza is an equestrian statue of Felipe III. Make sure you spend a couple of hours wandering around the neighborhood that spills out from the Plaza Mayor; it's filled with small shops and — guess what? — *tapas* bars. See "Enjoying Madrid's Nightlife," later in this chapter, for my recommendations.

Location: You can find this plaza off of Calle de Toledo, just south of Calle Mayor.

Plaza de Toros de las Ventas

Few observers are indifferent to bullfighting. One of Spain's most representative traditions, it has passionate, die-hard fans as well as staunch opponents, who decry it as a barbaric anachronism. If you faint at the sight of blood, don't even consider attending a bullfight. I'm always surprised, though, how many people find themselves transfixed by the spectacle of man and beast pitting off in a ring. To aficionados, bullfighting is more art and ritual than sport. The uninitiated may have a hard time grasping that concept — after all, six bulls are put out to die each afternoon — but if you're up to it, Madrid is one of the top spots in Spain to witness the Spanish fascination with *matadors* and charging beasts. Its bullring, the Plaza de Toros de las Ventas, isn't the oldest in Spain (that honor goes to Ronda, in Andalusia), but it represents, along with Ronda and Seville, the pinnacle of Spanish bullfighting. Built in the 1920s, its tiles and Moorish-style arches are meant to evoke the *mudéjar* architecture so prevalent in the south of Spain. (For more on *mudéjar* architecture, see Appendix B.)

If you can't stomach a *corrida* (bullfight) or you land in Madrid out of season, you can visit the Museo Taurino (Bullfighting Museum), a modest place with portraits of famous *matadors,* jewel-encrusted capes and jackets, stuffed bull heads, and Goya etchings. You can see the outfit belonging to Spain's first female bullfighter, Juanita Cruz. Don't miss the bloody *traje de luces,* or suit of lights, that the legendary Manolete was wearing when he was gored to death. If that sounds like fun, you can visit the museum (free admission, open Tuesday to Sunday 9:30 a.m. to 2:30 p.m.), but you're not allowed inside the actual *plaza de toros.*

To see the bullring, visit during the bullfighting season (May to October) and choose either a *sol* (sun) or *sombra* (shadows) seat. A word of advice: spring for the more expensive sombra seat. You can roast like a suckling pig in the *sol.* For tickets to bullfights (which range from 425–13,000 pta./$2.30–72), visit the ticket booth at the Plaza de Toros de la Venta, or call ☎ **91-356-22-00** for information.

Museo Taurino, Calle de Alcalá, 237. ☎ 91-725-18-57. Metro: Las Ventas. Admission (museum): Free. Open: Mar–Oct, Tues–Fri and Sun 9:30 a.m.–2:30 p.m.; Nov–Feb, Mon–Fri 9:30 a.m.–2:30 p.m.

Puerta del Sol

The focal point of Viejo Madrid, this noisy and chaotic square is the heart that pumps shoppers, tourists, and traffic out to the smaller arteries of the city. Although it's not particularly distinguished in appearance, it is an essential feature of Madrid. Originally part of a wall that encased the Old Quarter, the Puerta del Sol (Gateway to the Sun) is Spain's ground zero; a marker indicates the square as the point from which all road distances in Spain are measured. One of the best known buildings in Madrid is the **Casa de Correos** (the original Post Office), built in 1768 by a French architect. A clock tower that was added in the nineteenth century tops it. The Puerta del Sol was the scene of many historical events, including an 1808 uprising against Napoleon in the War of Independence, an episode documented in Francisco de Goya's great and harrowing painting, *Dos de Mayo* (which now hangs in the Prado).

The Puerta del Sol is the equivalent of New York's Times Square. On New Year's Eve, Madrileños crowd the square to hear the chimes of the clock tower. Like Spaniards everywhere, they stuff 12 grapes into their mouths — one at the sound of each chime. Try it, and you're destined to wind up with a mouth of unchewed fruit and grape juice running down your chin. Perfect for that New Year's kiss.

More cool things to see and do

✔ **Sampling some smaller museums.** If the crowds at the Prado and Thyssen get you down, sample some of Madrid's excellent smaller museums, great in their own right but just off the prime tourism circuit (literally and figuratively). Not only are these terrific art collections; they're your ticket to glorious Madrileño mansions and palaces.

✔ **Visiting the Museo Lázaro Galdiano.** Calle Serrano, 122 (☎ 91-561-60-84; Metro: Rubén Darío or Núñez de Balboa). This museum is a quietly spectacular surprise. It's one of the Madrid's finest museums, housed in an immaculate nineteenth-century mansion in one of the city's newer northern neighborhoods. The superb private collection includes European old masters and applied arts from ancient times to the nineteenth century. You find lesser-known Goyas (from his black period), works by El Greco, Velázquez, Zurbarán, Ribera and Murillo, Limoges enamels, and Renaissance jewelry. The museum is open Tuesday to Sunday from 10 a.m. to 2 p.m., and closed holidays and the month of August; admission is 500 pta. ($2.75), but it's free on Wednesday.

✔ **Exploring Museo Sorolla.** General Martínez Campos, 37 (☎ 91-310-15-84; Metro: Iglesia or Rubén Darío). Check out the former studio and mansion of the celebrated Impressionist Joaquín Sorolla, who lived there in the early 1900s — it looks like the painter and his family left last week. The home is crammed with objects the artist collected in his lifetime and a generous selection of his works, including the luminous Mediterranean beach scenes for which he's best known (Sorolla was known as the painter of light). The museum is north of downtown, not far from Paseo de la Castellana. Free guided tours (in Spanish only) are available October through June. The museum is open Tuesday through Saturday from 10 a.m. to 3 p.m. and Sunday from 10 a.m. to 2 p.m.; admission is 500 pta. ($2.75), but it's free on Sunday.

✔ **Milling around Viejo Madrid.** One of the best ways to absorb the flavor of Madrid is to stroll the atmospheric streets of the Old City, where you uncover remnants of medieval Madrid and the city later built by the Habsburgs. A good place to start is in the **Plaza Mayor** (described earlier in this chapter). **Cava de San Miguel,** which you reach through the Arco de Cuchilleros, is a lively strip of *mesones* (cave-like restaurants) and taverns. Along Calle Mayor is **Plaza de la Villa,** Madrid's old town square. The cluster of handsome buildings dates to the fifteenth and sixteenth centuries. The oldest structure is the **Torre de los Lujanes,** a *mudéjar* (Moorish and Christian architectural mix) construction with a tall, minaret-like structure. **Casa de la Villa,** on the opposite side of the plaza, was built in 1640 and once housed both the town hall and city jail. **Casa de Cisneros** is a reconstructed sixteenth-century palace with a splendid Plateresque facade.

South of the plaza, beyond Calle Segovia, is **Plaza de la Paja,** a pretty and quiet space that was medieval Madrid's commercial center. On this plaza is Madrid's only Gothic building, the **Capilla del Obispo** (Bishop's Chapel). Nearby is the Moorish-looking fourteenth-century **San Pedro** church. Just east is a jumble of some of Madrid's most animated streets: **Cava Baja, Cava Alta, Almendro,** and **Calle del Nuncio.** Just about every address in this district, called **La Latina,** houses an appealing old tavern or *tasca.*

The *barrio* is one of Madrid's classic, working-class areas. The popular **El Rastro Fleamarket** (see "Shopping," later in this chapter) is held every Sunday along the warren of streets near **Calle de Toledo,** a lively thoroughfare that leads back up to the Plaza Mayor.

Getting all turned around in Viejo Madrid is easy, so don't get frustrated. The many taverns along the way make great pit stops for map study. Or, just stop in for a beer, and while you're there, ask the bartender or patrons for some assistance.

✔ **Drinking in the best of Bourbon Madrid.** Spain's "Art Avenue," **Paseo del Prado,** was the central axis of the Bourbon monarchs' royal expansion plan for the city. It was designed to be the center of arts and sciences (in fact, the Prado was originally scheduled to be a national science museum). Besides connecting Madrid's principal art museums (the Prado, Thyssen-Bornemisza, and Reina Sofía), beautiful nineteenth-century palaces and apartment buildings line the leafy promenade, which a fountain of Neptune bisects. North of the Prado, at Calle Alcalá, is **Plaza de Cibeles,** crowned by the ornate fountain of the Roman goddess Cybele, one of the city's most famous monuments. When *fútbol* fans get crazy after major wins, they usually wind up in Cybele's lap — and she never seems to mind. Two great buildings frame the Plaza: the **Palacio de Comunicaciones** (Main Post Office) on the Prado side, and **Banco de España** across the way.

Carlos III, continuing his makeover of Madrid, constructed the **Puerta de Alcalá** gateway to the city. In the eighteenth century, it marked the eastern border, but of course the city kept growing and growing. Today the massive granite monument's five arches are more like doors in the middle of a living room.

✔ **Making the most of Modern Madrid.** Upper-crust nineteenth-century apartment buildings and tonier-than-*tú* shops line Madrid's chicest neighborhood, **Barrio de Salamanca.** It extends from Puerta de Alcalá to Calle Ortega y Gasset and from Serrano to Plaza de Roma. If those *pesetas* are burning holes in your pocket, join the elegant *señoras* on their daily rounds of the barrio's antiques shops, fashion boutiques, and art galleries. If I had to choose, I say that Calle Serrano is the best for a nice day stroll.

Madrid's massive **Museo Arqueológico** (Archaeology Museum), Calle Serrano, 13 (☎ 91-57-79-12), is most notable for its cool replica of Spain's Altamira caves, festooned with prehistoric paintings of bison (a great place to duck in out of the summer sun) and the fourth-century B.C. Iberian bust of *La Dama de Elche.* The museum is open Tuesday through Saturday from 9:30 a.m. to 8:30 p.m. and Sunday from 9:30 a.m. to 2:30 p.m.; admission is 500 pta. ($2.75), but it's free Saturday starting at 2:30 p.m. and Sunday.

✔ **Strolling along Paseo de la Castellana.** A continuation of Paseo del Prado, this tree-lined promenade stretches from Plaza de Colón way out to Madrid's new northern neighborhoods. A prime strolling ground, Paseo de la Castellana explodes in summer with stylish outdoor terrace cafés and bars. If you want to join the parade of beautiful people and Spanish-style "yoopies" (yuppies), grab your cigarettes and toss a nonchalant sweater around your neck, but don't dare show up before 11 p.m. Unless you're a real night owl, the *copas* (cocktails) crowd will stay here way past your bedtime.

Missing Madrid's busiest artery, **Gran Vía,** is nearly impossible, if for no other reason than your hotel is likely to be on or near it. Bursting with a dazzling collage of cinemas, shops, hotels, strip shows, and neon and bright lights, the section from Plaza de Callao to **Plaza de España** is Madrid's Broadway. Frenetic and slightly seedy, it offers few if any classic sights, though it's a sight in itself. In the center of Plaza de España is a statue of Cervantes and his beloved characters, Don Quixote and Sancho Panza.

Taking the kids to the parks

North of the Royal Palace, the nicely landscaped **Parque del Oeste** (West Park) extends along the River Manzanares. Young fans of the movie *The Mummy* will enjoy the park's most attention-getting feature, the **Templo de Debod,** a fourth-century B.C. Egyptian temple that once stood next to the Nile. Adults, however, may think it odd to find such a thing marooned in the middle of Madrid. When the Aswan Dam flooded, a group of Spanish engineers rescued the temple; the Egyptian government thanked them by donating the structure to Spain. An aerial cablecar, which you can find at Paseo del Pintor Rosales, s/n, connects Parque del Oeste to **Casa de Campo,** a 4,000-acre expanse of green, formerly royal hunting grounds. You can also reach the park by getting off at the Lago or Batán Metro stops. The park contains a lake (with rowboats), a pretty decent zoo (Parque Zoológico), and theme park (Parque de Atracciones) — making it a great place to take the kids if they (or you) tire of Madrid the museum city. The zoo (☎ 91-711-99-50) is open daily from 10 a.m. to sunset, and admission is 1,600 pta. ($9) for adults, 1,300 pta. ($7) for children 3 to 8, and free for children 2 and under. Kids will especially like taking the *teleférico* (aerial cable car, ☎ 91-541-74-50) there. The ride is 515 pta. ($2.75) round-trip. The cable car runs daily 11 a.m. to 9 p.m March through October, and from November through February, it runs only on weekends from noon to 9 p.m.

And on Your Left, the Prado: Seeing Madrid by Guided Tour

Sometimes the most hassle-free way to see a city in a short period of time is on a guided tour. If you don't have much time and want someone else to worry about getting around, the following tours can give you a good overview of the city.

Bus tours

The Patronato Municipal de Turismo (City Tourism Office) offers an extensive series of historical and cultural tours by bus and by foot throughout the year. The list of topics and places covered is much too long to detail here; ask at any tourism office about the **Discover Madrid** program and scheduled visits or call ☎ **91-588-29-06.** (Bus tours run 950 pta. ($5) adults, 750 pta. ($4) students and seniors.)

Big yellow double-decker tour buses operated by **Sol Opentours** (☎ **91-52-211-20;** Internet: www.solopentours.com) run a non-guided circuit in Madrid, with 15 pickup and drop-off points, including Plaza de España, Puerta del Sol, the Prado Museum, and Plaza de Colón (9 a.m. to 7 p.m. daily). The buses run daily from 9:30 a.m. to 7:30 p.m., and cost 1,600 pta. ($9) for adults and 800 pta. ($4.50) for children. You can purchase tickets on board the bus, which are valid for an entire day (the entire circuit lasts 90 minutes).

Madrid Visión organizes multi-language city bus tours (with headsets). They depart from Gran Vía, 32, but you can get on or hop off anywhere along their route. The sightseeing tour costs 1,700 pta. ($9). If you stay on the bus, the tour lasts about a half-hour. For more information, call ☎ **91-302-45-26.**

Walking tours

Guided walking tours of Viejo Madrid, in English, are available every Saturday at 10 a.m. and 12 p.m. through the Municipal Tourist Office. Walkers leave from the tourism office at Plaza Mayor, 3; the price is 500 pta. ($2.75) for adults, 400 pta. ($2.20) for seniors, children ages 4–12, and students. Call ☎ **91-588-29-06** or 91-588-16-36 for more information. Tours are in Spanish unless there's a large English-speaking group. If your Spanish is of the rusty high school variety or nonexistent, make sure to check the group's composition ahead of time.

Suggested One-, Two-, and Three-Day Sightseeing Itineraries

If you're not overcome with jet lag, on **Day One** you almost certainly want to start with one of Madrid's big hitters: the Prado Museum or the Royal Palace. At either, your objective should be to get there early, before the crowds (though you may find a line at either when the doors open). If you spend the morning at the Prado, you can then stroll the Paseo del Prado/La Castellana, stroll in Retiro Park, and catch lunch either around Puerta del Sol or the Chueca district. If you begin with the Palacio Real, you're in position to have a few *tapas* as well as lunch in Viejo Madrid. Spend the afternoon on a relaxed tour of Viejo Madrid, including the Plaza Mayor and perhaps visiting the Monasterio de las Descalzas Reales (check the odd opening hours carefully).

On **Day Two** in Madrid, take in whichever of the major sights I listed in Day One that you couldn't work in to your schedule. If you're a certified art head, plan on checking out another of the Big Three art museums (either the Thyssen or the Reina Sofía). Others may want to head to the sophisticated Barrio Salamanca, for some of Madrid's best shopping.

On **Day Three,** you can either hit a smaller museum or two, such as the Lázaro Galdiano or Sorolla, check out more of Madrid's green spaces, or examine a neighborhood — Viejo Madrid, Latina, or Chueca in depth or plan an excursion to Aranjuez or El Escorial (or slightly farther afield, such as Toledo or Segovia). If you have limited time in central Spain, a day trip makes the most sense.

Shopping in Madrid

Madrid is where Spaniards from the rest of Spain go to spend their money (much like how Brits go to London to shop and Americans stock up in New York). As Spain's largest city, Madrid has more of everything, from the chicest designer clothing stores to a healthy supply of all the regional handcrafts you find (usually at cheaper prices) throughout Spain.

If you're traveling beyond Madrid, you may want to acquire some of your loot — at least as far as artisanry is concerned — in other towns. Of course, you may not want to lug it around the country with you, so if you're departing from Madrid, you can always leave shopping until the end.

I describe Madrid's well-defined primo shopping areas in the following sections, but for a true Madrid experience, hit the famous weekly flea market, **El Rastro,** on Sunday mornings (see the "Run to *El Rastro*" sidebar, later in this chapter).

Madrid's best shopping areas

The old center, near **Puerta del Sol,** especially the pedestrian-only streets Preciados and del Carmen, is a dense concentration of shops of all kinds, from little mom-and-pop places to the mega-department stores found in all major cities. Waves of souvenir shops and others selling accessible silver and jewelry surround **Plaza Mayor.** The glamour of **Gran Vía,** once Madrid's most exclusive shopping avenue, has given way to a more utilitarian stores selling downtown fashion, shoes, bookstores, and specialty food and wine shops. Just north of Plaza de España, **Calle Princesa** is a main shopping drag with a little bit of everything, but mostly clothing and shoe stores. **Mercado Puerta de Toledo,** south of Plaza Mayor, used to be the old fish market, but it's been recast as a slick shopping center, a full catch of restaurants, boutiques, and antique stores. **Barrio Salamanca,** just north of Retiro Park and east of Paseo de la Castellana, ought to have a doorman at the entrance. This elite district is home to Madrid's most upscale boutiques. If you want the latest and chicest in designer wear, jewelry, and home furnishings, and you don't need to ask the price, check out Calles Goya and Serrano and the small streets that feed into them. Calle Claudio de Coello has some of the best art and antiques dealers.

If you're shopping with a mission, you need to plan your attack around Spanish shopping hours, which for the most part continue to respect the midday lunch closing (by and large, only malls stay open all day). Shop hours are generally Monday through Friday, 9 or (more likely) 10 a.m. to 1:30 p.m. or 2 and 4 or (more likely) 5 to 8 p.m. On Saturdays, they're open from 9:30 a.m. or so to 1:30 p.m. On Sundays, even compulsive shoppers have to take the day off.

What to look for and where to find it

In Spain, the law coordinates sales, with twice-annual sell-offs of inventory that all begin at the same time: the second week of January and the last week of July. Signs announcing *rebajas* (sales or rebates) are plastered over store windows. Prices continue to drop when stores move from first to second and finally, ultimate *rebajas*.

From antiques to wine, you'll find no shortage of ways to spend your money in Madrid. The following stores are some of my favorites.

Antiques

Check out El Rastro, the flea market for odds-and-ends, on Sundays. Calle de las Huertas is also a good area to conduct your hunt.

At **Centro de Arte y Antiguedades,** Serrano, 5 (☎ **91-576-96-82;** Metro: Serrano), you find a number of dealers under one roof (of an attractive old building), some with very fine and very unusual items.

Books

Between the Atocha Train Station and the Botanical Gardens, just east of Paseo del Prado, is a weekend open-air book fair, with new, used, and rare books for sale. If you're in Madrid at the end of May and beginning of June, check out the **Feria del Libro de Madrid** (Madrid Book Fair), which virtually takes over Retiro Park.

Crisol is a bookstore chain with numerous outlets across the city; they have a decent selection of books in English. Among their branches: Paseo de la Castellana, 90 (☎ **91-344-09-67;** Metro: Colón) and Goya, 18 (☎ **91-575-06-40;** Metro: Goya).

Run to *El Rastro*

Even if you're not a shopper, don't miss **El Rastro,** the best-known flea market in Spain, south of the Plaza Mayor. Every Sunday, the unruly market spills over from the long and narrow Calle Ribera de Curtidores into several adjacent streets. It's gotten more commercial and less funky in recent years, but it's still as much a cultural visit as shopping excursion. Once mostly an antiques market, today it has fewer rarities and more run-of-the-mill items: clothing, jewelry, art, animals (!), and, of course, monumental piles of junk. Be careful in the crowds, though: Put your wallet in your front pocket and hold your bag or camera tight to your chest. A lot of jostling goes on, and pickpockets know it's one of their best chances to target tourists. During the week, antique shops in the area are open, though prices aren't exactly what you call flea-market bargains.

El Rastro is open Sundays from 9 a.m. to 8 p.m., but many sellers take off by mid-afternoon. To get there take the Metro to the La Latina stop.

VIPS is an all-purpose chain that often heavily discountes art and architecture books (in both Spanish and English). VIPS stores are seemingly everywhere; but the two you're most likely to pass are Gran Vía, 43 (no phone; Metro: Gran Vía) and Serrano, 41 and (no phone; Metro: Serrano).

Crafts

Artespaña, Hermosilla, 14 (☎ 91-435-02-21; Metro: Serrrano) is a government-run store with a large selection of crafts, especially items for the home.

El Arco de los Cuchilleros Artesanía de Hoy, in the Plaza Mayor (No. 9) (☎ 91-365-26-80; Metro: Sol), may be a mouthful, but it's also hands down the best place to go for crafts from all over Spain. From Spanish fans to embroidered shawls, jewelry, hand-blown glass, and ceramics, you'll find it here — as well as a staff that speaks English.

Check out the enormous selection of hand-painted ceramics at **Antigua Casa Talavera,** Isabel la Católica, 2 (☎ 91-547-34-17; Metro: Santo Domingo), including attractive pieces from Valencia and Talavera, and tiles.

Cigars and tobacco

Attention cigar-smoking Americans: You're sure to light up when you visit **Tabacos Bejarano,** José del Hierro, 39 (no phone), which sells *Habanas,* or Cuban cigars. Treat yourself to them while you're in Spain, because you can't take them with you when you return to the U.S.

Department stores

FNAC, Preciados, 28 (☎ **91-595-61-00;** Metro: Santo Domingo)is a French store, specializing in books, music, and magazines, and it offers occasional in-store performances.

Marks & Spencer is an English department store chain with high-quality items and a terrific food store that's spreading across Spain. A Madrid branch is on Serrano, 52 (Metro: Serrano). However, the granddaddy of Spanish department stores, with an encyclopedic inventory, is **El Corte Inglés,** Preciados, 3 (☎ **91-379-80-00;** Metro: Callao or Sol).

Fashion

Adolfo Domínguez, Serrano, 96 (☎ **91-576-70-53;** Metro: Serrano), from Galicia, is one of Spain's top designers for both men and women. His stores are elegant, but not ridiculously expensive.

Ermenegildo Zegna, Serrano, 21 (no phone; Metro: Serrano) is an upscale menswear designer who has gained international renown.

Loewe, Gran Vía, 8 and Serrano, 26 (☎ **91-577-60-56;** Metro: Gran Vía and Serrano), is a leather heaven (for everyone except the cow), and since 1846, the quintessential Spanish luxury clothier. Loewe's offers great luggage and handbags, if price is no object for you.

Roberto Verino Claudio Coello, 27 (no phone; Metro: Gran Vía or Serrano), is a top designer with clothes for both men and women.

Zara has surprisingly hip but affordable fashions for both sexes. Look carefully at materials and washing instructions, though, because some pieces are suprisingly delicate. There are two branches, at Hermosilla, 16 and Gran Vía, 32 (☎ **91-575-64-45** and **91-522-97-27;** Metro: Serrano and Gran Vía, respectively).

Gifts

If you or your family and friends are fans of Lladró, the famous Spanish porcelain figures, you can pick them up at the source, **Lladró Tienda Madrid** Serrano, 68 (☎ **91-247-71-47;** Metro: Serrano).

With an incredible selection of hats (many very imaginative) and souvenir items (such as swords and shields), **Casa Yusta,** Plaza Mayor, 30 (☎ **91-366-50-84;** Metro: Sol), has protected heads for more than a century.

Fans, those elegant accessory items that no stylish Spanish woman is without, make great gifts, but if you're in Madrid in summer, buying one for yourself is wise. **Casa de Diego,** Puerta del Sol, 12 (☎ **91-522-66-43;** Metro: Sol), has more fans than you've probably ever seen, from cheap to exotic, and a good selection of shawls, too. If you're a really big fan of fans, you can find even more fans at **Almoraima,** Plaza Mayor, 12 (☎ **91-365-42-89;** Metro: Sol).

Jewelry

At **Perlas Majorica,** Gran Vía, 39 (no phone; Metro: Gran Vía.), you can buy those fabulous faux pearls from Majorca. (And I promise you, no can tell the difference.)

Music

Virgin Megastore, Serrano, 61 (☎ 91-310-41-10; Metro: Gran Vía), is one of the top places to pick up a flamenco or *rock en Español* (Spanish rock) recording to take home or stick in your headphones on your travels.

FNAC, Preciados 28 (☎ 91-595-61-00; B: Santo Domingo or Gran Vía), the big French bookstore and record chain offers a wide selection of international and Spanish recordings.

Madrid Rock, Gran Vía at Fuencarral (☎ 91-521-02-39; Metro: Santo Domingo or Gran Vía), is a Spanish chain that has most of what the big international stores have, but it also offers a huge selection in back of sale items — CDs between $5–$8.

Shoes

Try some shoes on for size at **Yanko,** Gran Vía, 40 (no phone; Metro: Gran Vía), a top Spanish shoemaker for both sexes.

Calzados Bravo has a nice selection of shoes for men and women, as well as luggage. There are branches at Gran Vía, 31 and 68; Princesa, 58; Goya, 43 (☎ 91-222-73-00; Metro: Gran Vía or Goya).

Malls

You find nearly 100 shops, featuring fashions, jewelry and household items, and a spate of restaurants at **ABC Serrano,** Serrano, 61 (☎ 91-577-50-31; Metro: Serrano), a magnificently restored nineteenth-century building where the daily newspaper ABC was produced.

Wine and cheese

Palacio de los Quesos, Calle Mayor, 53 (no phone; Metro: Sol) has everything you want in Spanish cheeses and wines, as well as *turrón* (a hard candy) and marzipan (an almond candy), which Spaniards are nuts about.

Majorca, Velázquez, 59 (☎ 91-431-99-09; Metro: Velázquez), is another great gourmet shop, where you can eat, as well as pick up Spanish wines for friends back home.

Enjoying Madrid's Nightlife

Madrid swings like no other city in Spain (or in Europe). If you're a creature of the night, you've come to the right place. If you can keep up with Madrileños, who pride themselves on how much they can party and how late they can go — when they sleep is anyone's guess — I take my hat off to you. In the nightlife and cultural capital of Spain you can find dozens of theaters and concert halls offering classical music, dance, and Spanish *zarzuela* (light comic opera), as well as wild discos and the entire spectrum of jazz, rock, alternative, and pop. On top of that, you can enjoy flamenco shows — some about as authentic as you come across in Spain and others targeted strictly at tourists — and everyone's favorite nighttime activity, *tapas* bar-hopping, raised to an art form in Madrid.

The night begins and ends late. In Madrid, afternoon extends to 8 or 9 p.m., and the language reflects that; when Madrilenos greet someone at that hour, they say *buenas tardes* (good afternoon), not *buenas noches* (good evening). Night doesn't really begin until after dinner, and because dinner can begin at 11:30 p.m. or midnight on weekends, it's obvious that "nightlife" more accurately means "early morning life" in the capital.

For up-to-date listings on what's happening in Madrid, get your hands on the weekly **Guía del Ocio,** available at newsstands, or the Friday editions of **El Mundo** or **El País.** For cultural questions of interest to tourists, call ☎ **91-540-40-10.** For information on clubs, discos, and concerts, as well as art exhibits, pick up a free copy of **In Madrid,** a monthly digest of the night stuff happening in Madrid.

Tickets for some venues are available only at their box offices. For tickets to most other cultural events, including bullfights, and soccer matches, contact **Localidades García,** Plaza del Carmen, 1 (☎ **91-531-27-32**) or **TEYCI,** Calle Goya, 7 (☎ **91-576-45-32**). **Corte Inglés** (☎ **91-432-93-00**) stores around the city also sell tickets to concerts. You can also call **Caja de Madrid** (☎ **91-558-87-87** or 902-488-488) and **Caixa de Cataluña** (☎ **902-38-33-33** or 91-538-33-33) for theater tickets.

Tavern and tapas crawls

Since the first little wine shacks opened on "Little Taverns" street in medieval Madrid, locals have incorporated tavern-hopping into their daily routines. For visitors, trolling the old town's interminable taverns is one of the highpoints of Madrid. *Tavernas* and *mesones* (both names to describe very similar *tapas* bars) are places to knock back small glasses of red wine, beer, or sherry, mix with boisterous company, and stave off a real meal with an assortment of *tapas*. *Tapas* come from the Spanish word *tapar,* meaning to cover.

In most places, you're given small snacks, or *tapitas* — olives, mussels, cheese, spicy potatoes, or *chorizo* (Spanish sausage) — as a bonus with your drink order. You can always order a more substantial *tapa* or *ración* (large portion). The idea is to pop in, stand at the bar, down a couple of shooters, offer a couple of unsolicited opinions on politics or soccer, and move on to the next place. Your visit can be a pit stop before heading home or on to a restaurant for dinner, or you can make it an all-night, increasingly loud and loose endeavor.

The best areas are around the **Plaza de Santa Ana, Plaza Mayor,** and the Latina neighborhood, especially the **Cava Baja** and **Cava Alta** streets. Here's an abbreviated list of places to check out, but your walks around town will no doubt uncover an appetizing place or two. Don't be afraid to pop in at places that look good.

More than 200 years old, and a classic of bullfighting ambience, **Taberna de Antonio Sánchez,** Mesón de Paredes, 13 (☎ 91-539-78-26; Metro: La Latina), is as authentic as they come. **Taberna Tempranillo,** Cava Baja, 38 (☎ 91-364-15-32; Metro: La Latina), is a friendly brick bar lined with wine racks (it has an amazing wine list). Located on one of Madrid's most frenetic *tapas* streets, it looks much more lived in than it is. The name **Taberna de Cien Vinos,** Calle del Nuncio, 17 (☎ 91-65-47-04; Metro: La Latina), means tavern of 100 wines, but it offers much more than that, including some great *tapas,* including roast beef and salt cod.

Casa Antonio, Latoneros, 10; ☎ 91-429-93-56; Metro: La Latina), a Madrid classic, has a zinc bar, Moorish tiles, and bright red doors. On nice days, the doors fling open and people spill out into the pedestrian street. You find an excellent assortment of *tapas,* like anchovies and homemade canapés at the very typical **Taberna de Dolores,** Plaza Jesús, 4 (☎ 91-429-22-43; Metro: Banco de Sevilla). **España Cañí,** Plaza del Angel, 14 (no phone; Metro: Sol or Antón Martín), a little tavern just a short distance from Plaza de Santa Ana, is modern, but authentic and lively; it makes a great pit stop. The flamenco on the sound system seconds its Andalusion look. Sit at the bar and have a *caña* (beer) and a tapa of *chorizo infierno* (literally, "hell's hot sausage") or *salmorejo,* a gazpacho-like cold soup native to Córdoba.

The row of cave-like bars built right into the wall along Cava San Miguel outside the Plaza Mayor transport the eighteenth century to the present (or you back to the eighteenth century). *Tapas* bars early in the evening, they get steadily more raucous as the night wears on. Most feature a guitar player or two and alcohol-fueled singalongs. The house speciality at **Mesón del Champignon,** Cava de San Miguel, 17 (☎ 91-559-67-90; Metro: Sol), is as the name implies: garlicky mushrooms that are stuffed, grilled, salted, you name it. **Mesón de la Guitarra,** Cava de San Miguel, 13 (☎ 91-559-95-31; Metro: Sol) is named for the ever-present Spanish guitar. This is the kind of tavern you expect to find in Madrid; it's almost always hopping with boisterous patrons, and wine and song flow freely.

Opera and classical music

Madrid's performing arts companies — including the Ballet Nacional de España, Orquesta Sinfónica de Madrid, and Orquesta Nacional de España — are among the best in Spain or even Europe. Look also for the world-famous flamenco troupe of Antonio Canales, Ballet Flamenco Antonio Canales.

Madrid's opera house, **Teatro Real,** Plaza Isabel II, s/n (Metro: Ópera), has had a tortured history of delays, interruptions, fires, and even a stint as a gunpowder arsenal. Closed various times, but most recently from 1988 to 1997, it was finally rescued and given a state-of-the-art lease on life. You may quibble with the showy, nouveau antique design — handsome but cheesy faux-wood columns, for example — but you can't argue with the sophisticated stage technology in place. Until Barcelona's Liceu reopened at the end of 1999, the Teatro Real was the most technologically advanced opera house in Europe. Madrileños, starved for big-ticket productions, bought up virtually every ticket for the first season for programs such as *Carmen, La Bohème,* and *Tannhäuser.* Ballet and concerts are also held at the Teatro. For tickets, visit the box office or call ☎ **91-516-06-06;** Fax: 91-516-06-51. For general information, call ☎ **91-516-06-60.** The box office is open Monday through Saturday, 10 a.m. to 1:30 p.m. and 5:30 to 8 p.m. If there's a performance on Sunday, the box office opens two hours before (generally at 6 p.m.). Guided tours of the sleek opera house (in English if there's a large enough group) are held on Tuesday through Friday at 1 p.m. and Saturday and Sunday from 10:30 a.m. to 1:30 p.m. (500 pta., or $2.75).

Opera takes the stage from January to July at the **Auditorio Nacional de Música,** Príncipe de Vergara, 146 (☎ **91-337-01-00;** Metro: Cruz de Rayo), and there are excellent classical music concerts from October to June. At **Teatro Calderón.** Calle Atocha, 18 (☎ **91-632-01-14;** Metro: Tirso de Molina), you can enjoy such well-known operas as Rossini's *The Barber of Seville.*

A visit to **Teatro Lírico Nacional de la Zarzuela,** Jovellanos, 4 (☎ **91-524-54-00;** Metro: Banco de España), is a chance to see *zarzuela,* the traditional form of light comic opera indigenous to Madrid. The singing is in Spanish, but you needn't know the language to enjoy the show.

Theater and musicals

Madrid is the *teatro* (theater) capital of Spain, but, logically, nearly all productions are in Spanish. If you don't speak Spanish and wish to see theater, you're best off opting for a performance of *zarzuela,* in which the language doesn't much matter. For other theater productions, you need to be relatively fluent in Spanish.

Teatro Albéniz, Calle Paz, 11 (☎ **91-531-83-11;** Metro: Sevilla), has theater as well as dance and an occasional *zarzuela* (light opera). The **Teatro Nuevo Apolo,** Plaza de Tirso de Molina, 1 (☎ **91-429-52-38;** Metro: Tirso de Molina), often presents popular international musicals, such as *Chicago.* Though you may think you can only see comedies at **Teatro de la Comedia,** Calle Príncipe, 14 (☎ **91-521-49-31;** Metro: Sol), groups here also perform classic Spanish works by playwrights such as García Lorca and Lope de Vega. Your Spanish needs to be fluent to understand complex, lyrical works like theirs, however. **Teatro Español,** Príncipe, 25 (☎ 91-429-03-18; Metro: Sol). The municipal Spanish theater program offers a wide variety of Spanish plays.

Bars and pubs

Two areas thick with back-to-back bars and cafés, many appealing to the young and rowdy, are **Calle de las Huertas** (Metro: Antón Martín), between the Plaza Mayor and Paseo del Prado, and the area around **Plaza Dos de Mayo,** in the Malasaña district (Metro: Tribunal). **Plaza de Santa Ana** (Metro: Sol or Antón Martín) is also extremely lively and flush with barhoppers most nights of the week.

Bar Cock, Calle de la Reina, 16 (☎ 91-532-28-26; Metro: Gran Vía or Banco de España), is a stylishly understated, urbane, and smoky place that features high ceilings and high-priced cocktails. It seems to attract a disproportionate number of models, actors, and public relations sorts. Another chic hangout is **Teatriz,** Hermosilla, 15 (☎ 91-577-53-79; Metro: Velázquez), a former theater turned restaurant and bar. The attention-demanding décor is the work of Philippe Starck. On a totally different note is **Cervecería Alemana,** Plaza de Santa Ana, 6 (☎ 91-429-70-33; Metro: Sol or Antón Martín); this beer hall is on an altogether different plane, with plenty of light, beer, and a young, cheerful crowd.

Tavern and *tapas* talk

Tapas are the small snacks on a little saucer plate, which, once upon a time, were used to cover the opening of your drink. The art of moving from one bar to another in search of snacks, Spanish grazing, is called *tapeo.*

All you need to make your way around a tavern or *tapas* bar is the shortest of Spanish vocabularies — and you may not even need these, because bartenders usually have few problems with the English words for beer and wine. Accompanying your requests with *por favor* (please) goes a long way to getting what you want.

A beer is *una cerveza* ("oo-na thair-*bay*-tha") or *una caña,* a draft ("*oo*-nah *con*-ya"). *Un vino tinto* is a glass of red wine. White wine is *vino blanco.* If you want to try a famous Spanish sherry, ask for *un jerez.* A dry sherry is simply *un fino.* And when you're ready to move on and want the check, say ¿*Me cobra, por favor?* ("may *koh*-bra, pore fah-*vohr?*"). You may or may not get a cash register receipt.

With a cool 1930s look, **Chicote,** Gran Vía, 12 (☎ **91-532-67-37;** Metro: Gran Vía), is one of Madrid's enduring classics, and one of its most famous cocktail bars. Hemingway dug it; he and many other writers and artists and drank here often in pre-Spanish Civil War days. The waiters are extraordinary genteel, and they should be given the high price of the drinks. Likewise, elaborately tiled **Los Gabrieles,** Echegaray, 17 (☎ **91-429-62-61;** Metro: Tirso de Molina), brings the flavors and sounds of Andalusia to Madrid. In a neighborhood thick with bars, its cellar once housed a *bordello.*

Cafés and terrazas: Let La Marcha begin

Outdoor cafés and bars (known as *terraces*) are a Spanish specialty — an opportunity to talk loudly, gesticulate with abandon, and check out the flow of people strutting their stuff. In Madrid, locals do these things about as well as anybody. Linger over a café or beer and do the same (though you can keep gesticulations to a minimum if you fear spilling your drink). Outdoor cafés are also a good option for nonsmokers, because in many Madrid bars, you may be the only one who's not chain-smoking.

Check out Plaza Mayor and Plaza Santa Ana for relaxed, traditional cafés that get going in early evening. In the heat of summer, the *terrazas* (open-air bars) along Paseo de Recoletos and Paseo de la Castellana really sizzle. The famous Madrileño *marcha,* the all-night party, begins at terrace cafés and then moves to the clubs and discos. If you want a primer on the latest fashions favored by Madrid's elite, just park yourself at any of the bars under the trees and settle in as the parade begins.

For more relaxed, traditional cafés that get going in early evening, check out Plaza Mayor and Plaza Santa Ana, or either of the following options. **Café Gijón,** Paseo de Recoletos, 21 (☎ **91-521-54-25;** Metro: Banco de España), is a revered institution (especially for the literary set) that dates back to the late-nineteenth century. And on historic Plaza de Oriente, near the Royal Palace and Opera House, the **Café de Oriente,** Plaza de Oriente, 2 (☎ **91-541-39-74;** Metro: Ópera), stands, built on the remains of a seventeenth-century convent. Sit in the palace-like interior or on the apppetizing sidewalk terrace.

Stoking a fire for flamenco dancing

Flamenco is as identifiably Spanish as bullfights and the glorious Iberian sun, so it's only natural that most visitors arrive in Madrid determined to see an authentic flamenco show, called a *tablao.* Flamenco may have been born in Andalusia, but some (or most) of its greatest practitioners reside in Madrid. Most shows are firmly directed at tourists, but that doesn't mean they're kitschy productions. The quality of dancing is generally excellent.

Several of Madrid's flamenco shows offer dinner theater options, but you're better off eating at a real restaurant first and suffering only the cover and drink minimum (2,500–5,000 pta./$14–$31). Dinner is far from their top priority, but the clubs tend to charge as if they're serving the choicest gourmet. The shows start late (generally around 11 p.m.), so you can easily get dinner elsewhere first.

Café de Chinitas is perhaps the best known of the Madrid clubs, with excellent shows and costumes. Its dinner and show runs 9,500 pta. ($53); the show only (with one drink included) is 4,300 pta. ($24) (Calle Torija, 7; ☎ 91-547-15-02; Metro: Santo Domingo).

One of the liveliest places in town, the **Corral de la Morería** has a good, slick flamenco troupe in action. The one-drink minimum/cover charge is 4,000 pta. ($22); dinner and a show runs you 10,000 pta. ($55) (Calle Morería, 7; ☎ 91-565-81-46; Metro: La Latina).

Casa Patas doubles as a tavern and restaurant, with flamenco shows at the back (Monday to Thursday at 10:30 p.m., Friday and Saturday at midnight). Shows are less glitzy, more intimate, and more affordable (2,500 pta./$14) than the two clubs listed previously (Cañizares, 10; ☎ 91-369-04-96; **Metro:** Antón Martín).

Live rhythms: Jazz, Latino, and rock

You didn't think that flamenco was it, did you? Madrid also offers a bunch of cool little clubs to hear live jazz and Latin music (which was hot in Madrid long before anyone in the U.S. started shaking their bon-bon to "Livin' La Vida Loca"). Check out the following clubs:

✔ **Café Central,** an attractive, sophisticated jazz café near Plaza de Santa Ana, has nightly piano, jazz quartets, and the occasional singer-songwriter (Plaza del Ángel, 10; ☎ 91-369-41-43; Metro: Antón Martín).

✔ **Populart** is always packed and the bar schedules live performances that range from jazz and blues to reggae and samba (Calle de las Huertas, 22; ☎ 91-429-84-07; Metro: Antón Martín).

✔ **Café del Cosaco** is owned by the same folks that run the Russian restaurant El Cosaco. This cozy little place is located just off Plaza de la Paja. The bar features eclectic live music shows, popular with the young and hip arts crowd (Calle Alfonso VI, 4; ☎ 91-365-27-18; Metro: La Latina).

✔ **Oba-Oba,** Jacometrezo, 4 (no phone; Metro: Callao), has live music, mostly Brazilian and Latino, most nights of the week.

✔ For alternative rock shows by Spanish bands, check out **Siroco,** which rocks 'til 5 a.m. Thursday to Sunday (Calle San Dimas, 3; ☎ 91-593-30-70; Metro: Noviciado).

Late-night munchies

In Madrid, the town that never wants to go to bed, an undying tradition is to top off the night (which is way into morning) with *chocolate con churros*. Churros are deep-fried pieces of dough, served piping hot. They're accompanied by cups of thick, rich hot chocolate — for dunking, of course. *Churrerías* usually open around 4 a.m., perfect for late-night partyers hungry for something other than alcohol, smoke machines, and bone-rattling rhythms. You won't believe how crowded these places can get at 6 a.m. A good place to add some much-needed grease and chocolate to your pre-dawn diet is at **Churrería de San Ginés,** on Pasadizo de San Ginés, between Calle Mayor and Arenal in the heart of Viejo Madrid.

Disco fever

Discos haven't died in Madrid, but they're predominantly young (very young) affairs. The blinding lights and ear-splitting sound systems don't get cranking until midnight. And you've got to show up (or still be there) at 3 a.m. if you want to see the action at full throttle. The music's changed, but the craziness, smoke, and general sense of abandon remain the same.

One of the city's longest-running discos is **Pacha.** Closed for awhile, it reopened to another huge following (Calle Barceló, 11; ☎ 91-446-01-37; Metro: Tribunal).

You've gotta see the scene in **Palacio Gaviria,** a wildly Baroque nineteenth-century palace place, to believe it. In the "13 Elizabethan lounges," you find everything from full-throttle disco to ballroom dancing and chic, secluded cocktail corners (Calle Arenal, 9; ☎ 91-526-60-69; Metro: Puerta del Sol).

Angels of Xenon ain't subtle: It has a whopping dance floor, bubble and smoke machines, and go-go dancers. If you're into techno, you'll dig the thumping bass lines (Calle Atocha; ☎ 91-369-38-81; Metro: Antón Martín).

If Angels is a bit too mod for you, try **Siroco's** tattered 60s feel. DJs cue up rock and pop hits of the 80s and 90s and some jungle, but shy away from trance-inducing techno beats (Calle San Dimas, 3; ☎ 91-593-30-70; Metro: Noviciado).

Exploring outside of Madrid

One of the highlights of visiting Madrid is getting out of town. That may sound odd, but just outside the capital are some of Spain's greatest hits, equal in their own way to the drawing power of Madrid. If you're really limited on time and not planning to rent wheels, you can zip in and zip out of **El Escorial,** a beautifully austere sixteenth-century monastery; **El Valle de los Caídos,** Franco's shrine to the war dead; or **Aranjuez,** the grand summer palace and gardens of the Bourbon monarchs. Both are in Madrid province and make easy half-day trips from the capital. More than two dozen trains depart daily from Madrid's Atocha, Nuevos Ministerios, and Chamartin train stations. During the summer, extra coaches are added. For schedules and information, call ☎ **91-328-90-20.** With just a bit more time, you can do one or more of the Central Spain biggies: **Segovia, Toledo,** and **Salamanca** — three of Spain's most enjoyable, historic spots. They're no more than a couple of hours from Madrid. (Turn to Chapter 15 for more information.)

If you don't feel like doing the planning (or driving) yourself, and you don't mind sticking to a group's timetable, three major players operate no-hassles day trips to the major sights outside of Madrid, (El Escorial and Aranjuez and the Valley of the Fallen), as well as to Toledo, Ávila, and Segovia (see Chapter 15). Prices for day tours range from 5,000 pta. ($27.50) to 12,000 pta. ($66). Prices generally include roundtrip transportation, some museum admissions, and a guided tour. Contact any one of the following:

- ✔ **Juliatur,** Gran Vía, 68 (☎ **91-559-96-05;** Metro: Plaza de España)
- ✔ **Pullmantur,** Plaza de Oriente, 8 (☎ **91-541-18-05;** Metro: Ópera)
- ✔ **Trapsatur,** San Bernardo, 23 (☎ **91-541-63-20;** Metro: Santo Domingo)

El Escorial, an austere monument to a king

Felipe II was Spain's austere monk-monarch. Known as "The Wise King," he created a Hispanic Empire, but he was also a cold tyrant and an unbending religious fanatic. **San Lorenzo de Escorial,** his legacy and sacred retreat in the foothills of the Sierra de Guadarrama Mountains, is monumental, gray, and spectacularly severe. It was intended as a "city of God," where mass was heard day and night.

Yet the somber exterior of this mega-monastery, built between 1563 and 1584 and termed the eighth wonder of the world in its day, hides a real treasure trove of artistic wealth. Beyond the fortress exterior is a museum of art diplaying the royal Hapsburg collection; a marble mausoleum holding the remains of Spanish monarchs; and a royal library containing Felipe's extraordinary collection of manuscripts and tens of thousands of priceless books, arranged beneath a ceiling of brilliant frescoes.

To live like a king at El Escorial — at least during Felipe's reign — didn't mean living large. Although public areas are suitably grand, Felipe's royal living quarters are utterly monastic — quite the opposite of the lavish apartments the Bourbon kings later installed at El Escorial. To get as close as he could to heaven, Felipe requested that his private room, "his humble cell," overlook the massive dome of the basilica.

If you've got a morbid streak, you'll love the royal pantheon beneath the altar of the church. There, almost all of Spain's monarchs are buried, including Felipe II and his father, Carlos V. The small, round, marble room is lined with neat stacks of black marble and bronze sarcophagi. As long as you're in the spirit, check out the galleries of deceased princes and princesses, in addition to illegitimate royal offspring, many of whom were mere infants when they died.

The museum holds numerous Titians, as well as paintings by Ribera, Zurbarán, and El Greco. El Greco's *The Martyrdom of St. Maurice* is one of the artist's acknowledged masterpieces. Don't miss two frescoes in the basilica: one of heaven, over the choir, and another by Titian, which depicts the live roasting of St. Lawrence — San Lorenzo, after whom the monastery is named. (More tidbits for the macabre crowd.)

If you're in Spain during the summer months, you have little choice but to deal with hordes of tourists streaming out to El Escorial, one of the most popular visits in the Madrid area. Try to go either very early or very late in the day; you may get lucky and run into fewer people. El Escorial (☎ **91-890-59-03**) is open October through March, Tuesday to Sunday from 10 a.m. to 5 p.m.; April through September, Tuesday to Sunday from 10 a.m. to 6 p.m. Admission is 850 pta. ($4.75).

El Escorial is located 49 km (30 miles) northwest of Madrid. Take either a train or bus to El Escorial. From Madrid's Atocha station, trains leave throughout the day, from 5:48 a.m. to 10:17 p.m. A one-way ticket is 370 pta. ($2) or 740 pta. ($4) roundtrip. The trip takes about an hour. By bus, **Empresa Herranz** (☎ **91-890-41-22**) leaves about every 20 minutes, from 7:15 a.m. 10:45 p.m., with returns as late as 9 p.m. Monday through Friday, 9:30 p.m. on Saturday and 10 p.m. on Sunday. Buses leave from the Intercambiador de Montcloa Station (Metro: Moncloa).

Valley of the Fallen

Just beyond El Escorial is the infamous **Valle de los Caídos** (Valley of the Fallen). Francisco Franco, Spain's unwavering dictator for 40-odd years, is buried just 8 miles north of El Escorial — as close to the royal burial site as he could manage. The colossal monument erected there is the kind of place Franco would force Spanish school children to visit were he still alive and in power. But he isn't, and you don't have to feel obligated to pay homage, either.

Franco used the forced labor of Republican prisoners of war to build a memorial to victims of the Spanish Civil War (only political protests succeeded in widening the tribute to include the dead on both sides).

Franco was probably less concerned with the fallen, though, than he was with his own fate. His monument to himself is a massive, 500-foot-tall cross that crowns a basilica carved into rock. You can take a cable railway to the base of the cross, for a great view of the surroundings, but unless you're especially interested in Franco and Civil War Spain, don't consider Valle de los Caídos a must-see.

The memorial (☎ 91-890-56-11) is open daily April to September, from 9:30 a.m. to 7 p.m., and October to March from 10 a.m. to 6 p.m. Admission is 650 pta. ($3.50). **Empresa Herranz,** which runs the buses to El Escorial, offers a same-day package that includes a visit to the Valley of the Fallen. Call ☎ 91-890-41-22 for additional transportation information.

The summer palace at Aranjuez

Visitors to Madrid beeline to Aranjuez with the same single-minded purpose that Bourbon monarchs did: to beat the heat. In the midst of Central Spain's arid plains, this royal summer palace near the meeting of the Tagus and Jarama rivers is a lush oasis of 700-plus acres of cool, shaded gardens, fountains, sculptures, and leafy trees imported from Spain's former colonies in the Americas. Aranjuez was prized by the royals for its fresh produce, including asparagus and strawberries. In mid-summer, you may think you've landed at Wimbledon: Vendors set up shop along the roadside, selling strawberries and cream. (There's even a tourist-oriented old steam train traveling from Madrid: *Tren de las Fresas,* or the Strawberry Train.)

The immense palace you see is not the same as the one favored by Ferdinand and Isabella, the legendary Catholic monarchs. Twice razed by fire, the palace had to be entirely rebuilt in the 1870s. Still, it remains extravagant. The **Porcelain Salon,** bathed in colorful tiles depicting Chinese scenes, may remind you of Madrid's Royal Palace — the tiles are from the same royal pottery factory. However, the standout features at Aranjuez are the serene gardens, particularly the **Jardín de la Isla** (Island Garden) and **Jardín del Príncipe** (Prince's Garden), romantic parks that inspired one of Spain's most famous pieces of music, Joaquin Rodrigo's *Concierto de Aranjuez.*

In the mile-long **Jardín del Príncipe** (Prince's Garden) at Aranjuez, you find the luxurious, curiously named **Casita del Labrador** — the Worker's Cottage (yeah, right; how many workers do you know that have mini-palaces with Greek busts, marble floors and brocaded floors?). Obviously, this isn't just any old house. Queen María Luisa invited her young lover, the Prime Minister Godoy, here for romantic trysts (her husband, King Carlos IV, was *loco* (crazy), so the cheatin' queen didn't even try to conceal her dalliances).

Aranjuez (☎ 91-891-13-44) is open Wednesday through Monday, 10 a.m. to 6 p.m. from April to September and Wednesday through Monday,

10 a.m. to 5 p.m. from October through March. Admission is 500 pta. ($2.75) for adults and 250 pta. ($1.40) for students and children. The palace is located 47 km (29 miles) south of Madrid. You can hop a bus or a train for Aranjuez. A couple dozen **Empresa Autominibus Urbanos** (☎ 91-530-46-06) buses depart from Estación Sur de Autobuses (Metro: Méndez Álvaro). The trip takes an hour and costs 390 pta. ($2.15). On Sundays, there are far fewer buses. Trains leave from Atocha station (Metro: Atocha RENFE) every 20 minutes or so; the trip costs 370 pta. ($2) one-way, 740 pta. ($4.10) roundtrip.

Fast Facts: Madrid

Area Code

The area code for telephone numbers within Madrid is **91**. You must always dial the prefix.

American Express

Plaza de las Cortes, 2 (☎ **91-322-54-45** or 91-322-54-28; Metro: Banco de España).

ATMs

Automatic teller machines are widely available throughout Madrid; most banks have 24-hour ATMs. You can find such branches along Gran Vía and Calle Serrano in the Salamanca neighborhood.

Currency Exchange

You can find currency exchange offices at the Charmartín rail station and Barajas airport. Major Spanish banks include La Caixa, BBV, and Banco Central Hispano.

Doctors

To locate an English-speaking doctor or report a medical emergency, dial ☎ **112**.

Embassies/Consulates

The Embassy of the United States is located at Calle Serrano, 75 (☎ **91-577-40-00**; Metro: Núñez de Balboa); Canada, Núñez de Balboa, 35 (☎ **91-431-43-00**; Metro: Velázquez); United Kingdom, Calle Fernando El Santo, 16 (☎ **91-319-02-00**; Metro: Colón); Ireland, Claudio Coello, 73 (☎ **91-576-35-00**; Metro: Serrrano); Australia, Paseo de la Castellana, 143 (☎ **91-441-93-00**; Metro: Cuzco); and

New Zealand, Plaza de la Lealtad, 2 (☎ **91-523-02-26**; Metro: Banco de España).

Emergencies

For general emergencies, dial ☎ **112**. For medical emergencies, call ☎ **061** or visit or call a 24-hour first aid station: Calle Navas de Tolosa (☎ **91-521-00-25**); Avenida Del Paseo de Extremadura, 147 (☎ **91-464-76-32**); or calle Gobernador, 39 (☎ **91-420-03-56**). For **a 24-hour pharmacy, call** ☎ **098**. For the municipal police, dial ☎ **092**. For a fire, ☎ **080**.

Hospitals

To locate a hospital, dial ☎ **112**. For medical emergencies, visit or call a 24-hour first aid station: Calle Navas de Tolosa (☎ **91-521-00-25**); Avenida del Paseo de Extremadura, 147 (☎ **91-464-76-32**); or Calle Gobernador, 39 (☎ **91-420-03-56**).

Information

For general Madrid information, call ☎ **901-30-06-00**. Municipal Tourism Offices are located at Plaza Mayor, 3 (☎ **91-366-54-77**; open Mon–Sat 10 a.m. to 8 p.m.; Sun and holidays 10 a.m. to 3 p.m.); Duque de Medinaceli, 2 (☎ **91-429-49-51**; open Mon–Fri 9 a.m. to 7 p.m., Sat 9 a.m. to 7 p.m.); Puerta de Toledo Market, 1-6 (☎ **91-364-18-75**; open Mon–Fri 9 a.m. to 7 p.m., Sat 9:30 a.m. to 1:30 p.m.); and Barajas Airport (International Arrivals Terminal; ☎ **91-305-86-56**; open Mon–Fri 8 a.m. to 8 p.m., Sat 9 a.m. to 1 p.m.). You can calling ☎ **902-20-22-02** or 901-30-16-00 to get telephone tourism information.

Internet Access/Cyber Cafés

If you want to net surf or need to send e-mail, try one of the following cafés or computer centers (though it's wise to check with the tourism office, because these tend to come and go with regularity): Cestein Centro de Navegación (Calle Leganitos, 9–11; ☎ **91-548-27-75;** Metro: Plaza de España); El Escribidor.es (Ponzano, 93; ☎ **91-553-56-37;** Metro: Cuatro Caminos); La Casa de Internet (Luchana, 20; ☎ **91-446-55-41;** Metro: Bilbao); or Cybercafe Lasser (Rosario, 21; ☎ **91-365-87-91;** Metro: Latina). Prices range from 200 pta. ($1.10) to 800 pta. ($4.40) per hour.

Mail

The Central Post Office is located at Palacio de Comunicaciones, Plaza de la Cibeles (☎ **91-396-20-00**). It's open Mon–Fri 8:30 a.m. to 9 p.m. and Sat from 8 a.m. to 8 p.m. The yellow sign *Correos* identifies branches of the Post Office.

Maps

A free street map covering the whole of Madrid is available at Tourist Information Offices at the airport, train stations, and in the city. The map is sufficient for virtually all city travel. You should also pick up the pocket-sized map of the Metro subway system, available free at any Metro station.

Newspapers/Magazines

Most European newspapers are sold on the day of publication, as are the Paris-based *International Herald Tribune* and European edition of *The Wall Street Journal. USA Today* is also widely available, as are principal European and American magazines.You can find all of these at the many kiosks along Gran Vía or near Puerta del Sol. Spanish-speakers should check out the weekly

entertainment information magazine *Guía del Ocio* (Leisure Guide), which lists bars, restaurants, cinema, theater, and concerts.

Pharmacies

Pharmacies (indicated by neon green crosses) operate during normal business hours but there is always one in every neighborhood that remains open all night and on holidays. The location and phone number of this *farmacia de guardia* is posted on the door of all the other pharmacies. You can call ☎ **098** to contact all-night pharmacies.

Police

For municipal police, dial ☎ **092.** For national police, ☎ **091.**

Safety

Madrid has a reputation of having some of the highest crime rates in Spain, though street crime is normally limited to pickpocketing and breaking into cars with items left in the seats. Exercise extra care along Gran Vía, Puerta del Sol, Calle Montera (known as a heavy red light district), the Rastro flea market, and areas with lots of bars (and rowdy drunks), such as Huertas and Latina. The presence of so many people out at all hours of the night is generally cause for reassurance rather than fear. Also, be especially careful of tourist scams near the art museums on Paseo del Prado.

Taxis

If you need to call a cab, taxi companies include Tele-Taxi (☎ **91-445-90-08**), Radio Teléfono Taxi (☎ **91-547-82-00**) and Radio Taxi Independiente (☎ **91-405-12-13**).

Telephone

For general telephone information, call ☎ **098.** For national telephone information, dial ☎ **009.** Madrid's area code is **91,** and you must dial it before all numbers.

Chapter 15

Castile: Around Madrid

. . . .

In This Chapter

▶ Setting out on side trips from Madrid

▶ Visiting Segovia's fairy-tale castle and 2,000-year-old Roman Aqueduct

▶ Discovering Salamanca, Spain's oldest university town

▶ Taking in the views at Toledo, El Greco's city on a hill

. . . .

Castile is the Spain most first-time travelers expect to find: a place of walled cities rising on the plains, grand castles and cathedrals, historic palaces and universities — the Spain of Roman conquerors and medieval kingdoms. Segovia, Salamanca, and Toledo match those expectations and then some, so it's a little surprising that so many people rush by these historic cities in frenzied day trips from Madrid. Sure, they're close together and accessible from the capital, but a very enjoyable Spanish vacation can easily take in these three places — all named UNESCO Heritage of Mankind cities — and nothing more. They also make for an excellent driving tour.

Segovia, Salamanca, and Toledo are all places whose beauty is immediately apparent. But to discover the depths of their appeal, you need to do more than a quick drive-by. These centers of learning, government, and religion, serious cities in stone and wood, are surprisingly pleasant places to spend some time. Consider these cities not just as add-on side trips from Madrid, but as destinations deserving of the same attention you'd give Granada (see Chapter 18) or Bilbao (see Chapter 13). A relaxed pace reveals the towns of Central Spain to be more than handsome museum pieces.

Just the Facts: Castile

Segovia and Salamanca are part of what was once the kingdom of Old Castile (which is now more commonly called *Castilla y León*), northwest of Madrid in central Spain. Toledo, for all its ancient roots, is part of the region of New Castile, or *Castilla y La Mancha,* southwest of the capital.

- ✔ **The way to go.** Segovia, Salamanca, and Toledo are all between one and three hours by car, train, or bus from Madrid.

- ✔ **Como se dice? Talking the talk.** There are no tricky secondary languages in Central Spain — just the king's *castellano* (Spanish).

- ✔ **What's for dinner?** This landlocked region goes big for meat and game — suckling pig, oven-roasted lamb, partridge, and sausage and beans. It's the kind of hearty, straightforward cooking that old inns serve in clay bowls.

- ✔ **The forecast.** The parched plains of central Spain — pay no mind to what that old song said about rain on the plains — are given to extremes: blisteringly hot in summer, brutally cold in winter. Think Dallas, Texas with snow.

- ✔ **When to go.** Spring and fall. Summer brings not only heat waves, but oceans of fellow tourists, overrunning some of the quiet beauty of towns like Segovia and Toledo. The region, though, is popular most of the year; high season is mid-March through the end of October, generally, and low season (with slightly lower hotel rates) is from November through mid-March. (Though in Toledo, December is also high season.) Many hotels jack up their prices for Easter week.

- ✔ **How long before moving on?** People often try to squeeze in these side trips from Madrid on madcap bus tours of only a day or so. Segovia and Toledo each require full days, and really reward overnight stays. You can best see Salamanca, the farthest from Madrid, in a couple of days. To visit all four, you need a minimum of four days by car, but that's zooming through at warp speed.

Major Attractions in Castile

My advice concerning attractions in Castile is simple: Do as much as you have time for, without blowing through anything. Almost everyone hits the towns of Castile after spending a few days in Madrid, which is the ideal way to organize a trip to central Spain.

You see lots of castles, military fortresses, and the remains of walled cities in Castile. The region was known for its warlike ways — it was fought over by the Visigoths, Moors, and Christians and spent nearly all the Middle Ages being attacked and sacked. In fact, even the name of the region relates to its warmongering ways: Castile is a derivative of *castillo,* the Spanish name for castle.

Castile is home to a fourth UNESCO Heritage of Mankind city. Ávila, one-time home to Saint Teresa, is known to have the greatest medieval walls in Europe. Space constraints prevent me from including Ávila in this book, but truth be told, apart from the eleventh-century city walls, there's not much to hold your interest. Ávila is en route to Salamanca if you're driving in from Madrid or Segovia (see Getting to Salamanca, later in this chapter), so pop in if you're interested before continuing on.

Segovia

Less touristy than Toledo, but nearly as rich a representative of the golden era of Old Castile, Segovia ("suh-*go*-vee-ah"), 91 km (54miles) northwest of Madrid, is one of the most picturesque cities in Spain. The city has one of the most impressive settings you'll find in Spain or anywhere: It rises like a mirage upon a limestone elevation from the dry plains. Its nearly 2,000-year-old Roman Aqueduct, an awesome construction of perfectly laid stones in a mile-long series of arches, is one of the most ingenious architectural feats on the continent. The city also has other big sights — the cathedral and the fantasy-world castle El Alcázar — and lots of charming little surprises in its Old Quarter. Look for the following attractions in Segovia:

✔ The **Roman Aqueduct,** a triumph of superior engineering and a symbol of the city

✔ **El Alcázar,** a castle crowning the city on the hill

✔ The **Catedral de Segovia,** the last great Gothic cathedral in Spain

Salamanca

Pristine Salamanca, 204 km (127 miles) northwest of Madrid, is a great university town, and was Spain's center of enlightenment in the Middle Ages. The entire Old Quarter, made up of university buildings, palaces, monasteries, and convents, is the finest collection of Renaissance and Plateresque golden sandstone buildings in Spain. (For more on Plateresque architecture, see the "Salamanca architecture 101" sidebar, later in this chapter.) In Salamanca, you find the following attractions:

✔ The **University of Salamanca,** the writer Cervantes' alma mater and a draw for students all over the world

✔ The **old and new cathedrals,** glowing examples of Gothic and early Renaissance architecture

✔ **Plaza Mayor,** a splendid gathering place, one of Spain's most stately public squares

Toledo

Toledo, 68 km (42 miles) southwest of Madrid, is on nearly everyone's must-see list for a reason. Its setting, high on a hill on the plains of central Spain, is incomparable, the subject of a thousand paintings, including favorite son El Greco's. The labyrinthine city looks like a complex castle surrounded by a moat, the *Río Tago* (Tagus River).

Each of its crooked atmospheric streets, packed with Moorish mosques, Jewish synagogues, Christian cathedrals, and stately palaces, is a rich Spanish history lesson. Before the Spanish Inquisition forced non-Catholics to flee Spain, Toledo was the capital of a tolerant, multicultural Spain. Look for the following sights in Toledo:

✔ The **cathedral,** opulent and spectacular, one of Spain's greatest

✔ **El Greco's** magisterial painting *The Burial of Count Orgaz,* as well as the artist's house/museum

✔ The last remaining **synagogues** of the city's influential medieval Jewish community

Experiencing Segovia

Segovia is, as the Spanish say, *encantador* — enchanting. In addition to its top draw, the nearly 2,000-year-old Roman Aqueduct, the city has other big sights — the cathedral and El Alcázar — and lots of charming little surprises in its Old Quarter. You'll want to spend most, if not all, of your time in the historic center, near the cathedral and castle.

Arriving in Segovia

Driving to Segovia is a breeze, and it's a scenic drive. Take the A-6 northwest from Madrid toward León. The Segovia turnoff (north on N-603) is signposted. If you're only visiting Segovia, though, a car's not necessary to explore the city.

La Sepulvedana (Paseo de la Florida, 11; ☎ 91-547-52-61; Metro: Príncipe Pío) buses leave Madrid for Segovia (a 90-minute ride) every half hour Monday through Saturday, beginning at 6:30 a.m. with the last return at 9:30 p.m. (10:15 p.m. on Saturday). On Sundays, service is hourly, with returns every half-hour between 4 and 10:30 p.m. One-way fare is 765 pta. ($4.25); same-day roundtrip is 1,230 pta. ($7). The **Segovia Bus Station** is at Plaza de la Estación de Autobuses, 1 (☎ 921-42-77-07).

The train takes half an hour longer than the bus, but I find it more comfortable and relaxed. You also have a better view of beautiful mountain terrain as you climb up to Segovia. From Madrid, nine trains a day depart from Atocha station (Metro: Atocha RENFE) between 6 a.m. and 8 p.m. They arrive in Segovia two hours later. The last train back to Madrid leaves at 8:55 p.m. One-way costs 630 pta. ($3.50); roundtrip, 1,135 pta. ($6). The **train station,** at Plaza del Obispo Quesada s/n (☎ 921-42-07-74), leaves you a good ways from the Old Quarter. You either need to take a taxi or bus (No. 3 to Plaza Mayor), or walk about 20 minutes.

Castile

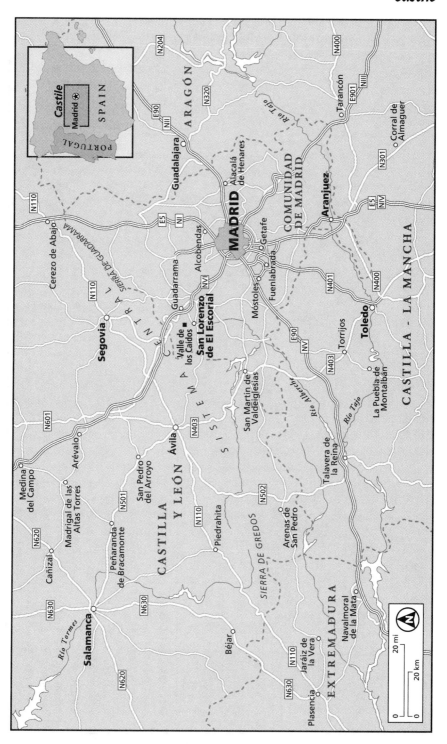

Segovia

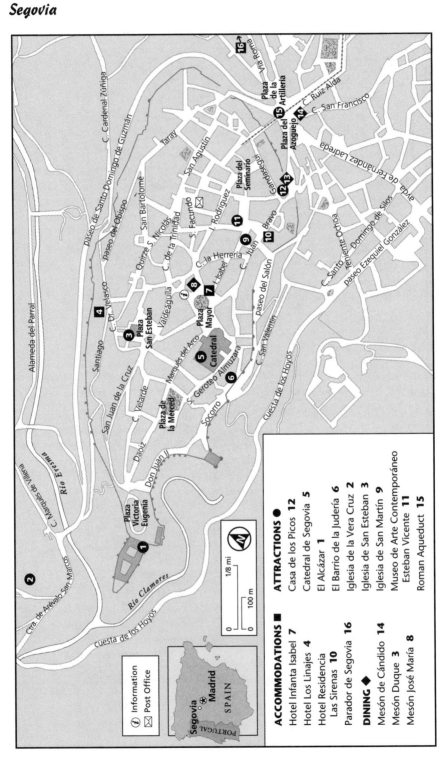

ACCOMMODATIONS ■
Hotel Infanta Isabel **7**
Hotel Los Linajes **4**
Hotel Residencia
    Las Sirenas **10**
Parador de Segovia **16**

DINING ◆
Mesón de Cándido **14**
Mesón Duque **3**
Mesón José María **8**

ATTRACTIONS ●
Casa de los Picos **12**
Catedral de Segovia **5**
El Alcázar **1**
El Barrio de la Judería **6**
Iglesia de la Vera Cruz **2**
Iglesia de San Esteban **3**
Iglesia de San Martín **9**
Museo de Arte Contemporáneo
    Esteban Vicente **11**
Roman Aqueduct **15**

Information
Post Office

1/8 mi
0
0   100 m

SPAIN
PORTUGAL
Madrid
Segovia

Getting around Segovia

Segovia's Old Quarter is pretty small. Your own two feet are the best way to get around, unless you stay at the Parador de Segovia, which is a couple of miles out of town and requires a taxi or car. To get a perspective of the city from beyond the walls (writers have long said that it forms a giant ship on the horizon), you either need to put on some long-haul sneakers or hire a cab if you don't have a car.

If you need a taxi, you can either catch one at the stop next to the Roman Aqueduct (pretty hard to miss!) or call ☎ **921-44-50-00.**

Staying in Segovia

Most people drop in on Segovia, rush around, and then bolt back to Madrid or on to their next stop. It's too bad, because Segovia's quiet Old Quarter is a special place to stay overnight. With the Roman Aqueduct, the cathedral, and El Alcázar (the storybook castle on the edge of the hill) all brilliantly illuminated at night, the city transmits medieval allure like few others. And for a small place, it's got a fair share of charming hotels. In fact, it's really pretty hard to choose among the following.

Hotel Infanta Isabel
$$ Old Quarter

You can't ask for a better location. This small nineteenth-century charmer is right on the central Plaza Mayor. It has an attractive Victorian décor, great service, and very large doubles — some with small terraces and breathtaking views of the plaza and Cathedral. With pretty curtains and other elegant touches like white painted furniture, the rooms are very reasonably priced — one reason this place is packed in high season.

Plaza Mayor. ☎ 921-46-13-00. Fax: 921-46-22-17. Parking: (nearby) 1,000 pta. ($5.50). Rack rates: 12,600–14,700 pta. ($70–$82) mid-March–Nov; 10,000–11,700 pta. ($55–$65) rest of year. AE, DC, MC, V.

Hotel Los Linajes
$$ Old Quarter

This personal, mid-size hotel (53 rooms) is the place to experience the charms of old Segovia. On a side street in the San Esteban part of the Old Quarter, the hotel occupies a seventeenth-century palace that belonged to a noble Segovian family (although much of the hotel is new construction). It's got a lovely lobby and central patio, and some rooms have priceless panoramic views over the Eresma River and the Parral monastery. (Asking for these is worth it.) About half the hotel underwent renovation in early 1999; rooms have nice wood furnishings and well-equipped baths. This is a peaceful place, which makes the small disco the hotel operates down some stairs out back oddly incongruous.

Calle Dr. Velasco, 9 (on the northeast side of town, near the Hospital de Misercordia and Puerta de Santiago). ☎ *921-46-04-75. Fax: 921-46-04-79. Internet:* www. hotelcity.com/spain/loslinajes. *Parking: 900 pta. ($5). Rack rates: 10,500–12,500 pta. ($58–$69). AE, DC, MC, V.*

Hotel Residencia Las Sirenas
$–$$ Old Quarter

Inexplicably named for mermaids, this is the best bargain hotel in town. Right in the heart of the Old Quarter, it's a short walk from the Plaza Mayor and Cathedral and across from an animated square, Plaza de San Martín. Enter through a simple door and find a long charcoal-colored marble floor and marble staircase at back. The whole place is well maintained; rooms have a lot of light and are decently furnished for the price. Rooms in the back of the hotel look out over the countryside to the Sierra de Guadarrama.

Calle Juan Bravo, 30. ☎ *921-46-26-63. Fax: 921-46-26-57. Internet:* http:// interhotel.com/spain/es/hoteles/4056. *Parking (nearby): 1,000 pta. ($5.50). Rack rates: 7,500–9,000 pta. ($42–$50). AE, DC, MC, V.*

Parador de Segovia
$$$ 2 miles northeast of Segovia

It's not convenient, but the views are out of this world. This spacious and tranquil *parador* (historic government-run hotel), tucked into a hill 2 miles north of the city, has a commanding perspective of the whole of Segovia — from the aqueduct to the medieval walls and the cathedral and castle. At night, all are beautifully illuminated, and you have to tear yourself from taking in the monumental city long enough to get some shut-eye. By day you can hit the pool, which has the same magnificent views as the rooms. The place is startlingly modern and very comfortable, if not romantic and palatial like some *paradors.* Rooms are large, with tiled floors and contemporary furnishings. Most have lovely views of the city down the hill. If you have a lot of time and want to take a leisurely approach to the city, this is a great choice. However, if you're here to see the Old Quarter in a day or so, or you wish to walk around the city at night, the inconvenience of having to drive or take a taxi down into town makes the Parador much less attractive an option.

Carretera de Valladolid, s/n (3 km northeast of Segovia along N-601, the Carretera de Valladolid; drive or take a taxi). ☎ *921-44-37-37. Fax: 921-43-73-62. E-mail:* segovia@parador.es. *Internet:* www.parador.es. *Parking: Free. Rack rates: 18,500 pta. ($103); inquire about special discounts for families with children. AE, DC, MC, V.*

Dining in Segovia

Segovia's the place for *cocina castellana* (Castilian cuisine) — roasts, hearty soups, sausages, and beans. The city's Old Quarter has a handful of restaurants that do it right, as well as look the part of classic Castilian *mesones* (inns). For more on Spanish dining customs, including meal-times, costs, and tipping, see Chapter 1.

Eating like a Castilian

Central Spain is no place for vegetarians. Everywhere you turn, you see wood ovens fired up, roasted *cochinillo asado* (suckling pig), and *cordero asado* (roast baby lamb). These and other dishes haven't changed much since the Middle Ages; try also *sopa castellana* (a broth with ham, vegetables, eggs, and bread), *cocido castellano* (a chickpea-based stew), and *perdiz* (braised partridge, especially popular in Toledo). If you're looking for a little something to tide you over, try *morcilla* (blood sausage) and *queso Manchego* (sheep's milk cheese that's hard when mature) — both are excellent accompaniments to a glass of red wine.

Drinking like a Castilian

The region of Old Castile, particularly the Valladolid area around the River Duero, has been gaining a reputation for producing some of the finest wines in Spain. Though red wines from Spain's Rioja region are better known (see Chapter 13), in recent years the reds from Ribera del Duero vineyards are quite literally on everybody's lips. The region produces not only Spain's most expensive wine, Vega Sicilia, but also more affordable, yet also superb, vintages from wineries like Pesquera and Mauro. They're deeply colored, smooth, and frequently oaky wines. Look for them in restaurants in Castile and throughout Spain. Valdepeñas reds, produced south of Toledo, are also quite good.

Mesón de Candido

$$$ **Old Quarter   CASTILIAN**

A meal at Candido's, right beneath the towering Roman Aqueduct, is pretty much an obligatory stop on the Segovia tourist circuit. Dalí, Hemingway, and even Tricky Dick Nixon have all dined on suckling pig here. The famous place has been an inn since the 1700s, and five generations of the Candido family have run the place for almost the entire twentieth century. The restaurant was declared a national monument in 1941. But that doesn't mean you get a crummy tourist menu. Happily, this is still one of the best places to eat in Segovia. Try to score a window seat on the second floor for dream-like views of the Aqueduct, illuminated at night. Oh, and the food: Start with a *sopa castellana* or *pimientos de piquillo rellenos de setas* (red peppers stuffed with mushrooms). If you don't have the classic *cochinillo* (roasted baby pig), you can always try *jabalí* (wild boar) or fresh grilled salmon.

Plaza Azoguejo, 5 (right next to Aqueduct). ☎ 921-42-59-11. Reservations required. Main courses: 1,300–2,800 pta. ($7–$16). AE, DC, MC, V. Open: Daily for lunch and dinner.

Mesón Duque
$$ Old Quarter   CASTILIAN

If you climb the main street from the Roman Aqueduct to the Old Quarter, you pass this classic *mesón* (tavern retaurant) on the left. Loaded with dark wood beams and knick-knacks, this must be what grandma's house would look like in the heart of Old Castile. The cozy inn has been serving Segovian specialties since 1895. Start with the *judiones de la Granja con bacalao* (kidney beans with cod) and follow it up with one of the Castilian roasts, which the house cooks about as well as anyone else in town.

Calle Cervantes, 12 (on road leading from the Aqueduct to the Old Quarter). ☎ 921-46-24-87. Reservations recommended. Main courses: 1,200–2,800 pta. ($6–$16); menú del día 4,000 pta. ($22). AE, DC, MC, V. Open: Daily for lunch and dinner.

Mesón José María
$$$ Old Quarter   CASTILIAN

One of the newer restaurants in town, José María has a hopping *tapas* (appetizer) bar in front that's usually packed with a mix of animated locals and tourists. The restaurant's in back, through an arch. One wall is a model of the Roman Aqueduct, its arches filled with wine bottles — a cute if touristy touch. If you've already had the Segovian roasted lamb or suckling pig at another inn, this is a good place to try something else, because the chef clearly has more than just roasts in mind. The stuffed fish *dorada cantábrico* (Golden Bream — a type of fish), crammed with garlic and mushrooms, is very tasty. There are other appetizing fish dishes, too, but the leg of lamb stuffed with mushrooms and truffles is tempting.

Calle Cronista Lecea, 11 (just off Plaza Mayor). ☎ 921-46-11-11. Main courses: 1,200–2,500 pta. ($6–$14). AE, DC, MC, V. Open: Daily for lunch and dinner.

Exploring Segovia

You won't have any trouble finding Segovia's top tourist attraction, the monumental Roman Aqueduct. The old walled quarter of Segovia rises above it. The cathedral and El Alcázar are the other premier attractions. Old Segovia is also rich in Romanesque churches and monasteries and cool little plazas.

Until the mid-1990s, cars were allowed to pass through the arches of the 2,000-year-old Roman Aqueduct in Segovia. Pollution from auto emissions was causing serious deterioration to the landmark, though, and Segovians finally mustered the political will to prohibit vehicular traffic from passing through — but not around — the Aqueduct. Although most locals recognize the value of protecting the ancient symbol of their city, that doesn't stop them from complaining about the congestion that the rerouting has caused.

The top attractions

Catedral de Segovia
Old Quarter

Called "the grand dame of Spanish cathedrals," this massive but delicately drawn limestone church was Spain's last great Gothic cathedral. Begun in 1525, it rises gracefully on the Plaza Mayor, right across from the spot where Isabella was named Queen of Castile in 1474. Inside are 23 ornate chapels, including one by José Churriguera, the architect of Salamanca's famed new cathedral (see the "Salamanca architecture 101" sidebar later in this chapter), a magnificent carved choir, and gorgeous stained-glass windows. This is actually the second church built on this spot; the cloisters, which you can visit, date from the first church. Allow an hour or so to tour the grounds.

Plaza Mayor. ☎ *921-46-22-05. Admission: Free to cathedral; 250 pta. ($1.40) to cloisters and museum. Open: 9 a.m.–7 p.m. (summer), 9:30 a.m.–6 p.m. (winter).*

El Alcázar
Old Quarter

Finishing off Segovia's trio of great monuments is its fairy-tale, turreted castle at the edge of the old town. The ancient fortress may, like the aqueduct, be Roman in origin, but it more likely dates from the twelfth century. At any rate, it was wholly reconstructed in the fifteenth century. It was a favorite residence of the Castilian monarchs during the Middle Ages. In 1862 a great fire destroyed much of the castle, so what you see is largely restoration work. The real highlight is climbing the Tower of John II, once a state prison. The 400 steep, one-way steps leave teenagers huffing and puffing and complaining, but if you're in decent shape, don't miss the amazing 360-degree view from the top of all of Segovia and the *meseta* (plateau) and mountains beyond. Plan on spending an hour or so at the Alcázar.

Plaza de la Reina (from the cathedral, walk straight along Marqués del Arco and continue along Daoiz; you run right into the Alcázar). ☎ *921-46-22-05. Admission: 400 pta. ($2.20). Open: 10 a.m.–7 p.m. (summer), 10 a.m.–6 p.m. (winter).*

Roman Aqueduct

One of Spain's most sensational sights and the subject of a thousand travel posters, Segovia's aqueduct is one of the greatest surviving examples of Roman engineering. The granite aqueduct, constructed in A.D. 90 (although some contend that it dates to 1 B.C.), has nothing but the force of physics holding its massive blocks together — no mortar, no clamps. Yet it has remained standing for nearly 2,000 years. Designed to carry water from the Ríofrío River in the mountains 10 miles away, the Aqueduct has 166 perfectly designed arches (35 were destroyed by the Moors in the eleventh century), 20,000 blocks, and 120 pillars. The structure reaches a height of 95 feet (in the Plaza de Azoguejo, where you'll probably view it) and stretches about two-thirds of a mile. As impressive as it is as a feat of engineering, the Aqueduct is also uncommonly beautiful. The way it frames the city is quite extraordinary. Make sure you check out the sight of the Roman Aqueduct fully illuminated at night against the black Segovian sky. Half an hour is sufficient to walk around and have a good look.

More cool things to see and do

✔ **Traipsing through old town.** Segovia is a charming town, and if you have time to do more than visit the top three showstoppers that draw all the tourists, a nice walk around the Old Quarter puts everything in perspective. The pretty **Plaza Mayor,** a lively place filled with cafes and *tapas* bars in summer, is the place to start. From there, proceed down Infanta Isabel and over to Canalejas. You come to the twelfth-century **Iglesia de San Martín,** one of Segovia's 40 Romanesque churches, notable for its handsome porches and carved portal. Plaza de San Martín is also a very pleasant little square, lined by attractive mansions. Across the way is the elegant house known by its Renaissance origins as **Casa del Siglo XV** ("fifteenth-century house").

The **Museo de Arte Contemporáneo Esteban Vicente,** back across Plaza de San Martín on Plazuela de las Bellas Artes, is an art museum housing more than 100 works of the Spanish artist Vicente, best known for his association with the New York School of Abstract Expressionists. (The museum is open Tue–Sat 11 a.m. to 2 p.m. and 4 to 7 p.m.; Sunday, 11 a.m. to 2 p.m.; admission is 400 pta./$2.20.) If you walk down Calle Grabador Espinosa, you come to the **Casa de los Picos,** a Renaissance mansion known for its armored-looking exterior. Finally, take Obisbo Gandasequi to San Agustín, turn left, and go straight on La Trinidad. Beyond the Episcopal Palace on Calle Valdeláguila is the handsome Romanesque **Iglesia de San Esteban,** with an impressive tower and a neat side gallery.

The little Romanesque San Miguel church didn't occupy its present spot just off the Plaza Mayor some 500 years ago. Back then it sat right *on* the Plaza Mayor. Though Segovia looks unchanged since the heyday of the Spanish empire, in fact a number of churches and buildings were taken down and reconstructed, stone-by-stone, in other locations in the city. Happily for workers, the massive Roman Aqueduct was not one of the structures that had to be moved.

Toledo wasn't the only medieval melting pot in Spain. In the thirteenth century, Segovia had a sizeable Jewish community, with at least five synagogues (Toledo originally had ten). The Jewish Quarter, **El Barrio de la Judería,** or Sefarad Segovia, is located behind the cathedral, along the old wall going toward the castle.

✔ **Venturing beyond the town walls.** Writers have long described the view of Segovia from outside the Roman walls as that of a giant ship, with the Alcázar at its bow, the cathedral forming the main mast, and the aqueduct representing the helm. A good place to view this city/ship is from the *parador* up on the hill, or the Parque del Alcázar at the crux of the Eresma and Clamores Rivers. Just beyond this point is the curious little **Iglesia de la Vera Cruz,** one of the most interesting Romanesque churches in Segovia. Though an odd polygon shape on the exterior, inside it's perfectly round. Stand in the middle of the inner temple and test the weird echo your voice produces. The church is said to have been the place of secret rites of the Knights Templar in the thirteenth century, although some modern historians doubt this claim. The church is open Tue–Sun 10:30 a.m. to 1:30 p.m. and 3:30 to 6 p.m.; closed in November. Admission is 200 pta. ($1).

Shopping in Segovia

Segovia's on the day-trip tour circuit, and the streets around the Plaza Mayor and cathedral are well stocked with shops clamoring for your tourist bucks. Several have good-quality crafts items, including the ironwork, pottery, and embroidery for which Segovia is known. For a unique shopping experience, visit the **Monjas Domínicas** on Calle Capuchinos Alta, 2 (☎ **921-46-00-80;** open 9 a.m. to 1 p.m. and 4 to 6:30 p.m. daily). The Dominican nuns make fine handmade polychrome figures. Prices start at 3,000 pta. ($17) and go up to 600,000 pta. ($3,333) for a hand-carved and painted altarpiece.

To see the nuns' work, you enter a door and ring the bell; a disembodied voice from behind the wooden turnstile says *"¿Sí?"* ("Yes?"). A simple *"Hola"* ("Hello") will grant you admission into the showroom (the voice will say *"Pase, por favor,"* or "Come in, please"). Once inside, you stand alone before a selection of objects on display behind bars. At length, another sister comes out and turns on the lights. Indicate which item you're interested in, and she'll fetch it for you, allowing you to inspect it through the iron gate.

La noche: Segovia's nightlife

Segovia is a pretty quiet town at night. Much of what nightlife it does have centers on the *tapas* bars and cafés of the Plaza Mayor and Plaza de San Martín. Surprisingly, there are two good Irish pubs in town that pull a decent pint of Guinness: **Canavan's,** on Plaza de la Rubia, 2, and **Limerick,** on Escuderos, 5. Both are just off the Main Square.

Fast Facts: Segovia

Area Code

Segovia's area code is **921,** which you must dial before every number.

Currency Exchange

There are banks and ATM machines located around the Plaza Mayor in the Old Quarter and downtown on the main street near the Aqueduct, Avenida Fernández Ladrera, and along Calle Cervantes and Calle Juan Bravo.

Emergencies

For medical emergencies, call Ambulancias Segovianas, ☎ **921-43-00-28** or the emergency unit of the Red Cross ☎ **921-44-07-02.**

Hospitals

Hospital General de Segovia is on Carretera de Ávila, s/n (☎ **921-41-91-00**). Hospital Policlínico San Agustín is on San Agustín, 13 (☎ **921-41-93-04**).

Information

Two main tourism offices serve Segovia. One is right on the Plaza Mayor (No. 10); ☎ **921-46-03-34.** Another is next to the Roman Aqueduct, on Plaza del Azoguejo, 1. ☎ **921-46-29-06.** They're open daily 10 a.m. to 2 p.m. and 5 p.m. to 8 p.m.

Police

The police station is at Guadarrama, 26 (☎ **921-43-12-12**).

Post Office

Segovia's main post office is on Plaza del Doctor Laguna, 5 (☎ **921-46-16-16**).

Checking Out Salamanca

Salamanca ("sahl-ah-*mahn*-kuh") is Spain's City of Enlightenment. If that sounds like an intimidatingly academic place for a vacation, relax — this university town is also one of Spain's loveliest cities.

The great university, once one of the world's pillars of learning and the institution that taught the great Cervantes, still dominates the town. Don't be surprised if you hear a lot of English on the streets; Salamanca reigns among young Americans studying abroad in Spain, and the city is a gathering place for students from all over the world.

Salamanca merits — even requires — an overnight stay. It's too far from Madrid for an easy day trip, but more important than logistics, you need time to fully appreciate its romantic charms.

Arriving in Salamanca

A car is the easiest way to get to Salamanca. It's about three hours from Madrid, two hours from Segovia, and an hour and a half from Ávila. From Ávila, which you must pass through whether you're coming from Madrid or Segovia, take N-501 West.

Salamanca

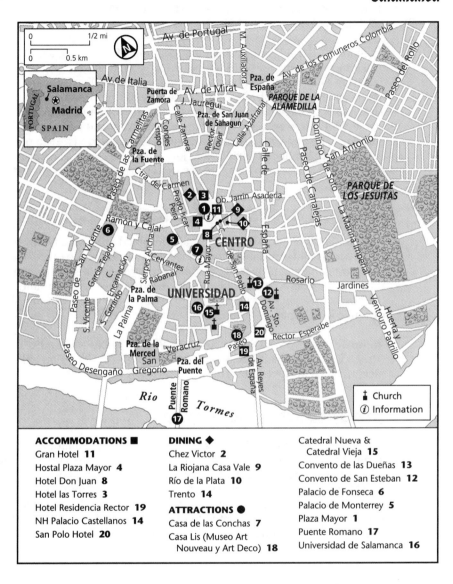

ACCOMMODATIONS ■
Gran Hotel **11**
Hostal Plaza Mayor **4**
Hotel Don Juan **8**
Hotel las Torres **3**
Hotel Residencia Rector **19**
NH Palacio Castellanos **14**
San Polo Hotel **20**

DINING ◆
Chez Victor **2**
La Riojana Casa Vale **9**
Río de la Plata **10**
Trento **14**

ATTRACTIONS ●
Casa de las Conchas **7**
Casa Lis (Museo Art
 Nouveau y Art Deco) **18**

Catedral Nueva &
 Catedral Vieja **15**
Convento de las Dueñas **13**
Convento de San Esteban **12**
Palacio de Fonseca **6**
Palacio de Monterrey **5**
Plaza Mayor **1**
Puente Romano **17**
Universidad de Salamanca **16**

Seven **Empresa Auto-Res** buses (in Madrid: Calle Fernández Shaw, 1;
☎ **91-551-72-00;** Metro: Conde de Casal) leave Madrid for Salamanca
daily beginning at 8:30 a.m., with the last returning at 10 p.m. The trip
takes 3 hours and 15 minutes. Returns to Madrid begin at 7:30 a.m., with
the last at 5:30 p.m. (7:30 p.m. on Friday and Sunday). The one-way fare
is 1,635 pta. ($9); same-day roundtrip costs 3,075 pta. ($17). You can
also use the express service, which takes 2 hours 30 minutes and costs
2,155 pta. ($12) one-way and 3,885 pta. ($22) roundtrip.

Buses also go to Salamanca from Segovia. The Salamanca bus station
(**Estación de Autobuses**) is located at Filiberto Villalobos, 71–85
(☎ **923-23-67-17** or 923-23-22-66).

From Madrid, trains leave Chamartín Station (Metro: Chamartín) at
9:30 a.m., 4:35 p.m., and 7:15 p.m. The 7:15 p.m. train doesn't run on
Saturday. On Friday and Sunday, an additional train leaves at 2:10 p.m.
The train arrives in Salamanca in 3 hours and 30 minutes after departure.
The first train back to Madrid leaves at 7 a.m. (9:10 a.m. weekends), the
last at 9:50 p.m. weekdays (5:45 p.m. on Saturday and 6:55 p.m. on
Sunday). The one-way fare is 1,625 pta. ($9); roundtrip is 2,925 pta.
($16). The Salamanca train station, located on Paseo de la Estación
(☎ **923-12-02-02**) is northeast of the Old Quarter. Take a taxi from there.

Getting around Salamanca

Salamanca is yet another thoughtfully designed Spanish city in which
you'll spend all your time in its Old Quarter — called the *casco antiguo*
or *zona monumental* (historic center). And, the city is small enough
that you only need to depend on your own two feet to get around. All
the hotels listed in the following hotel review section are within walking
distance of Salamanca's top sights.

Radio Tele-taxi (Don Quijote, 1–11; ☎ **923-25-00-00**) and **Radio Taxi**
(Paseo Canalejas, 49; ☎ **923-27-11-11**) both operate 24 hours a day;
pick up a taxi at the train station.

Staying in Salamanca

Salamanca has two excellent luxury hotels in historic buildings at
surprisingly reasonable prices, as well as several top-shelf budget hotels,
all within the *zona monumental* (historic center). Don't consider a
hotel that isn't within walking distance of the major monuments and
Plaza Mayor (this rules out the *parador,* which is outside the Old
Quarter and therefore not listed here). Salamanca doesn't have many
rooms, though, so it frequently fills up, especially during the month
of September, which is jam-packed with local festivals.

Gran Hotel
$$$ Old Quarter

You pay for location — right off the Plaza Mayor — at this formerly grand
1930s hotel. But, frankly, it's been left in the dust by newer and much
nicer (and cheaper!) hotels in Salamanca's historic core. And, several
budget hotels have locations that are the equal of this one. Rooms aren't
anything special. Consider this as a last resort if everything in town is
full up (but even then I'd ask for a discount).

Poeta Iglesias, 3 (one block south of Plaza Mayor). ☎ ***923-21-35-00.*** *Fax: 923-21-35-01. Internet:* www.madeinspain.net/hotelessalamanca/granhotel. *Parking: 950 pta. ($5). Rack rates: 15,000 pta. ($83) (with golf included 16,000 pta./$89). AE, MC, DC, V.*

Hostal Plaza Mayor

$ Old Quarter

Right across from the neat little San Martín church and a stumble home from the *tapas* bars of the Plaza Mayor, you can't ask for a better location, especially at these prices. Rooms are smallish, but nicely decorated, with wooden headboards and attractive curtains. Two of the 19 rooms have parquet floors.

Plaza del Corrillo, 20 (less than one block south of the Plaza Mayor). ☎ ***923-26-20-20.*** *Fax: 923-21-75-48. Internet:* http://interhotel.com/spain/es/hoteles/5951. *Parking: Nearby, 1,000 pta. ($5.50). Rack rates: 7,500 pta. ($42). AE, MC, V.*

Hotel Don Juan

$$ Old Quarter

A stone's throw from the Plaza Mayor and surrounded by the old city's monuments, this small family-run budget hotel is unexpectedly attractive. In a 200-year-old building, the comfortable, carpeted, and clean rooms have salmon-colored bedcovers, and hallways aren't the creepy corridors of most budget hotels — here they're done in marble and light wood. The small staff is exceedingly friendly. The small cafeteria on the first floor is a good place for a quick bite.

Calle Quintana, 6 (one block south of Plaza Mayor). ☎ ***923-26-14-73.*** *Fax: 923-26-24-75. Internet:* http://interhotel.com/spain/es/hoteles/4010. *Parking: Nearby 1,000 pta. ($5.50). Rack rates: 8,000–9,000 pta. ($44–$50). AE, MC, V.*

Hotel las Torres

$$ Old Quarter

Its modern, functional furnishings aren't the most luxurious, and are certainly a far cry from the architectural grace of the building, declared an artistic-historic monument, but the location on the Plaza Mayor is the envy of far more expensive hotels. The 44 decent-sized rooms are sparkling clean but nondescript. Some look out onto lovely Plaza Libertad and some overlook Plaza Mayor, one of the prettiest in all Spain. There's a first-floor restaurant/cafeteria that opens onto Salamanca's main square.

Plaza Mayor, 26 and Concejo, 4 (enter through cafeteria on Plaza Mayor or main entrance just outside the square). ☎ ***923-21-21-00.*** *Fax: 923-21-21-01. Internet:*

http://hotelcity.com/spain/torres. *Parking: Nearby, 1,000 pta. ($5.50). Rack rates: 11,900–15,300 pta. ($66–$85). AE, MC, DC, V.*

Hotel Residencia Rector

$$$ Edge of Old Quarter

The stunning stone Renaissance façade — you'll think you've stumbled upon a palace on the Salamanca sightseeing circuit — is only a prelude to the elegance within. This quiet and charming small hotel, a private mansion until 1990, is one of the finest I've stayed at in Spain. Details clearly matter here. Everything is perfect, from the elegant, warm-toned décor to the white-gloved breakfast and friendly attentions of the staff. I no sooner checked in than the woman at the desk kindly gave me a packet of information about Salamanca and informed me that the Plaza Mayor was "seven minutes walking distance down Calle San Pablo." The Rector's 14 enormous rooms are very tastefully decorated; the white marble bathrooms are spacious, and the linens and towels plush. Public rooms, including a small bar for guests only, have pretty antiques and stained-glass windows. For the level of comfort, service, and graciousness — five-star in every way — it's an excellent value. I can't wait to go back.

Calle Rector Esperabé, 10 (on edge of the Old Quarter; from Madrid Road, cross first bridge, go left around roundabout; hotel is on left facing old city wall). ☎ *923-21-84-82. Fax: 923-21-40-08. E-mail:* hotelrector@teleline.es. *Internet:* www.teleline.terra.es/personal/hrector. *Parking: 1,000 pta. ($5.50). Rack rates: 17,000–20,000 pta. ($94–$111). AE, MC, DC, V.*

NH Palacio Castellanos

$$$ Old Quarter

This new hotel, belonging to the Spanish NH chain, is one of its most luxurious. The hotel's obvious good taste is flashier if not quite as refined as the serenely elegant Rector. A fifteenth-century palace with a pretty central patio and colorful, modern furnishings in its 62 rooms, it's a good choice for those who find the Rector a little too quiet. The Palacio Castellanos is in the heart of the *casco histórico* (historic district), on a pretty main street that leads directly to the Plaza Mayor. The entrance faces the San Esteban convent.

Calle San Pablo, 58–64 (take Enrique Estevan bridge and pass Paseo del Rector Esperabé; the hotel is two blocks in on the left). ☎ *923-26-18-18. Fax: 923-26-18-19. E-mail:* nh@nh-hoteles.es. *Internet:* www.nh-hoteles.es. *Parking: 1,700 pta. ($9). Rack rates: 19,900 pta. ($110); weekend rate, 15,300 pta. ($85). AE, MC, DC, V.*

San Polo Hotel

$$ Edge of Old Quarter

This four-year-old hotel, just inside the Old Quarter, has a curious conceit: It occupies the site of the ruins of an eleventh-century Romanesque church, which have been incorporated into the modern hotel construction. It's a great idea in this ancient city, and if the execution isn't perfect, well, who's to quibble? The 40-room hotel looks as though plans to make it more luxurious were suddenly aborted, but it's still a fine mid-level choice. Rooms are a little cold feeling, but the views of Salamanca's cathedral are inspiring. Ask for a room with a view of the old town.

Calle Arroyo de Santo Domingo, 1–3 (at intersection of Avenida Reyes de España and Paseo del Rector Esperabé, just over river). ☎ */Fax:* ***923-21-11-77.*** *Parking: Free. Rack rates: 12,000–14,500 pta. ($67–$81); weekend rate 13,000 pta. ($72) (not available Easter, May, Aug, Sept and long weekends). AE, MC, DC, V.*

Dining in Salamanca

You can find all the restaurants in this section in Salamanca's Old Quarter, within walking distances of the hotels I reviewed in this previous section.

For quickie bites as you tool about Salamanca's Old Quarter, look for **Mesón Cervantes** (Plaza Mayor, 15; ☎ **923-21-72-13**) or **El Mesón** (Plaza Poeta Iglesias, 10; ☎ **923-21-72-22**), both of which serve good Castilian tavern fare. For *tapas,* pop in and out of the *tascas* (cave-like restaurants and taverns) on the Plaza Mayor, which is usually hopping with students.

Chez Victor
$$$ CONTINENTAL

Salamanca's top restaurant is like the city itself: elegant and refined without being at all stuffy. Chez Victor's owner is from Salamanca, but he trained in France, and his interest in delicate, subtle French preparations shows. The market-fresh vegetables and salads are a nice change in the land of lamb and suckling pig. Among main courses, the turbot (a flounder-like fish) in a hot vinaigrette and medley of peppers and zucchini is wonderful, as is the grilled monkfish on a bed of julienne zucchini. You find a number of terrific meat and game dishes on the hand-written English menu, including *magret de pato,* roasted duck with berries. Save room for the scary part: a separate dessert menu for chocolate lovers. Being one of them, I dived into the delectable *marquise de chocolate* and *café* (coffee).

Calle Espoz y Mina, 26. ☎ ***923-21-31-23.*** *Reservations recommended. Main courses: 1,800–3,400 pta. ($10–$19). AE, DC, MC, V. Open: Tues–Sat lunch and dinner, Sun lunch only; closed Aug.*

La Riojana Casa Vale
$$$ CONTINENTAL

Every city needs a thoroughly dependable, traditional restaurant that prepares the standard dishes that locals grew up eating. In Salamanca, that restaurant is Casa Vale. In the heart of the historic center, it's a great place for a simple, unfussy lunch or dinner. The list of choices is long and most everything is well done. You may try a *sopa castellana* (traditional Castilian soup) for starters and continue with sole stuffed with mushrooms and shrimp, with *lenguado rellendo de setas y gambas* (an essence of almonds) or *cabrito asado a las finas hierbas* (roast baby kid with fine herbs).

Calle San Pablo, 1 (just off Plaza Mayor). ☎ **923-21-31-23**. *Reservations recommended. Main courses: 1,800–3,000 pta. ($10–$17); menú del día 2,000 pta. ($11). AE, DC, MC, V. Open: Tues–Sat lunch and dinner, Sun lunch only; closed Aug.*

Río de la Plata
$$$ CASTILIAN

A charmingly plain little place, with just nine tables and a low ceiling at the back of a bar, Río de la Plata looks like a men's club. Two blocks from Plaza Mayor, it's intimate and cozy, and the white-jacketed waiters seem to know patrons by name. The menu is a long list of well-prepared favorites, like grilled hake, *solomillo* (beef sirloin), and roasted baby lamb. This basement restaurant with a fireplace (a great place to drop in on a chilly night) has been going strong since the 1950s.

Plaza del Peso, 1 (two blocks from Plaza Mayor). ☎ **923-21-90-05**. *Reservations recommended. Main courses: 1,100–4,500 pta. ($525–$31); menú del día, 2,500 pta. ($14). AE, DC, MC, V. Open: Tues–Sun lunch and dinner; closed July.*

Trento
$$$ INTERNATIONAL

A new entry on the Salamanca dining scene is this restaurant on the premises of the Palacio de Castellanos hotel (see review in the hotel section, earlier in this chapter). The attractive, modern décor works well in the magnificent fifteenth-century palace it occupies. The offering of fresh fish, including grilled sole with a medley of fresh vegetables, is continually good, as is the carefully selected wine list.

Calle San Pablo, 58–64 (one block from old and new cathedrals). ☎ **923-26-18-18**. *Reservations recommended. Main courses: 1,600–3,100 pta. ($9–$17). AE, DC, MC, V. Open: Daily lunch and dinner.*

Exploring Salamanca

You want to spend a day or so to fully appreciate this city's beauty. In the afternoon sun, Salamanca's sandstone spires and domes glow golden, and shadows drape across the city's red roofs and stately arcaded Plaza Mayor. The Old Quarter, with its exquisite Renaissance and Plateresque buildings, is a tangible reminder of Spain's Golden Age in the fifteenth and sixteenth centuries.

Salamanca architecture 101

Salamanca is a university town, but you could just as easily call it a living architectural museum. The Old Quarter is a remarkable palette of stone on stone. Nowhere else in Spain was stone molded into such a wealth of ornate detail. The old university façade is perhaps the greatest example of Plateresque work in Spain. *Plateresque* refers to a form of early Spanish Renaissance architecture in which rather somber facades are embellished by ornate stone carvings, their fine detail reminiscent of silver filigree. The term Plateresque is itself a reference to the art of silverwork (*platero* means silversmith in Spanish). The stone carving enlivens otherwise somber facades. Elements to look for include sculpted capitals andparapets, medallions, and round arches.

Churrigueresque architecture is named for three architect brothers — Jose, Joaquin, and Alberto — natives of Salamanca who worked throughout Spain but were especially busy in their hometown. The Churriguera style is like ornate Baroque architecture on speed — it knows no excess. It's applied principally in altarpieces, but Salamanca's handsome and harmonious Plaza Mayor is also the work of the brothers. Everyone seems to get the three brothers confused, though; some works are attributed to the wrong sibling, or, in the absence of identifying traits, merely to the entire clan.

The city and university together have cooked up a deal that allows you to visit four of Salamanca's sights for one price, 500 pta. ($2.75). These include the historic university building, the *Patio de Escuelas Menores* (Minor Schools' Patio and Museum), *Casa Lis* (the Art Nouveau and Art Deco Museum), and the Archbishop Fonseca College (also called the Irish College). Ask for the brochure and pass at the tourism office or your hotel, or call ☎ 923-12-14-25 for further information.

The Top Attractions

Catedral (Old and New)

Old Quarter

One cathedral just isn't enough for this monumental city. Instead of replacing the old cathedral, Salamanca built a new one next to it. In fact, you enter the old cathedral through the new one. The much larger new cathedral has a dazzling main doorway loaded with Plateresque stone work. (Try to see it in the afternoon sun, when it really sparkles.) The new cathedral began in the early sixteenth century but wasn't finished until 1733. Make sure you check out the ornate choir and Cristo de las Batallas chapel, the work of the Churriguera brothers.

The old cathedral, constructed in the twelfth century, is a mix of Romanesque and primitive Gothic. Though the church is literally overshadowed by the new cathedral next door, its rooster tower, the famous Torre del Gallo, gets plenty of attention. Inside, the most spectacular feature is the *retablo* (altarpiece) on the High Altar, which was being thoroughly restored in the first half of 1999. Hopefully, when you visit, you'll can see the bold altarpiece, attributed to the fifteenth-century artist Nicolás Florentino, which consists of 53 different paintings of the life of Christ. Also of note are elaborate Gothic tombs and chapels around the cloister that feature frescoes and gargoyles.

Don't leave before visiting the Patio Chico, a small courtyard that puts the old cathedral in perspective and provides a gorgeous view of the spires against the Salamanca sky. (You may have to circle around back if the door to the patio at the transept is closed when you visit.) Visiting the two cathedrals probably requires a couple of hours.

Plaza Juan XXII (two blocks from Paseo del Rector Esperabé). ☎ *923-21-74-76. Admission: 300 pta. ($1.75) (free Tues mornings). Open: New Cathedral, daily 10 a.m.–1 p.m. and 4–6 p.m.; Old Cathedral, daily 10 a.m.–12:30 p.m. and 4–5:30 p.m.*

Casa Lis (Museo Art Nouveau y Art Déco)
Edge of Old Quarter

If you walk along Calle Rector Esperabé, which borders the historic center to the south, you can't miss this stunning building with its bursts of bold stained glass. An immaculately restored nineteenth-century private mansion, it now houses the Art Nouveau and Art Deco Museum of Salamanca. The collection, with pieces from the late 1800s to the 1930s, includes porcelain and enamel, Lalique glass, Modernist paintings, jewels, furniture, and dolls. Don't miss the museum shop, not so much for the shopping, but for the view of the river and Roman Bridge through that amazing stained glass. Allow one to two hours here.

Calle Gibraltar, 14. ☎ *923-12-14-25. To get there: from Rector Esperabé, walk up the ramp and around the small street, Gibraltar, to the right. Admission: 300 pta. ($1.75), students and seniors 200 pta. ($1.10), free Thurs mornings. Open: Tues–Fri 11 a.m.–2 p.m. and 4–7 p.m.; Sat, Sun, and holidays 11 a.m.–8 p.m.*

Blood graffiti

Everywhere you look in Salamanca, but especially on the university buildings, names are stenciled in scarlet letters, an identifiably Old World academic font. Though today it's a clever marketing ploy, the script dates back to the fifteenth century, when graduating students proved their mettle by entering the bullring. Students proclaimed their victories (over the bull and, presumably, the university) by taking the bull's blood and painting the word *VITOR* (victor) on a university building, signing and dating their work.

Plaza Mayor
Heart of Old Quarter

I've been lucky enough to see most of Spain's great plazas, and Salamanca's grand main square is one of the finest. To get there, just follow the students and locals, most of whom don't go a day without ducking under its arches. Salamanca's Plaza Mayor is one of the biggest and most animated squares in the country, but what makes it special is the exquisite harmony of its architecture. Mostly designed by the Churriguera brothers, the architects so instrumental in giving Salamanca its renowned Plateresque look, the square was completed in 1733 — though the Baroque *ayuntamiento,* or town hall, was added about 20 years later. The other important building is the Royal Pavilion, where the royal family used to gather to view events in the square. The arcades' crowning medallions celebrate the lives of famous Spaniards like Columbus, Cortés, and Cervantes. The Plaza Mayor was once the scene of bullfights (as plazas were throughout Spain), but today it's a place to shop, watch the sun go down, and linger for long hours at one of the outdoor cafés, until your espresso buzz finally commands you to move.

Universidad de Salamanca
Old Quarter

In its heyday in the thirteenth through sixteenth centuries, Salamanca rivaled Oxford, Paris, and Bologna, the other great European centers of learning. Its university, the oldest in Spain, was founded by King Alfonso IX of León in 1218. It produced some of Spain's great academic figures, including Cervantes, St. John of the Cross, and the philosopher Miguel de Unamuno. The most spectacular building is the *Patio de las Escuelas,* or Old University façade. Erected in 1415, the building gained its glorious Plateresque frontalpiece sometime in the sixteenth century. The figures of Ferdinand and Isabella (Called the Catholic Kings) are surrounded by a riot of ornamentation — cherubs, crests, and creatures — which fills virtually every inch of the stone frontispiece. Go inside and take a look at the famous but plain lecture hall of professor Fray Luis de León, a sixteenth-century theologian who was imprisoned by the Inquisition for five years for translating the Biblical *Song of Songs* into Castillian Spanish.

Back outside, cross the Patio de las Escuelas and enter the Escuelas Menores patio, with its beautiful lawn and gorgeous arches. The museum here is known for its planetarium-like *Cielo de Salamanca* (Salamanca Heavens) fresco, painted in 1473. Allot a couple of hours to visit the university.

Patio de las Escuelas, 1 (at intersection of rúa Antigua and Compañía). ☎ *923-29-44-00. Admission: 300 pta. ($1.67) (free on Monday mornings). Open: Mon–Sat 9:30 a.m.–1:30 p.m. and 4–7 p.m., Sun and holidays, 10 a.m.–1 p.m.*

More cool things to see and do

✔ **Oohing and aahing on a house and palace tour.** Wedged in among Salamanca's myriad university buildings, convents, and churches are lots of fine mansions and palaces. **Palacio de Fonseca,** on Calle de San Pablo, was built in 1538 and has a beautiful interior patio; look for the figures on the second floor with the weight of the world on their shoulders. A famous house you pass often is **Casa de las Conchas** (House of the Shells), on Calle de la Compañía and Rúa Mayor. The façade of this sixteenth century Gothic mansion is decorated with steel grilles and protruding scallop shells — the symbol of the knightly Order of Santiago, a group to which the former owner belonged. Have a look at the central patio. A tourism information office and public library are now housed here. Massive **Palacio de Monterrey,** also on Calle de la Compañía, is one of Salmanca's most beautiful Renaissance palaces. Had it been completed, it would've been one of the largest private palaces in Spain (what you see is only one-quarter of the original plans). Still, the upper deck is a fabulous example of Plateresque ornamentation.

Casa de las Muertes (House of the Dead), on Calle Bordadores, gets its gruesome name from the tiny skulls that decorate its early sixteenth century façade. The owner ordered the skulls to commemorate his uncle, an archbishop. Nearby is **Casa-Museo de Unamuno,** where the renowned university professor and philosopher Miguel de Unamuno lived and then died in 1936. It's also a museum dedicated to the professor's life (open Tuesday through Friday, 9:30 a.m. to 1:30 p.m. and 4:30 to 6 p.m.; Saturday and Sunday, 10 a.m. to 1:30 p.m.; 300 pta.). Likewise, check out the **Torre del Clavero,** which is not a house or a palace, but did once belong to one. It's a turreted octagonal tower that was part of a now-disappeared fifteenth-century manse. The tower is on Plaza de Colón, just off San Pablo.

✔ **Bridging the gap.** Just beyond the old city is Salamanca's oldest surviving monument, the stone *Puente Romano,* or Roman Bridge, across the River Tormes. Constructed in the first century A.D., it still has 15 of its original 26 arches. Take a walk across, not only for the photo-op view of Salamanca, but also to check out the park below the bridge and alongside the river. The city has been working for years to finish it; on my last trip, a cool sculpture garden (with painted trees like the totems of some hip tribe) was installed near the bulldozers' paths, but nobody can tell me if it was permanent or a temporary piece.

✔ **Joining the faithful at Convento de San Esteban and Convento de las Dueñas.** After the old and new cathedrals, the two best religious buildings in Salamanca are these convents that face each other on Plaza del Concilio de Trento. **San Esteban** has a monumental Plateresque doorway, a robust stone canvas of delicate carving. Inside the church are impressive frescoes and a typically ornate José Churriguera altarpiece. **Convento de las Dueñas** is a Gothic construction with a lovely Renaissance cloister — the finest in the city and one of the best examples of the Plateresque style in Spain. Train your zoom lens on the freakish ghouls inhabiting the tops of the upper-story capitals. Convento de San Esteban (☎ 923-21-50-00) is open daily 9 a.m.to1 p.m. and 4 to 7 p.m. and admission is 200 pta. ($1.10). Convento de las Dueñas (☎ 923-21-54-42) is open daily 10:30 a.m. to1 p.m. and 4:30 p.m. to 7 p.m. and admission is also 200 pta. ($1.10).

Shopping in Salamanca

Salamanca isn't what you'd call a shopper's town, but it does have a few unique shops in the Old Quarter.

Antiqvaria is a cool little antique store with interesting books, watches, and silver. It's on Rúa Mayor, 43–47 (☎ 923-26-99). It has a branch called **Antiqvaria Rustic,** on Calle Palominos. **Mercatus,** on Calle Cardinal Plá y Deniel, is the university shop in this university town. It offers all kinds of gear and paper products with the ubiquitous, quasi-official Salamanca Academic lettering (see "Blood graffiti" sidebar, earlier in this chapter). **Tienda de Lis,** the gift shop of the Art Nouveau and Art Deco Museum (Casa Lis), has a good selection of nouveau and deco jewelry, books, and other items.

La noche: Salamanca's nightlife

Despite the U.N.-like presence of so many students, Salamanca is still small and has a fairly low-key night scene. On warm evenings, the **Plaza Mayor** is in a constant state of motion. The best way to counteract its hyperactivity is to stay still, preferably at an outdoor café, and watch everyone move faster than you. Rambunctious students fill **The Irish Rover** (Rua Antigua, 11), an Irish pub dressed up like a chic theater, which has lively jam sessions on Wednesdays. Latin flavor predominates at **El Savor** (Calle San Justo, 28), where you find Latin music and sweaty dancing from 10:30 p.m. to very late every night. (You can take Latin dance classes Monday through Friday from 8:15 to 9:30 p.m.) If sweaty isn't exactly your idea of an ideal evening, classical music concerts and *zarzuela* (light comic opera) are held at the **Palacio de Congresos y Exposiciones.** Call ☎ 923-26-51-51 for more information and a schedule of events.

Castile, and especially Salamanca, is famed for its *tunas* — the name given the roving bands of troubadours that stroll the streets serenading young women with songs of university life and love. Like characters who wandered out of a Velázquez court painting, the *tuneros* keep a great academic and musical tradition alive. With their ruffled collars, black velvet suits, and billowing capes, they look like something plucked from the seventeenth century — which, in a way, they are. Though they won't hound you like Mexican mariachis may, *tuneros*

work for tips. If you enjoy their performance and spectacle (which you're almost certain to), give them a couple hundred pesetas (a buck or so).

Fast Facts: Salamanca

Area Code

Salamanca's area code is **923,** which you must dial before every number.

Currency Exchange

There are ATM machines located around the Plaza Mayor in the Old Quarter and ATMs and banks along Avenida de Portugal and Paseo de Canalejas.

Emergencies

For medical emergencies, call Ambulancias Cruz Roja, ☎ **923-22-22-22.** For police emergencies, dial ☎ **092.**

Hospitals

Hospital Clínico Universitario is located on Paseo San Vicente, 108 (☎ **923-29-11-00**). The **Cruz Roja** (Red Cross) is found on the same street, Plaza de San Vicente, 1 (☎ **923-21-68-24** or 923-22-22-22).

Information

The main municipal Tourism Office is on the Plaza Mayor (No. 14) (☎ **923-21-83-42**). The province's office is located on Rúa Mayor, 70 (in Casa de las Conchas), ☎ **923-26-85-71.** They're open daily from 10 a.m. to 2 p.m. and 5 to p.m. From June 1 to September 30, an additional office operates at the train station.

Police

The police station is on Plaza Mayor in the *ayuntamiento* (city hall) building (☎ **923-27-91-38**).

Post Office

Salamanca's main post office is on Gran Vía, 25–29 (☎ **923-26-06-07**). A branch is located at Avenida Portugal, 75–77 (☎ **923-22-03-91**).

Touring Toledo

Toledo ("toe-*lay*-doe") looks like the set design of a Spanish spaghetti western — one in which Moors on horsebacks storm the citadel on the hill. Rising suddenly from the parched plains of La Mancha from a perch on a granite cluster high above the *Río Tago* (Tagus River), Toledo's cathedral spires and fortress turrets are visible for miles around. As spectacular as the setting is, what Toledo contains within its medieval walls is even more extraordinary. The fabled city of the painter El Greco, Toledo was where Spain's ancient cultures met and thrived.

Few cities live and breathe their history like Toledo. Captured by the Romans and later conquered by the Visigoths, Toledo became the capital of Spain in 1085, as well as a melting pot of Moors, Jews, and Christians in the Middle Ages. For several centuries it set the example for religious and cultural tolerance. Five hundred years after the Moors and Jews were expelled from Spain, Toledo remains a fascinating showcase of their achievements. Parts of the city — an intricate jumble of churches, synagogues, mosques, noble houses, and humble residences — are virtually unchanged since the sixteenth century.

The city's past is a rich tale of strategic conquests and interlocking cultures. The Romans captured Toledo in 192 B.C., named it *Toletum,* and built it into a strategic settlement. The Moors invaded Spain in 711 and headed straight for Toledo, capturing the city in 712. Under Moorish control it remained a cultured and rich city with a thriving Jewish community of 12,000, until the legendary general El Cid conquered it in 1085 for Alfonso VI. Toledo then became the capital of Spain, but the city fell into a steady decline after the Catholic crusades banished its Jewish and Muslim populations at the end of the fifteenth century. In 1561, Felipe II chose backwater Madrid as his administrative and political capital, cementing Toledo's second-tier status (but, ironically, probably preserving its medieval appearance).

Toledo ranks among Spain's top tourist destinations, and although it's not been physically corrupted like, say, the Costa del Sol (it's much too immutable for that), it suffers the impact of massive tourism unlike any other historic place in Spain. It's tiny, hilly, and hemmed in by medieval walls, and in summer, the massive groups and mammoth buses overwhelm the city's impossibly narrow streets and small churches, synagogues, and museums. Although Toledo remains the most obligatory side trip from Madrid (and one of the most important visits in the entire country), a peak-of-summer visitor who breaks out in hives at the thought of massive crowds and omnipresent tour buses may do well to take a detour to Segovia instead (or schedule a fall or spring visit).

If you stay overnight in Toledo, you get to enjoy the city late in the day and evening, when the day-trippers depart, and very early the next morning, before they come barreling in again. I recommend spending two days in Toledo, though surprisingly few visitors actually do this.

Arriving in Toledo

A car is the easiest way to get to Toledo, but driving within the city walls on the tiny, one-way streets is hair-raising. I suggest going by car only if you're planning to do a tour of other sights in Central Spain, such as Segovia or Salamanca. If you do drive, Toledo is only a quick hour from Madrid, on the N-401 south.

The bus is the quickest, cheapest, and most convenient way to get to Toledo from Madrid. **Galliano Continental** (Estación Sur de Autobuses; ☎ 91-527-29-61; Metro: Méndez Álvaro) buses leave Madrid for Toledo (a one-hour trip) Monday through Saturday every 30 minutes, beginning at 6:30 a.m. with the last return at 10 p.m. (No bus at 2 p.m.) Returns to Madrid are also every half-hour, though the first bus is at 5:30 a.m. On Sundays and holidays, the schedule is every half-hour from 8:30 a.m. to midnight. One-way fare is 580 pta. ($3).

Toledo

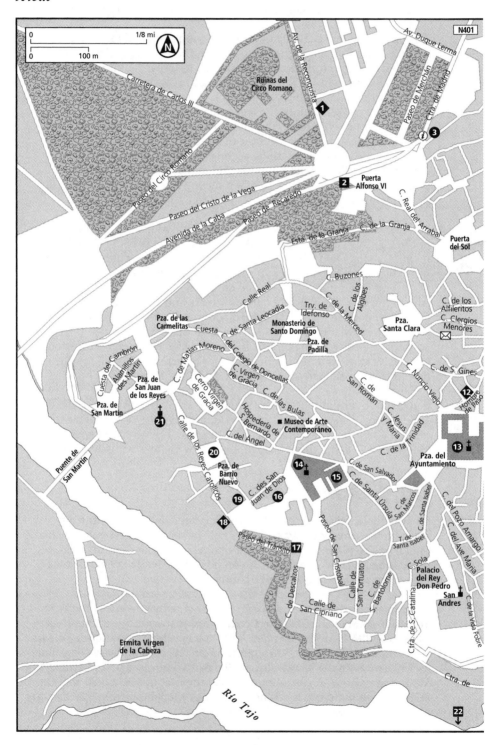

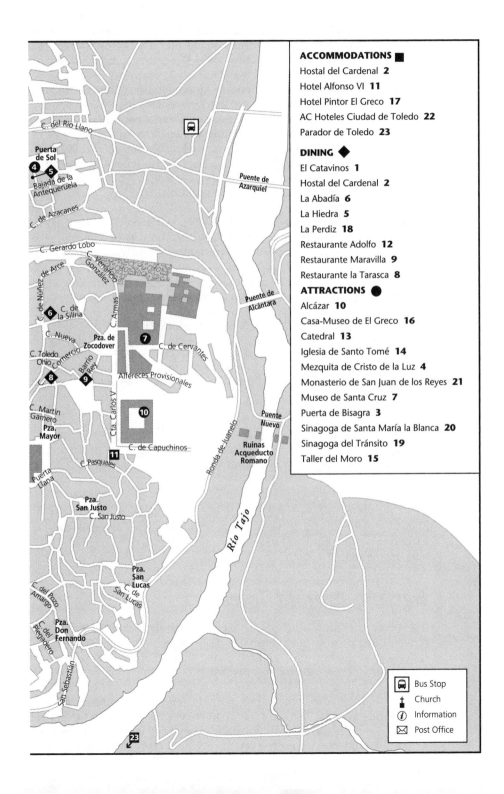

ACCOMMODATIONS ■
Hostal del Cardenal **2**
Hotel Alfonso VI **11**
Hotel Pintor El Greco **17**
AC Hoteles Ciudad de Toledo **22**
Parador de Toledo **23**

DINING ◆
El Catavinos **1**
Hostal del Cardenal **2**
La Abadía **6**
La Hiedra **5**
La Perdiz **18**
Restaurante Adolfo **12**
Restaurante Maravilla **9**
Restaurante la Tarasca **8**

ATTRACTIONS ●
Alcázar **10**
Casa-Museo de El Greco **16**
Catedral **13**
Iglesia de Santo Tomé **14**
Mezquita de Cristo de la Luz **4**
Monasterio de San Juan de los Reyes **21**
Museo de Santa Cruz **7**
Puerta de Bisagra **3**
Sinagoga de Santa María la Blanca **20**
Sinagoga del Tránsito **19**
Taller del Moro **15**

🚌 Bus Stop
✝ Church
ⓘ Information
✉ Post Office

The Toledo bus station (**Estación de Autobuses**) is next to the river, on Avenida Castilla-La Mancha (☎ **925-21-58-50** or 925-22-36-41). It's about ⅔ of a mile from the historic center. You can either walk (be warned: it's steep!) or take a No. 5 or 6 bus (the fare is 110 pta./60¢; pay on board).

The train from Madrid, which departs Atocha Station (Metro: Atocha RENFE), takes 75 minutes. It's a tad more expensive than the bus, but slightly less hectic. In Toledo, the train pulls into a cool, 1917 railway station, with a clock tower and keyhole arches. Several trains per day make the trip; the first leaves at 7:05 a.m. Monday through Friday (8:20 a.m. on weekends and holidays). The first train back to Madrid leaves at 7 a.m. (8:30 a.m. on weekends), the last at 9 p.m. Fare is 630 pta. ($3.50) one-way, 1,135 pta. ($6) roundtrip.

The **RENFE Train Station** (☎ **925-22-30-99**), on Paseo de la Rosa, is about a 20-minute walk from the Old Quarter. You can also take a No. 5 or 6 bus. There's no permanent taxi stop at the train station.

Getting oriented in Toledo

The good news is that Toledo is compact. The bad news is that it is as labyrinthine a place as you're likely to find. Its twisting, turning streets don't even make sense to locals (see "Fast Facts: Toledo" at the end of this chapter for a map recommendation). But, it's so loaded with important sights that even if you get lost you'll stumble onto something.

The city is on a hill and, the Tagus River bounds it on three sides. The southwest part of the city is the old **Barrio Sefardí** (Jewish Quarter), where you find the synagogues, El Greco house and museum, and the San Juan de los Reyes Monastery. The cathedral is almost in the dead center of old Toledo. Alcázar (the fortress) is high on the hill, just east of the cathedral.

The view El Greco painted of his city was from the south side of the Tagus River, looking northwest. If you have a car, the **Carretera de Circunvalación** (beltway) provides stunning views of the city and its amazing setting.

Getting around Toledo

If you drive to Toledo, ditch your car immediately and take advantage of the public parking at Puerta Vieja de la Bisagra (the Old Bisagra Gateway), at the entrance to the old city. Only a couple of hotels, mostly outside the old city, have parking.

Don't even think about venturing by car into the maddening maze of old Toledo's streets. The only way to make your way around the small historic center is on foot, and virtually everything you want to visit is within the medieval walls. The streets are incredibly steep, though, so make sure you don some comfortable, supportive walking shoes. A day spent walking in Toledo is like a rough day on a stair machine at the gym.

If your legs have had it and you need a taxi to rescue you or whisk you to the train or bus station, call ☎ **925-25-50-50.**

Staying in Toledo

Staying overnight in Toledo is a great idea — there's so much to see, and walking around the tiny, hilly stone streets wears out even the best-conditioned travelers. If you can afford the extra time, decline the head-spinning one-day tour.

Toledo has a smattering of good and affordable hotels, some with gorgeous views and others that really capture the city's special atmosphere. The hotels tend to be small, though, and because Toledo is one of the most popular spots in Spain, you need to make advance reservations. If you plan on going anytime between March and September, making phone reservations a month or two in advance is a good idea. The smaller the hotel, the greater the need for early reservations. Be aware that higher room rates are charged for Holy Week and the Corpus Christi festival in early June.

AC Hoteles Ciudad de Toledo
$$$ Across the river south of the city

One of the best new hotels in Spain and the top upscale choice in Toledo, the Ciudad de Toledo took some of the "wow" out of the *parador* down the road when it opened in October 1998. It has an equally coveted location, directly across the river from Toledo, and equally brilliant views of the city, but it's brighter and more cheerful. This hotel is one of the newest members of the AC family, which also includes the top-flight Santo Mauro in Madrid. A model of contemporary luxury and design, the 49 rooms have hip orange and green color schemes, with bathrooms done in brightly colored tiles. The prices are more than fair for a hotel of this caliber.

Carretera de Circunvalación, 15 (on beltway immediately south of Toledo; follow signs to Parador de Toledo). ☎ *925-28-51-25, central reservations* ☎ *902-292-293. Fax: 925-28-47-00. E-mail:* ciutod.direc@ac-hoteles.com. *Internet:* www.ac-hoteles.com. *Parking: Free. Rack rates: 16,000–20,000 pta. ($89–$111). AE, DC, MC, V.*

Hostal del Cardenal
$$ Edge of Old City

This relaxed and personal inn feels like an old Toledo home — it's the perfect hotel for the city. The former residence of an eighteenth-century cardinal, the small place is built right into the city's medieval ramparts, just around the bend from the Puerta de Bisagra. It has graceful Moorish gardens with trickling fountains and serene patios. Its 27 antique-filled rooms are very comfortable, if not lavish. The restaurant (see the restaurant reviews, later in this chapter) has long maintained an excellent reputation for classic Castilian cooking. For the price, this hotel is a steal, but the secret's out. It's so small that it's full most of the year.

Paseo de Recaredo, 24 (just west of Bisagra gate, off Avenida de la Cava). ☎ *925-22-08-62, reservations* ☎ *925-22-49-00. Fax: 925-22-29-91. E-mail:* cardenal@ macom.es. *Internet:* http://cardenal.macom.es. *Parking: Free. Rack rates: 9,450–12,600 pta. ($53–$70). AE, DC, MC, V.*

Hotel Alfonso VI
$$ Old City (near the Alcázar)

I was ready to write off this old-style Spanish hotel, right across from the Alcázar, until I saw the back rooms that face south. They have small balconies and views that gaze out across Toledo, the river, and the rugged countryside. Even though you're not looking up at the city on the hill (as you do from the *parador* or the Ciudad de Toledo hotels, across the river), the view is still extraordinary. The rooms are a little plain, perhaps (except for the shocking bright green curtains and bedspreads), but the place has an odd, yesteryear character. Wait until you get a load of the kitschy basement bar, done up in full medieval regalia with suits of armor and heavy stone arches. Bring on the grog and gruel!

General Moscardó, 2 (one block south of stairs to Alcázar). ☎ *925-22-26-00, reservations* ☎ *925-25-49-02. Fax: 925-21-44-58. E-mail:* info@hotelalfonsoVI. com. *Internet:* www.hotelalfonsovi.com. *Rack rates: 16,200–17,400 pta. ($90–$97), deals from 13,560 pta. ($75) for Internet reservation. AE, DC, MC, V.*

Hotel Pintor El Greco
$$–$$$ Old City (Jewish Quarter)

Similar in ambience to the Hostal del Cardenal but without the gardens, this small hotel also has a great Toledan feel. A seventeenth-century noble home and former bakery, it showcases lots of tiles, exposed brick, dark wood, and iron lamps. Rooms around the central courtyard are light and airy, and immaculately maintained, if oddly reminiscent of the American Southwest. One of the best things about the place is its location in the heart of the old Jewish Quarter. It's close to the El Greco museum and synagogues, and is remarkably peaceful.

Alamillos del Tránsito, 13 (one block southeast from Santo Tome Church). ☎ *925-21-42-50. Fax: 925-21-58-19. E-mail:* info@estancias.com. *Internet:* www. estancias.com. *Parking: public 700 pta. ($4). Rack rates: 14,700–18,000 pta. ($82–$100) (high rate Easter week only). AE, DC, MC, V.*

Parador de Toledo

$$$ Across the river south of the city

The *Parador* allows its guests to see Toledo as El Greco did. Overlooking the city, on a hill above the river, the views are regal. The handsome and fairly spacious rooms look and feel appropriately Castilian, with leather furniture, chests, and heavy, dark wood tables. But you'll probably spend most of your time (when not traipsing about the city) on the terraces and by the large pool. Most guests just can't get enough of the views. (A room with a view is well worth the extra $20.) This is one of the most popular *paradors,* so make your reservations early.

Cerro del Emperador, s/n (4 km; 2 miles from the center of Toledo; access from Carretera de Circunvalación). ☎ *925-22-18-50. Fax: 925-22-51-66. E-mail:* toledo@ parador.es. *Internet:* www.parador.es. *Parking: Free. Rack rates: 18,500 pta. ($103). AE, DC, MC, V.*

Dining in Toledo

El Catavinos

$$ Edge of Old City   CASTILIAN/SPANISH

I love this new, quirky place on the outskirts of Toledo's medieval core, just 5 minutes from the Bisagra gate. The owner is a photographer and hunter of wines, of which there is an ample choice (the name of the restaurant means *wine taster*). There's a bar downstairs, among the wine racks, and a simple dining room upstairs, decorated with Luis Martínez's photographs of Latin America on the peach walls. The menu, a dizzying array of midday and evening fixed-price meals that are excellent deals, is filled with good *comida casera* (home cooking). The grilled salmon was quite tasty, as was the *solomillo* (sirloin steak), served in a huge portion that came with fries worthy of a Belgian bistro.

Avenida de la Reconquista, 10 (just beyond Puerta de Bisagra, 10 minute walk north from Glorieta de la Reconquista, the roundabout on Avenida de la Cava). ☎ *925-22-22-56. No reservations necessary. Menús del día 1,200–3,000 pta. ($7–$17). MC, V.*

Hostal del Cardenal

$$$ Edge of Old City   REGIONAL

For many years one of Toledo's most respected restaurants, some locals report that the kitchen here has become a bit stagnant in recent years. Still, it's hard to go wrong in a setting this fine. Attached to the wonderful Moorish gardens of the Hostal (see hotel review, earlier in this chapter), the restaurant remains one of the most atmospheric places to dine in the old city. Oven-baked sea bass, lamb chops, and the local specialties, roast suckling pig and partridge, are well-executed standards. Be sure to take a stroll in the gardens after dinner.

Paseo Recaredo, 24 (just west of Bisagra gate, off Avenida de la Cava). ☎ *925-25-07-46. Reservations recommended. Main courses: 800–2,600 pta. ($4–$14); menú del dia 2,650 pta. ($15). AE, DC, MC, V.*

La Abadia

$$$ Old City CASTILIAN

I stumbled upon this friendly and nicely designed, slightly upscale restaurant/bar while hunting down a nearby synagogue. It's called "The Abbey" — appropriate in a city with such a roster of religious monuments. The restaurant serves solid Castilian fare like *judías con perdiz* (white bean and partridge casserole, a classic Toledo dish), patés, and venison. It's also a great place to drop in for *tapas;* the bar area is often packed with hungry, talkative nibblers. Fittingly, the Abbey serves a handful of Belgian abbey beers for those of you tired of red wine and sherry.

Plaza de San Nicolás, 3 (at intersection of Calle de Alfileteros and Núñez de Arce, next to San Nicolás church). ☎ *925-25-07-46. Reservations recommended. Main courses: 800–2,800 pta. ($4–$16); menú del día 3,450 pta. ($19). AE, DC, MC, V.*

La Hiedra

$$ Old City SPANISH

A cute and airy little place, with black-and-white tile floors, lots of tall plants, and an attractive patio, La Hiedra (the name means *ivy*) is easy to miss. It's just up the winding street from the Mezquita de Cristo de la Luz, an old mosque not far from the Puerta del Sol gate. The house specialty is *arroces* — rice dishes for two. If you're in an odd-numbered group, you can opt for the *merluza en salsa de almendras,* hake (a white fish) in almond sauce. Some diners report that the food can be a bit hit or miss — not always on a par with the creativity of the dishes.

Calle Cristo de la Luz, 9 (up street from Cristo de la Luz mosque, near Puerta del Sol gate). ☎ *925-25-56-89. Reservations recommended. Main courses: 1,100–2,600 pta. ($6–$14); menú del día 2,000 and 3,000 pta. ($11 and $17). AE, DC, MC, V.*

La Perdiz

$$$ Old City CASTILIAN

A good-looking but unfussy place owned by the same people that run the city's fanciest restaurant, Adolfo, La Perdiz (meaning *partridge*) is more down-to-earth than its upscale relative. In the heart of the Jewish Quarter between the synagogues Tránsito and Santa María la Blanca, its two dining rooms feature exposed brick and crisp white table linens. An excellent starter is the *croquetas de perdiz* (partridge croquettes), a house specialty. Follow that with one of the rice dishes (with shellfish, for example), roast suckling pig, or *albóndigas de bacalao* (cod balls), all solid entrees to fortify you for Toledo's challengingly hilly streets.

Calle Reyes Católicos, 7 (two blocks east of San Juan de Reyes monastery).
☎ *925-21-46-58. Reservations recommended. Main courses: 1,500–2,500 pta.*
($8–$14). AE, DC, MC, V.

Restaurante Adolfo
$$$ Old City   CASTILIAN

The place in the Old Quarter for well-to-do locals and discriminating
tourists, Adolfo occupies a handsome fifteenth-century building on a
little side street not far from the cathedral. It's a bit hard to find, just off
Calle Hombre de Palo one block north of the cathedral. Dine in one of
four quiet dining rooms with elegant place settings and solid beams over-
head. The kitchen is creative, pumping out original interpretations of
traditional dishes like *merluza al azafrán* (saffron-flavored hake). Game
is a specialty. The wine cellar, though, is the real star. Set in an eleventh-
century Jewish *cueva,* or basement, it's the best in Toledo. For dessert,
everyone raves about the marzipan; if you like the sweet almond paste,
you'll love it (it's lighter than most versions). When I last dined here, the
food was tops, but the service was pretty disappointing.

Calle de la Granada, 6 (one block from cathedral, off Hombre de Palo).
☎ *925-22-73-21. Reservations essential. Main courses: 2,200–3,600 pta. ($12–$20).*
AE, DC, MC, V.

Restaurante Maravilla
$$ Old City   SPANISH

Just off a cute little square, away from Toledo's roar of tourists, this small
dining room, decorated with colorful *azulejos* (tiles) is attached to a small
hotel, the Hostal Maravilla. Despite the name (which translates to
"restaurant of wonder"), the restaurant may not perform miracles, but
it's faithful to Toledo standards like quail and partridge. It also offers a full
range of fortifying pastas. More adventurous diners in this land-locked
capital opt for fish and shellfish. Locals pack the place for its good value.
Menus are available in English.

Plaza Barrio Rey, 7 (one block west of Cuesta de Carlos V). ☎ *925-22-85-82.*
Reservations recommended. Main courses: 800–2,500 pta. ($4–$14). AE, DC, MC, V.

Restaurante la Tarasca
$$ Old City   CASTILIAN

Just a couple short blocks north of the cathedral, on a busy street lined
with jewelry and craft shops, La Tarasca is a good place to duck in for a
solid lunch. There's a regular menu, but all anyone seems to order is the
menú del día (fixed-price meal). The décor is merely functional, but it's
a little nicer in back, away from the door. It quickly gets crowded with
sightseers and locals (there seems to be more of the latter), so try to beat
the 2 p.m. lunch rush, especially on weekends. You may start things off
with a pretty decent *paella* (a rice, meat, and seafood casserole), and

follow it up with *cordonices* (braised game hen) or trout. A glass of wine and dessert (flan or ice cream) is included in the menu.

Callejón del Fraile, s/n (off Calle de Comercio, two blocks northeast of cathedral). ☎ *925-22-43-42. Reservations recommended. Main courses: 700–2,400 pta. ($4–$13); menú del día 1,400 or 2,200 pta. ($8 or $12). AE, DC, MC, V.*

Exploring Toledo

In Toledo, separating the must-sees from the can-do-withouts is tough. In some ways, the distinctions are a bit arbitrary — the city is a fascinating whole with a long roster of complex parts. In any case, seeing everything in a single day is impossible. However, if that's all you have time for, consider only the main stops listed in the "Top attractions" section, later in this chapter. If you can spend the night and at least a second day in Toledo, consider visiting a couple of the locations detailed in the following "More cool things to see and do" section.

Before you set out to conquer Toledo, consulting a good map in addition to the one provided here (see "Fast Facts: Toledo," at the end of this chapter, for a recommendation) is essential. Toledo is a complicated maze of twisting streets that makes providing good directions nearly impossible. If your map reading fails you, ask a local. They may have to think about it, but most are more than happy to point you in the right direction.

The best place to start your tour is from the Puerta de Bisagra (where the Tourism Office is located). Pass through the massive gate and enter the twisting maze of Toledo's tiny streets. All the major sites I list are within the Old City.

The city of Toledo offers a package deal of 300 pta. ($1.70) to see four sights: the outstanding **Museo Santa Cruz, Taller del Moro, San Roman Church,** and the **Museum of Contemporary Art.** You can purchase the joint admission at any of those locations.

Beastly crowds

Plaza Zocodover is the busy central square where tour guides gather and check their rosters, barking off names, waving colored flags, and disciplining the troops for their next stop on the itinerary. In prime tourist season, the square, lined with shops hawking swords and souvenirs, can be a chaotic counterpoint to Toledo's quiet medieval secrets. Once you experience it, you probably won't be surprised to learn that Zocodover means "market of the beasts." It comes from the Arabic *Suk-al-bawab,* named not for the tourists, but for a medieval animal market that took place there.

The top attractions

Catedral de Toledo
Old City

Allow sufficient time to see Toledo's centerpiece, one of the most opulent, jaw-dropping Gothic churches in Spain. The massive asymmetrical structure makes a solid case for Toledo's religious importance in the Middle Ages. Begun in 1226, it wasn't finished until nearly three centuries later, in 1493 (the year after Columbus is credited with discovering America). On the outside, the cathedral is French Gothic; the interior mixes Spanish Gothic with Mudejar, Renaissance, and Plateresque elements. Right in the middle of the cathedral nave is the choir, a splendid example of wood carving on the lower choirstalls and alabaster sculpture on the upper tier. The *Alta Mayor* (High Altar) is a fabulous, brightly colored polychrome *retablo* (altarpiece) dripping in gold. The kings of Castile are buried here. Walk around the altar and look straight up. Curiously hung from the ambulatory is an almost ridiculously ornate marble sculpture, *Transparente*. A controversial sun roof (it's so incongruous, I don't know what else to call it) was cut to allow sunlight in to illuminate it. Before the opening was carved, the sculpture was almost impossible to see.

The sacristy (to the left of the main altar) holds a treasure trove of artworks, including El Greco's *Expolio (The Denuding of Christ),* as well as works by Titian and Goya. The Sala Capitular, to the right rear of the cathedral, is a mini Alhambra, with intricate *mudéjar* (Christian architecture employing Arab motifs and elements) ceilings and stucco doorways. In the Treasury is a wondrous sixteenth century *monstrance* — the receptacle used to display communion wafers or bread — that weighs nearly 400 pounds and is nearly 10 feet high. Despite the monstrous proportions, the faithful hoist and parade it through the streets of Toledo during the Corpus Christi celebration in June. Plan on spending one to two hours here.

Arcos de Palacio (just off Plaza del Ayuntamiento). ☎ *925-22-22-41. Admission: 500 pta. ($2.75). Open: Mon–Sat 10:30 a.m.–1 p.m. and 3:30–6 p.m., Sun and holidays 10:30 a.m.–1:30 p.m. and 4–6 p.m.*

Iglesia de Santo Tomé: El Greco's The Burial of Count Orgaz
Old City

The Church of Santo Tomé doesn't really qualify as a visit to a church; it's a required stop to see a single painting. However, that painting is one of the finest in Spain: El Greco's masterpiece, *The Burial of Count Orgaz.* The painting, created for the space where it still hangs today, is masterful in its color, contrast, and composition. It depicts the miraculous appearance of St. Augustine and St. Stephen at the burial of the Count, a church patron who paid for the construction of Santo Tomé. It's also a self-portrait: El Greco is seventh from the left at the bottom, staring straight ahead. Visitors often cram the small room, so try going as soon as it opens in the morning or just after lunch if you want to ponder the work in relative peace. Allow as long as you can stand looking at a stunning work in the company of lots of restless day trippers — about a half hour, allowing for the crowd.

Plaza del Conde, 2 (one block south of Calle del Ángel/Calle de Santo Tomé, in the southwestern part of the city). ☎ *925-21-02-90. Admission: 150 pta. (85¢). Open: Daily 10 a.m.–1:45 p.m. and 3:30–5:45 p.m. (summer hours, open until 6:45 p.m.).*

Monasterio de San Juan de los Reyes
Jewish Quarter

A Gothic monastery commissioned to commemorate the Spanish victory over Portugal in 1476, this was to have been the burial place of the Catholic Monarchs, Ferdinand and Isabela. (They were eventually buried in the Granada cathedral.) As you may guess, it's suitably grand, a gorgeous and surprising mix of Gothic and *mudéjar* architecture. The fine Gothic cloisters have a superb Moorish-style, wood-carved ceiling and brilliant stone carving. Peek out over the balcony for a view of some wild gargoyles. The monastery is in the extreme western portion of the city, near the Jewish Quarter. An hour here should suffice, though the cloisters are a place to linger.

Calle de los Reyes Católicos, 17 (just beyond the point where Reyes Católicos meets Calle del Ángel, about two blocks west of the Santa María la Blanca synagogue). ☎ *925-22-38-02. Admission: 150 pta. (85¢). Open: Daily 10 a.m.–1:45 p.m. and 3:30–5:45 p.m. (until 6:45 p.m. in summer).*

Museo de Santa Cruz
Old City

Built before the era of superstar architects, this museum is as notable for the building itself as what it displays inside. Given that it was a hospital for orphans and the indigent in the sixteenth century, the building is surprisingly sumptuous, with carved wood ceilings and rich marble floors. The museum can stand a little upkeep and better lighting, but its outstanding early Renaissance features, including a dramatic, ornamental stairway and Plateresque patio, are impossible to miss. The museum has a number of El Grecos, the most important being *La Asunción de la Virgen* (1613). Originally an altarpiece, this is one of the master's final works, painted just months before his death. Extending from ceiling to floor is the battle flag from Lepanto, the landmark 1571 victory over the Moors. Throughout the wings of the building, designed in the form of a Greek cross, are excellent sixteenth century tapestries, furniture, and decorative arts. You probably need a couple of hours at this interesting museum.

The Santa Cruz museum is one of the few sights in Toledo that remains open at midday (except Monday). Go at 2 or 3 p.m.; not only is it less crowded, but this way you can squeeze more activities into your day without too much dead time at lunch.

El Greco: Domenico the Greek

If anyone ever needed a nickname, it was Domenico Theotocopoulous. Spaniards simply called the Greek artist (who didn't adopt Toledo as his hometown until 1577, when he was already 36 years old) El Greco, or "The Greek." Toledo made him famous, and vice-versa. El Greco's *View of Toledo* is a lovely picture of the city on the hill, but the painter is considered one of Spain's greatest for his deeply spiritual portraits of saints and madonnas, depicted in an otherworldly elongated fashion.

Contrary to popular legend, El Greco almost surely did not suffer from an astigmatism. The ethereal figures, their forms reaching toward heaven, were a product of the artist's deeply spiritual vision. His portraits were meditative and almost hallucinatory. It's little surprise that his paintings found no favor at all at Madrid's Royal Court, where realism reigned supreme. However, his adopted city adored him, and El Greco found his place of divine inspiration in its melting pot.

El Greco's supreme artistic achievement, *The Burial of Count Orgaz,* depicted a burial ceremony so important that two saints miraculously appeared at it. But the artist himself met a less ceremonious end: he lies in the Santo Domingo Monastery, underneath a curious little museum run by the nuns there. You can view El Greco's remains by kneeling down and peering through a hole in the floor. The coffin is so small that it looks more like a toolbox.

If you want to see the tomb and the *retablos* (altarpieces) El Greco painted in the monastery, it's on Plaza Santo Domingo El Antiguo (☎ **925-22-29-30**). The hours are Monday to Saturday from 11 a.m. to 1:30 p.m. and 4 to 7 p.m., and Sunday from 4 to 7 p.m. only. Admission is 150 pta. (85¢).

Calle Miguel de Cervantes, 3 (one block east of the granite archway on Plaza de Zocodover). ☎ 925-22-10-36. Admission: 200 pta. ($1.10). Open: Mon 10 a.m.–2 p.m. and 4–6:30 p.m., Tues–Sat 10 a.m.–6:30 p.m., Sun, 10 a.m.–2 p.m.

Sinagoga del Tránsito
Jewish Quarter

This fourteenth-century synagogue was one of ten that once existed in Toledo, when one-fifth of the population was Jewish. The exterior is rather nondescript on the outside, but inside it's a wealth of elaborate *mudéjar* decoration. The two-story interior has a dazzling carved cedarwood ceiling and splendid stucco inscriptions in Hebrew. The upstairs balcony was reserved for women. Within the synagogue is the Sephardic Museum, which displays an interesting collection of tombstones, robes, and books, many dating prior to the expulsion of Spain's Jews in 1492. Allow from a half-hour to an hour.

Calle de Samuel Levi, s/n (just south of the Casa-Museo de El Greco, near the intersection of Paseo del Tránsito and Calle de San Juan de Dios). ☎ 925-22-36-65. Admission: 400 pta. ($2.20), free Sat afternoons and Sun. Open: Tues–Sat 10 a.m.– 2 p.m. and 4–6 p.m., Sun 10 a.m.–2 p.m.

Across the river: El Greco's view of Toledo

It's not uncommon to feel a little claustrophobic as you navigate Toledo's labyrinthine streets by foot, dodging cars and tour buses along the way. If you have a car, don't miss a drive along the Carretera de Circunvalación, the beltway that runs alongside the River Tagus around the city. Head east towards the Ermita de Nuestra Señora del Valle, a small chapel above the river, the *Parador del Toledo*, and the Roman Bridge, Puente de Alcántara. The views of the city are dazzling, especially at dusk — it's not hard to see why El Greco was so enamored of this view of his adopted hometown. A couple of bars and outdoor cafes have sprung up here, though few tourists seem to make the trip. If tourists do venture across the river, most go on up to the terrace at the *parador,* which is equally good (in fact the hill on which the *parador* sits is purportedly the hill from which El Greco painted *View of Toledo*).

If you don't have a car, at least walk out through the San Martín neighborhood, west of the old Jewish Quarter and over the San Martín Bridge (which dates to 1203), and take a look back at Toledo rising on the hill before you. Leave at least an hour (more if you catch the light just right as you gaze at the city).

More cool things to see and do

Toledo so overflows with worthy churches and monuments that they should draw your attention if you have more than an afternoon or single day in the city.

✔ **Touring the Alcázar.** Toledo's *Alcázar* (☎ 925-22-30-38), or citadel, on the hill is hard to miss, and not a bus tour goes by without stopping at it, but inside it's frankly a bit of a disappointment. Originally built by Carlos V in the sixteenth century (a conversion of the thirteenth-century fortress of El Cid, the famed Castilian warrior), it's been destroyed by fire and battle and rebuilt many times — most recently, after the Spanish Civil War. Restored and converted into an army museum, it now looks much as it originally did. Its large Italianate central patio is its most appealing feature, unless you're wowed by unending displays of weapons and uniforms. The Alcázar is located at Calle General Moscardó, 4 (climb ramp off Cuesta de Carlos V, near Plaza de Zocodover). It's open Tuesday through Sunday from 9:30 a.m. to 2 p.m. Admission is 200 pta. ($1.10).

✔ **Getting to know El Greco.** Though the name of this museum, **Casa-Museo de El Greco** (☎ 925-22-40-46), implies that El Greco actually lived here, he didn't. His actual home was destroyed long ago; this one merely resembles it. Although that sounds like a monumental tourist rip-off, the museum houses a hefty collection of El Greco's paintings, including one of a view of Toledo — but not the famous *View of Toledo,* which belongs to New York's Metropolitan

Museum of Art. The house part of the Casa-Museo was still under renovation at press time, as it has been for the past five years — the last word had it reopening in late 2000, but that didn't happen. The museum is located at Calle Samuel Levi, 3 (one block south of Calle de Santo Tomé; take Travessía de Santo Tomé). It's open Tuesday through Saturday from 10 a.m. to 2 p.m. and 4 to 6 p.m., Sunday 10 a.m. to 2 p.m. Admission is 400 pta. ($2.20), but it's free Saturday afternoon and Sunday, and also free for seniors.

✔ **Taking in another synagogue.** The twelfth-century **Sinagoga de Santa María la Blanca** (☎ 925-22-72-57), the oldest of ten that once existed in Toledo, is one of only two that remain. (See the Sinagoga del Tránsito review in the attractions section, earlier in this chapter.) A national monument, it has a Christian name because it was taken over by the Catholic Church in 1405. The synagogue has classic horseshoe-shaped arches, similar to those of the landmark Córdoba Mosque (see Chapter 16). The surprising Moorish design is owed to the Muslim craftsmen who were commissioned to build it. The crafty Moors also built the synagogue so that it faces Mecca (luckily, in the same direction as Jerusalem). The synagogue is at Calle de los Reyes Católicos, 4, just down street from (and east of) San Juan de los Reyes monastery. It's open daily from 10 a.m. to 1:45 p.m. and 3:30 to 5:45 p.m. (in summer it stays open until 6:45 p.m.). Admission is 150 pta. (85¢).

✔ **Walking through *Puerta de Bisagra,* the town gates.** There are actually two Bisagra gates to the city. The old gate, built in the eleventh and twelfth centuries, is the only one that remains of the original Muslim wall around Toledo. Its arch is clearly Moorish in style. The newer, Greco-Roman gate, just west of the original one, was completed in 1550. It's much grander and carries the Hapsburg coat of arms (at the time, Spain was part of the Holy Roman Empire, ruled by the Hapsburgs). The gate (either door No. 1 or door No. 2) is the best place to begin a walking tour of Toledo. Enter at the intersection of Calle del Cardenal Tavera and Avenida de la Cava (the north entrance to the city).

✔ **Admiring a legendary mosque.** You can't go inside the miniscule **Mezquita de Cristo de la Luz,** built in the tenth century, but it's well worth trying to stumble upon it on your walks through the city. The Moors built the square brick mosque, one of the oldest surviving in Spain, on the site of a Visigothic church. In fact, some original pillars remain, having been molded into Moorish arches. The mosque's name, "Christ of the Light," is attributed to a legend of the military general El Cid, who, on his way into Toledo to seize it from the Moors, knelt in front of the mosque. Later, according to the story, a lamp illuminating a crucifix (said to be left by El Cid) was supposedly uncovered inside a wall of the mosque, where it had been burning for some 300 years. The mosque is at Calle del Cristo de la Luz, just inside the walled town from Puerta del Sol, across from Convento de Carmelitas.

✔ **Visiting a Moorish mansion. Taller del Moro** (no phone), a fourteenth-century Moorish mansion, is best visited for the building itself, which has excellent carved Moorish porticos. You also find a small museum of tiles and Moorish crafts. The name of the building means, literally, "The Moor's Workshop." It's located at Calle del Taller del Moro, around corner from Santo Tomé church, down street from Plaza El Salvador. Hours are Tuesday through Saturday from 10 a.m. to 2 p.m. and 4 to 6:30 p.m., and Sunday from 10 a.m. to 2 p.m. Admission is 100 pta. (55¢); free Saturday afternoon and Sunday.

Shopping in Toledo

Toledo is a mecca for crafts shoppers. The city's distinctive black-and-gold *damascene* art, nearly as symbolic of Toledo as the Alcázar or the cathedral, is found everywhere within the Old Quarter. The art is an old Moorish practice of inlaying gold (and sometimes copper or silver) against a background of matte black steel. It's the rare tourist who doesn't go home with at least a ring, letter-opener, or some other *damascene* souvenir. (If you're not impressed with the merchandise, the relentless sales pitches you encounter will certainly run you down.) Damascene items can be handcrafted or machine-made. If it's cheap, it's machine-made; if you're looking for a heftier, better-crafted souvenir, visit one of Toledo's reputable shops that have artisans on the premises.

Toledo has also been known for its swords since the Middle Ages. Although swashbuckling tourists cart them off by the dozens, be warned that airport security will most likely consider them weapons. Embroidery from the small provincial towns of Lagartera and Oropesa is featured in many shops; embroidered blouses, napkins, and tablecloths make good gifts. You may also want to look for local pottery and traditional blue-and-yellow ceramics from Talavera. If you're driving, you probably already saw roadside vendors selling pottery and ceramics on the way in from Madrid. Their prices are often much better than the touristy shops in Toledo. Another good thing to score, if you have the taste for it, is Toledo's marzipan (*marzapan* in Spanish).

Aptly named **Calle de Comercio** is lined with dozens of shops, all featuring a wide array of Toledo damascene. Marzipan is available at several bakeries on or near Plaza Zocodover.

Damascene and swords

Braojos Arco de Palacio, 5 and Comercio, 44 (no phone), is one of the top places in Toledo for damascene objects and engravings. You won't find the cheap machine-made stuff at **Casa Bermejo,** Calle Airosas, 5. (☎ 925-22-03-46). You will, however, find a disciplined team of artisans that, in addition to creating excellent gift items, also cranks out ornamental swords and military dress items for West Point and the armies of several European countries. If your tastes are grander than the key chains, letter openers, rings, and earrings you see everywhere in Toledo, check out **Felipe Suárez,** Paseo de los Canónigos, 19 (☎ 925-22-56-15). It's got the entry-level goods, but its damascene artisans also create unique and very pricey art objects.

Marzipan

Pastelerías Santo Tomé, Calle Santo Tomé, 5 and Plaza Zocodover, 7 (☎ 925-22-37-63). Founded in 1856, this is one of the most famous marzipan bakeries in Toledo; it exports all over the world. **Casa Telesforo** (Plaza de Zocodover, 13; ☎ 925-22-33-79). The oldest of the old-time marzipan factories, Telesforo has been churning out highly decorative designs in sweet almond paste since 1806. **Pastelería Casado** (Cuesta del Alcázar, 11; ☎ 925-22-37-34). Next to Plaza Zocodover, this traditional Toledan bakery has been in business since the 1950s. There's also a crafts-and-gift shop at the same address.

La noche: Toledo's nightlife

Toledo, noisy and agitated by day, really calms down after the tour buses rumble back to Madrid. Early evening is a perfect time to meander around the city's crooked streets and quiet plazas. If you're up for more than a walk around town, drop in on any of these *tascas* for tapas and drinks: **La Abadía** (Calle Núñez del Arce, 1); **Ludeña** (Corral de Don Diego, 10); **El Trébol** (Santa Fé, s/n); or **La Venta del Alma** (Carretera de Piedrabuena, 35). Deserving special mention is **El Temple,** an amazingly cool bar in an eleventh-century Moorish palace once occupied by Alfonso VI. It has a great open central patio and slightly crumbling walls that resonate with the flavor of ancient Toledo. El Temple is on Calle Soledad, 2, about a block south of the Alcázar (☎ 925-21-04-31).

A few shopping detours

If you're a shop-a-holic, or just find the crafts of Toledo too good to resist, you may want to take a road trip or two. **Talavera de la Reina** is renowned for the blue-and-yellow ceramics it has produced since the 1400s. The town (71 km, or 44 miles, west of Toledo) is loaded with ceramics vendors, but so are the roads leading to town. You may score a better deal stopping roadside. To get there, take C-502 west from Toledo.

If your intended booty is embroidery, plan a mini-excursion a bit farther west to the small towns **Orpesa** (24 km, or 15 miles, from Talavera) and **Lagartera** (7 km, or 4½ miles beyond Orpesa). You'll have no trouble finding the richly embroidered table-cloths and other linens that local women create.

Fast Facts: Toledo

Area Code

Toledo's area code is **925,** which you must dial before every number.

Currency Exchange

There are ATM machines located around the Plaza Mayor. The Banco de España is located on Calle de la Plata, near the San Nicolás Church.

Emergencies

For medical emergencies, call Ambulancias Cruz Roja, ☎ **925-21-60-60** or 22-22-22. The municipal hospital emergency number is ☎ **061.** For hospital information, call ☎ **925-26-92-00.** For municipal police, ☎ **925-21-34-00;** for emergencies, dial ☎ **092.**

Information

The main tourism office is located at Puerta de Bisagra, s/n; ☎ **925-22-08-43.** Hours are Mon–Fri 9 a.m. to 6 p.m., Sat 9 a.m. to 7 p.m., and Sun 9 a.m. to 3 p.m.

Maps

In most Spanish cities, the maps at the tourism offices suffice — not in Toledo, however. You get either an illegible, photocopied map or a terribly oversimplified one. Do yourself a favor and purchase the 200-pta. ($1.40) map put out by Julio de la Cruz, at any newspaper kiosk or at many souvenir shops. It's large, clear, and has all Toledo's streets and sights clearly marked.

Police

Call ☎ **925-21-34-00** or ☎ **092.**

Post Office

Salamanca's main post office is on Calle de la Plata, 1 (☎ **925-22-36-11**).

Part V
Southern Spain

The 5th Wave   **By Rich Tennant**

"For tonight's modern reinterpretation of Carmen, those in the front row are kindly requested to wear raincoats."

In this part . . .

When most people close their eyes and dream of Spain, it's probably the rich images of Andalusia that spring to mind. The south is like an Iberian highlight film with accompanying soundtrack: bullfights in the hot sun; flamenco's passionate staccato rhythms; and dark-haired beauties with flowers in their hair and polka dots on their twirling dresses, fans waving in their delicate hands. The classic landscape of parched mountains, rolling chestnut hills, and olive groves as far as the eye can see also produces some of Spain's quintessential savory treats: gazpacho, sherry, olive oil, and robust green olives.

There's so much to see and do in Andalusia that you could spend a lifetime there, not just a vacation. Its scenery includes stunning Moorish monuments, like Granada's Alhambra and Córdoba's Great Mosque; sunkissed white villages perched on gorges and mountain tops; the sultry charms of Seville; and Spain's most developed stretch of beaches. No wonder Andalusians are always exclaiming *¡olé!* in the movies.

Chapter 16

Seville and Córdoba

● ●

In This Chapter

▶ Getting around Seville and Córdoba

▶ Keeping busy with festivals, monuments, museums, and bullfights

▶ Finding the best places to stay and dine, plus tips for perfecting the *tapas* crawl

▶ Getting out of town: Side trips to Roman and Moorish ruins

● ●

*T*he region of Andalusia is fairy-tale Spain, the clichéd-but-true land of summer heat, Gypsy passion, and a fascinating Arab past. In their heyday, the Moors (Arab and Berber conquerors of Spain) dominated most of Spain, but their empire took deepest root in the south.

In Córdoba, the Moors built the Mezquita, the Great Mosque — which, along with the Alhambra (see Chapter 18), is Muslim Spain's supreme achievement. Seville's immense cathedral, the third-largest in Europe, was constructed over the ruins of another great mosque, incorporating the dramatic minaret as a belfry. By the tenth century, Córdoba had become Europe's most advanced and populous city, a capital of high culture and learning. In turn, Seville was Spain's leading light in its sixteenth-century Golden Age, when the riches of the Americas flowed back through the city via the Guadalquivir River, and great artists like Velázquez, Murillo, and Zurbarán created the Seville School.

The Old Quarters of both cities are pretty jumbles of narrow alleyways lined with tiled portraits of saints and madonnas, potted plants and bougainvillea, and cool interior patios. Seville is unmatched in Spain for ambience, the kind of place where the scent of orange trees and the joy of living, not just working, move people to lyrical odes. Córdoba is clearly the great city that was, but it remains a fascinating, living, historical document. Above all, both cities represent Spain at its most folkloric. Popular celebrations are infectious, and the people are as radiant and nearly as warm as the blinding sun that beats down on their mythic part of Spain.

Just the Facts: Seville and Córdoba

Seville and Córdoba are two major cities in the southern region of Andalusia, one of Spain's most attractive and friendly areas. Seville, 548 km (340 miles) southwest of Madrid, is the capital of Andalusia; Córdoba is 403 km (250 miles) south of Seville.

- ✔ **The way to go.** Seville and Córdoba are within easy reach of Madrid, especially with the high-speed AVE train, which gets you to Seville in just under 2½ hours (Córdoba's a stop along the way, 1½ hours from Madrid).

- ✔ **The name game.** Seville in Spanish is *Sevilla* ("say-*vee*-yuh"), while Córdoba is pronounced the same in Spanish and English (though it sometimes is written Cordova in English). The region, Andalusia, is called *Andalucía* ("ahn-da-loo-*thee*-ah") in Spanish. Southern Spaniards are called *Andaluces* ("ahn-da-*looth*-ez").

- ✔ **¿Cómo se dice? Talking the talk.** The language is Spanish, but Spanish in Andalusia sounds unlike it does anywhere else in Spain. Southerners tend to swallow the ends of words and pronounce the "c" and "z" with a soft *"s"* sound, like they do in Latin America, rather than the lispy *"th"* sound you hear everywhere else in Spain. The language in Andalusia sounds different enough that Spaniards sometimes say that locals speak "Andaluz" (which, mimicking the habit of their chopping the last syllables off words, is pronounced "*ahn*-da-loo.")

- ✔ **What's for dinner?** Fried foods, cold soups, and slightly chilled aperitif wines rule the day in Andalusia. The best way to beat the heat is with a cold bowl of *gazpacho* ("gath-*potch*-oh"), a chilled tomato soup. *Pescaíto frito,* deep-fried fish, is served in nearly every bar and restaurant. As in Madrid, the pursuit of *tapas* and *copas* (all-hours snacking and drinking, respectively) is a local institution, but Andalusians insist that they invented the art of *tapas.* The *tapeo* (tapas crawl) in Seville and Córdoba is a joyous affair like nowhere else in Spain. Andalusian aperitif wines — *jerez* (sherry), from just south of Seville, and *montilla* ("mahn-*tee*-ya"), a splendid dry wine from Córdoba — are superb.

- ✔ **The forecast.** Get ready to sweat: Southern Spain is hot. Seville and Córdoba are two of the hottest cities in Europe (in summer, the only place hotter is the North African desert). Winter is mild, while spring and fall are warm but comfortable.

- ✔ **When to go.** The best time to visit Seville and Córdoba is April and May, when flowers are in bloom and the famous festivals, including Easter Week, possess the locals and transform their cities (although this is also the hardest time to get a hotel). If you can't make it then, fall and winter aren't bad, because the sun shines year-round. Unless you have a high tolerance for heat (that is, if you grew up surrounded by cacti), you're better off avoiding the sizzling summers. July and August are packed with heatstroked tourists; unless you're a masochist, avoid these cities then.

✔ **How long before moving on?** Seville has enough to see and do that you need a minimum of two days to take in its main draws, but you can comfortably spend a week in Seville, where the sultry pace is intoxicating. You can see the highlights of Córdoba in a long day.

Major Attractions in Seville and Córdoba

Seville and Córdoba form two of the three bases in Spain's southern triangle of Moorish influence (the other is Granada; see Chapter 18).

Seville

One of the most enjoyable and exuberant cities in Spain, Seville invades the senses. The boulevards are lined with orange trees, church bells overlap with the clop-clop of horses and buggies, and the smell of fresh flowers is everywhere. Charming palaces are painted deep ochre and blood red. Seville has inspired artists and musicians like few other cities; from the art of passionate, soul-baring flamenco to operas like *Don Juan, Carmen,* and *The Marriage of Figaro,* Seville has always been a place to sing about. You can get a taste of Seville in just a couple of days, but it's the kind of place that you want to return to over and over.

Seville is well known for the following attractions:

✔ The **Cathedral,** the world's largest Gothic edifice, and the belfry, **La Giralda,** a minaret in a former life

✔ **El Alcázar,** the fantastic fortress/royal residence, where kings and queens entertained lovers and enemies

✔ **Barrio de Santa Cruz,** the colorful, quintessential Andalusian neighborhood

✔ **Parque de María Luisa** (Maria Luisa Park), a green oasis, lush enough to beat the heat

✔ Seville's unrivaled **spring festival season** — Easter and April Fair

Córdoba

You may find it hard to believe that Córdoba was once Europe's most enlightened and populated city. When the rest of the continent sank into the Dark Ages, Muslim Córdoba soared ahead, with libraries, universities, mathematics, and sophisticated architecture and trade. But

Thay what?

If you're unaccustomed to Spain's version of Spanish — called *castellano,* or Castilian — it may sound as though everybody has a lisp, pronouncing the letters "c" and "z" as "th." Zaragoza becomes "Thair-ah-*go*-tha." But in the country's deep south, especially in rural areas, many locals really do speak with a lisp. Even "s," which is plain old "s" everywhere else in Spain, is pronounced by some as "th" — so, *no sé* ("no say", I don't know) becomes "no thay."

the city in which Jews and Christians lived alongside the Moors saw its best days long ago. Once a city of one million, the provincial capital today has scarcely 300,000 inhabitants, becoming one of the few cities in the world to suffer so dramatic a population drop without an accompanying natural disaster.

But Córdoba's former greatness is instantly revealed when you slip behind the dreary exterior of the Great Mosque and are suddenly enveloped by one of the most awe-inspiring scenes in Europe: an unending horizon of overlapped, candy-cane striped arches.

Look for the following attractions in Córdoba:

- ✔ The **Mezquita** (Great Mosque) — one of Muslim Spain's great monuments
- ✔ **La Judería,** the old Jewish Quarter of whitewashed streets, lively bars, and artisans' shops
- ✔ Córdoba's spectacular flowered **patios** and May **festivals**

Spending Time in Seductive Seville

Seville, conquered by the Romans in the third century B.C., became one of Spain's most important Roman towns. After Rome fell, Spain was overrun by various barbarian invaders including the Visigoths and the Vandals. The Moors finally conquered Spain in the eighth century and ruled the city for more than 500 years, until the Reconquest in 1248. Seville prospered in the sixteenth century when by royal decree it became the gateway to the Americas (and the benefactor of all that loot flowing down its river). The city lived a grand Golden Age in the arts during the sixteenth and seventeenth centuries, but then gradually lost ground to Madrid and Barcelona.

Today, Seville is Spain's fourth-largest city, with a population of 800,000. Sevillanos have earned a reputation for working less and socializing more than any other region in Spain. There's little doubt that they love few things as much as gathering at bars for drinks and *tapas.* As an outsider, you may be inclined to believe that locals spend a good part of the day, and a good portion of their salary, just hanging out. But natives will tell you that they simply know how to live better than the workaholics up north.

Maybe it's the languid air of Andalusia, but *guiris* (foreigners) love Seville. And although Americans don't yet top the list of visitors to Spain, they are the number one group of tourists in Seville, ranking ahead of the Germans, French, and Italians for the past decade. Along with Salamanca, Seville is also the most popular place for American college students to spend a semester or full academic year.

Arriving in Seville

Seville is accessible by air, train, and bus from all major points in Spain, but in all likelihood, you'll cruise into Seville from another point in Andalusia or from Madrid. Probably the easiest way is to glide in on the superfast AVE train, though if you're hopping around Spain by plane, flying into Seville is easy.

By plane

Seville's international airport is **Aeropuerto Internacional San Pablo** (Autopista de San Pablo, s/n; ☎ **95-444-90-00**). The national airlines of several European countries fly into Seville, and daily flights arrive on Iberia from Madrid, Barcelona, Bilbao, and Valencia (Air Europa flies to Seville from Barcelona). The airport is 10 km (6 miles) north of Seville, on National Highway IV. The **Tourism Information Office** (☎ **95-444-91-28**) is open daily from 9 a.m. to 8 p.m.

From the airport to downtown, you can take a bus, a relatively short ride that goes to Alfonso XIII Hotel, on Puerta de Jerez (750 pta./$4). A taxi from the airport to the *zona centro* (anywhere near the Cathedral) should cost about 2,500 pta. ($14).

By car

Spain's big cities aren't great places to deal with wheels, so if you're just traveling to Seville (and Córdoba and Granada), and not planning on touring the surrounding country, skip the car. Driving to Seville from Madrid, take the N-IV (E-5), which veers right (west) at Bailén and passes through Córdoba. The easy trip is all highway from Madrid, but it takes more than five hours, depending on stops and your willingness to do as the Spaniards do and flout speed limits.

The A-92 highway connects Seville with Granada and the Costa del Sol. For roadside assistance, call ☎ **900-12-35-05**.

Seville

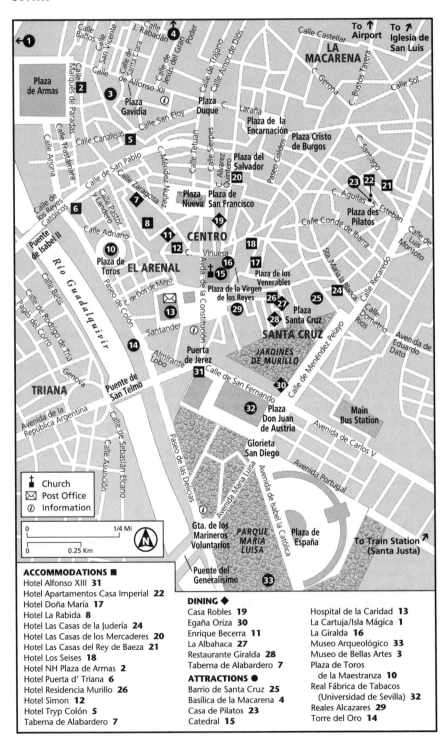

ACCOMMODATIONS ■
Hotel Alfonso XIII **31**
Hotel Apartamentos Casa Imperial **22**
Hotel Doña María **17**
Hotel La Rabida **8**
Hotel Las Casas de la Judería **24**
Hotel Las Casas de los Mercaderes **20**
Hotel Las Casas del Rey de Baeza **21**
Hotel Los Seises **18**
Hotel NH Plaza de Armas **2**
Hotel Puerta d' Triana **6**
Hotel Residencia Murillo **26**
Hotel Simon **12**
Hotel Tryp Colón **5**
Taberna de Alabardero **7**

DINING ◆
Casa Robles **19**
Egaña Oriza **30**
Enrique Becerra **11**
La Albahaca **27**
Restaurante Giralda **28**
Taberna de Alabardero **7**

ATTRACTIONS ●
Barrio de Santa Cruz **25**
Basílica de la Macarena **4**
Casa de Pilatos **23**
Catedral **15**

Hospital de la Caridad **13**
La Cartuja/Isla Mágica **1**
La Giralda **16**
Museo Arqueológico **33**
Museo de Bellas Artes **3**
Plaza de Toros
  de la Maestranza **10**
Real Fábrica de Tabacos
  (Universidad de Sevilla) **32**
Reales Alcazares **29**
Torre del Oro **14**

By train

Unless you're coming from small towns in Andalusia, where train service is infrequent, I recommend the more comfortable trains over buses, especially in the heat of the south. The fastest and easiest way to get to Seville from either Madrid or Córdoba is the **AVE High-speed Train,** which was inaugurated in 1992 for the World Expo in Seville. It's a little more expensive than slower trains, but oh how it goes. It makes the trip to Seville, with stops in Ciudad Real and Córdoba, in just 2 hours and 20 minutes. The one-way fare is 9,900 pta. ($55). The trip to Córdoba lasts just under a half-hour (7,200 pta./$40).

The AVE train from Madrid and Córdoba to Seville flies like a bird (not coincidentally, since that's what *ave* means in Spanish), and while it's the most expensive regular train service in Spain, it's also one of Europe's fastest and most comfortable. Making the trip even more tempting, certain trips and age categories can save you money on the AVE. A roundtrip ticket saves you 20 percent; a roundtrip for travel on the same day saves you 25 percent. Children ages 4 through 11 get a 40 percent *descuento* (discount), while seniors get 25 percent off.

If you can't catch the AVE, or you want to save a few *pesetas,* hop aboard a **Talgo 200 Train** (fast but not lightning fast like the AVE). It takes a little over three hours and costs 8,300 pta. ($46). The slowest regional trains, called *Estrella,* can take more than five hours, which is time you could be spending enjoying the south instead of just traveling through it.

Seville's AVE and regular train station is **Santa Justa** (Avenida de Kansas City, s/n; ☎ 95-454-02-02), just north of downtown. Major car-rental agencies are all located at Santa Justa, so picking up a car after arriving in Seville by train is a snap. Ticket and information offices for RENFE, Spain's national railway, are located at Calle Zaragoza, 29. (☎ 95-421-79-78; Internet: www.renfe.es).

Buses C1 and C2 go from the rail station to downtown Seville. A taxi should cost about 800 pta. ($4.50).

By bus

Seville has two major bus terminals: **Estación Plaza de Armas** (Avenida del Cristo de la Expiración; ☎ 95-490-80-40) and **Estación Prado** (Calle Manuel Vázquez Sagastizabal; ☎ 95-441-71-11). Twelve **Alsina** buses (☎ 95-441-88-11) per day travel to and from the Prado station to Córdoba (1,200 pta./$6), and nine Alsina buses leave for Granada (2,710 pta./$15) from the same station. Alsina also makes the trip to Málaga (10 buses; 2,245 pta./$12). **Amarillos** buses go to Ronda (four per day; ☎ 95-498 91 84; 1,235 pta./$6) from Prado. **Comes** (☎ 95-441-68-58; 1,300 pta./$7) buses depart from Prado station to Cádiz.

For bus schedules and information, call ☎ 95-442-00-11.

Fiesta time! Seville's popular festivals

Seville is renowned for its rituals and celebrations during **Semana Santa** (Holy Week), just before Easter, and **Feria de Abril,** the April Fair that erupts two weeks after Easter. During these two weeks, Seville is the most festive, most spectacular place in Spain. But if you're not in the mood for crowds, inflated prices, religious ceremonies, and vibrant color, plan to be somewhere else.

Semana Santa: Holy Week (the week before Easter) is one big march of processions throughout the city. Assemblies of men carry flower-bedecked, madonna-topped floats on their shoulders. They're accompanied by penitents in long robes and pointy hoods — to an American, the uncomfortable visual reference is the KKK (though these folks have a much different type of fanaticism on their minds). Mournful dirge music and candles complete the somber, almost spooky mood. Processions go on all week, but the best days are Holy Thursday and Good Friday. Thursday night is pretty spectacular — parades pass hourly. Don't miss **La Macarena,** not the dance, but the patron saint of bullfighters (see "More cool things to see and do" later in this chapter), or **El Gran Poder.** Macarena returns to her Basilica on Friday around 1 p.m. Pick up schedules of processions, particularly the pamphlet Sevilla en Semana Santa from the tourism office.

Feria de Abril: After the somber expressions of faith during Holy Week, Seville explodes during its annual April Fair, a festival of flamenco and sevillana dancing, drinking, horse parades, and wonderful costumes. Andalusian women, from little girls to elegant older ladies, are decked out in gay, brightly colored, and often polka-dotted flamenco dresses. Men, atop fine Andalusian horses, look like gentleman ranchers, with their broad-brimmed hats. The roots of the party are in fact agricultural — it accompanied annual livestock auctions in the mid-nineteenth century. The *alegría* (joy) is contagious, and it lasts all week.

Rocking El Rocío: One of Spain's most spectacular expressions of religious faith is the El Rocío pilgrimage, which takes place at the end of May in the province of Huelva (near Almonte and the Parque Nacional de Doñana), west of Seville. It's like a rowdy religious rave. Accompanied by flutes and tambourines, thousands of the devout travel on foot, on horseback, and in oxen-led carriages to the Almonte marshlands. The faithful, donning their best flamenco duds, take flowers and wax figures to worship at the Our Lady of El Rocío sanctuary. When the float of la Virgen del Rocío — the Virgin of the Dew — passes, mayhem erupts as everyone tries to lay a hand on her and be touched by her saintliness. For more information on this festival, see www.andalucia.com/festival/rocio.htm.

To find out this year's dates for **Semana Santa** (Easter), **Feria de Abril** (April Fair), and de Rocío contact the tourism office or visit the Web site www.andalucia.com. www.sevilla.org.

Orienting yourself in Seville

Seville sits right on the banks of the Guadalquivir River, which divides the city in two. The historic center of the city, which includes the

Cathedral, Barrio de Santa Cruz, and just about all the sights you want to see, is on the east side of the river.

Touring Seville by neighborhood

Though Seville is a large and complex city, its main *barrios* (neighborhoods) of interest to visitors are easy to get a handle on. The Old City grew up around the city's major monuments, which are among the most important in Andalusia: the **Cathedral** and **Giralda Tower;** the **Reales Alcazares** palace-fortress; and, immediately to its east, the **Barrio de Santa Cruz,** which is the ancient Jewish Quarter. **Parque María Luisa,** the major green space in the city, is south of here.

The major avenues running through the Old City are Avenida de la Constitución and Calle Sierpes. The *zona centro,* or modern center of Seville, proceeds outward from the Old City. The working-class, thoroughly authentic *barrio* Triana is across the river, as is La Cartuja, site of the 1992 World Expo.

Getting info after you arrive

The main **Andalucía Tourism Information Office** is located just down the street from the Cathedral, Avenida de la Constitución, 21 (☎ 95-422-14-04). You can find others at the **San Pablo Airport** (☎ 95-444-91-28) and **Santa Justa Train Station** (☎ 95-453-76-26). They're open daily from 9 a.m. to 8 p.m. **Municipal tourism offices** are at Plaza de la Concordia, s/n (☎ 95-490-52-67) and Costurero de la Reina/Paseo de las Delicias, 9 (☎ 95-423-44-65).

Getting around Seville

Though Seville is large, the principal areas of interest to most visitors are in a compact, walkable area. The Barrio de Santa Cruz, one of Seville's most enchanting neighborhoods, is almost entirely pedestrian. Almost all the hotels I recommend are within walking distance of the major sights. You should only need public transportation or a taxi to the airport or train station, or in the evening if you want to go over to Triana, across the river, to check out the bars, restaurants, and live music clubs there.

By bus

You have little need to take a bus, although it comes in handy for getting to the train station, **Santa Justa** (see "By train," earlier in this chapter). Bus Nos. 32, C-1, and C-2 go between downtown and the train station. For bus information, call ☎ 95-442-00-11. A single fare on the city buses costs 125 pta. (70¢).

By taxi

Taxis usually line up on Avenida de la Constitución, just outside the cathedral. You can also hail one anywhere on the street. To call a cab, call **Radio Taxi** (☎ 95-458-00-00), **Radio Teléfono Giralda** (☎ 95-496-00-00), or **Tele-Taxi** (☎ 95-462-22-22).

By car

If you have the time and the interest to explore some of the small towns, Andalusia is one of the top regions in Spain from which to rent a car and roll through the countryside or the coast. The major agencies in Seville are: **Avis** (Avendia de la Constitución, 15; ☎ 95-421-65-49); **Europcar** (Avenida Luis de Morales, s/n; ☎ 95-457-45-01); **Hertz** (Avenida República Argentina, 3; ☎ 95-427-88-87); and **Thrify** (Fernando IV, 3; ☎ 95-427-81-84).

By bike

If the horse-drawn carriages (see the section "And on your left, the Cathedral: Seeing Seville by guided tour," later in this chapter) are a little too clichéd for you, Seville is a great place to tool around by bike. You can pick up a day's bike rental at **Francisco Mora,** on Calle Cano y Cuento, 2 in Santa Cruz (☎ 95-441-19-59). Francisco's store rents out mountain bikes for 1,500 pta. ($8) a day. Another place to pick up a two-wheeled steed is **BiciBike** (Calle Miguel de Mañara, 11-B; ☎ 95-456-38-38). They provide half-day and full-day rentals.

Staying in Seville

Seville is one of the best places to stay in Spain. A number of hotels drip with local character, and at reasonable rates. All the hotels I recommend here are conveniently located within walking distance of most major sites in the old center of romantic Seville. (Several faceless international hotels are available as well, but for the most part they're removed from what you're going to Seville to see, and so I didn't include them.)

Note that prices rise significantly (as much as double) during Seville's famous Holy Week and Feria de Abril (April Fair) celebrations — basically, two weeks a year. The high end of the rates in the following section reflects those increases (but, because those rates distort the overall picture, I didn't base the dollar-sign ratings on those special rates).

The top hotels

Hacienda Benazuza

$$$$$ Sanlúcar la Mayor, on the outskirts of Seville

Hacienda Benazuza ("*Hath*-ee-enda Ben-ah-*thoo*-tha"), 10 miles outside of Seville, was once an Arab country house in the tenth century, and then a luxurious farmhouse on a hill of olive groves. Today it's one of the finest hotels in Spain. The gardens, with Moorish pools and fountains, are to die for. The restaurant, La Alquería, is also one of the best in the country. The downside? Well, the price. It ain't cheap, but this kind of serenity and luxury never is. One of the biggest names in Spanish cooking, Chef Ferrán Adría of the award-winning El Bulli restaurant in Catalonia, runs the restaurant. To get there from Seville, follow the signs for Huelva and go south on the A-49 highway; take exit No. 6. The hotel is on a hillside above the little agrarian hamlet of Sanlúcar la Mayor.

Calle Virgen de las Nieves, s/n, (Sanlúcar la Major) Seville. ☎ *95-570-33-44. Fax: 95-570-34-10. E-mail:* hbenazuza@jet.es. *Internet:* www.hbenazuza.com. *Parking: Free. Rates: 40,000–59,000 pta.($222–$328). Four nights' minimum stay required during Semana Santa and Feria de Abril. AE, DC, MC, V. Closed Aug.*

Hotel Alfonso XIII
$$$$$ Old City (near Parque María Luisa)

This Old World classic will break the bank, but if you've got a bank to break, it's the place to do it. The finest and most famous hotel in Seville, the historic Alfonso XIII ("Alfonso Tray-thay") is right up there with the Ritz and Palace — one of Spain's most distinguished and storied hostelries. When the Infanta (Princess) Elena got married in Seville a few years back, she and the entire Royal Family stayed here. A beautiful, imposing structure with the city's most prestigious address, it has opulent halls with marble floors, carved wooden ceilings, and Moorish arches and tiles. The 146 rooms are appropriately regal, as are the gardens and magnificent pool, but this indulgent palace isn't for everyone. As the kind of place where the rich and famous drop in and expect to be treated with deference, it seems a bit snooty to me. (Okay, maybe that's just sour grapes on my part.)

San Fernando, 2 (at Puerta de Jerez, junction of Avenida Constitución and San Fernando). ☎ *in U.S.,* **800-325-3535** *or 888-625-5144; 95-422-28-50. Fax: 95-421-60-33. E-mail:* hotel-alfonsoXIII@sol.com. *Internet:* http://sol.com/hotel/alfonsoXIII. *Parking: 2,200 pta. ($12). Rates: 55,500 pta. ($308) (68,000–75,500 pta./$378–$419 during Holy Week, Easter, and April Fair); weekends, 34,000 pta. ($189), including taxes and breakfast. AE, DC, MC, V.*

Spring has sprung: Guys in hoods

Don't make the mistake of visiting Seville during **Semana Santa** (Holy Week) or **April Fair** *(Feria de Abril),* the latter two weeks after Easter, unless you really mean to take part in the celebrations. The first is somber, with processions of penitents in long robes and spooky pointed hoods; the second is exuberant. Streets are jammed, hotels are packed, and while it's an exhilarating time to see Seville at its best, paradoxically, it's tough to see what makes the city great at other times of the year.

If you intend on coming to Seville for either celebration, make your reservations early — as much as a year (that's right, a year) in advance, especially for the choicest spots that I mention in the hotel listings.

Hotel Apartamentos Casa Imperial
$$$$ Edge of Old City, NW of cathedral

It seems absurd to call this impeccable, luxurious retreat an "aparthotel," with all the images of cheesy kitchenettes and bad carpeting that such a thing usually conjures — in fact, nothing is farther from the truth. Yes, all rooms have small kitchens and some have small living areas, but this is a lovely, refined version, and a great hotel solution for people wanting space and privacy. With four plant-filled, interior patios, brilliantly tiled staircases, small pools and fountains that kids will love, and boldly painted rooms, the three-year-old Casa Imperial is one of a kind. Near the Casa Pilatos, this fifteenth-century palace (which incredibly belonged to the *butler* of the Marquis of Tarifa) is charming and intimate, with great personal attention. As hard as it is to believe that Casa Imperial lies in the middle of bustling Seville, the hotel is perfectly in tune with the city's romanticism. The 24 apartments are popular with Germans, because the hotel is owned by a joint Spanish–German initiative.

Calle Imperial, 29 (one block north of Plaza Pilatos, off San Estéban). ☎ *95-450-03-00. Fax: 95-450-03-30. E-mail:* info@casaimperial.com. *Internet:* www.sol.com/casa-imperial. *Parking: 3,000 pta. ($17). Rates: 24,126–30,781 pta. ($134–$171) breakfast buffet included; Holy Week, Easter, and Feria de Abril, 48,252 pta. ($268). AE, DC, MC, V.*

Hotel Las Casas de la Judería
$$ Barrio de Santa Cruz

Secluded at the end of a small alley off the edge of the Santa Cruz neighborhood — the former Jewish enclave, la Judería — this is one of the best-value hotels in Spain. But the secret's out. The place is packed year-round, so book a room early. The hotel occupies a seventeenth-century palace of the Duke of Béja, the patron of Cervantes (the Duke actually owned a series of mansions here). The brightly painted palace — brilliant *Sevillano* yellows, whites, and blues — has a series of tranquil interior patios with gurgling fountains. The 57 rooms are impressively appointed, and are all different. They have handsome antique furnishings, and many have four-poster beds and small living rooms. Service is top-notch, although it can get a little hectic at check-in and check-out times. If you can't get in here, try at the other two, also top-rated, Casas hotels by the same group (reviewed next in this chapter).

Plaza Santa María la Blanca/Callejón de Dos Hermanas, 7 (difficult to find; near the church of Santa María la Blanca, on northeast border of Santa Cruz, down a tiny alleyway). ☎ *95-441-51-50. Fax: 95-442-21-70. Internet:* www.ibernet.net/lascasas. *Parking: 2,000 ($11). Rates: 15,000–35,000 pta. ($83–$194). AE, DC, MC, V.*

Hotel Las Casas de los Mercaderes
$$$ Zona Centro

Another in a winning family of character-driven Seville hotels in atmospheric palaces, this is a little smaller and only the slightest bit more
exclusive than its sister, Las Casas de la Judería. In the commercial center
of the city, between Plazas San Francisco and El Salvador, it's only minutes away from the Cathedral. The 47 rooms in this handsome white mansion with yellow- and blue-trimmed windows are set back from the street
on a small courtyard. The rooms are impeccably dressed; many have
small balconies overlooking perfect eighteenth-century Andalusian patio.
Guests are equal parts business travelers and vacationers.

*Calle Álvarez Quintero (3 blocks north of Cathedral, between Plazas El Salvador
and San Francisco). ☎ 95-422-58-58. Fax: 95-422-98-84. Internet:* www.ibernet.
net/lascasas. *Parking: 2,000 pta. ($11). Rates: 14,500–28,500 pta. ($81–$158). AE,
DC, MC, V.*

Hotel Las Casas del Rey de Baeza
$$$ Zona Centro

The latest addition to the Casas hotel family that revolutionized the Seville
hotel scene opened in April 1998. The other two Casas are three-star establishments; Baeza, a bit more removed from the tourist hordes than the
others, is the four-star leader of the group. The 44 spacious and warmly
attired rooms have large, modern, marble bathrooms, and a number feature living rooms. Rooms are on three levels off a central courtyard of
this eighteenth-century converted mansion. And if those views aren't
enough for you on a warm Seville day, try the ones from the rooftop pool.

*Plaza Cristo de la Redención (off Calle Santiago, between Corral del Conde and
Casa Pilatos). ☎ 95-456-14-96. Fax: 95-456-14-41. E-mail:* baeza@zoom.es.
Internet: www.ibernet.net/lascasas. *Parking: 2,000 pta. ($11). Rates:
17,000–32,000 pta. ($94–$178). AE, DC, MC, V.*

Hotel Los Seises
$$$ Old City

Tucked away on a small street behind the Cathedral, Los Seises ("*say-
says*") has one of Seville's quintessential views — from the rooftop pool,
La Giralda (the cathedral tower) is just a few hundred yards away. Los
Seises makes a valiant effort to preserve the original structure of the sixteenth-century palace it once was and update it with touches of moder-
nity, the latest trend in Seville hotels. Although this concept isn't
perfectly achieved, and the hotel doesn't rise to the level of Casa Imperial
or the three Las Casas hotels, it's still one of the city's best. Double rooms
are sleek, well-appointed, and very large, with foyers and sunken sitting
areas. Most people find the hotel charming, and a relatively good deal,
given its small size (42 rooms) and unbeatable location. The Pope did
(yes, his Holiness was a guest).

Calle Segovias, 6 (2 blocks north of the Cathedral, off Placentines). ☎ *95-422-94-95. Fax: 95-422-43-34. E-mail:* seises@jet.es. *Internet:*www.infosevilla.com/ hotel/los-seises. *Parking: 2,000 pta. ($11). Rates: 18,000–37,000 pta. ($100–$206). AE, DC, MC, V.*

Hotel Puerta d' Triana

$$ Old City

This little place on busy Reyes Católicos is a complete surprise. Although the government rates it at two stars, its elegance matches that of higher rated places, and at a bargain price. It has ornate public rooms, and, although the 65 guest rooms can't compare (they're considerably plainer than rooms in the top-rated hotels), they're still large and comfortable (though I think they should lose the matching wicker sets of headboards and chairs). With this location, near the Plaza de Toros and within walking distance of the Cathedral, it's hard to do better if you're looking for a budget hotel — this one, odd bird that it is, even includes breakfast in the price.

Reyes Católicos, 5 (3 blocks north of Paseo de Cristóbal Colón). ☎ *95-421-54-04. Fax 95-421-54-01. Internet:* http://interhotel.com/spain/es/hoteles/ 4120. *Parking: Discount at nearby garages available. Rates: 10,600–16,500 pta. ($59–$92). AE, DC, MC, V.*

Hotel Tryp Colón

$$$$ Northern edge of Old City

One of Seville's long-time classics, built for the 1929 World's Fair, the Colón makes a grand statement. Its lavish lobby reeks of Old World comfort, and, although there are plenty of newer options in the region, it's still a great place to stay if you like your hotels big and busy. Near the bullfighting ring, the Colón is in a happening part of town with a lively nightlife. It's changed management repeatedly, but the service maintains its five-star status.

Canalejas, 1 (one block north of Reyes Católicos). ☎ *95-422-29-00. Fax: 95-422-09-38. E-mail:* hotel@tryp.es. *Internet:* www.sol.com. *Parking: 2,200 pta. ($12). Rates: 30,565–46,200 pta.($169–$257); weekend rate 14,700 pta. ($82). AE, DC, MC, V.*

Taberna del Alabardero

$$$ Zona Centro

Consider yourself lucky if you score one of the seven exquisite doubles at this gorgeous little four-star place. Forget about Easter and April Fair, because they're booked at least two years in advance, but as long as you don't plan on scoring one then, who knows? In a meticulously restored nineteenth-century mansion that belonged to the poet J. Antonio Cavestany is a gorgeous arcaded central patio, where breakfast and afternoon coffee are served. The rooms, on the third floor of the mansion, are named for places in Spain. They're all top-of-the-line elegant, with rich fabrics, bold flower patterns, and hot tubs, though each is different in configuration and decoration. As you may expect in a place so small, the service is very personal and friendly. If that isn't enough, the restaurant by the same name is one of the city's finest (see the review, later in this chapter).

Zaragoza, 20 (four blocks northwest of the Cathedral, near Maestranza bullfighting ring). ☎ ***95-456-06-37.*** *Fax: 95-456 36 66. E-mail:* hotel.albardero@esh.es. *Internet:* www.esh.es. *Parking: 1,900 pta. ($10). Rates: 18,000–30,000 pta. ($100–$167) continental breakfast included. AE, DC, MC, V.*

Seville's runner-up hotels

Hotel Doña María

$$$ **Old City** This small family hotel is a great alternative if you don't mind frilly bedspreads and curtains; it has a nice terrace with a small pool and dreamy views. It's also right across the plaza from the giant Cathedral, the heart of Seville. Kids can watch the horses line up with their carriages along the plaza. *Don Remondo, 19.* ☎ ***95-422-49-90.*** *Fax: 95- 421-95-46. Internet:* www.hoteldmaria.com. *Rates: 20,000–28,000 pta. ($120–$168) double.*

Hotel La Rabida

$–$$ **Old City** This former nineteenth-century casa noble (aristocratic mansion) on a quiet street is a real find in the budget category. *Castelar, 24, four blocks west of the Cathedral.* ☎ ***95-422-09-60.*** *Fax: 95-422-43-75. Internet:* hotel-rabida@sol.com. *Rates: 9,300 pta. ($55.80) double.*

Hotel NH Plaza de Armas

$$$ **Zona Centro/River** This ultramodern and impersonal businessman's hotel has none of the particular Andalusian charm of the other places I've listed. *Marqués de Paradas, s/n, two blocks east of river and Puente del Cachorro.* ☎ ***95-490-19-92.*** *Fax: 95-490-12-32. Internet:* www.nh-hotels.com. *Rates: 15,500 pta. ($93) double; 19,400 pta. ($117) suite.*

Hotel Residencia Murillo

$–$$ **Barrio de Santa Cruz** This hotel is a bargain for this neighborhood, with a kitschy medieval lobby complete with suits of armor and a framed, 1965 letter from the Mayor of St. Louis, Missouri. Rooms are spare and kind of dark, but with an idiosyncratic charm. *Calle Lope de Rueda, 7–9, around the back side of Plaza Santa Cruz.* ☎ ***95-421-60-95.*** *Fax: 95-421-96-16. Internet:* www.sol.com/hotel-murillo. *Rates: 7,100–8,900 pta. ($42.60–$53.40) double; 8,800–11,200 pta. ($52.80–$67.80) triple.*

Hotel Simon

$ Old City A former eighteenth-century private mansion, this is Seville's best bargain at the budget level, which is great if you're bringing in the whole family, with elegant public rooms, a beautiful interior courtyard, and stately dining room; rooms are all different and have nice antiques; the place is usually full. *Calle García de Vinuesa, 19, two blocks west of the Cathedral.* ☎ *95-422-66-60. Fax: 95- 456-22-41. Internet:* hotel-simon@sol. com. *Rates:12,000 pta. ($72) double.*

Dining in Seville

Rather than divide the Seville dining scene into "Top Restaurants" and "Runners-Up," as I did with the hotels, I arrange things in this section a little differently. A more natural division here is between restaurants where you can enjoy a sit-down dinner and more informal *tapas* (appetizer) joints. At many of the latter, there's no rule against sitting down — if you're lucky enough to score a coveted seat — but it's an entirely different way of assembling a meal. I love snacking my way across Spain, but the joy of eating at bars and restaurant counters and front rooms in Seville is something special. Even the sit-down places have *tapas* bars in front, so if you arrive at one and it looks dead or too pricey go with Plan B: A *tapas* crawl!

For more on Spanish dining customs, including mealtimes, costs, and tipping, see Chapter 1.

Enjoying the top restaurants for a sit-down meal

Casa Robles

$$$ Zona Centro ANDALUSIAN

Around since the 1950s, Casa Robles is as unpretentious and straight-forward as its name, which means "oak house." Focusing on top-quality and super-fresh meat, fish, and vegetables, the brothers Robles continue their presence among Seville's elite restaurants. The family-owned place has an enthusiastic following among locals, and it always seems to be bustling. The fresh fish always catches my eye; check out *lubina con naranjas* (a white fish with *Sevillana* oranges), or baked hake enlivened with strips of Serrano ham.

Calle Álvarez Quintero, 58 (two blocks north of the Cathedral). ☎ *95-456-32-72. Reservations recommended. Main courses: 1,200–2,800 pta. ($7–$15); menú del día 3,000 pta. ($17). AE, DC, MC, V. Open: Daily lunch and dinner.*

Egaña Oriza

$$$$ Zona Centro BASQUE/INTERNATIONAL

If you're only traveling in the south of Spain and you won't have a chance to sample authentic Basque cooking anywhere else, make a beeline here.

And if you've come directly from Bilbao, you may have even more reason to check out Seville's best Basque restaurant, which just happens to be its top-rated dining room. A husband-wife team comes up with the innovations at this swank place catercorner from the city's most prestigious hotel, the Alfonso XIII. The restaurant's stylish décor, in a restored mansion just off the Murillo Gardens, is as inspired as the menu. And as for the menu, start off with *salmorejo* (the thick Cordoban version of gazpacho) with oysters and serrano jam and follow it up with *lubina con crema de patata al azafrán* (silky sea bass with a saffron-potato cream sauce). Savory game and meats, such as duck and wild boar, are given interesting accents, including wild cherries, plums, figs, and apple puree. Like all Basque cooking, which depends upon the freshest and best-quality ingredients and the inspiration of a talented chef, eating here isn't cheap — but it's worth it!

San Fernando, 41 (at entrance to Murillo Gardens). ☎ *95-422-72-11. Reservations required. Main courses: 2,700–5,900 pta. ($15–$33); menú del día 5,200–9,600 pta. ($29–$53). AE, DC, MC, V. Open: Mon–Fri lunch and dinner; Sat dinner only; bar, daily 9 a.m. –midnight; closed Aug.*

Enrique Becerra
$$$ Zona Centro (El Arenal)   ANDALUSIAN

At this friendly place just around the corner from Plaza Nueva and Seville's Cathedral, even first-time visitors are welcomed like members of the regular crew, and it's got a slew of regulars. A cozy spot that feels more like a tavern than a restaurant, it's got a hopping *tapas* bar (with stools!) in front with an impossible-to-choose lineup of clams, stuffed mushrooms, and more, and an attractive back dining room with deep yellow walls, dark beams, and leaded glass. If you sit down, you can try *bacalao gratinado con salsa de espárragos* (crispy codfish with asparagus sauce), or *cordero asado a la miel relleno de espinacas y piñones* (roast lamb with honey and stuffed with spinach and pine nuts). The wine cellar is one of Seville's most select.

Gamazo, 2 (three blocks west of the Cathedral, off Calle Castelar in El Arenal district). ☎ *95-421-30-49. Reservations recommended. Main courses: 1,600–2,600 pta. ($9–$14); menú del día 4,250 pta. ($24). AE, DC, MC, V. Open: Mon–Sat lunch and dinner.*

La Albahaca
$$$$ Barrio de Santa Cruz   BASQUE/FRENCH

One of the prettiest restaurants on the prettiest square in the prettiest neighborhood in Seville, La Albahaca has a lot going for it. It's in a lovely Andalusian mansion built in the 1920s, with several dining rooms, a terrace, lots of greenery, and colorful tiles. Because of its location, it gets the upscale tourist trade, who enjoy the Basque chef's crepes stuffed with mushrooms and *foie gras* (fattened goose liver) in Port wine sauce, and great salads for starters. You can choose partridge braised in sherry or beef sirloin with *foie gras* for the main course, among many other options.

Plaza de Santa Cruz, 12 (several blocks east of the Cathedral, in heart of Santa Cruz district). ☎ *95-422-07-14. Reservations recommended. Main courses: 2,000–3,500 pta. ($11–$19); menú del día 4,000 pta. ($22). AE, DC, MC, V. Open: Mon–Sat lunch and dinner.*

Restaurante Giralda

$ Barrio de Santa Cruz   SPANISH

This little place hardly competes with some of the illustrious restaurants on these pages, but sometimes you're in shorts and sneakers, and all you want is to get off your feet and eat a substantial, cheap meal, and, this may just fit the bill. Don't be disapppointed; the eats here are basic all the way, and everything is geared toward tourists. But the surroundings, an old Sevillana house with a tile-covered patio, have charm. So save your money for a nice dinner, and for about $6, you can get a filling, unspectacular lunch — gazpacho, paella valenciana, flan — and get back to the business of sightseeing.

Calle Justino de Neve, 8 (just off Callejón del Agua in Santa Cruz district). ☎ *95-421-51-13. Reservations not necessary. Main courses: 750–1,800 pta. ($4–$10); menú del día 950 pta. ($5). AE, MC, V. Open: daily for lunch and dinner.*

Taberna del Alabardero

$$$$ Zona Centro   SPANISH

If you are lucky enough to sneak a coveted room at this tiny hotel (reviewed earlier in this chapter), you can saunter downstairs to dine at one of the city's hottest restaurants. Even if you're not sleeping here, though, you can join the king, president, and just about everybody else that eats here. In a sumptuous nineteenth-century palace with dark wood, mirrors, and oil paintings, there are five dining rooms (four private, for all those famous folks). The kitchen is the work of the owner, Luis Lezama, who is also a priest, and the head chef, Juan Marcos. The menu is eclectic, offering delicacies like red fruit soup with mascarpone cheese, Sanlúcar prawn carpaccio, lamb sweetbreads, and a tournedos of fresh cod. Every year (going on five years now) in February, the restaurant celebrates its utter Spanishness with *semana de arroz* — rice week, which glorifies the art of *paella* (a casserole of rice, seafood, and meat). Taberna del Alabardero is near the bullfighting ring, and about a 15-minute walk from the Cathedral.

Zaragoza, 20 (four blocks northwest of the Cathedral, near Maestranza bullfighting ring). ☎ *95-456-06-37. Reservations essential. Main courses: 1,600–2,800 pta. ($9–16). AE, DC, MC, V. Open: Daily, lunch and dinner; closed Aug.*

Hamming it up

Spaniards are wild about ham; *jamón serrano* (cured ham) pretty much qualifies as a national obsession. But Spaniards go absolutely crazy over *jamón de Jabugo*. Jabugo is a tiny town in the mountains of Andalusia, in the province of Huelva, and famed for producing the most delectable cured ham in all Spain. Aficionados of Iberian ham, dry and sliced razor thin, claim it's Spain's greatest delicacy. As such, it doesn't come cheap; a *ración* (portion) of thin shavings of the stuff can cost as much as $20.

Experiencing the best tapas bars

If you've been to other Spanish cities by the time you stroll into Seville, or you've read the other dining sections of this book, you know that *tapas* are a fundamental feature of the Spanish dining scene. But in Seville, *tapas* are a joyous popular religion. They aren't as fancy and filling as they are in the Basque Country, but they're hands down the best way to get a handle on Seville and the charming, universally friendly people who delight in nothing as much as popping into bars, sampling squid, prawns, blood sausage, and cured ham along with a great aperitif wine like a *fino* (a type of dry sherry), as well as chatting up bartenders and newly made friends. I've spent days in Seville without ever so much as sitting down to a proper meal — but I always ate exceedingly well. Sevillanos go on *tapeos* at 1:30, 3:30, 8 p.m., and until midnight or later — basically, until the bars run out. Even breakfast (*tostadas* — toast, with pate or *sobrassada* sausage spread) is just another excuse for hitting *tapas* bars. Meals at *tapas* bars generally fall into the inexpensive or moderate range ($–$$).

By the way, kids are sure to love this form of eating (all snacking, all the time), though you may have to pick and choose carefully among the *tapas* (octopus may not go over so well).

The best way to dive into a Seville-style *tapeo* (*tapas* crawl) is to choose a *barrio* (neighborhood), loosen your belt, and start eating. To wash it all down, ask for a *caña* ("*kahn*-ya", draft beer), *una manzanilla* (deliciously dry aperitif wine, like sherry), or a *vino tinto* or *vino blanco* (red or white wine, respectively). The following haunts are divided into three neighborhoods that are ripe for snacking: Triana, Santa Cruz, and Zona Centro.

In Triana

Tourists seldom visit this rambling neighborhood across the Guadalquivir River. Too bad, because they're missing some of Seville's best *tapas* spots, as the locals well know. Check out these great *tapas* locations:

Rio Grande (Betis, s/n; ☎ 95-427-83-71) is a fancy full-scale restaurant with a great see-and-be-scene terrace overlooking the river. Skip dinner and go for *tapas* instead — anything made with fish is good.

Down the street, the main drag that lines the west side of the river, is **La Albariza** (Calle Betis, 6; ☎ 95-433-89-60). It has a stand-up bar with black wine barrels as tables. The bar area is pure Andalusian casual dining and is much more *auténtico* (authentic) than the restaurant in back. Lean on a barrel and order up *tortillitas de camarones* (yummy, tiny fried shrimp omelettes), great, huge pickled olives, and fried *boquerones* (white anchovies).

Kiosco de las Flores (Calle Betis, 1; ☎ 95-433-38-98) sits at the bend along the river, next to the Isabel II Bridge. A rarity, it has outdoor tables, where you can order full *raciones* of *jamón de Jabugo* (see the "Hamming it up" sidebar earlier in this chapter), only. Try *coquinas* (tiny sautéed clams), baby eels, shellfish salad, or *gazpacho* (cold tomato soup).

Sol y Sombra (Castilla, 151; ☎ 95-433-39-35) has a *taurino* (bull-fighting) culture and earthy *tapas*. It's a good place for razor-thin cured ham, *puntillitas* (garlicky beef tenderloin), and blood-red Rioja wine.

In Santa Cruz

Seville's cool old Jewish Quarter is a favorite of most visitors, and it's a good spot to *tapas*-hop in the early evening. You'll probably pass **Casa Román** (Plaza de los Venerables, 1; ☎ 95-422-84-83) repeatedly. It's perfect for a meat fix; try the *chorizo* (spicy pork sausage), Serrano ham, and other basics, such as a wedge of *tortilla española* (potato and onion omelette).

Hostería del Laurel (Plaza de los Venerables, 5; ☎ 95-422-02-95), also a small, historic hotel (see the sidebar "Did Don Juan win the bet?"), sets tables out in its delightful square. If you've pictured yourself a Don Juan or Carmen, sipping sangría and savoring cured meats, this place is tailor-made.

Modesto (Calle Cano y Cueto, 5; ☎ 95-441-68-11), a seafood restaurant, is more ramshackle than modest. Its lively downstairs *tapas* bar is popular with Sevillanos and tourists alike. The famous dish here is Tío Diego, a stir-fry of cured ham, shrimp, and mushrooms.

In Zona Centro (Central Seville)

In the central, commercial district of Seville, there are too many *tapas* haunts to keep track of. Check out the following, but if you see one with people hanging about the bar and out the door, that's all the information you need to pop in and enjoy.

Did Don Juan win the bet?

In pop culture, a Don Juan is an irresible stud, but it wasn't always that way. In the original story, written in the 1600s by Tirso de Molina (a priest who later received the honor of having a Madrid neighborhood and, er, Metro stop named after him), the legendary rogue roams Seville in search of willing — and unwilling — maidens. Don Juan challenges a friend to a bet of carnal proportions: who can seduce more women in a calendar year. The rivals meet up one year later to check their score-cards; Don Juan, with six dozen notches on his belt, is declared the winner, but he can't stop there. On a roll, he ups the ante, claiming that in just six days he'll seduce not only his rival's fiancee, but a nun as well.

Recall that a priest wrote the story of Don Juan. (Like he's gonna get away with steal-ing a nun's virtue.) The rapscallion's designs on Sister Doña Inés are the last straw for God, who strikes Don Juan down and condemns him to a sinner's life in hell.

Evidently that struck the nineteenth-century playwright José Zorilla as much too harsh a penalty, and too dark an ending. In Hollywood fashion, he rewrote the story. In his version, the rivals meet up at Hostería de Laurel in the Barrio de Santa Cruz (where you can go today and test your pick-up lines). Don Juan announces his assault on the holy church, but in the rewrite, he gets the girl (the one in the black habit) and rides off with her to life everlasting. So guess which version lived on? Of course, the one with the scandalous but happy ending.

- ✔ **La Tasca de El Burladero** (Canalejas, 1; ☎ 95-422-29-00) is the downstairs *tapas* bar of a well-known restaurant in the five-star Hotel Colón. The bar — with a long bar, stools, and even a number of squat tables — is popular with people on dates, families, and older couples on their way to the restaurant. The *tapas,* like *pez espada casera* (home-cooked swordfish), are small meals.

- ✔ Just a block back from Avenida de Constitución, **Casa Morales** (García de Vinuesa, 11; ☎ 95-422-12-42) is a classic old *tapas* bar that dates to 1850, and it looks like it hasn't changed a bit since then. You can get *chorizo* to go with your beer or wine here, but the best thing to do is to go across the street to **La Isla** (García de Vinuesa, 13; ☎95-422-83-55). La Isla is little more than a fry stand, but you can pick up a newspaper full of *pescaíto frito* (tiny fried fish), shrimp, or fish 'n' chips (priced by the kilo), and take 'em back to the bar. (Morales is one of the few places in the area that doesn't have a problem with BYOT — Bring Your Own Tapas).

- ✔ **Bar Giralda** (Mateos Gago, 1; ☎ 95-422-74-35), with old vaults that once formed part of Moorish bathhouse, is a famous student hangout. Boisterous and hip Sevillanos come for *pastel de puerros y espinacas* (leek and spinach pie) and *pimientos rellenos* (stuffed peppers).

✔ **Entrecárceles** (Calle Faisanes, 1; no phone), just off Plaza del Salvador, is a tiny nook of a place with hanging hams, a wooden bar, an old wooden refrigerator, and walls with peeling ochre paint. A tavern since 1894, it looks like a movie set. *Tapas* are written on a chalkboard and on tiles. Try *salmorejo* (the thick Cordoban version of *gazpacho*) with ham, *pimientos rellenos de carne* or *bacalao* (peppers stuffed with meat or cod), or *lomo al camembert* (pork loin with Camembert cheese).

✔ **El Rinconcillo** (Gerona, 2; ☎ 95-422-31-83) may be a little out of your way, but it's been a tavern since 1670. It almost goes without saying that the Little Corner is the oldest *tapas* bar in Seville. It has a gorgeous wraparound wooden bar (on which bartenders tally your tab in chalk), walls lined with *azulejos* (ceramic tiles), marble-topped tables, and tons of *tapas*. It's also very popular with the locals and has a regular cast of characters. I can still taste the *espinacas con garbanzos* (spinach with chickpeas).

✔ **Bodega Extremeña** (Calle San Esteban; ☎ 95-441-70-60) is a dark, atmospheric little place with hanging garlic and hams, near Casa Pilatos. It's got a range of cheap *tapas,* including *morcilla al vino* (blood sausage soaked in sherry), *huevos de cordoniz* (game hen eggs), and, for the really adventurous, *orejas en adobo* (I shouldn't tell you, but that's pig's ears in oregano and vinegar).

Exploring Seville

You can cover almost everything you want to see in a first or second visit to Seville — everything, in other words, that I've outlined here — on foot (if you have a car, leave it in the hotel parking). Seville's loaded with monuments, cathedrals, and other sights, but as important as any of them is the special character of the city — its hole-in-the-wall *tapas* bars overflowing with talkative patrons, fragrant orange trees, and the insistent sounds of flamenco song and dance spilling out into the street. Don't be so intent on seeing the sights that you miss picking up on what makes the city unique. Slow down, like *Sevillanos* do, and soak up the atmosphere.

Keep in mind as you wander the city that the sun in Andalusia can be scorchingly hot, with an average temperature of 93 degrees in summer. I recommend setting out early in the day, so that by the crucial overhead sun hours (11 a.m. to 2 p.m.), you won't rush around to hit the sights. Bring along a hat or cap and, especially in the summertime, remember to slather on the sunscreen. Bring along bottled water to prevent dehydration, and take frequent breathers — *tapas* stops are good ways to duck out of the sun — but watch your alcohol intake, because it acts as a dehydrator. Your last defense? Fool-proof deodorant.

The top attractions

Barrio de Santa Cruz

The labyrinthine Santa Cruz district, once a Jewish ghetto in the Middle Ages, became the fashionable neighborhood of Seville's aristocrats and nobility during the seventeenth century. The city's most colorful neighborhood, Barrio de Santa Cruz is Seville at its romantic best. Its winding whitewashed alleyways, with names like *Gloria* (Glory), *Vida* (Life), and *Ángeles* (Angels), are full of wrought-iron grilles, leafy plazas, and plant- and flower-filled patios. The area remains picturesque despite the hordes of tour-guide-led groups traipsing through in all major Indo-European languages. Visit the **Hospital de los Venerables Sacerdotes** (Hospital for Venerable Priests), a handsome old structure, founded in 1675 as an asylum for priests and flush with seventeenth-century Baroque art. The only way to see it, though, is to join a tour that's given only in Spanish. The language isn't really the problem; the guide I had was the least inspired, monotone bore I've seen. If you don't understand Spanish, you won't miss anything (the pamphlet in English gives you much more information anyway). The hospital chapel has impressive frescoes by the Seville painter Valdés Leal. Work your way along the *barrio's* streets until you find the **Plaza de Santa Cruz,** a pretty square with a Baroque cross at its center. South of the square are the Murillo Gardens, strolling gardens along Menéndez Pelayo. Allow the better part of a full morning or afternoon in Seville's most picturesque neighborhood.

Barrio de Santa Cruz begins just east of the Reales Alcázares; walk through the small passageway that appears to be a part of the fortress. You pass through a courtyard, the Patio de Banderas, and a small tunnel and enter the streets of Santa Cruz — beginning with the Callejón del Agua (Water Alley).

Hospital de los Venerables: Plaza de los Venerables, 8 (enter neighborhood east of Reales Alcazares; corner of Reinoso and Rueda). ☎ *95-456-26-96. Admission: 600 pta. ($3). Open: daily 10 a.m.–2 p.m. and 4–8 p.m., with hourly guided visits.*

Catedral
Zona Centro/Old City

Seville's massive stone Cathedral, built on the site of an ancient mosque, left no doubts about Christian intentions in Andalusia. Begun in 1401 (and, amazingly, finished only a century later), it was intended to make the largest possible statement about Spain's future religious and political rule. Before going in, circle the exterior to get a good look at its rose windows and Gothic flying buttresses. Enter through the **Patio de los Naranjos** (the orange tree courtyard, a holdover from the old Mosque, where worshippers performed their ablutions before entering to pray). Inside, the Cathedral's an impressive sight, with incredible proportions, great art works, and fantastic details in individual chapels. Don't miss the **Capilla Mayor** (Chancel) and its spectacular **Retablo Mayor,** an overwhelming altarpiece, the world's largest, of delicately carved gold leaf depicting the life of Christ. Behind it is the **Capilla Real** (Royal Chapel), with an ornate dome, the tombs of Alfonso X of Castile and his mother, Beatrice (Ferdinand's wife), and a Romanesque Virgin de los Reyes. The patron saint of Seville, this last figure is removed for the Feast of the Assumption every year and paraded through the streets for her cult of followers. Other highlights include the **Tesoro,** (treasury), with works by Goya and Murillo, and the showy nineteenth-century **Monument to Columbus** — a larger-than-life-size coffin held airborne by the kings of Spain's medieval kingdoms.

About the time the wrecking ball was smashing into the mosque previously on the site of the **Catedral,** the builders reportedly said, "Let us build a cathedral so immense that everyone, on beholding it, will take us for madmen." Those madmen went on to build the largest Gothic building in the world and the third-largest church in Europe (after St. Peter's in Rome and St. Paul's in London). Because of its size, plan on spending a couple of hours getting lost in it (and climbing La Giralda, the tower).

Plaza del Triunfo/Avenida de la Constitución (corner of Avenida. de la Constitución y Alemanes). ☎ *95-421-49-71. Admission: (including visit to Giralda Tower) 700 pta. ($4) adults, 200 pta. ($1.10) children and students. Open: Mon–Sat 10:30 a.m.–5 p.m.; Sun 2–6 p.m.*

La Giralda
Zona Centro (Cathedral)

The brick minaret that originally stood tall as part of the great mosque on this site was given gradual makeovers over the centuries and incorporated into the Cathedral. Your admission ticket to the Cathedral allows you to climb the neverending but, surprisingly, not-all-that-taxing inclined ramp of the belfry/minaret. Horsemen used to ride up the ramp to announce prayers, but you can go up just for the views, which kids will enjoy. Make sure to stay up long enough to hear the bells bong, and take your camera and a map of Seville so you can pick out the tiny neighborhoods and monuments below — the vistas are pretty incredible. The belfry, by the way, is named for its weather vane on top, a statue of faith.

Plaza del Triunfo. Admission: (included in Cathedral visit). Open: Mon–Sat 10:30 a.m.–5 p.m.; Sun 2–6 p.m.

Museo de Bellas Artes
Zona Centro

This handsome fine arts museum, a mini-Prado, is worth a visit even if you skip the art (okay, not really, but almost). A painstaking restoration has left this seventeenth-century former convent in beautiful shape, and its peaceful open-air patios, orange trees, and aged *azulejos* (ceramic tiles) are a great place to view art. Many of Spain's greats are here — works by the seventeenth-century Seville School's Murillo, Valdés Leal, and Ribera; Velázquez; and Zurbarán. Don't miss **Sala V** (Room 5), a room with frescoed domes and Murillo's terrific angels and saints.

Plaza del Museo, 9 (just off Alfonso XII, three long blocks west of Plaza Duque de la Victoria). ☎ *95-422-07-90. Admission: 250 pta. ($1.50), free for students and members of EU. Open: Tues 3–8 p.m.; Wed–Sat 9 a.m.–8 p.m.; Sun 9 a.m.–3 p.m.*

Reales Alcázares
Zona Centro

If you're not going to Granada to see the Alhambra (see Chapter 18), this jaw-dropping royal residence (plain on the outside but spectacular within) is the next best thing. An awesome display of *mudéjar* architecture (Christian architecture employing Arab motifs and elements), it's the kind of place you can lose yourself in for hours. A UNESCO World Heritage Site, and one of the oldest royal residences in Europe, it was built by master craftsmen from Granada, and is awash in delicately carved arches, brilliant tiles, and heavenly ceilings. In 1364 Pedro I (also called Pedro the Cruel) ordered its construction on a site variously occupied by a Roman acropolis, a Moorish castle, and the first Moorish fortress in Spain. The palace itself has an amazing history: A long line of monarchs married, gave birth, had affairs, and ruled here; traitors and enemies met untimely ends here; and Columbus and Magellan both came here to beg for royal approval for their expeditions.

Perhaps the finest rooms are the **Apartamentos de Carlos V** (Apartments of Carlos V), decked out in gorgeous tapestries and tiles; the **Salón de Embajadores** (Ambassadors' Hall), crowned by a world-class carved cupola of gilded wood; the **Patio de las Doncellas** (Patio of the Maidens), with rich, intricate plasterwork that rivals the Alhambra; and the **Patio de las Muñecas** (Dolls' Patio), which is small, charming and spectacularly intricate. Look for the two small faces, the dolls of the patio name, supposedly carved into a column (don't worry if you can't find them; I never could). The Moorish gardens are the equal of the sumptuous interiors, and a perfect place to relax amid lush terraces and fountains. You need a couple of hours at least to appreciate the intricacies of the buildings and gardens here.

Plaza del Triunfo, s/n (across from the Cathedral). ☎ *95-450-23-23. Admission: 600 pta. ($3); handheld audio tour to the Reales Alcazares is available in English for 400 pta. ($2.20). Open: Oct–Mar Tues–Sat 9:30 a.m.–6 p.m., Sun 9:30 a.m.–2:30 p.m.; Apr–Sept Tues–Sat 9:30 a.m.–8 p.m., Sun 9:30 a.m.–6 p.m.*

Royally cruel

Pedro the Cruel, who established his court in Seville, receives much of the credit for creating the **Alcázar,** the gorgeous royal residence (though the structure was considerably expanded and enhanced by later monarchs). But Pedro left his mark in other ways — primarily blood stains. In what became the appropriately named **Hall of Justice,** he murdered his brother, Don Fabrique, who conducted a brazen affair with Pedro's wife, Doña Blanca. On a different occasion, King Cruel dispensed with his dinner guest, the Emir of Granada, but not without first pocketing the Moor's fantastic uncut ruby and other priceless jewels. But what goes around comes around: Pedro was eventually assassinated by his own half-brother, Henry the Magnificent.

More cool things to see and do

✔ **Cooling off in the shade.** When Seville's unrelenting heat begins to barbecue your brain, bolt for (or more likely, stagger to) the park. The lushly shaded gardens of **Parque María Luisa,** designed in the late-nineteenth century along the Guadalquivir River, are the best thing this side of a cold bath. (In the dead of summer, you may be tempted to rip off your clothes and go screaming into the fountain, but don't — the punishing sun beats down on the tiles as if they were the sands of the Sahara.) In spring, the acacia trees and rose bushes are particularly fragrant, and the Arab-style fountains and ponds, punctuated with floating swans, are extremely romantic. Within the park is the **Plaza de España;** a massive semi-circular palace with decorative tiles commemorating each province in Spain, it was built for the 1929 Ibero-American Exposition. Though kids are always captivated by this huge structure, today, it's in a sad state of neglect. (Many of the tiles I took so many photos of 15 years ago on my first visit are now chipped and faded.) Kids still enjoy rowing boats around the moat and water still springs from the fountain, but the Plaza already seems like a relic. The park also houses the **Museo Arqueológico** (Archaeological Museum; ☎ 95-423-24-01; open Tuesday 3 to 8 p.m., Wednesday to Saturday 9 a.m. to 8 p.m. and Sunday 9 a.m. to 2 p.m.; 250 pta./$1.40). It's worth a visit only if you've plenty of time in Seville, or you just want to get inside for a while.

One of the best ways to visit the park is to hire a horse-drawn carriage, but if you're walking back to the center of town, take Avenida de María Luisa to San Fernando. On the southwest corner, across from the gardens of the Alcázar, is Seville's university, which inhabits the **Real Fábrica de Tabacos** (Royal Tobacco Factory). This factory is where the Gypsy seductress Carmen, best known as the heroine of Bizet's famous opera set in Seville, rolled cigars along with about 10,000 other Andalusian women.

Presumably, they sang and danced all the while. You're welcome to take a stroll through and see the grandeur that came with a nineteenth-century state tobacco monopoly.

✔ **Visiting Casa de Pilatos (Pilate's House).** North of the Cathedral, Pilate's House, Plaza de Pilatos, 1 (southeast section of the Old City; four blocks west of Menéndez Pelayo; ☎ 95-422-52-98) is a superb, two-story, fifteenth century Renaissance palace built by the Marquis of Tarifa. Without doubt one of the finest homes in Seville, it's bursting with grand architectural and artistic treasures: Greek and Roman busts, frescos, handsome painted ceilings, courtyard sculptures, walls plastered with colorful glazed ceramic tiles, and a carved dome *mudéjar* ceiling over the staircase. My father's fond of saying "They don't make 'em like they used to," so I brought him here to prove him right. Admission to the museum is 500 pta. ($2.75); to the patio and gardens 500 pta. ($2.75); to both, 1,000 pta. ($5.50). It's open daily 9 a.m. to 6 p.m. (from July to September daily 9 a.m. to 8 p.m.).

✔ **Picking a side at the bullfights.** One of Spain's oldest, grandest, and most important bullfighting rings — the oldest is a little farther south, in Ronda (see Chapter 17) — **Plaza de Toros de la Maestranza** ("my-eh-*strahn*-tha"), Paseo de Cristóbal Colón, 12 (intersection of Paseo de Cristóbal Colón and Adriano, across from river; ☎ 95-422-45-77), was inititated in 1761 and completed 120 years later. Not round, but oval, the stark white ring seats 14,000 people. As in all Spanish bullrings, you can buy the cheap seats in the *sol* (sun) or the more expensive ones in the *sombra* (shade). You'll understand the price difference once you sit through a bullfight in the intense Seville sun — you'll be virtually dead in the afternoon. Bullfights used to last all day, with 12 *toros* (bulls) meeting their maker (and almost as many horses — the steeds that brought in the *picadores* [horsemen who jab the bulls around the neck and shoulders to wear them down] — didn't wear protective gear until the 1920s, and many were fatally gored). Today only bulls — six during every bullfight — are slain.

The bullfighting season at la Maestranza begins the first week in April and lasts through October. You can download an advance schedule if you've got a *matador* of choice (www.realmaestranza.com) or pick one up from the tourism office when you arrive in Seville. Tickets are available at the box office or at kiosks set up in major tourist districts in the center. Admission is 400 pta. ($2.20); it's open daily 9:30 a.m. to 2 p.m., and 3 to 6 p.m.

The bullring tour includes a visit to the museum **(Museo Taurino),** which displays various *trajes de luces* (flashy "suits of lights" worn by matadors), photos of bull aficionados like Ernest Hemingway, and paintings of bull lore. You finish the group tour in the chapel, where the bullfighters come to pray to La Macarena, the patron saint of *toreros* (yes, she of the world-famous song and dance number).

✔ **Discovering La Macarena!** You can thank Al Gore for this one. Sure, the cheesy Spanish pop song *Macarena* topped the charts all over the world, but had it not been for the then-vice president's memorably wooden interpretation of the dance, we may well have forgotten it by now. Believe it or not, La Macarena's more than just a participatory dance number. She is one of Seville's most revered madonnas, a tearful patron saint of bullfighters, a favorite of Gypsies, and a legend when it comes to Holy Thursday's procession. You can see the colonial-looking **Basílica de la Macarena,** Calle Bécquer, 1 (Puerta de la Macarena, extreme north of Old City; intersection of Muñoz León and San Luis; ☎ 95-490-18-00), on the extreme northern ring of the Old City (the fastest way to get here is to take a cab along the outer ring: Colón to Torneo to Resolana Andueza). It's a bit of a hike, but if you're at all fascinated by the cult of madonna worship that's especially strong in the south of Spain, a visit here is obligatory. You can visit the Macarena museum, with its over-the-top processional floats of Our Lady of Hope (her official name) — one's covered in a forest of candlesticks, another's a shiny golden chariot. If you just want to see the famous crying virgin Mary, enter the church through the front door with the faithful. Admission to the basilica is free; to museum it's 400 pta. ($2.20). Both are open daily 9:30 a.m. to 1 p.m. and 5 to 8 p.m.

✔ **Traveling into the past.** La Cartuja, across the river from Seville's major downtown area, is where the 1992 World Expo was held. Nobody was quite sure what to do with the installations afterward, but they've finally been put to work as a theme park, and one with a sixteenth-century motif at that. **Isla Mágica** (Magic Island), Pabellón de España, Isla de la Cartuja (across Puente de la Barqueta Bridge, take bus C2 from city center; ☎ 95-446-14-93), travels back in time for the little ones. Rides and show themes include the *Amazon, Gateway to the Americas,* and *El Dorado.* The park also has a motion theater with seats that shimmy and shake like the vehicles on screen you're ostensibly piloting (it's pretty cool and realistic — the kids will love it!). Admission for adults is 3,300 pta. ($18) for the whole day or 2,300 ($13) for afternoon only; children 5–12 years and seniors 2,300–1,700 pta. ($13–$9); children under 5, free. The park is open March through November, daily 11 a.m. to 1 a.m.

✔ **Taking in the Torre del Oro.** One of Seville's enduring landmarks is this cylindrical tower built for defense purposes in 1220, toward the end of Moorish rule in Seville, on the banks of the Río Guadalquivir (near Puente San Telmo). Once completely sheathed in glimmering golden tiles (hence the name, Torre del Oro, or Tower of Gold), today the watchtower shelters a small naval museum. It's open Tuesday through Friday, 10 a.m. to 2 p.m., Saturday through Sunday, 11 a.m. to 2 p.m.; admission is 100 pta. (55¢).

✔ **Going to the hospital — for art's sake.** The Baroque seventeenth-century **Hospital de la Caridad** (Hospital of Charity), Calle Temprado, 3 (☎ 95-422-32-32) — established to care for the destitute, infirm, and criminal — contains a splendid chapel, a mini-museum of art. It houses works by the painter Juan de Valdés Leal, including his famous *Postrimerías,* and the sculptor Pedro Roldán, as well as a handsome altarpiece by Simón de Pineda. There are also a dozen paintings by native son Bartolomé Murillo. The hospital was built by Miguel de Mañara, reputed to be one of the models for the legendary Don Juan (building a charity hospital smells of a desperate act of penance for such a rogue character). It's open Monday through Saturday, 9 a.m. to 1:30 p.m. and 3:30 to 6:30 p.m.; Sunday 9 a.m. to 1 p.m. Admission is 400 pta. ($2.20).

And on your left, the Cathedral: Seeing Seville by guided tour

You can choose from two sightseeing bus tours in Seville. **Sevirama** (☎ 95-456-06-93) has stops at the Torre del Oro, Plaza de España, and Isla Mágica. It's one of those open-top, get-on-and-get-off buses (1,500 pta./$8; children under 12 free). **Sevilla Tour** offers bus multilingual tours in buses designed to look like trolley cars (☎ 95-450-20-99). A ticket is good for 24 hours, and you can pick up the bus at Torre del Oro, Plaza de España, Isla Mágica, and Cartuja (the Expo '92 site).

If your feet ache and you want to catch some rays from the top of an open-air bus tour of Seville, pick up one of the flyers for the Sevirama buses. Doing so saves you 200 pta. ($1.10) on the price of a hop-on hop-off ticket. The discount is easy to come by; you'll either have the flyer thrust into your face around the cathedral or in the Santa Cruz neighborhood. Meanwhile, the ad for Sevilla Tour in the free magazine *Welcome & Olé!* offers the same 200-pta. ($1.10) discount. Put the savings toward some sunscreen.

You can't miss the horse-drawn carriages lined up outside Seville's cathedral. They're a very popular way to clop-clop around Seville, and this attractive, romantic city is one of the most enjoyable places in Spain to get off your feet and behind a horse. If you've thought about it in other places like Córdoba and haven't hopped aboard, Seville's the place to do it, especially if you've got your sweetie by your side. Fares are posted and are non-negotiable (unless you find a rogue driver); they run 4,000 pta. ($22) for an hour (4,500–5,500 pta./$25–$31 during Holy Week, Easter, and the April festivals). Besides the stop in the plaza fronting the Cathedral, there are stops in María Luisa Park, Plaza del Triunfo, Plaza Virgin de los Reyes, and Torre del Oro.

Suggested one-, two-, and three-day itineraries

Make your first stop on **Day One** the Plaza del Triunfo and Plaza de la Virgen de los Reyes, which are lined with horse-drawn carriages waiting to squire you around Seville. Here you find the imposing **Cathedral** and its minaret-slash-belfry (which you can climb for unforgettable views), and the **Reales Alcazares,** the important royal residence. Those two sights and lunch will take up most of the day.

Day Two might begin with a walking tour of colorful **Barrio de Santa Cruz,** awash in bright colors, *tapas* bars, shops and the gaiety for which Seville is renowned. Don't miss the **Hospital de los Venerables Sacerdotes.** In the afternoon, check the excellent **Fine Arts Museum (Museo de Bellas Artes),** one of Spain's finest, and the lush **Parque Maria Luisa,** a good place to hide from the sun.

On **Day Three,** visit the famed bullfighting ring **(Plaza de Toros de la Maestranza)** and some of Seville's other churches, such as **Basílica de la Macarena.** You may also want to hop aboard one of the horse-and-buggies for a romantic clip-clop through the streets of Old Seville. If you have kids, trek across the river to **La Cartuja** and the **Isla Mágica** theme park. You may also spend a third day visiting one of the easy-to-reach day trip sites, such as Carmona or Italica. But most important, don't leave Seville without scarfing down lots of *tapas* and sherry.

Shopping in Seville

Seville's a joy for shopping hounds — as much for the joy of strolling, at which Sevillanos are peerless, as for the typically Andalusian goods that make great gifts.

Best shopping areas

The principal shopping districts are **Barrio de Santa Cruz,** for artisan's shops, antiques and trinkets; and **Zona Centro** (center, just north of the Cathedral Tower) — particularly the pedestrian streets **Sierpes** and **Tetuán.** The area west of the Cathedral, **El Arenal,** is packed with cool little antique shops, as are **Mateos Gago** and **Rodrigo Caro** in Santa Cruz.

What to look for and where to find it

Look for hand-painted ceramics, old *azulejos* (glazed ceramic tiles), antiques, and for women who want to play the part of charming Sevillana seductress, fans, embroidered shawls, and colorful flamenco dresses.

You either have to depend on your feet or taxis to get around Seville. Map out where you want to go; if anything looks too far (more than five blocks, say), hop in an inexpensive, air-conditioned taxi. And remember that shops are closed for long lunch breaks, often from 1:30 to 5 p.m. If you must shop at mid-day, head to **El Corte Inglés** department store (on Plaza Duque de la Victoria), which doesn't dare close or turn off the mega-watt air conditioning.

Antiques

A gregarious Sevillano family enterprise, **Felix e Hijo** (Felix and Son . . . and daughter and in-laws), Avenida de la Constitución, 20 (☎ **95-422-33-34**), deal in classical archaeological finds: Greek vases, Egyptian masks, and Roman mosaics. Not everything is impossibly expensive and impossible to lug home — you may just find that one piece that crystallizes Andalusia's storied past. In any case, Felix also arranges shipping. Mari Carmen, Felix's daughter, runs **Felix,** Avenida de la Constitución, 26 (☎ **95-421- 80-26**), specializing mostly in antique Andalusian posters — of the April Fair, bullfights, and hard-to-find deco advertising posters. The old posters of Semana Santa and Feria de Abril are fetching, with affordable prices to match.

Baked goods from on high

For pastries from heaven, check out what the nuns are baking. At **Convento de San Leandro,** Plaza de San Ildefonso, 1, the sisters sell *yemas de San Leandro* (egg yolk candies). You can get all kinds of airy pastries, some made especially for the Christmas holidays, at **Convento de Santa Inés,** Doña María Coronel, 5, and jams and marmelades at **Convento de Santa Paula,** Santa Paula, 11 (☎ **95-442-13-07**). During the month of December, visit the **Palacio Arzobispal** (Archbishop's Palace), Plaza Virgen de los Reyes across from the Cathedral, for a stupendous selection of *dulces navideños* (Christmas sweets).

Books

Three guesses as to what's sold at **English Bookshop,** Marques de Nervión, 70 (☎ **95-465-57-54**). If you need a traveling fix, check out the selection of novels and travel books, which are all in the English language.

Ceramics

El Postigo, Calle Arfe, s/n (☎ **95-421-39-76**), has one of the largest stocks of hand-painted ceramics in Seville, with a selection of pottery, planters, and other patio-perfect pieces. For hand-painted vases, tiles and plates with historic Andalusian patterns, check out **Martian Ceramics,** Calle Sierpes, 74 (☎ **95-421-34-13**). The selection's good, if not, out of this world.

Crafts

Artesanía Textil, Calle Sierpes, 70 (☎ **95-456-28-40**), is a great place for handwoven Andalusian blankets, table linens, and shawls. **El Bazar del Barrio** (The Neighborhood Bazaar), Calle Mateos Gago, 24 (☎ **95-456-00-89**), a cute shop in the Santa Cruz district, has everything from antique *azulejos* (glazed ceramic tiles) to watercolors of bullfighting scenes. The items are more carefully selected than what you find in souvenir shops.

Department stores

El Corte Inglés, Plaza Duque de la Victoria, 10 (☎ 95-422-09-31), is the megastore that dominates Spain like a fortress on the plains; you can get anything from flamenco dresses, dishes, and vacuum cleaners to shoe polish and CDs of flamenco artists. **Marks & Spencer,** Plaza Duque de la Victoria, 6 (☎ 95-456-36-56) is the quintessential British purveyor of all things well-made, practical, and not too expensive. Conservative, but not stuffy. (They make great cotton underwear).

Fans

Casa Rubio, Calle Sierpes, 56 (☎ 95-422-68-72), has a terrific selection of fans, from fancy hand-painted numbers to modern functional items that will keep you cool in the wicked Seville heat.

Flamenco dresses

You can find cheaper *trajes sevillanos* (flamenco dresses) and shawls, but you won't find any more exquisite than the hand-embroidered numbers at **Angeles Berral,** Calle Pajaritos, 7 (☎ 95-456-31-30), a small, personalized shop just a few doors down from Casa Pilatos. They're extremely elegant and tasteful (and pricey). Generations of Sevillanas have come to **Perdales,** Cuna, 23 (☎ 421-37-09), for the perfect, body-hugging costume to wow 'em at the April festivals (see the sidebar, "Fiesta Time! Seville's popular festivals"). The outfits aren't cheap (and I have a hard time figuring out when would be the right moment back home to wear one . . .), but if you need a showy number to go with your castenets and fan, this is the place. Don't forget the color-coordinated shoes.

For the ranch

For 20 years **Arcab's,** Paseo de Cristóbal Colón, 18 (☎ 95-421-81-30) has been a sturdy place to get a hand-tooled saddle, riding boots, and other items related to the majestic Andalusian horse (or your regular old Texas steed). For riding saddles, boots, spurs, buckles, blankets, leather pouches, and more, try **San Pablo,** Calle Murillo, 9 (☎ 95-422-56-34). This family-owned place has dealt equestrian accessories for half a century.

Fashion

Zara, Plaza Duque de la Vitoria, 1 (☎ 95-421-48-75), something akin to the Galician incarnation of Banana Republic, has affordable and hip fashions for men, women, and kids. (The menswear Zara is up the street, at Calle Tetuán.) Two of the hottest names in women's fashion are **Victorio & Lucchino,** Sierpes, 87 (☎ 95-422-79-51). Dresses by this Andalusian design couple are Spain's version of Dolce and Gabana, but more elegant and sophisticated and less modish.

Flea markets

Los hippies is what locals call these flea-market locations for leather goods, hippie fashions, costume jewelry, and heavenly junk. Wednesday and Thursday it's at Calle Rioja and Plaza Magdalena; Friday and Saturday in Plaza del Duque. On Thursdays, check out Feria Street and Calle Alameda for antiques, paintings, and furniture.

Music

Allegro, Calle Dos de Mayo, 37 (☎ 95-421-61-93), just beside the Teatro de la Maestranza, is a specialist in classical music. It also has a top-notch selection of Spanish music, including flamenco and zarzuela. You can give things a listen before buying. **Sevilla Rock,** Calle Alfonso XII, 1, is the place to come for cassettes for your rental car or musical souvenirs of Andalusia. You can find the latest in Spanish pop-flamenco or the hardcore *cante hondo* (deep-throated vocal) stuff (like the anthology of the great singer Camarón de la Isla).

Feeling the rhythms of Seville's nightlife

There are three things you shouldn't miss on a sultry Seville night: a rousing flamenco *tablao* (performance); outdoor cafés and bars (either near the Cathedral or along either side of the river) for people-watching, *tapas*-munching, and libation-quaffing; and live, combustible music, with rhythmic hand-claps, cries of *iolé!* and a palpable sense of community, at clubs where you see locals get down and dirty performing *sevillanas* (an informal gathering of singing, music, and dancing) — they leave the professional flamenco shows to the tourists.

For listings of what's on and what's going down, check out any of the following free publications that list nightlife options: *Welcome & Olé!, The Tourist,* or *El Giradillo,* available at tourism offices throughout the city.

Catching a flamenco show

El Arenal, Calle Rodo, 7 (☎ 95-421-64-92), produces one of the best flamenco song and dance shows in Seville. In the back room of a seventeenth-century building with small tables, the place and performances practically shout passionate Andalusia. Shows are 4,100 pta. ($22; dinner is extra) and run every night from 9 p.m. to 11:30 p.m., with a second show from 11:30 p.m. to 1 a.m. It's located between Dos de Mayo and Varflora, near the bullring and Paseo Colón.

Los Gallos, Plaza de Santa Cruz, 11 (☎ 95-421-69-81; Internet: www. infor.es/gallos), is in the heart of the old Jewish Quarter, Barrio de Santa Cruz. You'd think this would be unforgiveably touristy, but the flamenco's pretty pure, and the place is lively and intimate. Visitors love it, and you may even find a few locals in attendance. The show runs 3,500 pta. ($19), which includes the first drink. It's two blocks south of Ximénez de Enciso, along Santa Teresa.

Dressed up like a Seville patio, **El Patio Sevillano,** Paseo de Cristóbal Colón, 11 (☎ 95-421-41-20), popular with large tourist groups, forsakes the intimate, flamenco-focused program for one with exotic costumes and a wide range of Spanish music and dance. Three shows are performed nightly from spring through fall (two the rest of the year). Including your first drink, admission is 4,000 pta. ($22). It's near the Maestranza Bullring and Calle Adriano, on the east side of Quadalquivir River.

Flamenco fever flows through *Sevilla.* If you've been to see a flamenco troupe and want to learn how to stomp your heels dramatically and twirl your arms seductively, maybe a dance class is in order. **Estudio de Baile** (Dance Studio) **Mario** offers classes in flamenco, *danza española* (Spanish dance), and Sevillanas Monday through Friday from 11 a.m. to 1:30 p.m. and 6 to 9 p.m. The studio's on Calle Procurador, 20; ☎ 95-433-89-14. **Taller Flamenco** (flamenco studio) offers intensive, four-day music and dance classes in small groups. They're on Calle Siete Revueltas, 5 (☎ 95-456-42-34).

Clapping along to Sevillanas

Casa Anselma, Pagés del Corro, 49 (no phone), on the westside of the river, rocks with communal singing and camaraderie. Either get here obscenely early to get a table, or come around midnight, when it starts to get really steamy — and packed. The garrulous owner, Anselma, is a local institution and quite a singer herself. To get there, take a taxi; Casa Anselma is four blocks back from Calle Betis in Triana, on the west side of Guadalquivir River.

Along the river, an area packed with bars and great little places for an evening *tapeo,* you find **Lo Nuestro** (Our Thing), Betis, 31–A (☎ 95-472-60-10), where locals do — what else? — their thing: sing and dance and drink. To get there, walk across San Telmo Bridge toward Triana neighborhood; take the first right past the bridge, on the main street facing the river. The bar's about halfway down on the right side.

Making it a night at the opera

Seville's fancy, newish opera house, **Teatro de la Maestranza,** Paseo de Cristóbal Colón, 22 (☎ 95-422-33-44) is the place to catch a Seville-inspired production of *Carmen, The Marriage of Figaro,* or *The Barber of Seville.* There are also jazz concerts and recitals here. The box office is open from10 a.m .to 2 p.m. and 5 to 8 p.m. As you face the Guadalquivir River, the opera house is halfway between San Telmo and Isabel II bridges.

Enjoying the theater

On the northern edge of María Lusia Park is this handsome theater, **Teatro Lope de Vega,** Avenida María Luisa, s/n (☎ 459-08-53), which brings some of the best productions to Seville. I caught a great performance of García Lorca's *The House of Bernarda Alba* here recently. Productions are in Spanish only (but that doesn't appear to stop large contingents of foreign visitors from attending). It's near the intersection of Menéndez Pelayo, Avenida de Isabel la Católica, and Avenida de Portugal.

Surviving Seville bars

For a full roster of *tapas* bars, a superb way to spend an evening in Seville, see "Dining in Seville," earlier in this chapter. Plaza del Salvador is always hopping with *jaleo* (commotion). The tiny bars there (**La Antigua Bodeguita** and **Los Soportales**) spill out into the square, where there are rickety little tables and lots of beer-drinking, good-natured, good-looking young people.

Abades, Calle Abades, 13 (☎ 95-422-56-22) is a pub in the guise of a converted nineteenth-century Barrio de Santa Cruz mansion. This is lounge culture at its finest; slip into the rich living room and decadent ambience and enjoy a cocktail with other stylin' folks. To get there, take Mateos Gago east of the Cathedral and turn left on Abades. Perched on the banks of the Guadalquivir, **Bar Capote,** Paseo de Cristóbal Colón, 11 (☎ 95-421-41-20), is the place to down a few cocktails in the open air and perform your riverdance when a *señorita* (lady) or *caballero* (gentleman) catches your eye. It's next to the Maestranza Bullring, facing the river.

At **Bar Quitaspesares** (also called Taberna Peregil), Plaza Padre Jerónimo de Córdoba, 3 (☎ 95-421-89-66), proprietor Pepe Peregil is so gregarious it's contagious. His bar is packed with young and old, and there's usually a group gathered in back, with guitar and voices in full swing. Young women often get up and show off their *sevillana* dance moves. Pepe's place is a little removed from the city center, near the Church of Santa Catalina. To get there, take Calle Martín Villa (which becomes Laraña) east off of Sierpes, all the way to Plaza Ponce de León, just west of the plaza that the bar is on. Take a taxi there and back; it's much too far to walk. (If that's too far, check out his son's bar, **La Goleta,** on Calle Mateos Gago, 20, in Barrio de Santa Cruz.)

Side trips from Seville

A great way to get out of town is to board **Al Andalus Expreso,** a vintage luxury train whose 12 cars are straight out of the 1920s, and set out for the highlights of Andalusia. Along the way, you pass (in air-conditioned luxury) through the south's spectacular scenery — dry, rugged mountains and rolling olive groves. The Seville-to-Seville roundtrip pulls into **Córdoba, Granada** (see Chapter 18), and two of Andalusia's famed *Pueblos Blancos,* or white towns, **Ronda** and **Jerez** (see Chapter 17). There's also a Madrid–Madrid roundtrip, which takes in the major sights of Andalusia before returning to the capital. On either, you dine aboard in the luxurious dining car or in fine restaurants (frequently *paradors*). The price includes meals with wine, tours, visits, transfers, and taxes, but traveling in such princely style doesn't come cheap. Prices range from $1,339 to $1,584 per person (depending on cabin type), for seven-day, six-night trips. The train hits the tracks from April–Oct, skipping the extremely hot months of July and August. Visit the Web site, www.alandalusexpreso.com, or contact your travel agent or **Marketing Ahead,** a Spanish travel specialist in New York, at ☎ **212-686-9213;** Fax:212-686-0271. Otherwise, try one of the following recommended side trips.

The Roman ruins of Itálica

Before the Moors and the Visigoths, the Romans ruled Andalusia. The ruins of the Roman city of Itálica (☎ **95-599-73-76**), which was founded in 206 BC, are so close to Seville (6 miles) that you can almost walk there. Two of the most famous Emperors of the Roman Empire, Trajan and Hadrian, were born in Itálica, and the city was one of the Empire's most important in A.D. 2. The main feature is the elliptical amphitheater, which could hold 25,000 spectators and was the largest built by the Romans. The town had about 10,000 inhabitants at its height. Excavations are ongoing, and Roman mosaics continue to be unearthed and transported to the Seville Archaeological Museum. In summer, concerts and dance festivals are held here — an evocative bit of staging.

Itálica is 9 km (5 ½ miles) northwest of Seville. To get there by car, take Highway N-360 in the direction of Mérida. By bus, take the Santiponce bus that leaves from Calle Marqués de Parada near the Santa Justa rail station. The site is open Tuesday through Saturday, 9 a.m. to 5:30 p.m., Sunday 9 a.m. to 3 p.m. Admission is 250 pta. ($1.40).

Carmona, a crossroads of cultures

Carmona, a pretty, ancient walled city on a plateau an hour from Seville, has narrow whitewashed streets, a number of handsome, noble Renaissance homes, and a handful of churches and convents. It also has three Moorish fortresses. Carmona's fame rests on its reputation as one of the oldest inhabited places in Spain (Phoenicians and Carthaginians preceded the Romans). It has two landmark gates — the **Puerta de Sevilla** and **Puerta de Córdoba.** Have a peek at the Gothic **Iglesia de Santa María,** too. But the town's best sight may be the cool **Roman Necropolis,** where 1,000 former citizens are buried in underground tombs carved out of rock. Look for the impressive *Elephant* and *Seville* tombs. The necropolis is on the outskirts of town and clearly signposted. You can hit it on the way into or out of town.

Carmona is 32 km (20 miles) east of Seville. If you're coming into Seville from Córdoba (or, of course, going on to Córdoba from Seville), it's an easy stopover — just follow the signs from the N-V highway.

Carmona's also a great place to overnight, with two superb hotels. The **Parador Alcázar del Rey Don Pedro,** Alcázar, s/n (☎ **95-414-10-10;** Fax: 95-414-17-12; E-mail: carmona@parador.es; Rates 18,500 pta./ $103), one of the better ones in the *parador* system, has a Moorish patio, inviting pool, and stunning views of the countryside. **Casa de Carmona,** Plaza Lasso, 1 (☎ **95-419-10-00;** Fax:95-419-01-89; E-mail: reservations@casadecarmona; Internet: www.casadecarmona.com; Rates: 18,000–34,000 pta./$100– $189), is a small and elegant sixteenth-century mansion with cozy, luxurious rooms — each evoking a different era of Andalusian history — and a nice pool.

Fast Facts: Seville

Area Code

Seville's area code is **95,** which you must before every number.

American Express

Hotel Inglaterra (Plaza Nueva 7; ☎ **95-421-16-17**).

ATMs/Currency Exchange

There are banks and ATM machines along the main drag in the *centro,* Avenida de la Constitución, just behind the cathedral, and on Plaza Nueva.

Embassies/Consulates

Most Western countries have consulates in sultry Seville. Australia (Federico Rubio, 14; ☎ **95-422-02-40**); Canada (Avenida Constitución, 30, 2nd floor, No. 4; ☎ **95-422-94-13**); Ireland (Plaza Santa Cruz, 6, 6th floor; ☎ **95-421-63-61**); United Kingdom (Plaza Nueva, 87; ☎ **95-422-88-74**); and the United States (Pabellón de los EE.UU/Paseo de las Delicias, 7; ☎ **95-423-18-83**).

Emergencies

For medical emergencies, dial ☎ **061** or call the Cruz Roja (Red Cross; Avenida de la Cruz Roja) at ☎ **95-422-22-22** or Casa de Socorro

(First Aid), Menéndez Pelayo, ☎ **95-441-17-12.** To call an ambulance, call ☎ **95-442-55-65.** In case of fire, call ☎ **95-422-00-80.** For the police call ☎ **091.** For roadside assistance, call ☎ **900-12-35-05.**

Hospitals

Hospital Virgen del Rocío is on Avenida Manuel Siurot, s/n (☎ **95-445-81-81**). Hospital Universitario Virgen Macarena is found at Avenida Doctor Fedriani, s/n (☎ **95-424-81-81**).

Information

The main Andalucía Tourism Information Office is located just down the street from the cathedral, Avenida de la Constitución, 21 (☎ **95-422-14-04**). Others are found at the San Pablo airport (☎ **95-444-91-28**) and Santa Justa train station (☎ **95-453-76-26**). They're open daily from 9 a.m. to 8 p.m. Municipal tourism offices are at Plaza de la Concordia, s/n (☎ **95-490-52-67**) and Costurero de la Reina/Paseo de las Delicias, 9 (☎ **95-423-44-65**). Dial ☎ **010** (8 a.m. to 10 p.m.) for general information about the city, including transportation, in English as well as other languages.

Internet Access/Cyber Cafés

In some Spanish cities, it can be tough to locate a good cybercafé to be able to tap into your *correo electrónico* (that's E-mail to gringos) while traveling. Seville, though, with its rambunctious retinue of foreign students, has several places where you can surf on good machines. Web surfing generally runs about 400 pta. ($2.20) for a half-hour, 500–600 pta. ($2.75–$3) per hour. Check into Open Net (Calle Pavía, 8; ☎ 95-421-70-35), which is usually packed with study-abroad students. Open from 10 a.m. to 9 p.m. Mon–Sat, it's near the bullfighting ring. Another place to check out is Cibercenter (Calle Julio Cesar, 8; ☎ 95-422-88-99). In the center of Seville, it's just off Calle Reyes Católicos and is open 9 a.m. to 7 p.m. Mon– Friday, Saturday 10 a.m. to 2 p.m.and 3 to 7 p.m. and Sunday 10 a.m. to 2 p.m. Finally, a place with a couple of computers at back is Afalfa **10** (on Plaza Alfalfa, 10; ☎ 95-421-38-41). It's open daily, noon to 8 p.m., later on weekends.

Mail

Seville's Central Post Office is found on Avenida de la Constitución, 32 (☎ 95-421-95-85).

Maps

The Tourism Office distributes city maps that should be sufficient for most visitors.

Otherwise, check with the tourist-oriented shops right around the Cathedral.

Police

The municipal police station is at Avenida de las Delicias, 15 (☎ 95-461-54-50 or ☎ 092). The national police office is located at Plaza de la Concordia (☎ 95-422-88-49). The national emergency number in Spain is ☎ 006.

Safety

Seville has earned an unenviable reputation for talented thieves, who can spot a rental car with helpless tourists at the wheel at more than 100 paces. If you must park your car anywhere other than a guarded hotel parking garage (try to avoid doing so), don't leave anything of value in it — no cameras, no passports, no nothing. Seville, still part of the poorest region in Spain, is also one of Spain's biggest tourist draw. Be very careful in Seville; carry only the amount of money you expect to spend (or don't mind losing) that day, and keep it in your front pocket. Also be careful around the Santa Cruz district late at night (despite the blistering sun, it's preferable to do your sightseeing there during the day).

Taxis

Radio Taxi (☎ 95-458-00-00), Radio Teléfono Giralda (☎ 95-496-00-00), or Tele-Taxi (☎ 95-462-22-22).

Discovering Historic Córdoba

Unless you're here in May, when the city bubbles over with festivals, flowers, and *alegría* (joy), you may find unpretentious Córdoba a little rough around the edges. It's a city that obviously fell into decline and never quite recovered. Only during festival time will you need much more than a day or so to explore its major sights.

Founded by the Romans and the largest city of their Iberian empire, Córdoba was captured by the Moors in A.D. 711. The city thrived under the Muslims while the rest of Europe foundered. Córdoba was not only the independent *caliphate* (the office of the caliph, who served as the spiritual head of Islam) of the Moors and the spiritual and intellectual center of Western Islam, but also a place where Muslims, Jews, and Christians lived side-by-side. By the tenth century, Córdoba possessed Europe's greatest libraries (not surprising when you realize that only the Moors knew how to make paper), a superlative university excelling in mathematics and science, hundreds of mosques, and dozens of synagogues. It also had the only paved and lighted streets on the peninsula. The numbers are indeed impressive: At the height of the caliphate — Moorish rule — Córdoba had a population of nearly 1,000,000. The city had 300 mosques, 600 Arab baths, 60,000 noble mansions, 50 hospitals, and 27 schools. And, at a time when most of Europe was illiterate, the library contained more than a quarter of a million volumes.

Although Córdoba helped pull Europe out of the Dark Ages, the city's preeminence under the Moors didn't last long. The Christian Reconquest captured the city in 1236, and Córdoba never recovered its former glory.

Arriving in Córdoba

You'll most likely roll into Córdoba by road or rail from another point in Andalusia or from Madrid. However, you won't fly to the city; Córdoba has an airport, but no commercial routes use it. You have to fly into Granada, Seville, or Málaga, all at least 2 hours away.

By car

If you go by car, you drive along undulating olive groves, and a car is virtually the only way to see some of the *pueblos blancos* (white towns) efficiently. Driving to Córdoba from Madrid, take the N-IV (E-5), which veers right (west) at Bailén. The toll-free trip takes about three hours. (The same highway continues directly to Seville.)

The N-342 highway connects Córdoba with Granada, while the N-331 unites Córdoba with Málaga.

By train

The fastest and least complicated way to get to Córdoba from either Madrid or Seville is definitely the **AVE High-Speed Train.** It's also the most expensive method of public transportation, but I highly recommend it for its efficiency and incredibly smooth ride. From Madrid, the trip takes just over 1½ hours; from Seville, 25 minutes. Fifteen trains travel daily to both destinations. The one-way fare from Madrid is 7,200 pta. ($40) (from Seville, 2,800 pta./or $16). If you can't catch the AVE, or want to save a few *pesetas,* hop on board a **Talgo 200 Train** (fast but not superfast like the AVE). It takes about two hours and costs 5,200 pta. ($29) from Madrid (from Seville, it takes over half an hour and costs 2,300 pta./$13). Three TALGO trains per day travel between Madrid and Cordoba. The slowest regional trains, called **Estrellas,** can take nearly five hours. They're cheap, but you waste valuable time that you can spend seeing the south if you take them.

Córdoba

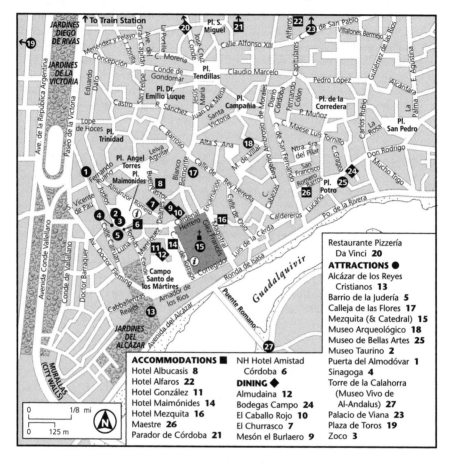

Restaurante Pizzería
Da Vinci **20**
ATTRACTIONS ●
Alcázar de los Reyes
Cristianos **13**
Barrio de la Judería **5**
Calleja de las Flores **17**
Mezquita (& Catedral) **15**
Museo Arqueológico **18**
Museo de Bellas Artes **25**
Museo Taurino **2**
Puerta del Almodóvar **1**
Sinagoga **4**
Torre de la Calahorra
(Museo Vivo de
Al-Andalus) **27**
Palacio de Viana **23**
Plaza de Toros **19**
Zoco **3**

ACCOMMODATIONS ■
Hotel Albucasis **8**
Hotel Alfaros **22**
Hotel González **11**
Hotel Maimónides **14**
Hotel Mezquita **16**
Maestre **26**
Parador de Córdoba **21**

NH Hotel Amistad
Córdoba **6**
DINING ◆
Almudaina **12**
Bodegas Campo **24**
El Caballo Rojo **10**
El Churrasco **7**
Mesón el Burlaero **9**

Look for the newest AVE trajectory, Córdoba to Málaga, expected to be
completed by the time you read this (construction began in November
2000).

Córdoba's main train station **(RENFE)** is northwest of the old town, at
Avenida de América, s/n (☎ 957-40-02- 02). The advance **ticket office**
is located at Ronda de los Tejares, 10 (☎ 957-47-58-84). For **AVE** train
schedules and information, call ☎ 957-49-02-02. In Madrid, the AVE
number is ☎ 91-328-90-20, and in Seville, ☎ 95-454-02-02.

By bus

Getting to Córdoba by bus is a simple enough proposition, until you
factor in the confusion of local bus stations. Each line has a separate
terminal scattered about the city. There are eight terminals in Córdoba;
several of them service Madrid (trips take about five hours). The separate terminals can make your trip a bit confusing, especially when the
train is so simple. I recommend taking the bus only if you're going to or

coming from a small town in which train service isn't available. Córdoba's busiest terminal is **Alsina Gräells** (Calle Diego Serrano, 14; ☎ 957-23-64-74), on the outskirts of town near Paseo de la Victoria. It has buses to Cádiz, Granada, Seville, and Jaén. **Ureña** (Avenida de Cervantes, 22; ☎ 957-47-23-52) serves Seville three times a day; the terminal's located a few blocks south of Córdoba's main train station, which is at the corner of Avenida de America and Avenida de Cervantes. The terminals **Priego** (Paseo de la Victoria, 29; ☎ 957-29-01-58) and **López** (Paseo de la Victoria, 15; ☎ 957-47-75-51) also service Madrid. For bus information to Seville, Málaga, and Granada call ☎ 957-23-64-74.

Orienting yourself in Córdoba

The provincial capital of Córdoba hugs the banks of the Guadalquivir River, which also flows through Seville, just 129 km (80 miles) to the southeast. The Old City, where you find the great Mosque and old Jewish Quarter, is north of the river, across the Roman bridge. Parts of the medieval Arab ramparts still stand on the fringes of the old town. The modern commercial and residential neighborhoods (and the RENFE train station) are north of the Old City, as Córdoba trails off into the foothills of the Sierra Morena Mountains.

Córdoba by neighborhood

Virtually everything you want to see in Córdoba is in or near the *centro* (historic center), which is along the river and around the Mezquita (Great Mosque). Immediately northwest of the Mezquita is the *Barrio de la Judería,* the old Jewish Quarter, Córdoba's most enchanting neighborhood.

Getting info after you arrive

The helpful **Andalusia Provincial Tourism Office** is located at Torrijos, 10 (☎ 957-47-12-35 and 957-49-16-77), right next to the Mezquita. A **municipal tourism office** is located at Plaza Judá Leví (☎ 957-20-05-22). They're both open daily from 9 a.m. to 8 p.m.

Getting around Córdoba

Córdoba's Old City is small and perfect for walking. In fact, many of the streets in this labyrinthine area around the Mezquita are pedestrian only. If you stay at one of the hotels a bit removed from the old center, you'll either need to cover substantial distances by foot or call upon the assistance of taxis and occasional buses.

By bus

You probably won't have much need for buses, unless it's from your hotel to the Old Quarter. For **bus information,** call ☎ 957-25-57-00 or 957-25-57-04. Your hotel can also indicate a nearby bus to the major sights in the old town.

By taxi

You find taxi stops on Avenida del Gran Capitán, Calles Cañero, Ciudad Jardín, Arcos de la Frontera, and Agustín Moreno, and the Plazas Colón and Tendillas. To order up a cab, call **Radio Taxi** (☎ **957-76-44-44** or 957-45-00-00). Taxis are inexpensive; unless you take one out to the ruins of Medina Azahara, no trip should cost you more than 1,000 pta. ($5.50).

By car

Wheels are the way to get the most out of your travels in Andalusia, especially if you plan on seeing more than just the three big cities of the south (Córdoba, Seville, and Granada). (If you only go to these, and don't plan to do any exploring, I advise against a car, because driving around the cities is difficult and potentially dangerous, with streets originally designed for the horse and buggy.)

If you want to rent a car to explore the countryside or the coast, the major agencies in Córdoba are: **Avis** (Plaza de Colón, 32; ☎ **957-47-68-62**); **Europcar** (Rep. Argentina, s/n and Camino de los Sastres, local 1; ☎ **957-2-34-60**); and **Hertz** (Avenida América, s/n, RENFE Railway station; ☎ **957-40-20-60**).

Horse for hire?

If you want to clop-clop around the Old Quarter, hire a horse-drawn carriage. You find carriage stops at Campo Santo de los Mártires (next to the Alcázar) and Calle Torrijos (next to the Mezquita). The atmospheric Old Quarter of Córdoba certainly makes the notion appealing, but on my last visit most of the horses looked a little anemic. If you're going on to Seville, I think you're better off getting a horse carriage there (if you must choose). The cost in both cities is about 4,000 pta. ($22) an hour, though some of the drivers in Córdoba may bargain with you out of high season.

Staying in Córdoba

Córdoba gets lots of day-trippers who file into the city to see the Mezquita (Great Mosque) and dash right out of town — which is probably why there's a somewhat limited hotel offering. It's a great place for budget travelers, though, with a disproportionate number of good, simple, and inexpensive lodgings near the Mezquita and old Jewish Quarter. At the upper end, choices are considerably slimmer. Prices go up, but not ridiculously so, during high season — April through May across the board, and September through October at some hotels.

Make your reservations far in advance if you want to stay in Córdoba during the popular May festivals.

Fiesta! Celebrating in Córdoba

Semana Santa (Holy Week) is intense in Andalusia and one of the greatest professions of faith in all Spain. Córdoba doesn't exactly take Easter lightly. And forget bunnies, chicks, and chocolate eggs; the worshippers crowding Córdoba's streets are waiting for the passing of 32 colorful ceremonial processions, including floats and penitents. Certain processions, such as María Santísima de la Esperanza (Holy Mary of Hope) and La Virgen de los Dolores (The Virgin of Sorrow) have enthusiastic, cult-like followings. Check with the Tourism Office for a schedule of processions and routes.

Córdoba is even more famous for its May festivals — if you can get a room (book at least a couple of months in advance), it's by far the best time for a visit to the city. **Las Cruces en Mayo** (May Crosses) marks the beginning of the month-long celebrations. Crosses are erected in patios and courtyards and decorated with potted plants, flowers, even shawls. Neighborhood associations, or *peñas,* also set up flamenco stages and small bars nearby — free-flowing wine is about as abundant as flowers in May. *Barrios* (neighborhoods) that traditionally sprout May Crosses are **San Agustín, Alcázar Viejo, San Lorenzo,** and **Santa María.**

After the decorated crosses, Córdoba's May party moves to courtyards, when the **Festival de los Patios Cordobeses** — a contest for best patio in Córdoba — consumes about 50 of them across the city. Such exuberant vegetation — red and green pots of roses, carnations, geraniums, jasmine, honeysuckle, and ivy — against the backdrop of stark, whitewashed buildings is a photo op at every turn. Some patios entered in the competition are communal neighborhood efforts, while others belong to palaces or convents.

Finally, the celebrations reach a crescendo with the **Feria de Mayo** (Mayfair), also called the **Feria de Nuestra Señora de la Salud** (Festival of Our Lady of Health). It's the grand finale, beginning around May 25 and bringing the month's festivities to a rousing close. Feria de Mayo is a smorgasbord of bullfights, flamenco, theater, and *casetas* (stages) set up by neighborhood associations for skits and performances. On generous display is the traditional Córdoban costume, with the *sombrero Cordobés* (wide-brimmed hat), Andalusian horses and, of course, lots of *fino* (fine) wines.

For more information on the best-decorated crosses, the most lavishly verdant patios, and other events, contact the Tourism Office at ☎ **957-47-12-35** or 957-49-16-77 (see "Getting info after you arrive," earlier in this chapter).

Hotel Albucasis

$$ Old Quarter

A quiet little hotel on an equally quiet little street in the Barrio de la Judería (the Jewish Quarter), the Albucasis does everything in its power to keep its cool in the Andalusian sun. The friendly, family-run hotel has a pretty, plant-filled courtyard, cool marble floors, and green-tiled bathrooms. The 15 air-conditioned rooms (only nine are doubles) are decently sized, with functional, sturdy furnishings. The common areas — a nice breakfast nook, a cozy sitting area, and the inviting patio — are excellent places to relax and share travel tales. Within echo range of the great Mosque's bells, the Albucasis is one of the city's best bargains.

Calle Buen Pastor, 11 (three blocks from Mosque, just off Deanes). ☎ *and Fax: 957-47-86-25. Parking: 1,900 pta. ($11). Rates: 12,000 pta. ($67). MC, V.*

Hotel Alfaros
$$$ Centro

A large, four-star hotel opened in 1992, the Alfaros pretends to be grand, playing up its neo-Moorish design as its clear historical connection to old Córdoba. The result, though, is mostly pretend-palace. The entrance — a garage on a narrow, busy downtown street 15 minutes north of the Mezquita — couldn't be less auspicious. The interior has the feel of an upscale tourist hotel in a modern Arab nation — Saudi Arabia, maybe. Alfaros has large and airy public spaces, with marble-and-stone floors, Moorish motifs, and a long, popular bar. The 131 rooms, while ample and comfortable, seem a bit of an afterthought, though. They're not constructed with the same quality materials and suffer from a lack of soundproofing. The hotel's finest feature is its courtyard pool; ask for a room facing it.

Calle Alfaros, 18 (three blocks from Plaza Colón). ☎ *957-49-19-20. Fax: 957-49-22-10. E-mail:* alfaros@maciahoteles.com. *Internet:* www.maciahoteles.com. *Parking: 1,600 pta. ($9). Rates: 14,500 pta. ($80) Jan to mid-March, July, Aug, Nov, and Dec; 18,000 pta. ($100) mid-March to June and Sept–Oct. AE, DC, MC, V.*

Hotel González
$–$$ Old Quarter

A small hotel in a restored sixteenth-century palace, this charmer feels perfectly Andalusian. It's just minutes from the Mosque, in the heart of the old Jewish Quarter, which is packed with historic monuments and bustling tourist-oriented shops. Though rooms are simple, they're also delightful, with colorful floor-to-ceiling drapes, antique furnishings, and tile floors (and air conditioning — which is a blessing in steaming Córdoba). The 16 rooms either overlook a pretty square, Plaza Judá Leví, or the hotel's equally pretty interior patio. Original artwork lines the central hall and corridors. The González is easily one of the top bargain places to stay in Córdoba. If you can't get in here, try the owners' other hotel, Hotel Mezquita, with similar facilities and identical prices (see the listing later in this section).

Calle Manríquez, 3 (off Herreros and Deanes, just west of the Mosque). ☎ *957-47-98-19. Fax: 957-48-61-87. Parking: 1,500 pta. ($8). Rates: 5,900–10,850 pta. ($33– $60). AE, DC, MC, V.*

Hotel Maimónides
$$$ Old Quarter

If what you care about is location, location, location, you can hardly do better than the Maimónides. Stumble out the front door and you run smack into the Mosque. And if it's the Mezquita you want to see, request a room with unequaled views of its rooftop (floodlit at night). That's probably enough to justify the price tag for some, but this once-grand hotel isn't up to the standards of the nearby Amistad. Even after it was finally renovated in the mid-1990s, rooms are still unexceptional, and bathrooms aren't exactly spacious. But the unpretentious Maimónides is a comfortable place to stay, and ideally positioned for short walks to not only the Mosque, but to the flamenco show down the street, and some of Córdoba's best restaurants in the Jewish Quarter.

Calle Torrijos, 4 (across from west side of Mosque). ☎ *957-47-15-00. Fax: 957-48-38-03. Parking: 1,600 pta. ($9). Rates: 15,200–17,000 pta. ($84–$94). AE, DC, MC, V.*

Hotel Mezquita
$–$$ Old Quarter

You can't get closer to the Mosque unless you sneaked in and slept inside (not something I recommend). It faces the main entrance of the great Mezquita-Catedral — hard to believe at these bargain prices. Its 21 immaculate rooms, all with individual air-conditioning units and satellite TV, are well-appointed; the antique furnishings, Moorish arches, and bold drapes and bedspreads give the hotel a funky charm. Some rooms have coveted views of the Mosque, while others overlook a cool, boldly colored central patio — a good place to hide from the heat of midday (unless you bolt straight for the air-conditioning). Like the Hotel González, which is owned by the same folks, this place has real Andalusian character at bargain prices.

Plaza Santa Catalina, 1 (off Calle M.G. Francés; on east side of the Mosque). ☎ *957-47-55-85. Fax: 957-47-62-19. Internet:* www.madeinspain.net/ hotelescordoba/mezquita. *Parking: nearby, 2,000 pta. ($11). Rack rates: 6,500–15,000 pta. ($36–$83). AE, DC, MC, V.*

Maestre
$ East of Centro

A ten-minute walk from the Mosque and Jewish Quarter, on two tiny, back-to-back streets overrun with *hostales* and *pensiones* (both informal types of guest houses), this is the best of the lot. It's a three-in-one establishment — hotel, hostel, and apartments — that hasn't stopped expanding since the mid-1970s. The hotel's the newest of the bunch, dating to 1992. Its 26 rooms are sparse and a bit dull, but they've got the basics: television, air conditioning, and small bathrooms. The lobby and interior courtyards, with Andalusian tiles and lots of greenery, are more comfortably outfitted than the rooms, so decide how much time you plan to spend in your room. If your answer's "not much," and that's about the amount you want to spend, you'll do fine here. If you've got a family in tow, check out the apartments, which feature one and two bedrooms, small kitchens, and eating areas.

Romero Barros 4–6 (small street off of Calle San Fernando, east of the Old City). ☎ **957-47-24-10.** *Fax: 957-47-53-95. Parking: 1,000 pta. ($5). Rates: 6,000–7,000 pta. ($33–$40). MC, V.*

NH Hotel Amistad Córdoba
$$$ Old Quarter

Occupying two former eighteenth-century mansions that face each other across a quiet plaza in the heart of the Jewish Quarter, this five-year-old hotel quickly leapt to the top of the heap, leaving old war horses Meliá Córdoba and Gran Capitán to the package tours. It's easily the choicest place to stay in Córdoba, and pretty fairly priced for this level of comfort. The neoclassical facades give way to a gorgeous central patio with Moorish arches and columns. Furnishings are cleanly modern, focusing on light woods, soft earthy tones, and occasional bright contemporary touches, like the royal purple chairs in the bar area. An upscale member of the Spanish NH hotel chain, it's next to the bullfighting museum and a just short shuffle from the old synagogue. The entrance that's cut right into the old Arab wall is a nice touch.

Plaza de Maimónides, 3 (off Calle Judíos in Jewish Quarter). ☎ **957-42- 03-35.** *Fax: 957-42-03-65. Internet:* www.nh-hoteles.es. *Parking nearby: 1,600 pta. ($9). Rates: 18,000 pta. ($100). AE, DC, MC, V.*

Parador de Córdoba (la Arruzafa)
$$$ Outskirts of Córdoba (in El Brillante)

Córdoba's large and thoroughly modern (except for the lack of daily maid service) *parador* (a historic government-run inn) is inconveniently located about three miles north of the historic quarter. It's not one of the *parador* system's best efforts — the NH Amistad in the Jewish Quarter beats it by a mile (see the previous review). You're best off staying here if Córdoba's heat and tourist hordes get to you; you can get away from it all with a dip in the refreshing pool or a volley on the tennis courts. The gardens are attractive and the panoramic vistas of the city are quite nice. The rooms aren't bad, though they don't rise above conventional. Try to get one with a balcony.

Avenida de la Arruzafa, 33 (3 miles north of city limits, in El Brillante neighborhood). ☎ **957-27-59-00.** *Fax: 957-29-04-09. E-mail:* cordoba@parador.es. *Internet:* www.parador.es. *Parking: free. Rates: 17,500 pta. ($97). AE, DC, MC, V.*

Dining in Córdoba

Córdoba has a small stable of good Andalusian restaurants, most of them clustered in and around the old Jewish Quarter. However, in contrast to the hotel scene, the city doesn't have too many good cheap places for dependable eats.

Eating like a Cordobés

The local cuisine, heavy on garlic and the olive oil in which Andalusia practically swims, concentrates on fried fish and stout meat dishes such as oxtail stew. Don't leave Córdoba without trying *salmorejo* ("sahl-moe-*ray*-ho"), a thick, tomato-based soup served cold. It's similar to gazpacho, but more like a puree and more substantial. On a hot day, it can feed you for lunch all by itself. You also find white gazpacho, or *ajoblanco* ("ah-hoe-*blahn*-koe"), made with olive oil, garlic, and almonds, topped off with grapes. *Rabo de toro* ("rah-bow day *toe*-roe," oxtail stew) is a staple in the Córdoba diet, as are *caldereta de cordero* ("kahl-day-ray-tah day core-day-roe," lamb) and *cochifrito de la sierra* ("koh-chee-free-toh day lah see-ay-rah," goat or mutton stew). Desserts show ancient Jewish and Moorish influences; try such pastries *pastel judío* ("pahs-*tell* hoo-*dee*-oh," a pastry made with citron preserves), *pestiños* ("pess-*teen*-yos," honey pancakes), and *buñuelos* ("boon-you-*ay*-los," fritters).

Drinking like a Cordobés

Although Andalusia's the place for *jerez* ("hair-*eth*," sherry), try the local variety, Montilla, an excellent dry and fragrant wine from the wine-producing region Montilla–Moriles. Perfect for *tapas, montilla* comes, like sherry, in several varieties: *finos* (fine and dry); *finos viejos,* also called *amontillados* (aged, fine wines); *olorosos* (aromatic wines); and *olorosos viejos* (aged aromatic wines).

Almudaina

$$$ Old Quarter   SPANISH/CONTINENTAL

The top-rated restaurant in Córdoba is also one of its most attractive. Almudaina is in a handsomely restored sixteenth-century mansion on a pleasing plaza, close to the Mezquita and Alcázar. There are six dining rooms, including a brick-walled and vine-covered central patio and elegant side rooms with lush drapes and chandeliers. Edelmiro Jiménez's market-based menu is continually changing, ranging from regional Cordobés dishes to French-inspired entrees. It's really hard to go wrong here; you may start with the excellent eggplant and *champiñones* (mushrooms), or the house foie gras, followed by *lubina* (sea bass) with shrimp and mushrooms. For dessert, the pear and nut mousse sounded great, but I was too stuffed to try it.

Jardín de los Santos Mártires, 1 (across Plaza Campo Santo de los Santos Mártires from the Alcázar). ☎ *957-47-43-42. Reservations recommended. Main courses: 1,800–3,800 pta. ($10–$21). AE, DC, MC, V. Open: Mon–Sat lunch and dinner; Sun lunch only; closed Sun in June–Aug.*

Bodegas Campo
$$$ Centro SPANISH/CONTINENTAL

A tavern and *bodega* (wine cellar) since 1908, this is one of the most inviting restaurants in Córdoba. The handsome, warmly rustic environment, decorated with vintage posters of the Córdoba May Festival, is flush with locals day and night. If you arrive early enough, have a drink in the *Sacristy,* a small atmospheric temple in back, past the wall lined by wooden wine vats signed by famous guests. Although wine is clearly an essential, the food is far from an afterthought. The kitchen of Javier Campos concentrates on local and regional dishes; for an appetizer, try the overflowing plate of *pescaditos fritos* (tiny fried fish, eaten whole), or the scrumptious *salmorejo* (a Cordobés version of gazpacho). *Solomillo ibérico* (sirloin steak) is a fine choice for the main course, if you've got a big appetite. Oh, and the cellar: It has a fine list of Spanish wine. Some are rather pricy, but the house red is excellent and a bargain.

Calle de los Lineros, 32 (one block in from Paseo de la Ribera along river; two blocks east of Plaza del Potro). ☎ *957-47-41-42. Reservations recommended. Main courses: 1,600–2,600 pta. ($9–$14); menú del día 4,750–5,000 pta. ($26–$27). AE, DC, MC, V. Open: Mon–Sat lunch and dinner; Sun lunch only; closed Sun in June–Aug.*

El Caballo Rojo
$$$ Old Quarter ANDALUSIAN/SPANISH

Córdoba's most famous and popular restaurant, El Caballo Rojo (The Red Horse) was a pioneer of Cordobés cooking, reviving ancient Moorish influences. Just yards from the Mezquita, this lively restaurant is one of the top spots to sample some classic Andalusian dishes, like *salmorejo* (cold, thick Cordobés *gazpacho*) and *rabo de toro* (oxtail stew), as well as inventive dishes, such as almond-and-apple white *gazpacho* and *rape mudéjar* (monkfish with raisins and pine nuts). The wine cellar is one of the most extensive in the city. The bar downstairs is always noisy with long-time regulars and tourists who've just stumbled in from the Mosque. Though that may make you fear for the worst, if you can handle the racket, you'll probably have a fun and even memorable meal here.

Cardinal Herrero, 28 (off Plaza de la Hoguera across from the Mosque). ☎ *957-47-53-75. Reservations recommended. Main courses: 1,600–3,400 pta. ($9–$19); menú del día 2,950 pta. ($17). AE, DC, MC, V. Open: Daily lunch and dinner.*

El Churrasco

$$$ Jewish Quarter   SPANISH

Right in the heart of the historic Judería, this is the place to come — as the name says — for *churrasco,* or juicy grilled meats. If the Cordobés sun has been beating on your head all day and meat sounds like a daunting proposition, start off with *ajoblanco* (white gazpacho) or artichokes in virgin olive oil, and see how your tastebuds warm to the idea. If you're not up to charcoal-grilled beef or pork loin, sample any of the tasty fish items, such as *rape a la oliva negra* (monkfish with black olives). The downstairs dining room, with the look of a Moorish courtyard, is more informal than the upstairs rooms. The bar at the entrance is a great place for a sherry or cold beer and tapas either before or instead of a meal.

Romero, 16 (two blocks west of the Mosque). ☎ *957-29-08-19. Reservations recommended. Main courses: 1,400–3,000 pta. ($8–$17); menú del día 3,000 pta. ($17). AE, DC, MC, V. Open: Daily for lunch and dinner; closed Aug.*

Mesón el Burlaero

$ Jewish Quarter   SPANISH/CONTINENTAL

Córdoba, surprisingly, doesn't have all that many good, cheap restaurants. For a bargain meal you can either sample some *tapas* or slip into this informal place at the end of an alleyway, just off Deanes — a five-minute walk from the Mosque. For a good, inexpensive lunch, you can't beat it — this is authentic Andalusian cuisine with few pretensions. There's a small outdoor patio and, indoors, simple checkered tablecloths. The daily specials are usually your best bet; among the frequent offerings are *salmorejo* (the local, thicker variety of *gazpacho*), oxtail, or pork loin.

Calleja la Hoguera, 5 (just off Deanes). ☎ *957-47-43-42. Reservations recommended. Main courses: 1,800–3,800 pta. ($10–$21). AE, DC, MC, V. Open: Mon–Sat lunch and dinner; Sun lunch only; closed Sun during June–Aug.*

Restaurante Pizzería Da Vinci

$$ Centro   ITALIAN/INTERNATIONAL

Tucked away in a *barrio* north of the historic Jewish Quarter, this isn't the straightforward pizza joint you'd expect from the name. Antonio Romero's restaurant does have an odiferous wood oven, and it does serve some excellent pastas, but he is equally focused on tempting roast meats, grilled and marinated fish, and nicely prepared salads. Da Vinci is the kind of good-value, neighborhood restaurant that's ideal for families — it has something for just about everybody, even grandma (if your grandma was like mine, stubbornly ordering spaghetti at seafood restaurants, and vice-versa).

Plaza de Los Chirinos, 6 (one block from Calle José Cruz Conde). ☎ *957-47-75-17. Reservations recommended. Main courses: 1,300–2,000 pta.($7–$11); menú del día 1,600 pta. ($9). V. Open: Daily lunch and dinner.*

Exploring Córdoba

Córdoba can't compare with Seville or Granada on the surface, because it has fewer attractions to detain most travelers. A day or day and a half is really all you need to explore the city's major sights. On the other hand, during festival time, you may never want to leave.

Córdoba's municipal museums, including the Reales Alcazares de los Reyes Cristianos (Royal Fortress and Gardens), Museo Taurino (Bullfighting Museum), and Julio Romero de Torres Museum (a collection of the Cordobés painter, on Plaza del Potro), are free on Fridays.

The top attractions

Alcázar de los Reyes Cristianos

Constructed on top of an old Moorish palace, the fourteenth-century Fortress of the Christian Monarchs, strategically located along the Guadalquivir River, served military and mercantilist purposes. For about eight years during the Reconquest, the Christian monarchs made the Gothic Alcázar their palace, and Christopher Columbus came here to schmooze and lobby the kings for funds to make his maiden voyage to the New World. The extensive gardens are truly regal, with a series of pools, water terraces, fountains, and palm and orange trees that reflect Córdoba's Moorish roots. Within the spare palace quarters (which once served as Inquisition headquarters) are archaeological finds from the area, including Roman mosaics and a sarcophagus from the third century. Below the Mosaics Room are steam baths that date to the time of the Moorish caliphate.

Two for the price of one

I'll leave you to draw your own conclusions about whether or not it was a heinous crime to insert a cathedral into the middle of the Great Mosque, thereby destroying the Mosque's perfect symmetry (and about a quarter of its pillars). Before the building of the Cathedral, one could see across the forest of pillars, surely a mind-bending optical effect. The Cathedral also destroyed the Mosque's perfect acoustics. (Even King Carlos V, who gave the okay to build the Cathedral, was dismayed upon seeing it. He reportedly exclaimed, "You have destroyed something unique to build something commonplace.")

Ironically, the building of the Cathedral may have saved the Mezquita. Of 300 mosques that once existed in Córdoba, the Great Mosque is the only one that remains, no doubt in tribute to its Christian church and treasures within, which precluded its sacking along with other remnants of Muslim Spain.

Flower Power: Calleja de las Flores

Córdoba is renowned for its stark, whitewashed houses enlivened by wrought-iron grilles, potted flowers, and windowboxes of colorful geraniums. Calleja de las Flores (literally, "little street of flowers") isn't much more than an alleyway just west of the Mosque (off Calles Blanco Belmonte and Victor Bosco), but it's a charming spot. Get your camera ready for the moment the Cathedral bell tower creeps into view, perfectly framed by the street's houses and arches. Other great *rincones* (corners) to spot Cordobeses' embrace of spring are domestic courtyards, which are often shared and gardened communal-style by a number of families. Annual contests are held to crown the best patios in Córdoba. Your best bet is to check with the Tourism Office, which organizes springtime visits to a number of them. Call ☎ 957-49-16-77 for additional information and tour times.

The fortress's imposing towers, the **Torre de los Leones** (Tower of the Lions) and **Torre de Homenaje** (Homage Tower), have been undergoing restoration for the past few years; with any luck, they should be open by the time you read this.

Calle Caballerizas Reales (between Guadalquivir River and Campo Santo de los Mártires). ☎ *957-42-01-51. Admission: 300 pta. ($1.75) or 425 pta. ($2.50) if towers are open. Open: summer, Tues–Sat 10 a.m.–2 p.m., 4:30–6:30 p.m., and Sun and holidays 9:30 a.m.–3 p.m.; winter, Tues–Sat 10 a.m.–2 p.m., 4–8 p.m. and Sun and holidays 9:30 a.m.–3 p.m.*

Barrio de La Judería

Córdoba's Jewish Quarter is a fascinatingand wonderfully alive area of impossibly narrow and crooked streets, ancient whitewashed houses with cool, colorful interior patios, and historic religious monuments. A stroll through the area is one of the highlights of Moorish Spain. When Córdoba was the largest and most advanced city in Europe in the tenth century, the cobbled streets teemed with silversmiths and craftsmen, and the residents — Jews, Christians, and Moors — all lived as they did in Toledo, in peace. Visit the **Sinagoga (Synagogue),** built in 1315 and the only Jewish temple in Andalusia that survived the tumult of the Inquisition and expulsion of Jews and Moors. If you're expecting cathedral-like grandeur, its utter simplicity will shock you: except for the stucco decorations, it's just a tiny, plain box. (An important Jewish community once thrived in Spain and built hundreds of synagogues, but the religious fervor of the Inquisition and Expulsion led to most Jews' publicly renouncing their faith or, more commonly, fleeing Spain. Only three synagogues remain in Spain: two in Toledo and the modest one in Córdoba.)

Pretty on the inside

Andalusian patios serve a very practical purpose — their construction at the center of the house, bathed in ceramic tiles and potted plants and vines, is essential for keeping the house cool. (The labyrinthine design of the Old Quarter, a Moorish innovation featuring houses close together on narrow streets, achieves the same cooling purpose.) But the patios' aesthetic flourishes also reflect a less pragmatic concern. At the heart of the Muslim religion is the notion that beauty is internal and should be kept private. Thus, most old Andalusian houses are simple on the outside; decoration is limited to the interior. The same concepts are apparent in Córdoba's Great Mosque. Notice how severe and unadorned its exterior is, compared to the unrestrained visual beauty concealed inside.

Across the street from the synagogue, but a world away, is the **Museo Taurino** — the Bullfighting Museum. Housed in a noble sixteenth-century house, Casa de las Bulas, it displays a replica of the famous bullfighter Manolete's tomb and other *toro* (bull) relics and memorabilia, including bulls' heads and the hide of the bull that gored Manolete to death. Four of Spain's greatest bullfighters, revered throughout the country, came from Córdoba and were known as the "four Caliphs of Córdoba."

Next to the museum is the **Zoco,** the old *souk,* or market area. Today it's again a market vying for your tourist dollars, with small shops dealing Córdoba crafts and jewelry. Just up the street from the synagogue is the **Puerta del Almodóvar** — Almodóvar's Gate. Nothing to do with Spain's hippest filmmaker, it's part of the original medieval entrance to the old Jewish Quarter. On the west side of the Judería are the remains of the old Arab city walls.

La Sinagoga: Calle Judíos. ☎ *957-20-29-28. Admission: 50 pta. (30¢); free to E.U. members. Open: Tues–Sat 10 a.m.–2 p.m. and 3:30–5:30 p.m.; Sun 10 a.m.–1:30 p.m.*

Museo Taurino: Plaza de Maimónides. ☎ *957-20-10-56. Admission: 425 pta. ($2.25); children under 18, free; Fri free. Open: winter, Tues–Sat 10 a.m.–2 p.m. and 5–7 p.m., Sun 9:30 a.m.–3 p.m.; summer, Tues–Sat 10 a.m.–2 p.m. and 6–8 p.m.; Sun 9:30 a.m.–3 p.m.*

Mezquita (Great Mosque)
Jewish Quarter (La Judería)

Córdoba's astonishing Mosque is one of Moorish Spain's greatest achievements, one of Spain's most enduring and treasured monuments, and one of the world's most remarkable mosques. It's brilliant, surprising, and it packs a historical wallop. You'd hardly guess its glory from the mostly plain exterior, though. The Moorish Emir Ab-ar Rahman I ordered it built in A.D. 786 at the height of power of al-Andalus — Muslim Spain (the Moors controlled all but a small sliver of northern Spain, in the present-day Basque Country). The Mosque was significantly enlarged over the next two centuries (the original mosque is only about one-fifth of the present structure), and in the sixteenth century, part of it was destroyed when, in an act of either *hubris* or revenge, Christians constructed a cathedral smack in the middle of the mosque. This juxtaposition may strike you as an abomination; at the very least, it stands as a fascinating document of Spanish religious and political history.

Enter through the **Patio de los Naranjos** (a large patio of orange trees, where the faithful prayed and cleansed themselves before entering the mosque). Even if you've seen pictures of the interior, the magical forest of candy-cane striped arches — a seemingly limitless horizon of dazzling harmony — will astound you. More than 850 columns and purely decorative arches of granite, jasper, and marble fill 19 aisles. Notice the capitals, which were rescued in large part from ancient (that is to say, *more* ancient) structures in Córdoba (the Mosque was built on the site of a Visigothic basilica). The mosaic tiles and marble that once covered the floors are now sadly gone, as are most of the polychrome ceilings, but the Mosque's grandeur resonates throughout. Wander in a delirious daze, but don't miss the *mihrab,* the wonderfully ornate prayer niche in the southeast corner of the mosque. A feast of carved marble, stucco, alabaster, and mosaics, it pointed to Mecca and was the most sacred part of the Mosque. Look up at its magnificent cupola.

The **Capilla Real** (Royal Chapel) and **Capilla Villaviciosa** (Villaviciosa Chapel), the first Christian components of the complex, are *mudéjar* (a hybrid of Moorish and Christian architecture) in style and were ordered by Ferdinand III in 1236, as part of the Reconquest. The ostentatious Italianate dome of the **Catedral** (Cathedral), begun in 1253, is a startling contrast to the mesmerizing quiet beauty of the Mosque. The Cathedral's saving graces are its magnificently carved mahogany choir stalls, which date to 1758, depict the Old and New Testaments, and pulpits, also beautiful works of carving.

Unfortunately, you won't get to enjoy the spectacular views of Córdoba and the Sierra from the top of the belfry; it remains closed for restoration, as it has for years.

In summer, the interior of the Mosque is heaven on earth, a blessed retreat from the sun (something the Moors surely considered when they designed it in Córdoba). But if you visit Córdoba in winter, even though the sun may shine brilliantly outside and you're decked out comfortably in shorts and sandals, it can get very chilly inside the Mosque. Like going to the movie theater on a blistering day, you're wise to bring a sweater.

Calle Torrijos, 10 (one block north of river). ☎ *957-47-05-12. Admission: 800 pta. ($4.50). Open: daily, winter 10 a.m.–5:30 p.m.; summer 10 a.m.–7 p.m.*

More cool things to see and do

✔ **Peeking in on patios.** Córdoba's known for its splendid patios, but outside of the May patio festival, finding and getting in to see the best ones is sometimes hard. For the best glimpse of aristocratic Córdoba, you have to venture a bit north of the Old Quarter. Tucked away in a busy commercial district, Palacio de Viana, Plaza de Don Gome, 2 (five blocks west of Calle Alfaros, southwest of Plaza de Colón — take bus to Plaza Colón; ☎ 957-48-01-34), is a sumptuous sixteenth-century palace, which locals call El Museo de los Patios — The Patio Museum. The mansion has 14 elegant interior patios, as well as halls decorated with rich furnishings, Goya tapestries, carved cedar ceilings, and rare tiles. Admission is 500 pta. ($2.75). It's open daily, 9 a.m. to 2 p.m. and closed the first two weeks of June (but you can still visit the patios).

✔ **Taking a magical history tour.** South of the Mosque, at the bend in the Guadalquivir River, are two important works of architecture dating to Córdoba's Roman and Moorish eras, Calahorra Tower and the Roman Bridge. The bridge isn't a quaint Roman artifact, but a heavily trafficked thoroughfare with 16 arches. The sad river, all but washed up now, mirrors the city's decline. The Romans used the river as a commercial waterway, and the Moors tapped into its power with waterwheels and mills (still visible from the bridge today). Cross the bridge (notice the shrine to St. Raphael, the archangel of Córdoba, about mid-way, which is usually decorated with flowers and lit candles) to approach the Calahorra Tower, built in the mid-fourteenth century to guard the entrance to the city. Today it houses an audiovisual museum, **Museo Vivo de Al-Andalus,** Puente Romano, s/n (☎ 957-29-39-29), with exhibits and a multimedia presentation on the three distinct religious and cultures upon which Córdoba is founded. While a good opportunity for kids to learn about Moorish Spain, the museum is probably best if you approach it like an escapist action flick on a hot summer day — a place of refuge. To get there, cross the Roman bridge just south of the Mosque. Admission is 500 pta. ($2.75) for adults, 400 pta. ($2.20) for children; the multimedia presentation is 650 pta. ($3.50) adults, 550 pta. ($3) children. The museum is open winter, daily 10 a.m. to 6 p.m. (Multivisión projection at 11 a.m. and 12, 1, 3, and 4 p.m.); summer, 10 a.m. to 2 p.m. and 5:30 to 8:30 p.m. (Multivisión projections are at 10:30 and 11:30 a.m., 12:30, 6, and 7 p.m.).

✔ **Hanging out in a plaza.** The attractively weathered square **Plaza del Potro** is best known for its historic inn, La Posada del Potro (Inn of the Colt), where Miguel de Cervantes, the author of *Don Quixote,* once stayed (the plaza figures into his epic novel). You can easily see that the inn was the kind of place where overnighters once pulled up on horseback and tied their steeds to the railing outside their rooms. Across the plaza, the **Museo de Bellas Artes de Córdoba** (Fine Arts Museum), Plaza del Potro, 1 (one block west of Calle San Fernando; a ten-minute-walk from the Mosque; ☎ 957-47-33-45), occupies a fifteenth-century charity hospital and has a small collection of Seville school painters and Cordobés artists. A number of outdoor cafes occupy the pedestrian street opposite the plaza and are good places to rest your legs and slurp an icy lemonade. Admission is 250 pta. ($1.40); free for members of the E.U. (European Union). The museum is open winter, Wednesday to Saturday 10 a.m. to 2 p.m. and 5 to 7 p.m., Sunday and holidays 10 a.m. to 1:30 p.m.; summer, 10 a.m. to 1:30 p.m. and 4 to 8 p.m., Sunday and holidays 10 a.m. to 1:30 p.m.

✔ **Digging up the past.** Most everything of interest in Córdoba relates to the city's multi-layered past, so a good way to explore those layers is to see what's been unearthed at Córdoba's **Museo Arqueológico** (Archaeology Museum), Plaza de Jerónimo Páez, 7 (between the Mosque and Plaza del Potro; ☎ 957-47-40-11). It occupies a handsome Renaissance palace and is a survey of the city's (which is to say, Spain's) history, with Roman, Visigothic, Muslim, Mudéjar, and Renaissance pieces. The diverse collection includes fantastic ceramics, mosaics, sarcophagi, and a terrific bronze stag that came from a fountain at the Medina Azahara palace (see "Side trips from Córdoba: A visit to the ruins of Medina Azahara," later in this chapter). The Moorish decorative arts are particularly well represented. Admission is 250 pta. ($1.40), free for members of the EU (European Union). It's open winter, Wednesday to Saturday 10 a.m. to 2 p.m. and 5 to 7 p.m., Sunday and holidays 10 a.m. to 1:30 p.m.; summer, 10 a.m. to 1:30 p.m. and 4 to 8 p.m., Sunday and holidays 10 a.m. to 1:30 p.m.

Bulls and horses

Toro, Toro, Toro: Córdoba's new Plaza de Toros (bullfighting ring), **Coso de los Califas,** is on the outskirts of town, on Avenida Gran Vía. Most big bullfighting events are in May (usually the last week), to coincide with the city festivals, but there are other scheduled bullfights in this *toros*-crazy town. Call ☎ **957-23-25-07** for information and tickets. Prices range from 1,000–12,500 pta. ($5.50–$69).

Horsing around: Andalusia is famous for its gorgeous, regal thoroughbred horses, and yousee them dolled up and on parade during the city's famous May Festivals. The **Club Hípico de Córdoba** has jumping tournaments, and there are horse-taming exhibitions at Caballerizas Reales, next to the Alcázar. If you'd like to hop up in the saddle yourself, visit the Club Hípico de Córdoba, Carretera de Trassiera, km 9 (☎ **957-35-02-08**).

A suggested one-day Córdoba itinerary

Head directly to the center of old town, near the river, and to the great Mezquita. Spend the majority of your time in Córdoba in the Mosque. On the way out, take a breather in the Patio de los Naranjos, and then head to the nearby Judería (Jewish Quarter). Visit the tiny fourteenth-century synagogue, the third major monument representing Córdoba's trio of faiths. Afterwards, see the lovely gardens of the Alcázar (fortress of the Christian Monarchs). If you're in Córdoba in spring or summer, the Calleja de las Flores will burst with color, with potted plants and brilliant geraniums adorning the whitewashed houses there. If you have time, wander the old Jewish Quarter, peeking in on patios, doing some shopping, and ducking in a restaurant or bar for *tapas* and sherry.

Shopping for Córdoba crafts

All these years after the Reconquest, Córdoba is still known for traditional Moorish crafts, such as handmade gold and silver filigree and embossed leather goods, known worldwide as Cordovan leather. All kinds of artisan shops featuring traditional Cordobés goods line (a bit too thickly for some tastes, perhaps) the Judería. A mark — a crowned lion and the name of the city — distinguishes the embossed Cordovan leathers.

Good souvenirs include *sevillana* dresses (the ruffly and frequently polka-dotted dresses worn by flamenco dancers and Andalusian women and girls during spring festivals), and *sombreros Cordobeses* (flat, wide-brimmed, black hats).

For handcrafts of all sorts, particularly jewelry, check out the **Zoco Municipal de Artesanía,** the old *medina* (Middle Eastern market) on Calle Judíos, just behind the bullfighting museum. It's open daily from 10 a.m. to 8:30 p.m. There are so many others, lining the streets Deanes, Romero, and the Plaza Leví that picking out just a couple is impossible. Browse the streets not far from the Mezquita.

If you're in the market for traditional leather goods from Córdoba, be careful of items advertised as embossed or handtooled Cordovan leather. Some of the sneakier shops may try to pass off inferior stamped leather from Morocco as the real thing. Nothing against Morocco, but the work is generally of lesser quality. Touch and inspect the product, and look for the lion symbol (though that too may be an imposter). Once you've seen the real stuff, distinguishing between it and the inferior imposters shouldn't be too hard.

For authentic leather goods, drop by the shop of talented artisan **Carlos López-Obrero.** His shop, specializing in hand-tooled leather and embossed leather products, is on Calleja de las Flores, 2 (no phone).

Taller Meryan, at the same address (☎ 957-47-59-02) is one of Córdoba's best shops and factories for quality embossed leather products.

La noche: Córdoba's nightlife

You're in one of the legendary cities of Andalusia, the old Moorish kingdom. So what to do at night? Simple. Join the waves of Cordobeses at taverns for tapas and the local spirits, and after that, be a tourist: Catch an animated flamenco show. If you're in Córdoba during the annual Guitar Festival (July), you won't want to miss seeing some great picking on the Spanish guitar.

Setting out on a tapas and tavern crawl

A *tapas* and tavern crawl in Córdoba is virtually irresistible. Here are a few local faves, great places to duck in out of the heat, have a *montilla* (similar to sherry) or *fino* (dry sherry) and order a small portion of Serrano ham, chorizo, *aceitunas* (green olives), or *queso* (cheese). These places are very casual and not the type where youl need reservations — plus, virtually no one speaks English here. There's no need to call ahead, and in accordance, I don't list phone numbers here. **Bodega Zoco** (Calle Judíos, s/n) is a fantastic underground stone catacomb of a place in the old *medina*. Go down the stairs at the back of the market into the relief of natural refrigeration. The *chorizo al vino* (sausage soaked in *montilla* wine) is a house specialty. Just up the street is **Bodegas Guzman** (Calle Judíos, s/n), an atmospheric place with wonderful 1920s and 30s posters from the May Festivals at the entrance and a crowd of regulars at the bar. **Bodegas Campo** (Calle de los Lineros, 32) is an excellent restaurant (see the listing in the restaurant section of this chapter) with a tiny bar at the entrance, but the real star is the sexy *Sacristía* (a *tapas* temple) at back, past the wine vats. **Mesón Juan Peña** (Calle Dr. Fleming, 1) has a terrific wine cellar, while the cinematic bar **Pepe el de la Judería** (Pepe of the Jewish Quarter; Calle Romero, 1) is a revered institution that's served drinks to generations of Cordobeses, and looks the part. Pick up a copy of the owner's book, *Cordobeses Ilustres* (Illustrious Cordovans). But the oldest-tavern-in-Córdoba award goes to **Casa Miguel** (Plaza Cirino, 7), serving great *tapas* since the early 1800s.

Performing arts: Flamenco and more

You're in the heart of Andalusia, and though the local flamenco scene is small, it's still one of the most traditional places in Spain to see flamenco dancing and emotional *cante hondo* (deep song). The place to be is **Tablao Cardenal,** Calle Torrijos, 10 (☎ 957-48-33-20), just across from the Mezquita. In a pretty open-air square, the group puts on a very respectable flamenco show that doesn't pander to tourists or try to wow them with cheap pyrotechnics. The sparks here are real. There are shows every night but Sunday and Monday at 10:30 p.m. The price is 2,800 pta. ($16), which includes your first drink. Reserving a spot in advance is wise, because it's popular, and once a large group shows up, there may be no more tickets. Try to score a seat as close to the stage as possible.

On occasion, you can catch flamenco at the **Gran Teatro de Córdoba,** but more often you find opera, classical music, and ballet. It's on Avenida del Gran Capitán (☎ **957-48-02-37**).

Jamming to fast-fingered guitar playing

Most Spanish guitar greats — such as Paco de Lucía and Tomatito — hail from Andalusia. Spanish classical and flamenco guitar derives, like most everything in southern Spain, from the region's indelible Muslim past. The playing evolved from the sounds of the classical Arab lute. Every July, Córdoba hosts the **Festival Internacional de la Guitarra** (International Guitar Festival), one of its most popular events. If you're here then, it's a great opportunity to see Spanish guitar maestros work their magic on the strings. From classical Spanish guitar to flamenco, you can see some of the fastest hands in the west, performing in great spots in the Old City — the gardens of the Alcázar, the Botanical Gardens, and the Gran Teatro (Grand Theater of Córdoba). The Spanish Tourism Offices abroad (see Appendix A) usually have their hands on a schedule several weeks in advance, or, once in Córdoba, ask for a schedule of performances at the Tourism Office.

Side trips from Córdoba: A visit to the ruins of Medina Azahara

If Córdoba's Great Mosque whetted your appetite for more remnants of the glorious Moorish domination of Spain, consider a short side trip to the ruins of **Medina Azahara,** or Medinat al-Zahara (☎ **957-32-91-30**). Built in the foothills of the Sierra Morena in 961 by the Caliph Adb ar Rahman III as a gift to one of his wives (judging by the opulence, she was a favorite), the palace was once a small, stunning city with 400 houses, 300 baths, a mosque, fortress, zoo, and luxurious gardens. Archaeologists believe that the palace was perhaps unrivaled in its opulence, with jewel-encrusted pillars, gold fountains, and quicksilver pools. The caliph supposedly had almond trees planted all the way to Córdoba — he liked the visual effect of the trees in bloom, which rolled out a snowy white carpet up to his dream palace. Just seven decades after its laborious construction (which required 10,000 men), the 300-acre compound was sacked and destroyed by the Almoravids, a group of Berbers with a political beef against the Al Mansur dynasty. The ruins of the grand hall, terraces, and living quarters, unearthed this century, merely suggest the grandeur of the palace-city on the outskirts of Córdoba, but they're worth a visit, even though they're surely not the posthumous record of his rule ar-Rahman meant to leave. Sections are being painstakingly reconstructed, though, and the Royal Palace doesn't require much imagination.

Medina Azahara is 8 km (5 miles) west of Córdoba at Kilometer 5.5. A car or taxi is pretty much essential (the bus leaves you about 2 miles from the palace). Take Avenida de Medina Azahara and C-431 west from Córdoba to Palma del Río. Admission is 250 pta. ($1.40). Hours are Tuesday through Saturday 10 a.m. to 2 p.m. and 4 to 6 p.m.; Sunday open 10 a.m. to 2 p.m. only. (Before heading out, check with the Tourism Office, because hours can vary.)

Fast Facts: Córdoba

Area Code

Córdoba's area code is **957**, which you must dial before every number.

Currency Exchange

You can find banks and ATM machines in the main shopping district in the Old Quarter near the Mezquita and along Avenida Gran Capitán in the modern business section of town (Banco de España, Banco Bilbao Vizcaya, and Banco BNP España are all located almost on top of each other on that street). A *casa de cambio* (exchange house) is Cambio de Divisas, Calle Cardenal Herrero, 30 (☎ **957-47-96-99**).

Emergencies

For medical emergencies, dial ☎ **061** or call the Cruz Roja (Red Cross) at ☎ **957-22-22-22**. For an ambulance call ☎ **957-29-55-70**. In case of fire call ☎ **080**. For a police emergency, call ☎ **091**.

Hospitals

Hospital Reina Sofía is located on Avenida Menéndez Pidal, s/n (☎ **957-21-70-00**). Hospital Los Morales is on Sierra de Córdoba, s/n (☎ **957-27-56-50**).

Information

The Andalusia Provincial Tourism Office is located at Torrijos, 10 (☎ **957-47-12-35** and 957-49-16-77), right next to the Mezquita. A municipal tourism office is located at Plaza Judá Leví (☎ **957-20-05-22**). They're open daily from 9 a.m. to 8 p.m.

Police

The municipal police station is at Campo Madre de Dios, s/n (☎ **957-23-37-53** or ☎ **092**).

Post Office

Córdoba's main post office is on Cruz Conde, 15 (☎ **957-47-81-02** or 957-47-82-67).

Safety

Córdoba is an exceedingly friendly and low-key town, but it's also a city that suffers perennially from unemployment and economic hardship. With the large number of tourists that traipse in and out, often along twisting, confusing streets, the city has gained an unfortunate reputation as a place where thieves prey on tourists — though it has always seemed safe to me. While there's no need to be alarmed, be careful if you venture beyond the Jewish Quarter and the area around the Mosque — areas with a noticeable police presence. Some parts west of Calle de San Fernando are uncomfortably deserted and perfect places for thieves-in-waiting. Leave valuables and extra money at the hotel safe, and try to carry things you don't want to lose on the front of your body.

Chapter 17

The Pueblos Blancos of Andalusia

. . . .

In This Chapter

▶ Enjoying Andalusia's *Pueblos Blancos*

▶ Driving through whitewashed medieval villages

▶ Exploring the leisurely south: Beaches and golf on Andalusia's famed coasts

. . . .

A ndalusia's *Pueblos Blancos* (white towns), small whitewashed villages clustered in the mountainous region between Seville and the sea, are southern Spain at its most mythical. Sprinkled throughout a dramatic landscape of olive groves and rugged, 5,000-foot limestone slopes are dazzling white villages improbably cleaved into rocky bluffs. Former defensive strongholds, their perfect whiteness is interrupted only by castle ruins and church bell towers.

The white towns of Andalusia look like entire North African villages uprooted and shipped by boat to the south of Spain. The Romans and Visigoths settled the region, but the Moors built these memorable medieval villages with impenetrable alleyways and thickly whitewashed houses. Ronda and Arcos de la Frontera are the largest white towns, with the best infrastructure for visitors. And they're within easy reach of Andalusia's famous sherry bodegas (wineries) in Jerez, the beaches of the Costa de la Luz, and mega-developed Costa del Sol.

Just the Facts: The Pueblos Blancos and the Coasts

Ronda and the other white towns are in the mountainous interior of Spain's southernmost provinces, Cádiz and Málaga. The only things farther south are the Andalusian coastlines and Africa. The white towns are mostly scattered about the Sierra de Grazalema Nature Reserve.

Andalusia

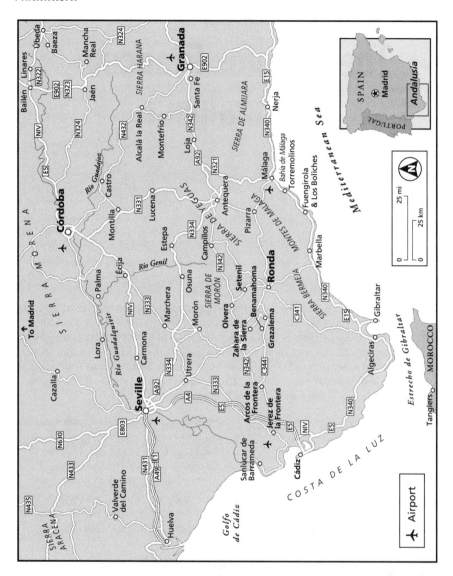

✔ **The way to go.** From any point in Andalusia, you can reach the white towns by car or rail, but they're a hike to get to if you're coming from another region of Spain. (Including them as part of a tour of southern Spain is best.) Likewise, you can easily reach the Costa del Sol and Costa de la Luz from Ronda and Arcos de la Frontera, respectively.

✔ **The name game.** Call the towns with long names by the first words in their names only. For example, Arcos de la Frontera is just "Arcos"; Jerez de la Frontera is "Jerez" ("hair-*eth*"); Zahara de la Sierra is "Zahara"; and Setenil de las Bodegas is "Setenil."

✔ **The forecast.** The white towns are mountain towns, so they're not as dreadfully hot as Andalusia's Big Three (Seville, Granada, and Córdoba). Winter is mild, while spring and fall are warm but comfortable. The southern coast is all about sun, getting more than 300 sunny days a year.

✔ **When to go.** The absolute best time to visit Ronda and the rest of the white towns is spring (March, April, and May), when flowers are in bloom across the valleys. If you can't make your trip then, fall is also nice and winter isn't bad, because the sun shines year-round. Likewise, the coasts are great year-round, but ridiculously crowded in summer.

✔ **How long before moving on?** The towns in this chapter are ideal for a driving itinerary. The only town where you really want and need to linger is Ronda. A peaceful place that you can see in half a day, Ronda makes a very enjoyable stopover. Arcos and Ronda are both good bases from which to set out and explore the white towns, so you may want to spend a night or more in either. Most of the small white towns are places to spin through, perhaps have lunch, and then move on.

Major Attractions in the Pueblos Blancos

Ronda and the Pueblos Blancos cover a relatively small area between Seville and the southernmost tip of Spain. The Gulf of Cádiz and the Mediterranean Sea surrounds this mountainous, agricultural region. Traveling by car, you really don't need all that much time to get around to a handful of the most picturesque white towns. Start either in Arcos or in Ronda and work your way from one to the other.

Ronda

The largest and perhaps most tourist-friendly *pueblo* (it simply has more infrastructure than any of the other white towns), historic Ronda is also one of the prettiest and most photogenic places in Spain. Here you find:

✔ **Puente Nuevo** is a daring 200-year-old bridge built over a sheer 300-foot drop, the **Tajo Gorge.**

✔ **Plaza de Toros** is Spain's oldest bullfighting ring, where legends have fought and eighteenth-century traditions still live.

✔ Sprinkled throughout the area are noble mansions, palaces, and **Roman baths.**

Pueblos Blancos

More than two dozen whitewashed villages dot the Sierra de Cádiz and the Sierra de Grazalema. The towns — which owe their distinctive look to the Moors, who inhabited this part of Spain for eight centuries — are themselves major attractions. Most have castles and cathedrals perched dramatically above the plains below. Look for these attractions in the Pueblos Blancos:

- **Arcos de la Frontera,** the westernmost of the white towns, is huddled atop a wedge of rock, high above the Guadalete River.

- **Jerez de la Frontera,** an easy side trip from Arcos, is the home of sherry and dancing Spanish horses.

- A driving route, which passes through a succession of small white mountain towns, each one prettier than the last.

The Costa del Sol and Costa de la Luz

The south of Spain has drawn beach worshippers for decades. You can choose between the relatively tranquil Costa de la Luz (Coast of Light) and self-indulgent, massively developed, and touristy Costa del Sol (Coast of the Sun). However, you don't have a choice about the weather — sunny and hot is the rule. Attractions in Costa del Sol and Costa de la Luz include:

- Rough, sandy **beaches** with strong winds

- **Golf courses** galore

- All the **nightlife** and beautiful people you can handle

Touring Arcos de la Frontera

Arcos de la Frontera (often shortened to Arcos), one of the prettiest of the Pueblos Blancos, is perched daringly on a red-rock promontory high above the Guadalete River. The town is so narrow at the top that squeezes down to a single street. Although there's little to see and less to do in Arcos, it is a good place to base yourself for the first half of a Pueblo Blancos tour. (Jerez de la Frontera also makes a decent base, but I like Arcos because it's smaller and less congested.) Arcos serves as a natural gateway to the villages; you can set out by car in the morning and do a loop of the western and southern white towns. Alternatively, it's a short trip to Jerez and a good starting point for travels to Cádiz and the Costa de la Luz.

Check out those bullboards

As you drive across the rolling landscape of the south, the oddest thing appears on the horizon: a Godzilla-sized black bull. Up close, you quickly realize that the anatomically correct bull is nothing more than a 30-foot-tall wood cutout of a bull — like a billboard without a product. In fact, that's exactly what it is. Several decades ago, Osborne, the famous winemaker in Jerez, erected bullboards across Spain to promote its sherries and brandies. When Spain outlawed all rural billboard advertising, nostalgic Spaniards, who grew up pointing out the bulls on car trips, protested and convinced Parliament to make an exception to the law. The government allowed the Osborne billboards to stand, officially designated National Historic Monuments, as long as they were stripped of all advertising.

Arriving in Arcos

To get to Arcos, you have to drive or take a bus; the closest train destination is Jerez de la Frontera, which is 20 miles away.

Driving to Arcos is easy, and, as a bonus, scenic. From Seville, take N-IV or A-4 south toward Jerez de la Frontera. Take the turn-off, N-342, east to Arcos. Arcos is 91 km (56 miles) from Seville; the drive should take just a bit over an hour.

Two buses a day (at 8 a.m. and 4:30 p.m.) go from Seville's Santa Justa Station to Arcos (the bus line is **Amarillos ☎ 95-498-91-84**) for a cost of 905 pta. ($5). You can also take buses from Cádiz and Jerez de la Frontera.

Getting around Arcos

Arcos is so small that you must rely on your feet to get you up and down the steep passageways and stairs. A rental car is the only practical way to get around from one Pueblo Blanco to another. (Unless, of course, you hate to drive and have oodles of money, in which case you can hire a taxi driver for the day.)

Staying in Arcos

You can find all the hotels listed here, with the exception of the farm stay, in Arcos's *zona monumental* (historic district).

Cortijo Fain

$$

Staying in the old Arab city of Arcos, high above the river, certainly has its charm. But if the tiny, whitewashed streets make you claustrophobic, check out Cortijo Fain, a beautiful *hacienda* in the midst of olive groves, just 2 miles from Arcos. The seventeenth-century farmhouse, brilliant white and adorned with purple bougainvillea, has a pretty pool in a garden setting. Rustically charming, it's the kind of place featured in fashion shoots. Cortijo Fain has only been a hotel for about a decade, and the ten rooms look more like an authentic country house than a hostelry. If you want to play country gentleman or dame, ask about horseback riding and retire in the evening to the well-stocked library. A two-bedroom setup is a good option for families.

Carretera de Algar, km 3 (from Arcos, take the road to Algar and look for signs). ☎/*Fax: 956-23-13-96. Parking: free. Rates: 12,000 pta. ($67). AE, DC, MC, V.*

El Convento

$–$$

Tucked into the historic district, down a tiny alleyway behind the *parador* (government-run hotel), this little find typifies the allure of the Pueblos Blancos. Built right into the Las Mercedarias Convent (hence the name), it only has 11 rooms, but they're a terrific value for the price, and they were completely renovated in 1998. The hotel, which has a fine restaurant (which shares the hotel's name and is reviewed later in this chapter) and rooftop terrace, offers great views over the gorge and countryside. Its charm and comfort has placed this hotel in high demand. Make a reservation as soon as you decide to spend the night in Arcos.

Maldonado, 2 (take Calle Escribanos from Plaza del Cabildo and turn right on Maldonado). ☎ *956-70-23-33. Fax: 956-70-41-28. Parking: 500 pta. ($2.75). Rates: 10,000–12,000 pta. ($55–$67) Mar–Oct; 7,000–9,000 pta. ($39–$50) Jan–Feb. AE, DC, MC, V.*

Hotel Los Olivos

$–$$

This attractive old two-story Andalusian townhouse with a pretty interior patio was converted into a lovely, small hotel. Its 19 rooms are comfortable, with wicker chairs and long, sheer curtains, but you may just want to spend all your time relaxing in the whitewashed patio and airy sitting rooms. Some rooms have splendid views of the olive groves beyond Arcos.

Paseo de Boliches, 30 (on main road into zona monumental). ☎ *956-70-08-11. Fax: 956-70-20-18. E-mail:* mmoreno0237@viautil.com. *Parking: 700 pta. ($4). Rates: 7,000–10,000 pta. ($39–$55). AE, DC, MC, V.*

Parador de Arcos de la Frontera (Casa del Corregidor)
$$$

You can't ask for a more dramatic location. This Parador, one of the more impressive in the chain, hugs the gorge, unleashing unbelievable views of the valley below that wows adults and kids alike. The building is on the site of the *Casa del Corregidor,* an eighteenth-century palace and seat of government. The hotel was given a makeover, and the rooms are modern with a cozy, American Southwest feel. Some of them have small balconies where you can sit and congratulate yourself for sitting on top of the world in southern Spain. The staff is uniformly friendly, which isn't always the case at paradors.

Plaza del Cabildo, s/n (overlooking gorge, next to the castle and Santa María church). ☎ ***956-70-05-00.*** *Fax: 956-70-11-16; E-mail:* arcos@parador.es. *Internet:* www.parador.es. *Parking: free. Rates: 17,500 pta. ($97). Inquire about discounts for families with children. DC, MC, V.*

Dining in Arcos

As with hotels, you can find the restaurants listed here in Arcos's *zona monumental* (historic district). In addition to what's listed in this section, the Parador de Arcos de la Frontera, described in the preceding section, has a handsome dining room serving regional specialties, with a fixed-price menu (lunch or dinner) for 3,500 pta. ($19).

Bar Alcaraván
$ TAPAS

If you're not really in the mood for a full sit-down meal, or you've already eaten at the other two main options that I mention in this section, drop into this amiable downstairs bar, which the cheerful owner says offers "the best *tapas* (appetizers) in town." He doesn't have a lot of competition, but you can assemble a fine meal from the *chorizo* (spicy pork sausage), *champiñones* (sautéed mushrooms), and *estofado de cordero* (lamb stew). The bar occupies tunnels, which may date to the tenth century, that run underneath the town's old Moorish castle (see the following section, "Exploring Arcos").

Calle Nueva, s/n (just behind castle). No phone. Tapas: 300–750 pta. ($1.75–$4). Open: daily for lunch and dinner; closed Sun evenings. AE, DC, MC, V.

El Convento
$$ ANDALUSIAN

Part of the hotel of the same name (see the review in the preceding hotel section), the restaurant's husband-wife team that also owns the Olivos Hotel in town saved the best for their kitchen. The restaurant is absolutely charming, and though tiny, has won several national culinary awards. They specialize in local cuisine that they say farmers in the area used to eat, which means game and meat dishes. For starters, try the *abajao* (asparagus soup for two). Main courses include lamb with aromatic herbs and *perdiz en salsa de almendras* (partridge in almond sauce). The wine cellar also has a few nice surprises.

Maldonado, 2 (take calle Escribanos from Plaza del Cabildo and turn right on Maldonado). ☎ *956-70-23-33. Main courses: 1,500–2,000 pta. ($8–$11). Open: daily for lunch and dinner. AE, DC, MC, V.*

Exploring Arcos

Arcos offers little to do, but the point of being here is to take in the spectacular site of this whitewashed village carved into a crag and the views down the gorge and over the countryside. The tiny alleys are fun to explore, but you can see the whole place in an hour. You can then plan your tour of the other white towns.

For photo opportunities, head to the **Balcón de Arcos,** an overlook in the *Plaza del Cabildo* — it literally hangs over the edge of the cliff. The old Moorish castle on the same plaza dates from the tenth century and the Ben Jazrum dynasty; it's been perfectly restored, but is off-limits to visitors (the owners live in it — lucky devils). The **Iglesia de Santa María** on the square is a church with a jumble of styles: Gothic, Mudéjar, Renaissance, and Baroque, with a splendid Plateresque façade (for more information on Spanish architectural styles, consult Appendix B). (Santa María is open daily 10 a.m. to 1 p.m. and 4 to 6:30 p.m., with guided visits Tuesday through Saturday at 10:30 a.m. Admission is 300 pta., or $1.75).

Walk down the main street out of *Plaza del Cabildo* to the **Iglesia de San Pedro** (on Calle San Pedro), which has a terrific Renaissance altarpiece, as well as paintings by Zurbarán and Ribera. Another great lookout point nearby for snapping pics is the **Mirador de Abades,** at the end of Calle Abades.

Before leaving Arcos for good, take the south exit from the city (toward Algar), which offers a gorgeous view of the gorge's sheer drop and the town above it.

A side trip to Jerez de la Frontera

Jerez de la Frontera (also called simply Jerez), lodged between the sea and the Sierra de Grazalema Mountains, is the Andalusian capital of wine and horses. It's the home of *jerez* (sherry) and the famous *Real Escuela Andaluza del Arte Ecuestre* — the Royal Andalusian School of Equestrian Arts. I suggest you visit one or two of Jerez's *bodegas* (wineries) and the horse school on a day's excursion from Arcos. If you're interested in hitting the coast, use the city as a base from which to explore Cádiz and the Costa de la Luz (in general, though, its hotels aren't that impressive; I prefer the three hotels in Arcos that I review previously in this chapter).

Arriving in Jerez

Jerez is a straight drive from Seville along N-IV or A-4. You should arrive in just a bit over an hour (it's 97 km, or 60 miles).

Two bus companies offer a total of 11 buses a day (from 5:30 a.m. to 8 p.m.) from Seville's Santa Justa station to Jerez. The lines are **Transportes Comes** (☎ 95-441-52-01) and **Linesur** (☎ 95-498-82-22). Both charge 875 pta., or $5, one-way. You can also catch buses from Cádiz and Arcos de la Frontera.

Likewise, you can take train service from Madrid and Seville. There are two daily high-speed TALGO trains from Madrid (2 hours, 10 minutes) leaving at 10:05 a.m.(9,000 pta., or $50, one-way) and 4:03 p.m. (7,800 pta., or $43, one-way). Twenty trains make the trip to Jerez from Seville; the TALGO train, which takes just under an hour, costs 1,500 pta. ($8) one-way; the regional Andalucía Expres train, a better deal, takes one hour and costs 895 pta. ($5) one-way. The **Jerez Train Station** is at Plaza de la Estación (☎ 956-43-23-19).

Getting info after you've arrived

The **tourist information office** is on Alameda Cristina, 7, just off Porvera Larga (☎ 956-33-11-50). Pick up a tour schedule of *bodegas* and a map plotting their locations. In summer, the tourism office is open Monday to Friday 9 a.m. to 2 p.m. and 5 to 8 p.m.; Saturday 9 a.m. to 2 p.m.; in winter it's open Monday to Saturday 9 a.m. to 3 p.m. and Saturday 5 to 7 p.m.

Checking out some bodegas

Spanish sherry — fortified wine — comes from Jerez. It owes its world-wide popularity to eighteenth-century British merchants who were searching for alternatives to French wines (which were virtually wiped out by disease). The oh-so-English names of several of the best-known wineries — Sandeman, Harveys, and Williams — reflect the British inter-est in sherry. A visit to one of the *bodegas* (there are about 100 in the area) introduces you to the varieties of sherry: *fino* (extra dry, light in color); *amontillado* (dry, full bodied and deeper color); *oloroso* (fra-grant, medium dry and gold colored); and *dulce* (sweet). *Manzanilla,* terrifically dry and so light it's almost ethereal, comes only from the town of Sanlúcar de Barramenda. At the tourist office, pick up a sched-ule of *bodegas* that permit visits. The price of the tour includes tastings.

Here are some wineries that you may enjoy:

✔ **González Byass,** Calle Manuel María González (☎ **956-34-00-00**), makes the ubiquitous *Tío Pepe* liqueur (that's the bottle with the *sombrero* on top). Tours costing 375 pta. ($2) are available Monday through Saturday from 10 a.m. to 1 p.m. on the hour, as well as at 6 p.m.

✔ **Domecq,** Calle San Ildefonso, 3 (☎ 956-15-15-00), Spain's oldest sherry winery (1730), offers tours Monday through Friday from 9 a.m. to 12:30 p.m., for 350 pta. ($2). Reserve in advance.

✔ At **Harveys of Bristol,** Calle Arcos, 57 (☎ 956-15-10-02), you can take a tour Monday through Friday at 10 a.m.or noon for a cost of 300 pta. ($1.75). No reservation is necessary.

✔ **Williams & Humbert Limited,** Calle Nuño de Cañas, 1 (☎ 956-34-65-39), which makes Dry Sack sherry, charges 300 pta. ($1.75), for its tours at 1:30 p.m., Monday through Friday. Reserve in advance.

Bring on the prancing horses

They prance, they dance, and they *piaffe, courvet,* and *capriole.* If you know what those high-stepping terms mean — or even if you don't — you may enjoy a visit to the **Real Escuela Andaluza del Arte Ecuestre** (Royal Equestrian School). The goal of training is for the horse and rider to commune in perfect synchronicity. From March to October you can see the dancing horses of Jerez every Thursday at noon. Tickets range from 1,500 to 2,400 pta. ($8–$14). On Mondays, Wednesdays, and Fridays, between 11 a.m and 1 p.m., you can see the training sessions and take a tour of the stables, stocked with beautiful Hispano-Arab horses. The school is at Avenida Duque de Abrantes, 11 (☎ 956-31-11-11; Internet: www.realescuela.org), just north of the old center. (Take Porvera north to Ponce, turn right and go two long blocks. The school is on the left side.)

Watching time go by in a museum

If you've seen the horses prance and you're too tipsy on sherry to drive home, pay a visit to Jerez's curious **Museo de los Relojes** (Clock Museum). In the **Palacio de Atalaya** (Watchtower Palace), several hundred interesting and beautiful French and English timepieces are on display — one of Europe's largest collections — and in working order. Hit

¡Salud! Sherry

If you haven't already discovered it, slightly chilled sherry is a great accompaniment to *tapas,* or appetizers. The best of the bunch in Andalusia are *finos* (very dry) and *manzanilla* ("mahn-tha-*nee*-ya"), complex and delicate, very dry aperitif wine — not, technically, a sherry. Both are made from the palomino grape and are best when served terrifically fresh — so you're in luck if you're in the area. Manzanilla comes from a single town, Sanlúcar de Barrameda, just up the road from Jerez. Locals drink sherry and *manzanilla* around the clock and not just as aperitifs. They pound them back with dinner.

A word of caution: If you're driving around Jerez visiting sherry *bodegas,* exercise some restraint when sampling; though they go down easy, these are fortified (very strong) wines.

Coastal links

Andalusia's loaded with golf courses, and a handful of hotels on the Costa de la Luz have agreements with (and discounts at) private golf clubs. The **Parador de Cádiz** has an agreement to the tune of 20 percent off, with the Club de Golf Novo Sancti Petri, 25 km (15 mi.) away. The **Hotel Montecastillo** (Carretera de Arcos, km 9.6; ☎ **956-15 12 00;** Fax: 956-15 12 09; doubles 18,500–35,200 pta., or $103–$196) in Jerez de la Frontera offers a 50 percent discount at the Jack Nicklaus-designed Montecastillo club it borders, as well as two others on the coast.

the museum at noon for a cool demonstration of synchronized chiming. You can find the museum just across from the Royal Equestrian School at Cervantes, 3 (☎ **956-18-21-00;** hours are Monday to Saturday from 10 a.m. to 2 p.m., and admission is 300 pta./$1.75).

A side trip to Cádiz and the Costa de la Luz

If you fear that a trip to the south of Spain is incomplete without *playa* (beach) and *sol* (sun), check out the western half of the Andalusian coast. The **Costa de la Luz,** Coast of Light (also called the Cádiz coast), is a short distance from Jerez.

 Although more ballyhooed than the Costa de la Luz, the Costa del Sol, southwest of Ronda, is an overgrown, overdeveloped resort for the rich and famous and for package tourists. It's the least interesting part of Andalusia, and the beaches really aren't all that great.

The relatively tranquil and unspoiled Costa de la Luz extends from Spain's southernmost tip to the Portuguese border, fronting the Bay of Cádiz. If you have limited time, the area of most interest is between Cádiz and Tarifa, a windswept coastline with fine, unpretentious beaches, dunes, the shelter of pine trees, and whitewashed fishing villages. If you want sand and sea, not scene, this area is where to go in the south. A car is the best way to explore the Costa de la Luz.

 Despite its history, the port city of Cádiz — purportedly the oldest inhabited city in the West, founded in 1100 B.C. by the Phoenicians — isn't really that interesting to most visitors. The best beach in the area is **La Victoria.** Up the coast (northwest), other beaches I recommend are **La Costilla** (in Rota) and **Regla** (in Chipiona). If you want to spend the night in Cádiz, the best place is the **Parador de Cádiz Hotel Atlántico** (Avenida Duque de Nájera, 9; ☎ **956-22-69-05;** Fax: 956-21-45-82), where doubles run 12,500 to 15,000 pta. ($69–$83). Its construction is modern, but it sits right on the coast. The **tourism office** is on Calderón de la Barca, 1; ☎ 956-21-13-13.

Between Cádiz and Tarifa are a couple of modest resorts, **Conil de la Frontera** and **Zahara de los Atunes.** At the southern tip of Spain, Tarifa has the dubious distinction of being the windiest city in Spain — little wonder that it's also the windsurfing capital. From here, Morocco is only about 14 miles across the Strait of Gibraltar. Morocco was a logical stronghold of the Moors, and a tenth-century Moorish castle is here. The town still retains a very palpable Arab flavor. Tarifa has an excellent, three-mile-long, white beach, **Playa de Lances.**

From Jerez de la Frontera, N-443 leads to Cádiz. N-340 leads east along the coast to Tarifa. Trains arrive from Seville (2 hours), Jerez (40 minutes), and Córdoba (5 hours). The train station (**Plaza de Sevilla;** ☎ 956-25-43-01) is on Avda. del Puerto, southeast of town. Buses go to Cádiz from all over the south, arriving at two terminals: **Comes,** Plaza de la Hispanidad, 1 (☎ 956-22-42-71) and **Los Amarillos,** Avda. Ramón de Carranza, 31 (☎ 956-28-58-52).

Fast Facts: Arcos de la Frontera

Area Code

Arcos' area code is **956,** which you must dial before every number.

Currency Exchange

You can find both a bank and an ATM machine around the main plaza on the way into town.

Emergencies

For medical emergencies, call the *Cruz Roja* (Red Cross), on Corregidores, 9; ☎ 956-70-03-55.

Hospitals

Servicio Andaluz de Salud has an outpatient clinic at Calle Calvario, s/n; ☎ 956-70-06-62.

Information

The tourism office (☎ 956-70-22-64) is right on the central square of the old town, Plaza del Cabildo (Cuesta de Belén, 1; within the Castle). The staff at the town's *parador* across the plaza is equally helpful.

Police

The police station is at Calle Nueva, s/n (☎ 956-70-16-52-12).

Post Office

Arco's main post office is on Paseo de Boliches, 24 (☎ 956-70-15-60).

Taking the Pueblos Blancos Route

You can easily see all the white villages in under a week, because they're that close together. However, spending a week on the route is probably overkill. In just a day or two, you can visit the four or five most picturesque (adding another day to your trip for Ronda). I recommend that you spend a night in Arcos and at least one night in Ronda, hitting the towns in between on one or two day trips. The only practical way to cover more than just Arcos and Ronda is in a car; with rented wheels (you're best off renting in one of the larger cities, such as Seville, Córdoba, or Granada). The region is as scenic as you'll find in Spain. In my last run through, I made many more stops on the side of the road to snap pictures than I did in the actual villages.

If you're a nature lover, you'll appreciate that the Sierra de Grazalema Nature Reserve runs almost the breadth of the route of the Pueblos Blancos, covering an area of more than 125,000 acres. It includes pine and oak forests and an important reserve for griffon vultures.

In Arcos de la Frontera or Ronda, pick up a brochure called a *Guía Práctica* (Practical Guide) to the Pueblos Blancos. It includes a map of the area that's plenty sufficient, and information on the towns that I don't have room to discuss here.

Several routes are available by which you can undertake a tour of the white towns. In this book, I only lay out one possibility for exploring the interior of the Cádiz and Malaga provinces: beginning in Arcos and winding up in Ronda. If you want to keep your kilometers down, consider staying in Ronda and doing a circular trip from there; the best of the white towns are closer to Ronda than they are to Arcos. Feel free to mix and match towns, rearrange the order, or explore some of the smaller places that I can't fully describe here. What you see and the route you take are almost entirely questions of how much time you want to dedicate to seeing the Pueblos Blancos. See Table 17-1 for driving distances around the Pueblos Blancos.

Table 17-1   Pueblos Blancos Driving Distances

Route	Distance
Arcos to Jerez	32 km (20 mi.)
Grazalema to Ronda	28 km (17 mi.)
Zahara to Olvera	32 km (20 mi.)
Zahara to Ronda	35 km (22 mi.)
Setenil to Olvera	13 km (8 mi.)
Olvera to Ronda	59 km (37 mi.)

The area of the Pueblos Blancos has been inhabited since prehistoric times, by the Iberians, Celts, Romans (in 1 B.C., the Romans founded Arcos de la Frontera and Ronda), Visigoths, and, more recently, the Moors. The Muslims, who dominated Andalusia for 700 years, did the most to shape these villages, as their winding, narrow alleyways, fortresses, and brilliantly whitewashed aspect attest. Berber farmers inhabited the villages, with their towns' castles suffering constant attacks from armies during the Christian–Muslim struggles for domination.

In the twentieth century, until roads to these mountaintop villages were laid down, the Pueblos Blancos continued as remote agricultural villages. Rugged sorts less savory than farmers took advantage of their strategic locations and inaccessibility. Smugglers, bandits, and even guerrillas fighting for the Andalusian resistance against fascist dictator Francisco Franco took up residence in the Pueblos Blancos.

From Arcos to Benamahoma

Take C-344 west from Arcos toward El Bosque. There you can either veer right and check out the leather-producing, industrial (but still white) town of Ubrique, or better yet, head to Benamahoma. A sun-kissed, tiny village with stone streets and whitewashed houses (what did you expect?) with wrought-iron balconies, its Arab origins are obvious. Orange and palm trees line the main street. Benamahoma is the kind of place where everybody stares at you, as if they expect you to bring the circus to town. No matter; have a quick look around and check out the white and tile-roofed church next to the tiniest of bullrings. (A little boy told me that the bullring was destroyed "by the bulls" and was no longer in use. I asked him how long ago it happened. "A long time ago," he said. "When I was four, and now I'm seven.")

From Benamahoma to Grazalema

Continue along C-344 west 18 km (12 miles) to Grazalema, which is perhaps the fairest of the white towns. Surrounded by craggy, olive-colored mountains on all sides, this immaculate town isn't merely *blanco* (white), it's *blanquísimo* (extraordinarily white). If you approach it on the road from Arcos, you'll circle above it and see unequalled views of its white houses, church steeples, and tile roofs. Spend a little time here, exploring its charming central square, three churches, outdoor cafés (perfect for lunchtime snacks), and wool and ceramic shops. There are a couple of full-fledged restaurants, pensions, and even a disco in Grazalema.

Besides the cafés, for a bite to eat, check out **Casa de las Piedras** (Las Piedras, 32; ☎ **956-13-20-14;** Fax: 956-13-22-38), which has excellent home cooking and rooms to for rent for 4,800 pta. ($27). Another place to have a look at if you want to spend the night is **Villa Turística Grazalema** (Calle El Olivar, s/n; ☎ **956-13-21-36;** Fax: 956-13-22-13; E-mail: tgasa@cadiz.org), a small hotel with great views and doubles for 7,500 to 8,500 pta. ($42–$47).

For the woolen blankets Grazalema is still famous for (though its once-thriving textile industry is nothing like it was), head to **Concha Pérez Coronel's** small shop (Anexo Plaza España, 18; ☎ 956-13-21-41) or **Artesanía Textil de Grazalema** (Carretera de Ronda; ☎ 956-13-20-08), on the road out of town to Ronda.

So much of Andalusia is dry and in perpetual need of rain, but rain frequently bathes the tiny whitewashed town of Grazalema. In fact, Grazalema has the distinction of having the highest annual rainfall in Spain. If you're here on a sunny day, or if you've been to the rainy northern region of the Basque Country, that annual rainfall statistic seems impossible, but it's true.

From Grazalema to Zahara de la Sierra

The road to Zahara de la Sierra (usually shortened to "Zahara") from Grazalema (14 km., or 9 miles along CA-531) is a bicyclist's dream and a motorist's nightmare. Passing along the Puerto de las Palomas ("Dove's Pass," 4,450 feet), the road winds along the mountain's edge, up one side and down the other, until it reaches a view of a blue-green reservoir stretching out among the olive groves. If the thought of the hair-raising road from Grazalema to Zahara de la Sierra makes, well, your hair raise on end, you can take a longer, less dangerous and ultimately less picturesque route: C-344 East to C-339 North, which leads to Zahara. If you have a steady hand, though, take the spectacular short cut, CA-531. And, as your driving teacher told you, go slowly and try to keep your eyes on the road.

The town of Zahara — stone streets and whitewashed houses (notice a trend here?) — is wedged into the side of the mountain, with an old tower perched on top, overlooking the water. The Moors founded Zahara de la Sierra, 511 meters (1,676 feet) above sea level, in the eighth century, and today it's a national monument. The main square is a good place to take a break and snack on a couple of *tapas* and a glass of *manzanilla*. Walk around toward the *mirador* (lookout), past the eighteenth-century Baroque church, and catch the stone path up the hill, where a ten-minute climb leads you through cacti and almond trees up to a medieval Nasrine castle. The views are sensational. Enter the spooky thirteenth-century tower **(Torre del Homenaje),** which is in excellent shape, at your own risk — it definitely seems like the kind of place where a hairy hermit will emerge from hiding. You can climb to the second floor sun terrace (which would make a great place for nude sunbathing).

The building that was being constructed when I last climbed the path looked like some guy's dream house, but it is actually an Archaeology Museum, built on the remains of the old church, Iglesia de Santa María de Mesa. By the time you read this book, it should be completed and open.

If you want to crash in Zahara, you can choose from a small hotel, **Arco de la Villa Paseo Nazarí,** s/n (☎ **956-12-32-30**), charging 7,500 to 8,625 pta. ($42–48) or two *pensions* (guest houses): **Marqués de Zahara** (San Juan, 3; ☎ **956-12-30-61**), charging 5,650 to 6,500 pta. ($31–$36) and **Los Tadeos** (Paseo de la Fuente; ☎ **956-12-30-86**) at low cost of 3,000 pta. ($17).

From Zahara to Setenil de las Bodegas

Leaving Zahara, you have a choice. You can either continue north to Algodonales or east to El Gastor. Both are nice, as are all these towns, but if you're in a hurry, continue past El Gastor to Setenil de las Bodegas.

Setenil, as it's known, is one of the most amazing villages in Andalusia — literally crammed into clefts of rock. You need to park the car at one end of the village and get out and walk. Look for Calle Herrería, one of the oldest streets in town. Once lined with blacksmiths' shops, its houses are wedged into the massive rock that forms their roofs. Talk about adapting to your environment. An elderly woman invited me into her small home, which had sloping cave walls that were painted thick white. Barbara García, who got around her *casas cuevas* (cave-house — that's literally what they're called in Spanish) on a wheelchair, told me that the house had been in her family for generations. (She thought her grandparents built it, but conceded that it could've been older still.) Setenil's Moorish fortress and twin-towered, sixteenth-century Gothic church **(Iglesia de la Encarnación)** sit high above the rock and white houses.

The road that leads north out of Setenil leads to a *mirador* and small church; take the turnoff for postcard views of the town and the cave houses below.

There's a single *pensión* in town if you want to spend the night under the rock ridges: **El Almendral** (Carretera Setenil-Puerto del Monte; ☎ **956-13-40-29**), charging 5,750 pta. ($32).

If you're as delighted as I am by town names that reveal their former lots in life, I have a good one for you. Just outside of Setenil is a tiny settlement, no doubt an agricultural one, called *Venta de Leche,* which means "Milk for Sale."

From Setenil to Olvera

The road between Setenil and Olvera is a dreamscape; it winds through olive groves and valleys that suddenly open up and reveal two perfect Pueblos Blancos laid out in the distance. The first is Torre Alhaquime; 4 km (2½ mi.) beyond it is Olvera, its Moorish tower and neoclassical church glued to the top of the mountain. Olvera, declared a national monument, was a Moorish stronghold and a key part of the Granada Nazari kingdom's defensive lines. It's easy to see why raiders had little success storming a settlement perched as high as this one. Head for a small plaza, where the town hall is located; then park your car and walk up. Next to the castle is **Iglesia de San José,** an unexpectedly large, colonial-looking, pale yellow and brown church (eighteenth-century) with a clock tower. Access to the twelfth-century castle is through a door across from the church. Its sign says it's open Tuesday through Thursday and Saturday and Sunday for visits from 9 a.m. to 2 p.m. Townsfolk assured me, though, that you can visit during the morning and afternoon every day but Monday, when it's closed.

Roaming around Ronda

Ronda clings to a cliff above a narrow 350-foot chasm, a dizzying ravine created by the Guadalevín River. Whitewashed houses and palatial mansions crowd the edges of the gorge. An audacious eighteenth-century bridge spans the drop and connects the Old Quarter with the new expansion, El Mercadillo. Ronda's precipice is spectacular, but as a vista it's got serious competition in the serene valleys and mountain ranges that extend on either side: the Sierra de las Nieves to the east and the Sierra de Grazalema to the west.

Beyond the beauty of its setting, Ronda is one of the oldest towns in Spain. Its perch was inhabited nearly 3,000 years ago and it was a Celtic, then Roman, and finally Moorish stronghold before Christian forces conquered it in the thirteenth century. The birthplace of modern bullfighting, Ronda is home to Spain's oldest and most beautiful bullring, and an old-fashioned annual festival to go with it.

Ronda exudes charm at every corner, from its ancient minarets to Arab baths and ornate iron grilles filled with potted plants. It's the one white town to visit if you don't have time for others. Mid-size Ronda (30,000 residents) is a perfect complement to Andalusia's Big Three (Seville, Granada, and Córdoba); if you're drawn to small-town charms, you'll likely find it one of the highlights of your trip to southern Spain.

Arriving in Ronda

Ronda is one of the few white towns accessible by means other than a car. You can hop a train from Seville, Córdoba, or Granada, and a bus from Seville, Arcos, and Jerez. If you're really pressed for time and not yet in Andalusia, you can even fly from Madrid or Barcelona — though you have to fly into Málaga, 60 miles away, and then catch a bus or train from there.

If you're going to Ronda by car, you can take any number of routes from other spots in Andalusia. Major highways bypass it, though, so you need to get off and take one of the smaller local highways. From Seville, take N-334 Southeast and head south, just after El Arahal, on

C-339, which leads directly to Ronda. From Granada, take N-342 West to Olvera, and C-342 South from there. From Málaga, take scenic C-344 directly to Ronda.

Trains arrive from Málaga, Seville, Córdoba, and Granada, as well as Madrid. From Madrid, the fare costs 4,700 pta. ($26; 9 hours); Seville, 2,155 pta. ($12; 3 hours); Málaga, 1,155 pta. ($6; 2 hours); Córdoba, 1,580 pta. ($8; 5 hours); and Granada, 1,730 pta. ($10; 3 hours). Note that a number of trains into and out of Ronda make stops and train changes in Bobadilla or Antequera.

Ronda's train station, **Estación de FF.CC.** (Avenida Alférez Provisional, s/n; ☎ 95-287-16-73), is on the northwestern edge of town, next to Avenida de Andalucía. The ticket office for **RENFE,** Spain's national railway system, is at Calle Infantes, 20 (☎ 95-287-16-62).

Buses from Seville, Málaga, Arcos, and Jerez travel to Ronda. **Los Amarillos** (☎ 95-231-59-78) travels to and from Seville and Málaga, **Portillo** (☎ 95-236- 01-91) also goes to Malaga. **Transportes Comes** (☎ 95-287-19-92) goes to Arcos, Jerez ,and Cadiz. The bus station **(Estación de Autobuses)** is on Plaza Concepción García Redondo, 2 (☎ 95-287-26-57), just down Avenida de Andalucía from the train station.

Getting around Ronda

Ronda is so small that using anything other than your own feet to get around is absurd. The areas of greatest interest to visitors are a handful of streets on either side of the gorge. If you're a competent rider, a great way to see the countryside that surrounds Ronda is via horseback (see "Exploring Ronda," later in this chapter).

If you arrive in Ronda without wheels but decide to rent a car in town to explore some of the other white towns, contact **Velasco** (Calle Lorenzo Borrego, 11; ☎ 95-287-27-82). If you need a cab to get to the train or bus station, call **Parada de Taxis** at ☎ 95-287-23-16 or pick one up in front of the Plaza de Toros (bullring).

Staying in Ronda

All of Ronda's hotels are conveniently located, with the possible exception of the Reina Victoria, which is farthest from the bridge. High season in Ronda is March to October; low season is November to February. Some hotels charge supplements for local Feria de Pedro Romero and the *corrida goyesca* (first week of September), as well as Easter Week, in April. (For more on these festivals, see "A calendar of special events" in Chapter 2.)

Hotel Don Miguel

$$

The Parador's not the only hotel with a great perch over the gorge. This hotel abuts the back side of the river gorge, which some bedrooms overlook. Rooms are fairly simple, but they're comfortable enough — a decent alternative if you want a dramatic view but don't want to pay the dramatically higher prices at the Parador across the street. The hotel, which has been around almost 30 years, is expanding into building No. 13 on the same street (with the same views); the new rooms should be complete by the time you read this text. Definitely get a room overlooking the gorge. The hotel restaurant, with a balcony clinging to the cliff, is quite good (see the review for Don Miguel, later in the restaurant section of this chapter).

Villanueva, 4–8 (on north side of gorge, across from Plaza de España). ☎ *95-287-77-22. Fax: 95-287-83-77. Parking: 750 pta. ($4). Rates: 9,500 pta. ($53). AE, DC, M, V.*

Hotel La Española

$$

Another good low-cost hotel in Ronda, this former dirt-cheap *pensión* got a makeover in 1998. The location is perfect — just two minutes from the gorge and Plaza de Toros — although you won't get gorge views. The comfortable rooms are nicely (for the most part) decorated with either deep-green or ochre walls, with piped-in music, minibar, and cheesy antique phones; doubles offer a view of gardens and the distant mountains beyond Ronda. Rooms have full baths (singles, showers only) and air conditioning. The downstairs restaurant has a nice covered terrace.

José Aparicio, 3 (on street between bullfighting ring and Plaza de España). ☎ *95-287-10-51. Fax: 95-287-80-01. E-mail:* laespanola@ronda.net. *Internet:* www.ronda.net/usuar/laespanola. *Metered parking: nearby. Rates: 12,000– 13,000 pta. ($67–$72). AE, DC, M, V.*

Hotel Reina Victoria

$$–$$$

This old British-style hotel, inaugurated in 1906 just after the building of the British rail line from Bobadilla to Algeciras, was once the swankest game in town. Today, eclipsed in service and installations by the Parador, it has a slightly dilapidated feeling, more like a museum than a hotel. The gardens, terraces, and pool, though, are still first-rate. Tour groups and English visitors still appear to enjoy the musty, old world decor and Nordic look of the place — sloping roofs, high chimneys, and bold green and white paint. But to me, it just seems out of place in this town with such distinct Roman and Moorish roots.

The German poet Rainier Marie Rilke once camped out for an extended period of convalescence here (in 1912) — in its day, Ronda's finest hotel.

Like a good-luck charm, or evidence of a more distinguished past, the hotel has maintained Rilke's room (as a small museum, not as a hotel room), but the staff is a little nasty about letting nonguests in to view it.

Calle Jerez, 25 (in modern part of town, ten-minute walk west of gorge). ☎ *95-287-12-40. Fax: 95-287-10-75. E-mail:* reinavictoriaronda@husa.es. *Internet:* http://infotur.tsai.es/infotur/ronda/htreivic. *Parking: free. Rates: 15,000–18,500 pta. ($83–$103). AE, DC, M, V.*

Hotel San Gabriel (Su Casa en Ronda)

$$

A family-owned and operated small hotel in a gorgeous 1736 mansion, San Gabriel is my favorite place in Ronda and one of my favorite hotels in Spain. Not only that, but it's perhaps the best deal I came across in all my recent travels in Spain. A labor of love created by a father, his sons and daughter, this Ronda family worked for 15 years to meticulously select the antiques for every nook and cranny of every welcoming room and complete the painstaking restoration before finally opening it in December 1998. They're so bent on it seeming home-like that they've incorporated "Your House in Ronda" into the name. Every detail is perfect, cozy, and utterly charming. Located in the artistic and historical center of Ronda, just a five-minute walk east of the gorge, it has Moorish accents, antique leaded and stained-glass windows, an antique carved central staircase, and even a TV salon with seats salvaged from Ronda's first theater. Each of the 16 rooms is different in its decor; my favorites are No. 4, 9 (a very *suite* deal), and 15, a charming top-floor, bi-level room.

José M. Holgado, 19 (just off Calle Armiñán, next to Plaza del Gigante). ☎ *95-219-03-92. Fax: 95-219-01-17. E-mail:* info@hotelsangabriel.com. *Internet:* www.hotelsangabriel.com. *No parking (though usually able to park free on street). Rates: 11,000 pta. ($61). AE, DC, M, V.*

Parador de Ronda

$$$

You can get dizzy staying at Ronda's national Parador. The hotel's backed right up to the edge of the gorge, next to the stunning bridge that spans its gulf. The hotel, built in 1994, is modern and extremely comfortable — exactly the reasons some locals have criticized it, for not doing a good enough job assimilating into Ronda's collection of old mansions and whitewashed houses. It's hardly a modern white elephant, though, and most visitors find the Parador a luxurious, even handsome, place to stay. It's also one of the friendliest *paradors* I've stayed in. Many of the 78 nicely appointed rooms have small balconies. Many also have unrivalled views of the 500-foot fall of the gorge and the bridge, which is illuminated at night, or the gorgeous mountainous countryside beyond. Make sure your room is one with a view.

Plaza de España, s/n (western side, right next to new bridge over gorge). ☎ *95-287-75-00. Fax: 95-287-81-88. E-mail:* ronda@parador.es. *Internet:* www.parador.es. *Parking: 1,200 pta. ($6). Rates: 15,000–18,500 pta. ($83–$103). Inquire about special discounts for families with children. AE, DC, M, V.*

Dining in Ronda

Casa Santa Pola

$$ SPANISH/ANDALUSIAN

A handsome new restaurant overlooking the gorge, near the Casa del Rey Moro, Casa Santa Pola has terra-cotta-colored walls and deep red tablecloths — very elegant surroundings for such an accessibly priced restaurant in a great setting. The dining rooms have Moorish-style arches and red brick, with Moroccan lamps. The menu is varied, but sticking with basics like *sopa de mariscos* (shellfish soup), the nice selection of salads, *cochinillo* (roast suckling pig), and *paellas* (a casserole of rice, seafood, and meat) may be a good idea. Behind the beautiful eighteenth-century front door of the Casa Santa Pola is an antiques museum with some extraordinary furnishings.

Calle Santo Domingo, 3 (first street left — east — off of Calle Armiñán; next to Casa del Rey Moro). ☎ *95-287-92-08. Reservations recommended. Main courses: 950–2,000 pta. ($5–$11). Menú del día 1,300–2,050 pta. ($7–$11). Open: daily for lunch and dinner. AE, DC, M, V.*

Don Miguel

$$–$$$ SPANISH/ANDALUSIAN

This restaurant, attached to a small hotel by the same name (reviewed earlier in this chapter), has one distinct advantage: location, location, location. Don Miguel's terrace dining area swings out over the river gorge — a pretty spectacular site for a meal. You can also sit in the large indoor dining rooms if the sun's beating down or if it's chilly outside. A great surprise — in a place that may rest on its location, the kitchen is one of Ronda's best. Try the oxtail stew or the partridge casserole.

Villanueva, 4 (right next to the gorge, on east side; across from Plaza de España). ☎ *95-287-10-90. Reservations recommended. Main courses: 1,200–2,400 pta. ($7–$14). Menú del día 2,400 pta. ($14). Open: Mon–Sat, lunch and dinner; Sun, dinner only. Closed first three weeks of Jan. AE, DC, M, V.*

Restaurante Pedro Romero

$$ ANDALUSIAN

Ronda has long been considered the cradle of Spanish bullfighting; if you miss seeing a *corrida* (bullfight), you can always come here, just across the street from Spain's oldest Plaza de Toros. Named for a legendary Ronda bullfighter (who is said to have slain nearly 6,000 bulls during his career), the restaurant is all taurine ambience — posters of bullfights, photos of matadors and, of course, stuffed bulls' heads line the walls. The simple surroundings have quite a bit of charm, touristy though they may seem. Logically, it's a place for meat — *rabo de toro a la Rondeña* (Ronda-style oxtail), lamb, veal, and rabbit. Start off with a house garlic soup.

Virgen de la Paz, 18 (next to Post Office, across from bullring). ☎ **95-287-11-10.** *Reservations recommended. Main courses: 1,300–2,500 pta. ($7–$14). Open: daily for lunch and dinner. AE, DC, M, V.*

Restaurante Tragabuches
$$$ CREATIVE ANDALUSIAN

The best restaurant in Ronda is a stylish new venture that's pretty uptown for this laid-back town. The downstairs back dining room (much preferable to the staid front room) has clean white walls and bubblegum-colored tablecloths and seat covers. This is evidently not your typical Spanish *mesón* (inn). The chef, Sergio López (a winner of the Best Young Chef in Spain award), is as daring as the decor. Dishes are creative and very successfully elaborated. I had a thick potato soup with salt-cured ham followed by oxtail raviolis with a puree of chestnuts. Also tempting was the sea bass with white beans and blood sausage. A tasting menu — a sampling of many dishes from the kitchen's repertoire — is available, but is only available if everyone at you're the table orders it (4,000 pta., or $22 per person). The wine cellar has some very well-chosen bottles, especially those under the heading "the great wines of Spain."

Calle José Aparicio, 1 (between Plaza de España and Plaza de Toros). ☎ **95-219-02-91.** *Reservations recommended. Main courses: 1,500–2,600 pta. ($7–$14). Open: daily for lunch and dinner. AE, DC, M, V.*

Exploring Ronda

Spain's oldest bullfighting ring, **Plaza de Toros de la Real Maestranza de España,** built in 1785, is one of its most storied and most beautiful. Constructed of limestone with double arches and 136 Tuscan columns, it's linked forever in the minds of Spaniards to the legend of Ronda native Pedro Romero, who is considered the father of modern bullfighting. A different kind of celebrity graced its sands a couple years back when Ronda's ring was the stage for a *matador* romance music video by Madonna.

Across the Plaza de Toros is the **Museo Taurino** (Bullfighting Museum), one of the better ones in Spain and a big hit with the kids. Its exhibits include bulls' heads, suits of lights worn by Romero and other matadors, and a second floor dedicated to foreigners involved in *toros* — including photographs of Orson Welles, and the paintings and suit of John Fulton, a Philadelphia-born bullfighter and artist who lived most of his life in Seville. Pedro Romero, the eighteenth-century killer of nearly 6,000 bulls, was the inspiration for Francisco de Goya's remarkable series of etchings

A few bits of bull trivia

Bullfighting: Not Just for Squares. Ever wonder why a bullring is called a *plaza de toros?* It's because bullfights used to take place in the middle of the town square (plaza). They're no longer held in those plazas — even the smallest Spanish towns have bullrings — but the name stuck.

A Welles-Chosen Friend. The great American film director Orson Welles, the legend behind *Citizen Kane* and *The War of the Worlds,* was, like novelist Ernest Hemingway, a great fan of Spanish folklore — and in particular bullfighting. He befriended the great Ronda bullfighter Antonio Ordóñez to such an extent that Welles was later buried on the *matador's* country estate outside of Ronda.

on *Tauromaquia.* The first week of September, Ronda hosts a *corrida goyesca,* a festival that recreates the atmosphere of an eighteenth-century bullfight in honor of Romero. Men and women decked out in fancy dress ride through the streets on horse carriages, and bullfighting aficionados come from all over the world to see classical exhibitions.

Museo Taurino: Plaza Teniente Arza (right off of Virgen de la Paz). ☎ 95-287-41-32. Admission is 400 pta. ($2.20) (purchase ticket from small shop outside). Open: daily, 10 a.m. to 6 p.m.

More cool things to see and do in Ronda

Ronda is more than just a bullfighting town, though it is the primary attraction. A number of other activities will entertain you while you're in town.

✔ **Meandering through magnificent mansions.** Ronda is the site of several exceptional aristocratic homes open to visitors. **Casa del Marqués de Salvatierra** is a noble Renaissance palace with intricate iron grilles and pre-Colombian figures (sticking their tongues out) adorning its rich Baroque facade. The mansion has remained in the hands of a single family and its descendents since 1475. The original Marquis Salvatierra was a well-traveled *conquistador* who, with orders from the Catholic monarchs, arrived in Ronda to engineer its capture from the Moors. The palace was constructed from a group of fifteenth-century Arab houses — a gift to the Marquis after the conquest of Ronda. The mansion has has wonderful gardens and interior details. The family that owns it still vacations here in the month of August, when it's closed to the public. The palace (Marqués de Salvatierra, s/n; ☎ 95-287-12-06; 300 pta./ $1.75) is open 11 a.m. to 2 p.m. and 4 to 7 p.m.; closed Thursday and Sunday afternoons. You have to knock at the heavy wooden door and wait for the attendant to answer; small-group tours are only in Spanish.

Just across the street is **Casa del Rey Moro** (Moorish King's House), an improbably named eighteenth-century palace with an unusual feature that you have to see to believe. Within the palace is a fourteenth-century water mine, a secret military structure carved out of the gorge by the Moors. Descend the poorly lit, zigzagging, and damp staircase into the depths until you finally reach the bottom of the ravine. Along the way, you pass the former Weapons Room, a secret escape exit, and the Room of Secrets, where the acoustics of the tiny room reportedly protected confidential conversations. It's said that the Moors employed Christian slaves to bring water up from the river. Fortunately, you don't have to do anything more than make the long climb back to the top of the never-ending steps and then emerge to enjoy the sumptuous gardens (designed in 1912) and the terrific views of the gorge and countryside. Casa del Rey Moro is being transformed into a hotel by the owners of the luxurious Casa Imperial in Seville; it should be magnificent when finished. The palace (Cuesta de Santo Domingo, 17; ☎ **95-218-71-00**) is open daily 10 a.m. to 7 p.m.; admission is 600 pta. ($3) adults, children 300 pta. ($1.75).

On the other side of the gorge are two other handsome homes with spectacular views south of Ronda. They're open daily 9 a.m. to 6 p.m. The fourteenth-century **Palacio de Mondragón** (Plaza de Mondragón, s/n; ☎ **95-287-84-50**; 250 pta./$1.40) was built by the Moorish king of Ronda, Abomelic, in 1314 and later inhabited by the Catholic monarchs Ferdinand and Isabel. In Moorish style, the palace has several interior courtyards adorned with mosaics and beautiful arcaded patios. It also has some of the best views in the city, looking back at the river gorge. The mansion today houses a small Natural History Museum, of less interest than the house itself. The mansion is open Monday to Friday, 10 a.m. to 6 p.m., Saturday and Sunday, 10 a.m. to 3 p.m. (adults, 250 pta., or $1.40; students and seniors, 100 pta., or 55¢; free for children under 14). Nearby, the **Casa de Don Juan Bosco** (calle Tenorio, 20; ☎ **95-287-16-83**; 150 pta., or 85¢) is most notable for its lovely terrace, with a beautiful fountain and views to die for.

✔ **Soaking up the Moorish past.** Ronda's thirteenth-century **Baños Árabes** (Arab baths), east of Marqués de Salvatierra (☎ **95-287-38-89**), are remarkably well preserved — perhaps the finest surviving example in Spain. From above they don't look like much, and the first chamber is just a series of open-air arches. But, the two main chambers, with star-shaped openings that allow light to stream through, and perfect horseshoe arches, are a thing of real beauty. A nearby aqueduct carried water from the point where the two rivers converge. You can reach the baths from the staircase that leads down through the Puerta de Felipe V, just beyond the Casa del Rey Moro and Palacio Salvatierra. They are open

Wednesday through Saturday, 10 a.m. to 2 p.m. and 3 to 5:30 p.m.; Sunday, 10 a.m. to 2 p.m.; Tuesday, 3 to 5:30 p.m. Closed Monday. Admission is free.

✔ **Walking on Ronda's wild side.** *Tajo* means "sheer drop," and Ronda's vertiginous ravine certainly is that. The views from the eighteenth-century **Puente Nuevo,** a spectacular feat of engineering across the gorge, are exhilarating. But if you've got the time and energy, don't stop at just staring down one side and then the other. A path from the Plaza de Campillo, in the old town, leads down to the bottom of the ravine, through almond trees and pink blossoms, for stunning vistas of the bridge from the bottom up (at sunset, the bridge is bathed in honey-colored light). A less strenuous walk through the Alameda del Tajo (Tajo Promenade), north of the bullring, is nearly as exhilarating. A perch hangs out over the cliff, providing great views.

A walk on the east side of the gorge leads to the eighteenth-century **Felipe V Gate;** the **Puente Viejo,** the old Roman bridge; and the **Puente Árabe,** the Arab bridge. A walk south from there, past the Arab baths, passes through the old Jewish Quarter and Ronda's ancient ramparts. Look for the Renaissance **Carlos V Gate** and thirteenth-century **Almocábar Gate,** part of the ancient walls and old entrance to the city.

The countryside beyond Ronda is perfect for more adventurous hikes, too. If you bring boots or very sturdy sneakers, check with the tourism office for information about trails that lead out into the surrounding *serranía* (mountains).

✔ **Enjoying Ronda by horseback:** The ravine and countryside beyond Ronda are tailor-made for wonderful trail riding. The company **Picadero "La Granja"** (Camino de los Molinos; ☎ 95-287-59-56) offers several routes, lasting from one hour to two days. For more information, visit the office at Plaza de España, 3. The *parador* also offers a number of excursions. Stop by the parador or call (☎ 95-287-75-00) for more information. One of the routes offered by both is a day-long adventure to the **Cueva de la Pileta,** a cave with remarkable prehistoric paintings, about 15 miles outside of Ronda. Horseback riding generally ranges from 4,000 pta. ($22) for an hour to 12,000 pta. ($67) for the entire day.

Ronda's remote ravines and mountains have long provided refuge to bandits, smugglers, and rebels. Some of the legendary figures roaming the hills in the sixteenth, seventeenth, and eighteenth centuries were Diego Corrientes, El Tempranillo, Pasos Largos, and El Tragabuches (the last of whom Ronda's best new restaurant honors). If you want to know more about Ronda's bandit past, take a look at the kitschy **Museo Bandolero** (Bandit Museum), on calle Armiñán, 65 (☎ 95-287-77-85; 350 pta./$2). It's open 10 a.m. to 8 p.m. in summer ('til 6 p.m. in winter). You don't have to worry anymore, though; Ronda is safe as can be (except for those pesky brats who stole my bike saddle last time I was there).

Shopping and nightlife in Ronda

Except for the daily rounds of tour buses, Ronda is a pretty quiet town. If you're looking for some action after dinner, check out the cluster of streets across from *Plaza de España* and the bullring; they're lined with unpretentious bars and cafés. Look around *Plaza del Socorro* and *Plaza de Abela* and the streets *Villanueva, Nueva,* and *Los Remedios.*

Those same streets are where you can find most of Ronda's shops. For antiques, check out **El Portón** (Manuel Montero, 14; ☎ 95-287-14-69) and **Muñoz Soto** (San Juan de Dios de Córdboba, 34; ☎ 95-287-14-51). A cool little gift shop, with toys and home items, is **El Pensamiento Ronda** (Calle Espinel, 16; ☎ 95-287-21-93).

Side trips to Málaga and the Costa del Sol

Málaga ("*Mah*-lah-gah"), the birthplace of Pablo Picasso and Antonio Banderas (now there's a pair of Latin lovers), is a pleasant port city that doesn't get too caught up in the resort glitz of the rest of the Costa del Sol. Andalusia's second-biggest city has a tropical feel. Its attractive waterfront promenade, *Paseo del Parque,* is lined by palm trees and jacarandas and is always full of strolling Spaniards.

The Costa del Sol is all about glitz, and unless you're fascinated by glamour and ostentatious shows of wealth (and lots, truth be told, of *gente bella,* or beautiful people), I don't recommend spending much time along Spain's overrated "Sun Coast." Though it enjoys more than 300 days of sunshine a year, to me it's the least interesting part of Andalusia. Crowds of Spanish and international vacationers dominate Costa del Sol; around Marbella and its luxo port, Puerto Banús, the crowd is mainly chic jet-setters awash in privilege. From Málaga to Sotogrande, pizza joints, t-shirt shops, crummy discos, and high-rise monstrosities — little different from Cancún or Miami Beach (except the beaches aren't nearly as good) — clog the coast. Regrettably, the best time to visit the Costa del Sol was about three decades ago.

However, if you still like the sound of the Costa del Sol (or if you just got a spectacular package deal), the best places to visit are **Marbella** and **Nerja.** A Mediterranean beach resort known throughout Spain and most of Europe, **Torremolinos** (10 miles west of Málaga) is a long line of concrete hotel boxes shuttling inexpensive package tours in and out. It's a poster child for the horrors of coastal development. Torremolinos is full of *gringos* (English-speaking foreigners or tourists), but not the glitzy gang you find down the road in Marbella. Tourism is big business; the town has 35,000 beds and more than 300 restaurants. I really don't recommend a stay here (bet you couldn't tell).

Tales from the bridge

Ronda's Puente Nuevo (New Bridge), a daring work of engineering, updated the old Roman and Arab bridges, which still exist just east along the ravine. Completion of the new bridge took two tries. The first, whose construction began in 1735, collapsed six years later, and 50 workers plummeted to their deaths at the bottom of the gorge. A new version of the new bridge began in 1751 and was finished in 1793. The persistent rumor that its architect either fell or jumped to his death from the bridge, though an interesting tale, isn't true. What is accurate is that the section of the bridge just above the middle semicircular arch served as a prison in the nineteenth century. If you walk along the narrow promenade next to the *parador,* you can clearly see the door and window below street level.

Getting to and around Málaga and the Costa del Sol

Málaga is 93 km (58 miles) southeast of Ronda. By car, take the interior road C-344 from Ronda (if you want to go along the coast, you have to drop down to San Pedro de Alcántara via C-339 and then head east on N-340). By train, you can take direct routes from Ronda (2 hours; 1,155 pta., or $6) and from Madrid (5 hours). (**Estación de Renfe:** Strachan, s/n; ☎ 95-221-41-27). By bus, **Los Amarillos** (☎ 95-218-70-61) and **Portillo** (☎ 95-287-22-62) both make the trip from Ronda. **Estación de Autobuses:** Plaza de los Tilos, s/n.

Málaga also has an international airport, 5 miles southwest of the city, if you prefer to fly there from a major Spanish (or European) city. From the airport into town, take a bus, train, or taxi. From the airport, the bus runs from 6:30 a.m. to midnight daily (30 minutes to city center; 135 pta./75¢; ☎ 95-221-02-950). Regular trains from the airport serve the city of Málaga (15 minutes; 150 pta., or 85¢), as well as other Costa del Sol destinations. To a number of towns in Costa del Sol or Málaga province, taxis are the only direct service.

Driving to **Marbella** and other points along the Costa del Sol is a snap. From Ronda, take C-339 south and head east on coastal road N-340. It's a total of 60 km (37 miles). From Málaga, head west along N-340 for 67 km (42 miles). Some 20 buses per day travel between Málaga and Marbella.

Málaga

The highlight of a visit to Málaga is a stroll along the promenade, stopping for ice cream or *tapas* and fresh seafood. You'll have plenty of company, as it seems to be the city's great pastime. Among the city's more traditional sights include the eleventh-century **Alcazaba** (Moorish fortress), Plaza de la Aduana (☎ 95-221-60-05). Admission to the Alcazaba museum is 50 pta. (30¢); it's open Tuesday through Saturday, 9:30 a.m. to 6 p.m. (winter), 9:30 a.m. to 8 p.m. (summer). The **Catedral de Málaga,** Plaza Obispo (☎ 95-221-59-17), is a peculiar mix of sixteenth-century architectural styles. Admission is 300 pta. ($1.75); it's open Monday through Saturday 10 a.m. to 1 p.m. and 4 to 6:30 p.m. The **Museo de Bellas Artes** (Fine Arts Museum), Calle San Agustín, 8 (☎ 95- 221-83-82), has works by Andalusian greats like Zurbarán, Ribera, Murillo, and Picasso. Admission is 250 pta. ($1.40); the museum is open Tuesday through Friday, 10 a.m. to 1:30 p.m. and 5 to 8 p.m., Saturday and Sunday, 10 a.m. to 1:30 p.m. Also in town is Picasso's childhood home, **Casa Natal de Picasso,** Plaza de la Merced, 15 (☎ 95-221-50-05). It's open Monday through Saturday, 10 a.m. to 2 p.m. and 4 to 8 p.m.; Sunday, 11 a.m. to 2 p.m. Admission is free.

Málaga's tourism information office is located at Pasaje de Chinitas, 4 (☎ 95-221-34-45). If you've flown into Málaga's International Airport, a tourism information office is there to help (☎ 95-204-84-84).

If you want to stay overnight in the Málaga area, the two *paradors* are your best options. In the historical quarter of Málaga, facing the Alcazaba, is **Parador de Málaga Gibralfaro,** Monte Gibralfaro (☎ 95-222-19-02; Fax: 95-222-19-04; E-mail: gibralfaro@parador.es; Internet: www.parador.es; doubles, 17,500 to 19,000 pta., or $97 to $106). Located next to the Gibralfaro Castle, it has splendid views of the harbor. Take the coastal road, Paseo de Reding, which eventually becomes Paseo de Sancha. Turn left onto Camino Nuevo. The other parador, 6 miles from Málaga, is a golfer's delight, wedged between a fine golf course and the Mediterranean. **Parador de Málaga-Golf,** Carretera de Málaga (☎ 95-238-12-55; Fax: 95-238-09-63; E-mail: malaga@parador.es; Internet: www.parador.es; doubles, 17,500 pta., or $97).

Marbella

The Costa del Sol's most stylish and monied resort, **Marbella** is where the most tanned go to lounge on yachts and play golf at exclusive clubs. As upscale as it is, Marbella still has one of the cheesiest public works I've ever seen: an overpass-slash-welcome gate with huge block letters spelling out M-A-R-B-E-L-L-A above the road into town. Despite that introduction, the red-paved old town is spotless and pretty enjoyable (even if expensive as heck). The two invariably packed beaches in town are **La Fontanilla** and **El Fuerte.**

After you're suitably bronzed, night is the time to shine. Wear white and lots of jewels and head to Marbella's innumberable bars and discos. If you own a yacht (or want to meet someone who does), you're in the right place in **Puerto Banús.** The chic places to party late are **Discoteca Olivia Valere** (Ctra. Istán, next to the mosque) and Oh!, in the **Hotel Don Carlos** (Ctra. Cádiz, km 198.5). If you didn't bring the right duds (if you didn't pack your very best jewelry, then you didn't, trust me), you can always drop in on the more relaxed *tapas* bar scene. The Old Quarter of Marbella is loaded with taverns and *tapas* bars.

Ay, Caramba! Overexposure

Almost all of Spain's beaches burst with bared bosoms. But bared buttocks — that is, totally bare — are a rarity. If you're dying to shed your shorts or bikini bottoms, a couple of places along the Costa del Sol let you get a tan without unsightly lines. **The Costa Natura** (Nature Coast) housing development (km 151 Málaga–Cádiz road, 3 km. from Estepona; ☎ **95-280-15-00**) has swimming pools, sports facilities, and shops where you can let it all hang loose. Less contained are authorized nudist beaches, which belong to the **Andalusian Nudist Association** (call them at ☎ **951-25-40-44**). The Costa del Sol nude beaches are: **Trópico de Europa** and **Cantarriján**, both near Almuñécar (east of Málaga, near Motril).

Marbella's Tourist Information Office is at Glorieta de la Fontanilla, s/n (☎ **95-277-14-42**) hours are Monday through Friday, 9:30 a.m. to 8 p.m., and Saturday 9:30 a.m. to 2 p.m. Another tourist office is on Plaza de los Naranjos (☎ **95-282-35-50**; same hours).

Teeing off in the area

The land of the rich, famous, and retired, the Costa del Sol is littered with golf courses. Between Málaga and San Roque are more than three dozen courses, including the famous club in Sotogrande, Valderrama, where the Ryder Cup (which pits the U.S. against Europe in team golf) was played in 1997. Many hotels along the coast have discount or free deals with clubs. If you're not staying at one that does, contact the tourism offices in Marbella or Málaga to see which golf clubs allow visitors to tee it up.

Staying in Marbella

If you want to snob-knob with the fashionable and spend the night in Marbella, pull your fancy rental up to **Marbella Club,** Boulevard Príncipe Alfonso von Hohenlohe, s/n (☎ **800-448-8355** in the U.S., 95-282-22-11; Fax: 95-282-98-84; Internet: www.marbellaclub.com; doubles, 34,500–58,000 pta. ($192–$322), a member of the Leading Hotels of the World association, with bungalow-style rooms. More affordable is **Hotel El Fuerte,** Avenida del Fuerte, s/n (☎ **800-448-8355** in the U.S., or 95-286-15-00; Fax: 95-282-44-11; Internet: www.hotel-elfuerte.es; doubles, 9,300–25,300 pta., or $52–$141), right on the beach and surrounded by gardens, with a shaded pool across from a lagoon. Both hotels have deals with golf courses — Marbella Club allows guests to play for free at three different clubs.

Nerja

About 30 miles east of Málaga, Nerja ("*nair*-hah") has good beaches, a whitewashed Mediterranean feel, and a charming seaside promenade. Its biggest attraction, though, is outside of town: the **Cueva de Nerja,** a huge prehistoric cave inhabited 25,000 years ago. Accidentally discovered by a group of kids about 40 years ago, it's full of well-illuminated stalactites and chambers, and is large enough to host, incredibly, a summer festival of concerts and ballet. The cave is located in the hills above Nerja, on Carretera de la Cueva, s/n (☎ 95-252-95-20). Hours are daily from 10 a.m. to 2 p.m. and from 4 to 6:30 p.m. Admission is 650 pta. ($3.50) for adults, 300 pta. ($1.75) for children 6 to 12. Children 5 and under are free. Buses depart hourly from Muelle de Heredia in Málaga from 7 a.m. until 8 p.m. Return buses are also hourly until 8:15 p.m. The journey takes about one hour.

The best place to stay in Nerja is the **Parador de Nerja** (Calle Almuñecar, 8, Playa de Burriana-Tablazo; ☎ 95-252-00-50; Fax: 95-252-19-97; E-mail: nerja@parador.es; doubles, 15,000–19,000 pta., or $83–$106). The hotel is perched on a cliff and has great views of the sea, coast, and distant mountains. You can take a lift down to the beach.

Fast Facts: Ronda

Area Code

Ronda's area code is **95,** which you must dial before every number.

Currency Exchange

You can find banks and ATM machines along the main drag in town, Calle Virgen de la Paz. An agency that will change money for you is Agrotur (Virgen de la Paz, s/n; ☎ 95-287-62-38).

Hospitals

Hospital La Serranía is located on Carretera de Burgos, km 1 (☎ 95-287-15-40). Hospital Ronda is at San Vicente de Paúl, s/n (☎ 95-287-70-40).

Information

The tourism information office is on Plaza de España, 1 (☎ 95-287-12-72), next to the Parador. It's open Mon–Fri, 9 a.m.–2 p.m. and 4–7 p.m.; Saturday–Sunday, 10 a.m.–3 p.m.

Police

The municipal police station is at Plaza Duquesa de Parcent, s/n (☎ 95-287-13-69). The national police are located at Avenida. Jaén, s/n (☎ 95-287-10-01).

Post Office

Ronda's Central Post Office is on Virgen de la Paz, 18–20 (☎ 95-287-25-57).

Chapter 18

Granada

● ●

In This Chapter

▶ Getting around Granada

▶ Choosing a place to stay — from sumptuous villas in the old Arab Quarter to quiet hotels within the Alhambra Grounds

▶ Keeping busy in Granada

▶ Striking out on side trips

● ●

*E*ver since the nineteenth-century American author and diplomat Washington Irving happened upon the abandoned Alhambra, the monumental red palace-fortress of the Moors, and reintroduced it to the Western world, most travelers to Spain have put Granada at the top of their must-see list.

Spain's magical mix of east and west — its Arab and Christian cultures — comes into sharpest focus in Granada. The last Moorish capital on the Iberian Peninsula, Granada was the seat of the Nasrid Dynasty, part of a fragmented *al-Andalus* (the name given to Muslim Spain). The Moors built the Alhambra in the foothills of the snowcapped Sierra Nevada, overlooking a broad, fertile valley. The Alhambra was the Islamic definition of an earthly paradise, and its murmuring fountains and regal, elegant palaces were testament to the kingdom's power and sophistication.

The Moors crossed into Iberia via the Straight of Gibraltar in 711 and settled at the base of the Sierra Nevada mountains. After Córdoba — then the Muslim capital — fell in 1031, Granada gained influence and importance among the fragmented Muslim kingdoms. In 1238, Mohammed ben Sasar founded the Nasrid dynasty, and his kingdom stretched from Gibraltar to the eastern coast of Spain. After nearly eight centuries of Moorish presence in Spain, King Boabdil, the last ruler of the dynasty, turned over the keys of Granada to the Catholic kings, Ferdinand and Isabella, in 1492, ending Muslim rule.

Granada's favorite son and Spain's great modern poet Federico García Lorca was deeply enamored of this city, its magical setting and the lingering legends of the Moors. "Only sighs glide/on the waters of Granada," he wrote. As a visitor to the city, you can wade into its Moorish past and trace Lorca's life, which ended tragically in Granada.

Granada

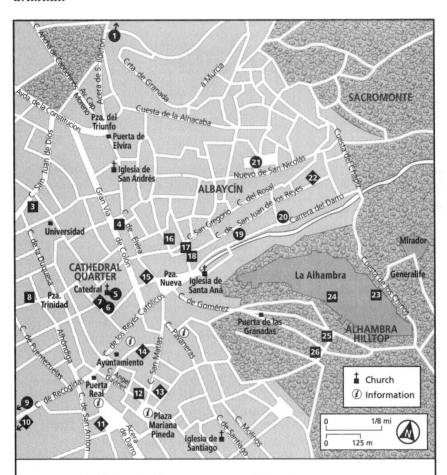

ACCOMMODATIONS ■
Alhambra Palace **26**
América **23**
Casa del Aljarife **16**
Hotel Carmen de Santa Inés **17**
Hotel Los Jerónimos **3**
Hotel Palacio de Santa Inés **18**
Hotel Reina Cristina **8**
Meliá Granada **12**
NH Hotel Inglaterra **4**
Parador Nacional
 de San Francisco **24**
Washington Irving **25**

DINING ◆
Alhabaca **13**
Antigua Bodega Castañeda **15**

Chikito **11**
Mirador de Morayma **22**
Parador Nacional
 de San Francisco **24**
Real Asador de Castilla **14**
Restaurante Sevilla **7**
Las Tinajas **10**

ATTRACTIONS ●
Bañuelo (Arab Baths) **19**
Capilla Real **6**
Catedral **5**
Mirador de San Nicolás **21**
Museo Arqueológico **20**
Monasterio de la Cartuja **1**
Huerta de San Vicente **9**

Just the Facts: Granada

Granada, one of the principal cities of Andalusia, is the capital of the province also named Granada. The province, in the southeastern part of Spain, extends from the Sierra Nevada mountain range down to the beaches of the Costa del Sol (for more on the Costa del Sol, see Chapter 17).

✔ **The name game.** You don't have to say *Granada* with a soft "d" ("Grah-*nah*-tha") for people to understand you, but please note that there's no "ham" in *Alhambra*. This star of Granada has a silent "h", as in "All-*ahm*-bra." The old Arab Quarter is called *Albaycín* (frequently spelled *Albaicín,* but always pronounced "all-buy-*theen*").

✔ **What's for dinner?** Eating in Granada is not the all-out pleasure it is in other provinces of Andalusia, but the basics are reliable: seafood from the Mediterranean coast, cured ham from the mountain villages of the Sierra Nevada, and, of course, gazpacho (chilled tomato soup).

✔ **The forecast.** The weather is hotter than you-know-what in summer and cool, even downright cold, in winter. Granada sits at an altitude of 2,200 feet, so nights are much cooler than days.

✔ **When to go.** One time you absolutely should not go to Granada is in July and August. You'll wilt; it gets blisteringly hot, something like Death Valley in California. The best time to visit Granada is spring, followed closely by fall. The winter can be pleasant but cool — you can see the snow-topped peaks of the Sierra Nevada in the background of the Alhambra, which is good news if you're a skier. However, don't come between Christmas and New Year's — the Alhambra is closed.

✔ **How long before moving on?** You need at least half a day to see the Alhambra, so plan to spend at least a couple of days in the city.

Arriving in Granada

Granada is a convenient destination, no matter where you're coming from or how you choose to arrive.

By plane

Granada's **Armilla airport** (☎ **958-24-52-00**) is 17 km (10.5 miles) south of the city, on Carretera Málaga, s/n. Daily flights arrive from Madrid, Barcelona, Majorca, Valencia, and the Canary Islands. Armilla isn't a huge or complicated airport; you can find a tourism information office as well as an ATM machine.

A shuttle bus (☎ 958-27-86-77) goes back and forth between the airport and Plaza de Isabel la Católica. (It returns to the airport Monday through Saturday at 8:15 a.m., 9:15 a.m., and 5:30 p.m.; Sunday at 5:30 p.m. and 7 p.m.) Travel time from the airport to downtown is under 45 minutes. Taxis, lined up outside the terminals, charge about 3,000 pta. ($17) to the center of Granada.

By car

National highway N-323 connects Granada to the north, including Madrid, via N-IV/E-5, and the southern coast. From Córdoba, take N-432 and from Seville, A-2.

By train

Express trains (called TALGO) from Madrid to Granada take about six hours. Three trains per day go from Granada to Madrid (3,800 pta., or $21). Trains also pull in from and return to Barcelona, Valencia, Málaga, Seville, and Córdoba.

The **RENFE** (Spain's national train service) **train station** (☎ 958-27-12-72; Internet: www.renfe.es) is at Avenida de los Andaluces. The ticket office is downtown at Calle de los Reyes Católicos, 45 (☎ 958-22-31-19).

By bus

Granada's main bus terminal for national departures is **Paseo Estación de Autobuses de Granada,** located at Camino de Ronda, 97 (☎ 958-18-50-10). Six buses per day come in from Seville (the trip takes 3½ hours and costs 2,715 pta./$15) and Córdoba (3 hours; 1,765 pta./$10), while three buses per day arrive from Ronda (3 hours; 1,110 pta./$6). You can also take a bus from Cádiz, Málaga, and Guadix. Contact **Alsina Graells** (Carretera de Jaén, s/n; ☎ 958-18-50-10) for routes and additional information.

Orienting Yourself in Granada

Granada seems congested and not especially appealing on your way in from the web of highways outside the city to Gran Vía de Colón, the city's principal artery. Perpendicular to Gran Vía de Colón is the other main downtown artery, running north-south, Calle de los Reyes Católicos. Near their intersection is the Cathedral and most hotels, restaurants, and shops. The Alhambra sits atop a hill, northeast of Plaza Nueva, while the other neighborhood of interest, the Albaycín district, occupies the hill directly facing the Alhambra.

Granada by neighborhood

In relatively small Granada, three principal areas are of interest to visitors. The Alhambra Hilltop district and Albaycín district face each other on opposite hills, and the downtown area, which contains the Cathedral and most hotels, is wedged between them.

Alhambra Hilltop

The ancient Nasrid Palace complex sits regally on a hill overlooking all of Granada. The neighborhood has a small number of restaurants and hotels, but above all, this is where you come to enjoy one of Spain's most remarkable treasures: the magnificent Alhambra. Here you'll find

- ✔ **Alhambra** and **Generalife,** the majestic Moorish palace complex and summer retreat.

- ✔ **Parador Nacional de San Francisco,** within the Alhambra grounds — Spain's most popular parador (historic government-run) hotel.

Cathedral Quarter/downtown Granada

The *centro,* or downtown Granada, is congested but compact and easy to navigate. This neighborhood is the business center of Granada, where you find most hotels, restaurants, and shops. Look for the following attractions in the Cathedral Quarter:

- ✔ The **Cathedral,** Granada's great Christian monument.

- ✔ The **Royal Chapel,** where the Catholic monarchs are buried.

- ✔ Sights just beyond downtown: the **La Cartuja Monastery** and poet García Lorca's childhood home, **Huerta de San Vicente.**

Albaycín

The old Arab Quarter, an evocative warren of whitewashed houses and tiny alleyways climbing the hillside, begs you to explore it. This area has few conventional sights, other than the mesmerizing views of the Alhambra and Sierra Nevada mountains, but the whole *barrio* (neighborhood) is itself an attraction, an integral part of Granada. Today you can find a few small hotels with great character located here in historic villas. In Albaycín you find:

- ✔ **El Bañuelo,** the Arab baths.

- ✔ The old **Arab walls.**

- ✔ Nearby **Sacromonte,** the old gypsy neighborhood and flamenco caves.

Getting info after you arrive

You can find tourism offices at the airport, **Corral del Carbón** (Mariana Pineda, 12; ☎ **958-22-59-90,** open Monday through Friday, 9 a.m. to 7 p.m.; Saturday, 10 a.m. to 2 p.m.; Sunday, 10 a.m. to 2 p.m.); **Real de la Alhambra** s/n (in front of Palacio de Carlos V; ☎ **958-22-04-45,** daily, 10 a.m. to 5 p.m.); **Duque de Medinaceli,** 2 (☎ **91-429-49-51,** open Monday, 9 a.m. to 7 p.m. and Saturday 9 a.m. to 7 p.m.); **Plaza Mariana Pineda,** 10 (☎ **958-22-66-88,** open Monday through Friday 10:30 a.m. to 1:30 p.m. and 4:30 p.m. to 7 p.m., Saturday 10:30 a.m. to 2 p.m.); **Avda Andalucía** (Barriada de la Encina; ☎ **958-27-93-98,** open Monday through Friday, 9:30 a.m. to 2 p.m. and 4 to 7:30 p.m., Saturday, 9:30 a.m. to 2 p.m.); and **Carretera de Málaga** (☎ **958-27-93-98,** open Monday through Friday 9:30 a.m. to 2 p.m. and 4 to 7:30 p.m., and Saturday 9:30 a.m. to 2 p.m.).

Getting around Granada

Granada is relatively compact but congested (don't use your car to get around). It's a good walking city, but some of the hills may prove challenging. Try the following alternative methods for checking out Granada.

By bus

One of the best things to hit Granada in recent years is a tourist microbus that goes back and forth from the Alhambra to the Albaycín district. The red-and-white minibuses, popular with both locals and tourists, run every 15 minutes between 7 a.m. and 11 p.m. The fare is 120 pta. (67¢).

If you're visiting Granada for a few days, or you've got friends or family in tow, buy a half-price, ten-fare bus ticket for 680 pta. ($3.75). You can purchase tickets at *estancos* (tobacco stands — look for the "Tabacos" sign). On board, you can also buy a 15-ride ticket for 1,000 pta. ($5.50).

By taxi

To order a taxi, call **Radio Taxi** (☎ **958-15-14-61**) or **Tele-Taxi** (☎ **958-28-06-54**). Few journeys cost more than 1,000 pta. ($5.50). You can hail a cab in the street (the little green light on the roof means you can hop in) or pick one up where they line up (usually outside hotels, the Alhambra, and near the minibus stop on Plaza Nueva).

By car

Granada is congested and complicated to drive in; a car isn't necessary in town. However, if you wish to explore more of Andalusia, renting a rig is a good idea. Rental car companies include: **Avis** (Recogidas, 31; ☎ 958-25-23-58); **Budget** (Recogidas, 35; ☎ 958-25-05-54); **Europcar** (Avenida del Sur; ☎ 958-29-50-65); and **Hertz** (Luis Braille, 7; ☎ 958-25-24-19).

On foot

Granada is surprisingly small, but you need to save your feet for the Alhambra and getting around the hilly Albaycín neighborhood. Walking between Albaycín and most of the downtown sights is easy enough, though. Unless you're staying in a hotel that's tucked into the woods near the Alhambra, you need to take a bus or taxi to get there.

By bike

Hilly Granada may not seem like an ideal place to rent a bike and get around, but if the extended ramp up to the Alhambra looks like a heaven-sent workout to you, you can pick up a bicycle for the day at **Manolo Maxi Alquiler de Bicicletas,** Manuel de Falla, 12 (☎ 958-25-27-14; 1,000 pta./$5.50 per half-day).

Staying in Granada

Granada's hotel scene used to encompass the *parador* — the most sought-after reservation in Spain — and everything else. But Granada has added a few outstanding small hotels with real Andalusian character to supplement the flagship of the national *parador* network. Granada's a very popular destination, so make your reservations early — especially in the spring and early summer.

If you want to make sure you get a room either at the **Parador Nacional de San Francisco** (☎ 958-22-14-40) or **América** (☎/Fax: 958-22-224-25) — both within the actual grounds of the Alhambra — book at least three to four months (or more) in advance.

Christmas in Granada with the snow-capped Sierra Nevada mountains in the background may sound romantic, but you'll feel more like the Grinch if you arrive without realizing that the Alhambra, probably Spain's single greatest sight (at the very least it competes neck-and-neck with Madrid's Prado Museum for that honor) closes between December 25 and January 1.

The top hotels

Alhambra Palace
$$$ Alhambra Hill

With a location darned near as privileged as the Alhambra itself, this palatial reddish-pink hotel on the hill envisions itself as the perfect Moorish-style companion to the real Nasrid Palaces just minutes away, and for most visitors to Granada, it is. Built by the Duke of San Pedro de Galatino in 1910, it looks like an Epcot Center version of a Moorish citadel and includes all kinds of neo-Mudéjar touches (splashy tiles, arches, carved plaster walls, wood ceilings, and even a pseudo-minaret). But what it has above all else is a superb location — it's within walking distance of the Alhambra and has priceless views of Granada below. The 122 rooms at the Palace, popular with travelers and business visitors alike, are spacious and impressive without being stuffy. Try to get a room with a small balcony overlooking the city, and ask to see a few rooms if you can, because their size and appeal vary quite a bit.

Peña Partida, 2-4 (on southern face of the Alhambra hill; the next-to-last stop on Alhambra minibus leaves you 200 yards from entrance). ☎ *958-22-14-68. Fax: 958-22-64-04. E-mail:* alhambra@mailhost.euroflat.es. *Internet:* www.eel.es/alhambrapalace. *Parking: free. Rack rates: 22,500 pta. ($125) double. AE, DC, MC, V.*

América
$$ Alhambra Hill

Happily, the impossible-to-get-into Parador Nacional de San Francisco doesn't have a monopoly on beds inside the Alhambra grounds. You can instead choose to stay at this tiny, charming, and homey hotel in an old Andalusian house. The rooms are exceedingly simple, but the house has a lovely plant-filled patio and magnificent gardens all around. Management offers simple, home-cooked meals every day but Sunday. Given its location, (for which you pay through the nose at the Parador), the América is constantly booked. Reserve here at least three to four months in advance.

Real de la Alhambra, 53 (within Alhambra grounds; take Alhambra minibus to edge of grounds, or take a taxi directly to hotel). ☎ *958-22-74-71. Fax: 958-22-74-70. E-mail:* hamerica@moebius.es. *Internet:* www.lingolex.com/most. *Parking: 500 pta. ($2.75). Rack rates: 13,500 pta. ($75) double. Closed Nov 10 to the end of Feb. AE, DC, MC, V.*

Hotel Carmen de Santa Inés
$$ Albaycín

An old Arab *carmen* (villa with a concealed garden) that was expanded in the sixteenth and seventeenth centuries was fully renovated and transformed into one of Granada's loveliest hotels in April 1998. This hotel's nine rooms, all different, are replete with handsome antique furnishings, Arab carpets, and wonderful decorative touches; six of the rooms even offer views of the Alhambra (the others overlook the interior patio). Tucked into the tiny streets of the old Arab Quarter, Albaycín, the hotel is as charming as the neighborhood it inhabits. The hosts serve breakfast in the beautiful garden, amid fountains and fruit trees.

Placeta de Porras, 7, off San Juan de los Reyes, 15 (two short blocks northwest of Carrera del Darro and Iglesia de Santa Ana). ☎ **958-22-63-80.** *Fax: 958-22-44-04. Internet:* www.madeinspain.net/hotelesgranada/carmen. *Parking: 1,500 pta. ($8). Rack rates: 12,500–16,500 pta. ($69–$92) double. AE, DC, MC, V.*

Hotel Palacio de Santa Inés
$$–$$$ Albaycín

Owned by the same folks that run the Hotel Carmen de Santa Inés (see the previous review), this lovingly renovated small palace, until only recently in complete ruins, is one of Granada's top choices. Dating to the beginning of the sixteenth century, it was known as the *Casa del Padre Eterno* (House of the Eternal Father). Today, it is a luxurious five-year-old inn with modern art on the walls, silver chandeliers, a two-story Renaissance courtyard, and thick-wooden-beamed ceilings. The painstaking renovation restored important frescos on the walls of the patio, painted by a disciple of Rafael. The hotel's six double rooms and seven suites are charmingly decorated, full of interesting antique pieces, and all different. Rooms 3, 6, 7, and 12 offer views of the Alhambra, which is illuminated at night. Like its sister, this hotel is located in the attractively labyrinthine Albaycín district. If there's a difference between the two hotels, this Santa Inés is slightly less intimate that the the hotel Carmen de Santa Inés.

Cuesta de Santa Inés, 9 (one short block northwest of Carrera del Darro and Iglesia de Santa Ana). ☎ **958-22-23-62.** *Fax: 958-22-24-65. Internet:* www.eel.es/ granada/hoteles/sines/sines.htm. *Parking: 1,500 pta. ($9). Rack rates: 15,000–17,000 pta. ($83–$94) double. AE, DC, MC, V.*

Hotel Reina Cristina
$$–$$$ Cathedral Quarter

Granada's best mid-range alternative, the family-owned Reina Cristina is full of charm and history. The charm is evident in the personal service the hosts give every client, and the beautiful, plant-filled interior courtyard, which looks like what it was — part of a handsome private home — rather than a hotel lobby. As for history, the home was formerly owned by a family named Rosales and was frequented by Granada's favorite son, the celebrated poet and playwright Federico García Lorca. He was taken from this hotel by Franco's forces and shot just a couple of miles away. Despite that sad note, the hotel is cheerful and an excellent deal. The rooms aren't overly large, but they're very comfortable. The hotel is just minutes from the Cathedral and most of Granada's main sights. It also has an extremely nice restaurant and *tapas* bar (a bar serving Spanish hors d'oeuvres) on the premises, which is very popular with locals and guests.

Tablas, 4 (one block west of Plaza Trinidad, southwest of the Cathedral). ☎ *958-25-32-11. Fax: 958-25-57-28. E-mail:* cliente@hotelreinacristina.com. *Internet:* www.hotelreinacristina.com. *Parking 1,500 pta. ($9). Rack rates: 12,300–19,900 pta. ($68–$111) double. AE, DC, MC, V.*

NH Hotel Inglaterra
$$–$$$ Cathedral Quarter

In 1991, the Spanish hotel chain NH bought the Inglaterra (once a popular family-run place in need of a makeover) and transformed it into one of Granada's most charming hotels. Set back on a small but busy street off of the city's busiest thoroughfare, *Gran Vía de Colón,* the hotel has just 36 exceptionally clean rooms around a brightly colored central courtyard. The rooms have hardwood floors, furnishings with light woods, and boldly colored walls, bedspreads, and curtains. Definitely opt for an interior room, because the area is crowded with bar-hoppers spilling out into the streets.

Cetti Meriem, 4 (two blocks directly northeast of the Cathedral). ☎ *958-22-15-58. Fax: 958-22-71-00. Internet:* www.nh-hoteles.es. *Parking 1,600 pta. ($9). Rack rates: 15,500–24,000 pta. ($86–$133) double. Deals: weekends 15,500 pta. ($86), including breakfast. AE, DC, MC, V.*

Parador Nacional de San Francisco
$$$$$ Alhambra

If you're the sort who plans vacations far in advance, and you're certain of the date you're visiting Granada, you may have an outside shot at getting a reservation at Spain's most popular *parador.* There's good reason for this hotel's popularity: an ancient Moorish palace converted into a convent in the fifteenth century, the Parador is lodged within the grounds of the magnificent Alhambra. The serene hilltop gardens, with the snow-capped Sierra Nevada peaks and Albaycín district in the distance, may just be Spain's finest location. The look of the rooms almost doesn't matter, but the good news is that, although they're not over-the-top luxurious, they are full of good taste and handsome antiques. If you're dying to stay within the Alhambra, no doubt a magical experience at night, put down this book and send them a fax right now — if it's three to four months before you'll be arriving in Granada. If it's not, you can still take a shot.

Real de la Alhambra, s/n (within Alhambra grounds; take Alhambra minibus to edge of grounds or, better yet, taxi directly to hotel). ☎ *958-22-14-40. Fax: 958-22-22-64. E-mail:* granada@parador.es. *Internet:* www.parador.es. *Parking: free. Rack rates: 29,500–33,000 pta. ($164–$183) double. AE, DC, MC, V.*

Granada's runner-up hotels

Casa del Aljarife

$$ **Albaycín** This three-room *pension* (guest house) is in a stylish, homey seventeenth-century house on a charming square; call ahead and the owner will meet you at the bus or train station. *Placeta de la Cruz Verde, 2 in Albaycín.* ☎/Fax: *958-22-24-25.* E-mail: aljarife@granadainfo.com. *Internet:* www.lingolex.com/most.

Hotel Los Jerónimos

$ **Downtown/Central Granada** This is a pretty bare-bones option, but if you're looking to save money and aren't overly particular about creature comforts (you find few here), you won't find anything better at the price. *Gran Capitán, 1, across from San Jerónimo monastery and several blocks south of Gran Vía de Colón.* ☎/Fax: *958-29-44-61.*

Meliá Granada

$$$ **Downtown/Central Granada** This big, busy hotel in the busiest section of town (three blocks east of Puerta Real), is pretty generic but a reasonable business traveler's hotel. *Angel Ganivet, 7.* ☎ *958-22-74-00.* *Fax: 958-22-74-03.* E-mail: melia.granada@solmelia.es. *Internet:* www.solmelia.es.

Washington Irving

$$ **Alhambra area** If you just gotta be on the hill, near enough to taste the mystique of the Alhambra, but you can't get into the Parador or América, this is the place to come. The hotel has seen better days, but it's still a classic. *Paseo del Generalife, 2, just outside of Alhambra grounds.* ☎ *958-22-75-50.* *Fax: 958-22-88-40.*

Dining in Granada

Granada is not one of the best places in Spain, or even in Andalusia, to eat out. A provincial capital, it's pretty unimaginative in terms of dining opportunities. Most of the places you find to eat are simple, no-frills restaurants. You don't have to eat poorly, but your memories are much more likely to be of the Alhambra than of the meals in Granada. Making a meal of *tapas* (Spanish hors d'oeuvres) is a reliable choice.

Typical dishes in Granada, so close to the Sierra Nevada, Spain's highest mountain range, are hardy. Granada's version of the cold soup gazpacho, *gazpacho granadino,* is usually made with *jamón serrano* (cured ham); *habas con jamón* are small broad beans in olive oil and with thin slices of salt cured ham; and *tortilla sacromonte,* perhaps the most

famous dish in Granada, is a Spanish *tortilla* (omelet) made not with
the usual potatoes and onions, but with calf, pig, or lamb brains. Call
me fussy, but that's one tortilla I *won't* taste.

For more on Spanish dining customs, including mealtimes, costs, and
tipping, see Chapter 1.

Alhabaca
$$$ Cathedral Quarter   SPANISH

A simple and tiny establishment — it seats a little more than 20 diners —
on a quiet plaza near a number of bars and nightlife, Alhabaca is a bit like
a country inn in the big, bad city. It has bare white walls, simple tables
with white tablecloths, and the kitchen in full view. Dishes are simple,
but well prepared. A good starter is *salmorejo,* the thick, gazpacho-like
tomato soup from Córdoba. The main course I had, *merluza en salsa de
almendras* (hake or white fish in almond sauce), was equally good. For
dessert, the *flan de calabaza* (pumpkin flan) was a Spanish version of
pumpkin pie.

*Calle Varela, 17 (between Varela and San Matías, 5 blocks from Plaza de la
Mariana).* ☎ *958-22-49-23. Main courses: 1,000–1,900 pta. ($5.50–$10.50). Open:
Tues–Sat lunch and dinner; Sun lunch only. AE, MC.*

Antigua Bodega Castañeda
$ Cathedral Quarter   ANDALUSIAN

A lively, cheerful spot just off Plaza Nueva — splitting the distance
between the Alhambra and the Albaycín *barrio* — this long train car of a
place is half inexpensive restaurant, half rollicking *tapas* bar. There are
just 10 tables or so, so you'll probably have to wait — or just muscle up
to the bar like everyone else. Besides all manner of cheap *tapas,* sand-
wiches, and large salads, it specializes in *potajes* — a type of thick stew
in clay pots that's probably fortified Spaniards since the time of
Columbus. There are six types of *potajes,* including codfish and lentils
with *chorizo* (spicy sausage). A great place to stop before making your
way up the hill to the Alhambra, Bodgea Castañeda is also just a stone's
throw from the Moroccan-style tea rooms, where you can grab a fabu-
lous fruit shake for dessert.

Calle Elvira, 5 (just off Plaza Nueva). ☎ *958-22-63-62. Main courses: 650–1,500 pta.
($3–$8). Open: daily for lunch and dinner. AE, MC, V.*

Chikito
$$$ Cathedral Quarter   ANDALUSIAN

A classic with local diners and mostly Spanish visitors to Granada (portraits of the most famous line the wall of the lively *tapas* bar at the

entrance), Chikito (pronounced like it looks) is cutely named (the letter "k" doesn't exist in Spanish) but serious about food. A little too serious, perhaps. I recommend standing at the bar and downing some excellent *tapas* over sitting in the stuffier dining room. If you do sit down, choose from among *zarzuela de pescado* (seafood stew), breaded and stuffed veal, and oven-baked hake (a white fish similar to cod).

Plaza del Campillo, 9 (between Angel Gavinet and Acera de Darro). ☎ *958-22-33-64. Reservations recommended. Main courses: 975–2,875 pta. ($5–$16); menú del dia 1,975 pta. ($11). Open: Thur–Tues for lunch and dinner. AE, MC, V.*

Las Tinajas

$$$ Cathedral Quarter   ANDALUSIAN

A delightful *mesón* (inn) decorated with original art and lots of plants and flowers, Las Tinajas is the work of José Álvarez, a veteran of the Granada restaurant scene. The *tapas* bar is a popular and occasionally noisy spot, serving up a delicious variety of hors d'oeuvres. The kitchen consistently elaborates dishes with the freshest possible ingredients, such as *rollitos de lubina rellenos de langostinos y jamón ibérico* (sea bass rolls stuffed with prawns and salt-cured ham). The wine cellar is well stocked with Spanish favorites and a few surprises.

Martínez Campos, 17 (just off Recogidas, south of Puerta Real). ☎ *958-25-43-93. Main courses: 1,475–2,875 pta. ($8–$16); menú del dia 2,200 pta. ($12). Open: daily for lunch and dinner; Closed July. AE, MC, V.*

Mirador de Morayma

$$ Albaycín   ANDALUSIAN/SPANISH

A gorgeous private home, decorated with what appear to be personal effects, this is a great chance to experience an authentic Granada *carmen* — an Albaycín villa with stupendous gardens concealed behind high walls. You have to ring at an imposing black door — be patient, it may take a while for someone to let you inside. Wind your way through the gardens on the way to the restaurant at back; the views of the Alhambra on the hill are nothing short of amazing. (Legend has it that Morayma, the wife of the last Moorish king, Boabdil, was imprisoned here, reduced to gazing at the Alhambra from the opposite hill.) The popular restaurant has several separate dining rooms with idiosyncratic touches (pre-Colombian pieces, a shrine near the bathroom). The traditional menu is diverse and servings are ample; prices are reasonable. Try the *espinacas con almendras* (spinach with almonds) to start, and perhaps the *solomillo de cerdo* (pork sirloin) to follow it up.

Pianista García Carrillo, 2 (difficult to find; a few blocks down from and to the left of the Mirador San Nicolás). ☎ *958-22-82-90. Main courses: 1,400–2,900 pta. ($8–$16). Open: Mon–Sat for lunch and dinner. AE, MC, V.*

Parador Nacional de San Francisco
$$$ Alhambra SPANISH

The Parador hotel, housed in a fifteenth-century convent, is hard as heck to get into, and expensive when you do. A good alternative if you've landed somewhere else is to pop in (well, not exactly pop in — reservations are very necessary) for lunch or dinner to soak up some of the serene Alhambra ambience. The views of the rose gardens and the Generalife in the distance are unbeatable. At lunch time, the attractive garden terrace is open — a great place to dine if you're not here in the middle of a scorching Granada summer. The national parador restaurants are generally dependable, if not always exciting, but this may be the very best of the lot. Dine on Benito Ortiz's creative Andalusian specialties such as *rape mozárabe con piñones* (Moorish-style monkfish with pine nuts) or blood sausage lasagna in a sauce of leeks.

Real de la Alhambra. s/n. (within Alhambra grounds; enter western gate, where you do not have to pay to enter the Alhambra). ☎ *958-22-14-40. Reservations required. Main courses: 2,000–2,800 pta. ($11–$16); menú del día 3,700 pta. ($21). Open: Daily for lunch and dinner. AE, DC, MC, V.*

Real Asador de Castilla
$$$ Cathedral Quarter ANDALUSIAN

Welcome, meat lovers. An authentic Castilian *asador* (barbecue restaurant), this is the place to get thick ribs, lamb, and roast pig direct from the spit. On a small plaza near the old *Ayuntamiento* (City Hall), it does big weekend business with local families, who huddle around the *tapas* bar before moving on to more serious pursuits. There's also fresh fish and a series of *guisos caseros* — home-cooked stews thick with vegetables and, mostly, meat.

Escudo del Carmen, 17 (two blocks south of Plaza Isabel la Católica, off San Matías). ☎ *958-22-29-10. Main courses: 1,200–2,700 pta. ($7–$15). Open: daily for lunch and dinner. AE, MC, V.*

Alhambra pit stops

If you're starved after a full morning or afternoon at the Alhambra, and the snack bars inside won't fill you up, you can go across the street to **Jardines Alberto,** Alixares del Generalife, s/n (☎ 958-22-48-18). A restaurant in a relaxed garden setting, it offers some imaginative Andalusian dishes, including asparagus stuffed with anchovies and served with *salmorejo* (cold soup, Córdoba-style) and *rape mozárabe* (Moorish-style monkfish). Another likely location for post-Alhambra eats is Peña Partida, the street just down from the Alhambra Palace hotel. Just a five-minute walk from the Alhambra, Peña Partida is lined with chummy, informal restaurants that post their menus outside.

La Alhambra & Generalife

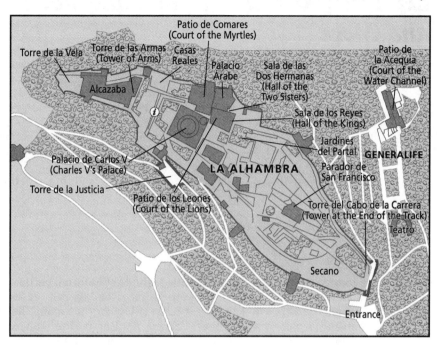

Patio de Comares
(Court of the Myrtles)

Torre de la Vela
Torre de las Armas
(Tower of Arms)
Casas Reales
Palacio Árabe
Sala de las Dos Hermanas
(Hall of the Two Sisters)
Patio de la Acequia
(Court of the Water Channel)
Alcazaba
Sala de los Reyes
(Hall of the Kings)
Jardines del Partal
GENERALIFE
Palacio de Carlos V
(Charles V's Palace)
LA ALHAMBRA
Parador de San Francisco
Torre de la Justicia
Patio de los Leones
(Court of the Lions)
Torre del Cabo de la Carrera
(Tower at the End of the Track)
Teatro
Secano
Entrance

Restaurante Sevilla
$$$ Cathedral Quarter   ANDALUSIAN

A classic in Granada, Restaurante Sevilla, named for that *other* city in Andalusia (see Chapter 16), has been around seemingly forever and is still going strong. The city's best-known restaurant, this two-story place is where the literary and musical elite used to dine back in the early 1930s. Today it's just as popular with Spaniards and a healthy portion of visitors who tramp through town. In summer, the restaurant fills the square next to the Royal Chapel with tables. Andalusian specialties reign. The four dining rooms are charmingly decorated with colorful Moorish-style *azulejos* (tiles). Open your meal with the inevitable gazpacho or *sopa sevillana* (a fish soup), followed perhaps by *cordero a la pastoril* (spicy lamb stew with herbs).

Calle Oficios, 12 (next to Royal Chapel). ☎ *58-22-12-23. Reservations recommended. Main courses: 1,300–3,200 pta. ($7–$18); menú del día 2,500 pta. ($14). Daily for lunch, dinner Mon–Sat. AE, DC, MC, V.*

Exploring Granada: The Alhambra and More

No matter how much time you have, make your first stop the Alhambra — unless weather reports call for clouds and rain. If at all possible, go on a sunny day, when the reflecting pools are brilliant and the views of the Albaycín district and Sierra Nevada are clear. You need at least a half-day — a full four to five hours — to fully see the Alhambra. In fact, I limit the "Top Attractions" in Granada to just three must-sees; they are crucial to getting a feel for this historic city, and they shouldn't require more than a day and a half to see. Any time left over is a bonus, and you can devote it to the second tier of attractions and things to do.

The top attractions

Albaycín

Granada's old Arab district, the site of the first Moorish settlement in Granada, is richly evocative of another time, when there were far more mosques than churches in the city. The Albaycín runs along the Darro River and a picturesque street, Carrera del Darro. The whitewashed neighborhood creeps up a steep hillside, full of quick twists and turns and ever-escalating steps, all the while keeping the Alhambra in its viewfinder. The entire district has been named a UNESCO Heritage of Mankind site. There are discoveries at every turn — *cármenes* (Moorish villas with orchards), quiet plazas, uneven cobblestone paths, tall cypress trees, and *aljibes* (cisterns).

The greatest discovery, though, may be the heart-stopping views from the **Mirador de San Nicolás Church.** A small plaza in front of the church looks directly across at the Alhambra, perfectly framed against the snow-capped ridges of the Sierra Nevada. A visit is best at sunset, when the Alhambra glows red, or late at night, when it is gorgeously floodlit. You may find yourself returning to this platform, a meeting place for young people and *gringos* (English-speaking tourists) in Granada, time and time again. Take Calle Zafra or Elvira to get there, but plan on getting lost amid the charming and serpentine streets. Bring good walking shoes and energy — there's a reason many of the Albaycín's streets begin with the word *Cuesta* (slope).

At the bottom of the hill, along the Carretera del Darro at Calle Bañuelo, is **El Bañuelo,** or Arab Baths. One of the oldest Moorish remnants in Granada (built in the eleventhh century, they predate the Alhambra), the baths are in surprisingly good condition, though they're not as elaborate or as large as those in Ronda (see Chapter 17). The baths (☎ 958-22-23-39) are open (to take a peek only) Tuesday through Saturday, 10 a.m. to 2 p.m. Admission is free.

Onward to the Alhambra

The easiest way to get to the Alhambra is to take a taxi or the red-and-white minibuses that shuttle back and forth between the Albaycín district and the hilltop palace complex (the nearest stop is below the hill, at Plaza Nueva). If you're the energetic sort, however, the steep uphill walk into the luxuriant shade of the woods surrounding the Alhambra is a magnificent way to make your way up. The walk doesn't take more than 20 minutes or so, but I don't recommend it for anyone but the most athletic (you need to save your energy to walk around the large grounds of the Alhambra and Generalife). To walk, follow the signs from *Plaza Nueva* to *Cuesta de Gomérez* uphill to *Puerta de las Granadas,* the first of two gates to the Alhambra. Keep going past the second; the ticket office is on your left (look for all the commotion). (Along the way, watch out for thieves masquerading as tour guides.)

Down the street is the **Museo Arqueológico** (Archaeology Museum), in the Casa de Castril, a stately Renaissance mansion. Its exhibits are of interest if you have a great curiosity about Granada's Muslim and Visigothic past, but they will be rather dull for others.

Museo Arqueológico: *Carrera del Darro, 41.* ☎ **958-22-56-40.** *Open Tuesday 3–8 p.m., Wed–Sat 9 a.m–8 p.m., Sun 9 a.m.–2 p.m.; 250 pta. ($1.40). Free to EU members.*

Catedral and Capilla Real
Centro/Cathedral Quarter

This ornate, powerful cathedral was Granada's sixteenth-century Christian answer to the Alhambra, an emphatic statement about the conclusive Reconquest of Spain from the Moors. The Catholic monarchs ordered it placed right in the middle of the Arab *medina* (marketplace). The cathedral started out Gothic in style, but wound up Baroque, with five massive naves, thick pillars, and a dramatic altar. In opposition to the light, delicate, elegant Alhambra, the cathedral is heavy, imposing, and grandiose.

The **Capilla Real,** or Royal Chapel, next door (off Calle Oficios), is where the Gothic marble tombs of the Catholic monarchs Ferdinand and Isabella lie behind the flourishes of a black-and-gold grille. When the last king, Boabdil, surrendered to Christian forces in Granada in 1492, the Catholic monarchs registered their greatest victory and almost immediately chose Granada for their eventual burial place. They are interred here along with their daughter Juana la Loca (Joanna the Mad) and her husband, Felipe el Hermoso (Philip the Fair). The chapel museum houses Queen Isabella's crown and Ferdinand's sword, as well as important paintings by Botticelli and others. Allot about an hour at the Cathedral and Royal Chapel. On your way out, peek into the **Palacio de la Madraza,** once the Arab university, directly across from the entrance to the Royal Chapel. Inside is a tiny, but spectacular *mirhab* (prayer niche).

Cathedral, Gran Vía de Colón, 5; chapel, Calle Oficios, 3 (one block southwest of Gran Vía de Colón). ☎ **958-22-29-59** and 958-22-78-48. Admission: cathedral, 300 pta. ($1.75); chapel, 300 pta. ($1.75); seniors 150 pta. (85¢), free to children under 10. Open: Mon–Sun 11 a.m.–1 p.m. and 3:30–6:30 p.m., Sun 3:30–6:30 p.m. April 1–Sept 30, 11 a.m.–1 p.m. and 4–7 p.m.

La Alhambra and Generalife
Alhambra Hilltop

Atop a wooded, ruddy hill is southern Spain's showpiece, the legendary Alhambra fortress and palace complex. Though its origins as a fortress date to the ninth century, the present citadel and walled fortifications of the Nasrid dynasty were begun in 1238, and the complex was enlarged throughout the thirteenth and fourteenth centuries — as the Moors solidified their hold on southern Spain — with palaces, residences, mosques, spectacular gardens, and a royal summer estate (the Generalife, adjacent to the Alhambra). After Christians retook Granada from the Moors, they added a convent and Renaissance palace to the Alhambra grounds in the sixteenth century. The whole complex fell into disrepair and, eventually, abandonment over the next hundred years or so, only to be rediscovered in 1829 by the American writer and diplomat Washington Irving. His *Tales of the Alhambra* succeeded in awakening the world's attention and prompting Spanish authorities to renew restoration of the palaces and grounds.

The Moors' intentions in constructing the Alhambra's were grand: nothing less than to create an earthly paradise. In its quiet elegance and harmony, its air of inscrutability and wonder, and its bewitching beauty, this sprawling compound was Muslim Spain's greatest achievement. The Alhambra's perfection attests to the splendor, power and architectural genius of the Moorish dynasty in Spain.

The Alhambra is Spain's single greatest sight and among the finest attractions in all of Europe. The palaces overflow with legend and intrigue — there are oft-told tales of harems and mass murders within their exclusive quarters. (It's no surprise that one of the palaces includes a room called the Hall of Secrets.)

Your Alhambra ticket (valid for one day only) allows you only a half-hour window of access to the Nasrid Palaces (you must enter at the time your ticket specifies, or lose your opportunity to see the finest part of the Alhambra, but you can stay as long as you wish after you enter). The Spanish government limits the number of people allowed to enter the Alhambra every day of the year. During peak visitation periods — primarily summer, but also at other vacation times such as Easter — you may not gain admission if you go late in the day. Try to go as early as possible, even though tour groups will be lined up, or try going during the extended lunch hour (2 p.m. to 4 p.m.). Even early in the morning, you may wait a couple of hours or more to enter. You may have some luck late in the day, after large groups have evacuated, but if the day's quota is filled, you'll be denied entrance after 4 p.m.

Enter the Alhambra complex at the end of the Cuesta de Gomérez and stroll along the gardens, where a *medina* (marketplace) once thrived. The first major building is the jarringly self-important fifteenth-century Renaissance **Palacio de Carlos V** (Palace of Carlos V, a Christian addition to the Alhambra grounds and stark stylistic contrast). It contains the **Museo de la Alhambra** (a newly redesigned museum devoted to the art of Al-Andalus) and a small **Museo de Bellas Artes** (Fine Arts Museum). You can either see the Carlos V palace first or save it until after you've seen the palaces of the Moorish kings, which deserve the bulk of your time. If you have time before your appointed hour, visit the **Alcazaba,** the fortress that is the oldest part of the Alhambra, begun in 1238. **Torre de la Campana** (the watchtower), the highest point of the Alhambra, is where the Catholic monarchs hung their banners after the Reconquest and installed a bell to regulate irrigation times in the fertile valleys below.

Restoration efforts altered the usual entrance to the Royal Nasrid palaces in early 1999 — normally you enter the **Sala del Mexuar,** but for the time being you first enter the **Palacio de Comares,** built by Yusuf I, and come upon the **Patio de Arrayanes** (Courtyard of Myrtles), a beautiful patio with a long, spectacular reflecting pool. Here are some of the palace's most remarkable *azulejos* (glazed ceramic tiles). Behind it is the **Salón de Embajadores** (Ambassadors' Hall), an ornately carved throne room built in the mid-fourteenth century. The dome represents the seven heavens of the Islamic cosmos. Make your way to the **Palacio de los Leones,** part of the royal family's private quarters and one of the most famous elements of the Alhambra. Built by Mohammed V, the palace is a festival of delicate marble columns with a gurgling fountain at its center; water trickles from the mouths of 12 lions. Here the delicacy of the plasterwork carving reaches new heights. At the back of the patio is the **Sala de los Abencerrajes,** a noble hall with a rich honeycombed ceiling where the last Moorish king, Boabdil, reputedly beheaded rivals (a legend that purports to explain the reddish, blood-stained color of the pillars). From here, wander around the lions' courtyard and back into the **Apartamentos de Carlos V** — quarters where Washington Irving stayed in the 1820s. His stay in the abandoned Alhambra was the basis for his famous book, *Tales from the Alhambra,* which publicized the great palaces to the world. Exit these parts and find the ruins of the oldest palace in the Alhambra, **Palacio del Partal,** with another large reflecting pool, and gardens that lead to the Generalife.

The **Generalife** ("hen-air-all-*ee*-fay"), also within the Alhambra's walls, was the country estate of the Nasrid kings. High above the city on 75 lush acres, it sings with murmuring fountains. The thirteenth-century complex is a series of magically serene courtyards and gently flowing waters, a place in which to lose yourself, as the swinging sultans and their harems surely did. The **Patio de la Acequia,** a closed Arab garden with a long, narrow pool lined by water jets forming delicate arches, is particularly fetching and photogenic. Don't miss a lovely walk on the footpath, **Escalera del Agua (Water Staircase),** along the upper gardens.

Some Alhambra sightseeing tips

An ideal visit to the Alhambra is a thoroughly peaceful experience. With the massive interest in visiting the palace complex, though, serenity can be tough to come by. Here are a few ways to save time and hassles:

✔ Purchase your ticket, up to three days in advance, by calling ☎ 958-22-09-12. Or get tickets Monday through Friday at the BBV Bank (Plaza Isabel la Católica, at the corner of Reyes Católicos) from 9 a.m. to 2 p.m. There's a 125-pta. (70¢) surcharge.

✔ Avoid the early morning if you dislike large groups. Tour groups on whirlwind tours of Andalusia line up at 8 a.m. — get out of their way, because they've got to be in Córdoba by noon!

✔ Lunch time is generally a good time to visit — most Europeans take long lunch breaks. (Try to get your timed entrance to the Nasrid Palaces between 2 p.m. and 4 p.m.) Better yet, come during the last hour of the afternoon session (winter, 5 to 6 p.m.; summer, 7 to 8 p.m.). This is a perfect time to visit, when the tour groups have moved on and most others still hanging around are tired. Note, however, that during the busiest times of the year, if you wait to get your ticket until late in the afternoon, you risk not getting admitted if the daily maximum is already filled.

✔ Rent a digital audiophone guide for a detailed explanation of the history of the Alhambra and some of the legends and tales associated with it. The tour is in several languages, including English, and it allows you to go at your own pace, repeating and skipping over passages if you like. It also gives you the great advantage of not having to read when you'd much prefer to look. And, at 500 pta. ($2.75), it's a bargain.

✔ Visit the Alhambra at night — a singular experience. Night is a great time to feel the silence of the floodlit palace, and hear the trickling fountains unmarred by groups shouting in French, English, Japanese, German, Italian, and Portuguese. However, you can only visit the Nasrid palaces (not including the Generalife). A nocturnal visit is best as a supplementary visit — if you've already seen it by day and found its beauty intoxicating. As your only visit, you miss too much at night, including the beauty of the reflective pools, the bright tile work, and the views of Albaycín and the Sierra Nevada.

Calle Real s/n. (Alhambra Hill). ☎ 958-22-75-25-26-27. (To reserve up to three days in advance, call Banco BBV ☎ 902-224-460 or ☎ 958-22-09 12; Fax: 958-21-05-84.) To get there: red Alhambra–Albaycín minibus from Plaza Nueva. Admission: Comprehensive ticket, including Alhambra and Generalife, 1,000 pta. ($5.50); seniors, 600 pta.; free for children under 8. Open: April 1–Sept 30, Mon–Sat 9 a.m.–8 p.m., Sun 9 a.m.–6 p.m.; Tues, Thur, and Sat night visits to Nasrid palaces only, 10 p.m. to midnight; Oct 31–March 31, Mon–Sun 9 a.m.–6 p.m. Museo de Bellas Artes (Fine Arts Museum, within the Carlos V Palace) is open Tues 2:30–6 p.m., Wed–Sat 9 a.m.–6 p.m., and Sun 9 a.m.–2:30 p.m.; 250 pta., or $1.40; free to EU members. The Museo de la Alhambra, Palacio de Carlos V, is open Tues–Sat from 9 a.m.–2 p.m.; free. The entire complex is closed Dec 25–Jan 1.

More cool things to see and do

✔ **Making time for tea.** The intense Moorish character of the Albaycín is palpable as you climb Calle Elvira . A couple of the district's streets, especially Caldería Nueva and Caldería Vieja, teem with *teterías* — Moroccan-style tea rooms with tons of tea varieties and a bohemian feel — and antique shops that reflect a *medina* (market place) past. Two *teterías* to try are **La Casa del Té,** Calle Calderería Vieja, 22 (☎ **958-21-01-79**); and **Tetería Nazarí,** Calle Calderería Nueva, s/n (☎ **958-22-06-82**).

✔ **Touring a monastery.** Northwest of town is **Monasterio de la Cartuja,** Paseo de la Cartuja, s/n (☎ **958-16-19-32**), which may be even more of a Catholic rejoinder to the city's Arab past than the Cathedral. Bathed in intricate stucco work, inlaid marble molding, cedarwood ceilings, wildly painted cupolas, and an eruption of glittery gold leaf, the Baroque cathedral is anything but subtle. See it after you've already visited the Alhambra; the contrast between the sweet harmony and simplicity of the Nasrid palaces and this ostentatious exercise is startling. The sacristy, with black-and-beige tile floors, mahogany chests, and a spectacle of carved stucco, looks like an optical illusion. To get there, take bus No. 8 or a taxi up *Gran Vía de Colón.* Hours are Mon–Sat 10 a.m.to 1 p.m. and 3:30 to 6 p.m., Sun 10 a.m. to noon and 3:30 to 6 p.m. Admission is 300 pta. ($1.75).

✔ **Getting a glimpse of the poet's life.** Federico García Lorca (1898–1936), Spain's greatest modern poet and playwright, was born in Granada, and his works bind him eternally to the city and its people. The internationally famous author of such works as *A Poet in New York, The House of Bernarda Alba,* and *Blood Wedding,* Lorca was a daring genius whose life was cut short by the Nationalist forces of dictator Francisco Franco. They captured the poet in Granada, took him to a field, and shot him.

Just southwest of downtown, García Lorca's childhood summer home, **Huerta de San Vicente,** *Calle de la Virgen Blanca,* s/n (within García Lorca park southwest of downtown, at the end of *Calle de Recogidas;* ☎ **958-25 84 66;** E-mail: huerta_san_ vicente@ imfegranada.es), is preserved as a museum. Although the view is now blocked by large apartment buildings, in his youth Lorca enjoyed unencumbered views of the Alhambra on the hill from here. Adorned with Lorca's art and personal effects — his bedroom and desk, where he wrote *Bodas de Sangre* (Blood Wedding), are almost monastic — it's a fascinating window on the life of one of Spain's greatest and most enigmatic literary figures. The tours are anything but staid house visits — the gentleman who leads the 30-minute walkthrough is a Lorca scholar, and he encourages visitors to read from Lorca's works as they wander the house. (A grasp of Spanish helps.)

To get there, you can take a 15-minute walk from *Puerta Real* down *Recogidas;* signs indicate a right turn (northwest) to park and *Huerta de San Vicente,* within. Hours are Tues–Sun 10 a.m. to 1 p.m. and 4 to 7 p.m. (April–Sept, it opens and closes one hour later in the afternoon). Admission is 300 pta. ($1.75); students under 9 and seniors, 150 pta. (85¢); free Wed.

If you're a fan of Lorca and you can spend some time in the region, you may want to explore his life by visiting three Granada homes essential to his work. In addition to *Huerta de San Vincente* — Lorca's summer home until his assassination in 1936 — you can see **Casa de Fuente Vaqueros,** where he was born, about 10 miles from Granada; and **Casa de Valderrubio,** in the town of Pinos Puente, the family's first summer home. For more information on the Lorca visitation route, contact any of the tourism offices in Granada (see "Getting info after you arrive," earlier in this chapter).

✔ **Exploring Sacromonte — but watch your pockets.** The hill called **Sacromonte** (Sacred Hill), northwest of the Albaycín, is famed for its gypsy caves carved out of the earth, touristy flamenco shows, and pickpockets who thrive on visitors to the first two. You can also check out a dilapidated abbey, **Abadía del Sacromonte** (☎ 958-22-14-45; Tues–Sun 11 a.m. to 1 p.m. and 4 to 6 p.m.; free). Plenty of people love to wander the streets on the hill, but its residents have earned a reputation for taking advantage of tourists. Therefore, I take caution recommending it, except for fearless visitors; you may want to visit Sacromonte as part of an organized flamenco outing in the evening (ask at your hotel or see "La Noche: Granada's Nightlife," later in this chapter).

✔ **Living the spa life.** Maybe your imagination ran wild visiting the ancient Moorish baths or the Alhambra, thinking about the luxurious bath-house life the sultans must have led. **Baños Arabes Al Andalus,** Calle Santa Ana, 16 (☎ 958-22-99-78; E-mail: aba@siapi.es; Internet: www.siapi.es/balnearios), a Granada spa, does its best to replicate the Arab baths. In fact, it has the fountains, colorful glazed ceramic tiles, and Moorish arches down pat. Clearly, this is not the sauna at your local YMCA. The spa also offers therapeutic massages and a tea room.

The land of carmens

The other major city in Andalusia, Seville, is known for its Carmen, the gypsy seductress and main character in the opera of the same name. But Granada has *cármenes* — Moorish country houses, tucked away in the old Arab Quarter, the Albaycín, that hide lush orchards and gardens behind high walls. In the sixteenth century, after the Reconquest depopulated the Arab Quarter, there was suddenly room to expand houses and transform them into mini country estates. From the outside, you would never suspect them to contain splendid gardens, but inside, the homes come alive with fragrant flowers, fruit trees, and Moorish-style fountains. Like the interior decorated patios found throughout Andalusia, the gardens spring from the Muslim philosophy of reserving riches and beauty for the interior — a philosophy that applies both to humans and their living quarters.

Shopping in Granada

Unsurprisingly, in this town where a Moorish accent remains so pervasive, the best crafts are those inherited from the Arabs, who were superb craftsmen. Look for *fajalauza* (glazed ceramics), wrought iron objects, leather goods, furniture with inlaid woods, and musical instruments — especially guitars.

Check out two areas first. The **Alcaicería,** right next to the Cathedral and Royal Chapel (off Calle Oficios), is the old Arab silk market. Today, it almost entirely showcases goods hawked at tourists, but you can still pick up some interesting Andalusian souvenirs. **The Corral del Carbón** (Mariana Pineda 12; ☎ 958-22-90-63; Mon–Fri 9 a.m. to 7 p.m., Sat–Sun 10 a.m. to 2 p.m.) an old commercial exchange, is one of the oldest Moorish structures in Granada. Currently it houses a number of artisan's shops. You can find similar shops, including most of Granada's antique stores, in the Albaycín district and particularly along *Cuesta de Elvira.* Another good street on which to espy crafts, including guitars, is **Cuesta de Gomérez** (leading to Alhambra hill). For ceramics, check out **Cerámica Fajalauza,** Camino de San Antonio, s/n; or **Céramica Aliatar,** Plaza de Aliatar, 18 (☎ 958-27-80-89).

Artesanía Albaicín, Calle del Agua, 19 (☎ 958-27-90-56), is one of Albaycín's most dependable places for tooled leather goods. It stocks the obligatory purses and wallets, and just about everything else you also find in a Moroccan *medina* (marketplace). **Casa Ferrer,** Cuesta de Gomérez, 26 (☎ 958-22-18-32), is the place for budding flamenco artists to go for authentic, handcrafted Spanish guitars; this family-owned shop has been around for more than a century. If you've got the bucks, you can get a fine instrument here (you can also get something more along the lines of a souvenir for $250 or so).

Cava de Puros Eduardo Ruiz (Carretera de la Sierra, near Paseo de la Bomba; ☎ 958-22-13-85) is a smoker's emporium with more than 20,000 Cuban cigars. Granada and its environs have plenty of good puffing places, but remember, you can't bring Cuban cigars back with you into the United States.

La Noche: Granada's Nightlife

In addition to what I list in this section, Granada usually has a respectable schedule of concerts, dance, and theater; ask at the tourism office for the current brochure of cultural activities. Other shows, including pop-flamenco artists and international dance troupes, are staged at the **Palacio de Exposiciones y Congresos,** by the river. For tickets and information, call ☎ 902-40-02-22.

Flamenco

The Sacromonte *barrio* is famous, or more accurately, notorious, for its flamenco *cuevas* — live music caves literally carved right out of the hill. Their popularity doesn't alter the fact that they're tourist traps — you won't see a local anywhere near these places — often nothing more than a well-oiled gypsy con game. Their sole purpose is to milk affluent tourists of their entertainment dollars — by means both straightforward and shadowy. Even with that caveat, having some fun at the *zambra* shows if you've got a sense of humor and your wits about you is not impossible (see the sidebar "*Sacro Monte!* (or, Holy hill! I've been robbed!)" elsewhere in this chapter for specific tips).

The shows are pretty interchangeable; most offer package deals that include transportation back and forth to your hotel, one drink and admission (around 3,500 pta./$19). Granada hotels are well stuffed with Sacromonte fliers, but a couple to look for are: **Zambra María la Canastera** (Camino del Sacromonte, 81; ☎ 958-12-11-83; small museum on site, Mon–Fri 4 to 7 p.m., Sat–Sun noon to 3 p.m.); **Cueva la Rocío** (Sacromonte, 70; ☎ 958-22-71-29); **Cueva la Zingara** (Camino del Sacromonte, 71; ☎ 958-22-22-71); **Cueva los Tarantos** (Camino del Sacromonte, 9; ☎ 958-27-24-92). **Casa Juanillo** (Camino del Sacromonte, 83) offers less touristy, fairly pure flamenco music and decent *tapas*.

Not in Sacromonte, but downtown, with a restaurant-show and late-night *sevillanas* (informal gatherings of Andalusian dancing and singing), is **El Corral del Príncipe** (Campo del Príncipe, 7; ☎ 958-22-80-88; closed Mon). The nightly 10 p.m. shows at **Jardines Neptuno** (Arabial, s/n; ☎ 958-52-25-33) are probably Granada's best, though they still pale in comparison to what you may see in Madrid, Seville, or Córdoba. Because you'll most likely arrive and leave late, and there's little late-night transportation, I recommend having a taxi take you directly to either of these. If taxis aren't waiting when you emerge, have the clubs call one for you.

Sacro Monte! (or, Holy hill! I've been robbed!)

The performances at the flamenco *cuevas* (caves) may seem high-priced to you, but you have to take care to avoid being ripped off in a more overt way. For starters: Don't bring any cameras or valuables to the Sacromonte district. Don't carry wads of cash — only as much as you're willing to blow that evening. Don't accept anything as part of the show — the castanets that you enthusiastically snap one moment will be added to your bill the next. Don't buy any souvenirs or, in general, anything beyond what is prepaid on your evening package.

Don't say I didn't warn you. If these words cause you consternation, check out the two flamenco shows that aren't in Sacromonte (see the nighlife section earlier in this chapter).

International song and dance

Granada's big annual music and dance party takes place at unusual theaters, which include some of the city's most wondrous, historic places — the Alhambra, Generalife, Cathedral, Royal Hospital, and San Jerónimo Monastery. The **International Festival of Music and Dance** is the last week of June and first of July. Call ☎ **958-22-21-11** for more information. For tickets, call ☎ **958-22-18-44** or purchase them directly at the Festival Ticket Office in the Corral del Carbón (calle Mariano Pineda, 12).

Bars and pubs

The Albaycín neighborhood is a lively quarter at night. Check out the picturesque street along the river, Carretera del Darro, where new watering holes continue popping up, complementing interesting old ones. **Bodegas Castañeda,** Cuesta de Elvira, 5 (☎ **958-22-63-62**), is a bar inhabiting old wine cellars, a great and lively place for *tapas* and drinks. The bar-restaurant **El Tragaluz,** Nevot, 26 (no phone), is a good, relaxed place for talking and occasional theater presentations. Folks with a rowdier impulse can pump it up at **Granada-10,** Cárcel Baja, 10 (☎ **958-22-40-01**), the city's best disco, with films and a wide-ranging crowd. It's open till the early morning hours.

Side Trips from Granada

From exploring caves to skiing the slopes, if you're hankering to get out of the city, the side trips outlined in this section may be just the ticket.

The Tourism Board of Granada wants you to get out of town. It's so intent on visitors seeing more of the province that they'll load you on a bus for free. A tourist bus with an accompanying professional guide carts small groups of visitors (an average of 20) off to destinations outside of the city, such as **Guadix, Alpujarras** (the southern face of the Sierra Nevada), and the **Tropical Coast.** The day trips take off in the morning and return to Granada the same day. There's no catch: the only requirement is that you have at least a two-night hotel reservation in Granada (the town). Simply call **Agencia Granavisión** at ☎ **958-13-58-04** and reserve your place.

Checking out the cave dwellers of Guadix

One of Spain's oldest settlements, **Guadix** ("*gwah*-deeks") is a place where people still live in caves. The town is perched on a 1,000-foot plateau, and the troglodyte dwellings are carved right into the rock — about all you see from the street is a whitewashed front door, chimney protruding from the ground/ceiling, and a jarring TV antenna. (Cave dwellers want their MTV, too; it looks like every cave has cable.) There's an entire neighborhood of *casa-cuevas* (cave houses); these oddities (there are about 2,000 of them) have existed here for half a millennium. On my last trip here, I asked an elderly gentleman to show me around his place. He explained that living in a cave was perfect; it was cool in the scorching summer and warm in the mountain winter. If you're shy about asking someone for a peek, visit the **Cueva Museo** (Cave Museum) on Plaza de la Ermita Nueva, which does its best to depict how underground people live.

In town there's also a sixteenth-century cathedral, by the same architect who worked on Granada's cathedral. You can also visit the Moorish **Alcazaba,** the eleventh-century fortress, and the **Mudéjar Iglesia de Santiago.**

By car, Guadix is 58 km. (36 miles) northeast of Granada on N-342. At least six **Autedia** (☎ **958-15-36-36**) buses per day make the one-hour trip to Guadix (550 pta./$3 one-way). The train from Granada takes about an hour and costs 760–835 pta. ($4.20–$4.60).

Going wild at the Sierra Nevada Nature Park

The Sierra Nevada mountain range contains a National Hunting Reserve and UNESCO-designated Biosphere Reserve, but most people know it as the site of some of Spain's best skiing. The Sierra Nevada (literally, "snowy mountain range") is Europe's southernmost ski resort. There are 14 snowcapped peaks higher than 9,800 feet, including the two highest mountains in Spain, and they're only about an hour's drive from Granada. Even if you're not a skier, the range is beautiful in summer; its proximity to the Mediterranean produces some lovely indigenous vegetation, and it's a great place for hiking, walking, and mountain biking.

The **Sierra Nevada Tourism Office** is located on Plaza de Pradollano, in the Edificio Telecabina (☎ **958-24-91-00**). Call ☎ **958-24-91-19** to gather information regarding the state of the snow and highways to the ski resort.

To get to the park, follow the road out of Granada to the *Sol y Nieve* Resort and Veleta Peak. For further information on the Sierra Nevada Nature Park and *Sol y Nieve* Resort, including how to get there if you don't have a car, contact the Visitor's Center and Information Office, Gran Vía de Colón, 36 (Granada); ☎ **958-29-30-63.**

During ski season (which sometimes lasts until June), you can check out the **Sol y Nieve** ski resort in Pradollano (2,100 m.). Ski lodges include **Meliá Rumaykiyya** (Dehesa de San Jerónimo, parcela 511, s/n; ☎ 958-48-14-00; Fax 958-48 00 32; doubles, 10,000–16,000 pta./$55–$89); **Nevasur** (Virgen de la Nieve, 17; ☎ 958-48-03-50; Fax: 958-48-03-65; doubles, 17,000 pta./$94); and **La General** (Pradollano, 10; ☎ 958-48-14-50; Fax :958-48-10-14; doubles, 11,000–14,500 pta./$61–$81).

Fast Facts: Granada

Area Code

The area code for telephone numbers within Granada is **958**. You must dial the prefix, even for local numbers.

ATMs/Currency Exchange

Banks and 24-hour ATM machines are on Plaza de Isabel la Católica and Puerta Real.

Emergencies

For medical emergencies, call ☎ **061**. Call the Red Cross *(Cruz Roja)* at ☎ **958-22-22-22**. For an ambulance, call ☎ **958-28-44-50** or 958-28-20-00.

Hospitals

Centro Médico Quirúrgico (Hospital Ruiz de Alda) is at Avenida Constitución, 100 (☎ **958-24-11-00**); Hospital de San Juan de Dios is on San Juan de Dios, s/n (☎ **958-20-43-00**).

Information

Tourism offices are located at the airport, Corral del Carbón (Mariana Pineda, 12; ☎ **958-22-59-90**; open Mon–Fri 9 a.m. to 7 p.m., Sat 10 a.m. to 2 p.m., Sun 10 a.m. to 2 p.m.); Real de la Alhambra s/n (in front of Palacio de Carlos V; ☎ **958-22-04-45**; daily 10 a.m. to 5 p.m.); Duque de Medinaceli, 2 (☎ **91-429-49-51**; open Mon–Sat 9 a.m. to 7 p.m.); Plaza Mariana Pineda, 10 (☎ **958-22-66-88**; open Mon–Fri 10:30 a.m. to 1:30 p.m. and 4:30 p.m. to 7 p.m., Sat 10:30 a.m. to

2 p.m.); Avenida Andalucía (barriada de la Encina; ☎ **958-27-93-98**; Mon–Fri 9.30 a.m. to 2 p.m. and 4 to 7:30 p.m., Sat 9:30 a.m. to 2 p.m.); and Carretera de Málaga (☎ **958-27-93-98**; open Mon–Fri 9:30 a.m. to 2 p.m. and 4 to 7:30 p.m. and Sat 9:30 a.m. to 2 p.m.).

Internet Access

Granada has a couple of places where you can check your *correo electrónico* (e-mail). Check out Net (Calle Santa Escolástica; ☎ **958-22-69-19**), between Campo del Príncipe and Plaza Nueva. It's open Mon–Sat 9 a.m. to 11 p.m. Another place is Madar Internet (Calle Calderería Nueva, 12; ☎ **95-422-88-99**), open Mon–Sat 10 a.m. to midnight, Sundays and holidays, noon to midnight. It's just off Elvira, at the edge of Albaycín. Each charges 400 pta. ($2.20) an hour. But check with the tourism office before you go, because these places across Spain have a habit of opening and closing at a moment's notice.

Police

For municipal police, dial ☎ **092**. For national police, ☎ **091**. The local police office is at Plaza Carmen, 5 (☎ **958-20-94-61**).

Post Office

The Central Post Office is located at Puerta Real, s/n (☎ **958-22-48-35**). It's open Mon–Fri 8:30 a.m to 9 p.m. and Sat 8 a.m. to 8 p.m.

Part VI

The Part Of Tens

The 5th Wave   By Rich Tennant

"I think we're close to the village Picasso grew up in."

In this part . . .

*W*hen people ask me to declare my absolute favorite sight, hotel, restaurant, or cultural experience in Spain — which friends, family, and strangers invariably do — I tend to stammer and stumble. Either Spain has too much to offer, or I'm too decision-challenged (I'm leaning toward the former). I guess that's why Top 10 lists exist. But rather than dump a series of personal "best of" lists on you — the winners I hope are evident throughout the book — I've narrowed it down to two. The first is a top experiences list, the second a collection of interesting odds and ends that amount to a sincere wish that you can discover for yourself what makes Spain such an intriguing place.

By the way, for those of you prone to count the number of items in Top 10 lists, I interpret the Top 10 concept rather loosely. In addition to having a tough time making decisions, I also can't count, it seems.

Chapter 19

Top Ten Can't-Miss Spanish Experiences

In This Chapter

▶ Dining and drinking in Spain

▶ Enjoying Spain's festivals and flamenco

▶ Examining the artistry and history of Spain

*T*icking off a Top 10 list of experiences in Spain is a tricky task, and one to which I succumb only under the duress imposed by my editors! (And at that, I couldn't stick to just 10; I sneaked in an 11th one.) To have a successful trip to Spain, by no means do you need to be able to check off all of the following items. In fact, it would probably be wiser to approach these as merely a sampling of the seductive experiences Spain has to offer, and go out and construct your own greatest hits list of top sights.

Popping Corks: Touring Spain, Wine by Wine

Oenophiles and casual imbibers alike are going to find Spanish wines richly rewarding, not to mention surprisingly affordable. You can enjoy a bounty of reds, whites, sparkling wines, and unique aperitifs, such as excellent dry sherries *(jerez)*, at restaurants across Spain. But an even greater pleasure is experiencing local wines in an authentic tavern or *tapas* joint, where knocking back little glasses of *vino* is a boisterous, popular affair — far from the stuffy atmosphere of wine snobs and rarified cellars. Look for fine vintages from the wine regions Rioja, Ribera del Duero, Penedès, and Priorato, and sparkling wines called *cava*. And be sure to sample popular Ribeiros and Albariños from Galicia, and *txakoli* ("*cha*-koh-li"), a fruity and fizzy white wine drunk in the Basque country. Or blow off all those unfamiliar names and ask for the *vino (tinto or blanco) de la casa* — the inexpensive house wine most of your fellow drinkers will be having.

No Bull: Experiencing a Bullfight

El toro, or bull, is a creature of mythic proportions in Spain and a pillar of Spanish popular culture. The bull is central to rituals Spaniards hold dear, such as Pamplona's annual *Encierro,* or Running of the Bulls — in which seasoned locals and foolish foreigners try to keep their footing on cobble-stoned streets, just out of reach of the hard-charging beasts — and *la corrida,* the bullfight, a sport-slash-drama that counts adherents every bit as faithful and passionate in Spain as soccer. Whether or not you are swayed by such demonstrations of macho courage, you are unlikely to forget your first experience of either one. Madrid (Chapter 14), Seville (Chapter 16) and Ronda (Chapter 17) are the best spots to take in a bullfight. Pamplona (Chapter 13) in July is the only place to witness the mayhem of a bull stampede through the streets.

Taking the Stroll Español

Spaniards tend to get antsy sitting around the house. Extraordinarily social creatures, they love to be outside, take in the sights and sounds, and carry on mobile conversations — face-to-face animated exchanges touching on gossip, politics, sports, and family — as they stroll through parks and boulevards. You'll see the *paseo* (stroll) in full stride in every Spanish city and provincial town, especially in the moments just prior to lunch or in the early evening before dinner. Some of the best spots to join the shuffling parade are the Paseo Nuevo promenade along the Playa de la Concha in San Sebastián (see Chapter 13); Barcelona's riveting La Rambla (see Chapter 11); the elegant Paseo de la Castellana and Retiro Park in Madrid (see Chapter 14); and in Seville, the narrow sunny streets of Santa Cruz neighborhood and the boulevards and gardens in María Luisa Park (see Chapter 16).

Grazing for Tapas

Spanish cooking has become as known throughout the world for *tapas,* the building-block hors d'oeuvres of restaurant and bar dining, as it has for classic dishes like paella (a rice, seafood, and meat casserole). A *tapeo* is akin to a pub crawl in Ireland or Scotland — a bar-to-bar treasure hunt, searching for and wolfing down finger foods that range from the endearingly simple, like a wedge of tortilla omelet, to the piled-high *pintxos* ("*peen*-chose," the Basque word for *tapas*) they serve in the Basque country. The best places to join in this quintessential Spanish sport are the backstreets of Viejo Madrid (see Chapter 14); San Sebastián's Parte Vieja (see Chapter 13); the old quarter of Bilbao (see Chapter 13); the rollicking taverns of Seville (see Chapter 16); and the small streets that fan out from Barcelona's pedestrian-only Rambla (see Chapter 11).

Feeling the Sound and the Fury of Flamenco

One of Spain's greatest cultural achievements is the passionate musical expression that belongs to one of its most maligned peoples, the *gitanos* (Gypsies). Flamenco dancing is a stunning display of grace and rhythmic fire, and the wail of flamenco *cante hondo* (deep-throated vocals) is a visceral people's song unlike any other. You can see a slick and colorful costumed production in any major city, but flamenco is best experienced in a small, dark club in Madrid (Chapter 14), Seville or Córdoba (Chapter 16 for both), where you can get close enough to see the sweat fly off dancers' arms and feel the hand-clapping and staccato dance steps like a bass drum in your chest.

Getting Lost in a Tangle of Time

Spain has a wealth of exceedingly fine museums, excellent repositories of Spanish art and history, but Spaniards live with their history on a daily basis. Wandering the crooked streets in a lively old quarter is among the most enjoyable history lesson you could have. The streets of Toledo may be impossible to make sense of, but they come alive with synagogues, mosques, and palaces — centuries of Jewish, Moorish, and Christian history. Barcelona's Gothic Quarter is a slightly spooky but vibrant warren of alleyways that once formed the core of a walled-in city. Salamanca's old quarter around the stunning Plaza Mayor is the place to relive the academic life and extracurricular activities of university students. Other great places to wander, get lost, and absorb a dose of history are San Sebastián's Parte Vieja and Seville's enchanting Barrio de Santa Cruz.

Dining 'til You Drop

In Spain, you *can* live on *tapas* alone, but nothing compares to the culinary artistry of a full-course *menu de degustación* (tasting menu) — a full-throttle dining experience — in the Basque Country. San Sebastián, a small resort city on a perfect bay, is Spain's dining leader, with more award-winning chefs than any other. Save your budget and appetite for a memorable meal at Arzak, Akelare, Martín Berasategui, Urepel or Rekondo. Bilbao runs a close second to San Sebastián. See Chapter 13. If you can't make it to the Basque Country, don't miss out on the next best thing — a Basque restaurant, either for a full meal or splendid selection of tapas, in any major Spanish city.

Appreciating Art for Art's Sake

Name the greatest artists of all time, and you'll count a significant, perhaps even disproportionate, number of Spaniards among them. And many of their masterpieces are on view across Spain, at some of the finest art museums in Europe. Madrid's Prado, endowed by kings to be the granddaddy of Spanish museums, has monumental works by Velázquez, El Greco, and Goya (as well as great Italian and Flemish works). Picasso's impassioned *Guernica* is on view down the street at the Reina Sofía, as are many other modern masters, including Juan Gris and Julio González. Barcelona boasts an impressive collection of Picasso's early works, single-artist museums dedicated to native sons Joan Miró and Antoni Tàpies, and a splendid collection of Romanesque and Gothic religious art at the Museu Nacional d'Art de Catalunya. Salvador Dalí's tortured genius holds surreal court at several museums in Spain, but the best place to get a taste of his unique gifts is his museum-theater in Figueres (Catalonia) and the home-museums he left behind in the Catalan countryside. Excellent art collections are also to be found in Seville (Museo de Bellas Artes) and Bilbao (Museo de Bellas Artes and the Guggenheim Bilbao, only a few years old but already a fixture on the Spanish and international art scene).

Succumbing to Modernista Mayhem

As the nineteenth century gave way to the twentieth in Barcelona, a creative coterie of architects produced their own take on art nouveau, and they produced an incredible number of visionary works of *modernisme*. Antoni Gaudí, Lluís Domènech i Montaner, Josep Puig i Cadafalch, and others changed the face of their native Catalan capital. Getting up close and personal with buildings that still startle today (and make you wonder how they ever got built . . . or almost built), including La Sagrada Familia, La Pedrera, El Palau de la Música Catalana, and the fantastically molded corners of the Manzana de la Discórdia, is a true architectural event. And it appeals to kids and people on whom architecture's never made that big an impression before. See Chapter 11.

Cruising El Campo

Touring the Spanish countryside, *el campo,* is a delight. You'll find small inns, simple and cheery taverns, and welcoming people. Hop in a car to experience places like the flat plains and medieval villages of the Empordà north of Barcelona (see Chapter 11) and the rolling olive groves and hilltop Moorish towns, the Pueblos Blancos, of Andalusia (see Chapter 17).

Partying at a Spanish Feria

Spain's renowned festivals run the gamut from rambunctious street parties (where people light firecrackers under each other's feet and throw wine and produce at each other) to somber religious rituals. Sacred or profane, they are a contagious pageant of color and tradition. Attending one of the biggies can mean extra headaches in terms of hotel rooms, crowds, and costs, but if this type of cultural immersion appeals to you, consider dropping in on Seville's Semana Santa and Feria de Abril; Córdoba's Festival de los Patios; Pamplona's San Fermín; Barcelona's La Mercé; or Fiesta de San Isidro in Madrid. If you can't make any of those, you're still likely to come upon a local patron saint's day that will give you a dose of Spain at its more popular and festive. For a full rundown of Spain's most popular festivals, see Chapter 2.

Chapter 20

Top Ten Things You Probably Never Knew About Spain

In This Chapter

▶ Discovering the appeal of fish and olive oil

▶ Digging up some tidbits on Picasso, Columbus, and other famous Spaniards

▶ Figuring out how the Basque people curse (or why they can't)

*M*aybe it's just a quirk of mine, but I often find the odd detail and insider vignette more enlightening than the big picture. If you're looking for more than the standard slide show to impress your friends after your trip to Spain, give these little-known nuggets a whirl.

And the Vote for Most Popular Goes to. . . .

Just how popular a destination is Spain? According to the World Tourism Organization, it now ranks number two (behind France) in the number of annual visitors — not just in Europe, but worldwide. In fact, Spain recently displaced the United States on that list. Although Spain's population has hovered around 40 million for decades, it receives some 50 million visitors annually.

Olive Oil Olé!

Spain is the world's largest producer of olive oil — a fact that won't surprise you once you've spent some time driving around Andalusia, a land of unending rolling olive groves (see Chapter 17). The region produces so much of this *aceite de oliva* (olive oil) that the Andalusians sell it to other countries, like Italy, who in turn bottle it and market it as their own.

I Bet He Got a Really Good Deal on the Rent

Antoni Gaudí, the famed and eccentric Catalan architect who popularized the wildly imaginative, fanciful building style of *modernismo,* dedicated 43 years of his life to building La Sagrada Familia — the legendary, unfinished oddity of a cathedral in Barcelona. During the last ten years of his life, absolutely consumed by the project's construction, he lived hermit-like in a tiny room on the premises until his death, in 1926. (He was run over by a local tram, leaving little in the way of blueprints for future architects to use to complete the temple.) See Chapter 11 for more on Gaudí and the Sagrada Familia.

That's $@#*7!%$ to You, Buster

Euskera, the language spoken by the Basque people of northern Spain, has puzzled anthropologists and linguists for hundreds of years. It seems no one can positively identify its origins. Yet the language is remarkable for another reason: It has no swear words. Even those completely fluent in Euskera have to dip into Spanish when they want to curse their heads off. The Basques themselves have an equally mysterious history. As one of the oldest ethnic groups in Europe, and with a language unrelated to any existing Indo-European tongue, some theorists believe them to be indigenous Iberians descended from Cro-Magnon man. Others have proposed — not entirely implausibly — that the Basques are the living link to the lost city of Atlantis. See Chapter 13 for more on the Basque region.

Salvador Dalí . . . the Bureaucrat?

The surrealist painter-cum-madman Salvador Dalí so loved La Pedrera, Antoni Gaudí's wild apartment house, that he envisioned himself holding public office there. But not just any public office. In his inimitable style, Dalí actually petitioned the Catalan government to create a new "Department of Public Imagination" in the building and to appoint him to oversee it. The government, not surprisingly, rebuffed his proposal. See Chapter 11 for more on La Pedrera, and Chapter 12 for more on Dalí.

Guernica, but Not Forgotten

Pablo Picasso painted his searing black-and-white portrait of war, *Guernica,* in protest of the 1937 Nationalist bombing (carried out by

Nazi warplanes) of the small Basque town of that name, during the Spanish Civil War. (Guernica is located just outside of Bilbao in Vizcaya province.) Picasso refused to allow the painting to be exhibited in Spain until Nationalist dictator Francisco Franco died. *Guernica* remained at New York's Museum of Modern Art, finally making its permanent home in Spain in 1980 after the deaths of both artist and dictator (1973 and 1975, respectively), and the return of democracy to Spain (in 1978). Picasso's masterwork first occupied an annex to the Prado Museum in Madrid; it now has its own gallery in Madrid's **Centro de Arte Reina Sofía** (see Chapter 14).

Here Lies Columbus — or Does He?

Christopher Columbus's massive coffin sits inside the Seville cathedral, but no one knows if the great explorer is, in fact, buried there. Disgraced and by no means a hero, he died, in Valladolid in central Spain, and his itinerant remains made journeys to Santo Domingo and Havana. See Chapter 16 for more on Seville.

How's That for Heritage?

Spain has more cities designated as UNESCO (United Nations Educational, Scientific, and Cultural Organization) World Heritage Sites than any other country. The eight cities are: Segovia, Salamanca, Toledo (see Chapter 15 for these three), Córdoba (see Chapter 16), Ávila, Santiago de Compostela, Cáceres and Cuenca (these last four were left out of this edition for space considerations). In addition to this roster of cities (whose old quarters were named in their entirety), other World Heritage Sites covered in this book include: Granada's Alhambra and Albayzín district (see Chapter 18); El Escorial palace and monastery (see Chapter 14); Gaudí's Casa Milá, Parc Güell, and Palau Güell, in Barcelona (see Chapter 11); the Cathedral and Reales Alcazares in Seville (see Chapter 16); and the *modernista* buildings Palau de la Música Catalana and Hospital Sant Pau, in Barcelona (see Chapter 11).

That Sounds Fishy to Me

Spain is the second largest per-capita consumer of seafood in the world (behind Japan). Even though Spanish waters produce thousands of tons of seafood each year, it's not nearly enough to feed the Spanish appetite for fish. So Spain, largely through importers in San Sebastián, buys from Norway, France, South Africa, and even South America.

The Original River Walk

Barcelona's famed boulevard La Rambla wasn't always a pedestrian-only street — in fact, it wasn't even a street. About 2,000 years ago, when Barcelona was a Roman settlement, the Rambla (the name means "riverbed" in Arabic) was a mountain stream. In the late eighteenth century, the stream was gradually filled in; elegant palaces and the city grew up around it.

Appendix A

Quick Concierge

● ●

American Express

Madrid: Plaza de las Cortes, 2 (☎ 91-322-54-45; Barcelona: Ramblas, 74; ☎ 93-301-11-66. Seville: Hotel Inglaterra, Plaza Nueva 7; ☎ 95-421 16-17; Granada: Calle Reyes Catolicos 31; ☎ 958-22-45-12)

ATMs

Automatic Teller Machines, or ATMs, are widely available throughout Spain, from large cities to rural villages. Look for signs that read *Cajero Automático* or *Cajero 24 Horas*. They dispense currency in pesetas — usually multiples of 5,000. You need a four-digit PIN (Personal Identification Number) to withdraw cash in Spain.

Business Hours

Banks are open Mon–Fri, 9 a.m.–2 p.m. Most offices are open Mon–Fri, 9 a.m.–2 p.m. and 4–7 or 8 p.m. Usual shop-opening times are 9:30 a.m.–1:30 p.m. and 4:30–8 p.m. Mon–Sat. Major shopping malls, department stores, and supermarkets stay open without a break from 10a.m.–9 p.m., or in some cases until 10 p.m. On a fixed number of Sundays in the year (approximately 12 in all), the large department stores and supermarkets open to the public. Along the coast, during the high season, shops generally stay open until well after 10 p.m. In restaurants, lunch is usually 1–4 p.m.; dinner 9–11:30 p.m. or midnight.

Customs

Officially, you're permitted to bring in items for personal use, including a video camera or two still cameras with 10 rolls of film for each, as well as a portable radio, cassette player, and laptop computer. Sports equipment for personal use (including skis, one bicycle, tennis racquets, and golf clubs) is also allowed. As for booze and tobacco, the maximum allowance per person is 200 cigarettes or 50 cigars or 250 grams of tobacco plus one bottle of wine and one bottle of any other liquor. Don't try to argue that you're bringing in firearms, narcotics, meat, or produce for "personal use" — your excuse won't fly.

Tourists can bring up to 1,000,000 *pesetas* (approximately $5,500) without declaring the amount in customs. You must declare any amount exceeding 1,000,000 *pesetas* upon arrival. Upon leaving Spain, tourists carrying more than 1,000,000 *pesetas* (or the equivalent in any other form of currency) must declare it.

Drugstores

To find an open *farmacia* (pharmacy) outside of normal business hours, check the list of stores posted on the door of any drugstore. The law requires drugstores to operate on a rotating system of hours so that there's always a drugstore open somewhere, even Sunday at midnight. See "Being Prepared If You Get Sick Away from Home" in Chapter 10.

Electricity

220 volts AC (50 volts) is common throughout Spain, although some older places may have 110 or 125 volts. Plugs with two round prongs are used in electrical outlets. Carry your adapter with you, and always check at your hotel desk before plugging in any electrical appliance. Traveling with battery-operated equipment is best.

Embassies/Consulates

If you lose your passport, fall seriously ill, get into legal trouble, or have some other serious problem, your embassy or consulate will probably have the means to provide assistance.

All embassies are located in Madrid: The United States Embassy, Calle Serrano, 75 (☎ 91-587-22-00, Metro: Núñez de Balboa), is open Mon–Fri, 9:30 a.m. to noon and 3–5 p.m.

The Canadian Embassy, Núñez de Balboa, 35 (☎ 91-431-43-00, Metro: Velázquez), is open Mon–Fri, 9 a.m.–12:30 p.m.

The Embassy of the United Kingdom, Calle Fernando el Santo, 16 (☎ 91-700-82-00, Metro: Colón), is open Mon–Fri, 9 a.m.–2 p.m. and 3:30–6 p.m.

The Republic of Ireland has an embassy at Paseo de la Castellana, 36 (☎ 91-576-35-00, Metro: Serrano); it's open Mon–Fri, 10 a.m.–2 p.m.

The Australian Embassy, Plaza del Descubridor Diego de Ordás, 3 (☎ 91-441-93-00, Metro: Cuzco), is open Mon–Thurs 8:30 a.m.–1:30 p.m. and 2:30–5 p.m., Fri 8:30 a.m.–2 p.m.

Citizens of New Zealand have an embassy at Plaza de la Lealtad, 2 (☎ 91-523-02-26, Metro: Banco de España); it's open Mon–Fri 9 a.m.–1:30 p.m. and 2:30–5:30 p.m.

The South African Embassy is at Claudio Coello 91 (☎ 91-436-37-80, Metro: Serrano), open Mon–Fri, 9 a.m.–1:30 p.m. and 2:30–5 p.m.

The following countries have consulates in Barcelona:

Australia (Gran Vía Carles II, 98, 10th floor; ☎ 93-330-94-96); Canada (Passeig de Gràcia, 77, Third floor; ☎ 93-215-07- 04); Ireland (Gran Vía Carles III, 94, Tenth floor; ☎ 93-330-96-52); New Zealand (Honorary Consulate: Travesera de Gracia, 64; ☎ 93-209-03-99); South Africa (Honorary Consulate: Teodora Lamadrid, 7–11, Edificio "Kerm; ☎ 93-418-64-45); U.K. (Avinguda Diagonal, 477; ☎ 93-419-90-44); USA (Passeig de la Reina Elisenda, 23; ☎ 93-280-22-27).

Emergencies

The national emergency number for Spain (except the Basque country) is ☎ 006; in the Basque country it is ☎ 088. See destination chapters for fire, police, and ambulance emergency numbers in individual cities.

Health

You don't need any special vaccinations to visit Spain. Although Spain isn't a developing country where you can't drink the water or trust the meat, you should still be prepared. Many ailments that travelers suffer are self-induced: too much drinking, too much sun, sore feet from too many museums, and so on. Be extremely careful of heat exhaustion, especially in central and southern Spain during the summer.

Information

Tourism information offices in every city are identified by a yellow box with a cursive, lower-case "i." See "Where to Get More Information," later in this appendix, for tourist offices abroad; consult individual destination chapters for local information offices. The number to dial for directory information is ☎ 1003, a service that will give callers information on all national and international codes.

Internet Cafés

Spain is still catching up to the U.S. and other countries on the information superhighway. Web surfing is popular, if not the daily tool it has become in the U.S. Many fewer Spaniards than Americans own personal computers, and telephone connection and usage rates are much, much higher than in America. Not only that, but the lines are often painfully slow. In most major Spanish cities you can now find *café internet* (cybercafés) — coffeehouses that double as places to sit down and log on — and Internet centers. Access can be slow and frustrating. The centers, cafes, and computers are improving all the time, but every once in a while, you'll sit down in front of a screen and be convinced you could get a message back home faster by chiseling it into rock and sending it by boat.

Internet cafes in Spain generally charge about 500 pta. ($3.50) per hour — not bad if you get a decent connection.

Because new Internet cafes are continually popping up and disappearing, your best bet for finding one — other than checking the "Fast Facts" sections in each destination chapter of this book — is to ask at the tourism office in each city. Or, if you want to check online before you go, do so at www.cybercaptive.com and www.netcafes.com.

Language

The official national language is Spanish, the third most widely spoken language in the world after Chinese and English. The Spanish in Spain is called *castellano* (Castilian), to differentiate it from the *español* spoken throughout Latin America. Spanish is spoken in every province of Spain, but local languages, which reasserted themselves with the restoration of democracy in 1975, are the official regional languages in certain autonomous regions. They are: Catalan in Barcelona and Catalonia; Euskera (the Basque language) in the Basque Country; Gallego (Galician) in Galicia; and Valenciano in Valencia.

Even if your Spanish is nonexistent, it's not usually too difficult to get by in Spain. People are helpful, and learning a few key phrases is a snap. English is spoken in most hotels and in many restaurants and shops. The best phrase book is *Spanish for Travelers* by Berlitz; it has a menu supplement and a 12,500-word glossary of both English and Spanish. Also, don't forget *Spanish For Dummies.*

Liquor Laws

The legal drinking age is 18. Bars, taverns, and cafeterias usually open at 8 a.m., and many serve alcohol until around 1:30 a.m. or considerably later. Generally, you can purchase alcoholic beverages in almost any supermarket.

Mail

Spanish Post Offices are called *Correos* ("koh-ray-os"). In every city you'll find a central post office as well as several branch offices, all identified by yellow-and-white signs with a crown and the words *Correos y Telégrafos*. Main offices are generally open from 9 a.m.–8 p.m. Mon– Fri; Sat 9 a.m.–7 p.m.; satellite offices generally have shorter hours (usually 9 a.m.–2 p.m.

Mon–Fri; 9 a.m.–1 p.m. Sat). You can purchase stamps at the post office or at *estancos* ("ay-stahn-kohs," or tobacconist stands — look for the brown-and-yellow sign that reads *Tabacos*). Rates are divided into four areas of the world, just like telephone calls: the E.U., the rest of Europe, the U.S. and Canada, and the rest of the world. Airmail letters to the U.S. and Canada cost 115 pta. (65¢) up to 20 grams, and letters to Britain or other EU countries cost 65 pta. (35¢) up to 20 grams. Postcards have the same rates as letters. Rates change frequently, so check at the local post office before mailing anything.

Postal service in Spain is still not the world's fastest, but it is improving. Allow about one week for delivery to North America, generally less to the U.K.; in some cases, though, letters take two weeks to reach North America. To speed things up, send a letter *urgente* ("oor-hen-tay;" express) or *certificado* (registered).

Maps

For the most part, you should be fine with the maps in this book and those distributed by the local tourism information offices. If you're driving around Spain, make sure you have a good road map; these are available at most bookstores and larger newspaper kiosks. To best negotiate the highways and byways of Spain (and for that matter, Portugal), purchase Michelin map number 990 (for a folding version). Michelin also sells more detailed maps of Spain (Nos. 441–446). Most large bookstore chains in the United States (such as Barnes & Noble) stock Michelin maps. Call Michelin's toll-free order number (☎ 800-423-0485) to order them.

Newspapers and Magazines

Most European newspapers are sold on the day of publication, as are the Paris-based *International Herald Tribune* and European edition of *The Wall Street Journal. USA Today* is also widely available, as are principal European and American magazines (such as *Time, The Economist,* and *Newsweek*). For Spanish-speakers or those willing to give it a try, the weekly entertainment information magazine *Guía del Ocio* (Leisure Guide) lists bars, restaurants, cinema, theater, and concerts.

Restrooms

In Spain, the restroom is called a *lavabo, aseo,* or *servicio* (often labeled WC, for water closet). The men's room is labeled *caballeros* (or just C), and the women's restroom is labeled *señoras* or *damas* (or just S). The best place for clean, safe public toilets are restaurants and well-lit bars (as a courtesy, order a coffee after using the facilities).

Safety

Random, violent crime rates are much lower in Spain than in the U.S.; murder is rare, and terrorism is more of a scary bluff than harsh reality. If you're careful and take reasonable precautions, you'll stay safe and enjoy yourself. With your valuables secure in a hidden money bag or belt, the worst that might happen to you is that the day's spending money in your wallet gets stolen.

Although it doesn't hurt to get some advance information and travel warnings before you go, State Department travel advisories (http://travel.state.gov) and other safety statistics sometimes make any place sound like a terrifying death trap. Overall, Spain is truly a safe place. Other than watching out for pickpockets and theft (especially when you have a rental car or are carrying expensive gadgets like cameras in touristy spots), you shouldn't have to worry much about safety at all. I exercise much more caution in New York than I ever did living in Spain.

However, pickpockets target tourists. Be especially careful anywhere that's crowded (buses, subways, train stations, street markets). Don't tempt thieves. Leave all your jewelry at home, and don't flash your wallet or valuables. When you aren't using it, keep your camera stowed away in a backpack or other nondescript bag (one that says "CANON A-1" in bold graphics reads like an advertisement to would-be Spanish thieves).

Any thief can tell a rental car by looking at the license plate. Don't leave *anything* in the car overnight, and when you're driving around by day, keep everything in the trunk so that when you get out, nothing is visible (pack the trunk before you start out for the day, because putting stuff in the trunk when you park and then walking away is a clear invitation to any thief who happens to be watching).

In Spain, nobody is likely to be physically threatening. If you're accosted, to avoid getting fleeced, just keep moving — and yell a forceful "No!" or "*Socorro*" ("so-*koh*-rro," Help!).

Smoking

Almost everyone in Spain smokes (perhaps it only seems that way; about half the population does), and they do it virtually everywhere. Some places have been designated as no-smoking, such as the Metro (subway) and public buses, but the posted signs often have little effect on Spaniards who view them as an unwanted intrusion into their inalienable right to smoke. Nonsmokers should be careful about reserving sections *no fumar* (no-smoking) on trains and buses. Don't bother asking for nonsmoking sections in restaurants; such places are extremely rare.

Taxes

A 7 percent value-added sales tax (known in Spain as IVA) is levied on all hotel and restaurant products and services. Visitors are entitled to a reimbursement of the 16 percent IVA tax they pay on most purchases (on a minimum purchase of 15,000 pta./$85). For more information on getting your refund, see Chapter 9.

Telephone

To call Spain, remember that it is six hours ahead of Eastern Standard Time. The same dialing instructions apply to sending a fax overseas. From the U.S.: dial the international access code, 011; Spain's country code, 34; the city code 91, 93, and the like; and the local number.

The Spanish telecommunications company, Telefónica, is today much better than it was as a state monopoly. Making local, long-distance, and international calls is easy, but tariffs for the last of these remain high — about twice as much from Spain to the United States as the reverse.

To phone home, use these country codes (after dialing the international access code from Spain, 00):

U.S. & Canada: 1; United Kingdom: 44; Ireland: 353; Australia: 61; New Zealand: 64; South Africa: 27

The easiest and most convenient way to place calls is to use phone cards (*tarjetas telefónicas,* "tar-*hay*-tahs tel-eh-*phone*-ee-kahs"), available in 1,000 pta. ($5.50) and 2,000 pta. ($11) denominations. They function like debit cards. The 2,000–pta. cards often carry a 100–pta. bonus. There are a handful of pay phones that admit coins only, but they are fast disappearing. Most accept both phone cards and coins. After you insert the card into the slot at the top left of the phone, a digital readout tells you how much money — *not* time — you have left on the card. Like a taxi meter in reverse, you can watch the *pesetas* tick down. Phone cards are available at any *estanco* ("eh-*stahn*-koh"), or tobacconist shop.

Whether you use coins or a phone card, making calls from Spanish pay phones is simple and convenient. There are *cabinas* ("kah-*bean*-ahs," or phone booths), identifiable by the big dotted I (for Telefónica) on the side, on virtually every corner and block in cities. I suggest that you pick up a phone card so you don't have to fumble around with coins and keep pumping them into the meter. To make a call, pick up the receiver, and wait for the dial tone. The display will say *Inserte monedas o tarjeta,* your cue to insert your card or at least 25 pta. in coins (you can feed the machine coins worth 5, 25, and 100 pta).

If you're making a local call, dial the two-digit city code first (even if you're calling the bar across the street, you have to dial the city code, 93 in Barcelona, 91 in Madrid, and so on.) and then the seven-digit number — firmly and deliberately. Go too fast, and the numbers may not register. Verify the number you're calling on the display. If you're using coins, a message comes

on to warn you that you're running low on phone fuel — an urgent signal to cram some more small coins into the slot. When you're finished with the call, hang up and collect either unused monies or your card. It's easy to forget the card — I've left more $11 cards in telephone booths than I wish to remember — so check to see that you've pulled it out of the slot before exiting the booth.

To make a long-distance call within Spain, the procedure is exactly the same because you have to dial the city prefix no matter where you're calling.

To make an international call, dial 00 and wait for the international dial tone. The connection rate will be several hundred pta., so if you're using coins, get ready: You'll be feeding them in as fast as you can talk. Dial the desired country code, city code, and number. If calling New York, you'd dial: 00 + 1 (U.S.) + 212 (NY) + 555-5555 (phone number). The number to dial for directory information is ☎ 1003. An English-speaking operator will furnish callers with information on all national and international codes.

Here are the basic toll-free access numbers you'll need to use your home long-distance calling card for calls while in Spain (make sure you check with your company before going — sometimes the charges are still very expensive). The following numbers will get you to an English-speaking operator: Sprint (☎ 900-99-13); MCI (☎ 900-99-14); AT&T (☎ 900-99-11).

Public telephone offices called *locutorios* are where you can place calls (long-distance and international) with the assistance of a clerk who will place the call for you. There are two major advantages if you come across a *locutorio:* You pay for the call afterwards (although not getting to see how much the call is costing you may not be an advantage), and it's usually infinitely quieter than making a *cabina* call on the street.

Unless it's an emergency, I don't recommend making even a local call from your hotel room. The markup (called a "surcharge") — up to several hundred percent — is outlandish. Make a few phone calls over the course of your stay and watch your room bill skyrocket. But whatever you do, do not make an overseas call from your room without a home-country calling card. Even using a calling card, don't be surprised if the hotel tacks on an additional surcharge for making supposedly toll-free connection calls. If they seem ridiculous to you — 75 ¢ to $1 per call — don't think twice about arguing the point when it comes time to pay your bill. One thing I've heard about, but never had to deal with myself in Spain, are hotels that block outgoing calls made via other carriers. If you can't get through to one of the 900 access numbers listed previously, ask your hotel if the number is blocked. If it is, tell them you will gladly change hotels — and write every guidebook on the planet to tell them of the hotel's discriminatory policy.

Sending faxes from your hotel can also be ridiculously expensive. It's much cheaper to find an Internet café and send an e-mail if possible.

Time Zone

Spain is one hour ahead of GMT, or six hours ahead of Eastern Standard Time in the U.S. Daylight Saving Time is in effect from the last Sunday in March to the last Sunday in September.

Tipping

Because a service charge is normally included in hotel and restaurant bills, tipping is not obligatory. However, it's customary to leave a few coins (about 5 percent of the bill) after service at a bar counter, and 10 percent on restaurant bills. Taxi drivers do not need to be tipped unless one gives you special service. Additional guidelines: Hotel porter, per bag, 100 pta.; lavatory attendant 25–50 pta.; tour guide, 10 percent of the cost of the tour.

Weather Updates

The best source for weather forecasts in Spain, assuming you don't have access to the Internet, is the local newspaper. You need to familiarize yourself with centigrade temperatures, however. Among the best Web sites to consult are: The Weather Channel (www.weather.com), which allows you to plug in any Spanish city destination and get a five-day forecast. With USA Today (www.usatoday.com-weather), you click on Europe and then Spain, and you can summon weather reports for Madrid, Barcelona, Seville, Granada, and Mallorca, as well as month-to-month climate reports on Barcelona, Bilbao, Madrid, and Seville. The Washington Post (www.weatherpost.com). Through *The Washington Post*'s weather link, you can get current temps and a four-day outlook for Barcelona and Madrid.

Toll-Free Numbers and Web Sites

Major North American Carriers

For the latest on airline Web sites, check www.air.findhere.com.

Air Canada
☎ 800-776-3000 in the U.S.
☎ 800-555-1212 in Canada
www.aircanada.ca

American Airlines
☎ 800-433-7300
www.americanair.com

Canadian Airlines
☎ 800-426-7000 in the U.S.
☎ 800-665-1177 in Canada
www.cdnair.ca

Continental Airlines
☎ 800-231-0856
www.flycontinental.com

Delta Airlines
☎ 800-241-4141
www.delta-air.com

Northwest Airlines
☎ 800-447-4747
www.nwa.com

TWA
☎ 800-892-4141
www.twa.com

United
☎ 800-241-6522
☎ 800-538-2929
www.ual.com

U.S. Airways
☎ 800-622-1015
www.usairways.com

European Carriers (National and Country-Affiliated Airlines)

Ireland
Aer Lingus
☎ 800-IRISH-AIR in the U.S.
☎ 020-8899-4747 in the U.K.
☎ 0645-737-747 in London
☎ 02-9321-9123 in Australia
☎ 09-379-4455 in New Zealand
www.aerlingus.ie

Spain
Iberia
☎ 800-772-4642 in the U.S.
☎ 800-363-4534 in Canada
☎ 020-7830-0011 in the U.K.
☎ 02-9283-3660 in Australia
☎ 09-379-3076 in New Zealand
www.iberia.com

Spanair
☎ 888-545-5757 in the U.S.
www.spanair.com

Air Europa
☎ 800-327-1225 in the U.S.
☎ 411-712-338-111 in the U.K.
www.g-air-europa.es

United Kingdom
British Airways
☎ 800-247-9297 in the U.S. and Canada
☎ 020-8897-4000 or ☎ 034-522-2111
in the U.K.

☎ 02-9258-3300 in Australia
www.british-airways.com

Virgin Atlantic Airways
☎ 800-862-8621 in the U.S. and Canada
☎ 01293-616-161 or ☎ 01293-747-747
in the U.K.
☎ 02-9352-6199 in Australia
www.fly.virgin.com

Major Car Rental Agencies
Avis
☎ 800-331-1212
www.avis.com

Budget
☎ 800-527-0700
www.budgetrentacar.com

Dollar (Europcar)
☎ 800-800-6000
www.dollarcar.com

Hertz
☎ 800-654-3131
www.hertz.com

National
☎ 800-227-7368
www.nationalcar.com

The following companies specialize in Europe (and Spain):

Auto-Europe
☎ 800-223-5555
www.autoeurope.com

Europe by Car
☎ 800-223-1516
☎ 800-252-9401 in California
☎ 212-581-3040 in New York City
www.europebycar.com

Kemwel
☎ 800-678-0678
www.kemwel.com

Where to Find More Information

Having picked up this book, you know that a trip to Spain begins long before setting foot on Spanish soil. You can take it a step further with just a phone, modem hookup, or plain old, low-tech snail mail. You can get tons of information about all things Spanish, large and small, from the Internet, tourism offices, and travel agents. Remember, though, that almost all of those outfits have a clear financial interest in luring you to their deal or their part of the world, so impartial information it's not.

The Tourist Office of Spain offers a comprehensive color brochure that you might want to have at your side, along with this book, as you begin to plan your Spanish vacation. For a free Spain Travel Planner, call ☎ 888-OK-SPAIN (888-657-7246).

Getting the official line

The Tourist Offices of Spain, with outposts in several countries, are good places to start. They put out monthly newsletters, have stock-rooms full of brochures put out by every regional government and tour organizers, information on the National Paradors (a government-operated chain of hotels usually in historic buildings — palaces and former monasteries and the like). They also have reams of information on Spanish culture and customs, and they operate a useful Web site, www.okspain.org, with links to all sorts of travel information. You can also get maps of most major Spanish cities and all regions from them.

By calling the toll-free number in the U.S. ☎ 888-OKSPAIN (888-657-7246), you can order the standard information package, with introductory information about Spain. For the Tourist Office of Spain nearest you, contact:

IN THE U.S.: Chicago: Tourist Office of Spain, Water Tower Place, Suite 915 East, 845 Michigan Avenue, Chicago, IL 60611. ☎ 312-642-1992; Fax: 312-642-9817. Los Angeles: Tourist Office of Spain, 8383 Wilshire Blvd., Suite 960, Beverly Hills, CA 90211. ☎ 213-658-7188; Fax: 213-658-1061. Miami: Tourist Office of Spain, 1221 Brickell Avenue, Miami, FL 33131. ☎ 305-358-1992; Fax: 305-358-8223. New York: Tourist Office of Spain, 666 Fifth Avenue, 35th floor, New York, NY 10103. ☎ 212-265-8822; Fax: 212-265-8864.

IN THE U.K.: Spanish Tourist Office, 57–58 St. James's Street, London SW1A 1LD. ☎ 0171-499-0901; Fax: 0171-629-4257.

IN CANADA: Tourist Office of Spain, 2 Bloor Street West, 34th floor, Toronto, Ontario M4W 3E2. ☎ 416-961-3113; Fax: 416-961-1992.

The U.S. State Department offers a consular information sheet on Spain with a summary of safety, medical, driving, and general travel information taken from official State Department offices reports. Check its Web site at http:travel.state.gov-travel_warnings.html, or contact the State Department at Overseas Citizens Services, U.S. Department of State, Room 2201 Sea Street, NW, Washington, D.C. 20520 (☎ 202-647-5225).

Surfing the Web

As popular a destination as Spain is, it's not surprising that online tourism resources are plentiful. But rather than just log on to a search engine, type in **Spain** and then have to make your way through an information cyberglut, I've compiled some of the best ones I've found. In addition to these, I provide you with other, more specific sites (including those of hotels) throughout the book.

The best Web sites to start with are those run by Spain's Department of Tourism and its National Tourist Offices abroad. Turespaña's Web site, www.tourspain.es, is the next best thing to the book you're holding in your hands. Open it up and click on leisure travel, adventure travel, or business travel. Its News feature has Spain news from around the world, including London ("Londres," with news relevant to U.K. travelers) and the U.S. The A-Z feature has good listings on things like "Accommodations" and "Sun and Beaches," but might be most helpful in its "Currency Converter" (which is up-to-date) and its "Temperature Converter" (just plug a Celsius temp in and it comes out in Fahrenheit degrees).

The U.S. Tourist Offices of Spain operate a Web site, www.okspain.org. It has "Before You Go" information (including U.S. air departures) and, in the "Press Corner," the current issue and back issues of the cyber version of the Office's monthly travel bulletin, *Travel Notes.*

Logging on to regional sites

For more specific information about individual regions in Spain, check out the following Web sites (but be warned that not all of them have their English-language versions up and running). Also, much of this Web surfing is for information junkies only; for almost everyone else, it will prove to be overly time-consuming given the relatively little yield you can reap.

For information about Barcelona, try www.bcn.es, www.barcelonaturisme.com and www.barcelona-on-line.es. Information about the Costa Brava and the city of Girona, as well as other parts of Catalonia, can be found at www.cbrava.es-girona. Mallorca web info is available at www.caib.es. For the Basque Country, try www.paisvasco or www.eskadi.net. Information on the city of Bilbao is at www.bilbao.net, and the other important Basque city, San Sebastián, has a Web site at www.donsnsn.es. For Pamplona and the rest of Navarra, the address to type in is www.cfnavarra.es. Specific information about Pamplona is found at www.pamplona.net. Galicia's regional tourism board has a good site, www.turgalicia.es. The Atlantic coast *rías* (fjords) have a site, too: www.riasbaixas.org.

Madrid's site is pretty disappointing given that it's the capital and largest city and focus of such tourism interest, but perhaps it will have improved by the time you read this. It's www.munimadrid.es. The smaller cities in Castile also have sites: www.avila.net, www.salamancaciudad.com, www.segovianet.com, and www.diputoledo.es. The south of Spain, Andalusia (Andalucía) has a main site, www.andalucia.org, and neither are Andalusian cities left out. Contact Seville at www.sevilla.org, Córdoba at www.ayuncordoba.es, and Granada at www.granada.org.

Some of Spain's greatest hits have their own Web sites. Pamplona's Running of the Bulls festival tramples the Web at www.sanfermin.com, while the St. James Pilgrims' Trail to Santiago, even though it's a millennium old, has a cyber site, www.xacobeo.es.

Locating hotel and train information

To look into a selection of Spanish hotels on the Internet, see the Web sites www.interhotel.com and www.hotelsearch.com. Both have comprehensive lists of hotels in every part of Spain and allow you to check availability and make reservations online. For the Spanish national parador system, visit the site www.parador.es.

For train information, including schedules and fares, call the 24-hour RENFE information and reservation number, ☎ 34-902-24-02-02 or visit the Web site, www.renfe.es.

Appendix B

A Guide to Spanish Art and Architecture

• •

*A*s you make your way around the country, consult the "crib sheet" I've assembled here to get a handle on Spain's most important artists and architectural styles.

Appreciating The Greats of Spanish Art

I have listed these painters chronologically, in the order of their birth.

Domenico Theotocopoulos (a.k.a. El Greco; 1541–1614). El Greco ("the Greek") was born in Crete, but settled in Toledo. He made his reputation in Spain as a painter of ethereal spiritual figures. Masterpiece: *The Burial of the Count of Orgaz* (in the church of Santo Tomás in Toledo).

José de Ribera (1591–1652). A Baroque painter of philosophers, martyrs and saints, Ribera was a powerful realist. Masterpiece: *The Martyrdom of St. Felipe.*

Francisco de Zurbarán (1598–1664). One of the greatest painters of the Seville School, Zurbarán was a master of light, which he shed on monks and madonnas. Masterpiece: *El Cristo Crucificado.*

Diego de Velázquez (1599–1660). Probably the first name of Spanish painting, the Seville-born Velázquez was a technical master and court painter who also depicted those without noble lineage, including dwarves and drunks. Masterpieces: *Las Meninas* (universally acclaimed as the greatest painting in the history of Spanish art (a judgment echoed by no less an authority than Picasso), *The Surrender of Breda, Las Hilanderas (The Spinners).*

Bartolomé Esteban Murillo (1618–1682). A painter of mystical scenes from the Seville School, Murillo painted traditional religious images as well as street characters. Masterpiece: *Immaculate Conception.*

Francisco de Goya (1746–1828). Perhaps the most versatile and prolific painter in Spanish history (at least until the appearance of Picasso), Goya was a court painter who produced fluid scenes of royalty and nobles, openly mocked the same figures, and painted bitter scenes of cruel war before descending into deaf despair (during which he produced his famous "Black Paintings"). His series of etchings on the art of the bullfight are Spanish classics. Masterpieces: *The Naked Maja* and *The Clothed Maja; The Second of May; Executions at Moncloa; The Family of Carlos IV.*

Julio González (1876–1942). A sculptor and abstract expressionist who worked with iron and collaborated with Picasso, González greatly influenced twentieth-century sculpture, including the likes of David Smith.

Pablo Picasso (1881—1973). Born in Málaga, Picasso spent formative years in Barcelona before moving to Paris and revolutionizing twentieth-century art. His name is synonymous with modern art. From his "Blue Period" and Cubism to Surrealist, politically motivated protest work, ceramics and sculpture, Picasso's genius was evident in anything he attempted — and he tried virtually everything. His output — thousands and thousands of paintings, drawings, etchings and sculptures — is unequalled. Masterpieces: *Les Demoiselles d'Avignon, Guernica.*

Joan Miró (1893–1983). The Catalan Surrealist who invented a unique and colorful language that seems childlike but is poetic and often charged with sexual symbolism. Masterpiece: *La Masia.*

Salvador Dalí (1904–1989). A Surrealist par excellence, celebrated enfant terrible and commercial wizard, Dalí was also a showman. He painted his dreams, such as melted clocks, and freaked out an entire generation. His married life, with the raving Gala, was as colorful as his art.

Antoni Tàpies (1923–). Perhaps the greatest living Spanish painter, this Barcelona painter and occasional sculptor is a fiercely independent abstract artist with a signature style of collage and thick and earthy, graffiti-influenced painting he calls *materia.*

Examining the Top Ten Spanish Masterpieces

According to a panel of art experts, the following were judged the top ten Spanish paintings of all time (in order of ranking, published in the Spanish magazine *La Revista de El Mundo,* in October 1995):

1. **Las Meninas** (Velázquez, in The Prado Museum, Madrid)
2. **Guernica** (Picasso, Reina Sofía Art Center, Madrid)

3. **Los Fusilamientos del 3 de Mayo** (Goya, The Prado Museum, Madrid)

4. **El Entierro del Conde de Orgaz** (El Greco, Church of Santo Tomé, Toledo)

5. **Les Demoiselles d'Avignon** (Picasso, Museum of Modern Art, New York)

6. **La Maja Desnuda** (Goya, The Prado Museum, Madrid)

7. **El Cristo Crucificado** (Zurbáran, The Prado Museum, Madrid)

8. **Vista del Jardín de Villa Médicis** (Velázquez, in The Prado Museum, Madrid)

9. **Bodegón** (Sánchez Cotán, The Prado Museum, Madrid)

10. **Paintings of Altamira** (Altamira cave paintings, Cantabria)

Following Spanish Architecture through the Years

What follows is a summary of the major periods in Spanish architecture, listed chronologically, with notes on the most recognizable features and most famous buildings for each style.

Roman (3rd–5th c. BC): The early conquerors of Spain were phenomenal engineers who left monumental roads, amphitheaters, and the massive aqueduct in Segovia.

Romanesque (10th–13th c.): An austere style, beautiful in its simplicity (though later examples often had profuse carving and ornamentation around portals). It was mostly applied to churches, which were built with round arches and massive, heavy walls.

Moorish (8th–15th c.): Geometric designs of brick with round horseshoe arches and spectacular decorative flourishes: *azulejos* (colorful glazed tiles), carved stucco, and calligraphy. Water is extremely important; fountains and gardens are ubiquitous. The greatest examples are in Andalusia (Granada's Alhambra, Córdoba's La Mezquita).

Mudéjar (11th–15th c.): Arab-style architecture and design created by Muslims who lived under Christian rule and used in Christian applications. The Reales Alcazares in Seville is a splendid example.

Gothic (12th–16th c.): Large-scale proportions, with high, airy chambers and naves, pointed arches, soaring buttresses and spires. Pillars take the place of thick walls, and flamboyant stained-glass windows replace murals.

Renaissance (16th c.): Classical Italian style imported to Spain in the 1500s, it focused on symmetry, with great columns and round arches. El Escorial, the royal palace outside of Madrid, is a prime example. In early Spanish Renaissance, called **Plateresque,** somber facades are enlightened by ornate carving, reminiscent of silver filigree. The Pórtico de la Gloria of Santiago's cathedral is its finest expression.

Baroque (17th–18th c.): A dramatic, swirling style of rich ornamentation and sculpture. It was designed to make a grand statement. **Churrigueresque** is an extreme Baroque style of the eighteenth century, named after a trio of brothers/architects from Salamanca. If Baroque intended to awe admirers, Churrigueresque meant to blow them away.

Modernismo: (also called *modernisme*, late 19th and early 20th c.): Catalan art nouveau, which boldly incorporated Gothic, Islamic and Renaissance elements. Spearheaded by Antoni Gaudí, whose Casa Milà is perhaps the finest example and whose unfinished church La Sagrada Familia is the best known.

A Glossary of Architectural Terms

Azulejos: Colorful, glazed ceramic tiles.

Bodega: Wine cellar.

Coro: Chorus stalls in the middle of a church nave.

Cortijo: (or Hacienda): Andalusian ranch or farm.

Masia: Catalan farmhouse.

Mirador: Balcony or belvedere with scenic views; also a glass-enclosed balcony of building.

Patio: Central courtyard, usually filled with potted plants (typical of Andalusia).

Plaza: Public square (Plaza Mayor is the town main square).

Reredo: Altar screen.

Retablo: Altarpiece.

Making Dollars and Sense of It

Expense	Amount
Airfare	
Car Rental	
Lodging	
Parking	
Breakfast	
Lunch	
Dinner	
Babysitting	
Attractions	
Transportation	
Souvenirs	
Tips	
Grand Total	

Notes

Fare Game: Choosing an Airline

Travel Agency: _____ Phone: _____

Agent's Name: _____ Quoted Fare: _____

Departure Schedule & Flight Information

Airline: _____ Airport: _____

Flight #: _____ Date: _____ Time: _____ a.m./p.m.

Arrives in: _____ Time: _____ a.m./p.m.

Connecting Flight (if any)

Amount of time between flights: _____ hours/mins

Airline: _____ Airport: _____

Flight #: _____ Date: _____ Time: _____ a.m./p.m.

Arrives in: _____ Time: _____ a.m./p.m.

Return Trip Schedule & Flight Information

Airline: _____ Airport: _____

Flight #: _____ Date: _____ Time: _____ a.m./p.m.

Arrives in: _____ Time: _____ a.m./p.m.

Connecting Flight (if any)

Amount of time between flights: _____ hours/mins

Airline: _____ Airport: _____

Flight #: _____ Date: _____ Time: _____ a.m./p.m.

Arrives in: _____ Time: _____ a.m./p.m.

Notes

Sweet Dreams: Choosing Your Hotel

Enter the hotels where you'd prefer to stay based on location and price. Then use the worksheet below to plan your itinerary.

Hotel	Location	Price per night

Menus & Venues

Enter the restaurants where you'd most like to dine. Then use the worksheet below to plan your itinerary.

Name   **Address/Phone**   **Cuisine/Price**

Places to Go, People to See, Things to Do

Enter the attractions you would most like to see. Then use the worksheet below to plan your itinerary.

Attractions	Amount of time you expect to spend there	Best day and time to go

Going "My" Way

Itinerary #1

☐ _____
☐ _____
☐ _____
☐ _____

Itinerary #2

☐ _____
☐ _____
☐ _____
☐ _____

Itinerary #3

☐ _____
☐ _____
☐ _____
☐ _____

Itinerary #4

☐ _____
☐ _____
☐ _____
☐ _____

Itinerary #5

☐ _____
☐ _____
☐ _____
☐ _____

Itinerary #6

☐ _____
☐ _____
☐ _____
☐ _____

Itinerary #7

☐ _____
☐ _____
☐ _____
☐ _____

Itinerary #8

☐ _____
☐ _____
☐ _____
☐ _____

Itinerary #9

☐ _____
☐ _____
☐ _____
☐ _____

Itinerary #10

☐ _____
☐ _____
☐ _____
☐ _____

Notes

Index

FOR DUMMIES
BOOK REGISTRATION

Register This Book and Win!

We want to hear from you!

Visit **dummies.com** to register this book and tell us how you liked it!

✔ Get entered in our monthly prize giveaway.

✔ Give us feedback about this book — tell us what you like best, what you like least, or maybe what you'd like to ask the author and us to change!

✔ Let us know any other *For Dummies* topics that interest you.

Your feedback helps us determine what books to publish, tells us what coverage to add as we revise our books, and lets us know whether we're meeting your needs as a *For Dummies* reader. You're our most valuable resource, and what you have to say is important to us!

Not on the Web yet? It's easy to get started with *Dummies 101: The Internet For Windows 98* or *The Internet For Dummies* at local retailers everywhere.

Or let us know what you think by sending us a letter at the following address:

For Dummies Book Registration
Dummies Press
10475 Crosspoint Blvd.
Indianapolis, IN 46256

BESTSELLING
BOOK SERIES